The Economist *Guide*

UNITED STATES

The Economist *Guide*

UNITED STATES

Hutchinson

Published by Hutchinson Business Books, an imprint of Century Hutchinson Limited 20 Vauxhall Bridge Road, London SW1V 2SA

Guidebook information is notoriously subject to being outdated by changes to telephone numbers and opening hours, and by fluctuating hotel and restaurant standards. While every care has been taken in the preparation of this guide, the publishers cannot accept any liability for any consequences arising from the use of information contained herein.

Where opinion is expressed it is that of the author, and does not necessarily coincide with the editorial views of The Economist newspaper.

The publishers welcome corrections and suggestions from business travelers; please write to
The Editor,
The Economist Guides,
Axe and Bottle Court,
70 Newcomen Street,
LONDON SE1 1YT

Series Editor Stephen Brough
Assistant Series Editor Brigid Avison
Editors John Farndon (*first edition overview*);
Lisa Cussans (*first edition travel*)
Jane Carroll (*second edition overview*);
Moira Johnston (*second edition travel*)
Designer Alistair Plumb (*first edition*);
Alison Donovan (*second edition*)
Production Controller Shona Burns
Researchers Tina Norris, Frances Roxburgh, Andrew Shaw
Indexer Fiona Barr

Contributors *Overview* Steve O'Connor, Lynn Feldman, Lisa Gandy, Robert Heller, Richard McKeogh, Jim Murphy, Pamela Sparr, Jack Stephenson;
Travel Michelle Beardon-Mason, Michael Berryhill, Suzanne Stone Burke, Bob Case, Tom Derr, Nadine Epstein, Eileen Evans, Rick Eyerdam, Laura Garner, Teresa Sullivan Gubbins, Steve Higginbottom, Joanna Hoffman, Caryl Jaeggli, Elizabeth Jewell, Iris Jones, Susan Kaye, Mary Lance, Katherine Larkin, Herbert Livesey, Catherine Lynch, Virginia McLean, Pat Maloney, Chris Michie, Jilian Mincer, Joe Poliforni, Paul Siegel, Tittle Gottlieb and Associates, Leslie Tweeton, Carla Waldemar, Tina Winn, Deborah Wise.

First edition published in Great Britain 1987
Second edition published in Great Britain 1990

British Library Cataloguing in Publication Data

USA. - (*The Economist guides*)
1. United States - Visitors' guides
917.3'04927

ISBN 0-09-174348-6

Maps and diagrams by Eugene Fleury (*first edition*);
adapted by Lovell Johns, Oxford, England (*second edition*)
Typeset by Tradespools Ltd, Frome, Somerset, UK
Printed in Italy by Arnoldo Mondadori, Verona

Contents

Glossary

ABA American Bankers' Association.
ABM systems Anti-Ballistic Missile systems. Their development was banned under a 1972 treaty with the USSR.
Arbitrage Trade in shares of companies involved in takeover struggles.
Bretton Woods US location of meeting in 1944 between 45 non-communist nations, leading to the creation of the International Monetary Fund (IMF) and World Bank.
CEO Chief Executive Officer. The effective head of a corporation.
CIA Central Intelligence Agency. Responsible for gathering intelligence from overseas.
cif Carriage, insurance and freight.
DIA Defense Intelligence Agency. Responsible for military evaluation of allies and potential enemies.
EC European Community.
FBI Federal Bureau of Investigation. Responsible for investigation of federal crimes and for some domestic counter-intelligence.
Fed, the The US Federal Reserve. An independent government agency which controls interest rates and the money supply.
fob Free on board.
FTC Federal Trade Commission. An independent commission set up to regulate competition and fight unfair business practices.
GATT General Agreement on Tariffs and Trade, which came into force in 1948. It is the world's major forum for negotiating the reduction of tariffs and other barriers to trade.
GNP Gross National Product. A country's Gross Domestic Product (the total value of its goods and services, normally valued at market prices) plus residents' income from investments abroad minus income accruing to nonresidents from investments in the country.
Gramm-Rudman targets Statutory annual limits to the US federal budget deficit. If the deficit exceeds the target, the Comptroller-General makes automatic cuts in spending across the board.
Group of Five (G5) Britain, France, Japan, the USA and West Germany.
GSP Generalized System of Preferences. A system agreed under the auspices of UNCTAD (UN Conference on Trade and Development) which gives developing countries certain tariff advantages for their exports of manufactured and processed goods to the developed countries.
Hispanics Spanish-speaking US residents and citizens from Mexico, Puerto Rico, Cuba and the rest of Latin America.
Junk bonds High-yield investment bonds in heavily borrowed companies. Often used to finance takeover bids.
NATO North Atlantic Treaty Organisation, founded in 1949 as an international collective defense organization linking a group of European states with the USA and Canada. France withdrew from NATO's military structure in 1966.
OAS Organization of American States. A political organization founded in 1948, embracing the USA and 30 Latin American and Caribbean states.
OECD Organisation for Economic Cooperation and Development. A forum for discussion and action on the world economy, founded in 1961. Members are the 24 industrialized democracies.
SALT Strategic Arms Limitation Talks. A series of negotiations between the USA and the USSR on nuclear weapons. SALT I lasted from 1969 to 1972; SALT II was negotiated by Carter but rejected by Reagan.
SDI Strategic Defense Initiative. Also known as Star Wars.
SEC Securities and Exchange Commission. An independent body regulating the buying and selling of stocks and bonds.
START Strategic Arms Reduction Talks. The successor to SALT II. It was suspended in 1983.
USTTA United States Travel and Tourism Administration.
WASP White Anglo-Saxon Protestant.

Using the Guide

The Economist Guide to the United States is an encyclopedia of business and travel information. If in doubt about where to look for specific information, consult either the Contents list or the Index.

City guides

Each city guide follows a standard format: information and advice on arriving, getting around, city areas, hotels, clubs, restaurants, bars, entertainment, shopping, sightseeing, sports and fitness, and a directory of local business and other facilities such as secretarial and translation agencies, couriers, hospitals with 24-hour accident and emergency departments, and telephone-order florists. There is also a map of the city center locating recommended hotels, restaurants and other important addresses.

For easy reference, all main entries for hotels, restaurants and sights are listed alphabetically.

Abbreviations

Credit and charge cards

AE	American Express
DC	Diners Club
MC	Mastercard (Access)
V	Visa

Figures Millions are abbreviated to m; billions (meaning one thousand million) to bn.

Publisher's note

The Economist Guides have been prepared for the international marketplace. They are designed to give foreign travelers an insight into local business practice as well as to provide invaluable information and detail for the national of the country concerned. For this reason, although some sections in the guide to the USA on local etiquette and customs may strike American readers as obvious, they highlight what will *not* be obvious about the USA and American business to foreigners.

Price bands

Price bands are denoted by symbols (see below). These correspond approximately to the following actual prices at the time of going to press. (Although the actual prices will inevitably go up, the relative price category is likely to remain the same.)

Restaurants

(three-course meal with a half bottle of house wine, coffee, tax and service at 15%)

[$]	under $20
[$]/	$20 to $40
[$]//	$40 to $60
[$]///	$60 to $100
[$]////	over $100
[$]/////	well over $100

Hotels

(one person occupying a standard room, including taxes and service)

[$]	under $75
[$]/	$75 to $125
[$]//	$125 to $175
[$]///	$175 to $225
[$]////	over $225
[$]/////	well over $225

INTRODUCTION

The USA enters the last decade of the century confident about the future but aware also that a changing world presents new and unfamiliar challenges. The Reagan administration saw a marked revival of national morale and posted an impressive record of economic growth. These achievements helped to elect President Bush as Reagan's successor, and bequeathed to the nation a climate of optimism about the future.

Far-reaching, unexpected initiatives by the Soviet Union put foreign affairs at the top of the new administration's agenda. Although sometimes apparently overwhelmed by the pace of *perestroika* diplomacy, Washington and the American public sensed that the traditional policy of containment, which had dominated security doctrine since World War II, had perhaps at last fulfilled its purpose and had to be adapted to a changed world situation.

President Bush's America is still the world's leading economy by a long way. Yet since the 1970s at least, great strides made by such competitors as West Germany and Japan have not only closed the gap, but successfully invaded the US market itself. Americans, who in the 1950s and 1960s had enjoyed the highest standard of living in the world, by the 1980s had slipped into fifth place. The steady and sustained boom in the US economy, moreover, has in itself created problems, of which the vast twin deficits – in government spending and foreign trade – are seen as a threat to continued stability.

Years of recession

Economic performance first became a pressing public issue in the 1970s, when, for the first time since the war, the underlying growth of the US economy began to slow. The Carter administration tried to help US exports by allowing the dollar to slide, but succeeded only in accelerating inflation and bringing growth almost to a standstill. At this time, too, imports from Japan began to make deep inroads into the US domestic market. From 1970 to 1985, for example, US imports of Japanese cars rose by six and a half times.

As the recession deepened and the USA faced embarrassment over the failure to retrieve US hostages held in Iran, Americans elected as president the robustly patriotic Ronald Reagan to restore their ailing fortunes. Reagan came to power in 1981 promising to recapture an earlier sense of security, revive progress and restore national self-confidence. President Reagan's solutions to the nation's malaise were partly a dose of traditional Republican nostrums – greater defense expenditures, reduced government spending on social programs and increased reliance on the marketplace – and partly something entirely novel. A sharp reduction in personal taxation, he argued, would transform the supply-side of the economy by providing individuals with much greater incentives to work and succeed. A wave of entrepreneurial activity would lead to faster growth, raising government revenues enough to offset the impact of the tax cuts.

The Reagan years

The verdict on the Reagan years is mixed. Supporters of "Reaganomics" can point to some notable successes. Although GDP actually fell by 2.5% in 1981–82, it grew by as much as 7% in 1983–84 before settling down to a stable, sustained 3%. An annual inflation rate of 13.4% in 1980 was more than halved – and then kept in check. The federal deficit is huge, but overall government deficit spending in the USA is, proportionately, comparable to that of most other developed economies. Industrial productivity showed steady improvement, increasing by as much as 10% between 1984 and 1988. Under the pressure of foreign competition, machine tools, steel and automobiles were important examples of industries which trimmed unit costs and improved productivity to reassert their position in the market.

Such achievements, however, were not without cost. The pace of expansion has meant a voracious appetite for investment (about $900bn a year) which sucks in foreign funds and thus swells national indebtedness. The federal deficit stubbornly resists control. The visible trade gap was cut from a record $165bn in 1986 to $135.5bn by March 1989, but at least some of the encouraging growth in exports and competitiveness in the international marketplace results from weakness in the dollar and thus may be difficult to maintain in the future. Millions of jobs were created during the boom of the Reagan years, but most were in the relatively low-paid service sector, which did little to disseminate the real achievements of the economy throughout the population.

The prospects for growth

President Bush inherited a strong economy which was in its seventh year of stable growth. Continued expansion will eventually require new physical plant and even more advanced management of human and technological resources. At this point in such a sustained boom, the trick is to maintain the pace of growth while keeping the economy from wobbling out of control. The administration will be called upon to produce a credible strategy for controlling both the federal deficit ($155bn in 1988) and the foreign debt ($684.5bn at the end of 1988). It will also have to deal with growing reservations about the once-sacred policy of free trade and with increasing demands for better access to foreign markets, as expressed in the Omnibus Trade and Competitiveness Act of April 1989.

The climate for business is favourable in the USA: capital is easily available, unions can be cooperative and open, and competitive dealing is the general rule. With its advanced technological base and continued R&D investment, the economy can expect continued steady growth through the rest of the decade. As always, Americans put their trust in the future and focus attention on the present. The past they consign to historians.

The Economic Scene

Natural resources

Endowed with a wealth of commercially-exploitable natural resources matched by few other nations, the USA is among the top four world producers for a vast number of primary products, ranging from corn to aluminum. It also remains among the leading exporters of many basic food and mineral products. But the US resource base is not without its problems, and many sectors – notably farm products and oil – are facing real difficulties as a fluctuating world situation undermines economic viability. The need to guarantee supplies of vital oils and minerals remains a key factor in American foreign policy.

Agriculture

US farms account for barely 2% of GNP and employ little over 3% of the work force, but their output is vast, and US farm production is rivalled only by that of the Soviet Union. More than enough of most basic commodities is produced to satisfy home need, and the US is able to export 40% more agricultural produce than it imports. Exports of American grain continue to dominate the world market, despite the severe drought in 1988, and in the late 1980s the USA still accounted for three-quarters of the soybean trade, half of the corn (maize) trade and a quarter of world wheat exports.

US farm production and the world (1986): principal crops

	US as % of world	
	Prod'n	Exports
Wheat	10.8	31.3
Corn for grain	44.0	70.1
Soybeans	53.9	72.3
Rice	1.4	18.8
Tobacco	8.8	16.1
Vegetable oil	13.6	6.2
Cotton	13.8	25.8

Source: *Statistical Abstract of the United States, 1988.*

Cattle remain the most valuable of all agricultural products, and on the great ranches of the western USA and the smaller farms of the South and Midwest, millions of beef cattle are raised, while the Northeast has thousands of dairy farms.

The corn and soybean industry is centered in the Midwest, where many hogs are also raised, while the vast prairies of central USA are covered by acre upon acre of wheat. The Southeast is the focus of tobacco farming, and cotton is grown mainly in the South and Southwest. The other main crops are hay, sorghum (the Great Plains), oats, potatoes, barley, rice and sugar beet.

The demise of the small farmer In the years since World War II, US agriculture has become increasingly capital-intensive, and rising production costs have driven more and more small farmers out of business. The number of farms has more than halved since 1950 – in 1988 there were fewer than 2.2m – while average farm size has more than doubled to over 450 acres/180ha, although the total area of farmland has contracted slightly. Large agribusiness units dominate the US farming scene, and in the early 1980s farms with annual sales of over $500,000 accounted for a third of all farm sales.

Farm crisis After a boom in the early 1980s, which saw farm production and profits hit new records, US farms have run into trouble. Falling world grain prices and over-production have devastated many small farmers in the

Midwest, while the rapid decline in agricultural land values since 1982 has hit all farmers. Those who bought land on credit at higher prices at the beginning of the decade are now facing huge repayments on land that has dropped in value by over a third, and many US banks have been placed in real difficulties by the spiralling losses on agricultural debt, estimated at $150bn in 1988. The parlous state of the farming community was exacerbated by the 1988 drought.

Forestry

Almost a third of the land surface of the USA is still covered by forests, although the total forest area is shrinking steadily. In 1977, there were 728m acres/295m ha of forest, of which 483m acres/195m ha were commercially exploitable. More than 60% of US timber production is concentrated in the states of the Pacific Northwest, notably Oregon, Washington, Alaska and northern California, while the forests of the South produce wood pulp and nearly all US turpentine, pitch, resin and wood tar. In 1987 the USA was producing more than 2.8 trillion board feet/860bn metres of sawn timber, yet it still had to import almost $14bn worth.

Fishing

Despite the thousands of miles of coast, the USA is not a major fishing nation, and it now imports almost as much fish as is caught by its fishermen. In the late 1980s, the US catch was worth some $3bn a year, of which about a third was caught in the Gulf of Mexico – notably in the form of menhaden, oysters and shrimps – a quarter in the Pacific (anchovies, crab, salmon, tuna) and about a sixth in the Atlantic (cod, flounder, haddock, hake and herring).

Minerals

The USA is blessed with commercially exploitable reserves of virtually every major mineral, and it leads the world in the production of lead, while only the Soviet Union exceeds the US output of copper. The USA is also a major producer of iron ore, gold, molybdenum, silver and zinc. The main zinc deposits lie in the Appalachians and the interior plains, while most other mineral ores are mined in the Rocky Mountains. Although it imports more than 90% of its manganese, bauxite, alumina and cobalt, and a majority of its tin, nickel, potash, tungsten and zinc, the USA is less reliant on foreign sources than most leading industrial nations, and the Federal Emergency Management Agency (FEMA) ensures there is always an adequate strategic stockpile of vital minerals. The proximity of Canada, the country's major supplier of minerals, further reduces the USA's vulnerability to disruption of supplies.

Energy

Extensive deposits of coal, natural gas, petroleum and uranium make the USA less dependent than most industrialized nations on imported energy. In fact, its oil and natural gas output is exceeded only by that of the Soviet Union, and its coal output only by China. US producers were hard hit by the fall in oil prices in 1986, which rendered many small wells in Texas and Louisiana uneconomic. The weakness of oil prices since then has also meant a reduction in exploration activity. No substantial new reserves have been found, so oil production is likely to decline, with a consequent increase in reliance on imported oil, which supplies over 40% of the country's needs. But the USA is virtually self-sufficient in coal, which provides over half its electricity, and all but self-sufficient in natural gas, which generates a further 11% of its electricity. The nation's great rivers, such as the Colorado and the Columbia, provide hydroelectric power. It is the USA's rich energy base, combined with the abundant mineral supplies, that has underpinned its industrial success.

Human resources

There are some 246m people living in the USA today, making it the fourth most populous country in the world, after China (1.06bn), India (766m) and the Soviet Union (275m). But the 1980s have seen a slackening of the vigorous growth – fueled by high birth rates and wave upon wave of immigration – that has trebled the population this century. Now the expansion of the American population is settling down to a steady 1% a year, compared to 1.7% in the 1950s.

An ageing nation

Americans are getting older; two significant changes in the nature of US society – the decline in birth rate and the increase in life expectancy – have raised the average age of the US population to over 30. And demographers predict that it may reach 36 by 2000.

Fewer children As the birth rate has declined steadily over the last 25 years or so, from a peak of almost 25 per 1,000 population in the 1950s to less than 16, so the number of children has also dropped. Now only 25% or so of the population are under 18 – compared with 35.7% in 1960.

More elderly people Improvements in health care and lifestyle are helping Americans to live longer. The average American man now expects to live to be well over 70, while women expect to live almost to 80. The number of people over 65 has almost doubled (to about 30m) during the last 30 years, and it is estimated that by the end of the century more than 35m Americans – more than 13% of the country's population – will be in the over-65 age group.

Observers have expressed considerable doubts about how the country will be able to support such large numbers of economically inactive people and provide all the extra care elderly people need. Even under the budget-cutting Reagan administration, expenditure on health, social security and Medicare has had to increase at almost twice the rate of inflation. But there are a number of positive spin-offs – booming sales of pharmaceuticals and "eventide" homes for the prosperous retired.

Shifting population

The USA is a vast country, and more than 98% of the land area is classified as rural. Yet 75% of Americans now live in towns, and the current plight of many farmers has renewed the steady drift from country to city and city suburb that has characterized this century.

The most densely populated area remains the Northeast, where vast conurbations and suburbs sprawl into one another to form an almost continuous belt of urban development. But the American population has always been unusually mobile, and as the traditional manufacturing industries in the Northeast and Midwest have declined, more and more Americans have moved West and South, homing in on the high technology industries in the sunbelt states of the South and the Mountain West. The populations of western states like Nevada, Utah, Arizona and Wyoming have shot up over the past decade, while Texas has become the third most populous state after California and New York. Los Angeles, meanwhile, is set to take over from New York by 2000 as the USA's largest city.

Florida is also showing dynamic growth as more and more people respond to its excellent location for business and travel to Latin America and as many of the growing population of elderly Americans decide to live out their last years in the sun. In the 1980s, the population of Florida rose by more than 2m.

Immigration

All but a few (6%) of the American population were born in the USA, yet this is a land of immigrants, and there are few Americans who cannot trace their family back to foreign settlers within half a dozen generations or so. Throughout its history the USA has received refugees, fleeing from poverty, war or political persecution – from the poor farmers and peasants who came in their millions from northwest Europe (especially England, Ireland and Germany) during the 19th century, to the well-publicized Soviet defectors of recent years. Not all came voluntarily: half a million Africans were brought as slaves during the 18th and 19th centuries to work on the plantations. But each group has added its own particular culture and outlook to the American scene.

Today immigration is estimated officially at about 600,000 a year and contributes around 20% of the annual growth in population (twice as much as in the 1950s).

Asians Among the most recent arrivals are the Vietnamese "boat people," and it is believed that there are now more than 750,000 people from Vietnam, Cambodia and Laos living in the USA. Each year, many arrive from other parts of Asia, too, notably the Philippines and South Korea, swelling the Asian-American population, at latest count, to well over 3.5m.

Latin Americans But by far the largest influx comes from Latin America, notably from Mexico, and every year 250,000 "Hispanics" enter the USA legally; many thousands more enter illegally. Most of them head for the West Coast and Texas.

Illegal immigrants Until 1965, the USA barred entry to Asians, but allowed a certain quota of immigrants from most European and American nations. The 1965 Immigration Act, however, abandoned quotas and cut the annual limit to 170,000. Although the Refugee Act of 1980 raised the limit to 320,000, there are still many people who are prepared to risk the consequences of entering the country illegally. Illegal immigrants from Cuba arriving in Florida make headline news, but it is the millions of Hispanics who slip undetected across the southern border of the USA who make up the largest "fugitive" population group. Conservative estimates put the illegal Mexican population alone at more than 5m.

Americans abroad Only during one period have Americans emigrated to any extent. That was during the Depression years of the 1930s, when more people left the country than entered it. Today, the largest group of Americans overseas are the 2.1m military personnel at bases around the world.

Race and work

White people make up about 85% of the population while 12% are black – mainly descendents of slaves from Africa – and 3% other races. The black population is much younger (only 8% are over 65, compared with 13% of the white population) and is growing almost twice as fast as the white population. It is expected that the black population will reach 35m by the end of the century. The two other fastest growing racial groups are the 18.8m Hispanics and the 3.6m Asians. Experts estimate that the Hispanics, who can be of any color, now form 7.5% of the population and will total 25m by 2000.

Discrimination continues to be a big issue, and blacks are still at a considerable disadvantage in the job market. Nonetheless more and more are finding jobs and moving away from the ghettoes into more affluent areas of the big cities. Black-owned businesses have risen since 1970 from 185,000 to more than 235,000. In many ways, it is now the Hispanics who are suffering the most acute discrimination, and it is they who provide the cheap, exploited labor in California and Florida as well as New York, not only on the fruit farms but in the semi-conductor industry.

International trade

The sheer size of the US economy means that the USA remains by far the world's largest trading nation and dominates the international trade scene, exporting to and importing from 180 different countries. The impact of trade on the economy is proportionally smaller than for virtually any other developed nation – accounting for about 10% of the US GNP compared with 20-25% for Japan and the Western European nations. But US exports still total more than 10% of world exports, while the US market takes 15-20% of world imports. The current account deficit rose sharply in the early 1980s, together with the value of the dollar. The decline of the dollar in the latter part of the decade restored export competitiveness and helped to close the deficit. However, the surge in US foreign debt and the consequent outflows of interest on that debt, mean a return to a surplus on current account is likely to be long and painful.

Spiralling deficit

The rapid escalation in the trade deficit dates back to the middle of President Reagan's first term in 1982, and many commentators have laid the blame squarely at the door of "Reaganomics," a fiscal policy that, through tax cuts, boosted personal income at the expense of capital investment and generated a huge federal deficit. With domestic interest rates and the exchange rate both high, American exporters lost their competitive edge, while rising levels of personal spending encouraged a massive growth in imports. In the early 1980s, imports to the USA were worth around $270bn, and the trade deficit hovered above the $40bn mark. By 1987, imports had soared by over a half, and the trade deficit had reached $160bn. Exports actually dropped in the years 1982-85 by more than $20bn. That was partly a result of the overvaluation of the dollar. After the Group of Five (G5) agreed in September 1985 to bring down the value of the dollar, the competitiveness of US producers improved and exports grew rapidly. The cheaper dollar also made imports more expensive. But the trade gap will remain a major problem.

Manufacturing exports tumble
Americans are acutely sensitive to the fact that it is in manufacturing that the turnaround in trade is most marked. From 1981 to 1985, the USA's manufacturing exports actually dropped by 14%, while imports climbed more than 70%. The USA swallows up more than a quarter of the world's manufacturing exports. After an $11bn surplus in manufacturing trade at the outset of the 1980s, by the end of the decade the USA was confronting a deficit in manufactured goods of well over $120bn, despite the recovery in export competitiveness. In cars and trucks alone the USA was running a trade deficit of more than $50bn, while there were negative balances of over $10bn in each of clothing, audio and video equipment, consumer goods, and iron and steel.

The Eastern invasion It is the South-East Asian countries which have made the most dramatic inroads into the US market. Japan is now the USA's major source of imports, with more than a $90bn inflow of goods per year. But Japan takes only $40bn worth of US exports, leaving a $50bn deficit. Taiwan now has the second largest trade surplus with the USA, exceeding even that of the country's major trading partner, Canada.

Protectionist pressure The US belief that the trade shortfall with Japan is not wholly due to relative competitiveness led the Bush administration to name Japan as the first country to be investigated for unfair trade practices under the Super 301 provisions of the 1988 Trade Bill. The bill gives the president substantial powers to negotiate the removal of such barriers to free trade, with the threat that the USA may in turn impose restrictions on exports from those countries it believes are not engaging in free trade. Nevertheless the USA already has import barriers and voluntary agreements to control trade in many key sectors.

The dollar After the 1985 agreement to depreciate the dollar, the G5 was then able to steady the dollar at a lower level through much of 1987. But since then the dollar has risen and, although this may be good for US morale, it threatens the price competitiveness that the earlier depreciation had achieved. There is also the threat of another fall in the dollar if the world financial community lost faith in the ability of the administration to solve the country's underlying economic ills.

Trading partners

The 1980s have seen the focus of America's trade shift radically away from the traditional European base toward the Pacific Ocean. Remarkably, Japan has all but taken over from Canada as the USA's major supplier, capturing a better than 20% share of US imports, and despite voluntary quotas it seems likely that imports from Japan will continue to rise. At the same time, South Korea, Hong Kong and especially Taiwan have consolidated their status as trading partners at the expense of the Western European nations. Taiwan now ranks as the USA's fourth most important supplier, only just behind West Germany and having overtaken Mexico. The EC accounts for over a quarter of US exports, and the moves there to complete the internal market by 1992 are viewed with some suspicion by Washington. The fear that a "Fortress Europe" might be detrimental to US interests has heightened tensions between the community and the USA. US exports to Latin America have been hit by the economic problems in Mexico, Brazil and Argentina. Although trade with the Eastern bloc and with the developing countries is on the rise, the thrust of US trade policy will continue to be the pursuit of wider access for US exporters in its existing major markets.

Main US trading partners (1988)

Exports to	%	Imports from	%
Canada	22.9	Japan	20.1
Japan	11.6	Canada	18.8
Mexico	6.5	W Germany	5.9
UK	5.7	Taiwan	5.6
W Germany	4.4	Mexico	5.2
Taiwan	3.7	S Korea	4.5
S Korea	3.3	UK	4.0
N'lands	3.1	France	2.7
France	3.1	Italy	2.6
Australia	2.6	Hong Kong	2.3

Source: *Survey of Current Business*

Key exports

Despite the vast increase in manufacturing imports into the USA in the 1980s, manufacturing remains the dominant sector in the US export trade. Machinery, manufactured goods and transport equipment together made up more than 70% of US exports by value in 1988, and the USA was the origin of 20% of the world's manufactured exports – compared with 18% for West Germany and 16% for Japan. Moreover, the USA is strikingly successful in certain fields – notably the aircraft and defense industries, where the main challenge comes from Europe, not Japan. Boeing and McDonnell Douglas have spearheaded an American aviation export drive so effective that the USA now has a trade surplus of more than $11bn in the aircraft business. But in sectors where the Japanese competition is most intense, US successes are counterbalanced by even more striking Japanese success. Although the USA's computer exports have continued to rise, imports have grown even faster, so its trade surplus has declined since the early 1980s. And in sectors such as clothing, where low labor costs are paramount, even the depreciation of the dollar in recent years has failed to protect competitiveness against exports from Third World countries.

But it is the decline of farm product exports from the USA that is perhaps the most significant trend, for as world food import markets shrink and world food production continues to rise, the USA is fast running out of lucrative destinations for its food exports. US food exports are still worth almost $30bn a year, but their share of US export trade is now well below 10%. Already, competition from Europe, Argentina, Australia and New Zealand for access to the massive Soviet market has hit American grain exports. And soon South Korea, Thailand and Indonesia may try to knock the USA from its perch as top supplier to Japan, the only substantial food importer in the non-communist world.

Key imports

In a nation as dependent upon personal mobility as the USA, it is perhaps hardly surprising that transport dominates the import scene. Car and truck imports soared during the 1980s to become the largest single sector, accounting for almost one-fifth of all US imports by value at over $80bn. Fuel, the second largest import, made up a further 10% of the import total. These two categories alone accounted for well over half the trade deficit, and the Reagan administration encouraged Japan to limit voluntarily car exports to the USA to prevent the deficit from rising still higher. Officially, however, voluntary restraints no longer exist.

The other major imports are machinery, clothing and footwear, and agricultural products. Significantly, food imports now regularly exceed food exports.

Main commodities traded 1988

	Exports ($bn)	Imports ($bn)
Food, beverages & live animals	30.9	24.2
Crude materials, oils & fats	26.6	14.2
Mineral fuels	8.2	41.1
Chemicals	32.3	19.9
Motor vehicles & other transport equipment	46.7	79.7
Machinery	88.4	117.3
Total incl. others	309.4	441.6

Source: Department of Commerce, *Survey of Current Business*

Trade in services

In the past, healthy sales of services abroad helped to offset the massive deficits created by the swelling imports of merchandise into the USA. Exports of services now account for more than 40% of the USA's foreign earnings. Business services are particularly lucrative, and fees and royalties paid on goods made overseas earn the USA billions of dollars a year. Insurance, banking and financial institutions are also major money-spinners, together with construction and engineering services. However, there has been a slump in profits in travel and transportation, and the USA has come to rely more and more for its services trade surplus on net gains in interest, dividends and profits from the US multinationals' massive overseas assets. But the increasing amount of foreign-owned US assets led to a rapid rise in the outflow of interest, dividends and profits, from $63bn in 1985 to $106bn in 1988. The consequence has been a smaller surplus on the services balance, and there is now the prospect of a deficit. Allied to the traditional outpayments of transfers to the rest of the world, this means the US current account can return to surplus only if there is a return to a trade surplus.

The nation's finances

For the first time since before World War I, the USA has become a debtor nation, and its indebtedness to the rest of the world dwarfs that of Brazil, Mexico and other "problem" debtors. Its capital requirements have been easily financed, because the US economy is still an attractive haven for overseas investors. But those inflows of capital have brought their own problems – instability in the dollar as "hot money" moves in and out, and a domestic backlash against the substantial investment in US companies and real estate by overseas buyers. The federal budget deficit is also a problem, and one that will increase as the Gramm-Rudman targets for the budget deficit become more difficult to meet. Without a cut in the federal deficit and a rise in personal savings, the external deficit will continue to overshadow the domestic economy.

Capital pressures

Throughout the 1980s, the swelling US trade, payments and federal deficits transformed the economy into a financial "black hole," sucking in money from all over the world. It is now heavily dependent upon foreign capital and maintains high interest rates to obtain a steady flow of money into the country, aided in recent years by increasingly liberal financial laws (such as the repeal of withholding tax in 1984). Japan now has almost twice as much capital invested in the US economy as the USA has invested in Japan.

For financial observers in the USA, one of the most worrying factors has been not the rise of capital inflows into the country but the collapse of capital outflows, which have plummeted from $121bn in 1982 to $33bn in 1985. In the latter half of the 1980s investment overseas recovered, but was dwarfed by the huge inflows of foreign capital needed to finance the current deficit. High interest rates at home are partly to blame for this reversal. But many banks have been scared off putting their money overseas by Third World countries unable to service the interest on loans. In fact, bank failures have become a real concern in the USA, and the Federal Deposit Insurance Corporation (FDIC) estimates that a tenth of the USA's 13,000 commercial banks are facing difficulties.

Macroeconomic indicators

	1984	1988
GNP at market prices ($bn)	3,765	4,862
Real GNP growth (%)	6.8	3.9
Consumer price inflation (%)	4.3	4.1
Exports *fob* ($bn)	224.0	321.6
Imports *cif* ($bn)	346.4	459.6
Balance of payments ($bn)	-107.1	-135.1
Public external debt ($bn)	192.9	330.0

Source: Economist Intelligence Unit

The dollar

Since the Bretton Woods Conference of 1944, the US dollar has been the world's major reserve currency, and it continues to be the reference point for most international financial deals. Japan, for example, holds nearly all its huge foreign investments in dollars – $640bn of them – and refuses to make the yen an international trading currency. Even without its vast economy, the pervasiveness of the dollar would enable the USA to wield enormous influence over the world financial scene.

When the Reagan administration first came to power, it seemed determined to learn from the mistakes of the Carter administration. The Carter approach, by allowing the

Origins of GNP 1987

market prices	% of total
Agriculture, forestry & fishing	2.1
Mining	1.9
Construction	4.8
Manufacturing	18.9
Transport & utilities	9.0
Distributive trades	16.4
Finance, insurance, etc	17.1
Government	11.8
Other services	17.5
Rest of the world	0.7
Total	100.0

Components of GNP 1988

market prices	% of total
Personal consumption	66.4
Non-residential investment	10.0
Residential investment	4.7
Federal expenditure	7.8
State & local expenditure	12.0
Exports: goods & services	10.7
Imports: goods & services	-12.6
Stockbuilding	1.0
Total	100

Source: Economist Intelligence Unit

dollar to slide, stimulated exports but helped to create "stagflation" – a depressed economy combined with accelerated inflation. Under Reagan, the dollar's ailing fortunes were revived by high interest rates and a less strictly regulated financial climate, and by 1984 its IMF trade-weighted index had climbed to over 150 (1980 = 100). But since then the dollar has fallen, eventually stabilizing at around its 1980 level. The administration is faced with the problem that another crisis of confidence could send the dollar even further down.

Expanding economy Despite its debt and export problems, the US economy continues to expand, driven by rising personal consumption. At $5,000bn, the USA's GNP is already huge – three times the size of Japan's, six times the size of West Germany's and eight times the size of the UK's. But it is still growing at just under 3% a year in real terms, and most commentators expect this expansion to continue until the end of the decade, though at a reduced rate. Forecasting GNP growth, however, generates enormous contention, for the credibility of the administration's budget plans, among other things, depends on the GNP forecast. The administration's forecast of GNP growth is habitually more optimistic than independent forecasts.

Federal financing

President Reagan came to power pledging to cut the deficit on goverment finances. But the Reagan years saw the US federal deficit escalating to unprecedented levels, as tax cuts sliced millions of dollars off receipts while the administration continued to spend heavily on defense. Standing at $78.9bn in the fiscal year 1981, the federal deficit swelled to more than $220bn in 1986, and the national debt has now surged to over $2,500bn – double the 1981 figure. Interest payments on the debt alone were expected to swallow up a seventh of the federal budget in 1989.

Beating Congress The budget for the following year (the fiscal year starts on October 1) is prepared by the Office of Management and Budget (using expenditure estimates prepared by each government department) and is submitted to Congress in January. As a result of President Nixon's attempts to sidestep congressional control of finance, Congress has acquired considerable power over the budget, and the budget committees in both House and Senate are now the most important in the legislature.

With the Democrats in control in Congress, the Republican administration has to exert all its powers of persuasion to push its budget proposals through the committees, and its success rate is low. Intense pressure from "special interest" lobbies can greatly alter the initial proposals.

Gramm-Rudman targets In an attempt to cut the spiralling federal debt, the administration in December 1985 agreed to the Gramm-Rudman-Hollings budget plan. This is designed to balance the budget by fiscal 1993, by enforcing manadatory automatic cuts in spending if deficit targets are not met each year. The weakness of the GRH legislation is that the cuts are based on the deficit forecast prepared by the administration. So far, a combination of good economic growth and optimistic forecasting has meant that major reductions in spending programmes or mandatory cuts have not been necessary. Any major slowdown in the economy could take the forecast deficit outside the GRH limits; if that were to occur, Congress and the White House might find the scale of cuts needed to meet GRH requirements politically uncomfortable, and the GRH limits might be amended upwards.

Where the money comes from The bulk of US government money (around 80%) comes from personal taxes and social insurance, while most of the rest comes from corporate income tax (around 10%) and customs duty (about 5%). But the Reagan administration tried to reduce the overall burden of taxation on both individuals and corporations, in the belief that tax cuts would stimulate the economy. In its first term, corporate taxes were cut to the point where they contributed only just over 8% of the federal budget. Now the emphasis is more on cuts in personal tax, particularly for high earners. In 1987 sweeping changes in the tax structure were introduced to "simplify" income tax and shift the burden back onto the corporations, mainly through the removal of investment subsidies.

Where the money goes The USA spends more money on weapons and the armed forces than any other country in the world (about $300bn a year) and defense swallows up more than 25% of the entire federal budget. The Reagan administration virtually doubled defense expenditure in its first term, and only persistent opposition in Congress has thwarted plans to boost it still further.

To finance tax cuts and defense spending the welfare budget has been heavily pruned. Income security has now been pared down to 12% of the budget (from 14% in 1980), helped by a decline in the unemployment rate from 9.5% in 1982 to just over 5% in 1989. Social security spending is static at around 20%, despite the steady growth in the elderly population. Education has suffered particularly savage cuts.

Federal Budget receipts

	1980	1990 (est)
Individual income tax	47.2	44.1
Corporation tax	12.5	11.1
Soc insurance tax	30.5	37.0
Excise taxes	4.7	3.3
Estate & gift tax	1.2	0.8
Customs duties	1.4	1.7
Misc receipts	2.5	2.1
Total	100.0	100.0

Federal Budget expenditure

	1980	1990 (est)
National defense	22.7	26.3
Social security	20.1	21.4
Health & Medicare	9.4	12.8
Income security	14.7	11.9
Education	5.4	3.4
Veterans' benefits	3.6	2.6
Transportation	3.6	2.5
Others	15.0	7.9
Interest	8.9	14.8
Offsetting receipts	-3.4	-3.6
Total	100.0	100.0

Source: Office of Management and Budget.

The Industrial Scene

Industry and investment

The single most salient fact about American industry is that it no longer enjoys the uncontested world economic hegemony that it maintained during the 1950s and early 1960s, and which peaked in 1966, the height of the nation's post-war boom. This fall from glory continues to color everything from national politics to the attitude of Americans toward foreign investment and visiting foreign executives.

Decline in manufacturing

Still the world's leading industrial nation, the United States remains a dominant force in the global economy. Its GNP, at almost $4,500bn, is nearly two-thirds as much again as that of Japan, its nearest rival. And, although the heady days when the USA held a 25% share of the world market for manufactured goods are gone, it retains around 14%, compared with Japan's 8%. Yet for over a decade America has gradually lost ground in comparison with virtually every other industrialized country. The American standard of living, once the highest in the world, is now only sixth, behind that of Switzerland, Japan, Norway, Denmark and West Germany (although the OECD argues that, after allowing for the cost of living, US incomes are as high as any). More significantly, the 1980s have seen the United States afflicted with a swelling trade deficit, which reached a record of $160bn in 1987 despite efforts to lower the value of the dollar.

The real significance of America's trade deficits, however, lies not in their size but in their composition. In 1980, when the United States had a $10bn trade deficit with Japan, its largest imports in dollar value from that country were cars, iron and steel plates, truck and tractor chassis, radios, motorcycles, and audio and video tape recorders. Its major exports to Japan were soybeans, corn, fir logs, hemlock logs, coal, wheat and cotton.

In other words, from the perspective of its main competitor, the United States seemed little more than a source of agricultural products.

Readjustment In many ways, what has been happening to the USA has been less a decline than a reaction to an artificial situation. At the end of World War II the United States, with a huge and intact industrial base and IOUs from most of the industrialized world, found itself in a position of world economic supremacy; in a sense, however, it had only been set up for a fall. It was simply a matter of time before America's rapidly rebuilding European and Asian debtors became vigorous competitors – with the stiffest competition coming from the nations that had had to do the most rebuilding.

What went wrong

A measure of the complexity of America's industrial problems is the wide divergence of opinion among scholars, analysts and politicians as to their causes.

Going soft Many on the right blame excessive government intervention. Welfare payments have sapped the Puritan virtues of Americans, they say, while high taxes have undermined incentives for managers and entrepeneurs. Unions, too, are blamed, for making America's basic smokestack industries uncompetitive by forcing through huge concessions in pay and conditions in the early 1960s. Others look for more complex causes, attributing the decline to the inevitable waning of the technological revolution that radically transformed the world during the middle part of this century.

Quick fix American management, too, has been criticized for adopting a shortsighted, "quick-fix" approach to declining profits. Faced with growing competition from the re-emergent economies of Europe and Japan, it is argued, the managers of America's basic industries have panicked and backed out of the contest. Instead of funding R&D and plant modernization – which might have allowed their industries to retain a competitive edge – managers diverted their declining profits into mergers, takeovers and other kinds of non-productive, but stock market-pleasing, investments. In this way the managers saved their own jobs, but consigned the industries in which their companies had made their name to impoverishment and decline.

Leveraged buy-outs and junk bonds

The end of the 1980s saw a surge in leveraged buy-outs and the issuance of so-called junk bonds. This process accelerated after the October 1987 "crash," when many companies saw the chance to buy their own stock at what they regarded as low prices and thus increase their earnings per share. The critics of such financing point out that the substantial increase in the indebtedness of US industry is fine when the economy is booming, but that a recession would interrupt cash flow and thus create substantial difficulties for the companies. The popularity of junk bonds derives from their high yield, which generally compensates for their greater rate of default. "Junk" is in fact a misnomer, since these bonds are often issued by companies which are perfectly sound, but which have not achieved debt ratings from Moody's or Standard & Poors'. One study shows that companies that issue such high-yield securities grow faster than the rest of the manufacturing sector and, despite taking on workers at a higher rate than in the rest of the economy, also have faster-growing labour productivity. The proponents of these bonds argue that the need to pay substantial amounts of interest concentrates managers' minds on making the best use of resources – be that selling off subsidiaries that are not performing or cutting out activities not essential to the efficient running of the enterprise (see *Financial markets*).

Growth industries

Ever since the turn of the century, the focus of the American economy has been shifting away from manufacturing toward the service industries. But after World War II, the pace of this shift accelerated rapidly. In 1948 the goods-producing industries (agriculture, mining, manufacturing and construction) produced 46% of America's GNP; the service inudstries (including trade, communications, banking, entertainment, social services) accounted for the other 54%.

Services Now, the service sector's share is more than 66%. The "post-industrial society" may be said to have finally arrived in 1981, when, for the first time, there were more Americans employed in services than in manufacturing.

High technology Clean, sophisticated and expensive, the "high-tech" industries are seen as one of the great hopes for America's industrial future. Between 1982 and 1985, when all other exports fell 10% in volume, the export of high-tech goods such as computers, telecommunications equipment, chemicals, aircraft, plastics and drugs rose by 30%. Indeed, America's high-tech industries have never had a negative balance of trade, and are the group most likely to benefit from the decline of the dollar from its highs of the 1970s.

Productivity While America's fall may have dented its ego and standard of living, there is reason to believe that the US economy will emerge, not weaker, but stronger, leaner and hungrier. For example, while

American productivity may not be increasing as rapidly as that of other industrialized countries, its advance is not insignificant. Manufacturing productivity rose by 4.7% a year during the 1980s, compared with 1.7% in the rest of the non-farm economy, with the biggest rise coming in the oldest and hardest-hit industries.

The fall in the dollar in 1985-87 prompted a massive surge in manufactured exports, with US producers able to increase their market share in almost all sectors.

Vast resources The most efficient American industries may never be able to undersell foreign competitors whose labor costs are a tenth or a twentieth of their own, but the USA still has the world's largest economy and has vast human, technological and natural resources. The USA will probably never regain the uncontested industrial hegemony it enjoyed after the war, but it is a long way from becoming a decadent, depressed and ineffectual has-been.

Foreign investment

Even if many Americans remain sceptical about their country's future, those from abroad still give it the thumbs up. The continued strength of the US economy led foreign investors to increase their direct and portfolio investment in the USA through the latter half of the 1980s. Indeed, the country needed their capital to finance its substantial current account deficits.

However, that surge of investment interest led in turn to fears of the "selling of America", fears that too much of the country's industrial might was being sold on the cheap to foreign buyers. Statistics claim that some 16% of US GNP is produced by foreign-owned assets, and that over one-third of the real estate in Los Angeles, Washington and Houston belongs to foreigners.

Some states have passed ordinances preventing the purchase by non-residents of substantial parcels of land (see *Law*).

A debtor nation

Total foreign direct investment in the USA totalled $329bn at book values at the end of 1988. Of that, some $121bn was invested in manufacturing, the rest in other sectors and real estate. Add foreign ownership of securities and bank deposits, and the total rises to $1,786bn. Total US assets abroad were only $1,254bn, leading to the claim that the USA was the world's largest debtor nation, owing about $532.5bn to the rest of the world. All that has happened, however, is that non-US companies are now doing what American firms have been doing for years – buying into strong companies in good markets. Total US investment abroad at the end of 1988 was $327bn, so that the net position was only slightly negative: a shock for Americans, who for years have been used to their country enjoying a strong net foreign asset position. However, despite the concern about foreign control of US industry, Morgan Guaranty estimates that it exceeds 30% only in chemicals and 20% only in the non-metallic minerals and primary metals sectors and the proportion of foreign economies owned by US companies is still much higher than the share of the US economy held by foreigners. Thus the British, the biggest foreign investors in the USA, with holdings equivalent to 1.7% of US GNP, have in turn 6.6% of their economy controlled by US firms.

The backlash The groundswell of opinion against foreign investment began to emerge with the 1988 Trade Act, which includes the "Exon-Florio amendment," calling for the review of any foreign investment with national security implications. It made itself felt again in 1989, when the Foreign Ownership Disclosure bill commanded much support in Congress. This bill proposes a ruling whereby foreign holdings of shares in US companies would have to be declared to the Securities and Exchange Commission.

Leading companies

International Business Machines

Perhaps America's most admired company, IBM makes everything from typewriters to photocopiers. But its most important product is still the computer. It remains pre-eminent in the mainframe sector, although that sector's importance has declined in the face of competition from personal computers and workstations. IBM has been able to establish its leadership in the personal computer field, despite strong competition from Compaq and Apple. It now has a range of machines, from mainframes through mid-size computers down to PCs, virtually all of which run on the same operating system. It is also strong in the software market, in line with its policy of moving into high-margin segments of the computer business.

Exxon

Formerly Standard Oil of New Jersey, Exxon is the most substantial fragment of the oil empire founded by John D. Rockefeller in 1870 and split up by the Supreme Court in 1911. Exxon is the world's largest driller, refiner and distributor of petroleum products, although it is being fast caught by Shell. Nevertheless, it has more than 40 refineries in over 20 nations and subsidiaries or affiliates in a further 58. Altogether, Exxon derives 65% of its oil and 75% of its sales from abroad. The company also has important interests in chemicals, minerals, electrical equipment, telecommunications, computers and even real estate.

General Electric

GE is best known as a manufacturer of lightbulbs and appliances, but its acquisition of RCA in 1985 brought it NBC, the largest US television and radio network. It also owns the investment bank Kidder Peabody. In the 1980s it sold off many of its subsidiaries to concentrate on some 14 core businesses. Among those are aircraft engines (where it is the world's largest company), plastics, engineering automation and medical diagnostic imaging equipment. It is still one of the world's largest companies in its traditional businesses of lighting, home appliances and defence electronics.

American Telephone & Telegraph

When AT&T's monopoly over the US telephone service was curtailed, by an order to divest its local telephone subsidiaries, it lost about two-thirds of its $80bn assets. In exchange, the company was allowed to move into new products, including computers and office equipment, but these have failed to make any significant contribution to profitability. Over 90% of the company's profits come from its long-distance telephone business, where it is still supreme in the residential sector, but facing severe competition in the more profitable corporate sector.

Philip Morris

The Philip Morris management has diversified the original tobacco business by some major acquisitions. In 1985 it acquired General Foods for $5.8bn, and topped that in 1988 with its $13.1bn takeover of Kraft. That has left the company with some of the world's major brand names in food – Birds Eye, Maxwell House, Sanka, Kraft, Miller Beer. Its food business is now the third largest in the world, even though less than 20% of 1987 sales came from that sector. Despite the declining importance of tobacco to the company's total sales, this still provides the bulk of its profits, thanks to the success of its Marlboro brand.

Merck

The world's leading pharmaceutical company, Merck has the highest price/earnings ratio among the top ten. Vasotec, its anti-hypertension product, is number five in the top-selling drugs worldwide, and Merck has another five in the top 50; altogether 15 Merck products have sales in excess of $100m each. Its research effort (at $500m annually, employing 4,600 people, the largest in the industry) has produced several new products, such as Prinivil, Mecavor and Zocor, which are expected to maintain the company's predominance through the 1990s.

E.I. Du Pont de Nemours

Du Pont is generally known as the developer of such chemical and fiber products as Teflon, Dacron and Lucite. Recent notoriety has come from its pre-eminence in the production of chlorofluorocarbons (CFCs). The company, having recognized the threat to the ozone layer from CFCs, has led the way in seeking an environmentally friendly alternative. Du Pont is the world's fifth largest manufacturer of chemicals, from which it earns good profits. But it has suffered from weaknesses in its other activities, such as oil and gas and biomedicines. Its purchase of Conoco in 1981 was designed to guarantee supplies of feedstock, but the subsequent oil price fall has meant only small returns on its $7.8bn investment.

General Motors

In 1988, GM's sales were $110bn, but it is a measure of its problems that it had a market value less than Merck, a company with one twentieth of its sales. Those problems are overcapacity, Japanese competition and a perceived decline in quality. GM used to make half the cars sold in America, and only in 1988 did it recognize that a market share of one third was a more realistic goal. So it closed factories and shed a quarter of its white collar workers. As it entered the 1990s it still needed to cut capacity, perhaps by as much as 1m cars annually. It also needed more flexibility, with its one-plant, one-product strategy inappropriate in a rapidly changing market.

Leading US companies

	Market capital $bn	1988 Sales $bn
IBM	65	60
Exxon	55	87
General Electric	49	39
AT&T	38	35
Philip Morris	32	32
Merck	28	6
Du Pont	26	33
General Motors	25	110
BellSouth	24	14
Ford Motor	24	93

Source: *Business Week*

BellSouth

BellSouth, an amalgamation of two former Bell System local telephone service subsidiaries, South Central Bell and Southern Bell, came into being as a part of the court-ordered break-up of AT&T. Since then it has proved to be one of the more internationally oriented of the "Baby Bells," with ventures in Europe and China. It also wants a major share of the emerging US cellular telephone market, and in 1988 made a well-publicized but ultimately abortive takeover bid for Mobile Communications Corporation of America. It also has a 20% share of the Yellow Pages market, often competing in other companies' territory.

Ford Motor

Ford was able to gain market share in the late 1980s, in contrast to GM, although it too faced increasingly stiff competition from imports and the US plants of Japanese companies. But it still had to close some factories, and it also cancelled an ambitious $5bn project to build a new family of trucks and vans. Instead it was spending substantial sums on revamping its capital equipment in an attempt to cut costs and improve quality. Ford also has a strong presence in Europe, with 10% of the car market and an even higher share of the commercial vehicle sector.

Telecommunications

Radical new departures in the US telecommunications business have followed the end of the giant American Telephone and Telegraph Company's 70-year monopoly of the telephone service in 1984. With AT&T facing competition in the long-distance telephone market, call rates have been driven down by 50% since deregulation. Its former subsidiaries, the "Baby Bells," have been active in developing the US cellular telephone services. Some of them, and AT&T, want to enter the electronic publishing field or to move into cable television. Since AT&T is only now beginning to react to this increased competition, the telecommunications industry will continue to see substantial changes.

The monopoly is broken

After battling the Department of Justice for close to a decade to protect its monopoly, AT&T finally succumbed in 1983. But the blow struck by the trustbusters was far from fatal. Although AT&T lost the 24 regional subsidiaries that provided the cheap local telephone service, it retained its most profitable division – its long-distance service – and was freed to move into new spheres of activity such as making computers (see *Leading companies*).

Baby Bells Consolidated into seven regional companies ('Baby Bells") providing local telephone services, the subsidiaries cast off by AT&T have also profited from the deal. Local rates formerly pegged artificially low are now allowed to float gradually upward and AT&T and other long-distance providers pay the Baby Bells fees for connecting local users to long-distance lines.

Despite government concern that the Baby Bells may exploit their protected status to subsidize other lines of business and undercut competition, they are already beginning to compete directly with their former parent in long-distance service and equipment manufacturing. They have also moved aggressively overseas, into cable television, cellular networks and equipment sales. Wall Street likes them: six of the Baby Bells, together with AT&T, are in the top 40 companies, in terms of market capitalization.

The independents

AT&T's monopoly on long-distance telephone calls was brought to an end as long ago as 1969, and there are now more than 50 independent companies providing a long-distance service.

Fierce competition has pushed down AT&T's share of the long-distance market, especially in the more profitable corporate sector. But AT&T has reacted by investing in fiber optics to improve quality and lower transmission costs. So, too, have its major competitors, MCI and US Sprint. These three dominate the long-distance sector, with the other companies either small systems or merely re-selling chunks of discounted service from the larger carriers.

At the local level, there are still some 1,400 independent suppliers of local telephone services. These range in size from the company servicing its local community, to GTE ($16bn sales in 1988) and United Telecommunications (4m subscribers).

Cellular take-off

The fastest growing sector is the cellular network, with the country divided into operating areas with two licensees – in each case the local Baby Bell and another company. Although this second company is often another Baby Bell (Southwestern Bell in Chicago, for example) the leader in this sector is McCaw Cellular Communications.

Oil and chemicals

The fortunes of the US oil and chemical industries are deeply intertwined. Du Pont, the nation's premier chemical producer, owns a major oil company, Conoco, while Exxon, the giant of oil firms, owns a chemical company which is in the top 15 world chemical firms and one of the world's largest producers of ethylene. Both industries now face the 1990s with some trepidation; the oil majors because they fear the recent strength of the oil price will not last, while the chemical companies fear a world slowdown that will leave the industry with excess capacity once again.

Oil

The United States' oil industry is big business. More than half the top 20 US companies in the Fortune 500 list are in oil, and the biggest oil company, Exxon, has yearly sales dwarfing the GNP of many countries. But the see-sawing world oil prices in the 1980s have had a traumatic effect on the US oil business.

Domestic crisis Companies reliant on US production were devastated by the sharp downturn in prices in 1986. Many US fields were developed in the 1970s, when the oil price rose at one time to $40 a barrel; they proved uneconomic once the price fell. US wells still lift only 14 barrels a day on average, compared with 5,000 barrels a day for Gulf wells. For "stripper" wells, which lift under ten barrels a day and make up about 11% of total US production, costs can run up to $15 a barrel, more than the price a barrel was fetching at certain times in 1986. Large numbers of stripper wells and heavy-oil producing properties were shut down, and the number of producing wells fell by 5%. The number of new completed wells drilled has also fallen, so that as older wells become uneconomic to run, the volume of US production (already 13% below its peak) is likely to fall further. Nevertheless, the USA remains a substantial force in the oil market, with domestic production representing 16% of world output, outweighed by domestic demand equal to a quarter of world output. The US economy uses almost as much oil as Western Europe and Japan combined, and its imports represent a quarter of total oil trade. However, its reserves are down by one third on their historical peak.

Scraping the barrel The downturn in home production and the 1986 collapse of oil prices have accelerated the cuts in capital expenditure by US oil companies, started when oil prices first began to fall in the early 1980s. There was no major recovery in those expenditures even when prices recovered. Intimidated by the activities of corporate raiders, the oil companies have been redirecting resources away from exploration and redevelopment into the hands of shareholders. They have achieved this in two principal ways: by large-scale buy-outs of other oil companies (Chevron bought Gulf and Texaco bought Getty); and by repurchasing shares (as with Atlantic Richfield and Exxon). The debt thus incurred is often reduced by sales of assets. The oil companies are also reversing the largely disastrous 1970s trend towards diversification and abandoning other operations such as hard minerals, petrochemicals, coal, synthetic fuels and insurance.

Downstream boom In contrast, the downstream end of the petroleum business, refining and marketing, is still buoyant. Lower prices and the reluctance of US tourists to go abroad because of terrorism and the lower dollar have boosted domestic demand for gasoline, helping integrated companies that both produce and distribute to ride out the crisis better than those that only produce.

Chemicals

Throughout the 1970s, the chemical industry, like the oil industry, anticipated a future of surging demand and profits. Like the oil industry, it was disappointed. Chemical companies coped with falling demand in the early 1980s by slowing down production to keep pace. But by the mid-1980s the overcapacity built up by the industry during the previous decade began to drag on profits. Until then the chemical companies would have achieved a better return on their investment by buying US Treasury securities.

However, the subsequent surge in economic growth both at home and in the rest of the world helped to boost demand for chemicals and thus also to raise prices and profits.

World position The US chemical industry has sales of around $250bn, and is responsible for some 15% of world exports of chemicals. The industry boasts five of the top 20 chemical companies by sales. It does even better in productivity stakes: there, seven out of the top ten companies are American.

US firms use fewer employees than their European counterparts, while in Japan many of the functions carried out by US company employees are performed by the trading houses. Profitability and margins generally are also higher in the USA than in the rest of the world, although often more variable. The US companies' research and development is also improving: the number of marketable chemicals discovered each year doubled during the 1980s.

A cyclical industry Having made a return to profitability, however, the industry may be laying the ground for a further cutback in profits later on. Additions to capacity now may be merely the cause of lower profits in the future. If all announced increases in US capacity in ethylene (a standard indicator of chemical fortunes) are actually set in place, then overcapacity is almost certain to arise.

Since the US market has many more buyers than the European market for most chemicals, the forces of demand and supply are more likely to impinge on the US industry than they do in Europe, where the industry is much more integrated.

Saudi competition The major chemical firms recognize that they are at a long-term disadvantage compared with the hydrocarbon-rich countries of the Gulf. Saudi Arabia, for example, has given high priority to the completion of 12 large plants which will enable it to meet 5% of the world's petrochemical demand. The result is that, to avoid competing directly, the American chemical industry is generally moving in the direction of specialty chemicals and away from basic petrochemical production.

But the trend is not total: although Du Pont and Monsanto are moving into pharmaceuticals and agricultural chemicals, Dow has stayed in (and made substantial profits from) commodity products.

The environmental lobby The US public has an extremely ambivalent attitude toward the chemical companies. On the one hand, household products such as Dow's Saran Wrap (plastic wrap) and American Cyanamid's Simonize car wax are familiar and widely used. On the other hand, chemical companies have been criticized for causing air pollution, for improperly dumping toxic wastes and for manufacturing war chemicals. Nearly all the chemical companies have had confrontations with environmental groups and federal regulators. Although not always strictly enforced, the laws designed to curb environmental pollution have considerable public support, and chemical companies are sure to fall under increasingly stringent restrictions on the manufacture and transportation of their products, at least within the boundaries of the United States.

Pharmaceuticals and biotechnology

By far the world's largest drug seller, the USA still holds almost a quarter of the world's pharmaceuticals market. Nearly half of the world's top 30 companies are American. But the increasingly lengthy process of obtaining government approval for new drugs, together with the $5bn spent by the industry on R&D, has not been reflected in substantial numbers of new products. The industry is under threat from generic drugs, but it is fighting back by pressing for some prescription drugs to be made freely available over the counter (OTC). New, more flexible laws and new fields of activity, especially biotechnology, may breathe new life into it.

Pharmaceuticals

For more than a decade the US pharmaceutical industry's profits have been rising at least 50% faster than those of all other industries. The steady increase in the number of Americans 65 years old and older has already been a big boost to the pharmaceutical industry; senior citizens make up 12% of the population, but account for 25% of all prescription drug sales. The number of physicians increased by 30% during the 1980s with the greatest growth in such specialties as family practice, in which a large proportion of prescriptions are written.

Soaring development costs In the past, drug prices lagged behind the general inflation rate, but in the 1980s they soared, increasing by as much as six times the Consumer Price Index. This rapid rise in prices has provoked congressional criticism of the industry for – in the words of Representative Henry A. Waxman, of California – "increasing its profits at the expense of the sick, the poor and the elderly." The drug makers protest that they are forced to raise prices because of the increasing cost of new product development.

Counting failures, it now takes an average of eight years and over $100m to bring a new drug successfully on to the market. Much of the added time and expense is the inevitable result of the increasing complexity of new drugs. But the stringent requirements of the US Food and Drug Administration have also contributed. The FDA requires drug makers to test their products first on animals, then on healthy human volunteers, and then on large samples of the population the drug is intended to treat. Drug companies claim that testing now eats up half of their products' 17-year patents, and so half the time when they have the exclusive right to market the drug, free of competition – the "useful life" of the drug. Congress, fearing that the United States is losing its long-standing competitive edge over Japan and Western Europe, came to the aid of the drug companies in the mid-1980s by enacting a law that will extend the patent life for new drugs for an additional five years. However, although the USA still provides more new drugs to the world market than any other country, it is being caught by Japan and West Germany. The number of US products in the top 50 best-selling drugs worldwide in 1987 was 20, three fewer than in 1986 .

Generic drugs – drugs no longer in patent – are now seen as the future money-spinners of the pharmaceuticals industry. Since the original version of the drug has already been thoroughly tested, it is comparatively easy for generic manufacturers to get FDA approval. Unencumbered by the developer's massive R&D, approval and advertising expenses, the generic manufacturer can market its copy for a tenth of the price of the original. Sales of generic drugs were worth about $6bn in 1987, and one estimate projects a 17% real rate of increase to $13bn (1987 prices) by 1992. The drugs due to come off patent by 1992 accounted for $5bn in sales in 1987. Factors driving the growth of generic drugs sales include pressure from politicians and insurers to reduce the cost of health care, and favourable legislation such as the 1984 Waxman-Hatch Act, which has eased the approval procedure for generic drugs. Insurance companies, and employers who provide medical coverage for their employees, are now encouraging patients to ask their doctors to write prescriptions for generic drugs. The Blue Cross and Blue Shield health insurance plans in California, Florida, Iowa and Michigan are offering incentives to choose generics.

The drug companies have been fighting competition from generics partly by pricing their patented drugs higher to maximize profits during the patent life and partly by entering the market themselves. Major brand-name manufacturers such as Parke-Davis, Pfizer, Smith Kline and French and Wyeth Laboratories have all moved into the generic business. Another avenue has been heavy advertising of prescription drugs to consumers, putting doctors under pressure to prescribe in line with patients' wishes.

Biotechnology

Slower to take off than initially anticipated, biotechnology remains the most exciting and potentially profitable division of the pharmaceuticals industry. From a base of virtually zero in 1980 the market for genetically engineered drugs and chemicals had expanded to $500m by 1988, but early forecasts of $5bn sales by the early 1990s appear over-optimistic. Although there has been extensive biotechnological research into pesticides and other chemicals, the bulk of activity is in the pharmaceutical area.

There are about 15 biotechnology-based drugs on sale, the leaders being Activase, developed by Genentech against blood clots, and Roferon, developed by Hoffman-LaRoche for the treatment of cancer. A further 80 formulations were undergoing clinical trials or awaiting government approval in 1989. The initial excitement about biotechnological development of drugs has been dampened because of the need to go through the same lengthy trial process as mainstream pharmaceutical preparations.

At present there are some 300 US firms involved in commercial biotechnology, about half of them in just four states: California, Massachusetts, New Jersey and New York. The total expenditure on biotechnology research is estimated at $2bn annually, and some $3bn has ben raised to start up new companies. By far the majority of firms are small and were established after 1975, with a flurry of new starts between 1979 and 1983. But about 100 of the firms are older, more established pharmaceutical and chemical companies, such as Bristol-Myers, Eli Lilly and Hoffman-LaRoche, which have slid into the field by establishing in-house research groups, or by funding research and engaging in joint ventures with smaller firms. Alliances with large corporations have recently become the dominant mode of financing for small biotech firms, which often have difficulties meeting their huge R&D costs on their own. One of the problems for biotech firms is that patent protection for biotechnological preparations, which by their nature must be derived from naturally occurring substances, has yet to be firmly established.

Monoclonal The industry's biggest commercial success to date is monoclonal antibodies. Sales of monoclonal products bring in more than $130m and are expected to earn $2.5bn by 1990.

Other fields Biotechnology has considerable potential too in less publicized fields than drugs. Breeds of farm plants resistant to drought, disease and herbicides as well as toxic waste-eaters for the chemical industry, are all being developed.

The motor industry

In the past the greatest threat to the US automobile producers came from Japanese imports. Now there are more Japanese manufacturing plants in the USA than there are domestic producers, and it is these "transplant" operations that have taken market share from both the domestic Big Three and from European imports. That process is expected to continue in the future, and the prospect has forced domestic producers to cut back on capacity and costs, and to look for other ways to improve development and marketing. So the Big Three are essentially out of entry-level cars and the Japanese and the Europeans are becoming stronger in the luxury market. This leaves the mass market as the battle ground between domestic producers and a still substantial level of imports.

Modernization

The mid-1980s saw US automobile manufacturers energetically modernizing and automating plants to bring down unit costs to a level at which they could compete with the Japanese. But in recent years the problem has been that even a booming market was unable to absorb all the capacity from the domestic producers. General Motors, in particular, took some time to come to terms with the drop in its market share from a traditional one-half of the market to one-third. Now that they have accepted that the old times are past, the US-owned companies are adapting to the new market.

General Motors' vision of a major expansion of its productive capacity and sales has been abandoned; before 1993 it may have to lose 100,000 employees and close perhaps five or six major plants. It may also have to accept that dispersing its marketing effort between five brand names, for virtually identical cars, may be counter-productive. Some of the most famous brand names in US industrial history may have become merely an echo of the past by the time GM's rationalization is over.

Ford has give up its strategic target of overtaking GM; instead it is concentrating on becoming the lowest-cost producer in the USA. That would be no mean achievement, for the best plants in the United States are as efficient and as profitable as any in the world. Ford's target is to cut $5bn off worldwide operating costs by 1992, and US operations will have to contribute a substantial part of that saving.

Chrysler has already been through the cost-cutting phase in the early 1980s, under Lee Iacocca, after the company had seemingly been going bust, and a further rationalization after the takeover of American Motors. Its grip on market share in the car market looks shaky, but it has done well in the offroad and family van segments. And its previous cost cutting means that its breakeven volume is half of what it was 10 years ago.

Cost cutting Besides rationalizing their plants, US car makers are making cuts right across the board. They are buying an increasing proportion of their parts abroad, and now they are also importing and selling vehicles made by minority-owned affiliates in low-wage countries.

Diversification Car makers are also diversifying. GM has always had a big finance subsidiary, but now Chrysler has moved into finance to become one of the nation's largest money companies by purchasing E.F. Hutton Credit Corp and Bank of America's Finance America Corp. It has also bought Gulfstream Aerospace Corp, while GM holds Hughes Aircraft Co and Electronic Data Systems. As one industry wag put it, GM is becoming a lot more General and a lot less Motors. Ford has bought First Nationwide Financial

Corp, holding company of the ninth largest savings and loan association.

Saturated market

The US car market made huge advances during the 1980s. Sales increased from 8m vehicles in 1982 to a peak of 11.5m in 1986, and productivity hit new record levels. But this buoyant situation may have made the car makers, especially GM, overconfident; and while the car market has remained above 10m vehicles annually – 10.6m were sold in 1988 – the US firms (particularly GM) have been plagued by overproduction and the consequent need to offer expensive sales incentives to shift production. The situation was slightly eased by the closure of Volkswagen's US production, but that has been more than compensated for by the steady growth of Japanese transplant production.

Immigrant plants

Originally designed to circumvent the voluntary restraint agreements on Japanese exports to the USA, the capacity of Japanese production plants in the USA has moved to 14% of total domestic production. Some of that output has been exported to Europe (some even to Japan), but the bulk has been used to boost the Japanese firms' market share in the USA. The strategy has been so successful that Honda and Toyota are now not far behind Chrysler, and may possibly overtake it by the mid-1990s.

Already Japanese cars (imports and domestic production) take a quarter of the US market, and that proportion can be expected to rise. The Korean manufacturer Hyundai has also opened a US manufacturing plant, and there are Japanese-US joint ventures.

Mazda, which has built a plant in Michigan, has a joint marketing deal with Ford, while Toyota has successfully combined with GM to build the Chevrolet Nova.

Prospects

The entire automotive industry, regardless of individual successes, is heading for a squeeze produced by forces beyond its control. The driving age population of the USA will grow at only a 0.8% annual rate in the 1990s, as opposed to 2% a year in the 1970s and 1% annually in the 1980s. This slackening trend, coupled with the slow growth of personal disposable income, means that car sales in the United States will probably hover around the present level of 10–12m a year. There is still a threat of overcapacity in the US market in the 1990s.

The number of different models of cars and lightweight trucks on the American market has risen from 190 in the mid 1970s to over 250, and the prospects are for an even greater variety in future. As the competition between domestic and foreign producers intensifies, the consumer is likely to be assailed by a wide range of incentives to buy, and increasing choice.

Low maintenance is also held out as a carrot to the consumer. The auto industry publicity mills are already talking about the 1990s as "the decade of the defect-free car!" when cars, apparently, will become as reliable as televisions and computers. But the Big Three may well find an increasing proportion of their profits stemming from non-automobile businesses.

Trucking future

In the truck market, the prospect that may transform the industry is the "standardized truck." At present, buyers of medium and heavy trucks can customize their vehicles by specifying which components from a wide variety of manufacturers go into their assembly. The standardized truck would reduce the buyer's options but also lower the truck's price by 25%. It is a Japanese and European innovation, however, so if consumers like it, US truck makers could suffer.

Defense and aerospace

The US defense industry is a leading supplier of arms not just to its domestic military but to the rest of the world, while the civil aerospace sector is a major supplier to the world's airlines. Aerospace exports account for 10% of exports, with about 40% of that represented by civil aircraft. US tank manufacturers lead the world, as do US supersonic aircraft and missile suppliers.

US government budget allocations for defense spending fell in real terms in the last four years of the 1980s. The pressures to cut the overall budget deficit, together with the easing of some East-West tensions, leave defense spending vulnerable. A consolation for the sector as a whole, though not for individual companies, is that the civil aerospace market boomed just as military spending cooled.

Military spending

Restrictions on the overall level of the defense budget have forced the Pentagon to change its spending patterns. The cost of an all-volunteer army, plus a greater emphasis on conventional weapons, means multi-billion dollar weapons systems are no longer given precedence. In the past such systems have failed to do the task intended, and there have been scandals over the cost of spare parts. The Pentagon now gives greater emphasis to updating existing planes and missiles, which has meant substantial opportunities for the defense electronics and avionics sector.

Rationalization expected The lack of orders for new planes and missiles was a substantial shock to US aerospace contractors, since 60% of their business came from Uncle Sam. Manufacturers are now much more likely to face cancellation of programmes, or purchases spread over a longer period. The industry expects substantial rationalization, with some major companies merging with others, or even going out of business altogether.

The FSX project The threat US companies fear most is that from Japan, even though the latter has no major presence in the sector. There was considerable opposition to the insistence of the Japanese on developing their own fighter, the FSX, rather than buying off the shelf from US firms. The 40% US participation in the venture assuaged some of the criticism, but US companies remain wary of allowing too much technical know-how to be transferred to the Japanese.

Civil aerospace

The civil aerospace market is booming. Boeing forecasts that the world's airlines will spend $516bn over the period to 2005, for about 8,400 planes. The boom arises because of two factors: a general increase in purchases of aircraft by the airlines to boost their capacity to meet increasing demand for air travel, and the need for current fleets of ageing aircraft to be replaced.

Noise restrictions and other environmental factors, together with a trend towards larger aircraft as airspace in the USA and Europe becomes more congested, have led commercial airlines to step up their orders for new planes.

Space

The Strategic Defense Initiative, popularly known as Star Wars, has come under pressure from political opponents at home and abroad. Research funding continues for the project, though at relatively low levels. If the project were ever to come to fruition, then there could be $500bn-worth of contracts for the industry. But budget constraints and a thawing in relations with the Soviet bloc make that less likely. The research may nevertheless have benefits that spill over into other space programs. The Space Shuttle has resumed flights, and the greater civilian interest in space also promises considerable profits for US firms. Space revenues already account for 20% of sales and double-digit growth is expected.

The major companies

Boeing, the industry giant, has experienced a substantial upturn in sales. This has led in recent years to problems it does not usually face – a decline in quality control and late delivery of promised aircraft. Those problems should ease as its Seattle workforce of more than 100,000, many of them recent recruits, mature with the company.

It still has 60% of the world civil aircraft market, despite the challenge of Europe's Airbus Industrie. It has more than 5,000 aircraft flying, and airlines' long experience with Boeing products give it a substantial product edge. Its order book now stretches through to the end of the century, and it is already working on larger versions of its 767 and of its new 747-400.

McDonnell Douglas ranks number two behind Boeing in the US industry, but has a much higher reliance (65%) on orders from the military, through planes, missiles and space technology. That proportion is falling as the sales of its MD-80 and its MD-11 (due in 1990) expand with the general demand for civil aircraft. But keeping up with Boeing is not easy, and Douglas has sought cooperation with France's Matra, and its helicopter division with the UK's Westland. Industry rumours persist that Douglas will join with Airbus to develop a rival to the Boeing 747.

Lockheed moved out of the commercial aviation business in the early 1980s, but continued to make substantial sales to the military of its C-5A transport aircraft. Once that contract ended, the company found it difficult to maintain its former level of sales. It is still heavily involved in missiles and space technology and has expanded its electronics capability. It is also seeking links with European aviation companies.

Other major companies Rockwell, chief contractor for the Space Shuttle, is now enjoying a resurgence with the resumption of that program; it suffered when the end of its B-1B contract coincided with the hiatus in the shuttle program after the 1986 Challenger disaster that killed seven astronauts. General Dynamics, an airframe manufacturer, is also heavily involved in missile technology and the F-16 fighter program. Grumman was badly hit by budget cuts, after the cancellation of its A6 bomber and doubts about the F-14 project; its previous successes include carrier-based Tomcat fighter aircraft. Raytheon is a major contractor in the missile program and has the contract to modernize air traffic control systems. Northrop suffered from the slowdown of development of the B-2 stealth bomber. Martin Marietta is a leader in defense electronics, missiles and space technology, while General Electric's engine division has boosted its share of the commercial jet engine market at the expense of United Technologies' Pratt and Whitney division.

Helicopters

More than 40% of the world market for helicopters is to be found in the USA, with more than half of that coming from the military. The four major US manufacturers – Bell, Boeing, Sikorski and McDonnell Douglas – have been hit by the defense cuts. The cancellation of government funding for the revolutionary Bell/Boeing V222 Osprey tilt-rotor project underlined the uncertainty injected into the market by such cutbacks. But the sector can take comfort in the fact that the 3,000 obsolete helicopters held by the military will have to be replaced soon.

Computers and software

The computer industry has been dominated for years by the giant IBM, known as the "Big Blue," although a number of new companies have displayed spectacular growth for a time and have been greeted as its potential rivals. Some of those are now in trouble, and even IBM itself finds that it is no longer the leader in every sector, but merely one market leader among several. However, US companies still dominate the world market, although Americans worry that the Japanese will threaten their supremacy in the supercomputer field.

Computers

US computer companies have until now dominated the world industry. The sheer size of the American economy, and the substantial demand for computer power from both the government and the private sector, have given them a market base on which to build global domination. The competition between the US companies themselves has been intense, with firms such as Apple and Sun springing from nowhere to become major world companies. Meanwhile, several former stars, including Honeywell and NCR, are no longer in the top rank.

Growth in the mainframe market is now very sluggish, simply because many tasks previously performed by the larger computers can be done on smaller machines. Moreover, IBM's success in the past is such that many of its customers now have more capacity than they need. But IBM suffered because many of its machines could not be interconnected, and this became a liability as more and more businesses wanted machines which could exchange information.

IBM also failed to spot the market for personal computers (PCs), pioneered by Apple and others. Once it did come into the market with its own PC, and established a standard, then the phenomenon of "clones" was born – with other firms copying, improving, undercutting and eventually outselling IBM's machines. IBM has since recovered some ground with its new PS/2 range of PCs. That has not stopped the cloning in turn of the PS/2.

The next development was that of very powerful chips which offer high performance at low prices. They are typically used in engineering workstations, themselves used for computer-aided design/calculation.

The latest battle is over which operating system will become the industry leader. The MSDOS system, used in the early IBM PCs and their clones, and Apple's Macintosh system, are now threatened by IBM's OS/2 and by Unix. The latter is favoured by many firms, but their inability to agree on a common Unix system may allow IBM to retain the initiative. Compaq and others are also promoting the Extended Industry Standard Architecture as an alternative to IBM's ideas.

Computer companies

IBM "Nobody ever got fired for buying IBM" used to be the Big Blue's line. But until recently IBM, although still dominating the industry, seemed to be in difficulties. Profits fell in the mid-1980s and, even though they then recovered, the bulk came from its overseas sales rather than the US market. Part of the problem resulted from the increased pressure felt by IBM in the fast-growing PC market. It started a large-scale cost-cutting and re-investment program but it also opened its systems network architecture to non-IBM hardware and software.

Digital Equipment Corporation found its market niche provided by the lack of connectivity between IBM products. It has become the networking leader and in the process the number two company, with sales exceeding $15bn. Minicomputers provide the bulk of its equipment sales. It was able to challenge IBM on its own patch with the VAX 8800, while also moving into the intelligent workstations sector. But it still excels in putting applications which were formerly on mainframes on to its minicomputers.

Unisys, the company formed by the merger of Burroughs and Sperry, has suffered in recent years because of its reliance on the mainframe and mid-range computer market. The latter especially has been hit by the growth of the workstation sector, led by firms such as Sun or Apollo, and by the appearance of superminis which have aggressively high performance. The company may well decide that it has to grow, if necessary by acquisition, in order to survive.

Apple has recovered some of its shine after a bad patch in the mid-1980s when founder Stephen Jobs was forced out of the company. It still controls about one-eighth of the PC market worldwide, and its Macintosh series is much more attractive to businesses, especially in the area of desktop publishing.

Compaq computers are the pre-eminent examples of IBM-compatible machines. But the company was also the first to introduce a PC based on the Intel 80386 processor. That helped it to gain a reputation for technological leadership, and a competitive start on IBM in the high-performance PC sector that the Big Blue will find difficult to recover. Its lap-top products were also well ahead of the market, although there it faces the challenge of the Japanese makers, such as Toshiba and NEC.

Sun Microsystems has benefited from the rapid growth in the workstations market, which averaged 100% a year through the 1980s. Mainly used by engineers, scientists and financial analysts, workstations have the potential to be used for non-scientific applications and this has made Sun, and its major competitor Apollo, high-fliers in the computer world.

Falling stars As some makers have risen, so have others, including Data General, CDC and Wang declined. In fact, CDC finally left the supercomputer market and Wang has seen its pre-eminence in word processing undercut by the move to PC-based systems rather than mini-based systems.

Supercomputers

One of the major growth sectors in computing could be supercomputers. The US firm Cray Research now faces increasing competition from the Japanese companies in this area, and lack of opportunities for Cray to make inroads into the Japanese market is a potential source of friction between the two nations.

Software

The microcomputer software industry consists of a thousand or so small firms dotted mainly around San Francisco Bay area or along Route 128 outside Boston. Apart from Microsoft, the company that provided the operating system for IBM-compatible PCs, most are just one-product companies. Micropro International found that success in one field (with its "Wordstar" word-processing program) does not guarantee success in another. Lotus Development has had similar problems in developing a follow-up to its 1-2-3 integrated spreadsheet program. In the PC market, competition is forcing software companies to add more and more features to their best-selling programs, increasingly taxing the memory limits of the MSDOS operating system.

Copyright Apple Computer, in its lawsuits against Hewlett Packard and Microsoft, has argued that particular features of programs can be subject to copyright, though that battle is not yet over. Action has been threatened by IBM against any infringement of copyright of its OS/2 operating system.

The Political Scene

The government of the nation

With an electorate of more than 170m, the USA is the second largest democratic republic in the world. It is one of the oldest, too, and the modern American system of government is based on a constitution that is now 200 years old, having survived the growth of the nation from 18th-century colony to modern superpower. Crises of recent years – arising from the Vietnam War and from high-level political scandals – have had no effect whatever on the legal structure and operation of the government. Once more, history has shown that the nation's institutions have a resilience and flexibility matched in few other countries.

The Constitution

The Constitution of 1787 is a concise document just a few thousand words long. Yet it provides the basis for a vast and complex political structure that directly employs 3m people and is lobbied, analysed and reported by thousands more. Much of this complexity can be laid at the door of the Founding Fathers who, fearing that government power might be abused, divided it between many institutions, each limited in power by the others.

The result is that the US government is divided both horizontally – between law makers (the legislature), law enforcers (the executive) and law interpreters (the judiciary) – and vertically – between national (federal), state and local governments. All of these components of government play a part in the political life of the USA, but there is no doubt that the center stage is dominated by the federal government.

Americans make much of their democratic traditions, and are justly proud of the Constitution and Bill of Rights, which protect fundamental freedoms such as freedom of speech. But agitation for civil rights, gay rights, women's rights and similar causes demonstrates that the achievement of democracy is a task which each generation defines for itself, and cannot easily be measured by the often low turnout on elections day.

The president and the executive

As head of state and chief executive, the president has enormous symbolic significance – not least in presenting the public face of the US government to the outside world. Yet although the presidency has played an increasingly prominent role in US politics, the real power of the president is hedged by competing power centres (see *Reins of power*).

The road to the White House The president is elected for a term of four years and can serve a maximum of two terms. He (there have been no women presidents) and the vice-president are the only members of the US government elected from a nationwide constituency; this direct link with the public is an important part of the office's significance.

The election process is long and complex. In election years, the campaigns of the major candidates dominate the media from the early months of the year, when candidacy is announced, to the final elections in November. For the final stages of the election, there are normally just two candidates, one representing each of the major parties, Democratic and Republican. But spring and summer of election year are dominated by the battle for the party nominations, beginning in most states with the "primary" elections for delegates to the parties' national conventions, and culminating in the ballots at the convention which settle the issue.

With the candidate decided, the campaign for the election begins. Campaigns costing millions of dollars focus on "pivotal" states: the eight most populous, which together have 225 of the 270 electors. At the ballot box, the public do not vote directly for their chosen candidate, but for electors to represent them in the electoral college. The electoral college vote is largely a formality; electors cast their vote as they pledged before the public elections.

The administration When the voters elect a president, they are, in effect, electing an entire administration. As soon as he takes office, the president makes a clean sweep of the higher echelons of the bureaucracy, clearing out 2,000 or more, right from the cabinet down to assistant secretaries and below, in order to fill these posts with appointments of his own choice. This is not compulsory, but it has become the established way for the president to make the administration his own. During the changeover, anyone with any claim on the new president's gratitude will eagerly press for some reward – whether power or mere honorifics.

Departments of the executive The job revolution with each new presidency does not extend to the permanent civil service – 13 executive departments, each with responsibility for a particular sector, such as Defense or Education. And the enormous expansion of this bureaucracy over the last 50 years has rendered it a somewhat unwieldy instrument of power. Executive departments exist to do the president's bidding but, in practice, they must spend most of their energies discharging statutory duties and are thus seldom the dynamic or responsive resource that presidents are looking for. Like bureaucracies everywhere, that in Washington is often tolerated only grudgingly by both the population generally and its political masters.

The cabinet contains all the heads, or secretaries, of the departments. Although appointed by the president, they work closely with officials from their respective departments. Presidents sometimes find that cabinet members, responsible for running their own departments, are not so responsive as their own personal team which staffs the executive office. Cabinet secretaries, such as those for Defense, Treasury and State, wield considerable power and the entire cabinet may be consulted on overall policy matters.

The Executive Office has become the principal instrument of presidential government, and each incoming president appoints a large proportion of its 5,000-odd staff. Its relatively small size, and its closeness to the president, have given it a special place in the executive. The president now relies on it to provide information, analysis and policy recommendation – tasks once the responsibility of the civil service and the cabinet. Certain departments within the Executive Office – notably the National Security Council (NSC) and the Office of Management and Budget (OMB), responsible for preparing the federal budget – have assumed a pivotal role in US government. The president's closest friends and advisers are the White House staff. In constant contact with the president, and controlling access to him, the White House staff have considerable power and often provide his main link with the outside world.

Congress

The US Congress consists of two separate houses, the Senate and the House of Representatives, which sit at opposite ends of the Capitol building in Washington DC. Congress is the lawmaking body of the US government, responsible for initiating bills as well as voting them through. But strong presidents have always given a lead by preparing legislation they want to see enacted and working with like-minded members of Congress to secure its introduction and passage. External pressure groups, also, can approach members to introduce bills on their behalf.

In addition to lawmaking, the two houses have certain responsibilities peculiarly their own. The Senate, for example, must confirm or deny the president's appointments and ratify any treaty with a foreign power; laws concerning the raising of revenue must originate in the House.

The electoral connection The House of Representatives has 435 members, or "congressmen," elected every two years. The number from each state depends on its population; the allocation is adjusted automatically every ten years, after the census. The Senate, with only 100 members (two from each state), is the senior house, and many congressmen aspire to be senators. Election to the Senate is for six years, and each state sends two senators. A third of the seats in the Senate are up for election every two years at the same time as voting is held for the entire House.

Since two thirds of the Senators in each new Congress were also in the previous one, the Senate has always enjoyed a greater degree of continuity than the House. Moreover, because they were elected on a statewide basis, senators were, in the past, less vulnerable to the vagaries of political life in local districts, which could unseat a congressman after two years. But the demographic changes of the past 30 years – migration to the suburbs and dispersion to the sun-belt – have helped erode the stability of constituencies, and even senators are no longer secure. Members of Congress must now, as always, cultivate the local interest groups and sources of funds they need to keep their political careers afloat. But with the televising of congressional debates and the attention which pressure groups pay to their voting record, they are perhaps more aware than ever of the electoral reckoning two or six years down the line. Many critics believe that because this encourages members of Congress to place a higher priority on local than on national interests, Congress has become a somewhat ineffective body. In particular, they argue, the need for members to protect local interests has prevented it from dealing with the massive federal budget; for while members of Congress are happy to vote for tax cuts, nobody is willing to be seen supporting measures that would cut expenditure back home in the constituency.

The rise of committees Congress's committees have grown both in stature and number over the last 15 years. Now nearly all proposed legislation is sent to the relevant standing committee, which commissions a subcommittee to make a thorough investigation. After examining the subcommittee's report, the standing committee introduces the bill to the full house for further debate, or proposes amendments, or ditches it altogether.

The Supreme Court

In a nation that places a great deal of emphasis on democracy, the power wielded by the nine unelected justices of the Supreme Court may seem paradoxical. In deciding cases brought before it, the Supreme Court is able to review all the activities of federal and state governments and to rule whether laws are constitutional or not. The president is as subject to the court's rulings as any other official. During the Watergate scandal of the early 1970s, the Supreme Court overruled President Nixon's claim of "executive privilege" and forced him to yield incriminating tapes.

The Supreme Court, through its power to interpret the Constitution and federal law, has always played a crucial role in setting the legal framework for American life. It was the Supreme Court, for example, that not only brought to an end enforced racial segregration between black and white people but also initiated moves toward "affirmative action" and has faced difficult new problems related to abortion and the operation of the criminal justice system.

The reins of power

As the American political structure has grown in size, so has the complexity of its hierarchy. The president is the focus of attention and the head of government. But his real authority is circumscribed by politics and bureaucracy. So numerous now are the factions competing for power both within and without the official hierarchy that it is often hard to predict the outcome of any particular policy debate, no matter what the president's own electoral rhetoric may have prescribed. No wonder, then, that many observers have come to see the US government as a hydra.

The power of the president

The office of president has a special hold over the public imagination, and Americans have always expected the president to be not just an officer of government but leader of the nation. Presidents most admired are those considered "strong," such as Lincoln and Roosevelt, and those least admired are often criticized for being "weak," such as Jimmy Carter. Respect for strong presidents has always been tempered by fears of the abuse of power, and those deemed to have taken too much to themselves – most notoriously President Nixon – are usually brought to book. But there is no doubt that most Americans expect the president to play a decisive role in the political process.

Power under the Constitution The power granted to the president by the Constitution is, on the surface, very limited. The president is commander-in-chief of the armed forces and is vested with the authority to make treaties with foreign powers. As head of the executive, he is also expected to see that laws are faithfully executed. But he has no authority to make laws himself. And his power to control the finances of the nation is circumscribed by Congress, which controls taxation and government borrowing, and by such quasi-independent agencies as the Federal Reserve Board, which supervises the banking industry. The president can veto legislation passed by Congress but a two-thirds majority in both houses of Congress overrides a presidential veto.

Accrued power The real scope of the president's power, however, is not to be judged by the duties assigned by the Constitution, but by what has accrued to the office over the years, either through custom, statutory responsibility imposed by Congress or initiatives taken by incumbents. Two factors in particular have immeasurably enhanced the importance of the presidency since World War II: the explosive growth in the size and range of government services and the increasing significance of foreign affairs. Ironically, although both these developments have added to the influence of the presidency, they have actually made it harder for the president himself to impose his personal will. Also, in the wake of the Watergate scandal in the early 1970s, Congress has made strenuous efforts to limit his options still further.

Growing government services As the scope of government activity has grown, so have the demands upon the federal government. Until recently, Congress had neither the resources nor the expertise to cope. Up until the mid-1970s it delegated more and more to the president, who could cope – with the aid of a greatly enlarged bureaucracy.

For some time now, it has been the president's task to draw up the budget, devise new programs of legislation and set the policy agenda. Congress may throw out many of the president's proposals, or amend them drastically – but it is still the president who often provides the initiatives. Moreover, as legislation is extended into highly complex, technical areas, Congress has tended to leave details to be filled in by the executive; the use of "executive orders" – rules issued by the president which have the force of law – is increasing steadily.

Foreign affairs The USA's prominence on the world scene, plus the increasing impact of international events on domestic issues, have put foreign affairs at the forefront of US politics. The frequent need for speed and secrecy in foreign affairs has enabled strong presidents to make much of the running in this field. But it is in this field, more than any other, that Congress is now trying to limit the president's options – both through congressional committees which examine his conduct of foreign affairs and by cutting the funds he needs to pursue his foreign policy objectives.

The president's men The president has the entire civil service at his disposal to help him in his work. But the customary presidential distrust of the bureaucracy has meant that most presidents rely on a small coterie of close associates, often not only for advice but also to carry out policy. Yet career civil service officials are responsible for the operation of the government machinery and will make their views known up the line. In theory, the secretary of state has the foreign affairs brief. But as the control of the National Security Council (NSC) over foreign affairs has increased, so presidents have tended to turn to the national security adviser, who heads the NSC staff, not to the secretary of state, for advice. In fact, many secretaries of state have found themselves deliberately excluded from the president's inner sanctum. Shut out of the real decision-making process, most recent secretaries of state have found themselves in an invidious position. Six resigned between 1973 and 1983. The Iran-Contra scandal at the close of President Reagan's tenure revealed how far individual White House staffers are sometimes allowed to act on their own initiative.

A strong national security adviser can play a key role in foreign policy making; but not every holder of the office is as influential as Nixon's adviser Henry Kissinger. Many important foreign policy issues under Reagan seem to have been hammered out between the president, the secretary of defense and the director of the CIA, for example. On some occasions, a determined White House chief of staff can set the foreign policy agenda as effectively as the domestic one.

Political appointments One of the president's most effective ways of impressing his personality on the political scene is through political appointments. Not only are the appointments of cabinet secretaries and many other top bureaucrats within his brief – so, too, are ambassadors and Supreme Court judges (when the posts fall vacant). However, most of these appointments require the approval of the Senate, which is occasionally withheld. Political appointments inevitably reflect political preferences, but in the Supreme Court at least, presidents can get nasty surprises from their appointees. Political appointments are often made for reasons of political expediency rather than suitability for the job. For example, President Nixon tried to reverse the reformist tendencies of the Supreme Court by appointing the conservative Warren Burger as chief justice in 1969. In fact, Burger turned out to be considerably less conservative than Nixon expected. It is generally felt that President Reagan's appointments have finally turned the Supreme Court into a conservative force in American political life.

Congressional power

After allowing the balance of power within the US government to swing far toward the executive, Congress has made strenuous efforts to restore the balance over the last 15 years or so – most notably in foreign affairs. President Carter was embarrassed by Congress's rejection of the SALT II arms treaty, while President Reagan has found his plans to finance the Nicaraguan Contra rebels thwarted on several occasions. Congress's gradual surrender of influence to the "Imperial Presidency" in the years after World War II was partly due to its lack of expert staff but, since the mid 1970s, Congress has taken on more than 20,000 bureaucrats to provide the necessary expertise. Most significantly, it has set up its own Congressional Budget Office to give it the ability to scrutinize the president's budget proposals thoroughly.

The power of the committees The real power of Congress lies in its many standing committees and subcommittees, for Congress only rarely rejects the recommendations of these panels of experts. Of course, there is considerable jockeying for posts on the committees; chairmanships are especially sought-after, for the chairman sets the agenda. The chairman of the committee is always a member of the majority party – in recent years, usually the Democrats – and the balance of the rest of the committee reflects the balance of the parties within the corresponding house. Traditionally committee appointments followed the seniority rule, which gave priority to right-wing Democrats from safe southern seats. Moves to democratize the process in favor of younger members and those from the more volatile northern states have had only a marginal effect.

The Rules Committee Because the House of Representatives simply does not have the time to consider all the bills presented by committees, it relies on the 15-member Rules Committee to control the flow of bills. This committee thus has enormous power to decide which bills are considered and which are not.

Watchdog committees The watchdog committee, in combination with special investigating committees set up to find out the facts in situations such as the Iran arms scandal in 1986–87, are Congress's means of scrutinizing the executive and making sure that it is not overstepping its prerogative. These committees have considerable power to call on members of the administration to explain their actions.

Bureaucratic power

Although presidents often find the bureaucracy unresponsive to their requirements, and resistant to fine tuning, the sheer size and stability of the federal government establishment provides the machinery on which day-to-day-government depends. Within the bureaucracy lie years of expertise and considerable resources. Although meant to be separated from the world of politics, and protected in their jobs from politically motivated hostilities, senior officials in government service often have an institutional commitment to their department and its traditional policies. The pressure of large departments such as the Pentagon is especially difficult for the president to ignore. Moreover, although presidents may sometimes think they are making the decisions, the range of alternatives is actually established by the bureaucracy.

It is a mistake, however, to confuse the federal bureaucracy with its counterparts abroad, such as the British Civil Service or the French Grands Corps.

Lobbying

One of the most striking features of the US political scene in recent years is the enormous growth in number and influence of lobbying groups. Such pressure groups concentrate on a single issue, and single-issue politics is fast becoming the order of the day in Washington. Between 1960 and 1980 the number of specialist pressure groups in the USA grew by 60%.

In Washington alone, there are thousands of pressure groups, applying pressure on members of Congress, on civil servants and even on other pressure groups to get their views heard.

Professional lobbyists Increasingly, they are employing professional lobbyists to help them target the right person or agency – for the range of government agencies and departments, and of private influential organizations, can make it almost impossible for an outsider to decide whom to lobby.

Major pressure groups The most influential of the pressure groups tend to be those representing commercial and business interests, such as the National Association of Manufacturers. Big corporations have their own lobbying staff: General Electric's office in Washington employs more than 100 people, for example. Corporations and pressure groups orchestrate financial support for politicians through political action committees, which disburse funds to suitable members of Congress. Such financial resources ensure access to Capitol Hill.

Also influential are the professional associations, such as the American Medical Association and the American Bar Association – and, to a lesser extent now, labor organizations such as the AFL-CIO (see *Employment*). The farmers' lobby remains among the most powerful of all.

In recent years, public-interest lobbies have gained prominence. Few politicians can avoid taking note of the Sierra Club's line on environmental issues. For example, Ralph Nader, founder of Public Citizen, is well known to Congress committees which are working on "conscience" issues.

Revolving door Many American politicians feel that the relationship between congressmen and bureaucrats and the organizations their work brings them into contact with is sometimes just a little too close. The "revolving door" which allows experts in a particular field to switch easily between the private sector and the bureaucracy is a well-known feature of American political life. The Federal Reserve Board was described by one politician as a "wholly-owned subsidiary of the American Bankers' Association."

Defense muscle There is no doubt that business interests play a major role in government policy-making. The immensely powerful defense interest is sometimes referred to as the "iron triangle," a potent alliance in the Pentagon between the congressional defense committees and the multi-billion-dollar defense industry. (see *Defense and aerospace*.)

State power

A mistake many foreign visitors to the USA make is to underestimate the power of state and local government. Within certain limitations, states set their own taxes on top of the federal taxes, and draft their own laws regulating commerce, education, social services and the criminal justice system.

The role of the states came to be overshadowed by that of the federal government following President Franklin D Roosevelt's New Deal in the 1930s. But recently, encouraged by the Reagan administration, "federalism" has been experiencing something of a renaissance. And state governors, like senators, are natural candidates for the White House. Both Reagan and Carter were state governors immediately before becoming president.

Party politics

American politics is dominated by just two parties, the Republicans and the Democrats. Between them they hold every seat in Congress, every state governorship, and all but a few political posts at state and local level. Over the years, these two vast coalitions have accommodated a wide range of often conflicting attitudes and interests. But there are signs that the cohesion of the parties is weakening, and voters are increasingly crossing party lines to express their views on specific issues.

The Democrats

At least since President Roosevelt's New Deal in the 1930s, the Democrats have seemed a little to the left of the Republicans: the party in favor of high government spending, both to invigorate the economy and extend the welfare state. But few even of the more liberal leaders of the party would be considered anything but moderates in Europe, while some older members from the south are far to the right.

Traditionally, the Democrats have drawn support from an uneasy coalition of right-wing white southerners with northern city dwellers, union members and ethnic and religious minorities – while, among the party elite, financiers, lawyers and academics are prominent. The southern vote, dating back to the Civil War, used to be the most stable element in Democratic support and it was this, as much as the vote of the "little man," that enabled the Democrats to maintain a majority in both houses of Congress for most of the last 50 years while providing all but one president from 1933 to 1969. While they remain the largest party (in terms of membership) in the country, and continue to control Congress, the Democrats have failed in recent years to weld a winning consensus among their diverse constituency.

The Republicans

Despite their origins in the 19th century as the anti-slavery grouping, the Republicans are seen as the more conservative of the two parties, opposed to the welfare state and big government. Supporters include the more affluent sectors of society – notably big business and farming interests (except in the Deep South) and inhabitants of well-to-do suburbs. Their identification with the traditional values of small-town America has also earned them the backing of older white people of all classes. The "moral backlash" witnessed in recent years in certain parts of the country has tended to buttress the party's appeal.

The weakening of the parties

Over the past 30 years, voters' identification with a particular party has been waning, and now as much as a third of the electorate is believed to be casting its vote not on the basis of party loyalty, but on personality and, more importantly, on issues. Increasingly, they are also voting for members of different parties for different offices.

One reason for this change in voting patterns has been the weakening of the party organizations. The almost universal adoption of primary elections for party nomination in place of selection by the old political machines means anyone can try for nomination, regardless of party service or standing with party workers. As the incentive for joining and working for a party diminishes, so the grass-roots party organization has begun to disintegrate. Elections now tend to be more about candidates than parties, and, lacking the backing of a party organization, candidates have to conduct their own campaigns for nomination – hence the rise of political action committees which provide funds and run campaigns.

National security

Defending the national interest has been a top priority with all US governments since the war. Defense spending consumes about 27% of the federal budget and a tenth of the entire working and pensioned population depends on military expenditure to some extent. Many different government agencies deal with defense matters, often with their own agendas and priorities. Much of the subject is meant to be shrouded in secrecy, but in the USA more than in most Western democracies, an active press and a keen congressional interest in defense creates a lively debate and a plentiful supply of revelations. Vigorous discussion and criticism of the activities of US security agencies has made the whole issue of security highly controversial.

The nuclear deterrent

Since shortly after World War II, the nuclear deterrent has remained the centerpiece of the USA's defense against the perceived Soviet threat, and since the 1950s the USA has been involved in an almost continuous race with the USSR to maintain an effective nuclear deterrence deemed essential to balance the vast Soviet conventional force. The USA's nuclear force includes an array of ICBMs (intercontinental ballistic missiles) fitted with MIRVs (multiple independently targeted re-entry vehicles), intermediate and short-range (battlefield) nuclear delivery systems, nuclear-armed submarines with multiple-warhead Trident missiles and a fleet of bombers.

Strategic Defense Initiative
Popularly known as "Star Wars," the attempt to develop an effective shield against ICBMs was strongly pushed by President Reagan despite considerable reservations about whether the necessary technology was or ever would be available. Concern was also expressed about whether this initiative would undermine fragile traditional efforts at arms control and limitation, as represented by the Anti-Ballistic Missiles Treaty. Subsequent indications are that President Bush will not continue to emphasize this program, particularly in the light of new opportunities for negotiated arms reductions, including conventional weapons, which may arise from the Soviet review of security policies.

Arms control The tortuous history of arms control negotiation took a new turn with President Gorbachev's initiatives in the opening weeks of the Bush administration. In response to the USSR's agreement to remove its intermediate-range missiles in Europe, the USA agreed to take out the Cruise and Pershing weapons it had put in place, at European request, to counter them. Further unilateral Soviet force reductions, while still not affecting overall military disequilibrium, do offer the prospect of movement towards elimination of the capability for surprise attack, and perhaps of a real cutback in conventional forces. Although moving cautiously, the new administration knew that domestic opinion would expect it to make the best of any prospect of curbing the arms race at last.

The armed forces

In the wake of the Vietnam War, selective service (conscription) in peacetime was ended, though young men are required to register. But the US armed forces are still well over 2m strong, with around 780,200 in the army, 570,000 in the navy, 600,000 in the air force and 200,000 in the marines. More than 500,000 are stationed abroad, mainly in Europe and the Far East.

Rivalry between the services is intense, especially over procurement budgets. But there are moves to achieve unity of command by strengthening the Joint Chiefs of Staff (JCS) – consisting of the heads of the army, navy and air force plus the chief of staff to the secretary of defense – and by increasing the power of the JCS chairman.

Only Congress can declare war, and its control was strengthened by the War Powers Act of 1973. But presidents have launched the armed forces on numerous "policing" missions not requiring prior agreement from Congress. Such actions include the invasion of Grenada in 1983 and the 1986 bombing raid on Libya.

Intelligence

Intelligence is a key element in the USA's protection of its national security and there are at least 11 government agencies involved in the gathering and analysis of intelligence about threats to the national interest, both abroad and at home. Principal among these are the Central Intelligence Agency (CIA), the National Security Agency (NSA), the armed forces intelligence units, the Defense Intelligence Agency (DIA) and the Federal Bureau of Investigation (FBI).

The US Intelligence Board, headed by the director of the CIA, meets regularly to analyse the intelligence gathered by the various agencies. The secrecy of many intelligence-gathering activities inevitably means that the scope of operations of each of the agencies is often obscure – even to the congressional intelligence committees which, in theory, are supposed to be thoroughly informed of their activities. Revelations such as the involvement of the NSC staff in arms deals with Iran – without the knowledge or consent of Congress – ensure that their activities remain highly controversial.

The CIA is the most famous of the agencies concerned with gathering intelligence from abroad. It was created to provide a central focus for the various intelligence-gathering agencies and to ensure a dependable warning system for national emergencies. Nominally under the umbrella of the NSC, its budget is obscure, since many of its appropriations are hidden in the general defense budget. Much of its time is spent monitoring broadcasts and publications freely available. But it is the CIA's clandestine operations which receive most media attention. These include the collection of secret intelligence and – with notification to designated members of Congress – conducting covert action in pursuit of objectives as directed by the president.

The FBI has domestic counter-intelligence responsibilities, but its operations are mainly concerned with criminal investigation. With a budget of around $850m, and 20,000 plain clothes agents, the FBI investigates crimes against federal law: kidnaps, bank robberies and murders, as well as anti-trust and some civil rights violations and corrupt practices. It publishes a list of the "Ten Most Wanted Fugitives" and backs up state police forces with data from the computerized National Crime Information Center in Washington.

The police

The federal government has no authority to police the nation under the Constitution, and policing in the USA is organized on a state and local basis. There are some 450,000 police officers altogether, split between 40,000 separate police forces, more than half of which are one- or two-man units with no training. In addition, there are 75 federal law enforcement agencies, concerned with interstate crime.

The National Guard comprises the volunteer armed forces of the individual states. With a combined strength of 400,000, it comes under the command of the state governor. In peacetime, it is primarily an emergency unit dealing with floods and fires. In the 1960s and 1970s, however, it was called out to quell racial and student disorders.

International alignments

Opposition to communist expansion remains the keystone of US foreign policy, and is the dominating influence on the pattern of the USA's relationships with other nations. But the need to promote commercial interests adds another dimension to the USA's international alignments, and in recent years closer links have been forged with the rising economic powers of the Pacific Basin.

Security pacts

Until World War II, the USA traditionally kept itself free from permanent alliances, but has been the post-war leader in building up defensive alliances, seeing them as vital bulwarks against the expansion of communism.

NATO remains the most important of all the USA's strategic alliances, and provides the basic framework for the defense of the West against the Soviet Union. Formed in 1949, NATO includes the USA and Canada, and most Western European nations (but France withdrew from the military structure of the alliance in 1966).

The USA maintains major forward bases in Europe, with some 317,000 military personnel committed to the NATO structure. Although its intermediate-range ballistic missiles (notably the Pershing II) were removed in parallel with Soviet withdrawal of its SS-20s, nuclear arms which remain (mostly in Germany) have become a source of tension between Bonn and its allies. The possibility of an East-West agreed reduction in conventional forces will present a challenge to NATO planners in the years ahead, and may well lead the USA to review its own foreign military commitments.

ANZUS and South-East Asia The USA, together with Australia and New Zealand, in 1951 signed the ANZUS treaty which aims to preserve peace in the Pacific area. However, in 1984 the newly-elected Labour government in New Zealand decided to refuse to allow visits by US naval vessels carrying nuclear weapons and since then, no joint military exercises have taken place under ANZUS and the annual Council meetings have been replaced by US-Australian bilateral talks. The USA has important bilateral treaties with Japan, the Philippines (the site of its major Pacific bases) and South Korea.

Latin America The USA is particulary sensitive to the threat of a communist takeover in any of its American and Caribbean neighbors, and the Rio Treaty and the Organization of American States (OAS) – which unites 26 American nations – assumed new importance in the past decade. Instability in Central America, dangerous insolvency and the fragility of the democratic process throughout the area will continue to be sources of concern for US administrations in the future. Increasingly, the USA is turning to the OAS, rather than the UN, to settle problems in Central and South America.

The United Nations As the United Nations organization has grown (it now has more than 160 member nations) so US commitment to it has waned: UN policy on major issues is made in the General Assembly and here the huge Third World vote may thwart the USA. But the USA can still use its position as one of the five permanent members of the 15-member Security Council to veto any resolution it disapproves of.

Israel and the Middle East Support for Israel is a central component of the US Middle Eastern policy: a powerful pro-Jewish lobby and traditional national sympathies will ensure that it remains so, despite growing unease over Israel's Palestinian policy, its links with South Africa and its role in the US arms deal with Iran in 1986. Israel receives at least $3.5bn a year in economic and military aid, and the benefit of US diplomatic backing in many disputes with the Arab states. But the USA is keen to retain friendship with some, at least, of the Arab states. Egypt, for example, receives substantial military and economic aid. The whole pattern of US relationships in the Middle East, however, has been disturbed by the terrorism which is often directed against US civilians. Nations identified as supporting terrorism are strongly condemned, and the USA has threatened (and used) military force against some of them.

Revolutions

Successive administrations have adhered, in rhetoric and in practice, to the "domino" theory – the belief that if one country fell to communism, then all its neighbours would topple. This has sometimes led the USA to support right-wing dictatorships – or, in some cases, oppose dictatorships which seem ineffective bulwarks against communism. In the 1950s and 1960s, Korea, Europe and South-East Asia most engaged the concern of Washington. Central America, Africa and, above all, Afghanistan have been areas of more recent concern. The withdrawal of the USSR from Afghanistan, Cuba from Angola and Vietnam from Cambodia have been matched by popular disenchantment in the USA with covert action as a means of pursuing policy abroad.

Economic relationships

Trade and aid have played increasingly significant roles in shaping the pattern of US international alignments since World War II. Both trade and aid, for example, were behind the US drive to create the Organisation for Economic Co-operation and Development (OECD) in 1961. Most Western European nations are OECD members, together with the USA, Canada, Australia, New Zealand and Japan; and the OECD is one of world's major forums for discussion and action on the international economy.

It is the General Agreement on Tariffs and Trade (GATT), however, which has became the principal forum where the USA applies pressure on Europe and Japan not to erect barriers to US trade – and also justifies its own barriers to foreign trade.

Canada The USA's closest bond, both physically and economically, is with its northern neighbour Canada, which is its largest trading partner by a long margin. Every year, some $80bn-worth of trade crosses the Canadian-US border, the longest undefended frontier in the world. A free trade agreement was ratified in 1988, despite several problems encountered during negotiations, particularly from protectionist pressure from the US lumber lobby.

The North Pacific The growing economic power of countries such as Japan, South Korea and Taiwan – combined with demographic shifts at home from east to west, and the rise of the Alaskan oilfield – have shifted the focus of US interest toward the Northern Pacific basin. In the early 1980s, the volume of US trade across the Pacific exceeded that across the Atlantic for the first time. Diplomatic relations with Taiwan are smoother, and US business has moved strongly into communist China.

Europe The traditional links with the UK and Ireland, and to a lesser extent West Germany, still figure strongly in the US world outlook, and the high proportion of US investment in the UK underlines the "special relationship." Although the USA is not on such intimate terms with other members of the EC, it retains close economic ties with all of Western Europe.

Latin America US investment in Latin America is enormous, and the huge debts to US banks built up by some South American countries, notably Brazil and Mexico, ensure that Latin American affairs stay at the forefront of US economic policy.

The Business Scene

Government and business

Government intervention in the US economy has historically meant regulation but very little public production or provision of goods and services. Ronald Reagan's attempts in the 1980s to reverse a trend toward increasing business regulation may well have a boomerang effect in the 1990s.

Regulatory authority

Over the years, federal and state governments have awarded themselves broad powers to control the way business is done in the USA. Federal and state statute books contain a host of rules primarily designed to protect free enterprise and ensure fair competition. Some federal regulations are administered by departments within the executive branch. The Department of Commerce, for example, grants patents and registers trade marks. But the federal government has delegated much of its regulatory power to nearly 100 independent bodies.

Independent agencies The reason behind creating independent agencies was to remove their activities from partisan politics. Agency heads, and sometimes other top officials, are appointed by the president with the Senate's consent. To prevent any one president from achieving control over an agency, their terms of office are usually long and overlapping. Because of this, agencies can sometimes work against policies of the administration in power. Some are also criticized for protecting the interests of related businesses before those of the public.

The following are among the most important federal agencies.

Interstate Commerce Commission *(ICC)* The oldest of all the regulatory agencies, the ICC's main task is to oversee private railroads, bus and truck companies, coastal and inland waterway shipping, freight forwarding and certain interstate pipelines in the USA. Deregulation has cut much of the ICC's authority.

Federal Trade Commission *(FTC)* has a wide brief covering acquisitions and mergers, cartels and price fixing, fraudulent advertising and a range of other unfair and deceptive trading practices. It leaves most antitrust work to the Department of Justice, and concentrates on consumer protection. The FTC has limited power to enforce its codes and operates mostly by persuading business to adopt acceptable practices – though critics say it is often business that persuades the FTC.

Federal Reserve Board (see *Financial institutions*).

National Labor Relations Board *(NLRB)* The NLRB regulates labor practices between employers and labor organizations. It oversees the process of forming and recognizing a union and assists with collective bargaining when invited. Its autonomy and power were greatly diminished during the unsympathetic Reagan years and it remains weak under President Bush.

Securities and Exchange Commission *(SEC)* Established in the wake of the stock market crash of 1929, the SEC is Wall Street's watchdog. It plays a prominent role in policing the activities of America's wheelers and dealers and regulating public share offers and financial disclosures. Its powers to investigate infringements of regulations are extensive, and it can close a brokerage firm by revoking its license. In practice it resorts to this sanction only against smaller companies, but it has shown that it is willing if necessary to prosecute leading firms.

Environmental Protection Agency *(EPA)* A relatively young agency, the EPA engages in research, setting standards, monitoring outputs and enforcing environmental laws. Severely weakened by a series of discredited Reagan appointments, the EPA is trying to make a comeback. Despite Bush's appointment of the first avowed environmentalist at the helm, sparse funding and bureaucratic wrangles may limit its effectiveness.

International Trade Commission *(ITC)* The ITC is one of the agencies whose commissioners are explicitly bipartisan. It has quasi-juridical, research and fact-finding functions, advising the public and various branches of government about international trade issues. It is responsible for determining countervailing duty, antidumping and other unfair trade practices as they concern specific products and companies.

The Office of the United States Trade Representative *(USTR)* Although it is not considered an independent agency, the USTR lies outside the cabinet department bureaucracy. Created in 1974, the USTR's office consists of a relatively small staff who develop and administer overall trade policy and participate in multinational and bilateral trade negotiations. The head has cabinet-level status and the USTR's power has grown over the years as trade has become a more vital and complex isue.

The Antitrust Division is not an independent agency, but a part of the Justice Department which has responsibility for enforcing the USA's antitrust laws. During the past decade, the Department of Justice more liberally defined what was acceptable business practice, reducing the number of antitrust investigations and cases.

The public sector

Direct government involvement in providing goods and services is even more limited now than it was before Ronald Reagan took office. One of the few major publicly-owned corporations left is the Tennessee Valley Authority (TVA), which provides hydro-electric power and flood control in the southeastern part of the USA.

Although the vast majority of Americans are rather skeptical about the government's ability to meet their needs directly, sentiment is growing that the current free market approach to health care, housing, and child care is woefully inadequate.

Privatization Schemes for selling off public businesses, services and property will not be a hallmark of the Bush administration's budget proposals, as they were of Reagan's. Environmental concerns will make it difficult for the president to put more public land and other natural resources up for grabs. The only other privatization scheme in prospect – allowing a private company to take over some of the US postal service's operations – does not have much public support.

Role of states Deregulation and the "New Federalism" prevalent during the 1980s created both tremendous problems and opportunities for state and local authorities. They approached the challenge sometimes by following the federal government's lead, for example, by contracting with private companies to provide public services.

More often, however, they took a different path and introduced new regulations and incentives for business. States, in fact, have taken the lead in providing a host of subsidies and other incentives to encourage both foreign investors and exports.

State agencies All states have their own semi-independent agencies which can issue bonds, provide cheap loans and offer tax incentives to private corporations.

Power in business

Traditionally, corporate power has been almost exclusively in the hands of top management who were little influenced by outside shareholders. But in the 1980s, managers saw much of their independence eroded. The wave of mergers and acquisitions as well as the rise of institutional investors, "corporate raiders" and corporate responsibility groups, serve as new checks on management power and decision-making; many large companies have been forced to take on substantial burdens of debt to defend themselves against unwelcome takeover bids.

Corporate power

The sheer size of the largest US corporations enables them to wield enormous clout, in both the business and political worlds. Commanding revenues equivalent to the GNP of many nations, they are able to negotiate with government officials almost as if they were a foreign country; and the corporate lobby is the most powerful in the country (see *The reins of power*).

Few of the big corporations are now run by the entrepreneurs who were the heroes of US business in the past. There are exceptions, such as Ken Olsen who, in 31 years, built up the computer company DEC from next to nothing to one worth $14bn, and H. Ross Perot, the Dallas billionaire who sold his company EDS to General Motors for $2.5bn. But they are rare. Perot controlled his company by owning a majority of the shares; most heads of public corporations now find themselves answering to a dispersed and often passive group of institutional shareholders. Without much shareholder influence, the chief executive officers of the big corporations are able to exercise an authority that reaches far beyond the bounds of the company. But corporate managers' power is offset by corporate raiders who watch constantly for companies that are badly managed or possess under-exploited assets.

Investors, raiders and arbitrageurs

The merger and acquisition boom of the 1980s gave financial manipulators a new power and status in the US business world, but the frenzy seems to have peaked. In 1988, for example, US exchanges traded $1,700bn in equity and options: one-third less than the value of trades in 1987. Experts do not consider this a fluke, rather that the volume of trading and M&A activity, in particular, is settling down.

Corporate raiders Capturing the headlines, though not necessarily the most fundamental power, are the corporate raiders whose opportunistic bids so worry companies. Devices such as the "junk bond" (high-interest bonds which are rated below investment quality) have helped the boldest raiders raise enough money to make hostile takeover bids for large corporations, even when their own resources are limited. Corporations can be so unnerved by bids or threats of bids that they resort to drastic action to protect themselves. However, with the prosecution of the "father of junk bonds," Michael Milken, convictions of several other players, and changing economic conditions, the bloom is off the rose. The number of new junk bond issues reached a peak in 1986 and has subsequently declined. It was $31.5bn in 1989 against $40.2bn in 1986. Redemptions are also proceeding at a record rate.

Arbitrageurs The merger boom also brought to the fore the risk arbitrageurs, who buy and sell shares in companies involved in takeover struggles – or those likely to be. Although their real power is limited, the star players can make huge sums of money for their backers.

Revelations of extensive insider trading have eroded confidence in arbitrageurs, however, and individuals like Ivan Boesky have been discredited.

Investment banks The linchpins of the merger and acquisitions machine are the big investment banks. They are among the most dynamic and powerful financial institutions in the USA. The top five investment banks handle 61% of all underwritten corporate securities. Confidence in them has survived the first round of insider trading scandals, but more revelations and lawsuits may yet emerge.

Regardless of what happens on that front, their pre-eminence in corporate financing is being strongly challenged by the largest commercial banks as the US financial system continues its major restructuring (see *Investment banks and other institutions*).

Investors and money managers

Traders and brokers may steal the limelight, but the institutional investors are a quiet, important force in the market. Total assets under the management of institutional investors have grown dramatically during the 1980s, more than doubling between 1981-87 to $4,600bn.

Pension funds constitute the largest institutional player, with 44% of the total institutional holdings.

Influence All told, institutional players hold an estimated 43% of outstanding equities. Their ability to influence market conditions varies according to the particular security and market in the USA. While they are responsible for increasing the size of trades and turnovers in the New York Stock Exchange, for example, their share of trading volume has been declining. This is because they have been shifting their portfolio towards non-equity securities such as real estate and into private off-market investments such as leveraged buyout funds.

Institutional holdings in individual corporations have increased and are currently substantial, especially for the largest capitalized corporations. An examination of the ownership of the top 50 US companies ranked by 1987 stock market value, shows that 47 out of the top 50 had institutional ownership in excess of 33%, 41 in excess of 40% and 27 in excess of 50%.

Federal Reserve

"The Fed" is the most powerful financial institution in the country and its chairman is considered the most powerful person after the president. The key to its clout is the Fed's independent control of interest rates and the money supply. The Fed's board makes its own analysis of the state of the US economy and makes monetary policy decisions autonomously. This at times dismays Congress and the executive, which occasionally threaten to bring the Fed under control, but never do (see *Commercial banks*).

Business connections

The "old boy network" is far less pervasive and influential in the USA than in Europe.

In the larger cities, business executives strengthen their ties through exclusive clubs, college and university alumna associations and certain business organizations. One of these, the Business Round Table, established in 1972, constitutes one of the more exclusive networks. Nearly 200 CEOs are members.

In smaller towns, the Rotary, Masons, Elks, and Moose clubs serve similar functions.

Organized crime is big business in the USA. The Mafia's activities reach deep into such sectors as labor unions, gambling and the construction industry. Although periodic police crackdowns and mob inter-family killings may take key figures out of action, the Mafia remains a force to be reckoned with in the spheres it sees as its own preserve.

The business framework

The sheer scale of US business is staggering. At the last count, in 1986, there were 3.4m corporations, 1.7m partnerships and 14.8m sole proprietorships registered. The tradition is that business here flourishes in a climate of unrestricted free enterprise. There is some truth in this, and in many respects businesses are free to do as they like; on the whole, regulations are designed to promote competition, not stifle it. However, in the wake of lax regulation in Washington, states and local governments are increasingly stepping in to establish their own parameters for acceptable business behavior. North Americans are highly litigious and the amount of legal documentation needed to do business in the US is paralleled in few other major industrial nations.

Corporate America

The US business scene is dominated by the corporation, and in particular, the big corporation. In the 1930s, only 0.2% of US businesses had assets of more than $50m. Today there are several hundred companies worth billions of dollars. The top 500 manufacturers had $2,000bn in sales in 1988, representing 40% of the nation's GNP, and their profits were 90% of total after-tax non-financial profits made. In certain sectors, such as manufacturing and oil, the predominance of the giants is even more striking. Only in the retail, construction, and some service industries, do small and mid-range corporations have any real impact on the overall figures.

Chastened conglomerates? In the 1960s and 1970s, vast conglomerates were in vogue. Led by innovative, efficient managers, they successfully combined a disparate array of businesses to make large, profitable organizations that became models for others to emulate. Conglomerates like ITT, headed by the charismatic Harold Geneen, and the United Aircraft Company, headed by Harry Gray, seemed ready to sweep all before them. But they lost a good deal of appeal in the 1980s. Flexibility, entrepreneurship, increased competition and rapid market response became the watchwords of the day, and the behemoths found themselves at a distinct disadvantage. Many saw profits slump. They sold off fringe activities and/or "decentralized" in an attempt to inject new life into their operations.

Incorporation

The procedure for setting up a corporation in the USA is, in many ways, similar to that in other countries. The principal difference is that US corporations are organized in a particular state, and so are subject to that state's own, often idiosyncratic, incorporation laws (listed in the Martindale-Hubbell Law Directory). In fact, there are no federal incorporation laws.

Most US firms do business in more than one state, but this is not a problem. Once a firm is incorporated in any one of the 50 states, it can set up operations right across the country. Frequently, even the firm's headquarters are outside the state of incorporation. All operations are subject to state corporation laws – and to local taxes – but the firm only has to incorporate once. To operate in a state other than that in which it is incorporated, a firm generally has to file with that state's secretary of state its Certificate of Incorporation, a "good standing" certificate and other routine documents, together with a fee paid annually.

Where to incorporate Picking the right state in which to incorporate can be crucial, and most businesses consult a good corporate lawyer and/or accounting firm before making their choice. Choosing the wrong state can lumber a corporation with a charter that hamstrings future expansions or changes of direction. Moreover, the state's incorporation laws may have significant effects on shareholder rights, dividends, taxation, etc.

Although the obvious choice might be to incorporate where the company would do the most business, this does not always make sense. Strictness of incorporation laws, tax liabilities and other company-specific considerations may make another state more attractive. Many firms are drawn to states with the most liberal incorporation laws like New York, Maryland and Delaware.

Delaware is the most popular state for incorporation. One attraction is that there is no need for any of the incorporators to be a US citizen. Neither is there any need for directors to meet formally for board meetings; they can simply talk over the telephone. Delaware gives great freedom over the payment of dividends and allows firms to keep the minute book, stock transfer ledger and other books outside the state – unlike New York. For any individual firm, however, New York and other states may have advantages which outweigh the liberality of Delaware.

How to incorporate The basic procedure for incorporation is so simple that do-it-yourself incorporation kits are available from bookstores. These include a stock register, certificate book, minute book and, sometimes, local bylaws. Foreign owners and anyone who contemplates running a business of any size, however, should hire a lawyer for advice and to do the paperwork. It is best to obtain professional assistance to minimize the possibility of future legal problems.

Incorporation in most states is an inexpensive and swift process, accomplished usually in less than one week. The procedure involves filing articles of incorporation, detailing the company's name, its purpose, its life (usually perpetuity), its capital, its stock value (if any), its statutory office address and the number of directors. The information provided becomes public record. Once the charter is granted, the firm is generally required to add "Inc" or "Corp" to its name.

For manufacturing businesses, no capital is needed beyond that essential to start operations. But for financial enterprises, most states have a minimum capital stipulation. Usually, there must be at least three founders and three directors.

Foreign investors Foreigners find few unusual problems setting up a business in the USA. There are not many federal rules regarding foreign investment. While no generalized foreign investment registration or approval procedures exist at the federal level, foreign investors are required to notify the Department of Commerce once a transaction has been made. The Exon-Florio Amendment to the 1988 Omnibus Trade Bill requires advance notice of sensitive acquisitions. It is designed to allow the administration to block a bid by a foreign investor for a US company "in the national interest," and is ostensibly aimed at protecting firms which are major defense contractors, or are engaged in other sensitive work for the armed forces. However, the definition of "national interest" is very vague, and some have argued that even computer and software companies could be considered strategically sensitive, without any involvement in defense work.

The amendment was brought into play early in 1989, against the bid for Consolidated Gold Fields by the Luxembourg-based company, Minorco. The bid was stalled to the extent that it was eventually abandoned.

The president can review and restrict mergers, acquisitions and takeovers of US companies by foreign interests if he deems them harmful to national security.

Similarly, although some states have certain restrictions, they tend to be minimal. Some states restrict land ownership and in most states foreigners are not permitted to establish deposit banks. A few prohibit foreign participation in the liquor industry (see *Law*).

Interestingly, foreign corporations wanting to do business in a particular state are regarded in exactly the same light as American firms from another state. This is because, legally, a corporation is considered domestic only in the state in which it is incorporated. In California, a Delaware firm and a Japanese firm are both equally foreign.

Despite the simplicity of setting up a local branch, most foreign corporations conduct their business through local subsidiaries for legal and tax reasons. One plus for staying foreign is that a foreign corporation is allowed to use its own, rather than US, accounting practices. The advantage of this is that whereas US firms are obliged to regard property and preferred shares as debt, foreign firms may be able to present them as assets and equity. When, in 1986, Rupert Murdoch purchased six US television stations, he raised $1.1bn in preferred shares on the strength of News Corp Ltd's $101m profit by using Australian accounting practices; under the US system the company would have shown a $263m loss.

Foreign corporations with shares in US public firms are subject to the scrutiny of the Securities and Exchange Commission (SEC) and must file details of: executives' and directors' pay, transactions conducted between executives, directors and shareholders, changes in management, major acquisitions and the financial status of the company and its main subsidiaries.

Going public

Most of the biggest corporations in the USA are publicly owned, and every year thousands of US businesses go through the process of making their first or subsequent public share offering. The procedure is, in many ways, similar to that in countries like the UK, with rules about disclosures, acquisition, shareholders, shares, etc. But the amount of documentation is vast and much of it is dictated by federal securities laws.

Filing an offer When a company, foreign or domestic, plans to sell securities to the public it generally has to register with the SEC and obtain its approval before going ahead with the sale. Depending on the size of the company and offering, certain information is required. Usually a company has to disclose information about: properties and the nature of the business; management; certified financial statements made by independent public accountants; and the provisions of the security to be offered for sale and its relationship to the registrant's other securities. Registration statements and prospectuses become public immediately upon filing with the commission. It is unlawful to sell the securities before the effective date, which is usually 20 days after filing with the SEC. This gives the SEC time to examine the documents and decide whether to block the offering until it obtains more information from the company. Companies offering securities for sale also need to be informed about state laws for information disclosure, which vary a great deal from state to state.

Shares can be either common or preferred; preferred shareholders in most states have certain extra voting rights as well as receiving fixed interest. Shares can also be bearer or registered, though the preference in the USA is for registered shares.

In some countries, the company's merchant and investment banks publish the share offer. In the USA, the offerer must publish the offer and the company usually appoints a depository – typically a clearing bank – to handle all the money. New stock issues by large public companies are generally underwritten and managed by the "top bracket" houses while initial public offerings (IPOs) by new, unknown, companies are generally done by the smaller investment houses. While some offers need prodding along to ensure they are fully subscribed, there is much less of the hectic last-day rush so typical of share offers in other countries.

Once a company's registration statement has been declared effective, the Exchange Act of 1934 requires it to file periodic reports with the SEC unless certain conditions pertaining to closely held stocks and a small asset base are met. Various documents also must be filed if the company wants its securities traded in any of the stock exchanges.

Short-term profits Investors and stock analysts have shown an increasing interest in short-term capital gains instead of holding equity as a long-term investment. To protect themselves against raiders and boost their appearance as a healthy company, many managers have played into this trend and have abandoned any long-term perspective they may have had in search of short-term profitability and high stock prices.

Proprietorships

Unincorporated and owned by just one person, the sole proprietorship is the simplest form of US business organization and the most common. The operation of sole proprietorships is regulated at the state level. Virtually any individual may operate in this form. Various state and local permits and licenses are usually required before establishing the business. The range of one-owner businesses and professional practices is as wide and varied as the nation itself.

The real attraction of proprietorship is that the owner is in total control. He or she is also at liberty to draw income at will, and deduct a whole range of expenses from the tax bill. The one drawback of this type of organization is that all of the sole proprietor's assets (both personal and for the business) are at risk in any financial or legal proceeding.

Partnerships

In the legal and financial world, partnerships are perhaps the most common form of business set-up. There are two kinds: general and limited. Both are relatively simple and inexpensive to establish. General partners are jointly and severally liable for all the organization's debts and obligations; if the partnership goes bankrupt, creditors can claim against anyone specifically in the partnership agreement. Limited partners, on the other hand, can be held responsible only for those areas laid out specifically in the partnership agreement. However, in any partnership, at least one must be a general partner who has unlimited liability. There is no need for the general partner to be an individual; it could be a corporation. One quite common arrangement in the USA is for a few individuals to go into partnership as limited partners; they may also own a corporation which acts as general partner.

Mergers and acquisitions

In the mid 1980s, circumstances combined to send a wave of acquisitions and mergers surging through the US business world. Favorable tax laws, the laissez-faire attitude of the Reagan administration towards M&A, cash-rich companies with more money than productive ideas, and low stock prices for asset-rich companies, are some of the factors which created a hothouse climate for the M&A boom. This seems to have peaked, however, as companies have become more sophisticated in protecting themselves against corporate raiders. Startling revelations of insider trading on Wall Street, along with the poor performance of many debt-laden acquirers and the rise in stock market prices which eliminated asset undervaluation have also contributed to the changing pace. Now M&A activity is moving into the more friendly, strategic alliance direction (see *Law*).

The regulations Foreign and domestic corporations contemplating an acquisition or merger are subject to the same laws. Thirty-day prior notification to the Department of Justice and the Federal Trade Commission (FTC) is generally required if: 1) the company(ies) engage in commerce or an activity affecting commerce in the USA; 2) one firm has annual net sales or total assets of at least $100 million; 3) the other has annual net sales or total assets of at least $10 million; and 4) the acquiring firm purchases at least 15% or $15 million of assets or voting securities. If an investigation is warranted, only one agency will perform it. If the takeover is hostile, the acquirer may also be affected by state laws.

Historically, the US has been one of the more rigorous antimonopoly environments in which to operate. Treble damages, criminal prosecution of some offenses and the ability to bring private actions distinguish US antitrust law from many other nations. Two of the more important pieces of legislation in this area are the Sherman Antitrust Act and the Clayton Act, which respectively deal with monopolization rules and conspiracies and cartels. Antitrust laws have been interpreted more liberally in recent years. Under current guidelines, unless the acquirer and its target control more than 20% of the market and the top four firms in the industry control at least 75% of the market, there is unlikely to be any challenge.

The tender offer When someone is interested in acquiring control of a company through a tender offer or other stock acquisition (5% or more of the outstanding stock), they are required to disclose information about the bid in advance to the SEC. This disclosure is also required by anyone soliciting shareholders to accept or reject a tender offer. Under the US Securities Exchange Act of 1934, anyone wishing to acquire "beneficial ownership" of a public corporation has to notify within 10 days the SEC and the target company, disclosing the source of funds, and plans for control. No substantial corporate marriage – that is, one involving 15% of the voting shares at $15m or more, or 10% at $25m or more – can be consummated until the specified periods have elapsed. These are 15 days for a cash tender offer and 30 days for any other. During this time, the authorities may intervene and halt the merger, but only a minority are actually reviewed.

Tax

In the wake of the tax revolution begun by the Reagan administration in 1987, the entire corporate tax system has changed. The thinking behind the changes was inspired by the former administration's supply side philosophy, so that corporate tax rates have dropped from 46% to 34%. Many loopholes were closed in an attempt to ensure that all companies paid some taxes. Citizens were furious over revelations that many well-known, large and very profitable corporations paid no taxes for several years running. Preliminary information seems to indicate that the new laws were not entirely successful in this latter goal.

Tax regulations The present US tax system is the kind of complex mass of statutes, rulings and acronyms that provides accountants and lawyers with endless business. One of the problems is that tax regulations come from a plethora of different sources and each one has a different status. In addition to the federal codes, there are Treasury Regulations, most of which have the force of law, and occasional updates transmitted as Treasury Decisions. Through the Internal Revenue Service (IRS), the

Treasury also issues Revenue Rulings designed to clarify gray areas in the existing tax code. Further IRS announcements may follow an important court judgment. Finally, the IRS may deliver a private ruling to an individual tax payer.

Corporations and individuals are taxed at the federal, state and local levels.

Federal corporate taxes US corporations are taxed on their worldwide income from 15-34%. A federal alternative minimum tax (AMT) is intended to prevent a corporation with substantial economic income from using various deductions, exclusions and credits to eliminate its tax liability. The AMT is imposed at a rate of 20% and applies if it exceeds the ordinary tax for the year. Companies are also subject to a capital gains tax (maximum 34% rate) and withholding tax on dividends, interest and royalties paid to foreign recipients (generally 30%).

It is up to the corporation to assess its own income and estimate how much tax it should pay. Within two and a half months after the end of the year – which can be either calendar or fiscal – it must file a tax return on Form 1120 for the IRS.

State taxes Some 43 states impose a corporate income tax. The maximum rates range from Michigan's 2.35% single business tax to 12% in Iowa. Several have also adopted AMT systems. During the latter half of the 1980s, states were forced to grapple with escalating costs and insufficient revenues as part of the Reagan administrations's "new federalism" which devolved many service responsibilities onto states. Many were also hit by tremendous economic declines. In response, state legislatures have been altering tax policy. First attempts to boost revenues by taxing corporate income on a "unitary" basis, that is on all of a corporation's income, regardless of where it is earned, met with stiff resistance by foreign multinational corporations. Today only Alaska imposes mandatory worldwide unitary taxation. In four states (California, Idaho, Montana and North Dakota), worldwide is the norm but tax payers can opt for the "water's edge" approach (based on all US profits). Thirteen others require water's edge, and three others have other variations on this theme. Recognizing that the tax base must be expanded and the importance of the "service economy," states are contemplating various taxes on services, despite the fact that certain business lobbyists forced Florida to rescind such a policy.

Local taxes vary tremendously across the country. They are complicated by a host of incentives that states, counties and municipalities are willing to grant to new investors and by the fact that states and municipalities are still sorting out the fiscal implications for their budgets of the federal tax reform.

Tax deductions Certain expenses, including depreciation, interest, salaries and wages, bad debts, contributions to charity, and rents are allowed as deductions against gross income. The deductability of expenses like business meals, travel and entertainment is limited. There are now uniform rules for capitalizing indirect costs into inventory and for capitalizing long-term building, installation, construction and manufacturing contracts.

Foreign tax credits are allowed for foreign income taxes paid or deemed paid by the corporation in conjunction with receiving a dividend from certain foreign corporations. The credit is limited to the US tax on the foreign-sourced portion of the company's worldwide taxable income.

Anti-avoidance measures In addition to the AMT policy, the USA is tough on transfer pricing within multinationals. The IRS has considerable powers under section 482 to adjust the prices different sectors of the corporation charge each other.

Tax on dividends and interest Dividends, interest, rents, royalties and similar forms of income paid by US sources to foreign recipients are generally subject to a 30% withholding tax. Interest from bank deposits and portfolio debt investments, however, are normally exempt from this withholding tax. The 30% rate may be reduced by tax treaties between the USA and the country where the recipient of the income is resident. However, such income is not exempt from the tax if it is effectively connected with the conduct of a US trade or business of the recipient. Then it is subject to regular US tax.

Taxes on foreign corporations Taxes on branches of foreign corporations are as heavy in the USA as anywhere. Generally, the source of the income and the determination of whether it is "effectively connected" with a US business affects the methods and rate of tax. A Branch Profits Tax (BPT) is designed to eliminate the tax difference between operating a US business as a subsidiary or a branch of a foreign corporation. It is similar to the withholding tax on dividends, but applies to foreign companies operating a US branch and foreign corporations that are partners in a foreign or US partnership. Generally a 30% BPT is applied to the relevant earnings. The BPT may be reduced or eliminated if the foreign corporation is a "qualified resident" of a country that has an income tax treaty with the USA.

Business information and regulations

The US scene is well documented, with many specialist agencies providing basic data on corporations, their financial standing and shareholder structure. Published information is extensive, but more detailed inquiries can be commissioned from a wide range of suppliers. Many corporations also take advantage of the USA's freedom of information laws to obtain data on rival companies.

Official sources of information For detailed and specific information on business at a local level, the 14,000 state-run local industrial development institutions are generally very useful – although it is worth bearing in mind that their job is to attract business to their own area. They can be contacted directly or via intermediaries such as the *US and Foreign Commercial Service Office of the Department of Commerce*, 14th St and Constitution Ave, NW, Washington DC 20230 ☎ (202) 377-3641.

The Bureau of the Census in the Department of Commerce also produces extensive and up-to-date statistical information, summarized in the annual Statistical Abstract of the United States, which lists sources for an enormous range of other statistics. Contact: *US Government Printing Office* ☎ (202) 783-3238.

Statutory bodies The *Securities and Exchange Commission*, 450 5th St, NW, Washington DC 20549 ☎ (202) 272-2650 is the body to which all share offers and all acquisitions of more than 5% in any publicly-owned US corporation must be referred. But it is also a very useful source of information on competitors' accounts and on subjects such as corporate law.

Other important regulatory bodies are: the *Antitrust Division of the Justice Department*, 10th St and Constitution Ave, NW, Washington DC 20530 ☎ (202) 633-2401 which oversees monopolies and mergers, together with the *Bureau of Competition of the Federal Trade Commission*, 6th St and Pennsylvania Ave, NW, Washington DC 20580 ☎ (202) 523-3601.

Trade and industrial associations The *Chamber of Commerce of the USA*, 1615 H St, NW, Washington DC 20062 ☎ (202) 659-6000 is an umbrella group for the thousands of local organizations in the USA. Besides these, there are national associations for virtually every individual type of business, such as the American Manufacturers' Association and the American

Bankers' Association. Most of these are represented in Washington DC.

Private information sources on companies Information on companies is not so freely available from public sources in the USA as in some European countries. However, *Dun and Bradstreet International*, One World Trade Center, suite 9069, New York, New York 10048, provides precise accounts and prospects in every market for the 120,000 biggest businesses in the USA and can be commissioned for credit reports.

Other valuable sources of information on companies are the following publications: the *Directory of American Firms Operating in Foreign Countries*, Uniworld Business Publications Inc, 50 E 42nd St, New York, New York 10017; *Ward's Directory of the 55,000 Largest US Corporations*, Gale Research Corporation, Book Tower, Detroit, Michigan 48226. There are also the *Thomas Register of American Manufacturers & Thomas Register Catalog File* and the *American Export Register*, both published by Thomas International Publishing Company Inc, One Penn Plaza, 250 W 34th St, New York, New York 10119.

One of the leading credit rating agencies is the *Standard and Poors Corporation*, 25 Broadway, New York, New York 10004. Standard and Poors also publishes the definitive and invaluable *S & P Register of Corporations, Directors and Executives.*

Management consultancies
Management consultancy is booming in the USA. According to the American Management Consulting Association (ACME), there are more than 35,000 management consultancy firms in the USA, and the number is growing every year. The problem for those interested in using a consultant's services is the sheer number of firms competing to offer advice – and the fact that they all seem to sell similar services. However, many consultancy divisions attached to big international accountancy firms are now specializing in particular sectors, making the choice a little easier. Among the largest and most respected of consultancy firms are *McKinsey & Company Inc*, 55 E 52nd St, New York, New York 10022 ☏ (212) 909-8400; *Arthur Andersen*, 33 W Monroe St, Chicago 60603 ☏ (312) 580-0033; and the *Boston Consulting Group*, 780 3rd Ave, New York, New York 10017 ☏ (212) 319-7140.

Employment

With employment now over 115m, more Americans are working than ever before. But the labor force expands by 2% a year, and increasing numbers of women are looking for jobs. Although low levels of unemployment were a feature of the end of the 1980s, in the recession in the early part of the decade unemployment rates were twice as high; in many parts of the USA it is still an employer's market, with a fluid and flexible workforce.

Changing job base

Two trends are changing the US employment scene dramatically: the continuing contraction of traditional sectors such as manufacturing and the boom in the new service industries.

Factory jobs lost Before 1980, more Americans still worked in manufacturing than in any other single sector – although manufacturing's share of the job market had been shrinking for a decade. The 1980s saw manufacturing jobs fall, with the economic boom merely slowing the decline in the sector's relative share of total employment. Now only 19m work in manufacturing, compared with the 23m who work in the services sector and in wholesale/retail trade. If the government's projections are correct, by 2000 more people will be working for the state than in manufacturing. Despite staggering improvements in productivity in some industries, the loss of jobs has sapped the bargaining power of manufacturing employees, and their wages are falling farther and farther behind. Some have been forced to accept "givebacks" – that is, cuts in their wages and conditions.

New service jobs The lion's share of the 2m or so new jobs created each year is in services – notably office and administration and the restaurant/fast food business. Most are poorly paid jobs, such as secretarial work, and tend to be taken by women.

Fall in real incomes Behind the apparently healthy employment figures, with millions of new jobs created each year, lies considerable hardship. The jobs that have been lost are generally the well-paid skilled and semi-skilled manual jobs; those that have been created are part-time or poorly paid. Whereas only 20% of the new jobs created each year in the 1970s were in the lowest wage category, now 60% are. The sectors that have seen the fastest growth – retail, finance, services – are those with below-average earnings. Some 5m workers (including 4% of full-time workers) are paid the legal minimum wage or less. One-sixth of all families below the poverty level had a head of household working full time. More than a third of the 8m or so new jobs created in the 1980s were part-time.

The boom in consumer spending belies the fact that personal income growth in the USA is actually lagging behind inflation as wages in manufacturing fall, and more and more people take up low-paid service jobs. Real hourly earnings rose hardly at all in the 1980s, and Americans have sustained personal spending partly on credit and partly by virtue of the fact that many couples have dual incomes.

Labor laws

US labor law is founded on the fundamental doctrine of "employment at will," a traditional right which enables employers to hire and fire at will. Enshrined in this doctrine is the important principle that employers can terminate an employee's job at any time, without necessarily any justification – although employers rarely abuse this right. Employment is therefore on the basis of a short-term contract negotiated between employer and employee or by collective bargaining. This contract has to be drawn up and agreed afresh every two or three years.

Because the contract must spell out the terms and conditions of employment completely and is the employer's/employee's only form of security, contracts tend to be complex documents that are legally binding on both parties. Wildcat strikes are rare in the USA – for strikers would be in breach of contract. Instead, strikes tend to occur after the contract has run its course and is being renegotiated.

Playing straight Ever since the Wagner Act was passed in the 1930s, employers have been under a legal obligation to negotiate contracts in good faith. If a union, or employee, can prove that management is not playing it straight, they can take their claim to the National Labor Relations Board. The Taft-Hartley Act of 1947 placed a similar obligation on the trade unions.

Fair work standards The federal government sets a minimum wage for most non-agricultural employees subject to the Fair Labor Standards Act of 1938. The act covers all employees of enterprises engaged in interstate commerce and requires that employees be paid at time and a half for every hour worked over 40 per week. The law provides a basic reference point, but there are numerous ways it can be sidestepped to make sure that an employee is not covered by the act. In areas where jobs are hard to come by, the act is frequently abused.

At present, the minimum wage can be adjusted only by Act of Congress, and this is a cause of some concern among labor leaders and politicians on the left. Throughout the 1970s, when inflation climbed steeply, the minimum wage was increased almost every year. During Ronald Reagan's presidency, the rate was frozen at $3.35 an hour. Thus the minimum wage fell from a half of average earnings in the 1970s to a third in the late 1980s. Any revision of the minimum is resisted strongly by the Republicans, who argue higher minimum wages mean fewer jobs, and President Bush has vetoed minimum wage rises he considers too high.

Advocates of raising the minimum argue that an increase would not only alleviate the distress of some of the USA's poorest people but also address the "chump change" problem. This is the dilemma facing poor people who see little point in working for derisory wages when they can earn more on welfare or hustling in the streets, a dilemma particularly associated with inner-city black youths. Critics of an increase in the minimum wage believe it would drive up labor costs, leading to higher inflation and unemployment.

Equal opportunities Over the past 30 years or so, civil rights movements have put considerable pressure on employers to prevent them from discriminating against people on the grounds of sex, race, religion or age. But the prevalence of the doctrine of employment at will has meant that there is actually less federal legislation on the statute books than in many other Western industrialized nations. Instead, equal opportunities and rights are often protected by executive orders from the president and incorporated in the contract.

In theory, the combination of federal legislation, executive orders, favorable high court judgments and amendments to the doctrine of employment at will achieved by the civil rights movement should provide groups that suffer discrimination with a high degree of protection. In practice, many women and blacks still find it difficult to get well-paid jobs. Unemployment rates are more than twice as high for blacks as for whites. Women are faring only a little better and Hispanics much worse.

Nevertheless, there is considerable variation from state to state. In January 1987, for example, the Supreme Court upheld a woman's right under Californian law to return to work after maternity leave; within weeks, it denied the same right to a woman from Missouri.

The proportion of women in employment was only about 55% in the second half of the 1980s, compared with about 76% of men.

Protection for the elderly The 1980s saw a number of congressional measures banning companies from forcing active workers aged 65 and over to take payouts. Thirteen states, including populous California, Florida, New Jersey and New York, had already outlawed the mandatory retirement age. But from January 1, 1987, all private US companies were required to do the same, although the public sector has seven years in which to comply. Experts predict that ending mandatory retirement could mean at least an 18% increase in the numbers of over-70 workers by 2000. The average retirement age now stands at 63.

Labor relations

The USA's past is littered with industrial disputes as bitter and as violent as any in the world. But the 1980s saw the workforce, if not necessarily happier with their lot, at least less willing to fight about it. Rancorous disputes have by no means disappeared, but they are fewer in number and duration than they were a decade ago. Workers now tend to be more concerned to protect their jobs than to achieve increases in pay, and this has cut the number of major work stoppages from over 200 annually in the 1970s to less than 50 a year during the latter half of the 1980s.

However, the pattern of industrial relations is perhaps more varied in the USA than in any other Western industrialized nation. There are enormous differences even within the same industry. Pay negotiations, for example, are almost invariably conducted on a plant-to-plant basis, or at most a state-to-state basis, rather than nationally, even within the strongly unionized industries. In the shiny new high-tech factories of the Sunbelt and California, wages are high, unionization is rare, the lifestyle is attractive and industrial relations are as good as anywhere. In the traditional industries in the old industrial areas, though, hard times have meant that management and workers are often at loggerheads – although the more determined employers have been able to weaken union power.

The right to strike is a fundamental American freedom, but it is hedged around with numerous legal restrictions – restrictions that vary considerably from state to state. Perhaps the most significant qualification is the "cooling-off" period laid down by the Taft-Hartley Act, which stipulates the time that must elapse before the next step in the escalation of a dispute. The idea is that labor and management will have time to reach an amicable agreement. In practice, however, the cooling-off period often allows both sides the opportunity to draw up their battle lines.

Picketing is also a fundamental right, a form of free speech protected by the First Amendment to the US Constitution. But, like the right to strike, it is hedged around with restrictions.

The unions Union membership in the USA is low – barely a fifth of the workforce – and interest in unionization is on the wane. The combined membership of the umbrella organization covering the trade unions – the American Federation of Labor and Congress of Industrial Organizations (AFL-CIO) – was 13m in 1987, though there were 4m or so workers in non-affiliated organizations. Only three unions had more than 1m members – the United Automobile Workers (UAW), Food and Commercial Workers (FCW) and the American Federation of State County and Municipal Employees (AFSCME).

Unionism remains strong in the old traditional industries such as manufacturing and transport, but has hardly any influence in industries such as finance, services and the retail trade. And while the unions retain a powerful grip on the workforce in long-industrialized states such as New York, Michigan, West Virginia and Pennsylvania, their presence in Florida, Texas and Mississippi is weak.

Union recognition The sheer diversity of the American labor movement is striking; there are more than 175 national unions with 71,000 affiliated local unions, and 35 national employee associations with almost 14,000 local chapters. But only one union is recognized as having the right to negotiate contracts in each place of work. A minority of workplaces now have a recognized union, but when there is one the management is legally obliged to negotiate with it. To gain recognition, a union must send a petition to the National Labor Relations Board, which then organizes elections to establish the views of the workforce. If another union gains a foothold in a place where there is already a recognized union, it can insist on new elections to determine which union has the right to negotiate on behalf of the workforce.

Closed shops are outlawed in many states by right-to-work laws. Some states have enacted right-to-work laws to weaken unions and attract industry. But strong opposition from labor leaders has insured that none of the major industrial states has such laws.

Executive salaries

While their employees' wages have been stagnating, the salaries of US executives have surged ahead, and they are now among the highest in the world. Earnings of $1m a year are not unusual. The gap between European executives and their US counterparts is wide and getting wider.

Part of the explanation for this is that American executives get a larger proportion of their pay in performance-related bonuses, and corporate profits have risen strongly. As many as 73% of directors of US companies have performance-related pay, compared with only 42% in Britain. Significantly, the total earnings of US executives rose by an average of over 11% a year in the mid 1980s.

Personal taxation Until recently, the USA had a labyrinthine tax system with no fewer than 15 different rates of taxation, ranging from 11% of the earnings of the poorest-paid to 50% for those at the top of the pay scale. Critics attacked not only its complexity but its "punitive" top tax rate which, they felt, was holding back entrepreneurs. Others commented that few top executives paid their taxes anyway, since the system embodied all kinds of tax shelters.

The tax reforms instituted by President Reagan replaced this panoply of rates with just two, at 15% and 28%, thus giving US taxpayers the lowest top tax rate in the industrial world. But the reforms also did away with several deductions, particularly in the real estate area. Interest payments on car loans, credit card debt and instalment plan purchases are also no longer tax-deductible. Even so, average rates of income tax are estimated to have fallen sharply and Americans pay less income tax than their counterparts in Europe and Japan. But for most Americans, just filling out an annual tax return is still a complicated and tiresome chore.

Some 6m people with incomes below the poverty line pay no tax at all.

State taxes Besides federal taxes, Americans also pay tax to their own state, and state tax rates vary considerably within guidelines laid down by the federal government. New York, for example, is very heavily taxed, and New York Republicans have called for cuts, arguing that the tax rate impairs New York's ability to compete for industry and skilled workers.

Financial institutions: introduction

The combined forces of deregulation and volatile interest rates have set off intense competition in the world's most highly developed financial system, spawning esoteric new products and financial markets. As foreign intermediaries, borrowers and investors flock to the USA, American banks and securities firms are increasingly turning to overseas and global markets.

Recent developments

Securitization Bank loans are being replaced by credit in the form of securities, as large corporations – sometimes more creditworthy than the banks from which they borrow – turn to the less expensive commercial paper markets for short-term funds. Even companies with unimpressive credit ratings can now gain access to public markets by issuing junk bonds or pooling their own receivables and selling them to investors.

Adapting to change Prohibited from underwriting these securities, commercial banks have had to make do writing guarantees and letters of credit to back the issues. But not all securitization has hurt the lenders: by securitizing and then selling off portions of their own loan portfolios, banks and savings and loans institutions have been able to reshape their balance sheets, create liquidity, and generate fee income.

Product boundaries blurred Over the past decade, financial institutions have sidestepped many of the legal and practical constraints stopping them from treading on one another's turf. Securities firms have invaded commercial banking territory, laying claim to short-term corporate lending markets and siphoning consumer deposits into high-paying mutual funds (see *Investment banks and other institutions*).

Banks have retaliated by buying discount brokerages and offering alternative forms of long-term finance to corporations. Even insurance companies have entered the fray, selling investment products and making residential mortgage loans.

More risk, fewer profits Intense competition from inside and outside the financial sector has driven commercial banks to book riskier loans and pursue less desirable markets; meanwhile, investment banks have been forced to put ever larger amounts of capital at risk for their clients. Some financial products – such as large corporate lending and bond underwriting – have become overcrowded and unprofitable for many participants.

Technology Advances in computers and telecommunications have revolutionized the financial services industry. Widespread automation brings investors instantaneous market data and allows securities firms to handle record numbers of transactions in a fraction of the time possible a few years ago. Commercial banks now offer dozens of electronic services, such as home banking and point-of-sale retail payments systems. The number of automated teller machines has risen dramatically, and there are now over 70,000 nationwide.

Emergence of financial conglomerates Deftly skirting banking regulations, retail and manufacturing firms have used their consumer credit operations as springboards into the banking and insurance industries. Sears, Roebuck, one of the nation's foremost department stores, has over 60m credit card holders and through the acquisition of numerous subsidiaries it now sells mortgages, insurance, real estate, banking products and securities alongside the vacuum cleaners, toasters and dishwashers. American Express has become a diversified financial corporation with revenues of $23bn a year. Its market capitalization outstrips that of the nation's largest banks.

Commercial banks

Much of the legislation imposed during the 1920s and 1930s to ensure bank safety has been stripped away, spurring innovation, risk taking and – in some cases – imprudence. Rapid asset growth during the 1970s, particularly in lending to Latin America and to energy firms, left many banks with problem loans and questionable levels of capitalization. Bank failures in the late 1980s were at their highest rate since the Depression. Nevertheless, there are still more than 13,000 privately owned commercial banks, most of them small, local institutions with assets under $200m.

Federal Reserve System

The Federal Reserve (the "Fed"), composed of 12 district banks, acts as the nation's central bank and is responsible for carrying out national monetary policy, usually in tandem with the Treasury. The 1,500 privately owned member banks, which control 70% of the country's banking assets, are required to maintain sizeable interest-free reserves with the Fed.

Open market operations are the primary tool the Fed uses to control the amount of money and credit in the banking system. The New York Federal Reserve Bank buys and sells huge blocks of government securities on the open market. By altering the balance between the supply and demand for credit in the economy, the Fed effectively influences the interest rates that banks charge. The Federal Funds rate – the rate at which member banks borrow and lend money to one another – determines the rate banks charge their customers. The Fed can also intervene in foreign exchange markets, raise or lower reserve requirements and control the levels of bank lending – but these powers are rarely used.

Regulatory powers The Fed sets capital adequacy guidelines and monitors the activities of its members. Non-member banks are regulated by state authorities. In addition, member and most state-chartered banks are supervised and insured by the Federal Deposit Insurance Corporation (FDIC).

Principal activities

Commercial banks have traditionally supplied industrial firms with short- and medium-term loans, but long-term lending has grown as banks have attracted time deposits and issued bonds. Electronic information and management products, such as cash management services, are on the rise. Now there are no interest rate ceilings on checking and savings accounts, banks are having to pay market rates for consumer deposits. Even so, the relative stability of these funds and the high profit margins possible on consumer loans have led banks to invest more heavily in retail banking than ever before. Tight restrictions apply to non-banking activities, but commercial banks are free to operate in related businesses such as discount securities brokerage, credit cards and investment management.

Correspondent banking

To circumvent restrictions against interstate branch banking, banks have formed an elaborate network of correspondent relationships. Larger banks frequently provide data processing and other high fixed-cost services to smaller banks in exchange for fees or deposits. Correspondent relationships also enable banks to sell assets to other banks. But the interdependence of financial institutions has become a matter of public concern. The near collapse in 1984 of Continental Illinois, the nation's 10th largest bank, was precipitated by faulty loans it had bought from a small Oklahoma bank.

Payments systems Lacking a centralized giro system, the USA relies largely on bank-owned clearing houses to handle funds transfers and check-clearing. It generates twice the payments per capita of any other country and writes nearly two-thirds of the world's checks. The average check must clear three banks before being returned. Despite efforts to promote electronic funds transfers, paper-based transactions still account for more than 90% of all non-cash settlements.

Money center banks

Money center banks are the largest and most influential of all American banks. Besides traditional lending, deposit-taking and trust activities, money centers are active participants in the money and international capital markets, and in US government securities underwriting and trading. For regulatory reasons, most big banks are now owned by bank holding companies.

Citibank, a subsidiary of the bank holding company Citicorp, has set its sights on becoming the world's first global bank, offering a huge array of financial products to consumers and businesses worldwide. Domestically, it has been the most successful money center in building its consumer banking operations.

Morgan Guaranty, owned by J P Morgan, the most prestigious American commercial bank, serves an elite clientele of blue-chip industrial and corporate clients. Consumer banking is limited to a few thousand wealthy individuals. It is the only money center with an AAA bond rating and is consistently one of the most profitable large US banks.

Bankers Trust decided in 1979 to eschew retail banking altogether to become a self-styled "merchant bank". It has made impressive inroads into investment banking territory, establishing a hotly contested commercial paper operation and aggressively selling its loans to other banks.

Bank of America was, in 1980, the world's largest bank in terms of assets. But since then, its fortunes have been assailed by everything from third-world debt to farm loan problems. By late 1986, it was having to fight off a bid from the smaller Californian bank, First Interstate Bancorporation. It was slowly recovering at the end of the 1980s.

Regional banks

The largest regional banks and bank holding companies now equal many money center banks in size but typically rely more on consumer deposits than money market funding. In recent years, large regionals have been among the most profitable and fastest growing banks in the country. Following a 1985 Supreme Court ruling allowing interstate mergers approved by the states, a rash of mergers took place to shut out the New York and California money centers, and the USA could soon see some of the concentration of banking power shift away from New York into the hands of a few "super-regionals‘.

Foreign banks

Growth of foreign banks has been dramatic. Roughly 27% of the country's corporate and industrial loans are now on the books of foreign banks, compared with 10% in the mid 1970s. Japanese banks are the most aggressive, controlling 40% of foreign bank assets in the USA.

Thrifts

Savings and loans and savings banks are granted government charters to collect retail deposits and make residential mortgage loans. These "thrifts" hold half of US home mortgages. In the mid-1980s, after a decade of deregulation, volatile interest rates and blatant mismanagement, the industry incurred losses of $12bn. Bailing out government-insured thrifts might cost taxpayers over $100bn. Only half the 3,000 thrifts are expected to have survived by the mid-1990s.

Investment banks and other institutions

With a fraction of the staff and one-tenth the assets of commercial banks, securities firms provide American corporations with most of their external funding. Following the deregulation of fixed brokerage commissions in 1975, many securities firms went under, but low-cost competitors soon emerged, and today there are 9,000 securities brokers and dealers in the USA. As investors and issuers become more sophisticated, and global in reach, it is the New York investment banks – with their vast networks of issuer/investor contacts and massive capital bases – that are the dominant players.

Investment banks

The top New York investment banks are among the most aggressive, innovative, and profitable financial institutions in the USA. The top six underwrite 80–90% of all corporate debt and equity issued. As financial consultants, investment banks wield considerable power over corporate decision-making. While their basic business is acting as intermediary between investors and private or public concerns seeking medium- and long-term funds, investment banks have rapidly broadened their fields of activity. Leveraged buy-outs, corporate restructurings, advising on mergers and acquisitions, and making direct investments in companies (merchant banking), have become much more significant contributors to earnings than in the past. As a group, investment banks pay the highest salaries in the USA, allowing them the pick of top graduates from the country's best schools.

Merrill Lynch is the largest brokerage house in the USA and one of the nation's most broadly diversified financial services firms, with a major position in both retail and institutional investor markets. It underwrites a quarter of the country's debt and equity.

Salomon Brothers, once the world's top securities underwriter and trading firm, had lost its leading position by the end of the 1980s. The firm has begun devoting more of its energy to more profitable merchant banking business. Salomon is famous for its aggressive approach as well as the infighting of its employees.

Goldman Sachs is pre-eminent in commercial paper, mergers and acquisitions, and equity trading. The firm is one of the last old-fashioned private partnerships left on Wall Street, although it has recently sought external sources of capital. In a good year, a partner makes as much as $5m.

Other financial institutions

Mutual funds sell shares directly to investors; the money raised is then pooled and invested in a variety of securities by professional managers. With over 2,700 different funds, 50m investors, and assets of $800bn, the industry has burgeoned into one of the nation's largest financial services providers. A specialized type of mutual fund, the money market fund, grew rapidly in the late 1970s. It allowed small investors to participate directly in the high-yielding short-term debt markets at a time when regulations kept bank interest rates artificially low. Although these regulations have gone, money market funds retain much of their popularity.

Venture capital firms provide more than $2.8bn a year to promising young companies denied conventional financing. In return for investment capital, venture capitalists receive substantial equity ownership and stand to make large profits if their companies prosper and go public or if they are bought out by other companies.

Commercial finance and factoring firms typically cater to small- and medium-sized businesses, advancing them funds against accounts receivables, inventory, equipment or other assets.

The tax benefits of equipment leasing have made this a hot financing technique. With corporate lending markets drying up, many commercial banks are acquiring finance and factoring firms.

Consumer finance companies are the largest providers of consumer instalment credit after commercial banks. A number of manufacturing and retail firms have finance subsidiaries, notably General Electric, IBM and the nation's big three auto manufacturers.

Financial markets

The United States has the largest, most diverse and highly developed financial markets in the world. There are no exchange controls and, with the removal of the US interest-equalization tax, foreigners are encouraged to participate both as issuers and investors. About 80% of all securities are not listed on public exchanges but are traded directly between dealers in the over-the-counter market. New York is the center of most trading activity; Chicago is the leader in commodities and options.

Debt markets

Credit markets in the USA have grown dramatically in recent years, as equity financing has become less popular. The largest borrower is the US government, which accounts for $2,500bn of outstanding debt. Most of the debt is traded directly in the over-the-counter market.

Government agency securities Treasury bills, notes and bonds are sold at weekly public auctions held by the Federal Reserve. The market is served by roughly 40 primary dealers – one third of them owned by US commercial banks and seven by the Japanese – that purchase and make markets in the securities. There is also a vast secondary market, served by a few hundred brokers and dealers. Daily trading in government securities exceeds $100bn.

Government agency securities Agencies of the US government have issued or guaranteed more then $900bn of debt held by private investors. Over half is composed of securities backed by pools of residential mortgages. Markets in agency securities are maintained by the primary dealers. Turnover ranges from $15bn–20bn a day.

Corporate bonds and commercial paper US corporations issue more than $200bn a year in bonds. Large issues are usually sold directly to investors by a syndicate of investment banks, who then make secondary markets in the securities. The emergence of the "junk" bond since the early 1980s has allowed hundreds of corporations with low bond ratings access to public markets. Commercial paper – short-term promissory notes used to raise working capital – is fast becoming a leading source of short-term funds for major corporations. Trading in commercial paper exceeds $15bn a day.

Equity markets

There are 12 stock markets across the USA operating independently. Trading hours vary according to time zone but electronic communications systems allow certain issues to be traded simultaneously on several exchanges. All public trading is controlled and supervised by the Securities and Exchange Commission (see *Law, Government and business*).

The New York Stock Exchange (NYSE) is the largest organized securities exchange in the world, with more than 75bn shares listed and a market value in excess of $2,500bn. The value of securities traded exceeds $6bn a day. Most of the 1,600 listed companies are prominent domestic and foreign firms.

The American Stock Exchange (Amex) in New York has less stringent listing requirements and tends to trade issues of companies still too small for the NYSE. Over 800 companies are listed and the annual volume traded is over $30bn.

Regional exchanges account for only about 10% of US trading volume in listed securities. Typically they feature the issues of local firms. The largest regionals are the Midwest Stock Exchange, the Pacific Stock Exchange and the Philadelphia Stock Exchange.

NASDAQ is the market where over-the-counter, rather than listed, stocks are traded. More than one-and-a-half times the size of the London Stock Exchange, the National Association of Securities Dealers' Automated Quotation system is a computerized network that connects 500 firms making markets in 5,500 over-the-counter securities. Subscribers to the system include thousands of securities dealers, pension funds, and other financial institutions. The value of shares traded is nearly $500bn a year. NASDAQ handles three times as many foreign issues as the New York and American exchanges.

Other markets

Foreign exchange The global foreign exchange market has doubled in size in recent years and now has a daily trading volume exceeding $200bn. New York is second in size only to London, trading $50bn a day. Only 10% goes to finance international commerce and investment; the bulk is traded by banks and speculators betting on market movements and hedging foreign investments. About 80 commercial banks dominate the market, although investment banks and commodity firms have become increasingly visible.

Futures The USA has the largest and most active futures markets in the world. Contracts in anything from pork bellies to precious metals to financial and currency futures are bought and sold with ease. Contracts are highly standardized and markets are closely tied to the underlying commodities. As a result, most of the world's hedging is done in the USA. The Chicago Mercantile Exchange is the biggest futures and commodities exchange, followed by the New York Futures Exchange. Increasingly, financial futures outweigh old-fashioned agricultural commodities in volume and activity.

More stringent supervision

Since the mid-1980s federal authorities have mounted an aggressive campaign against manipulation of securities and commodities markets. A string of highly publicized convictions for insider trading has led banks and securities firms to invest millions to ensure compliance with securities laws. In the most celebrated case, Drexel Burnham – the leading underwriter of junk bonds – was fined $650m in December 1988.

Investors and investments

Pension funds and insurance companies and other financial institutions hold 60% of all outstanding securities and account for at least 85% of the transaction volume in every major securities market. Individual participation in the market has waned as investors have cut transaction costs by letting professionally managed mutual funds invest for them. Now, direct household ownership accounts for less than 40% of the $6,000bn–7,000bn worth of securities portfolios in the USA. Corporate equities and government debt constitute two-thirds of all American securities portfolios. The remainder is largely held in corporate and municipal bonds, and as mortgage-backed securities on the commercial paper market. Although total investment in foreign issues has risen sharply, these still account for less than 3% of the securities held.

Insurance

The US insurance industry writes 43% of the world's insurance business. Most life, property and casualty insurance is sold by private insurance companies, while government-sponsored and non-profit organizations fund 60% of health benefits. The industry is primarily regulated at the state level, with tight controls over both insurance and investment activities.

Life insurance

Americans buy more life insurance relative to the national income than anyone but the Japanese and Canadians. In 1987 there were 395m life policies in force, providing $7,500bn in total coverage, 41% being accounted for by group life insurance offered by employers.

Companies More than 90% of these are publicly owned; the remainder are mutual life companies, owned by policyholders. Mutual companies tend to be older and larger, controlling 50% of the industry's assets. The largest life company, Prudential, writes less than 8% of the nation's life insurance premiums.

Products With banks and securities firms competing for consumer investment dollars, life companies have had to design new products: universal life, the most popular, divides premium dollars between a high-yielding investment portfolio and a death benefit. And many companies now sell the same mutual funds and individual retirement accounts (IRAs) as banks and securities firms. Insurance companies manage two-thirds of US private pension fund assets.

Sources of income Over the past two decades life premium receipts have declined from 49% to 25% of total income, whereas investments of capital and reserves, spurred by higher interest rates, have grown to contribute nearly 30%, with annuities contributing about 20%. Companies have aggressively entered the real estate markets, both as developers and equity owners.

Prospects Price wars, the creation of interest-sensitive products, and competitive pressures on investment spreads have led to a steady decline in the profitability of individual life insurance. A wave of consolidation – similar to that sweeping the banking industry – could mean difficult times ahead for companies lacking size and/or marketing clout.

Property and casualty

Roughly 3,500 companies insure 93% of all homeowners and virtually all business in the USA. Property and casualty (P&C) underwriting has proven consistently unprofitable. Until recently, companies were able to achieve bottom-line profits by aggressively investing reserves and capital, keeping insurance rates low to allow for the healthy returns companies could get on idle funds. Declining interest rates and net underwriting losses of over $45bn in 1984 and 1985, however, pushed the industry into the red and set off the steepest-ever rise in insurance prices.

Premiums and losses About half of the $190bn P&C premiums written annually come from individuals – almost half of them to insure automobiles. Claims paid and claims adjustments absorb 80 cents of every premium dollar earned. Auto accidents are the leading cause of losses ($80bn a year), followed by theft ($15bn).

Lobbying for law reform Companies are pressing for extensive tort reform to combat the steep rise in out-of-court settlements. Limits on liability, awards, punitive damages and attorney's fees have already been imposed in some states. These gains may prove a mixed blessing if states also insist upon lowering the ceilings on rates companies can charge.

Accountancy

Accountancy in the USA is dominated by what used to be known as the "Big Eight" firms, which between them control 90% of the profits, revenues, income tax, and employment of the companies listed on the New York Stock Exchange.

The profession

An accounting career in the USA begins with the long and arduous study for the Uniform CPA (certified public accountant) examination. This qualification is essential because only CPAs can carry out audits.

The high potential earnings, and the increasing glamor of life at the top of the profession ensures that most CPAs set their sights on the Big Eight, which between them manage to interview approximately 150,000 graduates a year, and hire some 10,000. It may take as little as five years to achieve partnership in a small firm and as many as 12 in a large firm.

The American Institute of Certified Public Accountants (AICPA) helps keep up standards through peer and quality review programs. Quality review is mandatory for all AICPA-member firms which perform audits. Peer review is mandatory only for AICPA members which audit SEC companies and belong to the SEC practice section of the AICPA. The SEC (Securities and Exchange Commission) regulates certain publicly traded companies.

While this sets a lower limit on competence, the choice of an accountant is best made with advice from another professional, either a lawyer or management consultant. Firms working in the same field may also choose the same accountant – while they would never share an advertising agency, picking the same accountant means picking one who knows the field well.

Mergers

Mergers of accounting firms are in vogue. Large firms are merging to decrease costs and improve worldwide service. The first to merge were Ernst & Whinney and Arthur Young. The merger will make the combined firm, Ernst & Young, the largest in the USA. Deloitte Haskins & Sells and Touche Ross's US partners also approved a merger.

Changing roles

Preparing tax returns and auditing company books still provides accounting firms with the bulk of their income. But over the past decade or so they have been branching out into fields such as litigation support, merger and acquisition services, actuarial services, benefits and healthcare consulting, and management and information systems consultancy.

Consultancy Consultancy now accounts for a fifth of the total revenues of the "Big Eight". Arthur Andersen earns 37% of its total revenues from information and management consulting, for which it has established a separate division. Reorganization of the firm has meant that consultancy partners, who bring in more revenue per partner than their audit or tax counterparts, will now be compensated for their efforts.

Consultancy revenues for the other large firms range from 14% to 24% of total revenues.

Internationalizing The big firms in the USA have begun to have a more international outlook. All the major firms have developed US specialists to help clients take advantage of relaxed European barriers.

Marketing has become a major focus of the large firms. Firms now advertise in all the major newspapers and business magazines. Most local and regional firms have a marketing director in each office and have established public relations departments or committees.

Commissions and contingent fees
The Federal Trade Commission and the AICPA reached an agreement allowing CPAs to accept commissions and contingent fees. However, since individual states license and regulate CPAs, state boards of accountancy will have the final say as to whether CPAs will be allowed to start recommending investments for a commission.

Choosing an accountant

The large firms have the benefit of extensive resources and back-up facilities, and are clearly in a position to attract the best talent. But some businesses may prefer the more intimate relationship possible with smaller firms, many of which have extended their practice areas and can now provide consultancy services.

The letter of engagement Typically, an accountant will give a client a letter of engagement at the outset. The terms of this letter have to be examined carefully, for they outline the way the accountant will work. It is also important to establish just what is expected of the client.

Accountants' letters of engagement are essentially intended to establish the business relationship. But part of the letter will be designed to protect them against future litigation.

Litigation

Increasingly, the law is holding accountants responsible for failure to detect fraud or advise their client properly. In the 1984 case, the United States v Arthur Young, Supreme Court Chief Justice Warren Burger stated: "The independent auditor assumes a public responsibility transcending any employment relationship with the client."

In an effort to decrease litigation, the Auditing Standard Board issued a new "opinion," defining the auditor's role and responsibilities in which it specifies that company management, not the auditor, is responsible for the financial statements.

However, state courts have been upholding suits against accountants for negligence when the audit has failed to reveal potential problems. Accountants are also being sued for violation of the Racketeer Influenced and Corrupt Organizations law (RICO), a statute that provides for treble damages. The AICPA is lobbying to amend RICO statutes and state liability laws.

One result of all this litigation has been increases in fees caused by the soaring insurance premiums paid by accountants for litigation cover.

The big firms

KPMG Peat Marwick Peat Marwick merged with Main Hurdman in 1986. KPMG, the smaller firm, concentrates on rapidly growing medium-size companies, while Peat Marwick courts the larger, more established clients. Both are strong on audits.

Arthur Andersen Chicago-based firm that projects a clean-cut, Midwestern image. Andersen has the largest consultancy practice among the top firms and specializes in information systems consultancy. Andersen is the only leading firm to have two divisions: audit/tax and consultancy.

Ernst & Young The combination of Ernst & Whinney and Arthur Young makes a geographically strong and diversified firm. Ernst brings strong Midwestern and Southeastern practices. Arthur Young adds strength on the East and West coasts.

Coopers & Lybrand Coopers is one of the oldest and most respected auditing concerns and audit is still the mainstay of its practice.

Price Waterhouse Price cultivates a gilt-edged image and pays its partners accordingly. It still earns most of its income from auditing, but has begun to diversify into areas such as information systems consultancy.

Deloitte & Touche Both Deloitte Haskins & Sells and Touche Ross's partners have worked at streamlining their firms in the past few years. Both have been at the top in revenue percentage growth. The combined firm will have strengths in all areas.

Law

The USA inherited the English system of common law, with its reliance upon the courts to establish by precedent rules for resolving disputes. The judicial branch of the federal government consists of a system of courts headed by the Supreme Court, and each state has its own court system separate from the federal courts.

The legal profession

In 1950 there were fewer than 250,000 lawyers in the USA. By 1980, the number had grown to 500,000, and was set to double by the mid-1990s. Very large law firms are common, but many attorneys work alone in private practice, are employed as in-house counsel by companies, hold positions in government, or work in the judiciary or academia. Ten years ago no firm had revenues of more than $60m. By 1989 the earnings of more than 40 firms topped $100m.

Specialization As in-house corporate legal departments have grown to assume more of their respective companies' legal work, law firms have developed specialized niches and expertise in response to the need for sophisticated legal services, whether it be in bankruptcy, antitrust, contracts or patents.

Training starts with a three-year postgraduate course at one of the country's numerous law schools. Typically a law student is employed by a law firm while studying for the state bar exam. In most firms, it then takes 8–11 years to become a partner.

Litigation Litigation in the USA is a long process. Simply filing a suit and locating and bringing prospective witnesses to court may take more than a year. Appeals, both to state and federal courts, are frequent and accepted as normal. Although the Supreme Court is the ultimate court of appeal, it deals only with cases that involve the constitution, an act of Congress, a treaty or a right protected by federal law. There is no appeal against its decisions.

Aspects of business law

All companies doing business in the USA are subject to the laws of the federal government, the laws of each state in which they are doing business and the local laws, for example, of the municipalities in which their offices may be located.

There is no requirement that state or local laws be uniform, and even those laws described as "uniform" usually contain significant differences. However, the corporate, commercial and tax laws are generally similar enough. Corporations are governed by the laws of the state in which they are incorporated, and people usually form a corporation in the state in which they plan to do business (see *The business framework*).

Foreign investment The USA has a liberal attitude towards inward investment, but there are some laws at both the state and federal levels that affect certain types of foreign investment. Specialist advice should always be sought by foreign companies planning to invest in land, banking, maritime industries, energy-related activities (including mineral leases and electric power generation), outer-continental shelf activities, communications, aviation and aeronautics.

Antitrust There are stringent laws designed to prevent conduct that restricts competition. Restraints on competition are illegal if "unreasonable," which price fixing, division of markets, group boycotts and certain arrangements whereby the purchase of one product is tied to the purchase of another, have been judged to be.

Mergers and acquisitions are governed by the antitrust laws and may be prohibited if they are found to constitute unreasonable restraints of trade, illegal attempts to monopolize a particular market, or unfair competition.

Product liability The USA has led the way in legislation to hold manufacturers liable for injuries resulting from defects in their products. Product liability cases are numerous and often involve sizable awards of punitive damages; the principles governing liability and damages vary from state to state.

Securities regulation

The Securities Exchange Act of 1934 regulates all aspects of public trading of securities and extends investor protection beyond purchasers of securities. Set up to implement it was the Securities and Exchange Commission (SEC), at present one of the largest federal agencies (see *Financial institutions*).

Choosing a firm

A review of the country's top law firms is provided annually in surveys conducted by *The American Lawyer* and the *National Law Journal*.

The *Martindale-Hubbell* directory of attorneys provides a listing of US law firms by state and by city, with entries written by the firms themselves.

Leading firms	No lawyers/ partners	Gross revenues ($ million)	European offices
Skadden, Arps, Slate, Magher & Flom	830/157	290	London
Jones, Day, Revis & Pogue	746/269	211	Geneva, London, Paris
Baker & McKenzie	920/340	196	Throughout Europe
Gibson Dunn & Crutcher	493/174	190	London, Paris
Davis Polk & Wardwell	338/88	180	London, Paris
Shearman & Sterling	412/113	180	London, Paris
Sullivan & Cromwell	318/92	159	London, Paris
Latham & Watkins	368/133	153	None
Cravath, Swaine & Moore	270/64	151	London
Morgan, Lewis & Bockius	590/206	151	London
Vinson & Elkins	401/171	146.5	London
O'Melveny & Myers	382/124	144.5	London
Sidley & Austin	504/209	140	London
Fried, Frank, Harris,Shriver & Jackobson	307/97	136	London
Weil, Gotshal & Manges	376/90	134	None
Cleary, Gottlieb, Steen & Hamilton	293/92	130	Brussels, London, Paris
Simpson, Thatcher & Bartlett	313/84	122	London
Fulbright & Jaworski	394/171	117	London, Zurich
Pillsbury, Madison & Sutro	402/157	116	None
Paul, Weiss, Rifkind, Wharton & Garrison	316/84	114	Paris

Figues are based on the AM LAW 100 for 1988.

Advertising and PR

On Madison Avenue in New York City – the heart of the US advertising industry – it has often seemed as if the copywriters and creative directors of the big agencies could mould America's consumer culture at will. But as the demand for advertising has shrunk and consumers have become more choosy, the agencies have had to hone their sales pitch, learn to exploit new media, accept smaller fees, and expand their services. One way they have expanded is to become involved in public relations work. In fact, as workers, communities and legislators become more sophisticated and concerned about the impact that business has on the lives of people, the importance of good public relations has blossomed.

Advertising

Advertising is big business in the land of mass consumption. While corporate restructurings and the fall in the dollar hurt sales and earnings for both ad agencies and their corporate clients during the first half of the 1980s, ad revenues have rebounded since their nadir in 1985. Total advertising expenditures approached $119bn in 1988.

Auto, food and consumer service companies are the heaviest advertisers. (Philip Morris led the pack in 1988, spending $1.6bn).

Television While direct mail ads are the most profitable, the fastest growth in advertising is taking place in cable TV, which is seeing ad revenues increase by the order of 12% annually.

Network television remains the favorite medium, particularly for the biggest advertisers, but its hegemony is being severely undercut as the number of viewers declines. The big three networks are trying to hold on to advertisers' custom and charge them more by returning to the way they did business in the 1950s and 1960s: getting companies to sponsor a particular show.

Slowdown Advertising agencies face a big battle as the USA ages and economic growth slows. They are finding consumers elusive and markets intensely segmented.

Public relations

Being seen, and being seen in the right light, is extremely important to businesses in the USA, particularly if they produce mass consumer products, are in a sensitive industry, like chemicals, or their operating environment depends to a large extent on public trust or legislation. Companies, depending on their size, resources, and type of business, generally use a combination of in-house staff and outside consultants for their needs.

Public affairs These needs are increasingly diverse and complex. In fact, the whole notion has expanded and taken on a new name. Public affairs – which comprise public relations, community relations (including corporate philanthropy), and government relations – are now the professional catchwords.

Pleasing the community Companies are finding that they have new uses for PR. For example, in recent years, firms involved in greenfield investments and in acquisitions have learned painful lessons about the costs of not sufficiently tending to community sentiments via a good PR effort.

They are also finding that they need to do more than PR to stay ahead of the game. Many companies find that an intensive community relations program enables them to foresee problems. Community relations programs can also build community loyalty which can pay off in terms of a more loyal and productive work force, better business, and a more conducive legislative environment.

Importing and exporting

The USA represents the largest industrial and consumer market in the world, to be rivaled only by the EC after 1992. Combined with its traditional hospitality to the notion of free trade, the USA is an attractive target for exporters seeking to expand sales. Many overseas companies have met with success – as the persistently large trade deficit will testify. Fears about the trade deficit's long-term consequences and the competitiveness of US exports have prompted legislators and trade negotiators to get tough with foreign countries. This is affecting attitudes towards imports, exports and foreign investment.

General trading environment

The USA is a participant in a number of accords which influence trade between it and other countries: it has ratified a free trade agreement with Canada, designed to create a unified market between the two countries. Among other things, the agreement phases out all tariffs for products sold to the other partner, and reduces investment barriers. An earlier agreement with Israel is also designed to promote free trade between the two countries. The Caribbean Basin Initiative gives some duty breaks to imports from designated Caribbean and Central American nations, while trying to encourage US investment there. Many companies, particularly from Japan, make use of incentives in US trade law to build factories in Mexico (commonly referred to as "maquiladoras") and then ship the goods to the USA, reducing labor costs and duty costs, and avoiding possible quotas. Tax laws offer similar inducements to locate production facilities in Puerto Rico and then ship goods to the mainland.

GATT The USA is an active participant in the General Agreement on Tariffs and Trade (GATT) through which it tries to tear down trade barriers in other countries, while being accused of side-stepping GATT with a range of non-tariff barriers. The USA also has numerous agreements under the Multi-fibre Arrangement which strictly limit textile and apparel imports. Many types of goods from developing nations can enter duty free under the Generalized System of Preferences (GSP) program.

Importing

While most goods can freely enter the USA, import of certain articles is either prohibited or restricted. Some of the rules limit entry to certain ports; restrict routing, storage or use; or require treatment, labeling or processing as a condition of release from customs. Prohibited imports include: certain narcotics; obscene, immoral and seditious matter; and merchandise produced by convict or forced labor. Licensing is compulsory for arms and ammunition as well as imports from Cuba, Cambodia, Libya, Nicaragua, North Korea, and Vietnam. In fact, the licensing virtually prohibits imports from these countries. Some major types of imports requiring a license or permit are alcoholic beverages, animals and animal products, some drugs, agricultural goods, petroleum products and trademarked articles. Other products, such as steel, autos and textiles, are limited by annual quotas.

Tariffs The overall tariff burden is not high, about 4%. Most tariffs are levied ad valorem, but a few are still charged at a specific amount per unit. Duty rates vary according to country of origin, type of product, and other factors. Only certain products from countries meeting political and economic criteria can enter duty free under the GSP program. The list of eligible products is revised annually by the United States Trade

Representative. Most imports enter at somewhat higher, "most-favored-nation" rates. Traditionally only the Soviet Union and some Eastern bloc countries have not received MFN status.

As of January 1 1989, the USA adopted the Harmonized Tariff Classification System, in line with that used by many other major trading nations. While this has helped reduce problems associated with tariff classifications, the applicable duty can still be a matter of interpretation. Foreign exporters can get a formal advance notice of the applicable rate by applying to the US Customs Commissioner.

Non-tariff barriers The government has a wide array of legal means to protect domestic industry from injurious imports. The principal laws are those governing antidumping and countervailing duties, market disruption caused by imports from communist countries and procedures for retaliation against unfair trade practices.

Among the non-tariff barriers that may prevent or delay customs clearance of foreign goods are special labeling requirements (wool and fur products, alcoholic beverages) and compliance with Food and Drug Administration and Department of Agriculture regulations (live animals, plants, insecticides, food, beverages, drugs and cosmetics) are subject to special inspection. In general, all goods imported into the USA must be marked individually with the name of the country of origin in English.

The Buy American Act of 1933 provides that goods procured for use within the USA by the government should be of domestic origin, unless they are not produced in sufficient quantity or quality or unless US procurement is inconsistent with the public interest.

Samples generally can be brought into the USA duty free if they meet certain requirements, i.e., they are less than $1 in value and are brought in for purposes of generating sales. Textile products face the most stringent guidelines for falling into this duty free category.

Free trade zones The US Foreign Trade Zone (FTZ) program was created by special legislation in 1934. Companies may bring foreign and domestic merchandise into zones for a variety of purposes, including storage, testing, relabeling, displaying and manufacturing, for eventual sale in the USA or for re-export. All customs duties and federal excise taxes are deferred while merchandise is in the zone, and in many instances, these duties or taxes can be substantially reduced or eliminated by using the FTZ.

There are more than 145 FTZs and 110 subzones (for manufacturing operations) in use. A company interested in establishing a new FTZ or tapping into an existing one contacts the governor's office in the state or territory where it wants to do business. The special FTZ board designated to decide on the applications is generally liberal with its permission.

Agents It is not necessary to employ the services of a sales agent if the exporter is communicating directly with the US importer. A sales agent is helpful in dealing with the administrative hassles of the import process. In general, there are no problems or restrictions in retaining their services.

The establishment of sales subsidiaries does not cause any inherent difficulties from a US customs standpoint. However, exporters need to consult with several US agencies before taking this step.

Identifying import opportunities The USA is not one vast market, but rather a group of regional markets, each with its own climate, lifestyle, buying habits and industrial composition. Exporters need to keep this fact foremost in mind in planning a strategy for entering the US market. Sales should start regionally if a company does not have sufficient financial resources to mount a continent-wide advertising, promotional, sample and inventory program. If the product has not been absolutely tested in the market a strong patent position can hold the competition at bay; if it does not travel well (for example, if there are high freight costs) its use will be geographically limited.

All US embassies maintain a commercial library and generally have individuals available who are familiar with most import requirements. In the USA, the Department of Commerce and Census Bureau publish extensive data of use in carrying out marketing analyses. It may also be wise to consult one of numerous market research firms for assistance.

Licensing No government approval is needed for foreign licensing of technology in the USA, but US firms are subject to export controls on the transfer of certain technology abroad. US antitrust laws apply to licensing agreements. The Department of Justice's basic concerns are that a patent as a limited monopoly must not be indirectly broadened by contract and that the licensing of trademarks and know-how must not foster a monopoly.

Exporting

Export incentives Concern about continued trade deficits has led the USA in recent years to expand its programs to promote exports, though these are still not as wide-ranging as those in many other countries. The Department of Commerce provides a host of information services (including individual country market analyses), and both it and the Department of Agriculture maintain a network of service officers overseas to help US businesses promote their exports. The Export-Import Bank is one of the major sources of public funding for exports, and is beefing up programs for small businesses. Similarly, many states are taking their own steps to promote exports, through offering advice, financial and marketing assistance to US companies.

Tax shelter Tax laws also encourage exports by sheltering portions of export income. To be eligible, a company must have a foreign sales corporation which is incorporated outside the USA. It must maintain foreign operations with separate books, records and a director resident overseas, and be principally active in the sale of US products abroad.

Distribution

Deregulation and its result – increased competition – in the 1980s brought down distribution and travel costs and increased the range of distribution options available. These positive effects, however, may not always be long-lasting. Air rates, for example, are increasing as the number of companies in the industry dwindles. Indeed, mergers and other forms of corporate reorganization will dominate transport in the early 1990s and will have a strong influence on how and at what cost goods are distributed and retailed in the USA.

Road or rail?

Although the value of air freight is slowly increasing, its high cost means that only a tiny fraction of US freight is shipped by air. (Airlines captured only 4% of freight revenues in 1988, the same percentage as pipelines.) By volume (tons per mile) of goods transported, rail is most popular (37% of all freight handled in 1988). This is because rail is generally the most cost-effective means of transporting heavy bulk items long distances. Yet the trucking industry takes the lion's share of all freight revenues – 75%. Trucking companies responded more quickly to deregulation than the railroads. By slashing their rates they have been enlarging their market share in the past decade. By comparison, deregulation has had less impact on the railroads, simply because each company has a monopoly on a particular route.

Intermodalism Rather than choose one means of transporting goods, many companies use more than one method to minimize costs and maximize advantages. "Piggybacking" for example, combines the low cost of long-haul transport with the flexibility of trucking to the final destination. Piggyback freight is expanding at a rapid pace, estimated at more than 20% a year, helped by the long distances involved, which make this method of transport more economic. For example, trains carried 3m trailers and containers in 1980. By 1988 they carried 5.7m.

Wholesale progress

Wholesale distribution in the USA is a $2,200bn a year industry which employs more than 6m workers. It consists of three parts: manufacturers' sales branches; agents and brokers; and merchant wholesalers. The last category handles 70% of total trade, and has seen its share grow each year since World War II. Imports and exports is the single fastest growing segment, with volumes expanding by more than 10% annually since 1974.

This industry is generally reputed to be the most efficient and competitive in the world. Productivity of distributive workers is more than 50% higher than the US average. This is in part because US distributors have been in the vanguard of using computers and other sophisticated techniques of stock management.

In fact, many European distributors are coming to the USA to learn new techniques in preparation for the European single market after 1992.

Retailing

Retailers face an especially turbulent period in the 1990s with hostile takeovers, mergers, leveraged buy-outs and consolidations shaking their ranks. They are also facing the fact that manufacturers, dissatisfied with how retailers handle their products, are increasingly interested in going direct to the market by opening their own stores.

Technological, economic and demographic changes are also reshaping this industry. Large all-purpose retailers like Sears and Montgomery Wards are finding that the market is driving them towards increased specialization. At the same time, with more adult women working outside the home, consumers are demanding convenience. Retailers have responded in various ways. This can go in the direction of successful "total marketing" ventures like the Krogers supermarket chain's new combination store or Wal-Mart. This also lies behind the explosive growth in direct marketing. Some 5.3bn catalogues were distributed in 1981; by 1986, this figure had more than doubled to 11.8bn. For other retailers, it means emphasis on consumer service.

Carving a niche Retailers are finding that consumers have more sophisticated tastes as markets become globalized, and that they are demanding higher quality products. Many mass marketers are turning to "micro-marketing" – targeting ware to special, niche markets. High-tech techniques for production (like computer-integrated manufacturing); marketing (teleretailing, advertising in new electronic media); and keeping track of stocks are aiding this trend.

Business Awareness

In a country with no aristocracy but that of wealth, social status in the USA is conferred by success and, in particular, business success, and the values of the business world are openly endorsed across a broad spectrum of society. There is none of the distaste for the profit motive that colors attitudes to business in Europe – nor any envy of those who make money through business. Significantly, few Americans believe high-earners should be taxed heavily.

Of course, the dice are loaded in favour of certain sectors of society: those who earn the coveted MBA business degrees which provide the key to entry to the best jobs are from predominantly affluent backgrounds. But the belief that anyone can succeed, given the talent and the will, plays a large part in American attitudes to business. The rags-to-riches self-made man is the hero of the American business world. Nevertheless, it is rarely the entrepreneur who heads the USA's biggest corporations; it is the loyal company man or (very rarely) woman who has worked his/her way up steadily through the ranks.

In such a vast and cosmopolitan country, the variety is considerable, but as a rule, American executives are more insular and limited in outlook, even more naive than might be expected. Their huge home market cushions most executives who do not travel abroad on business from outside influences. This insularity is lessening, but it still colors the outlook of Americans working in the more secure sectors.

Working hours and attitudes

The US executive is, typically, a dedicated professional, prepared to work immensely hard to achieve personal and corporate goals. Social and family life are deeply cherished, and leisure interests outside business are common. But no external activities and commitments detract from the basic concentration on business and, above all, on business success.

Working discipline

The traditional image of US working practice is the well-disciplined office, in which managers do as they are told, are neatly dressed and sober at all times, do not argue with their superiors or gossip in the office, and acquiesce in a system that includes rapid and harsh dismissal. Although this image has softened a little over the past decade, it remains a characteristic feature of American business life.

High turnover US companies are far more ready to dismiss executives, both individually and *en masse*, than their European counterparts. In one recent year, for example, 56% of all large American companies were reported to have slashed large numbers of middle management; and in the five years up to 1986, according to *Fortune*, big companies dismissed a total of half a million managers. US companies can often be ruthless both in the treatment of people whose employment has been "severed" or "terminated" (they may be escorted out of the building by security guards, with scant time even to clear out their desks) and in the swiftness with which employees past their prime often find their services dispensed with.

Professionalism Most Americans accept harsh discipline pragmatically, acknowledging that it is an inevitable counterpart to a system that offers generous rewards and allows the talented and hard-working to climb swiftly to the top. The very brusque dismissal of older staff is accepted partly because it helps open the way to new young talent. Americans pride themselves on their professionalism, and dismissal is seen as just one facet of professional discipline. They take their work very seriously, and this seriousness has been reinforced by the wave of conservatism that characterized the years of the Reagan presidency. But the work ethic was strong even before Ronald Reagan came to power – although it varies in nature from the Puritanism of the Midwest to the frenetic rat race of New York City. As a rule, the US executive works as hard, and with as much concentration, as any in the world.

Working hours Normal working hours are 9am to 5pm, but there are innumerable exceptions. Regional variations are particularly marked. In manufacturing areas such as Detroit, for example, the hours are linked to plant operations; office work starts at 7am and ends officially at 3pm. In Chicago, executives generally start work around 8am and finish about 4pm. (Avoid, therefore, trying to catch a 4pm plane from Detroit or a 5pm flight from Chicago; the rush-hour traffic is horrific.) In Washington DC and other cities with severe traffic problems, working hours have been staggered in an effort to ease the rush-hour congestion. There is also considerable variation from industry to industry. Thus, brokers and other financial services people on the West Coast are at their desks by 7am, because that is when (10am) Wall Street opens on the other side of the country. Some may start even earlier, in time for the 8am nationwide conference call.

These hours are observed quite faithfully, but they are the minimum. Many US executives at all levels work very long hours. Such long hours are not compulsory, but they are essential for any executive who wants to succeed. As a rule, the higher an executive climbs up the tree, the longer hours he or she tends to work.

After hours While at the office, American executives tend to work hard, with the minimum interruptions. Lunches rarely last much more than an hour. The business breakfast provides a valuable extension to overfilled working days. Occasionally Saturdays will serve the same purpose. But there is usually a marked separation between working hours and leisure hours. Rather than staying in town to socialize with business colleagues after work, American executives generally go directly home. They also make a point of keeping weekends free for recreation; even if they play golf with business associates, the contact will be primarily social, not business.

Home calls

Despite their careful protection of leisure hours, US executives are also accustomed to interruption by business calls at home at weekends and in the evenings. Home telephone numbers will certainly be circulated to all managers' colleagues, and there is rarely any objection to relevant calls from outsiders.

Home computers Even if office hours do not spill over into the evenings, office work may, and many executives take work home. Over the past decade, ownership of personal computers has expanded enormously, and executives will often work at home on their PCs quite intensively. Familiarity with PCs is only one aspect of the American's deep knowledge of, and fascination with, the hardware and software involved in his or her job.

Vacations Vacations tend to be very short. Most executives get only two weeks a year, and only at the very top of the corporation do people take more. Even there, the maximum is four weeks. This is one of the reasons why Americans lay so much emphasis on their recreation at weekends and on public holidays – they simply do not have the long vacations enjoyed by executives elsewhere.

Regional variations

The USA is an enormous country with citizens of every national origin, and there is enormous variation in attitudes to business and business practices.

New York heat In Manhattan the drive for success and the pervasiveness of the business mentality are more marked than anywhere else in the USA. Life in Manhattan is fiercely competitive, and rivalry for everything, from multi-million-dollar merger fees to tables at fashionable restaurants is intense. Besides being supreme in financial services of all descriptions, Manhattan is the hub of corporate America, the capital of advertising, marketing and the media, the center of the legal world, the home of fashion, and much more besides.

Beyond the Big Apple Away from New York, business life tends to be less formal, less cosmopolitan and less obviously pressured. But the more relaxed ways in other regions should not deceive visitors into believing that achieving a successful deal will be any easier. American business is quite ruthless in its pursuit of profit, even in the small towns and state capitals where important headquarters may well be located. In the South, being a "good old boy" – sociable and expansive – is the keynote, and a handshake is much more than a casual greeting: it is a bond between friends. There is a deep sense of honor here, though, and people are taken at their word – flippancy might well be misplaced. The West Coast, on the other hand, is casual and modish, with the emphasis on youth and dynamism. Far from being frowned upon, unconventionality (within narrow limits) is often admired here – a strong contrast to the conservative Midwest, where tradition is strong and things are done by the book.

Corporate hierarchies

Informality is the hallmark of the US business manner. Even in institutions where the etiquette is most rigid, such as the big Wall Street banks, first names are used at every level. But this informality goes hand in hand with intense involvement in the affairs of the company – in its internal politics (which can be savage) as much as in its external sales.

The ladder of power

It is power, rather than status, on which US executives set their sights. Thus, membership of the executive committee, where power resides, is much more important than membership of the board, which has no executive role except to hire (and sometimes fire) the CEO, or chief executive officer.

Executive power The CEO is the most sought-after position in the US corporation. Whatever other titles the CEO may have – he or she could be either chairman or president – CEO is the title that indicates that it is he/she who makes the decisions, exercises the ultimate executive power and "calls the shots."

The board If the company has a chairman who is not the CEO, the chairman heads only the board, not the company or the management. But the board has fiduciary responsibilities to the shareholder and always reserves certain important decisions to itself – the appointment and rewards of the CEO, for example. In a large company, the board has several committees which exercise a number of key functions. A compensation committee, for example, may deliberate on senior salaries, bonuses and stock options, while the audit committee plays a central role in monitoring the integrity of the corporation's finances. The compensation committee is dominated by non-executives, who are drawn mostly from other large corporations. But like other committees, and the whole board, it seldom takes decisions that are not to the taste of the top excutives – especially the CEO.

The president The COO, or chief operating officer, may also be called the president. As the title indicates, he or she is responsible for operations, reporting to the CEO, who has wider strategic responsibilities.

Vice president Below the COO there is often a collection of vice presidents. Although much coveted, the position of the vice president can be highly ambiguous. A vice president who sits on the executive committee is probably called an "executive vice president," and has considerable powers. A "senior executive vice president" is even more important, but a "senior vice president" is usually inferior. Some vice presidents are powerful and influential figures within the company – on a par with finance directors in Europe – while others are merely junior executives. In advertising agencies and banks the title "vice president" is often bestowed on a large number of executives, simply because clients want to feel that a senior executive is handling their affairs. The key to a vice president's real status within the corporation often lies in additions to the title. The title may well have "and treasurer," or "and general counsel," or "engineering," or "public affairs" attached. This shows whether the vice president is head of a function or a division. The head of an important manufacturing subsidiary is often corporate "vice president and general manager."

Women in business

In recent years women have been making a determined assault on the doggedly masculine world of US business and have achieved some success. Women today are much more noticeable in decision-making positions in the major corporations and professional service firms, and in some sectors the proportion of women employed in middle management has risen to about 40%. But they still encounter considerable prejudice and resistance.

In particular, very few women have penetrated the highest levels of management, despite equal rights legislation which has been in effect for more than 20 years. One recent survey of 50 top US companies found only 2% of the executive positions held by women. Women, moreover, still feel disadvantaged and discriminated against: a recent Gallup Poll showed that 71% of them thought their chances of promotion were lower than those of men with equal ability.

Despite this, women are now much more conspicuous in US business, and there has been a subtle softening of its aggressively "macho" character – although it must be said that the women who have been able to make their mark are no less forceful than their male colleagues. Male chauvinism and sexual harassment are still widespread but tend to be covert rather than overt, and any foreign visitor who treats a US businesswoman patronizingly can expect not only her antagonism but the disapproval of many of her male colleagues. This is particularly true in industries such as publishing, where women are a major force.

There are now many women graduating from the business schools. In 1973 the number of women attending business school was only 9.2% of the total; today the figure is probably around 30%. At Harvard Business School, the proportion went to over a quarter in 1983 and has stayed around that level. More significantly, of 30 targets ranked high on headhunters' lists, two were women, according to a 1986 article in *Fortune*. But one worked in retailing and fashion, the other in newspapers; jobs in the top echelons of sectors such as manufacturing have been much harder to come by – although the need to conform with federal legislation has forced big US groups to be clearly seen not to operate discriminatory policies.

Companies can less and less afford the social costs of operating in a discriminatory way – not to mention the costs of lost talent: a loss clearly shown by women who, frustrated by big companies, are setting up on their own. The number of woman-owned businesses rose by 30% in a recent six-year span. Whether self-employed or company employee, the American businesswoman is as dedicated to her work as any man.

The business method

Visitors to the USA are often struck by the vigorous pace of American business. Briskness is not universal in US corporations; it goes against the leisurely grain of the Deep South. As a rule the American business person values dynamism and the "go-getter" is much admired. Yet ideas and fashions in American business are as mobile and changeable as the personalities – fixed ideas about US business are always being disproved by US business executives themselves.

Business thinking

Behind the briskness and dynamism of US business lies a surprisingly thoughtful attitude. American businessmen take their work far more seriously than their European counterparts. Typically, they are aware of current thinking on business methods and philosophy to a degree that is rare elsewhere.

Gurus and fashions The American manager is a great reader of business books and avidly follows the example of the latest management guru. Fashions such as the emphasis on innovation and enterpreneurial ability – "intrapreneuring" in the mid-1980s jargon – spread rapidly and last a few years before giving way to the next wave. By the end of the 1980s, the fashion was for "competitive advantage." It pays visitors to the USA to be aware of the management ideas currently in vogue. The ideas sometimes seem bizarre and are often ephemeral, but they should not be taken lightly; American business people take them as seriously as every other aspect of business life.

Introspection Equally symptomatic of the thoughtful approach of the American executive is the almost obsessional concern with every issue that affects the corporation or the individual manager. Managers today are deeply worried about, for example, the excessive aggression of the new MBAs graduating from business school, smoking by managers (some companies pay for managers to go on anti-smoking courses), and the role of "whistle-blowers" in alerting boards to corporate wrongdoing.

Control and direction

Paradoxically, in a business world that worships pace and dynamism, US corporations tend to go about their business with extreme deliberation. The phrase "paralysis by analysis" was coined in the USA, and exhaustive analysis will normally feature in any transaction or plan. The approach is encouraged by business school training, in which "numerate" or finance-based, disciplines predominate. Significantly, management methods based on statistical techniques originated in the USA, and it is in American business that they are still used most intensively. Every project is subjected to rigorous financial scrutiny, and

American managers are generally well-versed in operating budgets and tend to be trained in the most up-to-date management accounting methods.

Heroes and "bean-counters" Ironically, despite the attention paid to financial detail, it is not the financial controllers who are most admired in US business; a corporation's accountants are dismissively known as "bean-counters." Now, as in the past, it is the risk-takers, the entrepreneurs, who provide the American business world with its inspiration. The heroes of the day are the young adventurers who have powered the rise of Silicon Valley in California and made many fortunes in the process. They provide the model for many large and apparently sober-minded companies today. Nevertheless, even the most visionary apostle of the high-tech heroes ties business practice firmly to financial realities.

The search for talent

US business has a great deal of faith in individual talent, and corporations go to enormous lengths to establish whether a future manager has the right qualities for the job – and are prepared to pay the right person handsomely once found. Tough "pressure" interviews are common, and psychological testing, too, has been vigorously developed. The background of every candidate is studied with almost excessive thoroughness.

"Headhunting" Corporations looking for someone to fill an important executive post not only closely scrutinize candidates who apply to them, but also closely observe their rivals or other industries in search of the right person. When they have found their "man," they are quite prepared to offer substantial financial inducements to tempt him/her away. The services of headhunting consultancy firms, who prefer to be known as "executive search firms," are widely used, and these firms have become very influential. Secrecy is of the essence when headhunting, and many Americans consider it highly unethical. But it has become a marked feature of US business life. Ambition is a much-admired and often ruthlessly exercised quality, and headhunters exploit the pursuit of ambition in a highly-organized manner. Although managers may deplore some of the results of headhunters' work, they use their services frequently – one of several examples from the business world of lip-service being paid on issues of principle.

Job-hopping Criticism of headhunting centers on the way it encourages job-hopping, lessens corporate loyalty and pushes up salary levels. All three developments, though, are prominent features of US business life.

High-fliers Top salaries, in particular, have been rising very fast: those for CEOs, frequently well into seven figures, have been increasing at a much faster rate than average pay for executives lower down the line. This discrepancy is often strongly criticised in the media and is indicative of the present pressure on middle management and of the premium exacted by "high-fliers" for their frequent changes of job.

A fair fight?

On the face of it, competing businesses seem fairly friendly toward each other. But often the welcoming handshake conceals a deadly rivalry restrained only by the limits of what works. The past saw plenty of collusion in price-fixing, market-sharing and the like – and although these have long been highly illegal, it is clear that they have not vanished entirely. Far more common, however, is ruthless fighting for market share and other advantages. The thin line between industrial espionage and true market research is often crossed – examples even include flying spy planes over the plants of a rival company, or hiring a key employee solely for the secrets of that company that he or she may possess.

Most people in US business think of themselves as highly ethical, but their behavior tends to be ruled more by pragmatism than by any rigid moral code. It is hard to keep dishonesty and law-breaking altogether out of a system that makes the pursuit of wealth its central objective.

Managerial privilege Under the influence of the Japanese example, US managers have taken many initiatives designed to involve workers more in their work and to encourage a more open and democratic atmosphere on the shop floor. However, the enthusiasm of managers for this approach, in practice as opposed to theory, is less than wholehearted. Managers want to manage; and reluctance to share authority is most marked within company management itself. Power-sharing is rare, and insistence on the prerogatives and privileges of executive rank is conspicuous.

The meeting

The advent of advanced electronic means of communications has done nothing to lessen the American enthusiasm for face-to-face contact. Meetings of all shapes and sizes, from the business breakfast to the monster convention, take place in endless profusion.

Setting up a meeting First encounters with a potential client or customer may be set up by either side. Whoever proposes the meeting is likely to suggest the other side's office as a meeting place, but there is no firmly established protocol. Many kinds of location are acceptable, and convenience is usually the most important criterion.

"On-campus" meetings Most business meetings take place "on campus," in the company's own offices. Big corporations tend to have lavish rooms for any normal size of meeting, plus handsome and spacious offices for their senior executives. These often have a seating area designed for the informal conversations that are the basic form of business meeting. Executives may stay in shirtsleeves if they want to put the visitor at ease – but they usually come straight to the point, and expect visitors to do likewise.

Board presentations Because of the size and spread of US corporations, executives are accustomed to large-scale meetings – and also to inquisitorial, even brutal questioning in front of their peers. For presentations to the board or any other top executive meeting, technical standards are very high. It is therefore essential to prepare any presentation with great thoroughness, to try to anticipate awkward questions, to be fully armed with relevant facts and figures, and to spend whatever is necessary to obtain visual aids of "professional quality" – the two words that sum up the ideal, and often the reality, of US management.

"Off-campus" meetings With convenience and time at a premium, meetings often take place at airports, many of which have well-equipped business lounges. Similarly, US executives often arrange meetings in hotels or conference centers, either because their own office facilities are inadequate or occupied, or because secrecy is paramount. The "downtown" hotels, in the city centers, are kept in business by business – and are used by locals as much as by out-of-town visitors. "Convention" hotels can have 2,000 or more bedrooms, and their conference and allied facilities go far beyond the norm in Europe.

The large-scale meeting, of course, has to be off-campus. Conventions play an important part in American business life, whether they are in-house – typically, a sales convention for far-flung sales people, or the annual assembly of the company's managers in overseas subsidiaries – or huge rallies of executives from many firms in the same industry. These rallies commonly take place in resort hotels, in places like Florida, or even abroad, as well as in the huge convention hotels in New York, Chicago, and other major cities. Recreation and friendly camaraderie are usually to the fore at these gatherings; and social encounters play as important a part in the business relationship as more formal meetings. They used to be very "macho" affairs, and women found themselves isolated – but as more and more women join the executive ranks, the male club atmosphere is beginning to break down. Visitors should not be fooled by the emphasis on leisure; the purpose of these gatherings is as serious as anything else in US business.

Business meals

The social element in American business is strong, and dining or lunching together is often a vital part of the business relationship. In fact, more important deals are probably clinched over the dining table than over the desk.

The working breakfast, a symbol of the overriding dedication to business, is an American invention, popularized to overcome the problem of there being only one lunch in a day. Breakfast does not intrude into the working day, and being a simpler, less variable meal interferes with the conversation less than lunch does. The location is generally a hotel or club. The working breakfast has proved so valuable that some especially sought-after Wall Street tycoons schedule two "power" breakfasts, one after the other, with separate guests.

Business lunches can be as long and alcoholic and leisurely as in London and Paris, but this is by no means typical. The standard business lunch is often preceded – but not accompanied – by drinks, and even the preliminary cocktail is often waived nowadays in favor of mineral water. The menu is lighter (and the price often lower) than for dinner in the same restaurant, and executives rarely expect to be at table for more than an hour and a half; a little more than an hour is typical.

Dinner invitations are less common than those for lunch and are likely to be social rather than business occasions. Visitors from out of town are more often invited to dine than locals. American traditions of hospitality ensure that foreign visitors especially are rarely left to their own devices in the evening. This applies particularly in the many American cities where restaurants of a high standard are hard to find.

Asking visitors home either for dinner or for lunch at the weekend is a common practice. These invitations are important and should not be refused, even though the main ostensible purpose is usually social rather than business. Social relationships are an important part of US business life; the American executive is highly gregarious and likes nothing more than to introduce people to each other – and the friendliness is seldom artificial.

Company hospitality takes many forms. US corporations, for example, are much more heavily engaged in cultural or sports sponsorship than European firms and often use such events to entertain business guests. On the whole it is wisest to accept. The social mixing – whether at a museum private view, a football match or a charity gala – will help to cement the business connection. Company dining rooms, while perhaps less widespread than in Europe, can be very luxurious. In most firms – especially in manufacturing – executives do not have a separate dining room, so a private meal usually has to be held outside at a restaurant or hotel.

Making contact

American executives are usually very accessible compared to their counterparts elsewhere in the world, and it is usually clear from a person's title exactly what his/her role in the corporation is – with certain exceptions (see *Corporate hierarchies*). Finding the right contact is usually simple, and following up, if the meeting has any future, rarely presents problems.

Using the phone American business lives on the phone – often the public phone. Any public place, such as an airport, will have far more phone booths than can be found in other countries. The most ambitious travelling managers keep in touch not only by voice, but also by connecting up their portable computers. Credit cards can be used for phoning from many airports and hotels. However, most phones accept only US phone cards, and if you have a local subsidiary, it is worthwhile asking them in advance to arrange a phone card for you.

Letter writing As in all matters of business etiquette, the safest course is to veer toward the formal. First names are ubiquitous in America. But if that stage of familiarity has not been reached, "Dear Mr......:" is proper for men and, unless you know what title she prefers, "Dear Ms......:" for women. Note also that a *handwritten* "Dear Mr......:" is unusual in the US and may be regarded as an insult rather than a sign of respect. Always write to thank a contact for seeing you or for any entertainment. Keep letters short and to the point – US business letters are, for foreigners, often startling in their brevity. The safe ending for letters is "Sincerely yours."

Returning hospitality

Hospitality should always be returned, if possible. The principle is to reciprocate in kind. If invited to lunch at a smart restaurant, you should offer a meal in a similar establishment. Asking your host to dinner – with spouses, if they came to the original date – is perhaps the best response.

Gifts and commissions In many firms, this issue is taken out of the outsider's hands by detailed corporate policies. Most companies forbid the acceptance of any gifts of substance. Cash payments are totally out of the question. Although bribery and corruption are unfortunately sometimes found in American business, these are exceptions, not to be either expected or encouraged by visitors. Small gifts, however, are acceptable. If invited home, always take flowers, or chocolates. Bottles of drink are safe gifts for all purposes.

Dressing for business

The variations in US business dress are as extreme as those in management style and follow much the same pattern. Thus, the West Coast company that favors a very loose, collegiate, trendy management style also has casual dress as its uniform – say, jeans, sneakers, and tieless colored shirts. At the other end of the spectrum, Wall Street bankers tend to dress extremely conservatively in dark pinstripe suits. The safest course is to dress in a somewhat formal manner: suits of conservative shades for men – and very possibly for women too. The tailored suit used to be popular female business wear, a weapon in the battle to establish women as equals of men, but women's dress is softening nowadays. Women high in the executive rank tend to shun suits.

Exceptions to suits are found – for example, conservative sport jackets and slacks. But whatever the coat, a tie is nearly always worn with the shirt. Lower ranking executives in the West, at least, do favor more colors and patterns than, say, English executives and wear shoes that would not be found in some more old-fashioned business environments. But the overall effect should still to be subdued.

The business media

The USA has the most vigorous and comprehensive business press in the world – an inevitable reflection of the dominant force of business in the national life.

Newspapers and journals

The two leading business publications in the USA are indisputably the daily newspaper the *Wall Street Journal* (which has a national circulation) and the weekly magazine *Business Week*.

The WSJ is an institution central to US business life, and every American with more than a passing interest in the business world scans its pages each day for relevant news. Its daily "Heard on the Street" column inside the back pages is a must for investors. It looks oddly old-fashioned and lacks analytical depth in its ordinary financial and business news, but its features are outstanding, and its nationwide sale gives it great influence. *Business Week*, too, is highly respected – a light, digestible magazine that manages to be remarkably authoritative. It is concise, well-written and fast in spotting new trends.

Coverage in the heavyweight nationals – the *Washington Post*, the *New York Times* and the *Los Angeles Times* – varies but is generally sound and thorough. Weekly news magazines, such as *Time*, can be surprisingly informative and entertaining on business issues. *The Economist* is now also printed in the USA, to which it devotes much coverage.

Biweekly magazines The top biweeklies, *Forbes* and *Fortune*, are both large and rich. *Forbes* calls itself "the drama critic of American business." It has great stock market influence and reports more widely than the others, but its coverage is unsystematic, and it is of less use to business people in general than to investors. *Fortune* targets the top management audience and many of its in-depth analyses are excellent.

Local magazines and closely targeted publications are a relatively recent phenomenon and are the best introduction to the business scene in any of the big metropolitan areas. Some of the business monthlies have reputations beyond their immediate circulation area. Would-be and actual entrepreneurs are served by *Inc* and *Venture*. New York has a very glossy monthly, *Manhattan Inc*, which runs articles on the city's business heroes.

Financial coverage in the USA is extensive. The two leading Wall Street magazines are *Barron's*, a weekly from the WSJ stable, which is full of statistics and authoritative but has a punchy style, and *Institutional Investor*, a monthly which gives a broad coverage of the financial scene. There are also countless investment newsletters. Influential letters range from the broad *Kiplinger Letters* and *Boardroom Reports* to the myriad specialist publications such as the *Gallaher Reports*, which cover the Madison Avenue advertising community.

Trade publications for specific audiences are, by and large, the best in the world. Their coverage is the best way of finding out rapidly what is happening in any market.

Broadcast media

TV has an influence more pervasive than any other US medium, and many people in business make a point of watching the early evening TV news in particular. The early morning TV shows, such as NBC's *Today*, are also watched by many in the business community, while morning "drive-time" radio programs have large audiences, and standards of reporting (for example on stock market moves) are often high. Specialist business programs, such as the *Nightly Business News Report* and Public Broadcasting's *Wall Street Week* are also well thought of.

Cultural Awareness

A historical perspective

From the moment the first European settlers stepped on to the shore of the wilderness continent, inhabitants of the New World have seen America as a land of opportunity – a land where those with the will and talent to succeed can carve out their own niche in the world no matter what their background. Such is the American dream and, from the hardy pioneers who trekked westwards into the unknown in the 19th century to the entrepreneurs who "make it good" in business today, Americans have maintained an unquenchable faith in the future and themselves that has given American society a unique dynamism and restlessness.

Early colonists

When Christopher Columbus first "discovered" the New World in 1492, there were already more than a million Indians living in North America. But the Indians' culture and their past were swamped by the European colonists who followed in Columbus' wake across the Atlantic. Europeans called the newly discovered continent "America" after the Italian explorer Amerigo Vespucci, but it was the English, Dutch and French in the north and the Spanish in the south who made the first, pioneering settlements in the new land.

The first permanent English settlement, founded on Chesapeake Bay in 1607, was called Jamestown, after the British king. But Americans were rarely so deferential again. Among the earliest settlers were many Puritans braving the New World to practise their religion free from the opposition they faced at home, and for centuries America seemed the promised land for the poor and the persecuted of Europe.

Yet the relentless Anglo-Saxon expansion provoked conflict with the equally ambitious French and Spanish, resulting in New World squabbles echoing Old World animosities. Seventy years of intermittent wars ended by treaty in 1763, in England's favour. Canada and all the territory east of the Mississippi river became English. Twenty years later, they were lost.

Revolution and expansion

Until then, most colonists considered themselves loyal subjects of the Crown, serving in its armies against the Catholic kings. But in imposing what it regarded as postwar order, which involved taxation and enforcement of regulations designed to ensure the continued hegemony of English shipping and trade, Westminster hastened the inevitable revolution. The rebellious colonists voiced their defiance with a Declaration of Independence in 1776, and the British immediately went to war against their truculent offspring.

In the way of such uprisings, the colonists' fight was the rebellion of a minority, for a third of the population remained loyal to England and at least as many others held themselves aloof. But with the defeat of General Cornwallis in 1781 at Yorktown, Virginia, victory fell on their side. Independence achieved, the colonists set about welding the loose confederacy of 13 states into a united country and drew up the remarkable republican Constitution which still provides the country's basic laws and system of government.

The experiment in republican democracy began in 1787, and its territory almost immediately doubled when, in 1803, president Thomas

Jefferson bought from Napoleon the French territory west of the Mississippi called Louisiana.

The adolescent nation prematurely flexed its muscles with Britain again in the War of 1812, a three-year effort that left its borders exactly the same. But the following years saw the United States almost bursting with national pride and self confidence. Soon, pioneers and their families were loading covered wagons and heading west across the continent to seek a better life. Their struggles form the core of the mythology of American history and even today remain the inspiration for the pioneering spirit and restless mobility of the American people.

In their eagerness, however, the American settlers swept aside Indian and Spaniards alike, convinced of their own "manifest destiny" to conquer the continent.

Civil war

As the immigration rolled on, festering internal conflicts began to erupt and the long and bitter feud between the North, with its mixed economy, and the South, dependent on slave-worked plantations, exploded into violent conflict. For the southern states, it was the election of an anti-slavery, northern president, Abraham Lincoln, that was the final straw; they withdrew from the Union in 1861. The terrible civil war lasted four years, leaving an indelible scar on the national memory and the defeated South in ruins.

The victorious Union embarked upon a remarkable era of invention and technological development. A transcontinental railroad was completed in 1869. The telegraph was introduced, and in rapid sequence, electrical generating and distribution systems, the telephone, the radio, motion pictures, the phonograph, the airplane.

Boom and bust

Industry boomed as a result of this fevered creativity and America finally caught up with the Industrial Revolution that had begun in England over a century before.

The country developed rapidly, and with a domestic vitality that now equalled or surpassed that of other industrialized nations, American ambition once again spilled over its borders. Hawaii, Cuba, Puerto Rico, the Philippines and the vital Panama canal zone were all gathered under the US umbrella, and America at last began to see itself as a world power. Although it remained aloof for three years from the great war that embroiled Europe between 1914 and 1918, its isolationism evaporated in a paroxysm of jingoism in 1917 when over 2m Americans went to war across the Atlantic.

Throughout the early 20th century, American troops were routinely landed in Panama, Nicaragua, Guatemala and Mexico to install governments or put down unrest. Such actions were the source of persistent anti-American sentiments. At home, amendments to the Constitution in 1920 granted the female vote and prohibited the manufacture and sale of alcoholic beverages – which succeeded only in promoting lawlessness and the rise of organized crime. In a lighter vein was the boom in consumer goods, and the rise of the "dream palaces," the cinemas that seduced Americans with the dream of a better world. But the dream and the economic boom of the "Roaring 20s" were shattered with the collapse of the Wall Street stock market in 1929 and, hard on its heels, the Depression.

The Depression, which threw 13m out of work – combined with the drought that turned the Great Plains into a dust bowl – tempered the buoyant optimism that had been so much a part of the US culture, and undermined faith in the capitalist system. Franklin D. Roosevelt, elected president in 1933, introduced his "New Deal" and began to install the components of a partial welfare state.

The war and after

The Depression did not truly end until the USA began to gear up for World War II. Emerging five years later as the only participant whose homeland was unscathed, America was unquestionably the single greatest world power. But fear of communists and the Soviet Union grew, worsened by an anti-communist war in Korea. The "Cold War" abroad that followed was paralleled by a witchhunt for communist sympathizers at home. As the 1950s passed, and these tensions lessened, US trade and industry achieved new heights – building on a new technological base, and making the most of the gap left by the war-damaged economies of Europe and Japan – and Americans became prosperous as never before. As the USA became a richer place, it became one where the poor and the racially disadvantaged began to demand their share; in the 1960s civil rights marchers took to the streets, and the federal government launched a "War on Poverty."

The economic strains caused by the growth of the welfare state, and the political strains caused by a disastrous war in Vietnam, began to shake Americans' belief in themselves and their institutions. The exposure of abuse of government power in the Watergate scandal further deepened the malaise. It was not until the election of a robustly patriotic president, Ronald Reagan, in 1980, that the country began to "feel good about America" once more. Despite a federal deficit that is barely under control, a sustained trade imbalance and the political embarrassments of the Iran arms scandal, the people were as optimistic and confident in the late 1980s as their Constitution-writing forebears in the 1780s.

Chronology

1607 First English settlement at Jamestown.
1770 Protests against English taxes and regulations culminate in the "Boston Massacre."
1776 Declaration of Independence.
1781 Lord Cornwallis surrenders to Franco-American forces at Yorktown, Virginia.
1787 US Constitution completed.
1789 George Washington inaugurated as first president.
1812 War with Britain over maritime trade.
1836 Texas declares independence from Mexico. Fall of the Alamo.
1861 Abraham Lincoln elected president. Civil War begins.
1863 Emancipation of slaves proclaimed by Lincoln.
1865 The Southern Confederacy surrenders. Lincoln assassinated.
1870 John D. Rockefeller founds Standard Oil.
1896 Henry Ford makes his first car.
1903 First flight by Wright Brothers.
1913 Panama Canal opens.
1917 US enters war in Europe.
1929 Stock Market collapse triggers worldwide economic depression.
1932 Franklin D. Roosevelt becomes president.
1933 "New Deal" programme of social and economic reforms launched by Roosevelt.
1941 Japan attacks Hawaii. US enters World War II.
1945 World War II ends in Pacific.
1950 Joseph McCarthy embarks on campaign against communists. Korean War begins.
1953 Korean War ends in truce.
1958 USA launches its first space satellite.
1959 Alaska and Hawaii become the 49th and 50th states.
1962 USA confronts USSR over Cuban missile bases. USA sends troops to Vietnam.
1963 President John F. Kennedy assassinated.
1969 USA lands astronaut on moon.
1973 Watergate scandal exposed.
1974 President Nixon resigns.
1976 Bicentennial of independence.
1980 Ronald Reagan elected president.
1986 Iran-Contra deal revealed.
1988 George Bush elected president.

Beliefs, attitudes and lifestyles

Living in a country of very large distances and a wealth of personal options, Americans may well appear not only mobile, but restless: one out of five moves residence every year and a majority have called some 14 different places "home" in the course of their lifetime. A readiness to change is manifest in personal relationships as well, with half the marriages ending in divorce. Everyone is from somewhere else: being a native New Yorker in New York is thought to be worth remarking on. And everyone seems to be going someplace as well. With all their material wealth, most Americans are committed to the pursuit of happiness with an energy which often leaves them, as they are the first to admit, little time to enjoy the fruits of their success.

Family, church and community

For all the stresses it has suffered in the current generation, family remains the focus for Americans. Multiple divorce and complex custody arrangements, however, can often give it new and unusual forms. Few American families escape completely from the uncertainties of their role in times of rapidly changing social and moral standards. Many Americans may turn to psychology for help, but most will still look for guidance from organized religion. Protestantism in a profusion of sects – Episcopalian (the American version of Anglicanism), Methodist, Baptist, Dutch Reformed (Calvinist), Quakar and Unitarian – and the majority faith although Catholicism is the largest single religion. Fundamentalist churches, so called for their close and often literal reading of the Bible and accent on personal commitment, were once mostly in isolated rural communities, but now, thanks to the power of television and radio, command large followings over wide areas outside the major metropolitan centers. While religion forms an important strand of a shared cultural heritage in most countries and is part of social life even for nonbelievers, it is a very private matter for most Americans. The constitutional separation of church and state not only guarantees religious freedom to every persuasion; it scrupulously denies any of them a place in civic life. For many Americans today, religion still provides a link to earlier loyalties and the community they grew up in.

Class and race

Americans pride themselves on being free of class-consciousness. This does not mean, however, that distinctions are not routinely made between "them" and "us," or newcomers not scrutrinized for clues and signals of their standing, rank or status. Yet there is much to be said for the Americans' claim, for there are almost as many criteria for judging one's neighbor as there are groups or communities in the culture, and no consensus among them across the country or even across town. Americans are quick to respect or praise achievement: but they react very negatively to those who claim deference as a matter of right. If Americans feel a quiet pride in the "classlessness," however, they are often sensitive to the tragedy which racism has brought into their history, and still grapple with its legacy.

The legacy of slavery Held as slaves in a country which declared that all men were created equal, American blacks (as they prefer to be called) were released from bondage into a twilight world of legal citizenship but social oppression. In the name of civil rights, and in alliance with many white sympathizers, they have struggled since the 1950s to emerge from the figurative as well as literal ghetto to which racial prejudice had condemned them. They have made surprising progress in such a short time and against such deeply-ingrained resistance: black mayors have been elected not only in Chicago and Washington, but in major cities of the deep South and black congressmen represent constituencies which have not changed much since Reconstruction. Great universities and major corporations actively recruit blacks and "positive action programs" discriminating in their favor are an accepted part of up-to-date personnel practice. Yet the legacy of generations of poverty and exclusion from mainstream society is not easy to overcome.

The plight of minorities Blacks are not America's only targets of racial feeling. Mexican-Americans in the Southwest, Hispanics in Florida and New York, and Native Americans (indigenous Indians) have all felt the chill of inhospitality or the violence of outright hostility. The open display of racial prejudice is generally unacceptable and racial epithets are strictly taboo. But grumbling is sometimes heard about the growing bilingualism in New York and other cities and at the compulsory provisions which government and the business community have adopted.

The war of the sexes

The feminist revolution of the 1960s and 1970s, while not unique to the USA, was carried forward there with a characteristic readiness to follow the argument wherever it might lead. The feminist movement argued that the rights of women were not being served in a society where women earned 40% less, on average, than men and only 2% of management at or above the rank of vice-president are women. To the confusion of some men and the chagrin of others, they sought access to work – whether policewoman or astronaut – to which their skills entitled them, and vigorous campaigns bought at least the legal right to equal pay, if not the fact. But there was much more at stake than simply equal pay or equality in the job market. Many women felt they also had a right to the dignity men seemed to reserve for themselves, and in a fashion typically American, proceeded to demand it. They asked to be spared the tiresome and degrading belittlement which passes for flirtation in many settings. They believed that decision about abortion belonged to them, and was not the province of society's moral guardians. The feminist movement reached a highpoint in the mid 1970s, and its achievements were significant. But the vilification of women involved in the movement, and the positive advances made, have softened the approach in the 1980s, an era known by many women as "post-feminist." Moreover, the price of the changes can be high for liberated American women; conflicts between family responsibilities and career are not always easily resolved.

Sexual liberation With the example of the black and feminist liberation movements before them, homosexuals in recent years have also asserted their right to the respect of the community and equal treatment by law. In some communities, notably San Francisco, they formed political pressure groups which had to be reckoned with by anyone seeking office. Liberation from the sexual mores of small-town America or from the taboos of religious upbringing also brought pornography into the open market, merchandized by the underworld, perhaps, but distributed under protection from the First Amendment (guaranteeing freedom of speech). More recently, dark clouds have gathered over this proliferating liberation. It is now recognized that AIDS threatens tragedy to the population at large, and society waits nervously for medical technology once more to rescue it from one of the crueller caprices of nature.

Regionalism

Most generalizations about so large and varied a country are difficult to justify: this is only slightly less so when speaking about its individual regions. Thus the small-town, farm-based, conservative Midwest is also the home of historic American populism and suspicious of Eastern money and central government. The older states of the Northeast, home to the American establishment and its long established universities, also contains a major complex of cities which became the frontier for millions of immigrant pioneers from Europe. The South still savours its self image as a land of easy grace and elaborate courtesy, while others remember its history of racial and religious bigotry, its poverty and rural backwardness. Neither picture will make much sense to the visitor who sees the energy of cities like Atlanta, the cosmopolitanism of New Orleans, the Cuban and Caribbean influence in Miami, and a general political melée in which militant blacks, fundamentalist pastors and aggressive young entrepreneurs jostle each other for influence and power. The Southwest retains the scenery of the western films, but the cowboy ethos has been applied to herding oil wells and stock portfolios. Texas alone is larger than many countries in the world and richer than most, despite occasional difficulties caused by a weakening of world oil prices. The West Coast, oriented toward Asia as the East Coast is toward Europe, has been the center of radical politics and radical life-styles. Yet Orange County near Los Angeles is the heartland of American political conservatism, Silicon Valley the center of high-tech enterprise and the universities among the most respected in the world. All the images are true – but so are the contradictions: regionalism exists, but its character is a matter of interpretation.

Education

America was an early leader in the movement for universal free education. Today, while not a matter of constitutional guarantees, this benefit is viewed by most people as a kind of right and is required for all children by state law.

Schools

Education is entirely in the hands of the state and the local community and most of the bill is met at the community level. Education is free at public (tax supported) primary schools (the first eight or nine year-long grades) and secondary or high schools (four further years). Provision of schools for children younger than five years of age varies according to the finances and circumstances of the community. The overwhelming majority of American children attend such free schools but prestigious, fee-paying institutions are sprinkled about the country. In recent years, parents concerned about the quality of free schooling available in inner cities have turned to private schools as a solution.

Private or public, American schools are conceived as an educational service to the children, their parents and the community: parent power is not only accepted but welcomed through the local Parent Teacher Association attached to every school. Since education is regarded as a universal benefit, conscientious schools attempt to serve the needs and talents of each individual child rather than some abstract standard of intellectual excellence. The result may seem to foreigners a puzzling mix of frivolity (baton-twirling and driver education) with more recognizable disciplines of traditional learning. Where schools are well-run and well-supported by the community, the quality of public education rivals any in the world and can offer opportunities seldom available elsewhere.

College

After high school, students can move on to college, and over half of them do. With more than 3,500 colleges and universities to choose from, Americans have come to look on a bachelor's degree rather than high school graduation as the natural termination of school life. There is an institution for every taste: alongside the old, prestigious and rich establishments, such as Harvard, Yale, Princeton, Columbia and Amherst, there is a profusion of privately funded and state-supported schools that range from vast educational plants offering the most advanced training available, to small, intimate academies which emphasize personal instruction and a taste for the humanities. Although university education has become commonplace, it is an expensive proposition and represents a continuing drain on the finances of families with college-bound children. State universities charge fees far below those of their private counterparts where the bill for one student can easily soar into five figures and is rising every year. Loans, grants and scholarships, and part-time work are frequently required to meet the cost, but most Americans believe it is an acceptable price to pay for the cash value a degree is thought to have in the job market. The link which Americans tend to make between education and earning power is also reflected in their preference for the oversubscribed prestige schools. As the bachelor's degree becomes a commonplace of middle-class citizenship, more and more graduates are pursuing postgraduate study, particularly for professional degrees in law (JD) and business (MBA), but also for the less exploitable dignity of the PhD.

Living standards

America is a very rich country indeed and evidence of its wealth is spread through all regions. Measured by the availability of decent to excellent housing, the wealth of appliances and the ubiquity of the automobile, the middle majority may well be accounted affluent by any of the world's standards. Yet expenses of medicine, care for the aged and higher education can seriously erode the security of many families, and most balance their checkbooks carefully in a continuing pursuit of higher expectations.

Rich and poor

The allegation of materialism often made against Americans probably arises from the profusion of consumer goods available to them. In fact, most Americans tend to be consumers, rather than collectors, and even the home with two (or more) cars and a well-kept swimming pool may well lack the artifacts of material value which serve as evidence of affluence in other societies. Although there are certainly exceptions, most Americans shy away from conspicuous display; the fun of wealth is in winning it in the first place.

Despite its high proportion of millionaires, America's cities and rural areas often show the bitter aspect of poverty and squalor. Some urban ghettos are among the worst in the developed world, and jobless communities where the sun has set on once powerful industries are a depressing counterpoint to luxury skyscraper apartments and the vast stretches of comfortable, leafy suburbs. Neither its wealth nor its poverty provides a true yardstick for the measure of the "real" America: it is both.

Work and leisure

Americans not only believe in work, they give every evidence of enjoying it and have even invented the working breakfast in their impatience to get down to the day's business.

While the clear desk, the three-hour lunch and the short day are perks of advancement in some countries, the higher an American executive advances up the ladder, the harder the expected slog.

Sport Golf offers probably the most popular release and can be played on innumerable and often excellent courses. Tennis has witnessed a boom in recent years while Americans of both sexes have become enthusiasts of fitness and exercise. Basketball may continue to be the most attended sport, thanks to its place in the high school sports program, but professional baseball, and more important, professional football command the most devoted following. Foreigners will need explanations of the fine points to appreciate either, but any one of 200 million Americans will be glad to oblige.

Leisure pursuits Americans enjoy dining out – and tend to make an occasion of it regardless of the quality of the food. They are proverbially hospitable and invite the most recent of acquaintances to their homes as a matter of course. Such entertainment is, as a rule, a relaxed affair, in keeping with the unspoken American suspicion that formality is a brake on friendliness.

Vacations Getting away from it all is not difficult in a land of tens of thousands of lakes, vast expanses of excellent beach and areas of wilderness which would surprise those who are familiar only with the major cities. Many own a second home, or manage to rent one, where the family can retreat during the long summer holidays. The Labor Day weekend, which ends the school vacation, probably witnesses more families on the move than at any time since the barbarian invasions. As the children grow up and arrange their own holidays, many Americans embark on world travel. Europe is the usual first port of call, but few destinations are exempt from their benign curiosity.

Meeting and getting on

Most Americans like to think of themselves as both friendly and forthright, and try to live up to the image as best they can. Greetings are always extended warmly, hands are shaken firmly, and they remember other people's names. They will normally signal the invitation to call them by their first names and are likely to lead the way by example. Titles are seldom used, except by way of establishing responsibility, and titles are seldom used in direct address to members of one's own business family (but always to "Senator," "Commissioners," and so forth). Policemen are always addressed as "officer" and "sir" is used only when a most respectful formality (or its opposite) is intended.

Shyness and diffidence in others makes most Americans slightly uncomfortable and somewhat guilty for having failed to put someone at his ease. They do not mind a moderate tardiness at social events (in fact they normally count on it), but they do not like to waste business time unnecessarily either.

Smoking and drinking Both in homes and in offices, it is no longer possible to assume that smoking is acceptable. In recent years, too, the consumption of spirits seems to have declined and there is a heightened sensitivity to the needs of those with "a drinking problem." Outside the office, however, alcohol still provides much of the lubricant for conversation.

City by City

Introduction

The map below shows the cities featured in detail in the city by city guide and locates them in their time zones. There are four standard time zones in the continental United States. Reading from East to West they are Eastern, Central, Mountain and Pacific. Each zone is one hour earlier than its eastern neighbor, so that in California, for example, it is three hours earlier than in New York.

Each city guide follows a standard format: information and advice on arriving, getting around, city areas, hotels, clubs, restaurants, bars, entertainment, shopping, sightseeing, sport and fitness, and a directory of local business and other facilities such as secretarial and translation agencies, couriers, hospitals with 24-hour accident and emergency departments, and telephone-order florists. There is also a map of the city center locating recommended hotels, restaurants and other important addresses.

For easy reference, all main entries for hotels, restaurants and sights are listed alphabetically.

ATLANTA

Area code ☎ 404

Atlanta is the home of Coca-Cola and the economic center of Southeastern USA. Founded in 1837, the town was a main distribution point for troops, munitions and supplies during the Civil War (in which it was burned by General Sherman) – and later for building materials during Reconstruction – because three railroads converged here. Today, three interstate highways (75, 85 and 20) intersect at Atlanta, and Hartsfield International Airport is an important domestic and international hub. Major companies such as Subaru, Yamaha, IBM, Panasonic and Canon have manufacturing, distribution or headquarters here, alongside Cable News Network, Coca-Cola, Delta Air Lines, Georgia-Pacific, and Lockheed-Georgia. The city's banks – Citizens and Southern Corporation and SunTrust – are among the region's most important.

Atlanta was the hometown of Dr Martin Luther King. Today the city's government is predominantly black, and the rights of minority groups are now accepted.

Arriving

Hartsfield Atlanta International Airport

Hartsfield has two huge terminals, North and South, each with four concourses, A, B, C and D, at which domestic flights arrive. In addition, North Terminal has an international concourse.

Signposting throughout the airport is good and baggage trolleys are available free. A transportation mall connects the domestic concourses; if you arrive or leave on a domestic flight, use the mall's computer-controlled train for easy, rapid, free transport to and from all the domestic gates and baggage claim. Customs and Immigration take about 20mins normally – 30mins when more than three flights arrive simultaneously. North Terminal services include currency exchange, 9–5, multilingual information center, duty-free shops and restaurants. Airport information ☎ 530-6600.

Air freight carriers include *Airborne Express* ☎ 761-6497 and *Emery* ☎ 699-1171; they use the airport's separate air freight terminal.

Nearby hotels *Hyatt Atlantic Airport*, 1900 Sullivan Rd, College Park 30337 ☎ 997-2770 TX 544074 fax 991-5906. *Marriott Airport*, 4711 Best Rd, College Park 30337 ☎ 766-7900 fax 762-6355. *Ramada Renaissance*, 4736 Best Rd, College Park 30337 ☎ 762-7676 TX 7581801 fax 763-1913.

City link Downtown Atlanta is 9 miles/14kms south, a 30min drive on Interstate 85 North. There is a rapid transit link to downtown, or take a taxi.

Taxi Dependable companies include Yellow Cab ☎ 522-0200, Checker Cab ☎ 351-1111, American Cab ☎ 523-2227, and London Taxi ☎ 681-2280. Be wary of using others; some drivers have a limited knowledge of the city, drive suspect vehicles, and may overcharge.

Car rental Driving is the best way to get around if your business takes you out of downtown. Eight agencies have desks in the airport: Hertz ☎ 766-2205; Avis ☎ 530-2700; Budget ☎ (800) 527-0700; Alamo ☎ (800) 327-9633; National ☎ (800) 227-7368; General ☎ (800) 327-7607; Dollar ☎ (800) 421-6868; and Thrifty ☎ (800) 367-2277.

Bus The Atlanta Airport Shuttle ☎ 535-2177 operates a good service to downtown and outlying hotels, leaving Ground Transportation in the North Terminal every 20mins, 4.30am–12.30am for downtown hotels, 7am–9pm for Buckhead hotels.

Rail The rail link run by MARTA (Metropolitan Atlanta Rapid Transit Authority) now links the airport to the city-wide system. The exact fare or tokens (from vending machines) are needed.

Getting around

If your business is downtown, walking is easy and enjoyable. But if you have to go to any outlying area, drive or take a cab. Public transportation is excellent downtown and has recently been extended to include surrounding areas.
Taxi see *City link*.
Limousine *Sun Belt Limousine* ☏ 524-3400 is considered the most professional; 24hrs. *Classic Coach* ☏ 892-1746 is also highly respected.
Driving Rush-hour traffic – 7.30–9 and 4.30–6 – is congested, but the freeway system makes for easy movement at other times. Parking is limited around downtown office buildings, so leave your car at the hotel and walk – or use public transportation. See *City Link* for car rental companies.
Rail MARTA trains run every 9mins and will take you anywhere in the business district quickly and safely.
Bus MARTA's buses run every 15mins, and the drivers are courteous and knowledgeable.

Area by area

The sky line of this fast-growing city changes continuously as big new skyscrapers rise up in the center and the surrounding districts. Most major corporations are downtown, but the Perimeter is gaining prominence and prestige as office towers are built along Interstate 285, the multilaned superhighway circling the city. The

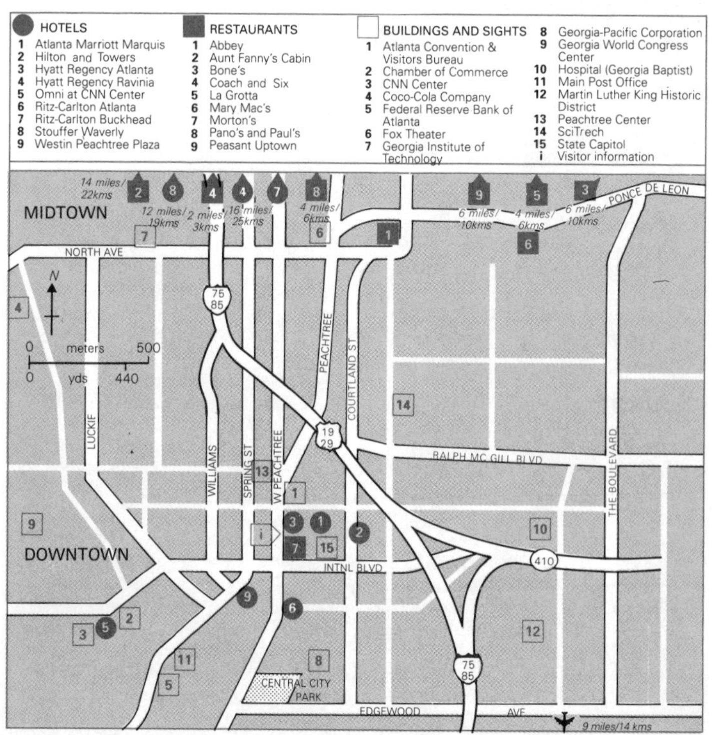

growth started at Perimeter Center, the intersection of I-285 and Ashford-Dunwoody. Cumberland, where I-285 meets Cobb Parkway (US-41), is a major office and retail center. Distribution companies have taken over the I-85 corridor into Gwinnett County, where Norcross is the area's high-tech center.

Downtown The area is bounded by Baker Street to the north, Memorial Drive to the south, Courtland Street to the east and International Boulevard to the west. Five Points is the center of the city's financial district. Peachtree Center, between Ellis and Baker Streets, is a high-prestige area for law and accounting firms and international banks.

Buckhead Once housing Atlanta's wealthy merchants only in summer, Buckhead is now both a business and residential area. The Governor lives here, and many of the estates and executive homes remain; others have given way to high-rises. The center for Atlanta's advertising and public relations firms, it has fashionable restaurants and nightclubs.

Midtown AT&T, BellSouth, Coca-Cola and IBM all have offices in Midtown, between 10th Street and Pershing Point. This is also the arts center of the city.

Hotels

Atlanta's development as a major convention city means there are plenty of hotels, many of which have also been recently improved.

Atlanta Marriott Marquis [$]////

265 Peachtree Center Ave 30303 ☎ 521-0000 [TX] 6712053 fax 521-0000 ext 6870 • AE DC MC V • 1,674 rooms, 5 restaurants, 1 bar, 1 coffee shop

Part of architect John Portman's 12-block urban village, this Marriott is a city landmark as well as its largest hotel. Its 48-floor indoor atrium is breathtaking. The city's major corporations, especially in the high-tech industries, use the Marquis for meetings and to house guests. Service and facilities are excellent. Medical services • pool, sauna, health club • 43 meeting rooms, clerical service.

Hilton and Towers [$]///

255 Courtland St NE 30043 ☎ 659-2000 [TX] 804370 fax 222-2865 • AE DC MC V • 1,250 rooms, 60 suites, 4 restaurants, 4 bars, 1 coffee shop

The Hilton and Towers is one of Atlanta's longest established business hotels. Nikolai's Roof restaurant atop the Towers is popular with Atlanta's chief executives. A complete business center has been added, including computer services, word processing, copy machines and secretarial help. Pool, tennis, health club, jogging, sauna • 49 meeting rooms, translation, teleconferencing, computer rental, recording facilities.

Hyatt Regency Atlanta [$]///

265 Peachtree St 30303 ☎ 577-1234 [TX] 542485 fax 588-4137 • AE DC MC V • 1,165 rooms, 53 suites, 4 restaurants, 1 bar, 1 coffee shop

A 23-story open atrium lobby, with live entertainment in the lounge, welcomes you to the Atlanta Hyatt. All rooms, recently renovated, have jacuzzis and minibars. Hairdresser • health club, pool • 27 meeting rooms.

Hyatt Regency Ravinia [$]///

4335 Ashford Dunwoody Rd 30346 ☎ 395-1234 [TX] 6827201 fax 395-7153 • AE DC MC V • 492 rooms, 41 suites, 2 restaurants, 1 bar, 1 coffee shop

This glass and granite de luxe hotel is used by top companies. The fully-glassed boardroom has a stunning panorama of the surrounding 10-acre forest. All rooms have desks and telephone-computer hookups. Ravinia is ideal for business in DeKalb, Cobb and Gwinnett Counties. Indoor pool, health club, tennis, jogging paths • 18 meeting rooms.

Omni at CNN Center [$]II
100 CNN Center 30335 ☏ 659-0000 [TX] 542380 fax 659-0000 ext 1149 • AE DC MC V • 430 rooms, 31 suites, 2 restaurants, 3 bars, 1 coffee shop
On the western fringe of the central business district, the Omni has a strong following of business travelers. Its rich wood-paneled lobby and comfortable rooms are welcoming. The Omni adjoins CNN Center, home of Cable News Network. The Omni Sports Arena is adjacent; the Georgia World Congress Center is next door. The hotel's Italian restaurant, Bugatti, is suitable for business lunches. Gift shops • health club in Center, with pool • 18 meeting rooms.

Ritz-Carlton Atlanta [$]II
181 Peachtree St NE 30303 ☏ 659-0400 [TX] 543291 fax 688-0400 • AE DC MC V • 432 rooms, 22 suites, 2 restaurants, 2 bars, 1 coffee shop
Just a block from Peachtree Center, the distinctive Ritz-Carlton is the choice of many discriminating business travelers for its elegant rooms and excellent service. Suites have crystal chandeliers, pianos and jacuzzis. Club-level floors have private access and concierge. The Restaurant and café are excellent for business and entertaining, and the piano bar is a hospitable sanctuary for unwinding after hours. Gift shops • arrangements with next-door health club, tennis, golf • 15 meeting rooms.

Ritz-Carlton Buckhead [$]II
3434 Peachtree Rd 30326 ☏ 237-2700 [TX] 549251 fax 233-5168 • AE DC MC V • 553 rooms, 28 suites, 3 restaurants, 2 bars, 1 coffee shop
In uptown Atlanta's most fashionable district, this Ritz-Carlton has a wide-ranging social and business clientele. The front entrance has crystal chandeliers and marble-faced pillars; fireplaces in the lobby lounge and main-level bar create a clubby ambience. The Café is very suitable for business luncheons, the Dining Room popular for dinner. Pool, sauna, jacuzzi, fitness center • 18 meeting rooms.

Stouffer Waverly [$]II
2450 Galleria Pkwy 30339 ☏ 953-4500 [TX] 701565 fax 953-0740 • AE DC MC V • 521 rooms, 21 suites, 4 restaurants, 3 bars
With spectacular views of the lush rolling North Georgia hills and a 14-story atrium, this hotel has very large rooms with handsome mahogany furniture. The Waverly is especially convenient for aerospace industry business in Marietta. There are good shopping centers close by. Health club, indoor/outdoor pools, sauna • 20 meeting rooms.

Westin Peachtree Plaza [$]III
210 Peachtree St 30343 ☏ 659-1400 [TX] 804323 fax 589-7424 • AE DC MC V • 1,074 rooms, 43 suites, 3 restaurants, 5 bars, 1 coffee shop
The Westin dominates Atlanta's skyline with its sparkling glass exterior, matched internally by marble floors. The Peachtree Ballroom accommodates up to 2,000, and is frequently used for meetings and parties by the city's largest corporations. The Sun Dial Restaurant is a favorite for social and business entertaining. On the tri-level dining area, the Savannah Fish Company draws lunch crowds from nearby law and accounting firms and the merchandise marts next door. The Georgia World Congress Center is an easy four-block walk up International Boulevard. Health club, pool • 39 meeting rooms.

Clubs

The *Capital City Club* ☏ 523-8221 is the center of Atlanta's business network. The men-only club comprises mainly chief executive officers, board chairmen, directors and presidents. The *Cherokee Town and Country Club* ☏ 993-4407 attracts a range of professions. The *Georgian Club* ☏ 952-6000 is mainly for executives of corporations around the Northern Perimeter. The *Atlanta City*

Club ☏ 522-0001 is for middle management from banking, accounting, advertising and public relations. The *Commerce Club* ☏ 525-1661 is used as a venue for business luncheons and meetings by its varied membership. *Horseshoe Bend Country Club*, *Piedmont Driving Club*, and *Dunwoody Country Club* are exclusive bastions of Atlanta society.

Restaurants

The city's business community is constantly on the lookout for new clients and contacts, and a new eating experience as well. In the main, when Atlantans leave business for the day, they are out to make profitable contacts, not talk shop, and so spread their culinary nets wide rather than patronizing two or three favorite restaurants.

Abbey [$]//
163 Ponce de Leon Ave ☏ 876-8532 • closed L • AE DC MC V • jacket • reservations essential
A good choice for entertaining clients in an unusual setting. In this church-turned-restaurant, the excellent food is served by attentive waiters wearing monks' robes.

Aunt Fanny's Cabin [$]/
2155 Campbell Rd, Smyrna ☏ 436-5218 • closed L Mon–Sat • AE DC MC V
International visitors enjoy the Cabin because it conjures up images of the era of *Gone With the Wind*; waitresses and waiters are clothed like slaves and servants before the Civil War. It also provides authentic "down-home Southern" cooking and true Southern hospitality.

Bone's [$]//
3130 Piedmont Rd ☏ 237-2663 • closed L Sat & Sun • AE DC MC V
The autographed caricatures of local and international celebrities indicate that Bone's has a following of business people and entertainers. The thick t-bones and spartan atmosphere of plain tables and chairs make it suitable for working lunches or easy-going evenings.

Coach and Six [$]////
1776 Peachtree St NW ☏ 872-6666 • closed L Sat & Sun • AE DC MC V • jackets for D • reservations essential
The Coach and Six is an Atlanta tradition, the restaurant you will be taken to when impressions count. Investment bankers, politicians, lawyers and professionals like the opulent surroundings for lunch as well as for evening entertaining. A wide ranging menu; homemade bread.

La Grotta [$]////
2637 Peachtree Rd ☏ 231-1368 • closed Sun & Mon • AE DC MC V • jacket for D • reservations essential
La Grotta is unquestionably the city's best Italian restaurant. Its cramped, modest quarters, below an apartment building in Buckhead, belie the quality of the food. La Grotta is popular with business groups for evening entertainment (but not for talking business). Another branch is at 647 Atlanta St, Roswell ☏ 998-0645.

Mary Mac's [$]
224 Ponce de Leon Ave ☏ 875-4337 • closed Sat & Sun • no credit cards • no reservations
Lawyers, bankers, politicians, secretaries, construction workers, and truck drivers all love Mary Mac's. Mary Margaret Lupo, a leader in the business community, can seat over 300 in her massive dining rooms. Fried chicken, creamed corn, collard greens, fried okra and cornbread, all make this a must if you want true Southern cooking. Your suggestion to take lunch here will be appreciated by locals, but do not plan a lengthy business discussion; guests are expected to enjoy a good meal, then give others the same opportunity.

Morton's $//
245 Peachtree Center Ave ☎ 577-4366 • closed Sat L, Sun • AE DC MC V • jacket requested
Heavy wooden tables and chairs and wooden plank floors recreate an atmosphere of America's prohibition era. Your order is taken by a waiter who rolls a cart to your table so that you may select your cut of Midwest prime beef or Wisconsin milk-fed veal. The menu also features fresh whole Maine lobster.

Pano's and Paul's $////
1232 West Paces Shopping Center, Ferry Rd NW ☎ 261-3662 • closed L, Sun • AE DC MC V
A highly regarded and award-winning restaurant in a shopping mall that serves American and Continental dishes in an elegant Victorian setting. For the more formal occasions.

Peasant Uptown $/
3500 Peachtree Rd NE in Phipps Plaza ☎ 261-6341 • AE DC MC V
An excellent choice for a casual business lunch or an intimate off-duty evening, the Peasant Uptown has a friendly atmosphere. Attentive waiters serve creative American dishes.

Bars

For quiet discussions, the best meeting places are those bars within the city's better hotels, such as the café/bar at the *Ritz-Carlton Buckhead*, which offers discreet jazz nightly.

Entertainment

Since the opening in mid 1989 of Underground Atlanta at Peachtree and Alabama Streets, containing 22 nightclubs and restaurants as well as 100 shops, downtown Atlanta is more lively at night. Many business people – local and visiting – go to Buckhead or the Perimeter where locals gather in fashionable bars and discos.
Theater and music The *Woodruff Arts Center*, 1280 Peachtree St NE ☎ 898-4444, houses a variety of arts groups and the High Museum of Art; the *Alliance Theater* ☎ 892-2414, the *Atlanta Ballet* ☎ 873-5811, and the *Atlanta Symphony Orchestra* ☎ 892-2414 are based here. The *Fox Theater*, 660 Peachtree St ☎ 881-1977, hosts such performers as Bob Hope and Carol Channing.
Nightclubs *Club Rio*, 195 Luckie St NW ☎ 525-7467, is Latin-style, with dancing on three levels (one with live entertainment). *Studebakers*, Courtyard of Tower Place, 3345 Piedmont Rd ☎ 266-9870, attracts those who want to dance the night away. *Dante's Down the Hatch*, 3380 Peachtree Rd NE ☎ 266-1600, and also at Underground, has a jazz trio; *Elan*, 4505 Ashford Dunwoody Rd NE ☎ 393-1333, is the favorite of middle and upper management. *The Punch Line*, 280 Hildebrand Dr NE ☎ 252-5233, features internationally famous comedians.

Shopping

Lenox Square in Buckhead is *the* center for shopping. The sprawling complex features Neiman-Marcus, Macy's, Atlanta-based Rich's and a host of fine specialty shops. *Phipps Plaza*, across Peachtree from Lenox, is anchored by Lord & Taylor's, but also has smart boutiques. The metro area is dotted with "regional" malls, such as *Gwinnett Place*, 30 miles north of downtown Atlanta on I-85 N; *Towne Center*, about the same distance up I-75 N in Cobb County; *Southlake* and *Shannon* malls in South Atlanta; and *Perimeter Center* (see *Area by area*). Rich's and Macy's also have downtown stores; and there are 100 specialty shops in Underground Atlanta.

Sightseeing

Atlanta sightseeing includes pre-Civil War homes – Albany, Madison, Thomasville – battlegrounds, museums and mountain landscapes in the Blue Ridge Mountains to the north.
Carter Presidential Center President Carter's library depicts his life and administration, as well as previous

administrations, in film, exhibits and documents. *1 Copen Hill. Open 9–4.45; Sun, 12–4.45.*
Cyclorama A 50ft-high, 400ft-circumference painting in the round, with three-dimensional figures, sound and light effects and narration of the 1864 Battle of Atlanta. *In Grant Park. Open 9–5.30.*
Kennesaw Mountain National Battlefield Park Kennesaw is the site of a crucial engagement in the 1864 Civil War Battle of Atlanta. *Old Hwy 41, Marietta ☎ 427-4686. Open 8.30–5.*
Little Five Points/Inman Park About 3 miles/5kms from downtown (Edgewood Ave NE), this residential and commercial area is a showplace of Victorian architecture. Atlanta entrepreneur Joel Hurt laid out this "garden neighborhood" and built the nation's first trolley line to his building downtown.
Martin Luther King, Jr Historic District A two-block area that includes the Nobel Peace Prize winner's birthplace and the Center for Non-Violent Social Change. *501 Auburn Ave ☎ 524-1956.*
Roswell Founded in 1830, this quaint little town has many pre-Civil War houses. Group tours can be arranged through the Roswell Historical Society. *227 S Atlanta St ☎ 992-1665.*
SciTrek New Science and Technology Museum with imaginative displays. *395 Piedmont Ave NE ☎ 522-5500.*
Wren's Nest The home of Joel Chandler Harris, creator of the Uncle Remus tales and characters – Brer Rabbit, Brer Fox, and others. *1050 Gordon St SW ☎ 753-8535. Open Tue–Sat, 10–5; Sun, 2–5.*

Guided tours

Atlanta Preservation Center ☎ 522-4345 has guided tours of the historic parts of the city. Stone Mountain, a 19thC community and the Park (see below), can be visited via the new Georgia Railroad Steam train ☎ 656-0769. Helicopter tours are available from *Dooley Helicopters Inc*, 2003 Flightway Dr, Chamblee ☎ 458-3431.

Out of town

Madison, Georgia A town containing homes so beautiful that General Sherman refused to burn them during the Civil War; 15mins east of Atlanta.
Stone Mountain Park On Highway 78, east of Atlanta, the world's largest relief sculpture – the mounted figures of Confederacy President Jefferson Davis and Confederate Generals Robert E Lee and Stonewall Jackson – is on the face of the largest known granite mass. Attractions include a laser show.

Spectator sports

Basketball, baseball and football are the main sports preoccupations.
Baseball The *Atlanta Braves* play at the Atlanta-Fulton County Stadium, 521 Capitol Ave ☎ 522-7630, from Apr–Oct.
Basketball The *Hawks* play at Omni Coliseum, 100 Techwood Dr ☎ 681-3600.
Football The *Falcons* appear at the Atlanta-Fulton County Stadium ☎ 261-5400.

Keeping fit

Fitness centers *Downtown Athletic Club*, 1 CNN Center ☎ 577-2120; *Holiday Fitness Center* at Lenox ☎ 233-5263; *Australian Body Works*, 4385 Roswell Rd NE ☎ 255-2217 and 5486 Chamblee Dunwoody Rd ☎ 393-0828.
Golf Visitors can play at *Georgia's Stone Mountain Park* ☎ 498-5717; *Adams Park*, 2300 Wilson Dr SW ☎ 753-6521; *Bobby Jones*, 384 Woodward Way NE ☎ 355-9049. Also at *Candler Park*, 585 Candler Park NE ☎ 371-1260; *Chastain Park* 216 W Wieuca Rd NE ☎ 255-0723; and *Pineisle Lake Lanier Islands* ☎ 945-8291.
Tennis *Bitsy Grant*, 2125 Northside Dr NW ☎ 351-2774, *Chastain Park*, 140 W Wieuca Rd NE ☎ 255-1993, *Piedmont Park* ☎ 872-1507 and *Stone*

Mountain Park ☎ 498-5728.

Local resources

Business services

The *Atlanta Chamber of Commerce* (see *Information sources*) can supply the names of suitable companies.

Photocopying and printing *Franklin's Copy Service*, Georgia World Congress Center ☎ 577-7444; *Tucker Castleberry Printing*, 226 Luckie St ☎ 525-8654; *AlphaGraphics*, 6 Decatur St ☎ 523-2679, offers self-service computer graphics and typesetting for reports and presentations; *Kwik-Kopy* gives quick turnaround and has several locations, including 100 Peachtree St NW ☎ 525-5700.

Secretarial *Barbara H Taylor* ☎ 581-1949, and *Business World* ☎ 392-4200 offer efficient service.

Translation *Inlingua Translation* ☎ 266-2661, *Berlitz Translation* ☎ 261-5062.

Communications

Long-distance delivery *Federal Express* ☎ 321-7566, *Airborne Express* ☎ 761-7199 and *Purolator Courier* ☎ (800) 645-3333.

Local delivery *Corporate Courier* ☎ 881-0098, *Dependable Courier Service* ☎ 763-1100, and *Righton-Time Delivery Service* ☎ 758-0550.

Post office The downtown office is at 100 Marietta St ☎ 525-2178.

Conference/exhibition centers

Facilities are provided at the *Georgia World Congress Center* ☎ 656-7600 and the *Georgia International Convention and Trade Center* ☎ 997-3566. Best and most convenient meeting arrangements are made through the hotels and the *Atlanta Convention and Visitors Bureau* ☎ 521-6688.

Emergencies

Currency exchange Available at the airport Mon–Fri, 9–7; Sat & Sun, 4–7, and at major downtown banks during normal hours.

Hospitals *Georgia Baptist Medical Center* ☎ 653-4136, *Northside Hospital* ☎ 851-8937, *Piedmont Hospital* ☎ 350-2222. *Georgia Dental Association* ☎ 458-6166.

Pharmacies *Reed Discount Drugs*, 14 Peachtree St NW ☎ 659-2046, and 55 Marietta St NW ☎ 688-0231.

Police 175 Decatur St ☎ 658-6600.

Government offices

Atlanta City Government ☎ 658-6000; *City of Atlanta Economic Development* ☎ 659-4567; *US Dept of Commerce* ☎ 347-7000; *US Customs* ☎ 763-7125; *Immigration and Naturalization* ☎ 331-5158.

Information sources

Business information The *Atlanta Chamber of Commerce*, 235 International Blvd ☎ 880-9000, helps with economic and demographic data; The *Business Council of Georgia* ☎ 223-2264 and *Department of Industry and Trade* ☎ 656-3590 are sources for state-wide information.

Local media The *Atlanta Journal* (morning) and the *Constitution* (afternoon) give local, regional and state coverage. The *Gwinnett Daily News* and *Marietta Daily Journal* concentrate on Gwinnett and Cobb County news, respectively. The *Atlanta Business Chronicle* is a weekly tabloid of local business news. For magazine coverage, *Business Atlanta* is aimed at the region's business leaders; *Georgia Trend* covers the state and Southeast.

Visitor information The *Atlanta Convention and Visitors Bureau*, 233 Peachtree St NE, Suite 2000 ☎ 521-6688, is the definitive source for tourist information. The *Georgia State Tourism Office* ☎ 656-3590 is also helpful.

Thank-yous

Florists *Blumenhaus Florist*, 1 Piedmont Center ☎ 237-6466; *Execuflower Service*, 5299 Roswell Rd ☎ 252-5151; *Peachtree Flowers*, 4280 Peachtree Rd ☎ 266-8800.

Gift baskets *The Butler Did It*, 3820 N Druid Hills Rd ☎ 255-8367.

BALTIMORE

Area code ☏ 301

Just 30 miles/48kms north of America's capital, Baltimore once had the reputation for being a dirty port and industrial city. Today, although still a major maritime and industrial center, it is a revitalized and rather sophisticated modern city. The Inner Harbor has been redeveloped, yet its port still has 43 miles/69kms of waterfront. It is there that Baltimore takes in ores, bananas and automobiles, and where it sends out grain, iron, coal, and steel. It is the headquarters of one of the world's biggest spice processors – McCormack; USF&G Insurance and Crown Central Petroleum have their national headquarters here as well. General Motors, Martin Marietta, Proctor and Gamble, and Black and Decker all have major plants in Baltimore and are important to the city's economy. Key growth sectors include bio-technology, centered at the Johns Hopkins Medical Center. Baltimore is not a tourist town, but the business visitor will be impressed by the scale of building and renovation.

Arriving

Baltimore–Washington International Airport (see *Washington*)

City link *Taxi* The center of Baltimore is just 15mins from the airport by taxi, 20mins during rush hours. The fare should run approximately $12.

Limousine A limo/van service to major Baltimore hotels for about $10 is operated by BWI LIM Service ☏ 441-2345.

Car rental Five firms are located at BWI: Avis ☏ 859-1680; Budget ☏ 859-0850; Dollar ☏ 859-8950; Hertz ☏ 850-7400; and National ☏ 859-8860.

Rail There is a daily Amtrak service to Washington and Philadelphia and other East Coast connections ☏ (800) 872-7245. Local commuter rail service is provided by MARC ☏ (800) 325-7245. A free shuttle bus service operates between the airport terminal and the rail station.

Getting around

Taxi Cabs are generally reliable and can be hailed in the street at any time. If you want to phone ahead, however, try *Diamond* ☏ 947-3333, *Yellow Cab* ☏ 685-1212, *BWI Airport Cab* ☏ 859-1100 or *Sun* ☏ 235-0300.

Limousine *Carey Limo* ☏ 727-7300, *Maryland Limousine* ☏ 850-4100.

Driving Parking is available at the Inner Harbor and downtown areas. For car rental information, see *City link*.

Walking The best way to get around downtown Baltimore is to walk. Driving is manageable, though not really necessary as the area is relatively small and there are skywalks from hotels to other major buildings.

Trolley *Baltimore Trolley Works* is part of the city transportation service. The trolleys run at approximately 7min intervals and stop about every two blocks along the Inner Harbor daily, 11am–7pm, and Charles Street, Mon–Sat ☏ 396-4259. Trolleys are also available for rent.

Bus For routes and times of the *MTA bus service* ☏ *539-5000.*

Subway For information on *Metrorail* ☏ 333-2700.

Area by area

Downtown The architecture of Baltimore combines the 20th century in the Charles Center–Inner Harbor area, the 19th century at Mt Vernon Place, and the 18th century at Fells Point, although much of the city was burned in the fire of 1904. Charles Center, the city's main business district, was the first stage in the downtown renaissance; its 33-acre complex has hotels, office buildings, apartments and restaurants. South

from the Center is the Baltimore Convention Center. At the waterfront, Harborplace's two pavilions contain more than 100 smart shops, boutiques and restaurants. Nearby are the World Trade Center, with its 27th-floor observation level, the National Aquarium and the Maryland Science Center. North of Charles Center is Mt Vernon Place, established in the early 1800s as the city's most prestigious residential district. The four-block area surrounding the 160ft Washington Monument has fashionable Victorian townhouses inhabited by many of the city's top executives. East from Inner Harbor, at the end of Broadway Street, lies Fells Point. Established in the mid-1700s, this once thriving maritime community is being extensively redeveloped.

Other areas For urban living, many executives choose Federal Hill, a neighborhood of renovated row houses, Mt Vernon and Roland Park. Fashionable suburban areas are Towson, Timonium and Cockeysville.

Hotels

With the revitalization of downtown Baltimore, major hotel chains such as Marriott, Omni, Stouffer, Hyatt, and Sheraton have built modern, business-oriented hotels to serve the Convention Center and the Inner Harbor. There are also some recently renovated smaller hotels which might be more suitable for a longer stay, especially if you prefer the comfort of a private apartment-like suite.

Admiral Fell Inn [$]/
888 S Broadway 21231 ☎ 522-7377 fax 522-0707 • AE MC V • 40 rooms, 1 restaurant, 1 bar
This small colonial inn at Fells Point is in fact three restored historic townhouses converted into a single hotel. Each room is handsomely decorated, and most have canopied beds. Service is efficient, the staff pleasant. There is a hot tub on the roof and an attractive pub in the lower level. A free van service takes guests anywhere in the city. Health club nearby • 1 meeting room.

Belvedere [$]/
Charles and Chase Sts 21202 ☎ 332-1000 fax 332-1422 • AE DC MC V • 100 rooms, 3 restaurants, 4 bars, 1 coffee shop
Restoration of Baltimore's grandest hotel began in 1976. Most rooms have full-service kitchens, and the hotel specializes in catering for meetings of 10 to 200. It has a distinguished restaurant, the John Eager Howard Room (see *Restaurants*), as well as the Owl Bar, where you can get a hearty meal in a more casual setting. The stylish lounge on the 13th floor has a splendid view. Hairdresser, shops • sauna, pool, racquetball courts, health club • 12 meeting rooms.

Cross Keys Inn [$]/
5100 Falls Rd 21210 ☎ 532-6900 fax 532-2403 • AE DC MC V • 148 rooms, 8 suites, 1 restaurant, 1 bar, 1 coffee shop
Just a 10min drive from downtown, the Cross Keys is quiet, almost suburban in atmosphere. It is situated next to the Cross Keys Village Square which has a bank, specialty shops and boutiques. The contemporary bedrooms have private patios. It is a good choice if you have business in the area, or in the nearby suburbs. Hairdresser • health club nearby, tennis • 10 meeting rooms.

Hyatt Regency [$]///
300 Light St 21202 ☎ 528-1234 [TX] 87577 fax 685-3362 • AE DC MC V • 459 rooms, 28 suites, 2 restaurants, 2 bars
This is Baltimore's top convention hotel, connected by overhead walkways to the Convention Center and Harbor Place. As befits a Hyatt, the lobby is spectacular, with glass elevators, greenery-filled atrium, a piano bar and a casual restaurant, Cascades. Rooftop Berry & Elliott's (see *Restaurants*) is more sophisticated, with harbor views. The Regency Club rooms are in the care of a concierge. Gift shop, beauty salon • health club, pool, jogging track, tennis • 19 meeting rooms.

Peabody Court [$]//
612 Cathedral St 21201 ☎ 727-7101 fax 539-7908 • AE DC MC V • 104 rooms, 39 suites, 2 restaurants
Baltimore's closest equivalent to a luxury European hotel is the recently refurbished Peabody Court at Mt Vernon Square. The rooms have an early-19thC European decor, with imported Directoire-style furniture. There are two fine restaurants: the Conservatory and the slightly more casual Peabody's (see *Restaurants*). Arrangements with nearby health club • 9 meeting rooms.

Sheraton Inner Harbor [$]//
300 S Charles St 21201 ☎ 962-8300 fax 962-8211 • AE DC MC V • 339 rooms, 20 suites, 1 restaurant, 1 bar

Specifically a business hotel, the Sheraton is well-equipped for meetings, and a skybridge links it to the Convention Center. The spacious modern lobby has an adjoining lounge. McHenry's offers American cuisine in a relaxed atmosphere; the glittery Impulse bar serves snacks. Pool, sauna • 11 meeting rooms.

Stouffer Harborplace $II
202 E Pratt St 21202 ☎ 547-1200
TX 9102508191 fax 539-5780 • AE DC MC V • 562 rooms, 60 suites, 1 restaurant, 2 bars
Located in the Gallery at Harborplace, this conveniently located hotel opened in 1989. It has grand views of the harbor and a rooftop garden. The rooms are well-equipped and spacious, with pleasant alcoves. On the Club Floor guests are pampered with extras (bathrobes), express check-in and check-out, private lounge and pass-key. Geared towards conventions, the hotel has the largest ballroom in Baltimore. Indoor pool, health club, sauna • 18 meeting rooms, with audio-visual equipment.

Tremont $II
8 E Pleasant St 21202 ☎ 576-1200 fax 685-4216 • AE DC MC V • 59 suites, 1 restaurant, 1 bar
A former apartment building, the all-suite Tremont is a favorite with sports and theater celebrities, who enjoy its privacy and the Downtown Athletic Club facilities available to guests. Corporate suites have a fully equipped kitchen and dining area; executive suites have kitchen, living room, dining room and separate bedroom with two queen-size beds. The celebrated 8 East (see *Restaurants*) is popular with the business community. Pool, sauna • 10 meeting rooms.

OTHER HOTELS

Holiday Inn-Inner Harbor $I *Howard and Lombard Sts 21201 ☎ 685-3500 fax 685-3500 • AE DC MC V.*

Society Hill $I *58 W Biddle St 21201 ☎ 837-3630 fax 837-4654 • AE DC MC V.*

Society Hill Government House $II *1125 N Calvert St 21202 ☎ 752-7722 fax 752-6278 • AE MC V.*

Tremont Plaza $II *222 St Paul Pl 21202 ☎ 727-2222 fax 685-4216 • AE DC MC V.*

Clubs

The *Maryland Club* ☎ 727-2323, established in 1896, is the old Baltimore all-male club into which the men of the city's "first families" are born. It serves lunch and dinner, but has no guest rooms. The *Merchants Club* ☎ 347-0505, a refurbished c.1905 building, and the *Center Club* ☎ 727-7788 are much used by local business people. *The Engineers Society of Baltimore* ☎ 539-6914, whose membership is about 40 per cent engineers, is another favorite dining spot for the local business community.

Restaurants

It comes as no surprise that good seafood, especially Maryland crab, is abundant in Baltimore. The city's revitalization has widened the variety of good restaurants available, and you can now choose from a range extending from the Conservatory's elegant European atmosphere to the bazaar-like cafés of the Inner Harbor and the ethnic foods of Little Italy. Baltimore is a city where business is often done over lunch and dinner.

Berry & Elliott's $II
Hyatt Regency Hotel ☎ 528-1234 • AE DC MC V
Overlooking Baltimore's Inner Harbor, this sophisticated restaurant offers Continental cuisine – seafood

and aged meat – as well as Cajun dishes all of which are often prepared tableside. A good choice for business entertaining.

Conservatory $////
Peabody Court Hotel ☎ *727-7101* • *AE DC MC V* • *jacket* • *reservations essential*
Sophisticated, glass-enclosed and affording a breathtaking view of midtown Baltimore, the Conservatory is one of the city's best restaurants; certainly it ranks as one of the most expensive. There is a chic bar where you can begin with cocktails before moving on to the superb French cuisine. The *prix fixe* dinner is first-class. Good for celebrating a special occasion.

8 East $//
Tremont Hotel ☎ *576-1200* • *AE MC V* • *jacket*
This small restaurant in the Tremont Hotel reopened in 1988 with a remodeled dining room and menu. Once French and expensive, it now serves "New American" cuisine at more moderate prices. Still a favorite of local executives.

Haussner's $//
3226-44 Eastern Ave ☎ *327-8365* • *closed Sun & Mon* • *AE DC MC V* • *no reservations*
Known for its eclectic art collections, this time-honored restaurant has long been a favorite of tourists and locals alike. The hearty, varied menu offers German specialties.

John Eager Howard Room $/
Belvedere Hotel ☎ *547-8220* • *AE DC MC V*
Evocative of the Federal period, with a 1780 portrait of the Revolution hero John Eager Howard hanging over a big stone fireplace, this restaurant has historically been the center stage for Maryland society. Its gracious service complements the Continental cuisine.

Peabody's $//
Peabody Court Hotel ☎ *727-7101* • *AE DC MC V*
Versatile and new, Peabody's nevertheless achieves something of a 19thC London gentlemen's club atmosphere. Prices are reasonable for very good Continental food; the desserts are fabulous. A good choice for a business lunch, it is also open all day from 7am until 10.30pm.

Prime Rib $//
1101 N Calvert St ☎ *539-1804* • *closed L* • *AE DC MC V* • *jacket*
The cosmopolitan atmosphere, white tablecloths, candlelight and attentive waiters are an attraction in themselves. But its steaks and, of course, prime ribs are the main reasons for the Prime Rib's popularity with visiting celebrities and the local elite.

Tio Pepe $///
10 E Franklin St ☎ *539-4675* • *AE MC V* • *reservations essential*
This popular Spanish restaurant in a townhouse basement specializes in excellent regional dishes, whole suckling pig and roast baby pheasant; and it does its own baking. It is always crowded.

Harborplace and Little Italy
At the Harborplace complex you can indulge in a unique gastronomic adventure with a splendid view of the harbor. With more than a dozen restaurants and cafés, as well as gourmet food shops in a traditional marketplace atmosphere, it is a great place to stroll, shop, dine, snack, sip and browse by the Bay.

Little Italy lies just two blocks east – an old established neighborhood, rich in cultural heritage, with such Italian favorites as *Sabatino's*, Fawn St ☎ 727-9414; *Da Mimmo*, 217 S High St ☎ 727-6876; *Velleggia's*, 829 E Pratt St ☎ 685-2620; and *Chipparelli's*, 237 S High St ☎ 837-0309.

Bars

Bars are not generally the place for business in Baltimore, but if you want somewhere to have a drink and a conversation, try the *Admiral Fell Inn Pub*, 328 S Broadway, Fells Point; or *8 East Lounge* at the Tremont Hotel. The bars and nightclubs in other hotels, strictly for socializing, include *Impulse*, at the Sheraton Inner Harbor; *Explorer's Club* at the Harbor Court, 550 Light St ☎ 234-0550; *Windows* at the Stouffer Harborplace; and *Thirteenth Floor* in the Belvedere.

Entertainment

Baltimore entertainment ranges from a pleasant night at the opera to the wide-ranging festivals of the Inner Harbor. For a complete listing of what's happening call ☎ 837-4636 or pick up a copy of the current *Baltimore Scene*. *Baltimore Box Office* is at the end of Pier 4 at the Inner Harbor ☎ 837-4636. The Inner Harbor provides all sorts of entertainment from tall ships and waterfront demonstrations to music festivals. In warm weather *Pier Six*, a 2,000-seat open-air pavilion, is a good concert spot.

Music Founded in 1857, and reputedly the oldest music school in America, the *Peabody Conservatory of Music*, 1E Mt Vernon Pl ☎ 659-8100, not only sponsors musical programs but also has a wonderful library. The *Lyric Opera House* ☎ 685-5806, at Mt Royal and Cathedral Streets, is another fine old building – a perfect setting for the Baltimore Opera, large musical productions and dance. The Baltimore Symphony has its season in the *Meyerhoff Symphony Hall*, 1212 Cathedral St ☎ 783-8110. The *Baltimore Arena,* 201 W Baltimore St ☎ 347-2010, stages everything from opera to rock.

Theater Stage productions are at the *Morris A Mechanic Theater* (Baltimore Center for the Performing Arts), Hopkins Plaza, Baltimore and Charles Sts ☎ 625-4230, and the *Center Stage*, 700 Calvert St ☎ 685-3200.

Shopping

Shopping in Baltimore today is not very different from what it was 200 years ago at the *Lexington Market*, 400 W Lexington St. All sorts of goods are sold in more than 100 stalls and shops. *Antique Row* is in the 700 and 800 blocks of N Howard Street, the 200 block of W Read Street and the 300 block of N Charles Street. Fells Point has the *Broadway Market* and many surrounding quaint shops. But the major downtown shopping area is Inner Harbor. *Harborplace* has a fine collection of shops in two buildings – Pratt Street and Light Street pavilions – offering everything from high-quality clothing and gourmet foods to handmade gifts from all over the world. *Hutzler's* department store is at the Convention Center Mall on Howard Street.

Sightseeing

To get a panoramic view of Baltimore, start at the *Top of the World*, World Trade Center, Pratt St ☎ 837-4515, which overlooks the city and its port.

B & O Railroad Museum *Pratt and Poppleton ☎ 237-2387. Open Wed–Sun, 10–4.*

Maryland Science Center and Planetarium *601 Light St ☎ 685-5225. Open daily, 10–5.*

National Aquarium This internationally known aquarium has 5,000 different species of marine life. *Pier 3, Pratt St ☎ 576-3800. Open daily, 10–5.*

US Frigate Constellation An enjoyable visit for nautical buffs. *Inner Harbor, Constitution Dock ☎ 539-1797. Open daily, 6–6.*

Walters Art Gallery Interesting and eclectic art collection, ranging from Greek artifacts to 20thC paintings. *Charles and Center ☎ 547-2787. Open Tue–Sun, 11–5.*

Guided tours

About Town Tours ☎ 592-7770 give walking tours of Inner Harbor and Federal Hill; *Baltimore Patriot* ☎ 685-4288 have 90min harbor cruises; *Clipper City* ☎ 539-6277 do a 3hr 30min sailing adventure. *Baltimore Rent-A-Tour* ☎ 653-2998; *Diversions* ☎ 486-3604; and *Widening Horizons* ☎ 829-0989 provide personalized tours.

Spectator sports

Baseball *Baltimore Orioles* play at Memorial Stadium, 33rd and Elbrise St ☎ 243-9800 or 338-1300. A new stadium opens in 1992 west of Inner Harbor.
Horse-racing *Pimlico Race Course*, 5201 Park Heights Ave ☎ 542-9400; *Laurel Race Course*, Laurel ☎ 792-7775; *Timonium Fairgrounds*, Timonium ☎ 252-0200.
Lacrosse *John Hopkins University*, 601 N Broadway ☎ 366-3300 ext 791.

Keeping fit

Fitness centers *Downtown Athletic Club*, 210 E Center St ☎ 332-0906, provides an indoor swimming pool, aerobics, tanning beds and weight-training equipment. Open to guests at many of the city's hotels. *Druid Hill YMCA*, 1609 Druid Hill Ave ☎ 728-1600; pool and fitness room.
Bicycling *Hotline* ☎ 333-1663 for information on bicycle trails.
Golf *Clifton Park Golf Course* ☎ 243-3500.

Local resources

Business services

The *Baltimore Area Convention and Visitors Association, 1 E Pratt St* ☎ 837-4636, the *Greater Baltimore Committee* ☎ 727-2820 and *Bedco* (Baltimore Economic Development Corporation) ☎ 837-9305 offer a wide range of services.
Audio-visual *Staging Connection* ☎ 953-3881.
Photocopying and printing *Day Speedy Printing* ☎ 539-8500, 24hr; *ASCO Duplicating Service* ☎ 327-2726; *A1 Copying* ☎ 752-0303.
Secretarial *HQ Services* ☎ 659-0055 provides secretarial and conference facilities.
Translation *Berlitz* ☎ 752-0767; *Academy of Language* ☎ 685-8383.

Communications

Long-distance delivery *Federal Express* ☎ 792-8200; *DHL Worldwide Courier Express* ☎ 247-6500.
Local delivery *Carl Messenger Service* ☎ 685-8700.
Post office Main office is at 900 E Fayette St ☎ 347-4425, 24hr.

Conference/exhibition centers

Baltimore Convention Bureau ☎ 659-7300 includes the *Festival Hall* ☎ 659-7000; *Baltimore Arena and Civic Center*, 201 W Baltimore St ☎ 347-2020.

Emergencies

Hospital *University Hospital*, 22 S Greene St ☎ 328-8667; for doctor referral ☎ 625-0022.
Pharmacy *Rite Aid*, Baltimore and Calvert Sts ☎ 727-9526.
Police 601 E Fayette St ☎ 396-2525.

Information sources

Business information The *Greater Baltimore Committee*, 2 Hopkins Plaza ☎ 727-2820, is the main force behind the city's renovation. Also prominent is *Baltimore Economic Development Corporation* ☎ 837-9305.
Local media The *Baltimore Sun* is a daily; the monthly *Baltimore* magazine is good for forthcoming events. *Harborplace News* ☎ 685-1804 stocks a wide range of newspapers.
Visitor information Baltimore Area Convention and Visitors Association, 1 E Pratt St, Plaza Level ☎ 659-7300; information site at Pratt and Howard Sts.

Thank-yous

Florists *Wilson's Harborplace Flower Market* ☎ 685-5565; *Fredrick Reitz*, 1309 W Baltimore St ☎ 685-9071; *Penny Lane* in Baltimore County ☎ 675-1700.
Gift baskets *Balloon Bouquets of Baltimore*, 2116 N Charles St ☎ 727-0909; *Sweet Craft Chocolatier* ☎ 332-0714; *Bayside Fruit and Nut Company* ☎ 332-1050; *Honeycomb* ☎ 752-2365; *Calico Cat* ☎ 962-8844; *Crabtree and Evelyn* ☎ 547-0668.

BOSTON

Area code ☎ 617

Boston – still often called the Hub, after Oliver Wendell Holmes's 1858 description of its State House as the "hub of the solar system" – is just as jealous of its commercial, cultural and social diversity as of its place as a crucible of American history. From colonial, mercantile beginnings, it has developed via shipping and manufacturing into a world leader in education, banking, mutual funds and insurance, medicine, publishing and high-tech. Home of the Kennedys and Harvard, cradle of Democratic politics and the Red Sox, Boston was once described as a society where the Lowells spoke only to the Cabots and the Cabots spoke only to God. Even in today's property-based economy, that is still how native Bostonians regard themselves and their city. It is a city firmly rooted in its past, where the descendants of the founding families – the Brahmins, as they came to be called – are still among the most powerful and influential voices in America.

Arriving

Boston Logan International Airport

All international flights arrive at Volpe International Terminal (E); domestic flights arrive at three others. It usually takes less than 30mins to clear Customs and baggage inspection.

The airport has five restaurants; more interesting, however, are the live lobsters sold throughout the airport which can be shipped on dry ice to any destination within the States. Many airlines provide executive lounges.

The international terminal has multilingual interpreters and currency exchange is available on ground level Mon–Fri, 8am–9.30pm, Sat & Sun, 11.30–9.30. A second currency exchange desk, in Terminal C, is open daily, 8–7. Air cargo ☎ 569-2727. General information ☎ 973-5500.

Nearby hotels *Logan Airport Hilton*, Logan International Airport 02128 ☎ 569-9300 fax 569-3981. *Ramada Inn–Airport*, 225 McClellan Hwy 02128 ☎ 569-5250 fax 569-9796.

City link Logan is only 2 miles/3kms from downtown and getting into the city is easy. Taxis are convenient, but for city center destinations the subway is quicker during peak hours 7–9, 4–6, and much cheaper.

Taxi Cabs line up outside each terminal. At non-peak times the journey should take no more than 15mins; fare about $10. During rush hours, traffic at the Callahan Tunnel can add at least 20mins.

Limousine service is available from all terminals.

Car rental Boston is a city where you do not need a car, unless your business is with some of the many high-tech firms along Route 128 (see *Area by area*). Rentals can be arranged at the ground level of all terminals.

Subway Take the free Massport shuttle bus to the "T" airport Blue Line subway station from which it is a 10–15min ride to Government Center/downtown Boston.

Bus A shuttle bus operator, Airways Transportation Co ☎ 267-2981, serves all major downtown hotels.

Getting around

Boston remains a city for walkers for two very good reasons – the street layout is complicated and parking is difficult.

Walking From anywhere in downtown Boston, a brisk 10–15min walk ought to take a visitor to most local destinations.

Taxi Boston cab drivers are notorious for asking passengers for directions to their requested destinations, and one-way systems sometimes make circuitous routes necessary. Cabs can

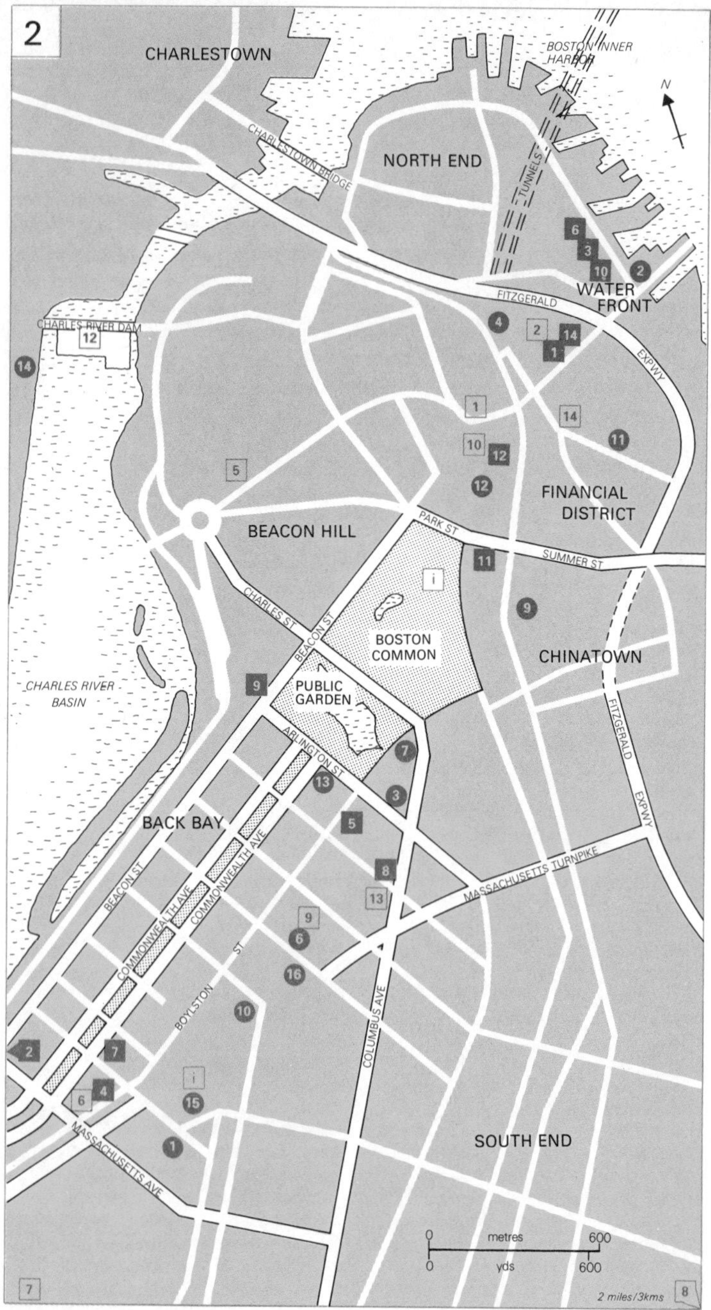
2
CHARLESTOWN
BOSTON INNER HARBOR
N
CHARLESTOWN BRIDGE
NORTH END
TUNNELS
EXPWY
WATER FRONT
FITZGERALD
CHARLES RIVER DAM
BEACON HILL
FINANCIAL DISTRICT
PARK ST
SUMMER ST
CHARLES ST
BEACON ST
BOSTON COMMON
CHINATOWN
CHARLES RIVER BASIN
PUBLIC GARDEN
ARLINGTON ST
FITZGERALD EXPWY
BACK BAY
MASSACHUSETTS TURNPIKE
BEACON ST
COMMONWEALTH AVE
COMMONWEALTH AVE
BOYLSTON ST
COLUMBUS AVE
MASSACHUSETTS AVE
SOUTH END
metres 0 600
yds 0 600
2 miles/3kms

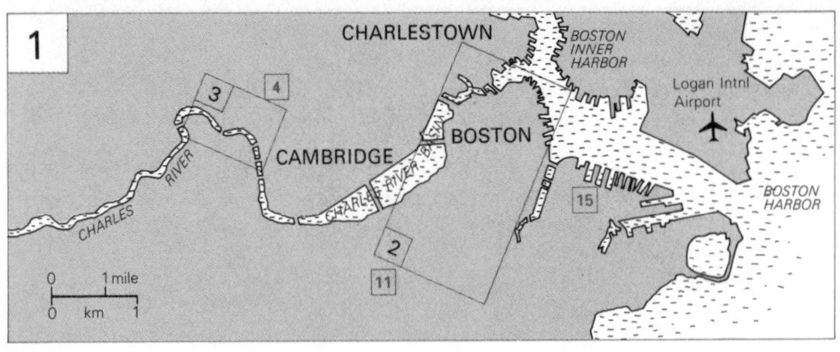

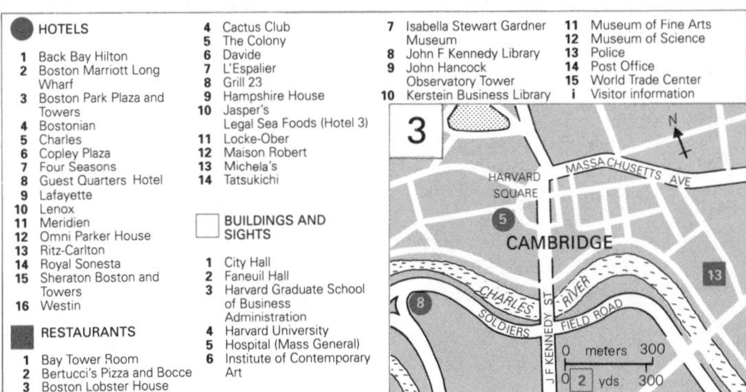

be flagged in the street but it is sometimes best either to phone ahead or use a hotel taxi stand. Reliable companies to try are *Boston Cab* ☎ 536-5010; *Checker Cab* ☎ 536 7000; *Red Cab* ☎ 734-5000.

Limousine *Fifth Avenue Limousine* ☎ 286-0555 caters to the city's corporate high rollers and rock stars; *Commonwealth Limousine Service* ☎ 787-5575 also runs a sophisticated fleet.

Car rental *Avis* ☎ (800) 331-1212; *Dollar* ☎ 367-2654.

Subway The MBTA, locally known as the "T," has four lines: the Red Line runs north–south, from Cambridge to Mattapan or Quincy; the Blue Line runs from the northeast into downtown; the Green Line has several branches operating from downtown to the west and southwest; and the Orange Line is a north–south line. Park Street Station is the major downtown transfer point for Red and Green Line trains; ☎ 722-3200.

Area by area

Downtown and Back Bay Boston's business life is centered on downtown – home of most financial, legal and political offices – and adjacent Back Bay, where the city's well-to-do live alongside the insurance companies, advertising and public relations agencies and retail stores in this traditional brownstone area.

The heart of Back Bay is bounded by Arlington Street, Massachusetts Avenue and Beacon and Boylston streets. The main thoroughfares are Commonwealth Avenue, for long one of the choicest and most expensive residential addresses, and Newbury Street, the city's most fashionable shopping district.

Fine houses in Marlborough and Beacon streets have now been transformed by Boston's young professionals, as rocketing costs forced the students who once lived there to move out to other more affordable areas in the west.

Despite development, downtown and Back Bay remain solid reminders of the city's past. The brick and granite buildings of Faneuil Hall and Quincy Market in downtown's Financial District date from the city's second mayor, Josiah Quincy, and one of the area's de luxe hotels is nothing less than the old Federal Reserve Bank.

The Waterfront, once a bustling popular seaport, now has luxury condominiums and retail stores; while in Back Bay's South End – home of Boston's gay community, as well as numerous well-heeled residents – brick townhouses and wrought-iron streetlamps are overlooked by the marble and glass of Copley Place.

Beacon Hill With its gas-lit streets, mansions and townhouses, Beacon Hill preserves an atmosphere enjoyed by 18thC Brahmins, whose descendants still dominate city life.

North End Traditionally the "wrong" side of the hill, North End houses mainly writers, academics, and intellectuals who choose to keep the Charles River between their homes and their Cambridge workbases of Harvard, MIT and Radcliffe.

Route 128, and the nearby cities, are dense with shiny buildings and corporate headquarters that the road has become known as "America's Technology Highway." At a time when California's Silicon Valley has been hit by slump, the western stretch of Route 128, between the towns of Needham and Burlington, is lined with headquarters or other premises of such firms as Prime Computer, Wang, Raytheon, Digital and Budd HN.

Cambridge is a blend of academic, art-oriented and corporate life, the headquarters of such enterprises as Lotus, Polaroid, Arthur D Little and Draper Laboratories. Its twin focal points – bustling Harvard Square and the tranquil Harvard Yard nearby – have been supplemented recently by the slick retail complex of Charles Square.

Other areas West of Boston are the wealthy, gracious tree-studded residential towns of Brookline, Newton, and Chestnut Hill.

Hotels

Traditional top hotels like the Ritz-Carlton and the Copley Plaza and newer competitors, such as the Four Seasons and the Westin, and dozens of other first-rate establishments provide amply for the needs of business visitors.

Back Bay Hilton [$]////
40 Dalton St 02115 ☎ 236-1100
[TX] *951858 fax 236-1506 • AE DC MC V • 340 rooms, 1 restaurant, 4 bars, 1 coffee shop*
A modern high-rise with a prime Back Bay address, this typical Hilton caters mainly and efficiently to the business community. Boodle's, a dining room specializing in mesquite-grilled steaks and seafood, is very popular among local executives. Pool, health club, access to golf and tennis clubs • 16 meeting rooms.

Boston Marriott Long Wharf [$]////
296 State St 02109 ☎ 227-0800
[TX] *928065 fax 227-2867 • AE MC V • 400 rooms, 2 restaurants, 1 bar*
Though sporting what is arguably the city's ugliest façade, this brick hotel has an ultra-modern interior (featuring painted steel pipes in the open lobby), a prime waterfront location, and is convenient to the financial district, Government Center and other downtown business addresses. Rooms on the seventh floor are equipped with large dining areas which can double as work spaces. Gift shops • indoor pool, health club • 17 meeting rooms, recording facilities.

Boston Park Plaza and Towers [$]//
50 Park Plaza at Arlington St 02116
☏ 426-2000 TX 94017 fax 426-5545 • *AE DC MC V* • *977 rooms and suites, 3 restaurants, 2 bars*
A well-located, family-run hotel which aims to provide all the services and shops the business traveler might need under one roof. The paneled Fox and Hounds restaurant and Plaza pub are popular meeting places; here as elsewhere the style is traditional. Airport shuttle, airline ticket offices, bank, shops, hairdresser • health club, access to Back Bay Racquet Club • 22-room conference center, 14 meeting rooms.

Bostonian [$]///
Faneuil Hall Mktpl 02109
☏ 523-3600 TX 948159 fax 523-2454 • *AE DC MC V* • *153 rooms, 6 suites, 1 restaurant, 1 bar*
Overlooking historic Faneuil Hall Marketplace, Boston's smallest luxury hotel aims at meticulous but unobtrusive personal service. There are two wings, the contemporary Bostonian wing and the more rustic Harkness wing. Rooms are small but well-decorated, with oversized baths, jacuzzis, and television sets concealed in armoires. The rooftop restaurant, Seasons, is one of the city's best for a quiet business meal. Lobby shops • use of nearby health club (pool and tennis) • 2 meeting rooms.

Charles [$]///
1 Bennett St 02138 ☏ 864-1200 TX 857417 fax 864-5715 • *AE DC MC V* • *299 rooms, 44 suites, 2 restaurants, 2 bars*
This personable Georgian-style hotel in Cambridge has a quaint New England flavor. With its antiques and four-poster beds, it draws an urbane, sophisticated clientele, many of them academics visiting the nearby Kennedy School of Government. All suites have small sitting rooms well-suited for business meetings, and those on the tenth floor have telephones equipped for computer modems. The hotel has a well-equipped third-floor conference center, and some floors are reserved for nonsmokers. Rarities, the hotel's sleek dining room, serves *nouvelle* dishes, and the live jazz at the Regattabar is the best in town. Smart shops • health club and salon with indoor lap pool, fitness center, aerobics studio • 12 meeting rooms with teleconference facilities.

Copley Plaza [$]///
138 St James Ave 02116 ☏ 267-5300 fax 267-7668 • *AE DC MC V* • *375 rooms, 26 suites, 2 restaurants, 3 bars, 1 coffee shop*
The Plaza opened in 1912 and is Boston's *grande dame*, complete with French period furnishings, carved mantels and gilded ceilings. Sited on Copley Square, it attracts an especially well-heeled clientele, and is a nucleus of high level business and social activity in the city. The Plaza Bar, with its tropical plants and Oriental screens, is a Boston institution, quiet enough for serious business talks. Hairdresser, beauty salon, jewelers, perfumery • 12 meeting rooms, Federal Express, translation, notary public.

Four Seasons [$]///
200 Boylston St 02116 ☏ 338-4400 TX 853349 fax 423-0154 • *AE DC MC V* • *288 rooms, 13 suites, 2 restaurants, 2 bars*
Rooms in this recently built status hotel are graced with cherry furniture and formal English chintzes; many have a separate work area off the bedroom. The brown oak, candlelit Aujourd'hui specializes in classical French cuisine updated for today's health-conscious travelers. Pool, weights, whirlpool, sauna, massage • 8 meeting rooms.

Guest Quarters Hotel [$]//
400 Soldiers Field Rd 02134
☏ 783-0090 fax 783-0897 • *AE DC MC V* • *310 suites, 1 restaurant, 1 bar*
A relative newcomer to the Boston scene, the city's only all-suites hotel is

well located for visitors with business in Cambridge. The 15-story atrium lobby makes for an impressive entrance. Suites have refrigerators and living rooms that can be used for meetings or entertaining. The Ambassador Grille serves *nouvelle cuisine* in a subdued country club-like atmosphere and is a good choice for quiet conversation. Nonsmoking suites • indoor pool, sauna, jacuzzi, arrangements with nearby health club • 8 meeting rooms.

Lafayette [$]///

1 Ave de Lafayette 02111 ☎ 451-2600 [TX] 853840 fax 451-0054 • AE DC MC V • 430 rooms, 41 suites, 2 restaurants, 1 bar

This 22-story Swissotel has four atriums, a central location and a Continental flavor. Its Le Marquis restaurant is one of the best hotel dining rooms in the city. Nonsmoking floor • pool • 12 meeting rooms.

Lenox [$]//

710 Boylston St at Copley Pl 02116 ☎ 536-5300 [TX] 928158 fax 267-1237 • AE DC MC V • 220 rooms, 2 restaurants, 1 bar

Run by the same family as the gargantuan Park Plaza, the Lenox has a totally different appeal. While maintaining the atmosphere of a comfortable private home, with antique furniture, fireplaces (in corner rooms), and many personal touches, it also caters to business needs (the *Wall Street Journal* is delivered daily to all rooms). 8 meeting rooms.

Meridien [$]////

250 Franklin St 02110 ☎ 451-1900 [TX] 940194 fax 423-2844 • AE DC MC V • 326 rooms, 22 suites, 2 restaurants, 2 bars

The Renaissance-style Meridien – located in the old Federal Reserve Bank – has 153 different room styles including loft bedrooms with downstairs living rooms. Julien serves creative cuisine in an Old World setting and the Meridien's bar has been described by *Boston Magazine* as "the best place to have a drink and make a deal." Gift and flower shops • health club with indoor pool, jacuzzi, aerobics, sauna • 8 meeting rooms, recording facilities.

Omni Parker House [$]///

60 School St 02108 ☎ 227-8600 [TX] 7103216707 fax 742-5729 • AE DC MC V • 541 rooms, 14 suites, 4 restaurants, 4 bars, 1 coffee shop

The home of Boston cream pie and Parker House rolls, this downtown hotel evokes a warmer atmosphere than most city hotels, from the mahogany walls and gilt ceilings down to the polished brass doors. Its financial district location makes the Parker House central to all downtown offices as well as Government Center. Downstairs, the Last Hurrah! is a turn-of-the-century saloon where local politicians meet for lunch and dinner; upstairs, the elegant Parker's serves Continental fare; and for after-dinner drinks, the quiet of Parker's Bar is ideal for talking business or relaxing. Nonsmoking rooms, florist, gift shop • 14 meeting rooms.

Ritz-Carlton [$]////

15 Arlington St 02117 ☎ 536-5700 [TX] 940591 fax 536-1335 • AE DC MC V • 202 rooms, 48 suites, 3 restaurants, 1 bar

Gentility and privacy reign supreme at the Ritz, where white-gloved elevator operators and call buttons for room service still matter. Guests are world travelers – Prince Charles stayed here during Harvard's 350th anniversary – and are treated accordingly. For years, professionals have flocked to the Ritz Bar, a local institution with an unobstructed view of the Public Garden and the best martini in town. The main dining room is the epitome of proper Bostonianism, and the downstairs café is *the* place for power breakfasts. Jewelers, gift shop, florist, dress shop • rooftop health club with sauna and massage • 10 meeting rooms.

Royal Sonesta [$]////
5 Cambridge Pkwy, Cambridge 02142 ☏ 491-3600 [TX] 275293 fax 661-5956 • AE DC MC V • 400 rooms, 12 suites, 2 restaurants, 2 bars
Guest rooms are crisp and contemporary in this expensively renovated Art Deco-style building overlooking the Charles River. The location provides easy access to Harvard, MIT and Mass General Hospital. Hairdresser, gift shop • pool, health club • 16 meeting rooms, computers, computer modems, software packages, copy center, business library.

Sheraton Boston and Towers [$]////
39 Dalton St 02199 ☏ 236-2000 [TX] 940034 fax 236-1702 • AE DC MC V • 1,250 rooms, 85 suites, 4 restaurants, 4 bars
Although lacking the cachet of Boston's more established hotels, the Sheraton's central location and its dining room, Apley's, combine to attract many visiting executives. Pool, exercise equipment, rowing machines, exercycles, jacuzzi • 41 meeting rooms, conference center, computers.

Westin [$]////
10 Huntington Ave 02116 ☏ 262-9600 [TX] 948286 fax 242-7483 • AE DC MC V • 804 rooms, 44 suites, 2 restaurants, 3 bars, 1 coffee shop
A far cry from the quaint or understated, the Westin has a convenient location, handsomely appointed pastel-colored rooms and a well-heeled professional clientele. Nonsmoking floor, florist, gift shop, jeweler • pool, health club • 23 meeting rooms.

Clubs

Socially, the legacy of the Brahmins continues to thrive in the *Somerset Club* and its male-only members – who are said to be responsible for the founding of the equally august *Union Club* ☏ 227-0589. The *Harvard Club* ☏ 536-1260 is also privileged, but women can join. Its downtown location offers a breathtaking view of the city. Playing second string to the Harvard at double the price is the *University Club* ☏ 266-5600, whose members are mostly Ivy Leaguers who didn't go to Harvard. Artists and writers go to the *Tavern Club*.

Restaurants

A city once known for fresh fish, baked beans and other native New England staples, Boston has in recent years experienced something of a culinary boom with the focus on first-rate ethnic and *nouvelle* establishments. For important business entertaining the top hotel restaurants are the safest choice.

Bay Tower Room [$]////
60 State St ☏ 723-1666 • closed L, Sun • AE DC MC V • jacket and tie • reservations requested
This dimly lit, 33rd-floor supper club provides an impressive setting for business deals either to be made or celebrated, though it is noted more for its sweeping views of the Boston Harbor than for its Continental cuisine.

Bertucci's Pizza and Bocce [$]
799 Main St, Cambridge ☏ 661-8356 • MC V
A Boston favorite, Bertucci's specializes in wood-fire-baked pizzas with toppings such as ricotta, roasted peppers and eggplant. Though family-oriented most evenings, this is a popular lunch spot for Cambridge business people and academics.

Boston Lobster House [$]////
256 Commercial St ☏ 720-1188 • AE DC MC V • jacket
With tuxedoed waiters and fresh-cut flowers, Sally Ling's Boston Lobster House has the grandeur of a Chinese palace, and cuisine to match. The

Newton Center ☎ 332-3600 branch is similarly upscale, but less expensive; there is a third at the Hyatt Regency Hotel, Cambridge ☎ 868-1818.

Cactus Club [$]II
939 Boylston St ☎ 236-0200 • closed L • AE MC V
Its sleek, pastel interior, Italian *nuova cucina* and sizzling social scene in the bar, helped this Art Deco-style restaurant carve a niche among both the conservative three-piece-suit set and the funkier arts and fashion crowd. Acoustics make conversation difficult.

The Colony [$]III
384 Boylston St ☎ 536-8500 • closed Sun, Mon • AE MC V • reservations essential
Modern cuisine based on traditional New England foods is served amid the refined trappings of a wealthy turn-of-the-century Brahmin home. Service is black-tie without being stiff; strong selection of wines.

Davide [$]I
326 Commercial St ☎ 227-5745 • AE DC MC V • jacket recommended, no pipes or cigars • weekend reservations essential
Davide's pretty setting and northern Italian fare have won acclaim from local restaurant critics and the waterfront business crowd.

L'Espalier [$]III
30 Gloucester St ☎ 262-3023 • closed Sun; Mon in summer • AE DC MC V • jacket required
You can expect the best in *nouvelle cuisine* and formal service at L'Espalier. Depending on mood and the type of deal being struck or celebrated, you can choose the ornate downstairs room or relax in the more club-like atmosphere above.

Grill 23 [$]II
161 Berkeley St ☎ 542-2255 • closed Sat and Sun L • AE DC MC V • jacket and tie • weekend reservations essential
The steaks and prime beef are the biggest draw, and the clubby atmosphere makes the Grill a good choice for business lunches. The clientele includes executives from nearby insurance companies, publishing houses and advertising agencies, as well as Back Bay shoppers.

Hampshire House [$]I
84 Beacon St ☎ 227-9600 • AE DC MC V • jacket • reservations essential
Brahmin in tone, this Victorian-style dining room is particularly inviting in winter, with its hospitable fireplace, window seats overlooking the Public Garden, and a menu that's as hearty and conservative as the clientele. The Oak Room Bar and Café serves lighter fare.

Jasper's [$]II
240 Commercial St ☎ 523-1126 • closed L, Sun • AE DC MC V • jacket and tie
Jasper White, one of the city's premier chefs, perfected his culinary skills at nearby Seasons (see *Hotel restaurants*). His menu is *nouvelle*, service is gracious and the atmosphere simple, contemporary and chic.

Legal Sea Foods [$]I
Boston Park Plaza and Towers Hotel ☎ 426-4444 • AE • no reservations
Legal's downtown branch (there are two others) is the restaurant Bostonians love to hate. They hate the long lines, the erratic service and the pay-first-eat-later policy. But they love the fish enough to keep going back. The working crowd who cannot afford to wait for a table often heads to the bar for chowder, raw oysters and clams.

Locke-Ober [$]II
3-4 Winter Pl ☎ 542-1340 • closed Sun L • AE DC MC V • jacket and tie • reservations essential
This is quintessential Boston, from the carved mahogany and floor-length white-aprons of the waiters, to the crystal sconces, leather chairs and Continental menu. This is where the

business elite meets to eat; private dining rooms on the 3rd floor are popular among local business executives and politicians from State House.

Maison Robert [$]//
45 School St ☎ *227-3370 • closed Sat L, Sun in summer • AE DC MC V • jacket and tie • reservations essential*
A good choice for business entertaining, this is the closest Boston gets to a real French "feel," and owner-chef Lucien Robert's cooking has been widely acclaimed. Located in the historic Old City Hall, the Bonhomme Richard restaurant is both pretty and proper, without being stuffy. Downstairs, Ben's Café provides a bistro-like setting and less expensive food; in summer a terrace café opens onto the old City Hall courtyard. There are also private dining rooms suitable for business meetings.

Michela's [$]//
1 Athenaeum St, Cambridge
☎ *225-3366 • closed Sat L, Sun • AE DC MC V • reservations essential*
Michela's Art Deco-style decor provides a cool meeting place for the food of northern Italy and southern California. Its first-rate classics include goat cheese lasagne and ravioli with squid ink. The restaurant is a favorite with the architects, engineers and computer programers of Kendall Square. Lunch prices are about half those from the dinner menu.

Tatsukichi [$]/
189 State St ☎ *720-2468 • closed Sat L, Sun • AE DC MC V*
Sushi and *sashimi* are the main specialties here, but the menu includes other Japanese dishes such as *tempura* and *teriyaki*.

Bars

The watering holes favored for business meetings are in the top hotels – *Parker's Bar* in the Omni Parker House; the *Plaza Bar*, at the Copley Plaza; the old Federal Bank vault at the Meridien; and the *Ritz* in the Ritz-Carlton. For the social crowd, there's a very lively scene. Back Bay's most stylish bars include the *Commonwealth Grille*, 111 Dartmouth St ☎ 353-0160, where you can gaze on the latest models, fashionable photographers and rock musicians; and *Joe's American Bar & Grill* (nr Newbury and Dartmouth St ☎ 536-4200), which is popular with ad agency boomers. Cambridge's beautiful people use the *Reggatabar* ☎ 864-1200 at the Charles Hotel and *Harvest*, 44 Brattel St ☎ 492-1115.

Hotel restaurants
Several of the area's best restaurants are in the city's de luxe hotels. Examples are *Seasons* on the rooftop of the Bostonian, *Boodle's* in the Back Bay Hilton, *Rarities* at the Charles, and *Aujourd'hui* in the Four Seasons. In the same league are *Café Fleuri* at the Meridien, *Le Marquis* at the Lafayette, *Parker's* in the Omni Parker House, and the genteel main dining room of the Ritz-Carlton.

Entertainment

Theater In recent years, Boston has evolved as a try-out town for Broadway shows. Major theaters include the *Shubert* ☎ 426-4520, the *Colonial* ☎ 426-9366 and the *Wang Center for Performing Arts* ☎ 482-9393. For local theater at its strongest, check out the *American Repertory Theater* ☎ 547-8300 and the *Huntington Theater Company* ☎ 266-3913.
Music Both the *Boston Pops*, starting their season in May, and the world-class *Boston Symphony Orchestra*, conducted by Seiji Ozawa, perform at Symphony Hall, 251 Huntington Ave ☎ 266-1492, from Oct–Apr; in July it moves to Tanglewood ☎ (413) 637-1600.
Nightclubs Most of Boston's

nightclubs are frequented by a post-graduate clientele. The city's premier disco is *Citi*, 15 Lansdowne St ☏ 262-2425, which features state-of-the-art everything, from lasers to acoustics. *The Jukebox*, 275 Tremont St ☏ 542-1123, is the best of the local 1950s and 1960s dance clubs; and the *Avenue Club*, 120 Boylston St ☏ 423-3832, caters to a very preppy crowd. For music, *Nightstage*, 823 Main St, Cambridge ☏ 497-8200, is the place for big names in blues and jazz.

Shopping

Back Bay is Boston's most stylish shopping district with elegant 19thC storefronts, art galleries, furriers and pricey boutiques along *Newbury Street*. The monolithic pink-marbled *Copley Place* is anchored by Neiman-Marcus and filled with such internationally known designer shops as Gucci, Tiffany's and Ralph Lauren. Nearby *Downtown Crossing* is Boston's oldest shopping center, with department stores Filene's and Jordan Marsh. At *Filene's Basement* you can buy anything from furs to Brooks Brothers suits at greatly reduced prices. *Faneuil Hall Marketplace* is the city's top tourist destination, with scores of bars, shops and restaurants. The food emporium is located inside the Quincy Market Building, where you can pick up everything from raw oysters to Chinese spare ribs. More of the same are in the adjacent *Marketplace Center*.

The Mall at Chestnut Hill, which includes Bloomingdale's, Filene's, Crate & Barrel and two high-class home furnishings stores (Adesso and Domain), is by far the best of the suburban malls.

In Cambridge, *Charles Square* has an interesting collection of small boutiques; and *Harvard Square* is packed with bookstores and gift and clothing boutiques. Also in the square are two small malls, The Garage and The Galleria, and the Harvard Coop, which sells all kinds of Harvard University paraphernalia and has one of the largest record selections in New England.

Sightseeing

Arnold Arboretum 265 acres of parkland with plants and trees (more than 7,000 varieties), and spectacular floral displays in the spring. *The Arborway ☏ 524-1718. Hours vary.*
The Freedom Trail A 2.5mile/4km marked walking tour of 16 historic sites from colonial and revolutionary times ending at the Bunker Hill Monument. *Start from Boston Common (trail information from the Visitor Center near Park St subway).*
Institute of Contemporary Art No permanent collection, but a changing range of imaginative temporary exhibits. The building – an old firehouse renovated by local architect Graham Gund – is worth seeing on its own merit. *955 Boylston St ☏ 266-5151. Open Tue–Sun, 11–7; closed Mon.*
Isabella Stewart Gardner Museum Rembrandts, Raphaels, Whistlers, Sargents and Matisses are displayed in the carefully preserved period rooms of a Venetian-style palazzo. *280 The Fenway ☏ 734-1359. Open 1–5.30, Tue to 9.30; closed Mon.*
John F Kennedy Library Films and exhibits depicting the life of the late President are featured in this contemporary waterfront museum. *Columbia Point on Dorchester Bay ☏ 929-4523. Open 9–5.*
John Hancock Observatory Tower In addition to the sweeping view of Boston, the 60th-floor observatory has a photo exhibit and a breathtaking film of the city taken from a helicopter. *Copley Sq ☏ 572-6427. Open 9–11; Sun from 10.*
Museum of Fine Arts The MFA's collections of European paintings – notably French Impressionists – and American art from the 18th and 19th centuries are particularly strong. There are 43 Monets in addition to canvases by Manet, Renoir and Pissarro. American artists represented include Winslow Homer, John Singer Sargent, Fitz Hugh Lane, Edward

Hopper and Mary Cassatt. There is also a vast collection of Asiatic and oriental art – T'ang Dynasty porcelain to Egyptian mummies. *465 Huntington Ave ☏ 267-9300. Open Tue–Sun, 10–5; Wed to 10; West and Evans Wings only Thu & Fri to 10.*
Museum of Science Astronomy, anthropology, medicine, music, electronics, computers and earth sciences are all represented. The Hayden Planetarium has a regularly changing program. *Science Park, on the Charles River Dam ☏ 723-2500. Open Tue–Sun, 9–5.*

Guided tours

Boat tours to Cape Cod and around the Harbor Islands are operated by *Bay State Cruises* ☏ 723-7800, the *Massachusetts Bay Line* ☏ 749-4500 and *Boston Harbor Cruises* ☏ 742-3313. *AC Cruise Line* ☏ 426-8419 offers whale watches and daily sailings to Gloucester in the summer. Jazz, classical, and contemporary musicians are the specialty of *Water Music Inc* ☏ 876-8742. Cruises last 3hrs.
Bus tours of Boston, Lexington and Concord are operated by *Brush Hill Tours* ☏ 287-1900 and *Gray Line Tours* ☏ 426-8805. Other excursions include Cape Cod, 57 miles/92kms south of Boston.
Walking tours of Boston are offered by various organizations including *Boston by Foot* ☏ 367-2345 and *Grand Tours* ☏ 482-7974.

Spectator sports

Baseball American League's *Red Sox* play at Fenway Park ☏ 267-1700.
Basketball The world champions *Celtics* play at the Boston Garden ☏ 227-3200 from Oct–Jun.
Football The *New England Patriots*, the region's only professional team, play at the Sullivan Stadium in Foxboro ☏ 543-1776.
Horse-racing Races every Mon, Wed, Fri and Sat year-round at *Suffolk Downs* ☏ 567-3900 in east Boston.
Ice hockey The *Bruins* face-off at the Boston Garden ☏ 227-3200.

Keeping fit

In good weather, Bostonians head for the Esplanade, a grassy knoll with clearly marked paths for bikers and joggers on the banks of the Charles River. Bicycles can be rented from *Community Bike*, 490 Tremont St ☏ 542-8623.
Fitness centers Many hotels have their own fitness centers or have arrangements with private clubs. Among the local clubs open to visitors are the *Boston Athletic Club*, 653 Summer St ☏ 269-4300; the *Boston Racquet Club*, 10 Post Office Sq ☏ 482-8881; the *Cambridge Racquet Club*, 215 1st St, Cambridge ☏ 491-8989; the YMCA, 316 Huntington Ave ☏ 536-7800; and the *YWCA*, 140 Clarendon St ☏ 536-7940.
Boating Instruction is provided at the *Boston Sailing Center*, Lewis Wharf, Boston Harbor ☏ 227-4198; the *Charles River Canoe Service* ☏ 965-5110; *Community Boating* ☏ 523-1038; and *Europa Windsurfing* ☏ 497-0309. The *Boston Harbor Sailing Club* ☏ 523-2619.
Golf The most prestigious clubs are the *Country Club* ☏ (617) 566-0240 in Brookline and *Pine Brook Country Club* ☏ (617) 894-3731 in Weston. Public courses include the *Fresh Pond Golf Club*, 691 Huron Ave, Cambridge ☏ 354-9130; the *Ponkapoag Golf Course*, Rte 138, Canton ☏ 828-7490; and the *Martin Golf Course*, Concord Rd, Weston ☏ 894-4903.
Tennis There are public courts at *Lee Pool*, Charles St (across from Mass General Hospital) ☏ 523-9746, and *Foss Park*, McGrath Hwy ☏ 727-9547.

Local resources

Business services

Firms which offer complete services, convenient locations and prompt turnaround include *Boston Mimeo & Stenographic Service Inc*, Broad St ☏ 482-4696; *Office Plus*, 6 Faneuil Hall Mktpl ☏ 367-8335; and *The Skill Bureau*, which has two locations,

at 129 Tremont St ☎ 423-2986, and 1384 Mass Ave, Cambridge ☎ 661 6699.
Photocopying and printing *Copy Copy* ☎ 267-9267 is at 815 Boylston St, across from the Prudential Center, and at several other locations; *Sir Speedy Instant Printing* ☎ 267-9711 is equally efficient with branches near Government Center, in the Financial District and in Brookline. Both companies offer pick-up and delivery.
Secretarial Reliable agencies include *Accountemps* ☎ 951-4000 and *Kelly Services* ☎ 542-4040.
Translation *Berlitz Translation Services* ☎ 266-6858 and *Linguistic Systems, Inc* ☎ 864-3900.

Communications

Long-distance delivery *Federal Express* ☎ 391-4760 or *Emery Worldwide* ☎ 542-0108.
Local delivery *Choice Courier* ☎ 787-2020. *Marathon Messenger Company* ☎ 266-8990 is Boston's most reliable bicycle courier system.
Post office General information ☎ 654-5083; the downtown office is at 647 Summer St ☎ 654-5327; the Back Bay office is at 390 Stuart St ☎ 654-5688.

Conference/exhibition centers

Facilities are provided at the *Bayside Exposition Center*, 200 Mt Vernon St ☎ 265-5800, which has meeting rooms for 4,000; *World Trade Center*, Commonwealth Pier ☎ 439-5000, has meeting rooms for 10–2,500 as well as a complete food and beverage service, advanced audio-visual systems and teleconferencing capabilities; and the *Park Plaza Castle*, corner of Arlington and Stuart ☎ 426-2000 ext 319, is a National Historic Landmark with towers, turrets, moats, and 20,000 square feet of exhibition space.

Emergencies

Hospitals *Mass General Hospital*, 55 Fruit St ☎ 726-2000; *Brigham and Women's Hospital*, 75 Francis St ☎ 732-5636; *Mt Auburn Hospital*, 330 Mt Auburn St, Cambridge ☎ 492-3500. Mass General does not accept credit cards. For dental emergencies, the *Mass Dental Society* ☎ (508) 651-7511 makes referrals. For doctor referral, call the *Mass Medical Society* ☎ 893-4610.
Pharmacies *Phillips*, 155 Charles St ☎ 523-4372, is open 24hrs.
Police Call ☎ 247-4200.

Government offices

US Dept of Commerce/International Trade Division ☎ 565-8576; *US Customs* ☎ 565-6147; *Immigration and Naturalization Service* ☎ 565-3879.

Information sources

Business information *Greater Boston Convention and Visitors Bureau* and *Chamber of Commerce*, Prudential Plaza, POB 490 ☎ 536-4100; the *Mass Office of Travel and Tourism* ☎ 727-3201 or (800) 632-8038.
Local media *Out of Town News*, Harvard Square ☎ 354-7777, carries the city's widest selection of international newspapers and magazines. *The Boston Globe* and *The Boston Herald* newspapers provide city and regional coverage. *The Globe* is Boston's white-collar daily with special business sections on Tue and Wed. *Business Magazine* is an authoritative monthly on the political, cultural and social scene. *New England Business* is a slick monthly survey of area powerbrokers.
Visitor information at Tremont St side of Boston Common and west side of Prudential Plaza, open daily, 9–5 ☎ (800) 858-0200. See also *Business information*.

Thank-yous

Florists *Winston Flowers*, 131 Newbury St ☎ 536-6861; *The Greenhouse*, 553 Boylston St ☎ 437-1050; *Victorian Bouquet Ltd*, 53 Charles St ☎ 367-6648. All accept credit card orders by phone.
Gift baskets *The Cheers Group* ☎ 242-9889 specializes in personalized corporate gift baskets.

CHICAGO

Area code ☏ 312

Birthplace of the skyscraper and fertile breeding ground of a whole school of modern architecture, Chicago is a city of skypunching buildings; it is no accident that the world's present tallest manmade structure is Chicago's Sears Tower. The Windy City – so named more for the hot-air rhetoric of its politicians than the gusts blowing from Lake Michigan – is America's Second City, after New York, but in temperament it is second to none. Still the nation's major railroad hub, it has seen economic decline on a massive scale, as the traditional steel industry died; it has experienced political upheaval and racial violence; crime is no stranger. But it is, as Carl Sandburg wrote, a big-shouldered city, where meatpacking has given way to hamburger merchandizing; where families like the Astors and the Pullmans have been replaced by the Crowns, Swifts and, wealthiest of all, the Pritzkers, of Hyatt. Its docks handle some 82m tons of freight a year; its airport 50m passengers. It has a gross product of $88bn, from industries as diverse as conventioneering and furniture-making, mail order and tool and diemaking, transportation and fast food. But it is also the city of the Chicago Symphony Orchestra and the world-renowned Chicago Art Institute; its university is an established intellectual, medical and scientific center, the home of nuclear physics and the Manhattan A-bomb Project. It is, too, a city of well-defined ethnic communities – Irish Bridgeport, Polish Albany Park and Hispanic Pilsen, for example – as well as areas of great wealth like North Shore. If the business pace is less frantic than Manhattan, it is no less intense and profitable.

Arriving

All international and most domestic airlines use Chicago's busy O'Hare International, 20 miles/32kms northwest of the Loop. An increasing number of domestic travelers, however, use the smaller Midway Airport, 8 miles/13kms to the southwest, and while corporate planes make use of the two major airports, more convenient is tiny Meigs Field, a mere 2 miles/3kms from the downtown Loop.

O'Hare International Airport

O'Hare, one of the world's busiest airports, has gone through a massive renovation. It has three terminals – 2, 3 and 4. Terminal 1 is United's domestic terminal; 2 and 3 are largely domestic, but they also handle Lufthansa, Swissair, Air France and British Airways. US airlines also use 2 and 3 for international departures. Terminal 4, a converted parking garage, is being used temporarily for all other international flights. A new internatiional terminal is due to be completed by 1992.

O'Hare does not suffer from chronic weather delays, but traffic volume is a major problem. During the afternoon and evening peak periods, departing planes are frequently backed up for more than an hour, and arrivals have to stack to wait for a break in traffic.

On the ground, passengers are guided smoothly through Customs (especially through the Green Channel if you have nothing to declare) and Immigration; the airport's signposting is especially good. For international flights, baggage pick-up is close to passport control, but it is a long walk from most gates to the domestic baggage claim areas. American Airways N7 gate is the closest to the cab ranks. Baggage trolleys can be rented for $1, and there are speedwalkers to parking garages and car rental desks. You can estimate 45mins from arrival hall to cab.

The airport is well-served for bars and restaurants, but most close at midnight. Repeat travelers patronize the restaurants in the O'Hare Hilton which is part of the 2/3 terminal complex. If you come into Terminal 4, the Hilton is across the road.

The interim international Terminal 4 has currency exchange facilities Mon–Fri, 8am–8pm. Mobile carts tour the domestic terminals 2 and 3 to meet incoming international flights ☏ 686-2200.

Nearby hotels *O'Hare Hilton*, O'Hare International Airport 60666 ☏ 686-8000 TX 9177360 fax 686-0405. Only a 15min indoor walk from the farthest gate, with excellent business facilities and suprisingly quiet despite its location. *Hyatt Regency O'Hare*, 9300 W Bryn Mawr Ave, Rosemont 60018 ☏ 696-1234 TX 282503 fax 696-1418. A 5min bus trip from the airport, with an extensive business service center (teleconferencing, secretarial, fax and telex facilities) and 41 meeting rooms.

City link *Taxi* For someone with a lot of baggage, the best way to get downtown is without doubt by cab, but traveling by road is a nightmare for much of the day and especially during rush hours – 7–9.30 and 3.30–7 – when the city's expressways are heavily congested. (Most European flights arrive just in time to meet that rush.) Driving then can take an hour or more; on Fridays two hours. Flights can be, and are, missed. Road repairs make the congestion worse by lane closures.

Yellow, Checker and independent cabs line up at the lower level of each terminal. Trips downtown cost at least $25, and off-peak travel time should be no more than 40mins.

Limousine Limousines are plentiful; see *Getting around*.

Car rental If you arrive during rush hours do not rent a car at the airport; there are plenty of rental car outlets downtown. Car agencies such as Hertz, Budget and National have booths at Terminals 2 and 3.

Bus The real alternative to a cab is the Continental Air Transport ☏ 454-7800 which provides service to many of the downtown hotels and costs about $7. But again you may have a walk of several hundred yards from your baggage claim area to its departure point.

Subway The quickest way downtown during rush hours for someone with little baggage and a good knowledge of the city is provided by the comfortable 24hr rapid transit rail link which takes about 35mins and costs $1. Pedestrian tunnels on the lower level of each terminal lead to the station. State and Washington or State and Monroe stations are close to most downtown hotels, but occasionally you may find it difficult to find a cab when you come up onto the street. As a general rule, the service is used by locals, though it is not recommended, especially at night.

Midway Airport

This no-frills airport is significantly smaller, less crowded and easier to get through than O'Hare. With only one three-concourse terminal, it has no international carriers, but Midway, Northwest, America West, Southwest and Chicago Air all operate domestic flights. Midway is popular with corporate and private planes, cargo companies and express mail services ☏ 767-0500.

City link A rapid transit link to Midway is still in the planning stages, but rush-hour traffic in this part of town is not quite as bad as that on the Kennedy Expressway; the trip downtown by cab should take about 20mins.

Taxi The trip to the Loop and Near North Side locations should cost no more than $16.

Limousine Stationed just outside the terminal entrance, United Limousine ☏ (800) 833-5555 will bring you to southerly destinations such as

cities in northern Indiana.
Car rental Major car rental firms like Budget, Hertz, Avis and National have booths at the airport.
Bus Stopping at all major Loop hotels, Continental Air Transport ☎ 454-7800 is fast and convenient and costs about $6; a shuttle to O'Hare is around $10. CW Limousine Service ☎ 493-2700 has vans to Hyde Park (the South Side home to the University of Chicago) and O'Hare.
Helicopter Aviation Red Carpet Services Inc ☎ 284-2867.

Rail station

Union Station An imposing structure just west of the Loop and the Chicago River, between Jackson and Adams Streets, Union Station is one of America's most famous old railroad terminals. It is a major Amtrak hub with trains leaving daily for all points east, south and west. Private sleepers and other first-class accommodations are available from Chicago. Amtrak information ☎ 558-1075. The Burlington Northern, Milwaukee Road, Norfolk and Western commuter lines also use Union Station. Although the building's exterior recalls the grandeur of the railroad's heyday, its interior is an uncomfortable mix of old and modern, but is currently undergoing renovation. First-class Amtrak travelers have their own waiting room across from the ticket counter; eating spots are generally undistinguished. The station is within easy walking distance of the Loop and is a short cab ride away from many of the centrally located hotels.

Getting around

Most major hotels are an easy walk or short cab ride from the Loop, the city's corporate headquarters, so renting a car is unnecessary unless your business takes you out into the suburbs. Whatever your means of transport, navigating is easy since the city is built on a simple grid system. Madison Avenue divides it north–south; State Street east–west. Each mile has 800 house numbers, so an address which begins 3200 North is near Belmont Avenue, 4 miles/6.4kms north of Madison. Halsted Street is 800 West, a mile west of State. (The system breaks down in parts of the South Side.)
Taxi Cabs are easy to find in major business districts, except when the weather is bad. There is also a convenient taxi stand at the south end of N Michigan, opposite the Wrigley Building – on the east side by the bridge. Most drivers are helpful and do not take advantage of visitors, though it is advisable to make sure they put the meter on at the start. If you are going to a suburb which is not contiguous with the city, ensure that the cab driver knows where you are going and check the price basis first, because meter rates do not always apply. To order a cab by telephone, call *Yellow and Checker Cab* ☎ 829-4222 or *American United Cab* ☎ 248-7600.
Limousine Chauffeured limousines are readily available and are often cheaper than taxis for long-distance trips. Two recommended limousine services are: *Carey Limousine Service* ☎ 663-1220 and *Chicago Limousine Service* ☎ 726-1035.
Car rental The major rental firms have offices both downtown and at the airport. If you decide to rent, the lowest downtown parking rates are at the municipal Monroe Street parking garage near Lake Shore Drive.
Public transport All subway lines originate in the Loop and some run between the lanes of major expressways, speeding by rush-hour traffic jams. Bus and el (elevated train) fares are about $1, and transfers are 25 cents; drivers accept bills.

Area by area

Chicago's business center is confined to the Loop, the LaSalle Street financial district and the Near North Side. North along Lake Michigan lies the Gold Coast, a prestigious

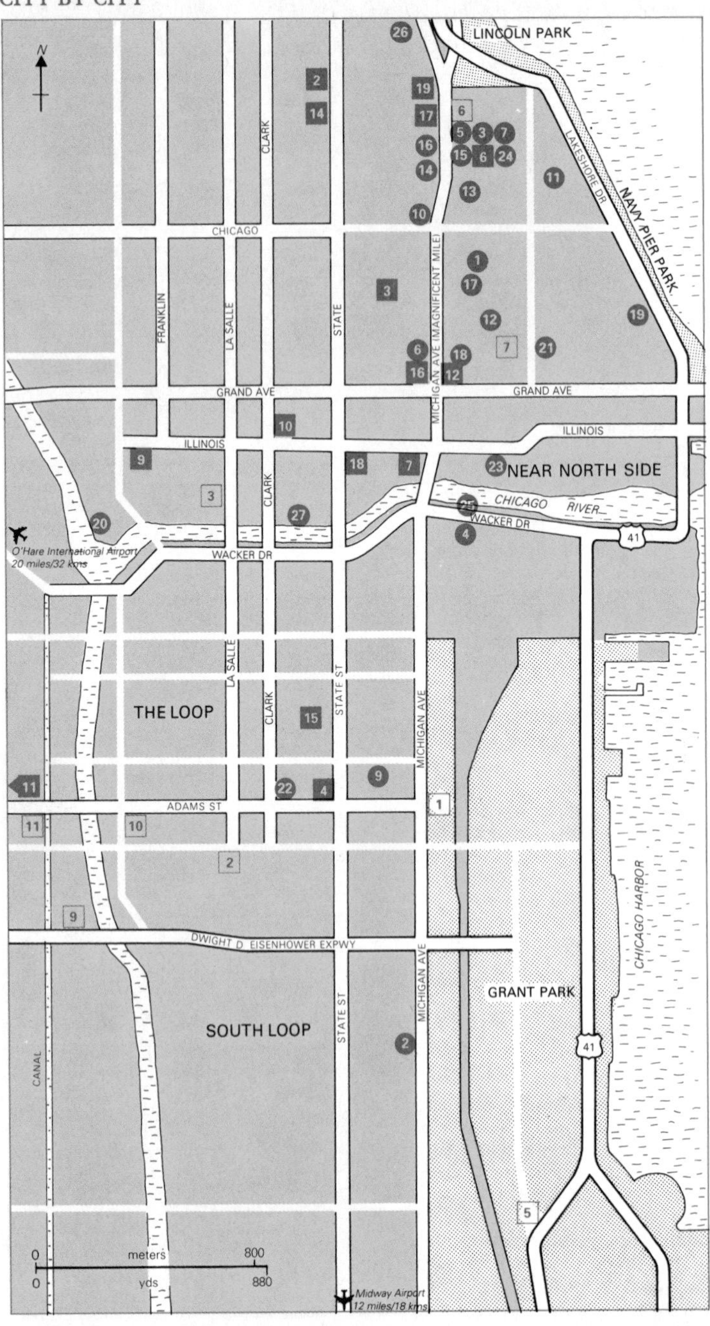

N
LINCOLN PARK
CLARK
LAKESHORE DR
NAVY PIER PARK
CHICAGO
FRANKLIN
LA SALLE
STATE
MICHIGAN AVE (MAGNIFICENT MILE)
GRAND AVE
GRAND AVE
ILLINOIS
ILLINOIS
NEAR NORTH SIDE
CHICAGO RIVER
WACKER DR
WACKER DR
41
O'Hare International Airport
20 miles/32 kms
LA SALLE
CLARK
STATE ST
MICHIGAN AVE
THE LOOP
ADAMS ST
DWIGHT D. EISENHOWER EXPWY
CHICAGO HARBOR
GRANT PARK
SOUTH LOOP
STATE ST
MICHIGAN AVE
CANAL
41
0
meters
800
0
yds
880
Midway Airport
12 miles/18 kms

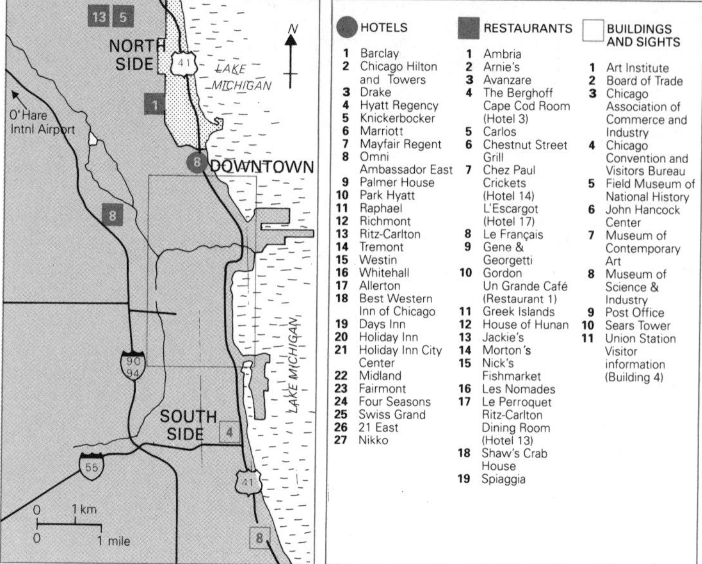

residential area for wealthy professionals. Lincoln Park, New Town and Old Town begin a few blocks farther northwest. Overlapping ethnic neighborhoods, each with their own commercial life and industrial pockets, are on the outskirts. Farther out are the suburbs, in Cook, DuPage, Kane, McHenry and Will Counties.

The Loop Technically, the Loop is the area within the imposing elevated track, but Chicagoans use the term loosely; often the Loop proper is seen as the area bounded by the river on the north and west, and stretching to 12th Street in the south, Michigan Avenue in the east.

There is also a newly-gentrified southern section known as South Loop, stretching from Van Buren to 12th. Newspapers and locals sometimes refer to the area north of Madison as North Loop. Most of the city's major office towers and complexes line Michigan Avenue, Dearborn Street and curving Wacker Drive. State Street – "that great street" – is now a major pedestrian shopping district. By night, however, the Loop is quieter, although an upper-class residential influx in the past decade has introduced new life. There are lakefront condominiums with dazzling views and new developments like the eye-catching River City, Dearborn Park and Presidential Towers in the south and west sectors. Several blocks away, La Salle Street is a canyon lined with massive buildings that house the city's banks and financial institutions. It is bounded on the south by the Chicago Board of Trade, the city's prominent commodity market.

Near North Side Anything north of the Chicago River and south of North Avenue is considered Near North, although there is no agreed single definition. Streeterville, the Gold Coast with its renovated robber baron mansions, and N Michigan Avenue's Magnificent Mile are home to many fashionable shops and restaurants. It is a bustling area, both day and night, especially around Rush and Division Streets with their bars, restaurants, and outdoor cafés. The ultra-rich live in beautiful old apartment buildings tucked away between the John

Hancock Building and Water Tower Place, the fashionable inner-city atrium mall. IBM Plaza, the Chicago Tribune Tower, the Sun-Times Building and the huge wholesale Merchandise Mart are all on the north bank of the Chicago River. Northwestern University's law and medical schools are here, although the University's main campus is in Evanston, the first suburb north of the city.

South Side Amid miles of Polish, Irish, Lithuanian and Black communities is Hyde Park, home of the University of Chicago and a middle and upper middle-class enclave. It is the city's most successfully integrated community. Farther south over the border in Indiana, steel mills spew smoke and yellow flames into the sky; but in southeast Chicago, the old manufacturing smokestack is dying fast.

O'Hare Airport area Many corporations have re-located to parts of the city and suburbs around O'Hare, creating a self-contained thriving business district. Major concerns like National Can (a division of Triangle) and Motorola line the Kennedy Expressway, and modern business complexes stretch along the Northwest and Tri-State tollways. The Zenith Corp. is on the Tri-State.

Suburbs Tax concessions have persuaded some big firms to move their headquarters to the suburbs. The Oak Brook area, west of the city in wealthy DuPage County, has attracted a number of major corporations; McDonald's and Waste Management have significant plants there. Their top executives tend to live along the affluent and exclusive 20 miles/32km North Shore. Mansions and palatial homes occupied by families of Crowns, Swifts and others dot the shoreline from Evanston north to Winnetka and Lake Forest all the way to Lake Bluff. In terms of increasing prestige and indicators of wealth and success, a ranking of suburbs would be Highland Park, Wilmette, Lake Forest, Kenilworth, Glencoe and, at the peak of the social scale, Winnetka. Barrington Hills, farther west, is also very exclusive.

Hotels

Many of Chicago's hotels are convention-oriented, but the city also has internationally acclaimed hotels, such as the Drake, Ritz-Carlton and the Mayfair Regent, as well as its share of smaller European-style hotels. All types offer a variety of convenience and comfort for business travelers, and the best have comprehensive business facilities. A new Sheraton opens late in 1990 or early 1991.

Barclay [$]////

166 E Superior St 60611 ☏ 787-6000 [TX] 270527 fax 787-4331 • AE DC MC V • 12 suites, 1 restaurant/bar

A small modern European-style hotel just off Michigan Avenue catering to executives. Its different sized suites are French Provincial in style; most have kitchens and many have conference areas, sunken living rooms and spectacular views of the Loop. The hotel's suites make it particularly useful for in-room business meetings; it is used by visiting headhunters for the same reason. The hotel – formed in 1980 – is named after the 40-year-old private dining club which it houses; guests automatically become members during their stay. Exercycles for use in suites • 5 meeting rooms.

Chicago Hilton and Towers [$]////

720 S Michigan Ave 60605 ☏ 922-4400 [TX] 797297 fax 922-5240 • AE DC MC V • 1,565 rooms, 148 suites, 3 restaurants, 3 bars

The flagship of the Hilton empire,

this gargantuan hotel underwent a $200m renovation a few years ago which gave the interior a much-needed face lift. Situated south of Chicago's downtown area, and with many of the city's best known cultural attractions nearby, its regal Grand Ballroom hosts many a political get-together. It has excellent business services. The hotel's restaurant, Buckingham's, is a popular business rendezvous. Nonsmoking rooms, shops • jogging track, pool, jacuzzis, weight training • 55 meeting rooms, word processors, computer rental and modems, business reference library, transcription, answering machines.

Drake [$]////
140 E Walton Pl 60611 ☎ 787-2200 [TX] 270278 fax 787-1431 • Hilton • AE DC MC V • 470 rooms, 65 suites, 3 restaurants, 2 bars
One of the great hotels of the 1920s, the Drake is the *grande dame* of Chicago's hostelries, catering equally to weary travelers, and society and business guests. (Nancy Reagan and Prince Charles have both been guests.) The Drake retains old-fashioned concepts of service and positively pampers guests staying on the exclusive 10th floor, refuge to numerous heads of state. Many of the rooms and suites have the best lake views in Chicago. The concierge has a reputation for being able and willing to do or arrange just about anything. The illustrious Cape Cod Room (see *Restaurants*) continues to get top marks as a fish restaurant; the Captain's Club and a glamorous bar area are also popular retreats. The Drake also has one of the city's best afternoon teas. Shops, hairdresser, florist • arrangements with nearby health club • 19 meeting rooms.

Hyatt Regency [$]////
151 E Wacker Dr 60601 ☎ 565-1234 [TX] 256237 fax 565-2966 • AE DC MC V • 2,019 rooms, 200 suites, 5 restaurants, 4 bars
The immensely popular Hyatt is a dependable favorite with executives both for its convenient downtown location and its extensive business services. The modern interior is done in true Hyatt style, with acres of glass, the sensation of sheer size, fountains and the trademark lobby waterfall. Jacuzzis are offered in some of the suites, as are open fires. Gift shops • arrangements with 2 nearby health clubs • 38 meeting rooms, teleconferencing.

Knickerbocker [$]////
163 E Walton Pl 60611 ☎ 751-8100 [TX] 206719 fax 751-0370 • AE DC MC V • 256 rooms, 27 suites, 1 restaurant, 1 bar, 1 coffee shop
Retaining the sumptuous and slightly flirty feel of the 1920s, the Knickerbocker's elegant lobby and guest rooms make a pleasant and much sought-after retreat from the hectic bustle of the city outside. The clientele is decidedly well-heeled and privacy is much valued. Its lobby houses the Limehouse Pub (see *Bars*), a delightful piano bar. Health club • 12 meeting rooms.

Marriott [$]////
540 N Michigan Ave 60611 ☎ 836-0100 [TX] 9102211360 fax 836-0100 ext 6139 • AE DC MC V • 1,173 rooms, 28 suites, 2 restaurants, 3 bars, 1 coffee shop
As its room numbers suggest, this Marriott is geared to conventions; but its address at the south end of North Michigan Avenue is convenient to the Loop and Gold Coast attractions alike. Nonsmoking rooms. Gift shop • indoor pool, health club, sauna, tennis • 34 meeting rooms.

Mayfair Regent [$]////
181 E Lake Shore Dr 60601 ☎ 787-8500 [TX] 256266 fax 664-6194 • AE DC MC V • Regent International • 174 rooms, 30 suites, 2 restaurants, 1 bar
An elegant Old World-style hotel more intimate and European than the Drake, the Mayfair Regent maintains a standard of comfort only achieved

by a guest-to-staff ratio approaching one-to-one. Recently refurbished, the ambience is more that of an elegant urban mansion than a hotel, with hand-painted Chinese murals and Louis XVI desks in the lobby, and flowers everywhere. Many rooms have lake views. Le Ciel Bleu is an undoubtedly elegant dining spot; the Palm, too, gets high marks as one of the city's traditional steak and seafood restaurants. Beauty salon • health club • 3 meeting rooms.

Omni Ambassador East [$]////
1301 N State Pkwy 60610
☎ 787-7200 [TX] 2212120
fax 787-9491 • AE DC MC V • 238 rooms, 50 suites, 1 restaurant, 1 bar, 1 coffee shop
Located slightly out of Chicago hotel land, the Omni Ambassador East compares with New York's Carlyle – super elegant, but uptown. It attracts a high society and show business clientele: expect jet setters, film stars and rock groups. Frank Sinatra is a frequent guest; Lauren Bacall and Humphrey Bogart honeymooned here. A considerable part of the building is comprised of residential suites. The Hotel restaurant, the Pump Room, has been a Chicago institution for over 60 years; booth number one is *the* place to be seen. Health club • 8 meeting rooms.

Palmer House [$]///
17 E Monroe St 6060 ☎ 726-7500 [TX] 382182 fax 263-2556 • Hilton • AE DC MC V • 1,750 rooms, 90 suites, 7 restaurants, 2 bars
The Palmer House ought to be the best business address in Chicago. This 1920s barn of a hotel, with its towering frescoed lobby, is host to Democratic Party functions and is magnificently situated in the heart of the Loop; it is but a step from the art museum. There are restaurants (nothing great, nothing awful) of every description and a good many shops. The staff at the serried ranks of check-in desks are efficient and courteous; the laundry works; the phones work; the rooms are comfortable and refurbished. But this is a Hilton convention hotel, and that sets the tone. It can take 30mins to get on one of the dozen or so elevators. So do not be fooled when you learn that statesmen stay here – they are in the very acceptable Towers complex, with its key-access elevators and special business facilities. Hairdresser, jeweler • health club, pool, steam room, massage, arrangements with nearby tennis club • 68 meeting rooms, teleconferencing, notary, translation, recording facilities.

Park Hyatt [$]/////
800 N Michigan Ave 60611
☎ 280-2222 [TX] 256216 fax 280-1963 • AE DC MC V • 255 rooms, 38 suites, 1 restaurant, 1 bar
Located just a few steps from Water Tower Place, the opulent Park Hyatt's lobby drips with Oriental rugs and *objets d'art*, a theme continued in the spacious guest rooms. Service is consistently good. The La Tour restaurant has a wine list with over 40 champagnes. A vintage Rolls-Royce is available for guest use, as is a $2,000-a-night penthouse complete with library and dining room. Nonsmoking floor • access to nearby health club • 6 meeting rooms.

Raphael [$]//
201 E Delaware Pl 60611 ☎ 943-5000 [TX] 206511 fax 943-9483 • AE DC MC V • 100 rooms, 78 suites, 1 restaurant, 1 bar
An elegant European-style small hotel at a good address off N Michigan Avenue, directly behind the John Hancock Building. Surprisingly, its comfortable suites cost less than rooms at other de luxe hotels. Its personalized service keeps guests coming back. A print of Raphael's *Madonna of the Chair* watches over the tiny chapel-like lobby; the lounge and restaurant are equally intimate. 3 meeting rooms.

Richmont [$]/
162 E Ontario St 60611 ☎ 787-3580 fax 787-1299 • AE DC MC V • 190 rooms, 13 suites, 1 restaurant, 1 bar
A useful alternative for someone on a tighter expense account, the Richmont has a quaint charm missing at the huge, modern convention hotels. Conveniently just off N Michigan Avenue, this intimate spot has a staunchly loyal following which gladly does without frills such as room service, to enjoy the quiet and cozy feel reminiscent of a small European hotel. Fitness center • 2 meeting rooms.

Ritz-Carlton [$]////
160 E Pearson St 60611 ☎ 266-1000 TX 20014 fax 266-9498 • Four Seasons • AE DC MC • 411 rooms, 84 suites, 1 restaurant, 1 bar
The Ritz-Carlton is the favored Chicago hotel of many. The combination of location, the remarkable atrium, a fine dining room and excellent Four Seasons service, together with large and well-furnished rooms, put the Ritz-Carlton, with its unusual 12th-floor lobby in Water Tower Place, in the top rank of international hotels. Security is among the city's best. Gift shop, hairdresser • health spa with pool • 6 meeting rooms.

Tremont [$]//
100 E Chestnut St 60611 ☎ 751-1900 TX 255157 fax 944-6300 ext 34 • AE DC MC V • 130 rooms, 9 suites, 1 restaurant, 1 bar
Yet another Chicago institution, the Tremont is a stone's throw from Michigan Avenue and has discreet European charm and old-fashioned elegance – as displayed by the collection of antique prints and Flemish vases. Guest rooms are unusually spacious, excellent for paperwork. Many have working fireplaces – a real status feature – and comfortable overstuffed chairs. The hotel restaurant, Crickets (see *Restaurants*) has several private rooms. The hotel prides itself on its special facilities for women executives. Arrangements with nearby health club • 4 meeting rooms.

Westin [$]///
909 N Michigan Ave 60611 ☎ 943-7200 TX 206593 fax 943-9347 • AE DC MC V • 697 rooms, 43 suites, 3 restaurants, 2 bars
Due in part to its excellent site on N Michigan Avenue, right in the heart of the Magnificent Mile, the Westin is always busy with executives, conventioneers and professional sports players. Although it is not considered a top business address, its ultra-modern interior and up-to-the-minute facilities make this one of Chicago's most popular convention hotels. Oversize beds and wet bars are available in most rooms. Health club • 18 meeting rooms.

Whitehall [$]///
105 E Delaware Pl 60611 ☎ 944-6300 TX 255157 fax 944-6300 ext 3422 • AE DC MC V • 223 rooms, 13 suites, 1 restaurant, 1 bar
This renowned independently owned hotel has the feel of a private club. Owner John B Coleman also has the Tremont, the New York Ritz-Carlton and the Ritz in Washington DC. Rooms show great attention to detail; several have jacuzzis. The Whitehall Club restaurant is open only to members and guests. Health club • 6 meeting rooms.

OTHER HOTELS

Allerton [$]// *701 N Michigan Ave 60611 ☎ 440-1500 fax 440-1819 • AE DC MC V.*

Best Western Inn of Chicago [$]// *162 E Ohio St 60611 ☎ 787-3100 TX 270337 fax 787-3100 ext 6240 • AE DC MC V.*

Days Inn [$]// *644 N Lake Shore Dr 60611 ☎ 943-9200 fax 649-5580 • AE DC MC V.*

Holiday Inn [$]// *Merchandise Mart Plaza, 350 N Orleans St ☎ 836-5000 TX HOLIDAY fax 906-3952 • AE DC MC V.* Right by the Merchandise Mart.

Holiday Inn City Center [$]// *300 E Ohio St* ☎ *787-6100* [TX] *HOLIDAY fax 906-3948.* • AE DC MC V.

Midland [$]// *172 W Adams St 60603* ☎ *332-1200 fax 332-5909* • AE DC MC V. Ideal for visitors with business in the financial district.

Among the newest hotels that have opened within the last few years there are the following:

Fairmont [$]/// *200 N Columbus Dr 60601* ☎ *565-8000 fax 856-1032* • AE DC MC V.

Four Seasons [$]//// *120 E Delaware Pl 60611* ☎ *280-8800 fax 280-9184* • AE DC MC V. In the top 40 floors of a downtown skyscraper; luxurious and well-equipped.

Swiss Grand [$]//// *323 E Wacker Dr 60601* ☎ *565-0565 fax 565-0540* • AE DC MC V.

21 East [$]//// *21 East Bellevue Pl 60611* ☎ *266-2100 fax 266-2103* • AE DC MC V.

Nikko [$]/// *320 N Dearborn 60610* ☎ *744-1900 fax 527-2664* • AE DC MC V.

Clubs

Most of Chicago's establishment lunching takes place within the city's private clubs, many of which are only just beginning to admit women, and even then only with restrictions. The clubs are central to business life in the city, and some of the rooms in the top clubs are stunning. The *Chicago Club* ☎ 427-1825 is the most prestigious; women are now admitted as guests. The (mainly Jewish) *Standard Club* ☎ 427-9100 is in the same league. In both clubs, your host will be part of Chicago society and active in charity work or the arts. The *Tavern* ☎ 263-1166 is a favorite with executives and many of the city's leading Democrats, media moguls and artists. The *Union League Club* ☎ 427-7800, nicknamed the Republican Club, is an alternative. Its wood-paneled dining room is a favorite with judges and lawyers. The *University Club* ☎726-2840 and the *Chicago Athletic Association* ☎ 236-7500 attract a wide range of professionals. Two private yacht clubs, the *Columbia* ☎ 938-3265 and the *Chicago* ☎ 861-7777, have dining facilities. The club with the best food is the *Mid-America* ☎ 861-1100, with a following among professionals in the media. Uptown clubs are the highly esteemed *Casino* ☎ 787-2100, dominated by women, providing good food, and more socially than business oriented; the *Raquet Club* ☎ 787-3200 is favored by the city's top families, particularly for Sunday brunch, and is used for business and pleasure. In addition, there are various executive lunch clubs in large office buildings – such as the *Metropolitan* ☎ 876-3200 in Sears Tower.

Restaurants

Chicagoans love to eat out. The business lunch is a valued tradition, and the best restaurants are jammed noon–1.30. Dinner is from 5.30–10, closing earlier in the winter. In the past few years a whole new crop of restaurants has sprung up, in addition to the city's classic eating institutions: outdoor cafés transform the city into a Midwestern Paris in summer, and the ethnic bistros reflect the city's mixed culture – Polish, Czech, Italian, Chinese, Serbian, Thai, Greek, German, Mexican, Indian, South American, and Vietnamese. Ask Chicagoans for their favorite spots away from the mainstream. Most of the restaurants listed here are on the Near North Side and on the North Side. North Loop and Loop restaurants are geographically the most practical for appointments at lunch time.

Ambria $ll

2300 N Lincoln Park West
☎ 472-5959 • closed L & Sun • AE DC MC V • jacket • reservations essential

Chicago's fashionable crowd makes reservations at least two weeks ahead to dine on excellent *nouvelle cuisine.* Set in the Belden Stratford Hotel just off Lincoln Park, Ambria has a plush, intimate atmosphere perfect for negotiations or celebrating the conclusion of important business deals.

Arnie's $ll

1030 N State St ☎ 266-4800 • closed Sat L • AE DC MC V •

Distinctive, plush and fashionable, Arnie's is a Chicago institution. Steaks, lamb and fish are the main fare. A good place to unwind, but not recommended for a quiet business dinner; nor is it particularly comfortable. Arnie's brunch is famous citywide.

Avanzare $l

161 E Huron St ☎ 337-8056 • closed L Sat & Sun • AE DC MC V • jacket preferred

In a high-rise lobby just off Michigan Avenue, Avanzare couples serious northern Italian cuisine with a relaxed, unflamboyant Continental atmosphere. This is a good spot for quiet business discussion, especially in the intimate, 10-table room upstairs.

The Berghoff $l

17 W Adams St ☎ 427-3170 • closed Sun • AE MC V • no reservations

Even when the wind chill factor is well below zero, there are lines outside the Berghoff at lunch time. For 85 years, waiters in white aprons and black jackets have served reasonably-priced German and American dishes, sandwiches and beer, and businessmen and lawyers have hobnobbed in its well-appointed bar and two huge dining rooms. Not a first-time choice for visitors wishing to entertain.

Cape Cod Room $ll

Drake Hotel ☎ 787-2200 • AE DC MC V • reservations advisable

Cozy, dark and comfortable, this New England-style seafood restaurant is on the street level of the Drake Hotel. It has red checkered tablecloths, wood floors, a chowder bar, and a happy hubbub. The Cape Cod is always full and remains one of Chicago's most desirable spots for dining.

Carlos $ll

429 Temple, Highland Park
☎ 432-0770 • closed L, Tue • AE DC MC V • jacket and tie • reservations essential

A small, intimate restaurant, Carlos' subtle *nouvelle cuisine* offerings more than make up for the 45min drive from the Loop. Owner Carlos Nieto is especially proud of his private sitting room and 10-person dining room upstairs, which has the simple, comfortable feeling of a private house, and is a fine place to entertain North Shore business associates. The wine list is long and expensive, but good.

Chestnut Street Grill $l

845 N Michigan Ave ☎ 280-2720 • AE DC MC V

A first-class modern fish restaurant, in Water Tower Galleria, with a splendid list of Californian wines. Unusually, you can drink vintage wine by the glass.

Chez Paul $l

660 N Rush St ☎ 944-6680 • AE DC MC V

This dark, rather earnest French restaurant in an elegant mansion is a favorite watering hole. There are hordes of businessmen here at lunch time.

Crickets $l

Tremont Hotel ☎ 280-2100 • AE DC MC V

Taking its cue from New York's 21 Club, on which its design and general ethos is loosely based, Crickets' *raison d'être* is not purely gastronomic. It has a fiercely loyal clientele of socialites (who may or may not also be business moguls) who love it because it's their place. Serious-minded gourmets find the food OK, but not exceptional; the wine list first class, but very expensive; the service reliable and gracious. So, Crickets is an institution; it's fun; it's good for the ego; but it's not Chicago's best restaurant by a long shot.

L'Escargot [$]//
701 N Michigan Ave ☏ 337-1717 • AE DC MC V • jacket
With its brasserie-style tone and not unreasonable prices, this L'Escargot in the Allerton Hotel is a very acceptable and genuinely French alternative in the good provincial class. It offers a set lunch and decent wines. Also at 2925 N Halsted ☏ 525-5522 where it is a big local favorite with Near Northsiders.

Le Français [$]////
269 S Milwaukee Ave, Wheeling ☏ (708) 541-7470 • closed L, Mon • AE DC MC V • jacket • reservations essential
Top executives, lawyers and doctors dine at the Liccionir's (ex-Carlos) charming cottage in this northwest suburb 35 miles/56kms from downtown. It is not the sort of place a business visitor is likely to have time to visit alone, but if you are invited there, you will be eating in one of the finest restaurants in the country.

Gene & Georgetti [$]/
500 N Franklin ☏ 527-3718 • closed Sun • AE DC MC V
Although many of Chicago's businessmen would claim G&G's provides the best and biggest steaks in town, its aggressively macho atmosphere rules it out for women dining together. Although not elegant, it has a loyal and extremely eclectic following. Actually getting your reserved table may be difficult if you are not known.

Gordon [$]//
500 N Clark ☏ 467-9780 • closed L, Sat • AE DC MC V
The warm atmosphere of this 1840s building is an unexpected bonus; the seafood and new American cooking are sufficient reason for choosing it. Both fun and businessy, it is a good place to unwind, enjoy a meal and still talk terms.

Un Grand Café [$]//
2300 N Lincoln Park West ☏ 348-8886 • D only; closed Sun • AE DC MC V • no reservations
Located next door to Ambria in the same hotel, and created by Mr Rich Melman (also responsible for Shaw's Crab House and PJ Clarke's – see *Bars*), Un Grand Café is a French bistro with excellent food. The crowd tends to be urbane and sophisticated, and the restaurant has become very popular as a casual chic place to dine. A 10min drive north of the Loop.

Greek Islands [$]/
200 S Halsted St ☏ 782-9855 • AE DC MC V • reservations for D Fri & Sat
At night, the Greek Islands has a jovial feel with casually dressed clientele interspersed with opera-lovers headed for the Lyric Opera just across the river. A popular lunch and after-work spot. Good traditional Greek food.

House of Hunan [$]/
535 N Michigan Ave ☏ 329-9494 • AE DC MC V • jacket preferred
In the heart of the busy Magnificent Mile, the House of Hunan is a convenient spot for a working lunch or dinner. The food is American Chinese; the atmosphere soft, cool and quiet; and the service good.

Credit card abbreviations

AE	American Express
DC	Diners Club
MC	Access/MasterCard
V	Visa

Jackie's $////
2478 N Lincoln Ave ☏ 880-0003 • closed Sun & Mon • AE DC MC V • reservations essential
Intimate, with closely set tables, this is not the place for private talks, but the food makes up for that. Intricate, oriental-influenced and decidedly *haute cuisine* is the hallmark of Jackie Etcheber's (ex Le Français) smart uptown restaurant. Jackie's is currently the top choice for many of Chicago's committed foodies.

Morton's $///
1050 N State St, Newberry Plaza ☏ 266-4820 • closed L, Sun • AE DC MC V
Morton's is fairly formal, but crowded and noisy. Its expensive steaks are said to be the best in the city, but the shellfish is also good.

Nick's Fishmarket $///
1 First National Plaza ☏ 621-0200 • closed Sat D, Sun • AE DC MC V • jacket preferred
Fresh seafood specialties and a Caribbean Islands atmosphere make this one of the top seafood restaurants in town. Fresh abalone and *mahi-mahi* top the list. Popular for business luncheons, but not in the same league as Shaw's.

Les Nomades $///
222 E Ontario ☏ 649-9010 • closed L, Sun, Mon • no credit cards • jacket and tie • Sat reservations essential
An intimate bistro-like private club in a signless red-brick brownstone. You have to be a member to eat here, says idiosyncratic Jovan Trboyevic; but he adds that most international visitors are welcome. If you are invited, you will not only enjoy your meal (with imaginative wines), but also know your host thinks highly of you.

Le Perroquet $////
70 E Walton Pl ☏ 944-7990 • closed L, Sat, Sun • AE DC MC V • reservations essential
Generally rated the tops, Le Perroquet is certainly one of Chicago's finest and most elegant restaurants – and its grandest. The *nouvelle cuisine* is served in a third-floor dining room, accessible only by private elevator. An invitation here means that your host is pulling out all the stops.

Ritz-Carlton Dining Room $////
160 E Pearson St, Water Tower Place ☏ 266-1000 • closed L, Sat • AE DC MC V • D reservations only
The Ritz-Carlton's dining room is certainly Ritzy and everything you might hope for from a grand hotel restaurant – even if it wouldn't be a committed gourmet's first choice.

Shaw's Crab House $///
21 E Hubbard St ☏ 527-2722 • D only Sat and Sun • AE DC MC V • L reservations only
Around the corner from the downtown IBM Plaza, Shaw's is a mélange of styles: formal 1930s decor and taped 1940s and 1950s jazz music. The seafood is strictly first-rate. Ensconced in Shaw's comfortable booths are top executives from Chicago's major television stations and partners of its most prestigious legal and financial firms. After work young professionals visit the adjacent Blue Crab Lounge.

Spiaggia $////
980 N Michigan Ave ☏ 280-3307 • AE DC MC V • closed L Sun • reservations essential
At one of the most fashionable addresses in the North Loop, the glass-dominated Spiaggia is consciously glamorous. The northern Italian cuisine includes everything from *vitello tonnato* – and lots of fish – to a locally famous thin-crusted pizza. Service, on the other hand, can be slow. Private dining rooms available.

Restaurant price symbols
For the meanings of the price symbols, see page 7.

Rib joints
Chicago is famous for tender barbecued pork and beef ribs. Two of the classier rib restaurants are *Carsons: The Place for Ribs*, 612 N Wells St ☏ 280-9200 (and at 8617 Niles Center, Skokie ☏ 675-6800), and *Randall's Ribhouse*, 41 E Superior St ☏ 280-2790. *Lawry's Prime Rib*, 100 E Ontario ☏ 787-5000 is considered among the best for rib roasts.

Deep-dish pizza
Chicago is the self-proclaimed birthplace of deep-dish pizza; stuffed with meats and vegetables of your choice, one or two slices are enough for most appetites. Try *Giordano's*, 747 N Rush St ☏ 951-0747; *Bacino's on Wacker*, 75 E Wacker Dr ☏ 263-0070; or *Pizzeria Uno* 29 E Ohio ☏ 321-1000, and *Pizzeria Due*, 619 N Wabash Ave ☏ 943-2400.

Bars
While most business is dealt with in the recesses of the city's private clubs, there are some local bars that attract a strong business clientele. Among the best are: *The Berghoff Café*, 17 W Adams St, which is conveniently located in the Loop. It is packed nightly with the off-duty business crowd; a bit too noisy for any serious conversation, but nonetheless a real Chicago institution dating back to 1898. The black-and-white tiled floor is often thick with bulging briefcases, making it difficult to walk the length of the bar. Excellent bar food. *PJ Clarke's*, 1204 N State Pkwy ☏ 664-1650, sister to the club of the same name in New York, is popular with the business community and politicians as well as the occasional athlete and actor. Like its New York counterpart, it has a rustic, turn-of-the-century look and is a popular after-work spot. *Gold Star Sardine Bar*, 666 N Lakeshore Dr, has an elegant, dark 1940s decor; regulars include personalities from CBS studios across the street. The plush couches and armchairs of the *Limehouse Pub*, 163 E Walton St ☏ 751-8100 in the Knickerbocker lobby (see *Hotels*), are often used for talking shop. *Miller's Pub*, 23 E Adams St ☏ 922-7446, is an unpretentious place with a late night license, food until 3am and a long bar. Its round tables are favorite haunts for Chicago football players and sports celebrities. *Benchers Fish House*, Sears Tower ☏ 993-0096, is an often-used spot for the local business force, while both *The Sign of the Trader*, 141 W Jackson in the lobby of the Board of Trade, and the *Broker's Inn*, 323 S LaSalle, are hotbeds of financial talk. *Bynion's*, 327 S Plymouth Ct near the Federal Bldg, attracts the fraternity of sedate lawyers.

Entertainment
Chicago's entertainment offerings are many and varied, as befits the cultural capital of the Midwest. To find out what's on, pick up a free copy of the *Chicago Reader*, Friday entertainment supplements to the *Chicago Tribune* or the *Sun-Times*, a *Chicago Scene* and/or *Chicago Magazine* at any newsstand.
Ticket agencies To book a show or concert, call either the box office or *Ticketron* ☏ 902-1919; major credit cards accepted. Half-price tickets are available for cash on the day of the performance at the *Hot Tix Booth*, 24 S State, Mon, 12–6; Tue–Fri, 10–6; Sat, 10–5 ☏ 977-1755 for information.
Theater and ballet The Chicago theater scene enjoys a growing national reputation. The *Goodman Theater* in the Art Institute of Chicago, 200 E Columbus Dr ☏ 443-3800 is known for fine performances of classic and new productions. Pre- and post-Broadway productions can be seen at the *Schubert Theater*, 22 W Monroe ☏ 977-1710, and at the *Arie Crown*, McCormick Pl at 23rd and Lake Shore Dr ☏ 791-6000. For

classics by such as Ibsen and Shaw, try the *Court Theater*, 5706 S University at the University of Chicago Hyde Park ☏ 753-4472.

The Maria Tallchief-directed *Chicago City Ballet* ☏ 988-4231 is highly regarded but has no permanent home of its own. A blend of jazz and ballet can be seen at the *Hubbard Street Dance Company*, 218 S Wabash ☏ 663-0853.

Music The renowned *Chicago Symphony Orchestra* plays at Orchestra Hall, 220 S Michigan ☏ 435-8111, in winter months. The *Lyric Opera Company* ☏ 332-2244 is at the grand Civic Opera House in the Loop, 20 N Wacker. Free outdoor concerts are given by CSO in Grant Park, near the Art Institute, at the Petrillo Bandshell in summer.

Blues Chicago is the world's blues capital. Two favorite North Side clubs are *Lilly's*, 2513 N Lincoln ☏ 525-2422 and *Kingston Mines*, 2548 N Halsted ☏ 477 4646, both open until 4am. *Cotton Chicago*, 3204 N Wilton ☏ 341-9787, is an upscale new club with an elegant bar. The *New Checkerboard Lounge*, 423 E 43rd St ☏ 324-9620, is in a rougher neighborhood but is still a favorite haunt of the Rolling Stones and BB King when they are in town.

Jazz Top quality jazz can be heard at midday or between 5–8pm at *Andy's*, 11 E Hubbard St ☏ 642-6805. For late night jazz with a touch of elegance, Joe Segal's *Jazz Showcase* in the Blackstone Hotel, 636 S Michigan Ave ☏ 427-4300 is the place. For up-to-the-minute information call ☏ 666-1881.

Cinema First-rate cinemas include those in *Water Tower Place* ☏ 649-5790 or the renovated *Chicago Theater*, 175 N State St. For arty offbeat movies, there is the *Fine Arts Theater*, 410 Michigan ☏ 939-3700; *Facets Multimedia*, 1517 W Fullerton ☏ 281-9075; and the *Biograph Theater*, 2433 N Lincoln ☏ 348-4123, where bank robber John Dillinger was gunned down by the FBI in 1934.

Nightclubs and comedy *High Hat Club*, 812 N Franklin ☏ 787-6333, is an Art Deco nightclub with jazz entertainment. The *Second City* comedy troupe has been host to many of the nation's finest comedians, giving them the opportunity to start out on the boards of its stage at 1616 N Wells ☏ 337-3992; make reservations well in advance.

Shopping

Though State Street has lost some of its former glory as the most famous shopping street in America's Midwest, it still is a thriving shopping center, lined with clothes and shoe shops and two of Chicago's prestigious department stores, *Carson, Pirie, Scott*, 1 S State St, and *Marshall Field's*, 111 N State St.

Clothing More exclusive shops have moved across the river to Michigan Avenue on the Near North Side. A walk down N Michigan Avenue's Magnificent Mile takes you past *I Magnin*, *Nieman-Marcus*, *Bonwit Teller*, *Saks Fifth Avenue*, *Burberry's*, *Gucci*, *Stanley Korshak* and many others. *Bloomingdale's* at last opened a branch at 900 N Michigan Ave only as recently as 1988.

Shopping malls *Water Tower Place*, 845 N Michigan, is a popular innercity atrium mall, named after the ornate original Chicago water tower standing nearby, one of the few buildings to survive the disastrous 1871 fire. Its seven floors house over a hundred shops, including *Lord & Taylor's* and another branch of *Marshall Field's*, as well as various children's shops, of which the best are *FAO Schwartz*, *Beagle and Company* and *Beauty and the Beast*. You can find sporting goods of every imaginable type at *Morrie Magees*, an eight-floor sports emporium at 620 N LaSalle Street.

Crafts *The Museum Shop* at the Chicago Art Institute, South Michigan at Adams St, sells jewelry, posters and art books; the *Illinois Artisan's Shop* on the second level of the State of Illinois Center is a good

place to find articles made by hand by local Illinois craftsmen.
Books *Kroch's and Brentano's*, 29 S Wabash, is the city's best bookstore and the country's second busiest after New York's 5th Avenue *Barnes & Noble*, with excellent, knowledgeable service and a regular stock of more than 125,000 titles.
Music *Jazz Mart*, 11 E Hubbard, has an extensive selection of tapes and records; *Rose Records*, 214 S State, covers the whole musical spectrum.

Sightseeing

Many Chicago skyscrapers are the background to sculpture and art by Picasso, Oldenburg, Chagall and Calder; look for it in the downtown plazas. The places listed below are all within easy reach of the business traveler and can be fitted into a busy daytime schedule.
Art Institute of Chicago Truly one of the world's finest art museums. With its notable collection of French Impressionists – including works by Monet, Picasso and Renoir – the Institute, right in the heart of downtown, is reason enough in itself to visit the city. Its new wing houses a fine collection of medieval and Renaissance art and its collection of prints is unique. You have to ask to see them, but where else would you be allowed to touch these magnificent works and wonder at the skill and craftsmanship from medieval times to the present day? Among its rarer exhibits is a collection of delicate and exotic paperweights, donated by a local real estate speculator, the late Arthur Rubloff. Other exhibits include the renovated old Stock Exchange Trading Room, now displaying Marc Chagall's stained glass; the Thorne Miniature Rooms; and a fine showing of Oriental and medieval art. Avoid weekends. *South Michigan at Adams St ☎ 443-3600. Open Mon, Wed and Fri, 10.30–4.30; Tue, 10.30–8; Sat, 10–5; Sun, noon–5.*
Chicago Board of Trade The grain market of the USA where you can watch the activities of the traders from a viewing gallery. *La Salle at Jackson St. Open Mon–Fri, 9–2.*
Field Museum of Natural History Exhibits include everything from precious stones and the origins of man to a Pawnee lodge and dinosaur skeletons. Architecture buffs would find the Stanley Field Hall, with its soaring coffered ceiling and superb Ionic capitals, worth visiting even if it were empty. *Roosevelt Rd and S Lake Shore Dr ☎ 922-9410. Open 9–5.*
John Hancock Center This imposing 100-story office and residential building has an observation deck on the 95th floor, providing an unbeatable view of the North Loop. Have a drink at Images, on the 96th floor, or a memorable, if expensive, meal in the city's loftiest restaurant, The 95th. *875 N Michigan Ave ☎ 751-3681. Open 9am–midnight.*
Museum of Contemporary Art Occupying an old bakery and housing seven galleries, this forum for untried and/or controversial exhibits of neon, video and avant-garde art includes works by Alexander Calder and Picasso. *237 E Ontario ☎ 280-2660. Open 10–5; Sun, noon–5; closed Mon.*
Museum of Science and Industry Chicago's top tourist attraction is an echoing cavern filled with gadgets, levers, computers and other hands-on devices which visitors can use to find out about scientific principles and the latest technological advances. Major drawing cards are the fullscale underground coalmine, a 16ft replica of a human heart, a half-acre model train set and the only German U-boat captured during World War II. *57th St at Lake Shore Dr ☎ 684-1414. Open Mon–Fri, 9.30–4; Sat, Sun and hols, 9.30–5.30.*
Sears Tower The 110-story Tower is still the world's tallest building (although construction started in 1989 on one of 1915ft, which will overtake it). On clear days the 103rd-floor offers magnificent panoramas of downtown, 1,300ft below. In clear weather you can see as far as the neighboring states of Indiana,

Wisconsin and Michigan. *233 S Wacker Dr* ☎ *875-9696. Open 9am–midnight.*
Water Tower The one remaining edifice from before the great fire which swept the city in 1871.

Guided tours
The Chicago Architecture Foundation, 330 S Dearborn ☎ 326-1393, organizes walking, bike, bus and river tours taking in many of the most significant examples of Chicago architecture. For an escorted tour of the city's cultural heritage, try *Culture Buses* ☎ 836-7000.

Out of town
Frank Lloyd Wright Home and Studio Foundation, 951 Chicago Ave, Oak Park ☎ 848-1976. One of America's leading and seminal architects, Wright designed 25 buildings in suburban Oak Park, just west of the city limits, 25mins from downtown. There is a tour of the whole area, which has a fascinating range of architectural styles. Around the corner is the childhood home of Ernest Hemingway, at 600 N Kenilworth. *The Indiana Dunes National Lakeshore* starts 65 miles/90kms south of the city along Lake Michigan. Magnificent sand dunes, some up to 70ft high, stretch all the way along the lake shore up into Michigan for a distance of about 100 miles/60kms. During the warm months there is a lovely nature walk through a preserved prairie.

Spectator sports
Baseball, football and horse-racing are the city's three prime spectator sports.
Baseball The *Chicago Cubs* play in ivy-covered Wrigley Field, 1060 W Addison St ☎ 281-5050; afternoon games are a popular diversion for well-heeled business types and city employees. Mayor Richard Daley was a keen fan of the *White Sox*, who play in Comiskey Park, 324 W 35th St ☎ 924-1000. Ticketmaster ☎ 559-1212.
Basketball The *Bulls* play in an exciting, but often unsuccessful, style at Chicago Stadium, 1800 W Madison St ☎ 733-5300.
Football The *Bears*, the city's new major obsession and source of pride, are based at 250 N Washington St, Lake Forest ☎ 663-5100 though they play at Soldier Field just south of downtown near the Field Museum.
Horse-racing Horse-racing remains a fervently attended sport in Chicago. The city has three tracks: *Hawthorne*, 3501 S Laramie, Cicero ☎ 780-7300; *Maywood Park*, North and 5th Avenues, Maywood ☎ 343-4800; and *Sportsman's Park*, 3301 S Laramie, Cicero ☎ 242-1121.
Ice hockey The *Black Hawks* have a stoutly loyal following despite their losing ways; games are at Chicago Stadium, 1800 W Madison St ☎ 733-5300 Oct–Apr.
Polo Prince Charles is an occasional player at international games at the Oak Brook Polo Club, 2700 York Rd, Oak Brook ☎ 571-7050.
Soccer *City Power*, the city's contribution to soccer, play at the Rosemont Horizon Sports Arena and at various outdoor locations. Ticket information ☎ 299-9000.

Keeping fit
There are dozens of health clubs in Chicago. Many hotels either have their own facilities or provide arrangements with nearby clubs, but the city is also tailor-made for outdoor activities. Swimming at the 28 miles/44kms of beaches and jogging along the lakeside paths in the parks and north and south of the city are just a few possibilities.
Fitness centers Most private clubs will let nonmembers use their facilities for a daily fee of around $15. Facilities range from swimming and jogging tracks to weightlifting and aerobics. The *East Bank Club*, 500 N Kingbury St ☎ 527-5800, is the city's most prestigious health club where Richard Daley Jr and well-known Chicagoans jog around the track. Guests must be accompanied by a

member. Other places for the exercise conscious include *Charlie Club*, 112 S Michigan Ave ☎ 726-0510; *Chicago Health and Racquetball Club*, 300 N State St ☎ 321-9600; *Combined Fitness Center*, 1235 N La Salle St ☎ 548-1300; *McClurg Court Sports Center*, 333 E Ontario ☎ 943-5220.
Beaches North Avenue Beach, Fullerton Avenue Beach and Oak Street Beach are particularly good for swimming and tanning, all within 10mins of the Loop.
Bicycling and jogging There are good jogging paths along the shore from the Loop south to 57th Street (not recommended after dusk) and from the Loop north to Evanston (about 11 miles/19kms – usually safe up to Wilson Avenue even at night). There are several concessions in Lincoln Park where bikes may be rented. Some hotels have rental bikes.
Golf It has been said that Chicago has more golf courses than any other major metropolitan center in the United States, but unfortunately the best are well out in the suburbs. Some hotels offer guest privileges at private clubs, and there are ten golf courses within the city, including *Waveland* in Lincoln Park ☎ 294-2274 (9 holes) and the 18-hole course at Jackson Park, 63rd and S Lakeshore Dr.
Raquet sports There are over 600 outdoor tennis courts, the most convenient of which are in Lincoln Park and the lakeshore just north. Many Loop-area health clubs also offer tennis and squash for a fee. For tennis information call *City-Wide Tennis* on ☎ 294-4790.
Sailing Fantastic sailing and outstanding views of the city are possible from the open water off Navy Pier, but nasty storms can kick up without much warning. Check weather ahead of time with US Coast Guard ☎ 353-0278.

Local resources

Business services

Most of the major hotels provide or can arrange basic business services for the visitor, but Chicago has no lack of firms offering extensive help for the traveling executive.
Audio-visual *Midwest Visual Equipment Co* ☎ 787-1644; *Rent Com, Inc* ☎ 678-7000; *Audio Visual Systems* ☎ 733-3370; *Show It Essanay* ☎ 733-3370.
Photocopying and printing *Paper Express*, 203 N La Salle St ☎ 407-0154, 24hr service, and *Instant Printing*, 200 S Clark St ☎ 726-6275, are both in the Loop.
Secretarial Dependable temporary agencies include *Kelly Services* ☎ 853-3434 and *Insta-Temps* ☎ 664-0622.
Translation *Interlingua* ☎ 782-8123, *Berlitz* ☎ 782-7778.

Communications

Long-distance delivery *Federal Express* ☎ 922-4921; *DHL Worldwide Express* ☎ 456-3200; *Emery Worldwide* ☎ 941-4620.
Local delivery The best service is generally had from *Arrow Messenger Service* ☎ 489-6688. Also reliable are *Chicago Messenger* ☎ 666-6800 or *Dash Messenger Service* ☎ 243-0987.
Post office The main post office is at 433 W Van Buren St ☎ 765-3210; post offices close early on Saturday.
Telex *Western Union/Telex* ☎ (800) 325-4176.

Conference/exhibition centers

Extremely large and only 5mins from the Loop is *McCormick Place-on-the-Lake*, 2301 S Lake Shore Dr ☎ 791-7000. *Rosemont O'Hare Exposition Center*, 9291 W Bryn Mawr Rd, Rosemont ☎ 692-2220, is close to the airport.

Emergencies

Hospitals *Northwestern Memorial Hospital*, Superior and Fairbanks ☎ 908-2000; AE MC V. *Resurrection Medical Center* (near O'Hare), 7435 W Talcott Ave ☎ 774-8000; MC V. *Michael Reese Hospital and Medical Center*, 31st and Lake Shore Dr ☎ 791-2000, emergency ☎ 791-2882; AE MC V. *Doctor Referral* ☎ 791-4444;

Pharmacies *Walgreen Drug Store*, 757 N Michigan Ave ☏ 644-4000 has a 24hr prescription service.
Police The two main downtown stations are at 1121 S State St (police headquarters) ☏ 744-4000 and 113 W Chicago Ave ☏ 744-8230.

Government offices

US Dept of Commerce/International Trade Division ☏ 353-6100; *US Customs/Commercial Importations–Personal Importation*, 230 S Dearborn St ☏ 353-6100; *Immigration and Naturalization Service* ☏ 353-7334.

Information

Business information The *Chicago Association of Commerce and Industry*, 200 N LaSalle St ☏ 580-6900, offers assistance in locating everything from audio-visual equipment to videotext directories. The *Chicago Convention and Visitors Bureau*, McCormick Pl on the Lake ☏ 567-8500 fax 567-8533 is the best source of convention information.
Local media There are two major daily papers, the *Chicago Sun-Times* and the larger *Chicago Tribune*. Both lean towards a conservative editorial line, although the latter leans slightly more to the center. The *Tribune* is known for its international coverage, the *Sun-Times* for city politics.

Rizzolis, a bookstore on the 3rd level of Water Tower Place, has daily papers from France, Italy, Germany and England, plus a good selection of foreign language books. Foreign papers are also available at the newsstand on the corner of Rush and Oak Streets. For magazines, *The Chicago Reader* and *Chicago Magazine* provide general information about the city, while Crain's *Chicago Business* is an invaluable source of local business news.
Visitor information *Chicago Tourism Council* ☏ 280-5740; *Chicago Convention and Visitors Bureau*, McCormick Pl on the Lake ☏ 567-8500.

Thank-yous

Florists *Floral Fashions*, 63 E Adams ☏ 427-2002; *A Lange Florist and Greenhouse* ☏ 848-4200.
Wine merchants *Sam's Wine & Liquors*, 1000 W North Ave ☏ 664-4394; *Zimmerman Liquors*, 213 W Grand Ave ☏ 332-0012.
Specialty shops *Marshall Field's*, 1 N State St ☏ 781-1000, has hand-dipped chocolate which they will send anywhere in the world; also their Frango mints make a good gift. *Let Them Eat Cake*, 948 N Rush St ☏ 863-4200, has *petits fours* and custom-made cakes.

CLEVELAND

Area code ☎ 216

Cleveland's traditional heavy industries – steel production, oil refining, shipping and railroads – were the foundations upon which men like John D Rockefeller, Samuel Mather and Marcus Hanna built their fortunes in the 19th and early 20th centuries, providing work for the thousands of immigrants whose children and grandchildren comprise much of the city's population today. The city still retains some elements of that smokestack economy, but it is also rapidly developing a service sector. The Cleveland Clinic – where the heart by-pass was developed – is one of the area's largest private employers, treating patients from around the world; Jones Day Reavis & Pogue, one of the country's biggest law firms, is headquartered here; AmeriTrust Corp. and National City Corp. are two of the Midwest's most important financial institutions; and Case Western Reserve University's polymer-chemistry departments work jointly with the region's buoyant plastics industry to create and develop new technologies and applications for its products.

Arriving

Cleveland Hopkins International Airport

CHI, 10 miles/16kms southwest of downtown, has three concourses (A, B and C) with a total of 42 gates radiating out from the central terminal. Movement from plane to cab is usually quick and trouble-free, thanks to good signposting. All passengers from outside the USA arrive at concourse A, Gate 9, and there is an international travelers' lounge across from Gate 6. Clearing Immigration and Customs generally takes 15mins – but may take 1hr if more than one flight arrives around the same time. General information ☎ 265-6000.

Dining facilities are sometimes quite cramped and offer only standard airport fare. Currency can be exchanged at the Society National Bank Mon–Fri, 10–2 (and at all major banks downtown). Free emergency translation services and document translations are available at the airport office of the Nationality Services Center of Cleveland ☎ 781-4560. Taxi stands, limousine pick-up and shuttle buses to rental-car lots are just outside the baggage-claim area.

Nearby hotels *Airport Marriott*, 4277 W 150 St 44135 ☎ 252-5333 fax 251-1508: very acceptable. *Sheraton Hopkins Airport*, 5300 Riverside Dr 44135 ☎ 267-1500 fax 267-1500 ext 447: very close to the airport RTA rail station from which it takes only 20mins to downtown.

City link *Taxi* Cabs are available outside the baggage-claim area. The fare to downtown is about $16.

Limousine Regular, scheduled service to downtown is provided by Airport Limousine Service ☎ 267-8282.

Car rental The normal 20min drive to downtown can take much longer during the morning rush 7.30–9.30, and even worse from downtown to the airport in the evening rush 3.30–7, but car rental is a necessity if business will take you outside the downtown area. Eight national rental agencies have desks or courtesy phones in the central terminal, near the baggage claim area. Avis ☎ 265-3700, Hertz ☎ 267-8900.

Rail There is a Regional Transit Authority (RTA) station at the airport: follow the signs from the baggage-claim area. Rapid Transit Trains take only 20mins to Public Square; the exact fare ($1) is required. This is the easiest, fastest and least expensive way to go if you have little baggage and are staying downtown.

Getting around

The city is bisected into east and west

by Ontario Street, which runs through Public Square, but the West Side is usually considered to be the area west of the Cuyahoga River. Streets (generally numbered) run north–south, avenues (all named) run east–west. Lake Erie lies to the north.

Walking If your business and hotel are both downtown, you can usually walk to your destinations just as easily as drive or take a cab.

Taxi Cabs are available only in front of major hotels, at the corner of east 9th Street and Euclid Avenue, and by phone; they are not allowed to pick up in the streets. *Yellow/Zone Cab* ☎ 623-1500 and *Americab* ☎ 881-1111 serve downtown.

Limousine *National Limousine Service* ☎ 289-0800 has cars with cellular telephones; *Century Limousine* ☎ 234-4097 provides 24hr service.

Driving If you have a car, you can find street maps and get advice in the Visitors Bureau Information Center, at the street-level main entrance to the Terminal Tower on Public Square. If possible, get a garage or parking lot space; police give tickets *and* tow away illegally parked cars downtown. *Budget* ☎ 433-1949.

Try to avoid the busy Interstates 90, heading east or west, and 71 and 77, heading south, during the evening rush. You can turn right at a red light, unless it is signed otherwise.

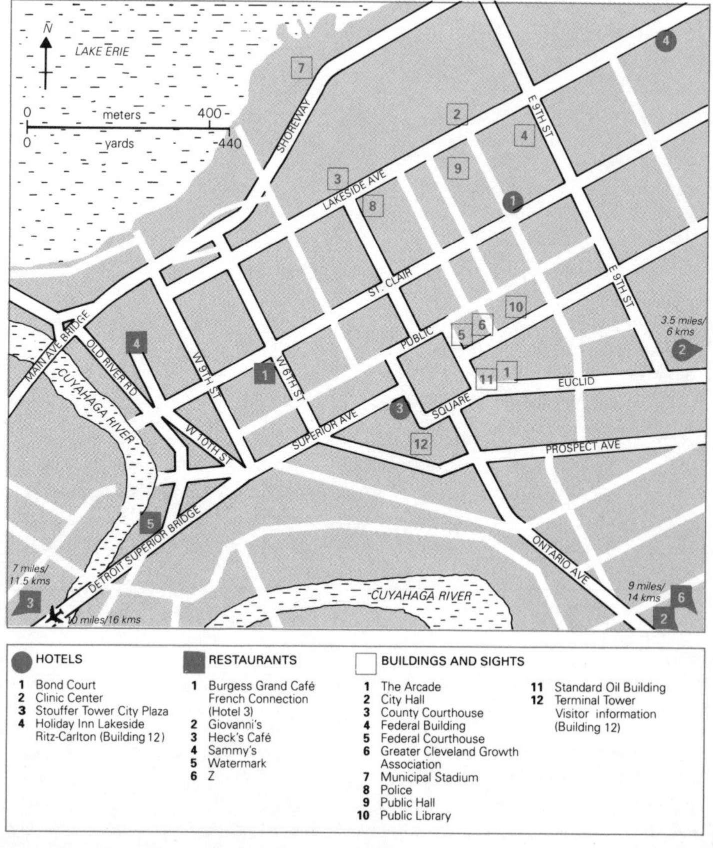

Bus and train *RTA* ☎ 621-9500 runs "loop" buses on routes covering most of downtown; schedules and route maps are posted at many stops and are available at an information center at 2019 Ontario Street, just south of Public Square.

Area by area

Downtown The skyline is dominated by the 52-story Terminal Tower and the new 45-story headquarters of Standard Oil, now BP America, both on Public Square – elegant and bustling by day; nearly deserted and possibly dangerous for lone pedestrians at night. A short walk up Euclid Avenue brings you to the Arcade, the 19thC marketplace transformed by glass and steel; at the intersection with E 9th Street, are most of the city's major banks and the headquarters of national law firms. Five blocks farther east is Playhouse Square, with many restaurants and three restored vaudeville theaters that are Cleveland's ballet, opera and repertory theater centers.

New office buildings and office/retail complexes have sprung up at the northern end of E 9th Street, near St Clair and Lakeside Avenues. Along Lakeside Avenue, from Ontario to E 9th, are city, county and federal government buildings, and the Cleveland Convention Center.

Six blocks west and a block north of Public Square lies the warehouse district, where sturdy 19thC buildings are being renovated for housing, office and commercial use. The Flats, in the Cuyahoga River valley, is a lively dining and entertainment area.

University Circle Farther east on Euclid, beginning at E 85th Street, are the Cleveland Play House Complex (designed by native Philip Johnson), the Cleveland Clinic and University Circle, an academic and cultural district.

West Side To the west of the Cuyahoga is Ohio City, an enclave of Victorian homes and distinctive restaurants. Running along the lakeshore through the West Side's suburbs are the yacht clubs and marinas of the boating set; to the southwest rapidly growing office complexes and high-tech industrial parks are taking over. The new International Exposition Center (I-X), a huge convention and trade-show hall, is also to the southwest, minutes from the airport.

Suburbs East of University Circle you will find Cleveland Heights, Shaker Heights, Hunting Valley and Gates Mills – Cleveland's classiest addresses.

Hotels

Because cabs are not available on the street, visitors – especially those with two or more appointments scheduled for the same day – would be wise to make proximity to destination their first criterion in choosing a hotel in downtown Cleveland. In general, hotel dining facilities are adequate, but sampling one or more of the area's growing number of good restaurants involves little extra effort or expense.

Bond Court [$]//

777 St Clair Ave NE 44114
☎ 771-7600 fax 771-5129 • AE DC MC V • 480 rooms, 40 suites, 1 restaurant, 2 bars, 1 coffee shop

One of the top downtown hotels, along with Stouffer Tower City Plaza. The Bond Court is very central and is especially convenient to the Convention Center, city and federal offices and many of the newer office buildings on the north side of downtown. Luxury multilevel suites have two work areas, multiple phone lines with computer modem facility and brass beds. 20 meeting rooms.

Clinic Center $/
2065 E 96th St 44106 ☎ 791-1900 fax 791-7065 • AE DC MC V • 348 rooms, 6 suites, 3 restaurants
The recently refurbished Clinic Center, always popular with medics and academics, now attracts a wider clientele. It is only a few minutes' walk from downtown Cleveland. Classics restaurant is a luxurious venue for a business or social meal. 7 meeting rooms.

Stouffer Tower City Plaza $////
24 Public Sq 44113 ☎ 696-5600 TX 752889 fax 696-0432 • AE DC MC V • 443 rooms, 49 suites, 3 restaurants, 2 bars, 2 coffee shops
Thanks to a recent $30m renovation, the Stouffer has regained its reputation as Cleveland's most elegant hotel in the best address; certainly it has the best restaurant, the French Connection (see *Restaurants*). The Stouffer is part of the Terminal Tower complex on Public Square, convenient to public transit, dining, and the entertainment district. The large suites have ample space for in-room meetings and business entertaining. Fitness equipment, indoor pool • 20 meeting rooms.

OTHER HOTELS
Holiday Inn Lakeside $/
1111 Lakeside Ave 44114 ☎ 241-5100 fax 241-7437 • AE DC MC V. Recently renovated, with indoor pool, sauna, weight room.
Ritz-Carlton W 3rd St (opening fall 1990). Luxury hotel in Tower City Center. Fitness center, pool • 5 meeting rooms.

Clubs

The *Union Club* ☎ 621-4230, oldest and most exclusive of Cleveland's downtown clubs, is a bastion of the establishment. Sometimes maligned as stuffy and insular, it nonetheless remains popular for business breakfasts, important lunches and even business meetings downstairs in the barbershop. The *Cleveland Athletic Club* ☎ 621-8900 has good fitness facilities and two dining rooms. It has reciprocal agreements with more than 50 other American clubs and is the preferred venue for noontime business-cum-racquetball encounters. The *Mid-day Club* is mostly professional; the spacious dining room (for breakfast, lunch and private dinners) offers a bird's-eye view of the city.

Restaurants

From the Mexican, Greek and Italian offerings you would expect to find in any cosmopolitan city, to authentic Hungarian, Thai and South American food, Cleveland offers the business traveler a very wide choice of cuisines. The establishments listed, which attract regular clientele, are recommended for business meetings or entertaining.

Burgess Grand Café $//
1406 W 6th St ☎ 574-2232 • AE MC V
This Victorian-inspired restaurant is especially popular with downtown business people for breakfast meetings. It has an all-mahogany bar in a renovated building in Cleveland's burgeoning warehouse district. The food is a mix of French and Italian.

French Connection $////
Stouffer Tower City Plaza Hotel ☎ 696-5600 • AE DC MC V • jacket
The smartly chic hotel dining room is one of Cleveland's best restaurants. Both the classic Continental cuisine – the menu changes seasonally – and formal service are good, and can be enjoyed from tables overlooking Public Square. Booths and discreet partitions provide privacy for business discussions.

Giovanni's $////
25550 Chagrin Blvd, Beachwood

☎ 831-8625 • closed Sun • *AE DC MC V* • *jacket*
This is Cleveland's best Italian restaurant – some say its best overall. Giovanni's has well prepared (sometimes tableside) northern Italian cuisine and an extensive wine list. An impressive choice for business entertaining. Plush and sympathetic, this is one of the city's restaurants where deals are often struck.

Heck's Café [$]//
19300 Detroit Rd, Rocky River ☎ *356-2559* • *AE DC MC V*
Housed in a former Art Deco movie theater 7 miles/11kms from downtown, Heck's offers a stylish location for entertaining convenient to the airport and the most interesting *nouvelle cuisine* on Cleveland's West Side.

Sammy's [$]///
1400 W 10th St ☎ *523-5560* • *closed Sun* • *AE DC MC V* • *reservations essential*
Known for its fish dishes and unusual sauces, its pastas, produce from its own 10th Street Market and its homemade sorbets, Sammy's is one of Cleveland's "in" places for business lunches and dinners. Located on the rejuvenated waterfront, it is fashionable and crowded every day, especially in summer. The raw fish bar and the view of the Cuyahoga River bring in the regulars and the visitors.

Watermark [$]//
1250 Old River Rd ☎ *241-1600* • *AE DC MC V*
An airy converted warehouse with an all-glass wall providing striking views of the Cuyahoga River. The menu features a number of mesquite-grilled dishes, seafood and some memorable desserts. Not far from Sammy's and with a similarly business clientele.

Z [$]//
Tower East, 20600 Chagrin Blvd, Shaker Heights ☎ *991-1580* • *closed L Mon & Sat, Sun* • *AE MC V*
A minimalist white decor in a building 20mins from downtown, designed by the founder of the Bauhaus School, Walter Gropius. Only abstract art adds the odd splash of color to a restaurant that is as sophisticated as its food. Voted Cleveland's top restaurant, the cuisine is Californian *nouvelle* (all entrées – fish, beef, veal and chicken – are grilled). The wine list is both extensive and expensive.

Bars

Cleveland is not especially noted for its nightlife except for the hangouts of the young professional crowd in the Flats, on the banks of the Cuyahoga River. For somewhere pleasant to enjoy a drink and a quiet business conversation, the downtown hotel lounges are best. For something more lively, however, try the suburbs.

Recommended bistros on Cleveland's East Side include *Gamekeeper's Tavern*, 87 West St, Chagrin Falls ☎ 247-7744, where drinks (and dinner) are served on an outdoor patio in the summer, indoors before a fire in cooler weather; *Nighttown*, 12387 Cedar Rd, Cleveland Heights ☎ 795-0550, a landmark watering hole and restaurant; *Noggin's*, 20110 Van Aken Blvd, Shaker Heights ☎ 752-9280, a popular East Side eatery whose bar features fresh seafood and interesting wines by the glass; and *Club Isabella*, 2025 Abington Rd, University Circle ☎ 229-1177, offering light fare and live jazz nightly 9–1.

On the Near West Side, you could try the *Ohio City Tavern*, 2801 Bridge Ave ☎ 687-0505, a former stagecoach stop and inn.

Entertainment

Theater and music Clevelanders are proud of the attention and money they have given to support classical music, ballet and dance. The *Cleveland Orchestra* plays weekends Oct–May at Severance Hall, 11001 Euclid Ave at E Blvd ☎ 231-1111, Jun–Sep at Blossom Music Center 1145 W Steels Corners Rd, Cuyahoga

Falls ☏ 566-9330. *Blossom*, 45mins out of town, where one can picnic casually on the lawn or sit in comfort in the pavilion, also hosts rock and pop during the summer. Big-name entertainment, ranging from comedy to jazz, can be seen in the round at the *Front Row Theater*, 6199 Wilson Mills Rd, Highland Heights ☏ 449-5000. A new entertainment facility, *Play House Square Center* ☏ 771-4444, comprises three restored historic theaters: the Ohio, State and Palace. The Center is used by Cleveland Ballet, Cleveland Opera, Great Lakes Theater Festival, a professional classical-repertory company with a summer-only season, and touring Broadway shows and modern dance troupes. With a Sep–Jun season, the country's oldest professional regional theater, the *Cleveland Play House*, 8500 Euclid Ave ☏ 795-7000, offers yet more high-quality dramatic fare.
Nightclub Try *Peabody's*, 2140 S Taylor Rd ☏ 321-4072 for folk.

Shopping

Two established department stores – *May Co* and *Higbee's* – are on Public Square, and there is an array of specialty shops in two downtown landmarks: *The Arcade*, 401 Euclid Ave, and *Tower City Center* in Terminal Tower. The most notable mall is *Beachwood Place* (Saks and other high-quality men's and women's fashion shops) on East Side at the intersection of Cedar and Richmond Roads, where you will also find the newly renovated and very posh *La Place* mall; equally exclusive is the *Galleria*; and, on the West Side, *Beachcliff Market Square*, an interesting mix of boutiques at 19300 Detroit Rd, Rocky River.

Sightseeing

Cleveland Metroparks Zoo
Revitalized in the past 15 years by such new exhibits as Birds of the World, African Plains and the Aquatic Center, this is something you can't do in 1hr, but it is worth visiting for longer if you have time. *3900 Brookside Pk ☏ 661-6500. Open daily 9–5; summer to 7.*
Cleveland Museum of Art Highly regarded around the world for its general collections, this is an excellent museum with an admirable collection of Picassos. Also worth seeing are the Old Masters and Oriental galleries. *11150 East Blvd, University Circle ☏ 421-7340. Open daily exc Mon; hours vary.*
Cleveland Museum of Natural History Ohio's largest natural science museum features permanent exhibits on dinosaurs, prehistoric American Indians and gemstones. *Wade Oval, University Circle ☏ 231-4600. Open Mon–Sat, 10–5; Sun, 1–5.*
Crawford Auto-Aviation Museum Two hundred beautifully restored antique automobiles and a smaller number of historic planes. *10825 East Blvd, University Circle ☏ 721-5722. Open Tue–Sun; hours vary.*
Municipal Stadium Home of the Cleveland Indians and Browns, the stadium is a monument to 1930s architecture. *585 W 3rd St.*
USS Cod This World War II submarine made seven patrols, mainly in the Pacific Ocean. *N Marginal Rd between E 9th St and Burke Lakefront Airport ☏ 566-8770. Open end-May–early-Sep, Mon–Fri, 11–4; Sat & Sun, 1–5.*
Western Reserve Historical Society Twenty period rooms recreate life in Ohio 1770–1920. *10825 East Blvd, University Circle ☏* 721-5722. *Tue–Sat, 10–5; Sun, 12–5.*
West Side Market One of the largest Old World-style indoor/outdoor markets, which has more than 100 traders selling everything from vegetables to baked goods and smoked meats. *Lorain Ave at W 25th St ☏ 664-3386. Mon & Wed, 7–4; Fri & Sat, 7–6.*

Guided tours

Executive Arrangements ☏ 991-8333 provide custom tours of Greater Cleveland by bus, van, limo or vintage car; *Holiday Boat Charters*

☏ 771-2628 take you on the water – Lake Erie or the Cuyahoga or Rocky Rivers; *North Coast Tours* ☏ 579-6160 have both standard and custom bus or walking tours; and *Trolley Tours of Cleveland* (May–Dec) ☏ 771-4484 offer 2hr tours of the city by trolley-bus.

Spectator sports

Cleveland is a busy sports city, with the emphasis on football. The offer of a seat in a corporate box at any of the sporting venues is a compliment.

Baseball *Cleveland Indians* play at Municipal Stadium, 585 W 3rd St ☏ 861-1200.

Basketball The *Cavaliers* are at the Coliseum, 2923 Streetsboro Rd, Richfield ☏ 659-9100.

Football The *Browns* kick off at Municipal Stadium, 585 W 3rd St ☏ 696-5555.

Horse-racing *Northfield Park Raceway* Rte 8, Northfield ☏ 467-4101, has harness racing; *Thistledown*, Emery and Warrensville Center roads, North Randall ☏ 662-8600, has thoroughbred racing Mar–Dec.

Keeping fit

Greater Cleveland has an abundance of parks providing an array of recreational activities for free or for a modest fee. Health club facilities are offered at most hotels, or they will have arrangements with a nearby club.

Beaches Public beaches can be found at Edgewater Park on the west and Euclid Beach on the east – part of the system of *Cleveland Lakefront State Parks* ☏ 881-8141.

Cross-country skiing Although primarily a preserve for 6,000 varieties of trees, plants and flowers, *Holden Arboretum* ☏ 946-4400 is also laced with cross-country ski trails.

Golf Among the many public golf courses in the area are those operated by *Cleveland Metroparks* at its Rocky River, Brecksville, Bedford and North Chagrin reservations ☏ 351-6300.

Jogging The *Cleveland Metroparks* have all-purpose trails for jogging, hiking and biking. Rocky River, Big Creek, Brecksville, Bedford, South Chagrin, North Chagrin and Euclid Creek reservations are also popular. For information ☏ 351-6300.

Tennis *Racquet Club East* ☏ 464-7122 in Bedford Heights is one of the few Cleveland tennis clubs open to the public which has indoor courts.

Local resources

Business services

Complete secretarial, word processing and answering services are available at *Executive Center*, 14650 Deroit Ave, Lakewood ☏ 221-2561; *Headquarters Companies* (pick-up and delivery), 23200 Chagrin Blvd, Beachwood ☏ 831-8220, and 25000 Great Northern Corporate Center, North Olmsted ☏ 777-0000; and *Statler Office Service*, 1127 Euclid Ave ☏ 566-8050.

Photocopying and printing *Original Copy Centers* ☏ 861-0620 (pick-up and delivery); *Kinko's*, 1832 Euclid Ave ☏ 589-5679, and 1990 Ford Dr, University Circle ☏ 229-5679; and *Kwik Print*, 1278 W 9th St ☏ 696-5000.

Secretarial Reliable temporary help can be obtained through *Kelly Services*, 7550 Lucerne Dr, Middleburgh Heights ☏ 243-8292, and *Olsten Services*, 2000 E 9th St ☏ 861-1900.

Translation *A Technical Translation Service*, 38355 Chimney Ridge Dr, Willoughby Hills ☏ 942-3130; *Berlitz Translation Services*, 815 Superior Ave NE ☏ 861-0950.

Communications

Long-distance delivery *Federal Express* ☏ 361-0872 and *Purolator* ☏ (800) 645-3333; for international deliveries, *DHL* ☏ *836-9130*.

Local delivery *Bonnie Speed Delivery* ☏ 696-6033; *Executive Delivery Systems* ☏ 861-4560.

Post office The downtown (and main) office is open Mon–Fri, 8–6.30 at

2400 Orange Ave ☏ 443-4096.
Telex and fax *Action Telex*, 20900 St Clair Ave ☏ 531-9111; and *An SOS Telex*, 1127 Euclid Ave ☏ 566-8050.

Conference/exhibition centers

Most of Cleveland's larger hotels offer conference and meeting facilities. *Clarion*, 35000 Curtis Blvd, Eastlake ☏ 953-8000, *Quail Hollow Inn*, I-90 and Rte 44, Painesville ☏ 352-6201, and *Aqua Marine Resort*, 216 Miller Rd, Avon Lake ☏ 933-2000, all provide a country-club setting for business meetings. The *Cleveland Convention Center*, 1220 E 6th St ☏ 348-2200, in downtown, has around 375,000 sq ft of space. The new *International Exposition Center* is at 6200 Riverside Dr ☏ 676-6000. For more information, consult the *Convention and Visitors Bureau of Greater Cleveland*, 3100 Tower City Center, 44113 ☏ 621-4110.

Emergencies

Hospitals The following hospitals operate 24hr emergency rooms: *Mt Sinai Medical Center*, 1 Mt Sinai Dr, University Circle ☏ 421-4000; *St Vincent Charity Hospital*, 2351 E 22nd St ☏ 861-6200; and *University Hospitals*, 2074 Abington Rd, University Circle ☏ 844-1000. For dental emergencies, call *National Dental Center*'s 24hr help-line ☏ 289-6900.
Pharmacies *Revco Discount Drug Center* is a major local chain with many locations open Mon–Sat till 10pm.
Police *Cleveland Police*, 1200 Ontario St ☏ 623-5000; *Cuyahoga County Sheriff* ☏ 443-6085.

Government offices

Cleveland City Hall ☏ 664-2000; *Cuyahoga County Administration* ☏ 443-7000; *Ohio Dept of Commerce/Real Estate Division* ☏ 622-3100; *US Dept of Commerce/International Trade Administration District Office* ☏ 522-4750; *US Customs* ☏ 522-7010; *US Immigration and Naturalization Service* ☏ 522-4770.

Information sources

Business information The *Greater Cleveland Growth Association*, 690 Huntington Building at E 9th and Euclid ☏ 621-3300, provides information about the local economy and business practices.
Local media The *Plain Dealer* is a daily morning newspaper with local, national and international coverage. The *Sun* newspapers are a chain of weeklies serving Cleveland suburbs. Crain's *Cleveland Business* is a bi-weekly business journal. *Cleveland Magazine* is a monthly general-interest publication. Another monthly magazine, *Northern Ohio LIVE* covers the arts, entertainment and dining-out. Cleveland's public radio station, *WCPN-FM* (90.3) features news and public affairs during the morning and evening rush hours.
Visitor information The *Convention and Visitors Bureau of Greater Cleveland*, 3100 Tower City Center ☏ 621-4110, operates a Visitors Information Center in the Terminal Tower, near the main entrance. Or call the Bureau's Fun Phone ☏ 621-8860 for a listing of current entertainment and special events.

Thank-yous

Florists *Alexander's Flowers* ☏ 292-4500; *Jones-Russell Florist* ☏ 621-8545; and *Segeln's* ☏ 791-8900 accept credit card orders by telephone.
Gift baskets *Cheese World* (imported and domestic cheeses) ☏ 371-8841; *Completely Nuts* (assorted nuts) ☏ 589-0666; *Feren Fruit Basket Co* (gourmet fruit and meats) ☏ 431-8700; and *Shaker Square Beverages Inc* (fine wines) ☏ 561-5100.

DALLAS

Area code ☎ 214

Despite the TV series, Dallas has been involved more in trade than in oil since it was established in 1841. Biggest among the city's major sources of revenue is its wholesale merchandise trade, which attracts more than half a million buyers a year to markets selling home furnishings, clothing and information-processing, among other products and services. Dallas is also a major defense electronics and armaments center, earning over $10bn annually. The area now has more than 400 high-tech firms, including Electronic Data Systems and Texas Instruments. It is home to chemical giants Valhi and Rexene, Kimberly-Clark, 7-up/Dr Pepper and, in the metals and building materials sectors, of National Gypsum, LTV and Tyler. It is a significant financial center and the headquarters of Southwestern Life, Southmark and the NCNB Texas National Bank. Established wealth outshines new money, and culture is important for the quality of life sought by its inhabitants. Conservative in politics, its city fathers owe their status more to family name than party allegiance. On the edge of the prairie, Dallas has extreme weather – over 105°F (30°C) in summer and ice storms in winter.

Arriving

Dallas/Fort Worth International Airport

Dallas/Fort Worth Airport is suitably gigantic for a Texan facility, with seven unconnected terminals arranged in a double row along International Parkway. The airport is midway between Dallas and Fort Worth – together known as the Metroplex – and is serviced by all major domestic and international airlines, as well as commuter and charter flights. International flights arrive at Terminals 2E or 2W; there are currency exchanges and Customs in both. For domestic travelers it should take about 30mins from arrival to leaving the airport – an hour if Customs and Immigration have to be cleared; information ☎ 574-6720.

An electric transport system, Airtrans, transfers passengers between terminals and to remote parking lots.

Nearby hotels *Hilton*, 1800 Hwy 26E ☎ (817) 481-8444 fax 481-3160. *Marriott*, 8440 Freeport Pkwy ☎ 929-8800 fax 929-1829. *Hyatt Regency Airport*, International Parkway 75261 ☎ 453-8400 fax 458-8668.

City link The trip into Dallas from the airport takes about 20mins, 30mins in rush hours, 7–9 and 4–6. To Fort Worth, allow 30mins, 50mins in rush hours. Bus, limousine, and taxi services to Dallas and Fort Worth hotels are near baggage claim areas at terminals 2E, 3E, 4E and 2W.

Taxi The best way to get into town, taxis are available 24hrs at all upper level exits. Fares to downtown Dallas and Fort Worth are about $25.

Limousine These should be reserved in advance: Texas Taxi ☎ 634-8294; Limousines by Jan ☎ 327-6616; and Royal Limousine ☎ 522-3290.

Car rental Getting out of the airport can be confusing; take a taxi downtown and rent there. However, three national agencies are open 24hrs with offices at the airport's north and south entrances: Avis ☎ 574-4130; Hertz ☎ 453-0370; and National ☎ 574-3400.

Bus Shuttle services to Dallas include The Link ($10), Tours by Stan ($7), Trailways and VIP Transport ($10). Shuttles to Fort Worth include Bluebird Transportation ($6) and Citran's Airporter ($6). Bus services generally run 8am–10pm. Pick-up points are clearly marked, but service can be infrequent (every half hour) and slow.

Getting around

Unless your business will keep you in the walkable downtown area, where there are plenty of taxis, a rental car is the best and most convenient method of getting around. Dallas is spread out, and it is criss-crossed by freeways and expressways.

Taxi Taxis cannot be hailed on the street; telephone in advance and allow 15–25mins for pick-up. Try *State Cab* ☏ 823-2161; *Terminal Cab* ☏ 350-4445 or *Yellow Cab* ☏ 426-6262.

Limousine See *City link*.

Car rental See *City link* for rental companies and telephone numbers.

Bus The bus system is not recommended, except on *Hop-A-Bus* downtown routes.

Area by area

Downtown The heart of Dallas's central business district is its downtown concentration of major banks, law and brokerage firms, and corporate headquarters. It includes business offices, historic sites, commercial buildings and arts institutions such as City Hall, the Public Library, the Museum of Art, Farmers' Market, JFK Memorial (and the Book Depository, from which the shot that killed Kennedy is thought to have been fired) and the original Neiman-Marcus store. Here is the 60-acre site on which the vast arts center is being built.

East Dallas Old-established neighborhoods in East Dallas – Swiss Avenue, Munger Place and Lakewood – have a wealth of historic buildings and parks. Most East Dallas residents have lived there for generations, though younger professionals are buying and restoring the old property.

Highland Park and the Golden Corridor Ten minutes north of downtown, the exclusive township of Highland Park is the city's top residential district, with a concentration of the city's founding families and old wealth. It also has the Southern Methodist University and Exall Lake. Other esteemed neighborhoods – such as Oak Lawn, Bluff View and University Park – plus restaurants, shops and office buildings, are strung along the North Dallas Tollroad, known as the Golden Corridor.

Far North Dallas As the tollroad

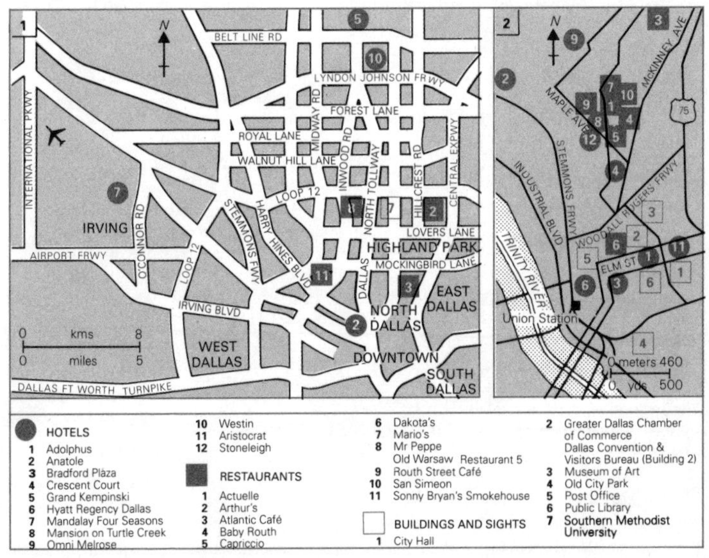

crosses Interstate 635 into Far North Dallas, chic new shopping centers and modern residential developments stretch northwards. Far North Dallas is the city's major area of new wealth, home of Dallas's population influx.

South and West Dallas South Dallas, largely a black community that includes Old City Park, and West Dallas, gateway to Texas Stadium in Irving, combines industrial development with mainly low-income residential neighborhoods. West Dallas also has two major business centers, the Infomart – a computer and high-tech facility – and Market Center – a large wholesale forum. Oak Cliff, just across the Trinity River, is being redeveloped; it is the home of the Dallas Zoo. On the city's western outskirts, midway between downtown and the airport, lies Las Colinas, an enclave of business headquarters, luxury hotels, country clubs and sleekly affluent residential areas.

Hotels

Because Dallas's major business locations are not confined to downtown, the hotels listed serve diverse working communities: downtown, Cedar Springs, Market Center, North Dallas, and Las Colinas.

Adolphus [$]////

1321 Commerce St 75202 ☏ 742-8200 [TX] 84530 fax 747-3523 • AE DC MC V • 415 rooms, 20 suites, 3 restaurants, 2 bars, 1 coffee shop

In the heart of downtown on the crossroads of Commerce and Akard, the landmark Adolphus is one of Dallas's most convenient addresses. Prominent guests include heads of state, international personalities and VIP entrepreneurs. An extensive concierge staff will provide for practically any need. The French Room is an opulent dining room, an excellent choice for an important meal. The Clark Hatch Fitness Center offers a full range of fitness equipment and activities. 20 meeting rooms.

Anatole [$]///

2201 Stemmons Frwy 75207 ☏ 748-1200 [TX] 730475 fax 761-7520 • AE DC MC V • Loews • 1,620 rooms, 145 suites, 12 restaurants, 8 bars

A magnet for much of the city's substantial convention trade, the Anatole dominates the skyline of Dallas's Market Center area and offers a good mix of business and sports facilities. The Verandah Club is an exceptionally elegant spa and health center. 58 meeting rooms.

Bradford Plaza [$]//

Jackson and Houston Sts 75202 ☏ 761-9090 fax 748-4359 • AE DC MC V • 117 rooms, 6 suites, 1 restaurant, 1 bar

An intimate European-style hotel offering privacy and quiet, the Bradford is conveniently sited in downtown's West End. Rooms are spacious; suites have desks and typewriters. 2 meeting rooms.

Crescent Court [$]////

400 Crescent Court 75201 ☏ 871-3200 [TX] 275555 fax 871-3272 • AE DC MC V • 188 rooms, 28 suites, 1 restaurant, 1 bar

The area's young business professionals have made Beau Nash one of the city's foremost business restaurants. The rest of this relatively new hotel measures up equally well. All rooms have three telephones and large desks; message service is prompt. There are 6 meeting rooms and 14-seat boardroom, equipped with the latest multimedia technology. Fitness center, pool.

Grand Kempinski [$]///

15201 Dallas N Pkwy 75248 ☏ 386-6000 [TX] 795515 fax 991-6937 • AE DC MC V • 529 rooms, 37 suites, 2 restaurants, 3 bars

This comfortable hotel is a good choice if you have business in North Dallas, and it is surrounded by shops, boutiques, restaurants, and nightclubs. The lobby concierge is on duty 24hrs. Health club, tennis • 24 meeting rooms, business center.

Hyatt Regency Dallas [$]//
300 Reunion Blvd 75207 ☎ 651-1234 [TX] 732748 • fax 742-8124 • AE DC MC V • 947 rooms, 49 suites, 2 restaurants, 2 bars, 1 coffee shop
Conveniently near the West End, this ultra-modern architectural landmark with its light-studded revolving tower is the choice of many visiting business travelers. Efficient, well-trained staff. Nonsmoking floors • health club, pool, tennis, jogging track • 25 meeting rooms.

Mandalay Four Seasons [$]///
221 S Las Colinas, Irving 75039 ☎ 556-0800 [TX] 794016 fax 554-0729 • AE DC MC V • 420 rooms, 9 suites, 3 restaurants, 2 bars, 1 coffee shop
A good choice for visiting executives based in Las Colinas, this modern hotel is convenient for the airport, downtown businesses, and Texas Stadium. It combines luxury, good business (especially convention) facilities and a prestigious address. Enjolie, its first-rate dining room, is often used for business entertaining. Health club, golf, tennis, pool • 12 meeting rooms, teleconferencing.

Mansion on Turtle Creek [$]////
2821 Turtle Creek Blvd 75219 ☎ 559-2100 [TX] 794946 fax 528-4187 • AE DC MC V • 129 rooms, 14 suites, 2 restaurants, 1 bar
The restored Sheppard-King mansion – an Italianate villa – comprises the hotel's excellent bar and restaurant area; the rooms were built in 1981. Filled with *objets d'art* and handsome reproduction furniture, the Mansion caters to an older, wealthier clientele. The visitors' register often reads like a Who's Who in America. The Mansion restaurant, thought by some to be the city's best, features American *nouvelle* dishes and attentive service. Pool, exercise facilities, arrangements with local country club • 8 meeting rooms.

Omni Melrose [$]/
3015 Oak Lawn Ave ☎ 521-5151 fax 521-5151 • AE DC MC V • 184 rooms, 1 restaurant, 1 bar
Though less sumptuous than the Mansion, the Melrose has spacious bathrooms, mahogany furniture, ceiling fans, and separate sitting areas in each room. Just to the north of downtown and only a few minutes from Market Center, it is popular with women executives. Personalized service. Arrangements with health club • 5 meeting rooms.

Westin [$]//
13340 Dallas N Pkwy 75240 ☎ 934-9494 [TX] 630182 fax 851-2869 • AE DC MC V • 430 rooms, 14 suites, 3 restaurants, 1 bar
Located in the Galleria Shopping Mall, the Westin is the most impressive place to stay in North Dallas. The Huntington Grill is a highly respected restaurant, and the excellent Sunday brunch in Zucchini's café is much patronized by locals. Health club, pool, nearby tennis, squash • 14 meeting rooms, express mail service.

OTHER HOTELS

Aristocrat [$]// *1933 Main St 75201 ☎ 741-7700 fax 939-3639 • AE DC MC V*. An intimate, all-suite hotel in eastern downtown, and near the arts district.

Stoneleigh [$]// *2827 Maple Ave 75201 ☎ 871-7111 fax 871-7111 ext 1213 • AE DC MC V*. This Cedar Springs hotel often has celebrity guests.

Clubs

The following are the most elite of all types of Dallas's clubs : *Bent Tree Country Club*, *Brook Hollow Golf Club*, *Cipango Club*, *City Club*, *Dallas Club*, *Dallas Country Club*, *Dallas Petroleum Club*, and *Northwood Club*.

Restaurants

Some of Dallas's best restaurants are in the big hotels. In particular, the Adolphus Hotel's French Room, Enjolie at the Mandalay Four Seasons and Turtle Greek's excellent Mansion dining room are nearly always filled with expense-account diners (see *Hotels*). Prices are high; expect to pay $40–$50 a person in the more elegant places, possibly going up to $80 or more. Many restaurants close by 10pm.

Actuelle [$]///
2800 Routh St, suite 125 ☏ *855-0440 • closed L Sat, Sun* • AE DC MC V
The newest entry in the current explosion of New American Cuisine establishments, this sleek restaurant in a gazebo-like pavilion overlooks the courtyard of the Quadrangle. A fine regional menu with touches of sophistication is masterfully prepared by one of the city's top chefs.

Arthur's [$]//
8350 N Central Expressway, Campbell Center ☏ *361-8833 • closed Sat L, Sun* • AE DC MC V • *jacket*
Renowned for its steak and seafood selections, Arthur's provides a formal dining atmosphere that is very popular for business entertaining. The maitre d' is sensitive to any need for privacy or prime seating.

Atlantic Café [$]//
4544 McKinney Ave ☏ *559-4441* • AE DC MC V • *reservations advisable*
Some locals swear the Atlantic Café serves the best seafood in this landlocked city. With an attractive setting of polished brass and dark wood trimmings, the restaurant's cozy booths are ideal for quiet conversation during lunch or dinner.

Baby Routh [$]/
2708 Routh St ☏ *871-2345* • AE DC MC V
An offshoot of the highly touted Routh Street Café, this casual restaurant attracts a fashionable crowd. Its *nouvelle* American dishes are best described as "country chic."

Capriccio [$]/
2616 Maple ☏ *871-2004* • AE DC MC V • *jacket*
This beautiful old Texan house has been effectively restored and now offers stylish comfort and better-than-average northern Italian dishes. An informal restaurant, Capriccio nonetheless sees a lot of business deals transacted over the *linguini* and *zabaglione*.

Dakota's [$]//
500 N Akard ☏ *740-4001 • closed Sat L* • AE DC MC V
Though a bit noisy for prolonged conversation, Dakota's is nevertheless a continuing success which draws Dallas's own VIPs as well as visiting celebrities. Serving a selection of grills – mainly steaks, chops and seafood – the below-ground restaurant is an impressive choice for client entertaining.

Mario's [$]//
135 Turtle Creek Shopping Center ☏ *521-1135* • AE DC MC V • *jacket*
Dishes from Northern Italy predominate in this lively restaurant, but French cooking also finds its way on to the menu. Homemade bread is an accompaniment to veal and beef that owes little to *nouvelle cuisine*.

Mr Peppe [$]/
5617 Lovers Ln ☏ *352-5976 • closed Sat L, Sun* • AE DC MC V • *jacket*
In this long-established but unpretentious café, the Swiss owner provides good French food and personal service at relatively modest prices. The noise level is rarely above a whisper – though it is not oppressively quiet.

Old Warsaw [$]//
2610 Maple ☏ *528-0032 • closed L* • AE DC MC V • *reservations essential*

With a darkly plush decor, classical music backdrop and a fine Continental cuisine, Old Warsaw was the city's ultimate dining experience in the not-so-distant past. Many of the old guard still consider it Dallas's top spot, and will be favorably impressed by an invitation to dine here.

Routh Street Café [$]//
3005 Routh at Cedar Springs
☎ 871-7161 • closed L, Sun, Mon • AE MC V • reservations essential
The best in Dallas according to many of the city's younger professionals, Routh Street Café offers a chic setting and Southwestern food with a *nouvelle* flair. The imaginative menu changes daily, and the all-American wine list has much to commend it.

San Simeon [$]//
2515 McKinney Ave at Fairmount
☎ 871-7373 • AE DC MC V
Sought out for its well-balanced dishes adapted from regional and ethnic traditions, San Simeon also wins honors for its impeccable service and superior wine list.

Sonny Bryan's Smokehouse [$]
2202 Inwood Rd ☎ 357-7120 • B and L only • no credit cards or reservations
A lot of restaurant reviews have proclaimed Sonny's the best barbecue joint – and one can see why. Ambience is next to nil, and the seating is either at a secondhand schooldesk or out in the car, but the ribs are excellent. Definitely an off-duty place, but well worth visiting for the experience.

Bars

The classier, more subdued bars are found mainly in the city's better hotels, restaurants and private clubs, such as the bar in the Beau Nash of the Crescent Court (see *Hotels*). Other good meeting places include North Dallas's *Gershwin's*, 8442 Walnut Hill Ln ☎ 373-7171, featuring solo vocalists; *Andrews*, 3301 McKinney Ave ☎ 385-1613, has exposed brick and Tex-Mex nibbles. There are also the *Hard Rock Café*, 2601 McKinney Ave ☎ 827-8282; *Plus Fours*, 2504 McKinney Ave; *Strictly Tabu*, 4111 Lomo Alto; and *SRO, 2900 McKinney Ave. The Grape*, 2808 Grenville Ave in East Dallas ☎ 828-1981, is a restaurant and a quiet wine bar for after-hours deal-making. Nearby on Greenville is the popular East Dallas wine bar, *St Martin's*.

Entertainment

Except for the hotels' numerous lounges and cozy bars and the permanently charged West End Historic District, streetlife in downtown Dallas fades with the setting sun. Greenville Avenue, Highland Park's Knox Street, Beltline Road in Far North Dallas and McKinney Avenue then come alive, offering dozens of bars, discos and nightclubs. In addition, Dallas has a varied selection of live theater, music and dance.

For information on what is available, call the *Cultural Arts Info Hot Line* ☎ (800) 385-1155 or check the "Weekend" sections in Friday editions of *Dallas Morning News* or the *Times Herald*. D magazine also has entertainment information.

Music, theater and dance The widely acclaimed *Dallas Symphony Orchestra* performs at the Music Hall, State Fair Grounds ☎ 565-9100, tickets ☎ 692-0203. For other musical events, the *Dallas Civic Music Association* performs in the McFarlin Auditorium at SMU ☎ 526-6870; *Dallas Grand Opera*, at 13601 Preston Rd ☎ 661-9750, tickets ☎ 691-7200; the *Dallas Opera* is at the Majestic Theater, 1925 Elm St ☎ 979-0123, tickets ☎ 871-0090; and *Dallas Summer Musicals*, State Fair Box Office, 6021 Berkshire Ln ☎ 691-7200. The Frank Lloyd Wright-designed *Dallas Theater Center*, 3636 Turtle Creek Blvd ☎ 526-8210, is headquarters for one of the city's oldest performing arts companies, while the *Arts District Theater* also stages DTC productions.

Live theater is also available at the *Dallas Repertory Theater*, NorthPark Center ☎ 369-8966; *Greenville Avenue Theater*, 2914 Greenville Ave ☎ 824-2552; *New Arts Theater*, 702 Ross Ave at Market St ☎ 761-9064; *Plaza Theater*, 6719 Snider Plaza ☎ 363-7000; *Theater Three*, 2800 Routh St ☎ 871-3300; and the *Southern Methodist University School of the Arts* ☎ 692-3146.

Nightclubs The best clubs include *Dick's Last Resort*, Ross and Record Streets in the West End Historic District ☎ 747-0001; it offers Dixieland jazz. *The Longhorn Ballroom*, 216 Corinth ☎ 428-3128, is the most authentic country dance hall. *Poor David's Pub*, 1924 Greenville ☎ 821-9891, presents oldies-but-goodies, such as Mary Travers. The best show in town is usually at the *Venetian Room* at the Fairmont Hotel, Ross and Akard ☎ 720-2020.

Shopping

Miracle Mile in Lover's Lane (Inwood Road to Douglas Avenue) has some of the city's most exclusive designer boutiques and three top specialty stores for women: The Gazebo, Lou Lattimore and Marie Leavell. Another area for top designer wear is *Highland Park Village*. Along *Oak Lawn*, Turtletique and Loretta Blum are favorites of Dallas women; Alexander Julian and Harrison's have good menswear. Two other popular men's shops – Marvin Brown and Pockets – are on *Greenville Avenue*.

Dallas's biggest and best shopping malls are all north of Northwest Highway (Loop 12), with hundreds of retail shops plus branches of most major national department stores. *NorthPark Center* has the largest Neiman-Marcus suburban branch store, as well as Lord & Taylor, The Carriage Shop and Ann Taylor. *The Galleria* also has Ann Taylor, plus Macy's, Marshall Field's and Saks Fifth Avenue. Nearby *Valley View Mall* has Bloomingdale's.

The renowned Neiman-Marcus and Sangar-Harris are both headquartered downtown, as is Brooks Brothers.

The *Farmers' Market*, 1010 S Pearl Expressway, is one of the largest outdoor markets in the country, with an eclectic assortment of produce and other Texan goods. Grand Prairie's huge flea market, *Trader's Village*, 2602 May Field Rd, operates at weekends, 8–sunset.

Dallas has a network of wholesale fashion outlets; a copy of *The Underground Shopper*, available at newsstands and bookshops, will guide the bargain hunter.

Sightseeing

Arboretum and Botanical Gardens Two former Dallas estates make up this 66-acre garden complex overlooking White Rock Lake. After touring the gardens, drive around the lake (9 miles/14.5kms). *8525 Garland Rd at Whittier ☎ 327-8263.*

Dallas Museum of Art The centerpiece of the new arts complex. Highlights include pre-Columbian art, Old Masters, modern American works, Oriental and Oceanic collections and the Reves Decorative Arts Wing. *1717 N Harwood ☎ 922-0220. Open Tue–Sat, 10–5; Thu, 10–9; Sun, noon–5.*

Dallas Public Library Photograph and art collections, special exhibits, recordings, listening centers, a cable television studio and an auditorium. *1515 Young St ☎ 749-4400. Guided tours (45mins) at 11 and 1, Sat; 3, Sun.*

DeGolyer Estate An historic mansion sits in the eastern part of the city. In nearly 43 acres bordering White Rock Lake, it has an art collection and beautiful grounds. *8525 Garland Rd ☎ 327-8263. Open daily exc Mon.*

Fair Park Home of the three-week long Texas State Fair each October, the fairgrounds are filled with Art Deco architecture, and provide a permanent home to many Dallas museums plus the Dallas Music Hall and the Cotton Bowl. The museums, including the Aquarium and the Museum of Natural History, are open

daily and most are free. *Grand Ave* ☏ *565-9931.*
Meadows Museum of Art owns a fine collection of Spanish art: more than 100 paintings by such artists as Velazquez and Goya. *Southern Methodist University* ☏ *692-2516. Open Mon, Fri, Sat, 10–5; Tue & Thu, 10–8; Sun, 1–5.*
Old City Park Historic homes and replica buildings – such as a doctor's office, depot, pioneer cabins, hotel, general store and school – recreate a semblance of early northern Texas communities. The park is close to downtown and has an excellent restaurant, Brent Place, serving lunch daily. *Gano and St Paul* ☏ *421-5141. Open Tue–Sat, 10–4; Sun, 1.30–4.30; closed Mon.*

Guided tours

Dallas Silver Cloud Tours, 4200 Herschel Ave ☏ 521-1664. *Execservice Unlimited*, 2701-A Fondren Dr, University Park ☏ 691-1166, specializes in custom group tours. *Gray Line of Dallas and Fort Worth*, 4110 S Lamar ☏ 824-2424, provides the most variety in daily, regularly scheduled city tours. *Kaleidoscope Tours*, 3131 Turtle Creek Blvd ☏ 522-5930, gives comprehensive and customized sightseeing area tours.

Spectator sports

Dallas is enthusiastically sports-minded, and local business deals are often settled at the Texas Stadium, where many companies hold corporate boxes.
Baseball The *Texas Rangers* ☏ 273-5100 play at Ranger Stadium, next door to Six Flags Over Texas, Apr–Sep.
Basketball The *Mavericks* appear at Reunion Arena, 777 Sports St ☏ 748-1808, Sep–Mar.
Football Dallas *Cowboys*, the city's favorite team, play at Texas Stadium, Texas 183 at Loop 12 ☏ 438-7676, also the site of the annual New Year's Day Cotton Bowl.
Rodeo The best venue is the *Mesquite* Championship Rodeo, Interstate 635 at Military Pkwy, Mesquite ☏ 285-8777; Apr–Sep, Fri and Sat at 8.30pm.
Soccer *Sidekicks Soccer* takes over Reunion Arena, Nov–Apr ☏ 658-7068.

Keeping fit

Fitness centers *President's Health & Racquet Clubs* have 14 locations in Greater Dallas providing gyms, swimming pools, indoor tracks and advanced training equipment. The *Turtle Creek President's Health Club*, 3232 McKinney ☏ 871-7700, is particularly prestigious.
Bicycling Locally popular bike trails skirt Bachman Lake on Northwest Highway and White Rock Lake on Garland Road; Turtle Creek Drive in Highland Park is also often used. Bicycle rentals are available from *Hundley Recreation Center*, 3240 W Lawther (at White Rock Lake) ☏ 823-6933, and *Inwood Cycle*, 3750 W Northwest Hwy ☏ 357-7625 (near Bachman Lake).
Golf Some of the best public courses are *Cedar Crest* ☏ 943-1004, *Grover Keaton* ☏ 388-4831, *Stevens* ☏ 670-7506 and *Tenison* ☏ 823-5350. Before reserving tee-off time, check with your hotel concierge to see if your hotel has guest arrangements with one of the local country clubs.
Horseback riding The following stables offer daily riding: *Benbrook Ranch & Stables*, south of Interstate 20 on Hwy 377 ☏ (817) 249-1176, and *Wagon Wheel Stables*, D/FW Airport ☏ 462-0894.
Tennis Tennis courts are scattered across the city in parks and near recreation centers. To find the public courts most convenient to your hotel and to make reservations ☏ 670-8745, Mon–Fri, 8.15–5.15.

Local resources

Business services

Photocopying and printing *Red-E-Print*, 8383 Stemmons Fwy ☏ 637-2532 (near Market Center); *Quik Print*, 1 Main Pl ☏ 741-1425,

also 750 N St Paul's Street (downtown). *Donia Printing*, 5217 Ross Ave ☏ 826-8911; *Minute Man Press*, 11617 North Central at Forest ☏ 363-2876 (North Central area). *Cliff's Printing & Instant Copy Shop*, 12720 Hillcrest ☏ 980-4714 (Far North Dallas).
Secretarial *Executive Secretarial Services*, Walnut Hill at Greenville ☏ 750-1111; *AMS Secretarial Service*, 6200 N Central Expwy, suite 226 ☏ 363-7824; *Capital Secretarial Services*, 401 Capital Bank Bldg ☏ 823-7950.
Translation *Berlitz*, 15340 Dallas Pkwy ☏ 387-4487; *Language Bank*, Dallas Council for Foreign Visitors, at the World Trade Center ☏ 744-3109.

Communications

Long-distance delivery *Emery Airfreight* ☏ 574-6300; *Federal Express* ☏ 358-5271; *Sky Courier* ☏ (800) 336-3344; *United Parcel Service*, 10155 Monroe ☏ 350-3342.
Local delivery *The Secretary's Choice*, 3720 Walnut Hill Ln ☏ 352-1732; *Wingtip Couriers*, 910 N Central Expwy ☏ 826-8690.
Post office *Main Post Office*, 400 N Ervay ☏ 767-5648; open Mon–Fri, 8–5. *D/FW Post Office*, at southwest end of the airport ☏ 574-2685 offers 24hr service for express mail; for other services Mon–Fri, 8–5.
Telex *Action Telex*, 6390 LBJ Fwy, Suite 105-E ☏ 661-2913; *Southwest Data Terminals*, 11052 Shady Trail, Suite 207 ☏ 956-7744.

Conference/exhibition centers

The largest facility is the *Dallas Convention Center*, 650 S Griffin St ☏ 658-7000, with banquet and meeting rooms, plus large areas for public shows.

Emergencies

Hospitals *Baylor University Medical Center*, 3500 Gaston; emergency ☏ 820-2501. *Medical City Dallas*, 7777 Forest Ln; emergency ☏ 661-7000, doctor referral ☏ 661-7072. *Presbyterian Hospital*, 8200 Walnut Hill Ln; emergency ☏ 696-7888, doctor referral ☏ 891-6060. *St Paul Medical Center*, 5909 Harry Hines Blvd; emergency ☏ 879-2790, doctor referral ☏ 879-3099.
Pharmacies *Eckesed*, 4311 Bryan at Haskell ☏ 824-4539; *Eckerd Drugs*, 2320 W Illinois Ave ☏ 331-5466; both are open 24hr.
Police (also fire and ambulance) 2014 Main ☏ 744-4444.

Information sources

Business information *Greater Dallas Chamber of Commerce*, 1201 Elm St, Suite 2000 ☏ 746-6600.
Local media The *Dallas Morning News* and the *Dallas Times Herald* are the two local dailies; a Southwest edition of *The Wall Street Journal* is also available. The monthly *D* magazine and the Chamber of Commerce's *Dallas Magazine* both contain helpful advice on sights, restaurants and entertainment.
Visitor information *Greater Dallas Convention and Visitors Bureau*, 1201 Elm St, Suite 2000 ☏ 746-6677.

Thank-yous

Florists *Biggerstaff Flowers*, 900 18th St ☏ 423-2501; *Bullard's Flowers*, 2800 Oaklawn ☏ 761-0190; *North Haven Gardens* (FTD), 7700 Northhaven Rd ☏ 691-6751; *Petals & Stems* (downtown) in the Fairmont Hotel ☏ 720-4009.
Gift baskets *Goodies From Goodman* (food), 12102 Inwood Rd ☏ 387-4804.

DENVER

Area code ☎ 303

A natural hub for business and government, Denver is the largest urban center in an eight-state area as well as Colorado's state capital. Although many of the city's petroleum-based businesses suffered from the oil recession, there has been an influx of high-tech companies along Colorado's Front Range, which extends from Fort Collins in the north to Colorado Springs in the south. The biggest employers in the metropolitan area include AT&T, Martin Marietta/Denver Aerospace, Mountain Bell, Adolph Coors, US West, Cyprus Minerals and IBM, and the state is now home to over 1,000 manufacturing and R&D firms, including Rockwell International, Digital Equipment, Hewlett-Packard, Martin Marietta, Cobe Labs and Tele-Communications.

Arriving

Stapleton International Airport

Stapleton has one main terminal with four unusually long adjoining concourses, and congestion can be extreme in the early mornings and evenings, and on Friday and Sunday evenings especially. Baggage trolleys are unwieldy; porters are stationed at baggage claim areas and at curbside check-ins. There are several restaurants and a 24hr cafeteria; currency exchange is in Concourse C, level 2 (6am–9pm). Couriers at the airport include *JCI* ☎ 363-6688, *Federal Express* ☎ 892-7981 and *Pony Express* ☎ 296-0619. Air cargo is handled by *Flying Tigers* ☎ (800) 238-5355. A new airport opens in 1993.

Nearby hotels *Airport Hilton*, 4411 Peoria ☎ 373-5730 fax 375-1157; *Registry*, Quebec St 80207 ☎ 321-3333 fax 321-3333; *Stouffer Concourse*, 3801 Quebec St ☎ 399-7500 fax 321-1966.

City link *Taxi* The quickest way to get downtown, only 6 miles/9.5kms northeast, is by cab – usually no more than a 15min drive, 30mins in rush hours (7.15–8.15 and 4.30–5.30). Cabs are available from the lower level by the baggage claim.

Limousine Stretch limos to downtown and southeast Denver locations are provided by Airport Limousine ☎ 398-2284, but you may have to wait more than 30mins for pick-up.

Car rental If your business will take you throughout the wide-ranging metropolitan area, it is best to rent a car. Major car rental companies have booths at the airport's lower level: Avis ☎ 398-5600, Budget ☎ 341-2277, Dollar ☎ 398-2323, Hertz ☎ 355-2244, National ☎ 321-7990.

Getting around

With the Rocky Mountains providing an unmistakable western orientation, Denver is quite easy to negotiate. If your business is mainly in the downtown area, walking and the free shuttle – which runs along the 16th Street Mall from Broadway Street to lower downtown – are by far the easiest ways of getting about. Traffic is not particularly heavy except during rush hours, and parking is readily available. East–west roads are generally avenues; north–south roads are streets. East–west numbering of addresses begins at Broadway, north–south at Ellsworth Avenue. The main north–south freeway is I-25; the east–west route is I-70.

Taxi Taxis do not cruise the streets, but can be found outside major downtown hotels. For a reservation, call *Yellow Cab* ☎ 777-7777 or *Metro* ☎ 333-3333.

Limousine *Prince Limousine* ☎ 295-7411 offers a 24hr service.

Car rental If you don't rent at the airport, local firms include *Alamo* ☎ 321-1176, *General* ☎ 320-1244, and *Thrifty* ☎ 388-4634.

Bus Not recommended; for information ☎ 778-6000.

Area by area

Downtown The downtown is slightly disorienting as it runs at a northeast–southwest diagonal to the rest of the city grid. As Denver's financial hub, 17th Street is thick with law firms, and oil company and major financial offices. The 16th Street Transitway Mall, a block south, has most of the city's department stores, boutiques and clothing stores and restaurants.

Lower downtown The western end of the downtown area, known as lower downtown, once the city's sleaziest district, has been extensively renovated and gentrified; it is now a choice retail area and is home to interior designers, architects and other creative businesses. Larimer Square's prestigious Victorian renovations attract shoppers and sightseers; the updated Tivoli Brewery shopping complex just off Larimer Street, a block from Larimer Square, is another smart shopping district. Sakura Square, on 19th Street between Lawrence and Larimer Streets, is the center of Denver's increasing Japanese community.

Capitol Hill East of downtown is Capitol Hill, once a most desirable residential site and today a mix of restored Victorian homes and small businesses, plus numerous government agencies and office buildings, and Restaurant Row, where you can find many of the city's newest and best restaurants. Though safe by day, the area has a high crime rate; take care after dark.

Cherry Creek North Near 1st Avenue and University Boulevard is the city's highest concentration of art galleries, chic restaurants and high-fashion boutiques. Nearby Polo Club, Country Club and Hilltop are prime Denver residential enclaves.

Denver Tech Center To the south is an area now known as the Denver Tech Center (DTC) because of its many high-tech businesses.

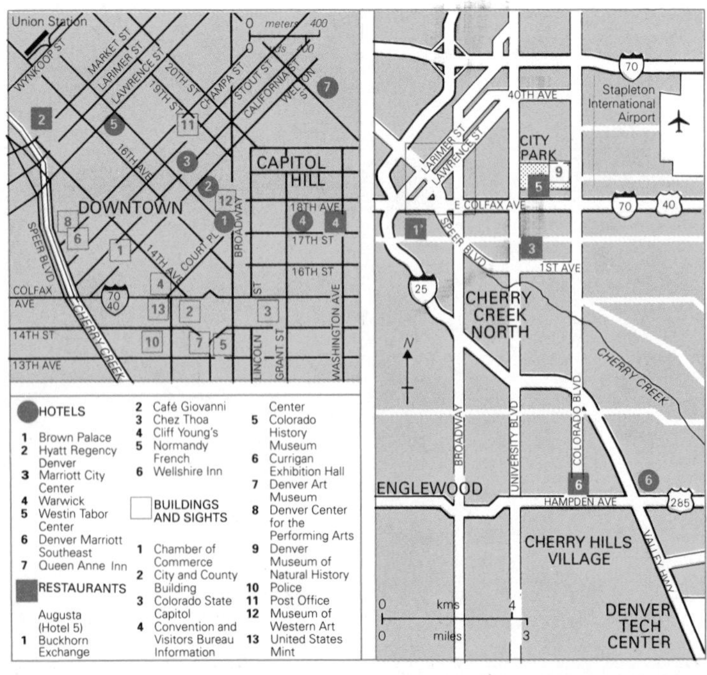

The suburbs
Cherry Hills Village, south of Denver, is the city's most affluent suburb, with expensive homes, open spaces and a criss-crossing of bridle trails. *Englewood* is a major commercial and activity center; *Lakewood*, to the west, is recreational and family-oriented. *Littleton*, 10 miles/16kms south of downtown, is the base for several national firms, such as Martin Marietta and the Manville Corporation. *Aurora* is the major employment center in the eastern metropolitan area.

Evergreen, 30 miles/48kms southwest, is a retreat where high-income executives enjoy mountain living. *Boulder*, 40mins northwest, is a university town – cultured, pricey, youthful and educated, with major high-tech businesses.

Hotels

Since 1892, the Brown Palace has been host to royalty, presidents, and celebrities. Today it faces stiff competition from several luxury downtown hotels.

Brown Palace [$]////
321 17th St 80202 ☎ 297-3111 [TX] 454416 fax 293-9204 • AE DC MC V • 230 rooms, 20 suites, 4 restaurants, 2 bars
The Brown is Denver's grandest hostelry. Because it is built as a triangle some rooms are spacious, others more cramped; ask not to be given a corner room. The Brown provides a high degree of personalized service, and its Victorian decor is both cozy and inviting. The Palace Arms is an elegant, formal restaurant. An excellent concierge takes care of most business travelers' needs. Gift shops, car rental • sauna, whirlpool, nearby health club • 11 meeting rooms.

Hyatt Regency Denver [$]///
1750 Welton St 80202 ☎ 295-1200 [TX] 452080 fax 292-2472 • AE DC MC V • 540 rooms, 27 suites, 3 restaurants, 4 bars
Close to the financial district, the Hyatt has great style. Rooms are exceptionally spacious and well-equipped, and have ample working space; suites are ideal for small meetings. The Marquis restaurant is quiet and highly valued by both local and visiting executives. Pool, tennis, jogging track, arrangement with nearby health club • 13 meeting rooms, teleconferencing.

Marriott City Center [$]///
1701 California St 80202 ☎ 297-1300 [TX] 9109312284 fax 691-3418 • AE DC MC V • 612 rooms, 2 restaurants, 3 bars, 1 coffee shop
The centrally located Marriott occupies the lower 20 floors of the ARCO Building. All rooms have good views of either the city or the Rockies. The hotel's restaurant, Mattie Silk's, is popular with the downtown business crowd. Pool, saunas, indoor tennis • 25 meeting rooms.

Warwick [$]///
1776 Grant St 80203 ☎ 861-2000 fax 832-0320 • AE DC MC V • 149 rooms, 43 suites, 1 restaurant, 1 bar
This hotel offers oversized guest rooms, all with a wet bar and private balcony. The refined restaurant is ideal for quiet dinners and business discussions. Pool, nearby health club • 9 meeting rooms.

Westin Tabor Center [$]///
1672 Lawrence St 80202 ☎ 572-9100 [TX] 4970844 fax 572-7288 • AE DC MC V • 420 rooms, 14 suites, 2 restaurants, 2 bars, 1 coffee shop
The Westin, the focal point of the Tabor Center retail and office complex, opened in 1985. Rooms are spacious, each with a refrigerator. The formal Augusta restaurant (see

Restaurants) is a local favorite with corporate executives. Health club, pool, sauna, racquetball courts, fitness center • 19 meeting rooms.

OTHER HOTELS

Denver Marriott Southeast [$]// *I-25 and Hampden Ave* ☏ *758-7000* [TX] *9109312595 fax 691-3418* • AE DC MC V. Near Denver Tech Center and convenient for the airport.

Queen Anne Inn [$]/ *2147 Tremont Pl* ☏ *296-6666* • AE MC V. Small, luxurious bed-and-breakfast establishment in a renovated Victorian house, near the central business district.

Clubs

The *University Club* ☏ 861-4267, the city's most prestigious club, and the *Denver Athletic Club* ☏ 534-1211 are popular dining spots for downtown business people. The beautifully decorated *Petroleum Club* ☏ 629-6440 offers spectacular views, but it does not buzz with the same activity as in years past. The *Metropolitan Club* ☏ 694-7344 caters largely to southeast Denver business people.

Restaurants

Although locally grown beef is still a favorite, it has been joined by more sophisticated Continental fare; California wines dominate most lists. All restaurants listed provide nonsmoking areas, and almost none imposes dress codes.

Augusta [$]//
Westin Tabor Center Hotel
☏ *572-9100* • *closed Sun & Mon* • AE DC MC V

One of Denver's best, this restaurant is popular both for business lunches and evening entertaining. The emphasis is on American cuisine – steaks, chops, roast beef, big salads, shrimp cocktails – with a rotisserie for duckling and rabbit. The decor is elegant Art Deco.

Buckhorn Exchange [$]/
1000 Osage St ☏ *534-9505* • *closed major holidays* • AE DC MC V • *reservations advisable*

Denver's oldest restaurant is an institution, its walls overflowing with western memorabilia, including period figurines, costumes, vintage photos and hunting trophies. Buffalo burgers, pot-roast sandwich, and elk steak are specialties. A good choice for working lunches, though slightly out of the downtown center.

Café Giovanni [$]//
1515 Market St ☏ *825-6555* • AE DC MC V • *reservations essential*

Occupying a Victorian warehouse in lower downtown, Giovanni's serves Continental cuisine to the cream of local society in opulent surroundings. Highly recommended for power lunches or dinners, or for first-class entertaining.

Chez Thoa [$]/
158 Fillmore St ☏ *355-6464* • *closed L Sat & Sun* • AE MC V

Between downtown and the Denver Tech Center, Chez Thoa offers elegantly presented French Vietnamese cuisine. It is especially popular with the younger business professionals in the area's numerous computer-based firms and is intimate enough for private conversation.

Cliff Young's [$]//
700 E 17th Ave (at Washington)
☏ *831-8900* • AE DC MC V • *reservations essential*

On the fringes of the Capitol Hill area, in Restaurant Row, Cliff Young's has great cachet and is an impressive choice for either lunch or dinner entertaining. Its wine list is extensive; its menu varied; its presentation impressive. Live violin and piano nightly.

Normandy French $/
1515 Madison at Colfax Ave
☎ *321-3311 • closed Mon and first week in Jul • AE DC MC V*
Styled after a French country inn, the Normandy has several small rooms, subdued lighting, a provincial French menu and one of Denver's largest wine lists. A good choice for talking business or entertaining.

Wellshire Inn $/
3333 S Colorado Blvd ☎ *759-3333 • AE DC MC V*
Between downtown and the Denver Tech Center in the luxurious setting of a former country club, the Tudor-style Wellshire overlooks an 18-hole golf course and is patronized by local executives who find its high-backed booths and private seating areas secluded. This is a good dinner spot, and its clubby bar is an excellent ice-breaker.

Bars

For after-hours business talk, local executives prefer the *Brown Palace*'s lobby bar which serves champagne and caviar 5–8pm. More low key is the hotel's dark and intimate *Ship Tavern*, a Denver tradition since the turn of the century. *My Brother's Bar*, 2376 15th St, is popular with younger professionals; good hamburgers.

Entertainment

For news of what's on, look at the *Rocky Mountain News* and the *Denver Post*, Friday editions.

Theater and music The *Denver Center for the Performing Arts*, 14th and Curtis ☎ 893-4000, is the major cultural center for the Rocky Mountain region. The *Helen G Bonfils Theater Complex*, part of the Center ☎ 893-4200, has its own repertory company. Avant-garde theater can be seen at *Germinal Stage Denver* ☎ 455-7108. The *Denver Symphony Orchestra* ☎ 592-7777 performs at Boettcher Concert Hall, Denver Arts Center. The *Corner Room* in the Oxford Alexis Hotel, 1600 17th St ☎ 628-5400, features live jazz.

Nightclubs The *Comedy Works*, 1226 15th St in Larimer Sq ☎ 595-3637, also serves dinner.

Shopping

Downtown shops are interspersed with office buildings along the 16th Street Mall, served by free, circulating shuttles. Along the route are major department stores such as *May D&F*. *Homer Reed*, 1717 Tremont Pl ☎ 298-1301, is a traditional men's clothing store. Generations of women have found designer labels and high fashion at *Montaldo's*, 1630 Stout ☎ 629-1111. Also downtown is *Kohlberg's*, 1720 Champa St ☎ 292-4578, with a good selection of Indian jewelry and crafts, and an Indian silversmith. Seventy shops, including *Brooks Brothers*, and 16 restaurants are enclosed in *The Shops* at Tabor Center ☎ 534-2141, an indoor retail complex on the 16th Street Mall. Two blocks south is *Larimer Square*, a one-block collection of boutiques and restaurants, housed in restored Victorian buildings on Denver's oldest street. The *Cherry Creek North* area, on 2nd and 3rd Avenues between Josephine and Steele Streets, is full of boutiques featuring high fashion, home decorations, jewelry and crafts. *Gart Brothers*, 1000 Broadway ☎ 861-1122, sells sports gear, and for the authentic cowboy accoutrements try *Miller Stockman*, 1409 15th St ☎ 825-5339, or *Sheplers* at I-25 and at Orchard Rd, Englewood ☎ 773-3311.

Sightseeing

The most important sights in the city are the Denver Art Museum, the Natural History Museum and the Larimer Square area. If you have a day to spare, visit the spectacular Rocky Mountain National Park, some 50 miles/80kms northwest.

Colorado History Museum This modern museum provides a panorama of Colorado's history. *1300 Broadway* ☎ *866-3682. Open Mon–Sat, 10–4.30; Sun, noon–4.30.*

Denver Art Museum This 28-sided, fortress-like structure has collections of Spanish-American and Southwestern art, as well as an outstanding collection of American Indian art. *100 W 14th St* ☎ *575-2793. Open Tue–Sat, 10–5; Sun, noon–5.*
Denver Museum of Natural History Dinosaurs that span entire rooms and lifelike dioramas are the principal attractions. It also has a four-story-screen IMAX theater. *Montview St and Colorado Blvds* ☎ *322-7009.*
Museum of Western Art One block from the Brown Palace Hotel, this private collection of Western paintings and sculpture includes works by Frederic Remington and Georgia O'Keefe. *1727 Tremont Pl* ☎ *296-1880. Open Tue–Sat, 10–4.30.*
United States Mint Throughout the summer, lines form for free, 20min tours of this mint which produces 5bn coins a year. *W Colfax Ave at Checokee St* ☎ *844-4952. Open Mon–Fri, 8–3.*

Guided tours

Bus tours *Gray Line* ☎ 289-2841 runs a 2hr 30mins bus tour of Denver's highlights. *Historic Denver* ☎ 534-1858 offers both driving and walking tours.

Out of town

West of Denver, off 6th Avenue, *Red Rocks Park and Amphitheater* offers a panoramic view of Denver and the plains. Farther west, off I-70, is the *Buffalo Bill Museum and Grave* ☎ 526-0747. About an hour out of Denver on I-25 is Colorado Springs and the *US Air Force Academy*, one of Colorado's most-visited attractions. In the same area are the *Cheyenne Mt Zoo*, the *Will Rogers Shrine*, and many special-interest museums.

Spectator sports

Baseball *Denver Zephyrs* appear at Mile High Stadium, off I-25 ☎ 433-8645.
Basketball NBA Denver *Nuggets* play at 1635 Clay St ☎ 893-3865.
Football The *Broncos* play at Mile High Stadium ☎ 433-7466.

Keeping fit

Denver's dry, sunny climate lends itself to a wide variety of outdoor sports. Most of the city's major hotels have in-house fitness facilities or arrangements with private clubs. Local clubs open to visitors include the *International Athletic Club*, 1630 Welton St ☎ 623-2100, and the *YMCA*, 25 E 16th Ave ☎ 861-8300.
Golf There are six municipal courses. Most scenic is *Wellshire* ☎ 757-1352 with 18 holes, rental equipment and a good restaurant and lounge.
Jogging paths border Cherry Creek and the Platte River; together they extend for some 20 miles/32kms.
Skiing Skiing begins within an hour west of Denver. Some of the closest resorts are *Loveland* ☎ 569-2288, *Keystone* ☎ 468-2316, and *Winter Park* ☎ 726-5514. Cross-country skiing is popular in the mountains (inquire at *Keystone* ☎ 534-7712 or *Snowmass* ☎ 923-2000) and – for the short time that snow remains on the ground in Denver – in the *Cherry Creek Reservoir* area as well.
Tennis The city has more than 150 public courts, including the 20-plus courts at *Gates Tennis Center* ☎ 355-4461.

Local resources

Business services

Two conveniently located firms that offer comprehensive, prompt services are *The Typehouse* ☎ 592-1369 and *Downtown Business Service* ☎ 698-5000.
Photocopying and Printing *City Wide Printing*, 520 W Colfax Ave ☎ 623-8193, *Hirschfeld Press*, 5200 Smith Rd ☎ 320-8500, and *Stop & Go Printing*, 1800 Glenarm Pl ☎ 296-7867; all will pick-up and deliver.
Secretarial Reliable agencies include *Kelly Services* ☎ 623-6262 and *Accountemps* ☎ 629-1010.
Translation *Berlitz Translation Services* ☎ 399-1845.

Communications

Long-distance delivery *United Parcel Service*, 5020 Ivy ☏ 439-3390; *Federal Express* ☏ 892-7981.
Local delivery *Speedy Messenger Service* ☏ 292-6000; *USA Direct Inc* ☏ 799-1819.
Post office General information ☏ 297-6000. The main downtown station at 1823 Stout St ☏ 297-6016 is open 7.30–5, the Terminal Annex ☏ 297-6455 24hrs.
Telex and telegram *Comspec Corporation* ☏ 773-3553 provides telex, TWX and E-Mail services; for telegrams contact *Western Union* ☏ (800) 325-6000.
Fax *Network Facsimile Service* ☏ 320-8444 is open 24hrs with pick-up and delivery.

Conference/exhibition centers

Denver's major conference facility is the downtown *Currigan Exhibition Hall*, 14th and Champa ☏ 575-5106. Next door, a 300,000 sq ft convention center opens 1990. The *Denver Merchandise Mart*, 451 E 58th Ave ☏ 292-6278, also hosts exhibitions.

Emergencies

Hospitals *Mercy Medical Center*, 1650 Fillmore St ☏ 393-3000; emergency ☏ 393-3600. *Rose Medical Center*, 4567 E 9th Ave ☏ 320-2121; 24hr emergency ☏ 3290-2455. Emergency dental treatment is available at *St Anthony Dental Service*, 4231 W 16th Ave ☏ 629-3648. For doctor referral call *Med Search*, a free service of St Joseph Hospital ☏ 837-7240.
Pharmacies *Medisave Pharmacy*, 2 S Broadway ☏ 388-3613, has a 24hr answering service, Mon–Fri, 9–6; Sat, 9–1.30; Sun, 11–3.
Police at 13th Ave ☏ 575-3127.

Government offices

US Dept of Commerce/International Trade ☏ 844-3246; *US Customs* ☏ 361-0716; *Immigration and Naturalization Service* ☏ 844-3526.

Information sources

Business information The *Denver Chamber of Commerce*, 1301 Welton St ☏ 894-8500, is a comprehensive source of business information.
Local media *The Denver Post* (business pullout Mon) and *Rocky Mountain News* are both morning dailies providing national, regional and local coverage. For magazine business coverage, see *Denver Business*; the *Daily Journal* publishes legal and construction news editions; *Colorado Business Magazine* covers area business developments. *Denver Magazine* profiles the city and its people, while *Colorado Homes & Lifestyles* features the state's architecture, leisure, and life-style.

The News Gallery, 13th and Sherman ☏ 830-2229, sells papers from around the country as well as a large selection of magazines. The *Tattered Cover Book Store*, 2955 E 1st Ave ☏ 322-7727, also has an extensive magazine rack. Denver's *Central Library* is only a few blocks from the heart of downtown at 1357 Broadway ☏ 571-2000.
Visitor information The *Convention and Visitors Bureau Information Center*, 225 W Colfax Ave ☏ 892-1505, provides special-event planning information, and an exhaustive collection of attractions brochures.

Thank-yous

Florists Credit card orders are welcome at the *Brown Palace*, 321 17th St ☏ 292-3893, and *De Miller* ☏ 399-3403.
Gift baskets *A Tisket A Tasket* ☏ 985-5297 accepts orders for personalized gift baskets, as does the *Brown Palace* ☏ 292-3893.

DETROIT

Area code ☎ 313

Detroit is dominated by the auto industry and its related suppliers and distributors. Chrysler, Ford, General Motors and Volkswagen of America have headquarters here, as do Allied Automotive and Fruehauf and Federal-Mogul. Non-related companies include American Natural Resources, Unisys, the Budd Company, K-Mart and Stroh's Brewery. The city's 20thC history is largely the story of carmakers, from the first Henry Ford and his contemporaries – Dodge, Olds and Fisher – to Henry Ford II, former first citizen, and Lee Iacocca, who saved Chrysler from extinction in the early 1980s. The city covers some 900 sq miles/2,300 sq kms. It is a major port and important financial center: NBD Bancorp and Comercia are based here. For the business visitor, it can be like having appointments in Cologne, Dusseldorf and Bonn during a single trip to the German Rhineland, such is the distance between Dearborn, Southfield and Troy, three of the major corporate and manufacturing areas. Only the financial center remains downtown near the busy Detroit River.

Arriving

Detroit Metropolitan Airport

The airport has two linked domestic terminals, with a Marriott Hotel between and concourses radiating out from each and from the connecting corridors. The usual food, bar, telephone, gift and other services are available in both terminals. Mutual of Omaha booths provide office and messenger services, desk space to rent, as well as insurance and currency exchange. The international terminal is separate. Information ☎ 942-3550.

Nearby hotels *Detroit Marriott*, Detroit Metropolitan Airport 48050 ☎ 941-9400 fax 941-9400 ext 7633. *Airport Hilton*, 31500 Wick Rd, Romulus 48174 ☎ 292-3400 fax 721-8870. *Holiday Inn*, 31200 Industrial Expressway, Romulus 48174 ☎ 728-2800 fax 728-2260. *Ramada*, 8270 Wickham Rd, Romulus 48174 ☎ 729-6300 fax 722-8740. *Sheraton*, 8600 Merriman Rd, Romulus 48174 ☎ 728-7900 fax 728-7900 ext 7100. All have courtesy pick-up services.

City link A car is really needed by anyone whose business is not confined to downtown. It is a 30min drive to downtown, 20mins to Dearborn, 40mins to Southfield, 60mins to Troy.

Taxi To get a cab, call as soon as you can – even before you claim your baggage. Reliable firms include Somerset Cab ☎ 689-7777 and Radio Cab ☎ 491-2600. Fares range from $17 to Dearborn, $25 downtown, $38 Troy.

Car rental All major companies have booths at the airport: Hertz ☎ 729-5200; Avis ☎ 942-3450; National ☎ 941-7000; Dollar ☎ 942-1905 and Budget ☎ 355-7900.

Getting around

The metropolitan area has an excellent highway system. Rush hours are 7.30–8.30, 4–5.30. A People Mover, consisting of an elevated track carrying automated cars, runs around the business district.

Taxi For short trips, taxis can be a useful alternative to driving yourself, but do not expect to hail a cab in the street: call ahead. *Checker Cab Co* ☎ 963-5005 has the largest fleet.

Car rental If you do not rent at the airport, major firms can be contacted easily from most business hotels. Parking is difficult and expensive downtown, but readily available elsewhere.

Limousine *Limousine Service* ☎ 471-0980.

Bus Services are limited and generally unreliable.

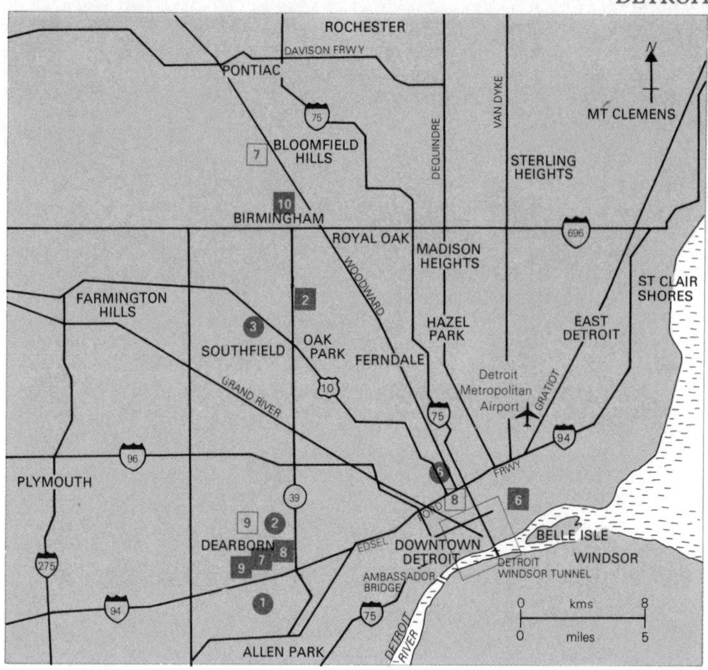

Area by area

Metropolitan Detroit has several business centers: downtown for conventions and financial firms; New Center, 3 miles/5kms north, home of General Motors; Highland Park, 3 miles/5kms farther, is Chrysler's base; and Dearborn, 12 miles/19kms west, Ford's administrative and manufacturing headquarters. Troy and Southfield are developing rapidly.

Downtown The downtown business area stretches half a mile north of the Detroit River between John Lodge and Fisher freeways, marked US-10 and Interstate 75 respectively. In this compact district are the Renaissance Center, the older established corridors of the Penobscot Building and the headquarters of American Natural Resources. Banks, utility companies, and accounting, insurance, legal and brokerage firms are downtown.

Other areas Ford World Headquarters is at Michigan Avenue and Southfield Road, *Dearborn*, with dozens of Ford offices nearby. *Southfield*, along Northwestern Highway, is home to Federal-Mogul and Allied; *Troy* has K-Mart's world headquarters on Big Beaver Road and elegant shops in Somerset Mall. *Birmingham*, due north of Detroit on Woodward Avenue, is the center of an affluent residential area. Many of the city's oldest families live in *Grosse Pointe*; chief executives tend to be in *Bloomfield Hills*; middle managers live west and northwest in Birmingham, Troy, West Bloomfield and Rochester.

Windsor, Ontario

Business travelers sometimes stay in or visit the small Canadian city of Windsor, a 5min drive in a tunnel under the Detroit River from downtown. Ford, GM, and Chrysler have plants there. Non-US visitors should check whether they need a visa to enter and that their US visa allows re-entry.

Hotels

Detroit has three major riverfront hotels in downtown – the Westin, Pontchartrain, and Omni – all near each other. In Dearborn there is the high-rise glass of the Hyatt Regency or the genteel warmth of the Dearborn Inn. The other suburban areas are served mostly by the chains and suite hotels.

Dearborn Inn [$]//
20301 Oakwood Blvd, Dearborn 48124
☎ 271-2700 fax 271-7464 • AE DC MC V • 234 rooms, 6 suites, 2 restaurants, 1 bar, 1 coffee shop
Ford executives who like old-fashioned comforts opt for this red-brick inn, built by Henry Ford in 1931 and added to over the years to create a reassuring hostelry set in ample grounds near Greenwich Village. It is still a centerpiece of Dearborn social life and is popular with many local business people for lunch or after-work cocktails in the Early American Room. The Snug bar is much favored. Bedrooms are small and filled with antiques, and the hotel's Georgian-style elegance and ambience are complemented by good leisure facilities. Gift shop • pool, tennis, arrangements with nearby health club and golf course • 12 meeting rooms.

Hyatt Regency Dearborn [$]//
Fairlane Town Center, Dearborn 48126 ☎ 593-1234 [TX] 235613 fax 593-3366 • AE DC MC V • 766 rooms, 42 suites, 3 restaurants, 2 bars, 1 coffee shop
Connected by monorail to the adjacent Fairlane shopping mall, this contemporary crescent-shaped hotel, with a 16-story atrium lobby and bronze-mirrored walls, is owned and frequented by Ford Motor Company. La Rotisserie offers fine food and good service, and Guilio's restaurant is much used by Ford and other office workers. There is dancing in the rooftop Rotunda at night. Gift shop, florist • pool, sauna, whirlpool, fitness center • 30 meeting rooms, audio-visual equipment.

Michigan Inn [$]/
16400 JL Hudson Dr, Southfield 48075 ☎ 559-6500 fax 559-3625 • AE DC MC V • 412 rooms, 12 suites, 2 restaurants, 1 bar, 1 coffee shop
On the edge of a large and slightly seedy shopping area, but with good freeway access, this full-service low-rise hotel is well-appointed, and its Benchmark restaurant has a fine menu. Southfield alternatives are chain hotels like the high-rise Holiday Inn and Hilton or suite hotels. Beauty salon, hairdresser, gift shop, florist • pool, tennis, putting green, sauna • 18 meeting rooms.

Omni International [$]//
333 East Jefferson Ave 48226 ☎ 222-7700 [TX] 5106002912 fax 222-6509 • AE DC MC V • 253 rooms, 18 suites, 1 restaurant, 1 bar
Smaller and more residential in feel than others in the city, this modern hotel is part of Detroit's attempt to revitalize downtown. It occupies 21 floors of the Millender Center and is connected to the Rennaissance Center by a skywalk. The restaurant, 333 East, is smart, with a menu featuring *nouvelle cuisine*. Pharmacy, hairdresser, beauty shop • tennis, jogging, racquetball, indoor pool, sauna, massage, weight training equipment • 4 meeting rooms.

Pontchartrain [$]//
2 Washington Blvd 48226 ☎ 965-0200 [TX] 8102215227 fax 965-9464 • AE DC MC V • Crescent Hotels • 385 rooms, 36 suites, 2 restaurants, 2 bars
The glass-sided "Pontch," as locals call it, overlooks the river and is close to the convention center on Jefferson Avenue. It gives first-class personal service, and its bars, seafood restaurants and Friday night rooftop jazz concerts are popular with downtown business people. Gift shop, complimentary executive limousine in the downtown area and to GM and Ford offices • health club/spa, pool • 9 meeting rooms, teleconferencing.

St Regis [$]//
3071 W Grand Blvd 48202 ☎ 873-3000 fax 873-3000 • AE DC MC V • Rank Hotels • 224 rooms, 18 suites, 1 restaurant, 1 bar
After a period of decline, this once-excellent establishment has been restored and now caters primarily for General Motors executives who can simply walk across the skyway bridge to GM World Headquarters. Its rooms have sleeping areas separate from their lounge/meeting spaces. The St Regis has an elegant dining room, and offers afternoon tea, Sunday brunch, a summer outdoor café (noisy, but pleasant), and evening piano music in the lobby. Its discreet bar is a favorite for after-business drinks. 4 meeting rooms.

Westin [$]//
Renaissance Center at Jefferson St Antoine 48243 ☎ 568-8000 [TX] 755156 fax 568-8146 • AE DC MC V • 1,400 rooms, 65 suites, 3 restaurants, 3 bars
Detroit's biggest and best for big conventions, and the tallest building in the city, the Westin is a popular choice for senior executives with business in the Renaissance Center. Labyrinthine passages lead off the vast and confusing atrium lobby to adjacent RenCen office towers. The 73rd-floor Summit restaurant revolves, and the main dining room, River Bistro, is very highly regarded.

The Café Rio provides Tex-Mex and Sunday brunch. The Westin has by far the best downtown business services, including word-processing and typewriter rental. Adjacent shopping mall (with post office) • health club, pool, sauna, outdoor jogging track • 27 meeting rooms.

OTHER HOTEL

Days Inn Detroit Downtown [$]

231 Michigan Ave 48226 ☎ 965-4646 fax 965-3163 • AE DC MC V. A 287-room high-rise on the trolley line five blocks north of the river and convention center.

Clubs

The finest Detroit clubs, catering to highly placed CEOs and executive VPs, are the *Detroit Athletic Club*, 241 Madison ☎ 963-9200, and the *Detroit Club*, 712 Cass ☎ 963-8600. Both offer dining, reading and meeting rooms; the former also has facilities for swimming and handball, and recently bowed to changing times and began admitting women members. Another old-line club, the *University Club*, 1411 E Jefferson ☎ 567-9280, is located in its own building and offers members a soothing, dark-paneled retreat where they can read by cozy fireplaces. A somewhat younger crowd can be found at the *Renaissance Club*, 200 Renaissance Center ☎ 259-4700, and the *Fairlane Club*, 5000 Woodview ☎ 336-4400. The latter, located in Dearborn, caters to the Ford upper echelon, while GM people are more likely to frequent the *Recess Club* in the Fisher Building ☎ 875-3554 across from GM Headquarters in downtown Detroit. For reporters, television and public relations people, the *Detroit Press Club*, 516 Howard ☎ 962-3090, provides a more informal atmosphere, and is the site of many of the city's press conferences.

Restaurants

Metropolitan Detroit has two distinct dining styles: international cuisine in cosmopolitan, often hotel-based, settings; and tiny neighborhood restaurants that reflect the varied heritage of the city's auto workers. Many restaurants are of the steak and chop variety.

Caucus Club [$]/

150 W Congress, 17 Penobscot Bldg ☎ 965-4970 • closed Sat L, Sun • AE DC MC V

Local executives meet here for chophouse-style food, a good wine list and prompt service in a warm, clubby setting. An old local favorite, on the ground floor of the Penobscot Building, the Caucus has always attracted a weighty business crowd.

Golden Mushroom [$]//

18100 West Ten Mile Rd, Southfield ☎ 559-4230 • closed Sun • AE DC MC V

Chef Milos Cihelka was the first Master Chef in the USA, and many community names come here to enjoy the low-calorie, low-cholestoral cuisine and excellent wines. It is just as renowned for its superb, calorie-packed pâté. Especially popular for business lunches in the Southfield area. The atmosphere is informal, and its mahogany booths ensure privacy.

Joe Muer Sea Food [$]/

2000 Gratiot Ave ☎ 567-1088 • closed Sat L, Sun • AE DC MC V • no reservations

The lines outside are testimony to the popularity of Detroit's oldest seafood restaurant. The atmosphere is informal and relaxing; the fish superb. They do not take reservations but serve cocktails as you wait.

London Chop House [$]//

155 W Congress St ☎ 962-0278 • closed Sun • AE DC MC V

This atmospheric basement restaurant

is where you are most likely to see Detroit's high flyers and international celebrities. It is a good place to impress downtown clients, and the Continental cuisine is much acclaimed.

Pontchartrain Wine Cellars [$]//
234 Larned ☎ 963-1785 • closed Sat L, Sun • AE DC MC V
This intimate downtown French-style bistro is usually packed with business people and leaders of Detroit's society set. The menu includes outstanding veal and seafood dishes, and the wines are excellent.

Van Dyke Place [$]///
649 Van Dyke ☎ 821-2620 • closed Mon D, Sun • AE MC V • reservations essential
You have to make a reservation at least six weeks ahead for dinner, a week ahead for lunch at this highly esteemed and elegantly restored mansion on the city's East Side. One of the city's best restaurants, with an extensive and choice wine list, the Van Dyke is an ideal place to celebrate a successful deal.

OTHER RESTAURANTS

Around the Fairlane Center and Ford World Headquarters in Dearborn are the *Kyoto Japanese Steak House*, 18601 Hubbard Dr ☎ 593-3200, and *Fairlane Charley's*, 700 Town Center Dr ☎ 336-8550, both popular local choices for informal meals. Ford people with business to discuss head to the quiet tables of the *Early American Room* at the Dearborn Inn, 20301 Oakwood Blvd ☎ 271-2700, or to the *Chambertin* in the Holiday Inn, 22900 Michigan Ave ☎ 278-6900. Residents of the affluent northern suburbs favor *Peabody's*, 154 S Hunter Blvd, Birmingham ☎ 644-5222, where they can unwind over a steak.

Bars

Business people who want to meet just for a cocktail or beer and a quiet talk tend to choose the bars in the city's hotels – whether it is a small booth in the atrium lobby of the *Westin*, a wing chair in the Golden Eagle lounge of the *Dearborn Inn*, the lobby of the *Omni*, or a corner table at the *Kingsley Inn*, 1475 N Woodward, Bloomfield Hills. But apart from the hotels, there are *Galligan's*, 519 E Jefferson, across the street from Renaissance Center, especially the roof bar in summer; *River Rock Café*, 673 Franklin, in Rivertown east of Renaissance Center, with a main floor bar and balcony bar for rock music lovers; and there is video music in the bar at *Monroe's*, 508 Monroe, atop Trappers Alley in Greektown.

Entertainment

The *Detroit Symphony Orchestra* plays at Orchestra Hall in the winter ☎ 567-1400, outdoors at Meadow Brook Music Festival on the Oakland University campus in Rochester in summer ☎ 370-2100. Major rock music events are held at *Cobo Arena* or *Joe Louis Arena* on the riverfront or north at *Pine Knob*. Broadway shows come to the *Fisher Theater* in the New Center ☎ 872-1000 or *Masonic Auditorium*, 500 Temple, downtown ☎ 832-2232.

Shopping

Three huge shopping centers dominate the suburban scene: *Fairlane Town Center*, Dearborn; *Twelve Oaks Mall*, Novi; and *Lakeside Center*, Sterling Heights. The *World of Shops* in the Renaissance Center has boutiques and shops selling everything from gourmet food to clothes; *Trappers Alley* at Festival Marketplace in Greektown has scores of specialty and novelty shops. *Maple Road*, in Birmingham, is one of the area's most pleasant shopping streets, with extravagant fashions and trendy cafés.

Sightseeing

For many business visitors based in outlying areas, sightseeing must include a trip downtown to see the modern development of Detroit's inner city. Farther afield, some travelers take advantage of Canada's proximity and attend the Shakespeare theaters in Stratford, Ontario, or go upstate to Ann Arbor, beautiful home of Michigan University.

Cranbrook Educational Institute Includes a science museum, art gallery and gardens. *500 Lone Pine Rd, Bloomfield Hills ☎ 645-3134.*

Detroit Institute of Arts Impressionist, Dutch-Flemish and African art, plus personal effects of Louis XIV and Diego Rivera murals of the auto world. *5200 Woodward ☎ 833-7900.*

Greenfield Village This 260-acre village, together with the *Henry Ford Museum*, comprise the biggest single indoor-outdoor museum complex in North America; to see everything would take at least two days. The village has the house where Henry Ford was born, Thomas Edison's Menlo Park laboratory, the Wright brother's bicycle shop and Harvey Firestone's farm, as well as a 16thC pilgrim house. *20900 Oakwood Blvd, Dearborn ☎ 271-1620.*

Spectator sports

Baseball The *Detroit Tigers* play at Tiger Stadium, Trumball at Michigan Ave ☎ 962-4000.

Basketball The *Pistons* appear at the Palace of Auburn Hills, 3777 Lapeer ☎ 377-8200.

Football The *Lions* kick off at the Silverdome, 1200 Featherstone, Pontiac ☎ 335-4151.

Horse-racing The two most popular tracks are *Hazel Park Harness Raceway*, 1650 East Ten Mile Rd, Hazel Park ☎ 398-1000, and *Ladbrokes Detroit Race Course*, 28001 Schoolcraft Rd, Livonia ☎ 525-7300.

Ice hockey Detroit's *Red Wings* play at Joe Louis Arena, 600 Civic Center Dr ☎ 567-6000.

Keeping fit

Most Detroit hotels have pools and either a fitness center or arrangements for guests with private health clubs. Some Dearborn hotels have guest privileges at the *Fairlane Club*, 5000 Fairlane Woods Dr, Dearborn ☎ 336-4400, including indoor and outdoor tennis courts.

Golf *Oakland Hills Country Club* is considered by some the area's best private club. Public courses include the *University of Michigan* course in Ann Arbor ☎ 663-5005; the *Oakland University* course north in Rochester ☎ 370-4150; and the *Rackham* in Huntington Woods ☎ 398-8430.

Jogging Downtown fitness fanatics congregate on Belle Isle, and there are frequent city marathons.

Sailing You can rent sailboats and motorboats at St Claire Shores.

Skiing When the snow is right, Mt Brighton ☎ 229-9581 is just a 1hr drive from downtown; an alternative is Alpine Valley, west of Pontiac ☎ 887-4183.

Local resources

Business services

Photocopying and printing There are copy shops all over downtown Detroit, but for pick-up and delivery contact *National Reproductions Corp*, 443 E Larned ☎ 961-5252, which has 12 offices metro-wide, with at least one providing 24hr service. In downtown, *American Speedy Printing Center*, 525 E Jefferson ☎ 963-3600, open Mon–Fri, 8.30–5.30.

Secretarial *Employers Temporary Services Inc*, 11220 Whittier Ave ☎ 372-7700; *Kelly Services Inc*, 100 Renaissance Center, Suite 1650 ☎ 259-1400.

Translation *Berlitz Translation Service* ☎ 874-2777 downtown; ☎ 642-9335 northern suburbs.

Communications

Long-distance delivery *Federal Express* ☎ 961-8771. *Purolator* ☎ (800) 645-3333 is popular for Canadian destinations.

Local delivery *Direct Delivery*, 34th floor, Book Bldg ☎ 595-7700, for same-day metro-wide deliveries. *United Parcel Service* ☎ 261-8500 is used by many firms for reliable next-

day local service, but they need 24hrs notice for pick-up.
Post office The main downtown office, 1401 W Fort ☎ 226-8675, has a 24hr stamp machine; Dearborn office, 3800 Greenfield Rd ☎ 337-4728. The Troy office, 2844 Livernois ☎ 689-6262, and the Southfield office, 22200 W 11 Mile Rd ☎ 357-3310, both have a 24hr self-service lobby.
Telex *Financial Exchange of Michigan*, 536 Shelby ☎ 962-7296.

Conference/exhibition centers

Cobo Hall, on the riverfront downtown at E Jefferson and Washington Blvd ☎ 224-1010, has 700,000 square feet of exhibition space, and expansion is under way. Contact *Detroit Civic Center*, 1 Washington Blvd ☎ 224-1010, or *Metropolitan Detroit Convention and Visitor Bureau*, 100 Renaissance Center, Suite 1950 ☎ 259-4333.

Emergencies

Hospitals *Henry Ford Hospital*, W Grand Blvd ☎ 876-2600, is in New Center area; for emergencies or doctor appointments ☎ 593-8100 in Dearborn, ☎ 254-1670 in Sterling Heights, ☎ 689-5200 in Troy and ☎ 661-4100 in West Bloomfield; AE MC V accepted. *Beaumont Hospitals* ☎ 551-5000 in Royal Oak and ☎ 828-5100 in Troy, accept MC and V.
Pharmacies *Perry Drugs* has metro-wide locations open daily; some are open 24hrs, including that at 5650 Schaefer Ave, Dearborn ☎ 581-3280.
Police City of Detroit, 1300 Beaubien ☎ 224-4400; Dearborn ☎ 943-2240; Oakland County Sheriff ☎ 858-5000; Wayne County Sheriff ☎ 224-2222; state police ☎ 256-9636.

Government offices

US Federal Information Center ☎ 226-7016; *US Customs information* ☎ 226-3158; *US Dept of Commerce/International Trade* ☎ 226-3650.

Information sources

Business information *Greater Detroit Chamber of Commerce*, 600 W Lafayette ☎ 964-4000, offers information about local companies and development prospects.
Local media *Detroit Free Press* is the city's morning daily favored by liberal readers; *Detroit News*, a morning and afternoon daily, is larger and more conservative. Both have daily business pages and Sunday business sections. *Metropolitan Detroit* and *Detroit Monthly* are magazines with good coverage of the city's dining and entertainment scene.
Visitor information *Metropolitan Detroit Convention and Visitors Bureau*, 100 Renaissance Center, Suite 1950 ☎ 259-4333. For a recorded list of current events ☎ 298-6262. For state information contact *Michigan Travel Bureau* ☎ (800) 292-2520.

Thank-yous

Florists *Floraline International*, 1 Parklane, Dearborn ☎ (800) 221-4417 provide a 24hr flower or gift basket service.
Gift baskets *Michigan Sampler Co*, 11849 E Seven Mile Rd ☎ 994-4331, takes telephone credit card orders.

FORT WORTH

Area code ☏ 817

Only 30 miles/48kms from Dallas, Forth Worth is developing from its traditional reliance on land, cattle and oil to high tech and has attracted the head offices of retailers Tandy and the Advanced Robotics Research Institute. It also houses the headquarters of Burlington Northern Railroad and AMR, both in the transportation business.

Arriving

Dallas/Forth Worth International Airport is about 40mins by cab northeast of Fort Worth. The "T" runs a bus service to downtown (see *Dallas*).

Getting around

Taxi Don't expect to be able to hail a cab; telephone ahead. Try *American Cab Company* ☏ 332-1919.
Limousine *CandleRidge Limousine* ☏ 292-5468; *Carey Limousine* ☏ (800) 214-263-7298; or *Barron Limousines* ☏ 263-8611 are the major firms.
Car rental Rental firms at the airport include: *Avis* ☏ 335-3211; *Budget* ☏ 336-6600; *Hertz* ☏ 332-5205; and *National* ☏ (800) 335-1030.
Bus The "T", the public transport service, has a free zone downtown and a low basic fare elsewhere ☏ 870-6200.

Area by area

Downtown is the central business district and where the best hotels are found. Landmarks are the glass Texas American Bank Tower; the Post Office; Texas & Pacific Railway Passenger Station; and the twin towers of the Tandy Corporation.
Northside Just 3mins north of downtown, this historic district once had the world's largest livestock market.
Eastside New middle-class, residential area on the I-30 artery to Arlington; headquarters of the Advanced Robotics Reseach Institute.
Southside Texas Christian University, the Colonial Country Club, and pockets of elegant residential development – old and new. Berkeley and Ryan Place in particular are monied residential areas.
Westside The city's oldest and most affluent residential areas – Westover Hills and River Crest – are here.

Hotels

All the hotels listed are downtown, with the exception of the Stockyards Hotel in Northside.

Hilton [$]/
1701 Commerce 76102 ☏ 335-7000 fax 335-7000 ext 7850 • AE DC MC V • 434 rooms, 4 suites, 3 restaurants, 2 bars
Overlooking the Water Gardens beside the Convention Center, the Hilton has been stylishly restored and has very professional standards of service. Executive floor, gift shop • indoor pool, jacuzzi • 19 meeting rooms.

Hyatt Regency [$]//
815 Main St 76102 ☏ 870-1234 [TX] 794826 fax 870-1234 ext 1555 • AE DC MC V • 514 rooms, 19 suites, 3 restaurants, 2 bars
Formerly the Hotel Texas, the Hyatt's old western-style exterior is complemented by a contemporary interior. The Business Center provides conference rooms for over 1,000, audio-video equipment, and secretarial assistance. Pool, health club • 18 meeting rooms.

Stockyards [$]/
109 E Exchange Ave 76106 ☏ 625-6427 fax 624-2571 • AE DC MC V • 52 rooms, 4 suites, 1 restaurant, 1 bar
The renovated Stockyards is popular with business travelers. Built in 1907, it has a grand oak staircase and a comfortable lobby, with leather Chesterfield sofas and handwoven rugs. 3 meeting rooms.

Worthington [$]//
200 Main St 76102 ☏ *870-1000 fax 332-5679* • AE DC MC V • *508 rooms, 70 suites, 3 restaurants, 1 bar*
A most elegant hotel geared to business travelers, it provides full concierge service, in-house translation and currency exchange. Pool, sundeck, health club, jacuzzi, sauna, roof-top tennis • 30 meeting rooms.

Clubs

Fort Worth's most exclusive country clubs are the *Colonial River Crest* ☏ 927-4200 or *Shady Oaks* ☏ 737-3333. Downtown there is the *Petroleum Club* ☏ 335-7571; *Fort Worth Club* ☏ 336-7211; the high-powered *Century II Club* ☏ 335-4851; and the *City Club* ☏ 878-4000.

Restaurants

Fort Worth is not a gourmet's paradise, but the following establishments supply good Tex-Mex, barbecue and Continental fare.

Angelo's [$]
2533 White Settlement Rd ☏ *332-0357* • *closed Sun* • *no credit cards* • *no reservations*
This Fort Worth institution, with its down-to-earth service, offers the best barbecue in town. Angelo's is an off-duty recommendation, a casual spot where you can be in, fed and out in 20mins.

Balcony [$]/
6100 Camp Bowie Blvd ☏ *731-3719* • *closed Sun* • AE DC MC V
Natives recommend this restaurant for its good Continental cuisine; best dishes include tournedos and fresh fish. Good for business *têtes à têtes*.

Carriage House [$]/
5136 Camp Bowie Blvd ☏ *732-2873* • AE DC MC V
The Carriage House is one of Fort Worth's oldest and most prestigious restaurants, and one of the few open for Sunday brunch. Continental food.

Joe T Garcia's [$]
2201 N Commerce ☏ *626-4356* • *no credit cards* • *no reservations*
Though the lines are always long at this casual Tex-Mex emporium, Joe T's is unbeatable for a relaxed evening. Fort Worth executives are as comfortable here as at the Carriage House, but because of the first-come-first-served policy, regard it as an off-duty spot or for a very relaxed business lunch or dinner.

Saint-Emilion [$]/
3617 W 7th St ☏ *737-2781* • AE DC MC V
A small restaurant with a good

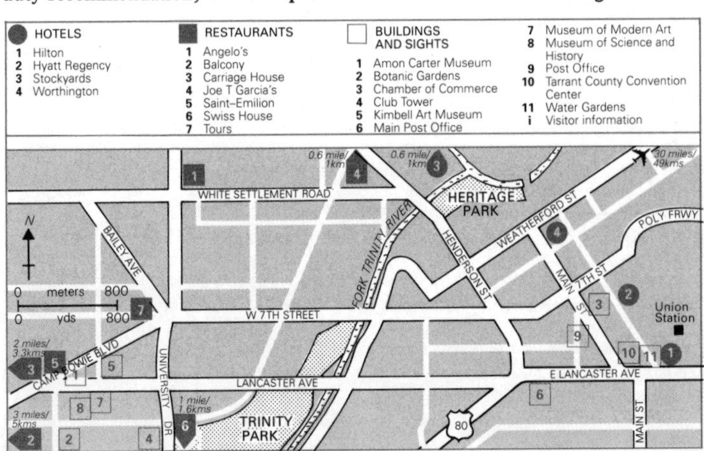

selection of grilled meats, including roast duck and lamb, plus an above-average choice of desserts. A quiet spot for business discussions.

Swiss House [$]/
1541 Merrimac Circle ☎ *877-1531* • *closed L, Sun* • *AE DC MC V*
A bastion of Fort Worth's establishment because of the good Continental food and cozy piano bar atmosphere. Another good choice for business.

Tours [$]/
3500 W 7th St ☎ *870-1672* • *closed Sun* • *AE DC MC* • *weekend reservations recommended*
Buried in a shopping center, Tours is a pleasant place for formal business dining. The menu is an interesting mixture of American, European and Mexican dishes.

Bars

For quiet conversation, you have to use the lounges of Fort Worth's major hotels; and the intimate piano bar at the Swiss House (see *Restaurants*) is also popular. *Billy Miners*, 150 W 3rd St, is more casual and lively. The *Caravan of Dreams*, 312 Houston St, part of a performing arts complex (see *Entertainment*), has an unusual and atmospheric bar.

Entertainment

Fort Worth has two major draws: the playhouse, *Casa Mañana*, 3101 W Lancaster ☎ 332-6221, which stages a range of productions, and *Billy Bob's Texas*, described as the world's best – and largest – country rock club. For what is on locally check the entertainment section of the *Fort Worth Star Telegram* or *Fort Worth Magazine*.

Music At the Tarrant County Convention Center, abbreviated to TCCC, 111 Houston, are *Fort Worth Ballet* ☎ 763-0207; *Fort Worth Opera* ☎ 737-0775; *Fort Worth Symphony Orchestra*, *Fort Worth Symphony Pops* and *Fort Worth Chamber Orchestra* ☎ 921-2676. *Cliburn Concerts* are played at several different locations ☎ 738-6509 or 738-6536. *Johnnie High's Country Music Revue* plays at the Will Rogers Auditorium, 3401 W Lancaster Ave ☎ 481-4518, every Sat at 7pm.

Nightclubs *Billy Bob's Texas*, 2520 N Commerce ☎ 624-7117, is a colony of 46 bars, indoor rodeo, restaurants, dance floor and VIP club. *Caravan of Dreams*, 312 Houston St ☎ 877-3000, has a jazz and blues club, theater and cinema. *White Elephant Saloon*, 106 N Exchange ☎ 624-1887, blasts country music – sometimes live.

Shopping

Sundance Square on Main Street downtown has book and video shops, boutiques and restaurants. *The Balcony of Ridglea*, 6333 Camp Bowie, has fashion boutiques. Major shopping malls are *Hulen Mall*, 4800 S Hulen St, and *Ridgmar Mall*, 2060 Green Oaks at I-30; on the Southside, there is the *Seminary South*.

Sightseeing

Amon Carter Museum Specializes in 19th and 20thC American art. There is also an extensive photograph collection. *3501 Camp Bowie Blvd* ☎ *738-1933. Open Tue–Sat, 10–5; Sun, 1–5.30; closed Mon.*

Botanic Gardens include 114 acres of rose gardens based on Versailles, and a Japanese Garden. *3220 Botanic Garden Dr* ☎ *870-7686. Open daily, 8am–sunset.*

Kimbell Art Museum Small but important collections of pre-Columbian sculpture, Oriental and African art, and European paintings. *3333 Camp Bowie Blvd* ☎ *332-8451. Open Tue–Sat, 10–5; Sun, 1–5; closed Mon.*

Museum of Modern Art A fine collection of modern 20thC art. *1309 Montgomery St* ☎ *738-9215. Open Tue, 10–9; Wed–Sat, 10–6.*

Museum of Science and History Contains an omnitheater as well as more usual museum exhibits. *1501 Montgomery St* ☎ *732-1631. Closed Mon.*

Spectator sports

Baseball The *Texas Rangers* play at Arlington Stadium, I-30 ☎ 273-5100, Apr–Oct.
Rodeo For weekly, year-round rodeo, *Kow Bell Indoor Rodeo* ☎ 477-3092 in nearby Mansfield; Sat and Sun 8pm for rodeo; Mon and Fri, bull riding.

Keeping fit

Fitness centers *Gym & Trim*, 6225 Sunset Dr in Ridglea ☎ 738-1986. *President's Health & Racquet Clubs*, 6833A Green Oaks Rd ☎ 738-8910, is in West Fort Worth.
Golf Visitors can play at *Meadow Brook*, 1815 Jensen Rd ☎ 457-4616; *Pecan Valley*, Ben Brook Lake ☎ 249-1845; *Rockwood*, 1851 Jacksboro Hwy ☎ 624-1771; and *Sycamore Creek*, 2423 E Vickery ☎ 535-7241.
Tennis *Mary Potishman Lard Tennis Center*, 3609 Bellaire Dr (on the TCU campus) ☎ 921-7960. The *McLeland Tennis Center*, 1600 W Seminary ☎ 921-1534.

Local resources

Business services

Photocopying and printing *The Printing Store*, 5821 Camp Bowie ☎ 731-1121; *Quik Print*, 600 Houston St Mall ☎ 336-6162.
Secretarial *Fort Worth Executive Center*, 777 Taylor St, Suite 8000 ☎ 336-0800; *Ridglea Telephone & Secretarial Service*, 5608 Malvey Ave ☎ 732-7151.
Translation *AAA Spanish Translation Service*, 4504 Wilson Ct ☎ 237-7588; *Berlitz Translation Services*, 1555 Merrimac Circle ☎ 335-4393.

Communications

Long-distance delivery *Federal Express* ☎ 332-6293.
Local delivery *Mail Call* ☎ 737-7151; *Metrocall Messengers* ☎ 572-4303; *Security Couriers*, 325 N Riverside Dr ☎ 831-6381 or (800) 442-6398.
Post office *Main Post Office*, 251 W Lancaster ☎ 334-2920; open Mon–Fri, 8.30–5.
Telex *Western Union* ☎ 335-8251; *Telequix* ☎ 265-1681.

Conference/exhibition centers

Fort Worth Tarrant County Convention Center, 1111 Houston St ☎ 332-9222; *Cowtown Coliseum*, 123 E Exchange Ave ☎ 625-1025; *Will Rogers Coliseum* ☎ 870-8150.

Emergencies

Hospitals *All Saints Episcopal Hospital*, 1400 8th Ave ☎ 926-2544; *John Peter Smith Hospital*, 1500 S Main ☎ 921-3431.
Pharmacy *Hall's Pharmacy*, 700 W Rosedale ☎ 877-3677; *open late Tue & Thu; Sat 9–2.*
Police (and fire) 350 West Belthag ☎ 274-2511, emergency ☎ 335-4222.

Government offices

Texas Consumer Credit Commission ☎ (214) 263-2016; *Small Business Administration* ☎ 334-3777; *Better Business Bureau* ☎ 334-3777.

Information sources

Business information *Fort Worth Chamber of Commerce*, 700 Throckmorton St ☎ 336-2491.
Local media The *Fort Worth Star Telegram* is the daily newspaper. For a magazine format there is *Aura Magazine*, *Fort Worth Magazine* and *The Longhorn Scene*.
Visitor information *Fort Worth Convention and Visitors Bureau*, 100 E 15th St Suite 400 ☎ 336-8791 or (800) 433-5747; *Fort Worth Visitor Information Center*, 123 E Exchange Ave. Other Visitor Information Centers are at the Museum of Science & History and the Sid Richardson Collection of Western Art, 309 Main St ☎ 332-6554.

Thank-yous

Florists *Gordon Boswell Flowers*, 1220 Pennsylvania ☎ 332-2265; *Petals*, 4919A Camp Bowie Blvd ☎ 738-0934.
Gift baskets *Coffee etc*, 6328 Camp Bowie Blvd ☎ 731-9069.

HOUSTON

Area code ☎ 713

Although Houston is one of the nation's busiest ports, a center for international finance, home of Texas Medical Center, NASA, dozens of major corporations and a wide range of manufacturing enterprises, the city's economy has been tied to oil and oil-related industries. The oil recession had a profound effect, changing Houstonian attitudes from permanent optimism to introspection. To counter its economic collapse, the city demanded relatively low taxes and no corporate or personal income tax. Developers cut rents to fill empty office space in exchange for long-term leases; housing is inexpensive and many developers from both inside and outside the city are investing in cheap real estate.

After the oil business went into decline, diversification became the trend. Scientific and biotechnological companies have started in Far North Houston; the Texas Medical Center continues to expand; and Clear Lake in southeast Houston is the home of the commercial space industry. Major firms include Texas Air, Cooper, Sterling, Compaq Computers and First City Bancorp; law firms Vinson & Elkins and Fulbright & Jaworski; engineering and construction companies Southdown, Tenneco and Baker Hughes; and the petroleum refiners Coastal, Union Texas, Shell and Pennzoil. It is a city where even the most important chief executive is likely to take a business visitor (especially one from abroad) home to meet his family or to his club.

Arriving

Intercontinental Airport Houston

IAH has three terminals, A, B and C, and a hotel between B and C. Each terminal has a 24hr bar and coffee shop and lounges for first-class passengers. Terminal A handles domestic, B and C international flights. The three terminals and the Marriott Hotel are linked by a free, 24hr "people mover." Clearing Customs takes 60–90mins. Currency exchange is available in each terminal. The white paging telephones provide 24hr multilingual information and information on air cargo.

Nearby hotels *Hilton Houston Airport*, 500 North Belt E 77060 ☎ 931-0101 fax 931-3523. *Hotel Sofitel*, 425 N Beltway 8 ☎ 445-9000 fax 445-9826. *Marriott Intercontinental Airport*, 18700 Kennedy Blvd 77032 ☎ 443-2310 fax 443-5294. *Sheraton Crowne*, 15700 Drummet Blvd 77032 ☎ 442-5100 fax 987-9130.

City link Depending on the time of day, road construction and weather conditions, it can take 45mins–2hrs to make the 22mile/35km journey into downtown Houston. Cabs, buses and limousines are available at the south exit of each terminal near the baggage claim area; rental cars are also available. Avoid the evening rush hour.

Taxi The fare to downtown Houston is about $25, though passengers may share a cab.

Car rental Rental cars are available at the west exit of the baggage claim area in each terminal. Companies include Avis ☎ 230-6800; Hertz ☎ 443-0800; National ☎ 443-8850; and Dollar Rent-A-Car ☎ 449-0161.

Bus An express bus service is run by Texas Bus Lines ☎ 523-8888 every 30mins to three stops for under $10: the downtown Hyatt Regency, the Galleria–Post Oak area and the Medical Center.

William P Hobby Airport

Accessible by either the 610 Loop or Interstate 45, Hobby Airport is 9 miles/14kms southeast of downtown and is used by domestic and commuter services.

City link *Taxi* The fare is about $15, journey time, 45–90mins.
Limousine Hobby Airport Limousine Service ☎ 644-8359 is available to downtown for $4.
Car rental Avis ☎ 641-9300; Hertz ☎ 659-8190; Ashbaugh ☎ 649-2929; and National ☎ 654-1695.
Bus Trailways operates buses half hourly to downtown.
Nearby hotel *Hobby Airport Hilton*, 8181 Airport Blvd 77061 ☎ 645-3000 fax 645-3000 ext 902.

Getting around

Three major arteries intersect Houston: Highway 59 and Interstates 10 and 45. (Houstonians often refer to freeways by their names rather than by their numbers.) Loop 610 circles the city and is often the best choice for getting quickly to your destination. If possible avoid major streets, especially Westheimer, and all freeways during rush hours (7–9, 4–6; Fri 3–7).
Taxi Taxi fares in sprawling Houston can be very expensive. You cannot hail a cab on the street, but the following companies are reliable: *Liberty Cab* ☎ 695-4321, *Yellow Cab* ☎ 236-1111 and *Cab-Jacks* ☎ 741-0000.
Car rental A car is essential for traveling in Houston. See rental agencies listed under *City link* for the two airports.
Bus Not recommended, because the system is not reliable enough, and can be confusing.

Area by area

Houston is sharply divided, with the Hispanic and black working classes living on the east side of town, close to the Ship Channel and manufacturing and construction sites. Southeast suburban towns such as Pasadena, Deer Park and Galena Park are where blue-collar workers live. The middle class has moved to the southwest, west and to the far northern suburbs. The major freeways are lined with office blocks.
The Loop The 610 Loop is a vital part of the freeway system, and serves as a geographical boundary, with homes, businesses and cultural activities designated as being inside or outside the Loop. Although most of the biggest corporations, banks and law firms are situated downtown, the Galleria–Post Oak district, just outside the Loop on the west side, is a major office and shopping area with the Transco Tower skyscraper its enormous landmark. Greenway Plaza, inside the Loop on Highway 59, is another important business and entertainment center.
Montrose and the Heights Inside the Loop are Houston's older, more established neighborhoods. Few live downtown, which is mainly deserted after dark. The Montrose area just west of downtown has the museums, galleries, top-class nightclubs and restaurants, as well as some sleazier zones. To the north of the city center is the Heights, where many grand 19thC houses have been restored.
River Oaks River Oaks, inside the Loop to the west of downtown, is the homebase of Houston wealth. Established in the 1920s, the area splendidly displays both the good taste and vulgarity of oil money.
Other areas Some small inner-city neighborhoods such as Courtlandt Place and the area around Rice University have been elegantly maintained, and are a little more subdued than River Oaks. Young professionals have gentrified the modest – though high-priced – homes in the neighborhood of West University Place. Many wealthy Houstonians prefer the Memorial area, with ranch-style houses on large, pine-filled lots to the west of River Oaks and outside the Loop. Other Houston professionals live to the southeast in Clear Lake, near the NASA complex. The area has good boating and fishing, yet is only a 30–45min drive to downtown and even nearer the petrochemical plants that line the banks of the 50-mile/80km Ship Channel, Houston's canal to the Gulf of Mexico.

Hotels

Houston hotels were hit hard by the oil recession. The once-grand Shamrock Hilton, now part of the expanding Texas Medical Center, and the downtown Sheraton have closed. But the hotels that have remained are geared to the needs of the business traveler.

La Colombe d'Or $////
3410 Montrose 77006 ☎ 524-7999
TX 272525 fax 524-8923 • AE DC MC V • 6 suites, 1 restaurant
In the Montrose Center, La Colombe d'Or is a refurbished mansion, with just six suites. Each has a separate dining room and all except the spacious penthouse are furnished with French antiques and open fireplaces. There is a well-stocked library and excellent restaurant, with Continental cuisine and an extensive wine cellar. The clientele is very distinguished.

Doubletree at Allen Center $///
400 Dallas 77002 ☎ 759-0202
TX 762544 fax 759-1166 • AE DC MC V • 353 rooms, 32 suites, 2 restaurants
Formerly owned by the French Meridien chain, the Doubletree is downtown across the street from the Public Library and close to City Hall. With marble floors, tapestries and exotic flowers, it still clings to its sophisticated French elegance. The dining room is a comfortable place for a working lunch. Business center, with secretarial services. Access to nearby health club • 6 meeting rooms.

Doubletree Post Oak $///
2001 Post Oak Blvd 77056
☎ 961-9300 TX 795315 fax 623-6685 • AE DC MC V • 455 rooms, 63 suites, 2 restaurants, 2 bars
In a parklike setting, the Post Oak has Oriental furnishings in the public areas; the rooms are country French in style, with telephones on the ample desks as well as by the beds.
7 meeting rooms.

Four Seasons $///
1300 Lamar St 77010 ☎ 650-1300
TX 784653 fax 650-8169 • AE DC MC V • 387 rooms, 12 suites, 3 restaurants, 2 bars
Convenient to the George R Brown Convention Center, the contemporary Four Seasons has become an

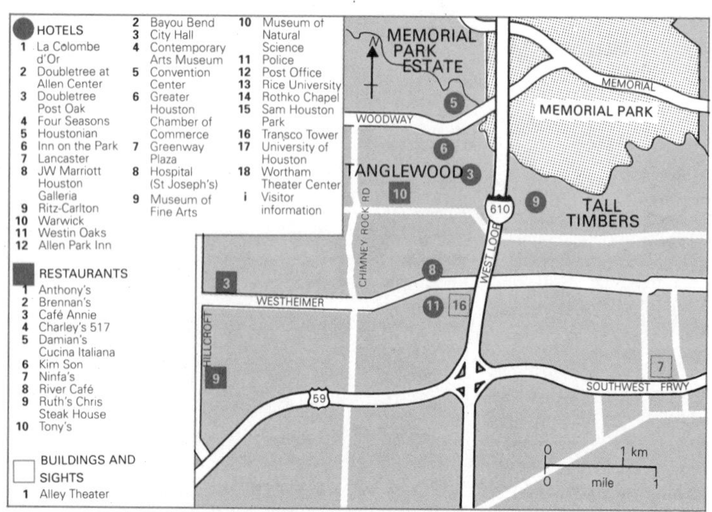

important downtown meeting place. Visiting politicians drop in on the city council's weekly breakfast club, which often meets in the De Ville restaurant. Business people use the quiet and comfortable first-floor bar and restaurant for lunch. Complimentary limousine service to downtown • pool, whirlpool, sauna, access to nearby health club • 12 meeting rooms, translation, teleconferencing, recording facilities.

Houstonian [$]////
111 North Post Oak Ln 77024
☏ 680-2626 [TX] 791810 fax 680-2626 ext 2744 • AE DC MC V • 250 rooms, 17 suites, 2 restaurants, 2 bars
The Houstonian Hotel and Conference Center was built for the fitness-conscious business traveler. On a wooded, 22-acre lot near the Galleria area, the Houstonian offers guests access to fitness center facilities including two swimming pools, racquetball, tennis and basketball, and a jogging trail. The Houston Press Club gathers in the second-floor bar Thursday evenings. 33 meeting rooms, computer rentals.

Inn on the Park [$]////
4 Riverway 77056 ☏ 871-8181
[TX] 794510 fax 871-0719 • Four Seasons • AE DC MC V • 344 rooms, 10 suites, 1 restaurant, 1 bar
One of the Four Seasons chain, this hotel is noted for its black swans and contemporary outdoor sculpture. Set slightly apart from central Houston and overlooking parkland, it has a fine *nouvelle cuisine* restaurant, an English pub and a health club with swimming, cycling and jogging, tennis and access to golf. 13 meeting rooms, translation.

Lancaster [$]///
701 Texas Ave 77002 ☏ 228-9500
[TX] 790506 fax 223-4528 • AE DC MC V • 85 rooms,-8 suites, 1 restaurant
When West Texas oilman T Boone Pickens comes to town to work on a takeover, he first takes over a suite at the tiny downtown Lancaster. The rooms are intimate and decorated with English charm, but each has three to four telephones and a sitting area adaptable for small meetings. The crowded Grill is a popular lunch spot. Computers are available on request. Access to nearby health club • 3 meeting rooms.

JW Marriott Houston Galleria [$]////
5150 Westheimer 77056 ☏ 961-1500

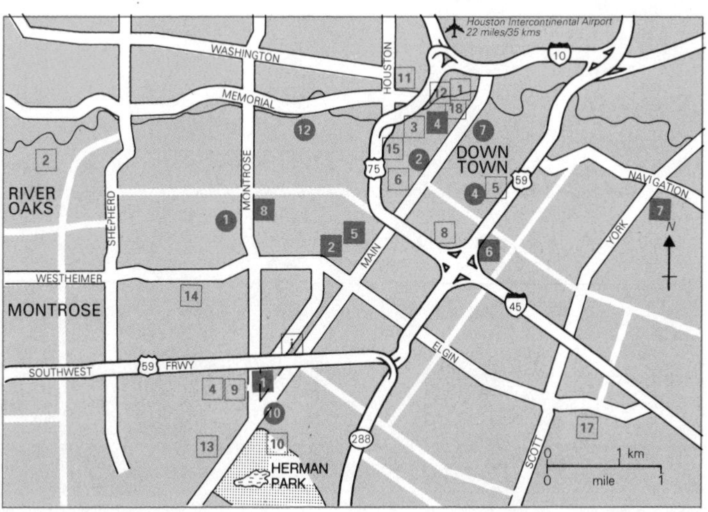

TX 755704 *fax 961-5045* • AE DC MC V • *476 rooms, 42 suites, 2 restaurants, 4 bars*
In the heart of the Galleria shopping district, this Marriott (previously the Inter-Continental) is another favorite with fitness enthusiasts. The hotel is decorated in marble and hardwood with art by contemporary Houston artists. Rooms have three phones, including one in the bathroom. The hotel aims to appeal particularly to businesswomen, with an emphasis on security. There are full-length mirrors, hairdryers and skirt hangers in each room. Drugstore, hairdresser, gift shops • health club, pool, tennis, sauna, whirlpool, racquetball • 9 meeting rooms.

Ritz-Carlton $////
1919 Briar Oaks Ln 77027
☎ *840-7600* TX *765536*
fax 840-7600 • AE DC MC V •
221 rooms, 27 suites, 2 restaurants
An intimate hotel decorated in marble, wood and French tapestries, the Ritz-Carlton offers excellent personalized service. Bankers from the nearby Galleria area often hold business breakfasts and lunches here; private dinners for up to eight can be arranged in the wine cellar. Formerly the Remington on Post Oak Park, it is adjacent to the heliport. 5 meeting rooms, law library, teleconferencing.

Warwick $///
5701 Main 77251 ☎ *526-1991*
TX *762590 fax 528-3128* • AE DC MC V • *250 rooms, 49 suites, 3 restaurants*
Across from the Museum of Fine Arts on the edge of Hermann Park, and a short cab ride to the Texas Medical Center, the Warwick is elegantly furnished, with European wood paneling and Aubusson tapestries. It is the first-choice for many visiting corporate VIPs, politicians and celebrities. Free facilities at the nearby Houston Health Club • 7 meeting rooms.

Westin Oaks $///
5011 Westheimer 77056 ☎ *623-4300*
TX *4990983 fax 960-6553* • AE DC MC V • *400 rooms, 20 suites, 2 restaurants*
The Westin's large rooms are decorated in earth tones and pastels; some are furnished with antiques and all have well stocked refrigerators. Useful for those with business in the Galleria, the hotel is within the huge shopping mall. Nonsmoking rooms • pool, health club, tennis • 11 meeting rooms.

OTHER HOTEL
Allen Park Inn $//
2121 Allen Pkwy 77019 ☎ *521-9321 fax 521-9321 ext 410* • AE DC MC V. About a mile from the downtown area; 24hr restaurant.

Restaurants

Houston restaurants tend to specialize in regional or ethnic foods: Creole, barbeque, seafood, Chinese, Vietnamese and Mexican. The emphasis is not so much on elegant service and elaborate recipes as on big servings, fresh ingredients, lots of liquor and wine, and a friendly, casual atmosphere.

Anthony's $//
4611 Montrose ☎ *524-1922* • *closed L Sat & Sun* • AE MC V
This Montrose lunch spot is the favorite of Houston's smart social set. Excellent antipasti, pasta and seafood.

Brennan's $//
3300 Smith ☎ *522-9711* • AE DC MC V • *jacket*
The Brennan family became famous for Creole food in New Orleans, and maintains its tradition in Houston. In a beautifully renovated brick house just south of downtown, the restaurant attracts many business diners. The seafood and the Sunday brunch are especially recommended.

Café Annie [$]/
5860 Westheimer ☏ *780-1522 • closed Sat L, Sun, Mon* • AE DC MC V
Even his competitors call owner-chef Robert Del Grande the most innovative restaurateur in town: his regional experiments include redfish baked in a sesame crust with coriander and Texas venison with chestnut ravioli. There is a quiet bar at the front, and the dining room tables are well-spaced.

Charley's 517 [$]///
517 Lousiana ☏ *224-4438 • closed Sat L, Sun* • AE DC MC V • *jacket*
A huge wine list, a gleaming, mirrored interior and the best lamb around attracts the business community at lunch time and theater, symphony and opera-goers in the evening. One of the few fine restaurants downtown.

Damian's Cucina Italiana [$]//
3011 Smith ☏ *522-0439 • closed Sat D, Sun* • AE DC MC V
This boisterous restaurant is not a fancy spot, but is still a favorite for casual business entertaining and top-class Italian food.

Kim Son [$]
1801 St Emmanuel ☏ *222-2461* • AE DC MC V
Vietnamese immigrants have introduced their cuisine to Houston. Kim Son, one of several Vietnamese restaurants, is large, modestly priced and slightly noisy; it is used by many Houston businessmen as well as Vietnamese locals. Recommended are barbecued pork with vermicelli, spring rolls with shrimp and fresh mint, and fresh crabs with lemon and black pepper.

Ninfa's [$]
2704 Navigation Rd ☏ *228-1175* • AE MC V
In a poor Hispanic neighborhood, this was the first of Ninfa Laurenzo's chain of popular restaurants, and is still preferred by many business people. The specialties are *tacos al carbon* with flour tortillas, washed down with powerful margaritas or Mexican beer.

River Café [$]/
3615 Montrose ☏ *529-0088 • closed Sat L* • AE DC MC V
The River Café is an established meeting place for artists and journalists, with a fine bar, plenty of elbow room and a mesquite grill that offers fish, steak and sausage with inventive sauces.

Ruth's Chris Steak House [$]//
6213 Richmond ☏ *789-2333 • closed Sat L* • AE DC MC V
With oil company logos plastered on the walls, this steak house was the independent oilmen's meeting place until the oil depression. It still offers massive pieces of well-marbled, aged beef and powerful martinis.

Tony's [$]///
1801 S Post Oak Blvd ☏ *622-6778 • closed Sat L, Sun* • AE DC MC V • *jacket and tie*
With its mixture of Continental and *nouvelle* dishes, its huge wine cellar (with over 100,000 bottles), and its resident gossip columnist (Maxine Messinger of the *Houston Chronicle*), Tony's is *the* place to be seen in Houston, and one that will impress any top-ranking client or business contact.

Clubs

The *Coronado* ☏ 659-2426 is the meeting place of the city's biggest names. The *Petroleum Club* ☏ 659-1431 attracts corporate oil executives. One of the city's oldest clubs, the *Houston* ☏ 225-1661, is often used for working breakfasts. Many lawyers belong to the *Ramada Club* ☏ 652-2932, and up-and-coming business people lunch at the *Houston City Club* ☏ 840-9001, a short drive from downtown at Greenway Plaza. The city's two most important country clubs are the *Houston Country Club* ☏ 465-8381 and *River Oaks* ☏ 529-8530.

Bars

Hotel bars are the business executive's favorites for a quiet drink. Of the independent bars, *La Carafe*, 813 Congress ☏ 229-9399, in one of Houston's few 19thC buildings downtown on Market Square, features Piaf and Streisand on the jukebox, and a varied clientele. *Grif's Inn*, 3416 Roseland ☏ 528-9912, is the Montrose sports bar. *Paradise Bar and Grill*, 401 McGowen ☏ 937-7772, on the edge of downtown, is a meeting place for professionals and liberal politicians. *Marfreless*, 2006 Peden ☏ 528-0083, offers classical music, sofas, dim lighting and elegant decor. *Cody's*, 3400 Montrose ☏ 522-9747, has a 10th-floor view and is a popular after-work spot. Houston is also the home of the "ice house," a beer joint that grows up around a tiny grocery store.

Entertainment

Houston has top-class companies in opera, ballet, symphony and theater, and the opening in 1987 of the twin-theater *Wortham Center*, Civic Center, 615 Louisiana ☏ 237-1439 or 222-4240, gave the opera and ballet a glamorous new base. It also has several comedy clubs, and a wide variety of touring performances. For information and tickets, contact *Showtix* ☏ 785-2787 or *Ticketron* ☏ 526-1709.

Theater and music The biggest and best theaters are the *Alley*, 615 Texas ☏ 621-0119, *Chocolate Bayou* ☏ 528-0119 and *Stages*, 3201 Allen Pkwy ☏ 527-8243. The *Houston Grand Opera*, the *Houston Symphony* and the *Houston Ballet* all have strong national reputations; contact *Showtix* ☏ 785-2787. The *Society for Performing Arts* ☏ 227-1111 showcases outstanding musical performers.

Nightclubs *Rockefeller's*, 3620 Washington ☏ 861-9365, attracts top rock 'n' roll and blues musicians; *Fitzgerald's*, 2706 White Oak ☏ 862-7625, is a rival, with a full range from country to jazz. *Anderson Fair*, 2007 Grant ☏ 528-8576, is a folk coffee house from the 1960s. The jazz upstairs at the *Blue Moon*, 1010 Banks ☏ 523-3773, takes place in a lively atmosphere.

Shopping

Houston boasts 13 shopping malls where you can visit up to 100 different shops under one air-conditioned roof. Major department stores include Macy's, Dillard's, Foley's and JC Penney. *El Mercato del Sol* is a mall specializing in Mexican goods.

On Westheimer and South Post Oak, is *Galleria*, the ultimate in Houston's upmarket shopping, the place to find designer clothes and jewelry, and its restaurants will revive the flagging shopper.

Outside of Houston, 20 miles/35kms north of the center, is Spring Texas. In Old Town Spring old homes have been restored and set up as a focus for the craft industry. Quilts and country-style goods are for sale. In Spring Town Market you'll find antiques, old jewelry and other "collectables."

Sightseeing

Visitors may enjoy seeing the island city of Galveston, an hour's drive away on Interstate 45, for its touristy Strand, the square-rigged ship *Elissa* and its wooden houses photographed by Cartier-Bresson.

Astrodome The world's first domed stadium is now the nation's smallest, but the guided tour is still popular; wear walking shoes. *8400 Kirby ☏ 799-9544. Tours daily at 11, 1 and 3.*

Bayou Bend The beautifully landscaped former home of philanthropist Ima Hogg is filled with American and Texan antiques. *1 Westcott Dr ☏ 529-8773. Tours (1hr 30mins) by reservation only.*

Contemporary Arts Museum The polished aluminium siding conceals exhibition space for contemporary artists of national and regional fame. *5216 Montrose ☏ 526-3129. Open Tue–Sat, 10–5; Sun, noon–6.*

Museum of Fine Arts The permanent collection features Italian Renaissance painting. There is a growing sculpture garden by Isamu Noguchi and a first-class photographic collection. *1001 Bissonnet* ☏ *526-1361. Open Tue–Sat, 10–5; Thu, 10–9; Sun, 12.15–6.*

Museum of Natural Science Displays of oil technology and the gem and mineral collection are the museum's high spots. *1 Hermann Circle Dr in Hermann Park* ☏ *526-4273. Open Sun & Mon, noon–5; Tue–Sat, 9–5.*

NASA–Lyndon B Johnson Space Center It is a 45min drive on Interstate 45 from downtown to rockets, spacecraft and moonrocks at the visitors' center; tours of Mission Control and the Skylab training room by reservation only. *2102 NASA Rd 1* ☏ *483-4321. Open 9–4 daily; guided tours hourly beginning at 10.*

Rothko Chapel This ecumenical chapel houses 14 paintings by the modern master Mark Rothko. Barnett Newman's sculpture, the *Broken Obelisk*, is outside. *3900 Yupon St* ☏ *524-9839. Open 9–6.*

Sam Houston Park Run by the Harris County Historical Society, the downtown park has six restored 19thC buildings filled with antique furniture and decorative arts. *Bagby and Lamar* ☏ *655-1912. Open Mon–Sat, 10–4; Sun, 1–5; tours every 30mins.*

Guided tours

The *Port of Houston* ☏ 225-4044 offers a free, 2hr boat tour of the Houston Ship Channel, artery of much of the city's wealth. Reservations are needed at least two weeks in advance.

Spectator sports

Baseball The *Houston Astros* play at the Astrodome, Interstate 610 at Kirkby Dr ☏ 799-9500.

Basketball The *Rockets* are at the Summit, 10 Greenway Plaza ☏ 627-0600.

Football The *Oilers* play at the Astrodome ☏ 797-1000.

Keeping fit

Fitness centers Most Houston hotels either have facilities or arrangements with a nearby club. The most prominent are the *Houstonian*, on the same lot as the hotel ☏ 680-2626; the *Texas Club*, 601 Travis (downtown) ☏ 227-7000; and the *Downtown YMCA*, 1600 Louisiana ☏ 659-8501. *Hank's Gym*, 5320 Elm, ☏ 668-6219, is for serious bodybuilders.

Basketball *Fonde Recreation Center*, Sabine at Memorial ☏ 247-1000, has the best pickup basketball games in town, with college and professional athletes occasionally taking part.

Bicycling Bicycles can be rented from *Recycled Cycles*, 7921 Westheimer ☏ 977-1393. There is a good bike path from the Sabine Street Bridge downtown along Buffalo Bayou.

Golf The central public courses are at *Memorial Park* ☏ 862-4033 and *Hermann Park*, 6201 Golf Course Dr ☏ 525-3388.

Jogging The most popular jogging track is a partially shaded 3-mile/5km loop in Memorial Park, 4 miles/6.5kms from downtown; another lines Buffalo Bayou from downtown. The heat and humidity can be overwhelming.

Tennis The best public tennis facilities are the municipally run *Memorial Park Tennis Center*, 600 Memorial Loop Dr ☏ 861-3765, with 18 courts, showers, lockers and a pro shop.

Local resources

Business services

Inside the Loop, *SRC Secretarial*, 5615 Kirby Dr ☏ 522-5926, offers 24hr service and a full range of typing and transcription. Also inside the Loop is *Legal Documents, Etc*, 4119 Montrose ☏ 529-4710. Hotels in the Galleria area frequently call *Nancy Sellers and Associates*, 770 S Post Oak Ln ☏ 961-3223. Full services plus conference rooms are available in the Galleria area at *Front Office*, an executive suite service at 1 Riverway ☏ 840-8611.

Photocopying and printing *Kinko's* offers cheap photocopying services downtown at 1430 San Jacinto ☏ 654-8161 and two other locations. *Kwik-Kopy* has offices downtown ☏ 659-1054, Galleria ☏ 960-9393 and at many other locations.
Translation *Berlitz Translation Services*, 3100 Richmond ☏ 529-8110; *ILS-International Language Service*, 2650 Fountainview, Suite 120 ☏ 783-1035.

Communications

Long-distance delivery *Federal Express* ☏ 667-2500; *Emery* ☏ (800) 443-6379; or *Purolator* ☏ 672-0941.
Local delivery *A & E* ☏ 225-0941 is one of the city's longest established services.
Post office The downtown office is at 401 Franklin ☏ 227-1474. For airport mail information call ☏ 226-3408.
Telex/telegram *Via Telex Company*, 9525 Katy Frwy (Interstate 10 W) ☏ 461-9849.

Conference/exhibition centers

Convention Center, 1001 Convention Center Boulevard ☏ 713-8000. For information, contact the *Greater Houston Convention and Visitors Bureau*, 3300 Main St ☏ 523-5050.

Emergencies

Hospitals *Hermann Hospital*, 6411 Fannin ☏ 797-4011; *Houston Northwest Medical Center*, Holcombe Blvd (at Fannin) 1960 West ☏ 440-1000; *Methodist Hospital*, 6565 Fannin ☏ 790-3311; and *St Joseph Hospital*, 1919 LaBranch ☏ 757-1000. For dental emergencies the *Houston District Dental Society* ☏ 961-4337 makes referrals. For doctors' referral, *Harris County Medical Society* ☏ 790-1838.
Pharmacies *Eckerd Drugs*, 2434 University ☏ 523-6611, is open 24hr. Another major chain is *Walgreens*, 822 Main (downtown) ☏ 223-1513.
Police 61 Reisner ☏ 222-3131; Highway Patrol ☏ 681-1761.

Government offices

US Dept of Commerce/International Trade Administration ☏ 229-2578; *US Small Business Administration* ☏ 660-4401; *Passport Assistance* ☏ 653-3160; *US Customs Entry of Merchandise* ☏ 226-2304; *US Customs Tourist Information* ☏ 443-5910; *Immigration and Naturalization* ☏ 653-3153.

Information sources

Business information The *Greater Houston Chamber of Commerce*, 1100 Milam ☏ 651-1313, and the *Houston Economic Development Council* ☏ 651-7200 provide city business and marketing data. To help businesses interested in relocating or expanding in Houston, the city has established the *One Stop Business Service* ☏ 663-7867.
Local media The *Houston Chronicle* and the *Houston Post* are the local daily newspapers. The *Chronicle* is larger and offers more complete coverage of business. The *Houston Business Journal* is a weekly all-business newspaper. *Guy's Newsstand*, 3700 Main ☏ 528-5731, and *Westheimer News*, 6427 Westheimer ☏ 781-7793, offer large selections of out-of-town publications. *Texas Monthly* magazine gives the most reliable and complete guide to what's on. *Ultra* covers the activities of the wealthy social set.
Visitor information *Greater Houston Convention and Visitors Bureau*, 3300 Main St ☏ 523-5050.

Thank-yous

Florists Houston's society florist is *Leonard Tharp*, 2705 Bammel Ln ☏ 527-9393. *The Empty Vase*, 2439 Westheimer ☏ 529-9969, does custom designs. *Basket of Flowers*, 1901 Avenue H ☏ 232-3747.

KANSAS CITY

Area codes: Missouri ☎ 816, Kansas ☎ 913

Once the major starting point for the wagon trains of settlers migrating west, Kansas City now ranks as the economic center of the American breadbasket. Agriculture, especially wheat, is big business, yet the city ranks second only to Detroit in car and truck manufacture. Other major industries include farm equipment, frozen food storage and distribution and greeting card publishing. The largest single employer is the federal government, which has many regional offices in Kansas City; the leading corporations are General Motors, Hallmark Cards, TWA and Ford. The metropolitan area, with around 1.5m residents, crosses the state line dividing Kansas and Missouri. Most of the financial corporations are in Kansas City, Missouri; the industries and factories are in Kansas City, Kansas. Johnson County, Kansas – about 20 miles/32kms from downtown – has become an important corporate area. Unless otherwise stated, area codes for ☎ numbers given are 816.

Arriving

Kansas City International Airport

Each of KCI's three C-shaped terminals has its own restaurant, shop and information booth. Baggage retrieval is adjacent to each gate on the same level of the building and it is only a short walk from disembarking to the terminal exits. Airport information ☎ 243-5237.

Nearby hotels *Kansas City Airport Marriott*, 775 Brasilia St 64153 ☎ 464-2200 fax 464-5613. *Airport Hilton*, 8801 NW 112th St 64153 ☎ 891-8900 fax 891-8030. *Holiday Inn KCI*, 11832 Plaza Circle 64153 ☎ 464-2345 fax 464-2543. *Ramada KCI Airport*, 7301 NW Tiffany Springs Rd 64153 ☎ 741-9500 fax 741-0655.

City link The airport is 25 miles/40kms, about 30–40mins by road northwest of downtown.

Taxi Except late at night, taxis are plentiful; 24 companies are licensed to operate from the airport. Agree a fare ($25–$30) before setting off. Reliable firms include Airport Transportation ☎ 421-7000.

Limousine Airport Limousine Service ☎ 921-6683.

Car rental Unless your business is confined to downtown, car rental is advisable; most major firms have desks at KCI.

Bus KCI Express ☎ 243-5950 operates to Kansas City and Johnson County. If your hotel is at the end of the route, the journey can take over 2hrs.

Getting around

Greater Kansas City follows a grid pattern; numbered streets run east–west, named streets north–south. Parking is both cheap and plentiful.

Taxi Cabs can be difficult to find on the street. Each company sets its own fare rate but rides are metred. Try *Metropolitan Transportation* ☎ 471-5000 or *Quicksilver* ☎ (913) 262-0905.

Car rental *Avis* ☎ 243-5760, *Budget* ☎ (913) 262-9090, *Hertz* ☎ 842-8484.

Bus *Metro Bus* ☎ 221-0660. For Johnson County ☎ (913) 469-8223.

Trolley *Kansas City Trolley* ☎ 221-3399 runs services between downtown, Crown Center, the Country Club Plaza, Westport and Barney Allis Plaza.

Area by area

Downtown The main business area lies just south of the Missouri River and east of the Kansas River and the state line. Legal, financial and related businesses are located here, as well as the main convention facilities. Several blocks south of route 70 is Crown Center, a prestigious development financed by Hallmark Cards

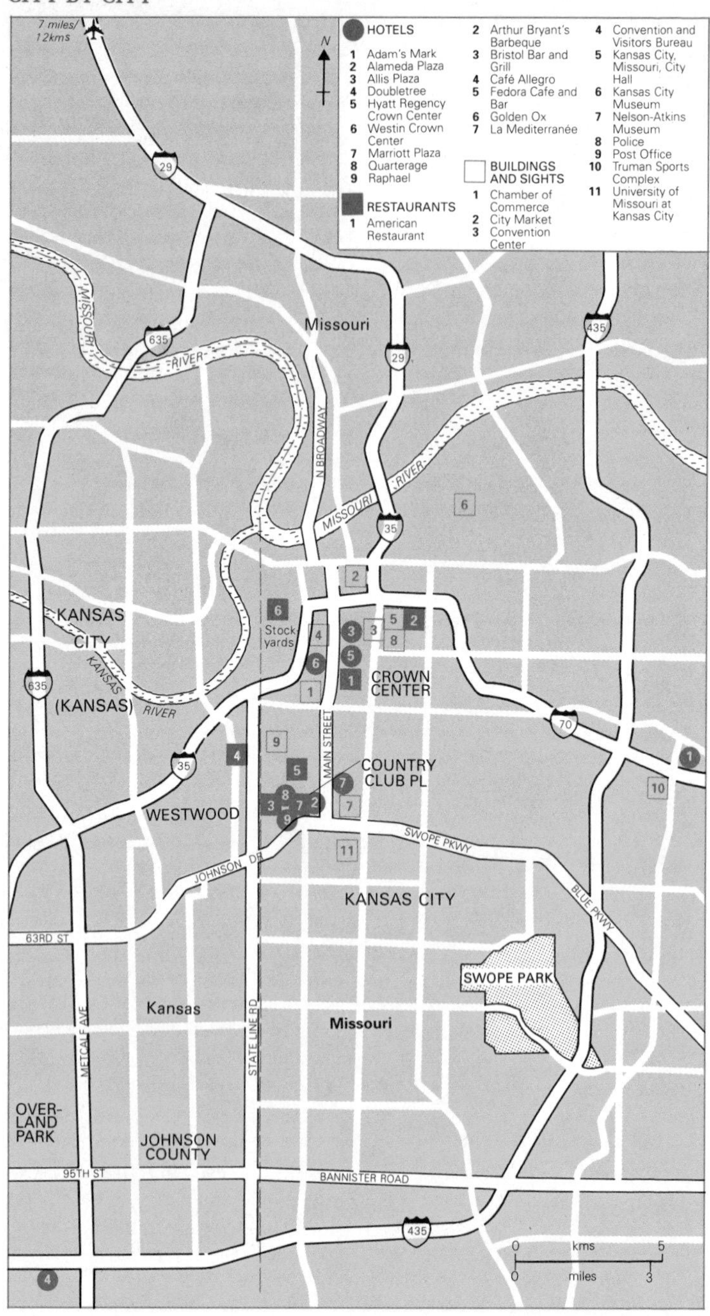

7 miles/ 12kms
N
HOTELS
1 Adam's Mark
2 Alameda Plaza
3 Allis Plaza
4 Doubletree
5 Hyatt Regency Crown Center
6 Westin Crown Center
7 Marriott Plaza
8 Quarterage
9 Raphael
RESTAURANTS
1 American Restaurant
2 Arthur Bryant's Barbeque
3 Bristol Bar and Grill
4 Café Allegro
5 Fedora Cafe and Bar
6 Golden Ox
7 La Mediterranée
BUILDINGS AND SIGHTS
1 Chamber of Commerce
2 City Market
3 Convention Center
4 Convention and Visitors Bureau
5 Kansas City, Missouri, City Hall
6 Kansas City Museum
7 Nelson-Atkins Museum
8 Police
9 Post Office
10 Truman Sports Complex
11 University of Missouri at Kansas City
Missouri
MISSOURI RIVER
N BROADWAY
KANSAS CITY (KANSAS)
KANSAS RIVER
Stock yards
CROWN CENTER
MAIN STREET
COUNTRY CLUB PL
WESTWOOD
SWOPE PKWY
JOHNSON DR
BLUE PKWY
KANSAS CITY
63RD ST
SWOPE PARK
Kansas
Missouri
METCALF AVE
STATE LINE RD
OVER-LAND PARK
JOHNSON COUNTY
95TH ST
BANNISTER ROAD
kms 0 5
miles 0 3

containing dozens of stores, restaurants, two luxury hotels, apartments and an office complex. Between route 35 and the Missouri River, City Market is where the region's farmers converge every Saturday.

Country Club Plaza About 3 miles/ 4.8kms south of Crown Center, this 14-block district, with its tiled roofs, pastel-colored buildings, wrought ironwork and fountains and modeled on Seville, Spain, is full of shops and restaurants. It is also an important business center and home to the Kansas City Board of Trade and the world's largest winter wheat market.

Westport Square The original starting point for wagons rolling westward, this area a few blocks north of Country Club Plaza has been extensively renovated and is now crammed with bars, restaurants and stores. It is very fashionable with the city's young professionals who have cultivated its casual atmosphere and established it as the center of Kansas nightlife.

Mission Hills Near to Country Club Plaza, this is Kansas's most exclusive, mansion-packed residential area. Close rivals are Country Club District, Roanoke and Rockhill.

Overland Park Quite a few telecommunications, insurance and engineering firms have been wooed across the state line to Overland Park in Johnson County. Together with nearby Leawood and Lenexa, it is also a residential area much favored by the young up-and-coming.

Hotels

Most of the de luxe, business-oriented hotels used by foreign visitors are downtown or in the Country Club Plaza area.

Adam's Mark [$]/

9103 E 39th St, Missouri 64133 ☏ 737-0200 fax 737-0200 ext 8600 • AE DC MC V • 370 rooms, 2 restaurants, 2 bars

Close to the Truman Sports Complex, this modern hotel is less formal and corporate-oriented than many, but it is nevertheless used for local meetings and conventions. Free shuttles to sporting events • health club, indoor and outdoor pools, tennis • 17 meeting rooms.

Alameda Plaza [$]//

401 Ward Pkwy, Missouri 64112 ☏ 756-1500 fax 756-1500 ext 114 • Ritz-Carlton • AE DC MC V • 390 rooms, 1 restaurant, 2 bars, 1 coffee shop

This very comfortable and elegant hotel overlooking Country Club Plaza was extensively renovated in 1989. Set in extensive gardens, it is extremely popular with local residents, especially for Sunday brunch. Health club, heated outdoor pool, tennis • 21 meeting rooms.

Allis Plaza [$]//

200 W 12th St, Missouri 64105 ☏ 421-6800 [TX] 442354 fax 421-6800 ext 4418 • AE DC MC V • 572 rooms, 2 restaurants, 1 bar

One of Kansas City's premier hotels, the Allis Plaza (formerly the Vista International) is beside the downtown Convention Center. The lobby, with its nine-tier waterfall, is a well-known local meeting place, as is the 12th Street Rag jazz club. The Harvest Restaurant attracts many corporate diners, and the executive lounges are well equipped for business visitors. Florist, gift shops, nonsmoking rooms • health club, indoor pool, tennis • 19 meeting rooms.

Doubletree [$]/

10100 College Blvd, Overland Park, Kansas 66210 ☏ (913) 451-6100 fax (913) 451-6100 ext 1966 • AE DC MC V • 357 rooms, 1 restaurant, 1 bar

Nestled among the trees, this spacious modern hotel in Overland Park caters to many regional conventions as well as local business people. Gift shop • indoor pool, racquetball, outdoor track • 11 meeting rooms.

Hyatt Regency Crown Center [$]//
2345 McGee St, Missouri 64108
☎ 421-1234 [TX] 434022 fax 435-4190 • AE DC MC V • 731 rooms, 2 restaurants, 1 coffee shop
The Hyatt is one of the city's most chic hotels. It has a popular lobby bar, J Patrick's Lounge, and the Peppercorn Duck Club serves some of the finest food in town. Nonsmoking floors, gift shop • health club, indoor pool, fitness center, tennis • 18 meeting rooms.

Westin Crown Center [$]//
1 Pershing Rd, Missouri 64108
☎ 474-4400 [TX] 426169 fax 391-4438 • AE DC MC V • 725 rooms, 49 suites, 3 restaurants, 3 bars
This de luxe hotel is part of the Crown Center Complex. Its lobby incorporates the limestone face of the hill upon which the hotel is built and features a winding stream, a five-story waterfall and tropical rain forest. It also has three lounges with live entertainment, and there is a panoramic view of downtown from Benton's Steak and Chop House. Nonsmoking floors, gift shop • health club, tennis, outdoor pool, putting green, fitness center • 8 meeting rooms.

OTHER HOTELS

Marriott Plaza [$]/ *4445 Main St, Missouri 64111 ☎ 531-3000 fax 531-3007 • AE DC MC V*. New hotel with good sports facilities.

Quarterage [$] *560 Westport Rd, Missouri 64111 ☎ 931-0001 fax 931-0001 ext 157 • AE DC MC V.*

Raphael [$]// *325 Ward Parkway, Missouri 64112 ☎ 756-3800 fax 756-3800 ext 2199 • AE DC MC V.*

Clubs

The most prestigious downtown dining club is the *River Club* at 611 W 8th St ☎ 221-5353. Others with business significance are the *Kansas City Club*, located in a stately 14-story building at 1228 Baltimore Ave ☎ 421-6789, and *University Club* at 918 Baltimore Ave ☎ 474-6000. Highly esteemed country clubs in the metropolitan area are the *Kansas City Country Club*, 62nd St and Indian Ln ☎ 362-8103; the *Carriage Club*, 5301 State Line ☎ 363-1310; the *Mission Hills Country Club*, 5400 Mission Dr ☎ (913) 722-5400; *Indian Hills Country Club*, Tomahawk Rd and Cherokee Ln ☎ (913) 362-6200; and *Blue Hills Country Club*, 777 W Burning Tree Dr ☎ 942-3292.

Restaurants

Many of the city's best restaurants are located in the Country Club Plaza. The city is best known for its steaks and barbecues.

American [$]//
200 E 25th St ☎ 471-8050 • closed L, Sun • AE DC MC V
Atop Crown Center, the American offers sweeping views of downtown and serves dishes such as Gulf shrimp creole, rock salt hobo steak and braised South Dakota pheasant in juniper sauce. The decor is modern, the atmosphere private and relaxed.

Arthur Bryant's Barbecue [$]
1727 Brooklyn Ave ☎ 231-1123 • no credit cards • no reservations
This unsalubrious restaurant is a "must" for devotees of pork ribs and brisket beef sandwiches. The secret of its success lies in Mr Bryant's unique spicy, peppery sauce.

Bristol Bar & Grill [$]/
4740 Jefferson Ave ☎ 756-0606 • closed L, Sun • AE DC MC V
A great place for oysters or broiled salmon, the Bristol, with its Victorian architecture and modern art, is a favorite of the city's young professionals for a brunch, snack or a

business meal. The back room is particularly striking, with a huge Tiffany leaded-glass dome.

Café Allegro [$]//
1815 39th St ☎ 561-3663 • closed Sat L, Sun • AE DC MC V
Much frequented by the city's upper crust, the Allegro has menus offering everything from Cajun to *nouvelle* American cuisine. A place for social rather than business entertaining.

Fedora Café & Bar [$]/
210 W 47th St ☎ 561-6565 • AE DC MC V
This Art Deco, European café-style restaurant, serving Continental cuisine, attracts the trendy business set in Country Club Plaza. Although fairly formal, it can be noisy.

Golden Ox [$]/
1600 Genessee Ave ☎ 842-2866 • AE DC MC V
Located in the center of the Stockyards, near Kemper Arena, the Golden Ox is a good choice for informal meals. Its steaks are said by many to be the best in town.

La Mediterranée [$]/
4742 Pennsylvania ☎ 561-2916 • closed Sat L, Sun • AE DC MC V
This restrained elegant restaurant in the Country Club Plaza is one of the best for private business meals. The cuisine is Continental, the wine list extensive.

Bars
The Country Club Plaza attracts an older and more formal crowd than Westport Square, which is very lively at weekends.

Entertainment
Kansas is known for its jazz, but theater, ballet and opera are all well supported. Information ☎ 474-9600.
Theater and music The *Midland Center for the Performing Arts*, 1228 Main St ☎ 421-7500, presents touring Broadway hits; the *Missouri Repertory Theater*, 4949 Cherry St ☎ 276-2704, performs year-round on the University of Missouri at Kansas City campus; the *Starlight Theater* in Swope Park, an outdoor amphitheater, features musical comedy and concerts May–Sep ☎ 333-9481. Drama and musical productions are staged at the *Music Hall* in the Municipal Auditorium, 1310 Wyandotte St ☎ 421-8000; the *Lyric Theater*, 11th and Central Sts ☎ 471-4933; and the *Folly Theater*, 300 W 12th St ☎ 842-5500. *Tiffany's Attic*, 5028 Main St ☎ 561-7921, and *Waldo Astoria*, 7428 Washington Ave ☎ 523-1704, are the city's two dinner playhouses.
Jazz Some of the most popular clubs are the *Bristol Bar & Grill* (see *Restaurants*) and those at the Westin, Allis Plaza and Hyatt hotels. Jazz Hotline ☎ 931-2888.

Shopping
Westport shopping area runs from Main St to Southwest Trafficway and from 39th to 43rd Streets. It has dozens of small boutiques, specialty stores and art galleries. *Country Club Plaza*, at 47th St and JC Nichols Pkwy, has more than 100 shops, top-name stores and boutiques. *Crown Center*, at Pershing Rd and Grand Ave, has three floors of boutiques, specialty shops and Halls, a fine department store.

Sightseeing
Harry S Truman Library and Museum Contains Truman's personal and official papers. *Hwy 24 at Delaware St, Independence, Missouri ☎ 833-1225. Open daily, 9–5.*
Harry S Truman National Historic Site The home of President and Mrs Truman. *219 N Delaware St, Independence, Missouri ☎ 254-2720. Open Tue–Sun, 8.30–5.*
Kansas City Museum The 72-room mansion formerly owned by the lumber giant RA Long, features regional history exhibits, a natural history hall and a planetarium. *3218 Gladstone Blvd ☎ 483-8300. Open Tue–Sat, 9.30–4.30; Sun, 12–4.30.*

Nelson-Atkins Museum of Fine Art An outstanding Oriental & European Old Masters collection and a fine restaurant. *4525 Oak* ☎ *751-1314. Open Tue–Sat, 10–5; Sun, 1–5.*
Stockyards One of the largest stocker and feeder markets in the US. *16th and Genessee Sts* ☎ *842-6800. Auctions Tue & Wed, 9am; Thu, 10am.*

Guided tours

Kansas City Sightseeing ☎ 833-4083 offers individual and group tours. *Missouri River Queen Boat Excursions* ☎ 842-0027 operate May–Nov.

Spectator sports

Baseball *The Kansas City Royals* play at Truman Sports Complex, I-70 and Blue Ridge Cutoff ☎ 921-2200.
Football *The Chiefs* are also based at Truman Sports Complex ☎ 924-9300.

Keeping fit

Parks and Recreation Department ☎ 444-3113.
Bicycling Bikes can be rented in summer at Swope Park.
Golf *River Oaks*, 140th St and US-71, in Grandview, Missouri ☎ 966-8111.
Jogging Tracks include *Penn Valley Park*, near Crown Center.
Tennis The city has more than 200 public courts.

Local resources

Business services

Executive Center ☎ (913) 341-2399; and *Executive Suites and Fairways* ☎ (913) 362-8321 for all services.
Photocopy and printing *Sir Speedy*, 1101 Grand St ☎ 421-7137, offers pick-up and delivery service; *Quik Print*, 910 Walnut ☎ 421-3780 and 2000 Main ☎ 421-2760.
Secretarial *Kelly Temporary Services* ☎ 561-3585; *AAA Secretarial Service* ☎ 531-4615.
Translation *Language on Wings* ☎ 842-2088; *Transintex* ☎ 331-1863.

Communications

Long-distance delivery *Federal Express* ☎ (913) 661-0255.
Local delivery *Express Delivery Service* ☎ 471-2340.
Post office The main office is at 315 Pershing Rd ☎ 842-2800.
Telex Western Union ☎ (800) 325-6000.

Convention/exhibition centers

Downtown convention facilities include the *Municipal Auditorium* and *H Roe Bartle Hall* at 13th St, Broadway to Wyandotte ☎ 421-8000; and just east of the state line is the *American Royal Center*, Wyoming Ave ☎ 421-6460.

Emergencies

Hospitals *St Luke's Hospital*, 4400 Wornall Rd ☎ 932-2171; *Menorah Medical Center*, 4949 Rockhill Rd ☎ 276-8000; *Research Medical Center*, 2316 E Meyer Blvd ☎ 276-4000.
Pharmacies *Revco Discount Drug Centers* and *Osco Drug Stores* have many branches: *Osco* is at 40th and Main Sts ☎ 561-9680.
Police 1125 Locust St, Missouri ☎ 234-5000.

Government offices

US Dept of Commerce/International Trade Administration ☎ 426-3141; *US Customs* ☎ 471-8530; *Immigration and Naturalization Service* ☎ 891-0603.

Information sources

Business information *Convention and Visitors Bureau of Greater Kansas City*, 1100 Main St, Suite 2250 ☎ 221-5242 or (800) 523-5953; *Chamber of Commerce*, 920 Main St, Suite 600 ☎ 221-2424.
Local media *Time For News* newsstand at 1310 Main St carries many out-of-town newspapers and magazines. *Kansas City Times* is the morning daily.
Visitor information See *Business information.*

Thank-yous

Florist *Fiddly Fig*, 6324 Brookside Plaza ☎ 363-4313.
Gift baskets *Crabtree and Evelyn of London*, 505 Nichols Rd ☎ 531-6468.

LOS ANGELES

Area code ☏ 213

Los Angeles is a sprawling giant of megalithic proportions, a bewildering array of individual communities crammed together in an area that covers nearly 400 sq miles/640 sq kms. Projected to be America's largest city by the year 2000, LA is a lotus land that began as a Spanish mission and became a last frontier, a mecca of opportunity. Americans and Europeans come to LA for the year-round sunshine, the variety of work and entertainment, and the liberal social attitudes. Others come for work – mainly in retail and service industries – from Latin America, Southeast Asia, Mexico and Iran. The population comprises just over half Anglo-Saxon, over a quarter Hispanic, and the rest black and Asian.

Aerospace, defense, real estate, finance and tourism are all major industries, but entertainment is dominant. Many of the big-name studios and networks are now part of megacorporations: Columbia was bought by the Sony Corporation in 1989; ABC is owned by Capital Cities; and NBC belongs to General Electric. Beyond the self-contained world that is Hollywood, oil, banking and real estate have played a large part in shaping Los Angeles. Atlantic Richfield (ARCO), the Getty Trust and Occidental Petroleum have their headquarters in the city, with landmark high-rises downtown, in Westwood, and in the San Fernando Valley.

Banking has made downtown LA the second-largest financial community in the USA, and its skyline is dominated by Bank of America, First Interstate, Security Pacific and Wells Fargo; a new Pacific Stock Exchange opened in 1986. Big names in real estate include Jon Douglas. Most recent money comes from Japanese developers eager to invest in land unavailable at home and Japanese bankers looking for US mergers. Hughes Aircraft, TRW, Northrup and Burroughs represent some of the area's contribution to the US defense program: Teledyne and Magnetek are major producers of electronic equipment.

Arriving

In addition to its international airport, Los Angeles also has four suburban airports: Burbank Airport to the north in the San Fernando Valley; John Wayne Airport south in Orange County; Ontario Airport (60 miles/96kms east); and the smaller Long Beach Airport to the south.

Los Angeles International Airport

Reconstructed for the 1984 Olympics, LAX has seven terminals clustered around a horseshoe layout; buses run between the terminals every 15mins. Along the right are West Coast airlines; the left side houses national airlines such as American and United; and at the top of the horseshoe is the impressive, glass-structured Tom Bradley International Terminal.

Some gates are a distance from the entrance/exit, and access from the street is complicated; it is better to have someone meet you outside the nearby baggage area on street level. Allow an hour to get through Customs and Immigration, double that during the peak travel season May–Sep. Business centers at Terminals 1 (☏ 646-4934), 4 (☏ 646-2929) and 7 (☏ 646-7934) provide mailing, secretarial, telex and notary services, computer rental, baggage storage and conference rooms for up to eight people. Airport information ☏ 646-5252.

Nearby hotels *Sheraton Plaza La Reina*, 6101 W Century Blvd 90045 ☏ 642-1111 fax 410-1267. *Marriott*,

5855 W Century Blvd 90045 ☏ 641-5700 fax 337-5358. *Hyatt*, 6225 W Century Blvd 90045 ☏ 670-9000 fax 641-6924. *AMFAC*, 8601 Lincoln Blvd 90045 ☏ 670-8111 fax 337-1883. All take major credit cards. At *Skytel*, a mini-hotel in the southmost part of the International Terminal, you can rent a tiny room by the hour to take a nap, shower, watch TV or make phone calls; reservations ☏ 417-0200.

City link LAX is 25 miles/40kms southwest of downtown LA; the drive takes 60mins, 45mins off-peak.

Taxi Cabs line up outside the baggage claim areas at all airport terminals.

Limousine The Celebrity Airport Livery ☏ (800) 235-3248 has vans and limousines for airport pick-up.

Car rental A car is a necessity in LA. All major companies have desks at the airport, and prices are no higher than in town. Pre-arrival reservation is advisable. Avis ☏ 646-5600; Budget ☏ 670-5151; Hertz ☏ 646-4861; National ☏ 670-4950. If you want something different, Budget ☏ 659-3473 rents Ferraris, Rolls-Royces and other exotic cars at prices to match.

Bus A Supershuttle fleet of vans patrols the airport regularly, providing an inexpensive door-to-door service to any LA destination. Use the Supershuttle phone in the baggage claim area or ☏ 777-8000 to make a reservation.

Getting around

Everyone drives in LA and although the city's freeway system is fairly efficient, rush hours (7.30–10am, 3–7pm) extend a 15min drive into a 45min crawl. Thirty freeways and 13 highways criss-cross greater LA, and virtually every part of the city is within 10mins of the freeway system. The freeways, especially routes 405 and 11, are often congested. If you get impatient on the 405, take Sepulveda Boulevard; Figueroa Street is a good alternative to Route 11.

Thomas' Road Guide, a spiral-bound book of detailed maps, is an indispensable aid for visiting drivers. Look out for pedestrians approaching crosswalks: you risk an instant penalty if you don't stop.

Taxi Some drivers are recent immigrants who speak little English, take circuitous routes and may charge whatever they think the market will bear. Finding a cab in the street is generally difficult, so it is quicker and more convenient to call *Celebrity Cab* ☏ 934-6700, *LA Checker Cab* ☏ 481-1234, or *United Independent Taxi* ☏ 653-5050.

Limousine Undoubtedly the most comfortable and efficient, although expensive, way to get around. *Music Express* ☏ 849-2244 is the best of the larger firms; *White Tie* ☏ 553-6060 is the city's largest service.

Bus Except for buses operating in the downtown area, public transportation is not useful for the business visitor.

Area by area

Dorothy Parker described Los Angeles as "63 suburbs in search of a city." These are the most important and distinctive of its myriad communities.

Downtown Originally an immigrant gateway to California, the area bounded by the Harbor Freeway and Los Angeles Street and between Sunset and Venice Boulevards now comprises the city's business (but not show business) heart. Landmarks include the moated Water and Power Building on 1st Street, residential Bunker Towers, the shiny Westin Bonaventure Hotel and the twin ARCO Towers. The southwest corner houses major offices of IBM, American Express and the real estate developer Grubb and Ellis. Flower Street is the center of banking and finance and the home of several corporations with Oriental and Middle Eastern connections. Seven blocks east at 9th and Los Angeles is the garment district, and farther east still are the produce and flower markets. Los Angeles Civic Center, which includes City Hall and the Court and Records buildings, is in the northeast corner

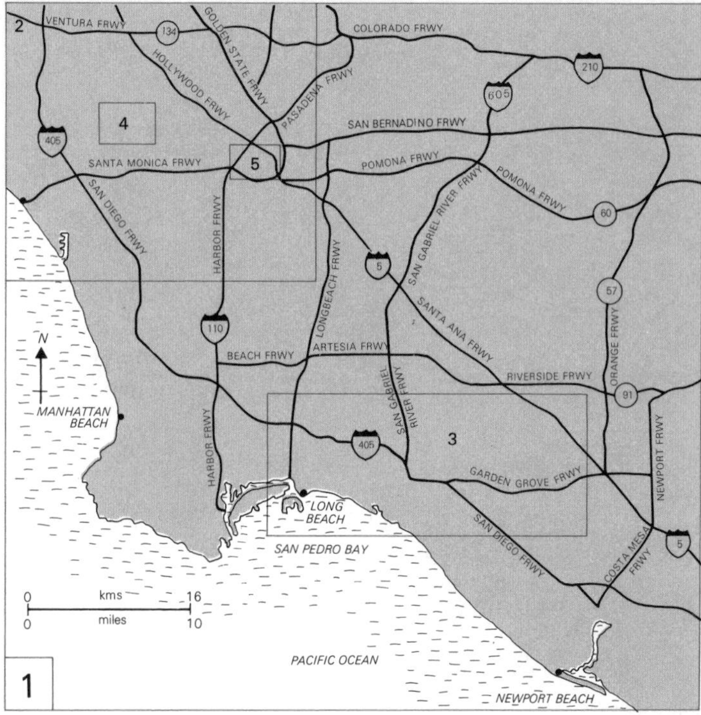

of downtown. Bordering it on the north and east are the ethnic communities of Chinatown, Little Tokyo and the Mexican area.

Mid-Wilshire Lying between downtown and Beverly Hills, mid-Wilshire has been colonized by some businesses, mainly legal, clerical and employment firms. Landmark buildings include Texaco, Pacific Telephone and Cannon Films headquarters. North of Wilshire, from Wilton Street to La Brea Avenue, Hancock Park and Larchmont Village are elegant, monied residential districts for prosperous downtown executives, with wide, tree-lined streets.

Hollywood Today's Hollywood is a far cry from the romanticized, illusionary image generally fostered. Since the Hollywood Freeway sliced across the city, the area has become principally one of sleazy shops and runaway teenagers. But some remnants of former splendor remain. Paramount Studios still preside on Melrose Boulevard, and Warner Holly Studios now occupy the old Goldwyn studios on Santa Monica Boulevard.

West Hollywood A city incorporated in its own right, West Hollywood is a burgeoning, prosperous business and residential area. It has a strong gay population, a busy art and design trade and talent agencies.

Beverly Hills Money – both the acquisition and the spending of it – is the key to Beverly Hills. There is no limit to how much you can spend or what you can buy. The area has little industry, but there are many lawyers, doctors and plastic surgeons, besides entertainment industry agents and the corporate offices of film companies.

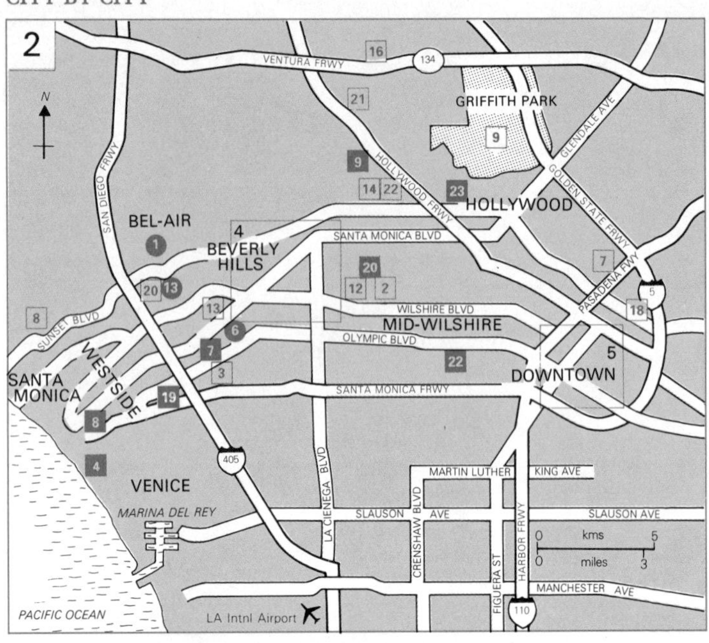
2
N
VENTURA FRWY
16
134
21
GRIFFITH PARK
9
9
HOLLYWOOD FRWY
GLENDALE AVE
GOLDEN STATE FRWY
14 22
23
HOLLYWOOD
SAN DIEGO FRWY
BEL-AIR
1
4
BEVERLY
HILLS
SANTA MONICA BLVD
20
7
PASADENA FRWY
5
20 13
12 2
8
SUNSET BLVD
13
WILSHIRE BLVD
18
6
MID-WILSHIRE
WESTSIDE
7
OLYMPIC BLVD
22
5
DOWNTOWN
SANTA
MONICA
3
19
SANTA MONICA FRWY
8
405
4
MARTIN LUTHER KING AVE
VENICE
MARINA DEL REY
SLAUSON AVE
SLAUSON AVE
LA CIENEGA BLVD
CRENSHAW BLVD
FIGUERA ST
HARBOR FRWY
0 kms 5
0 miles 3
MANCHESTER AVE
PACIFIC OCEAN
LA Intnl Airport
110

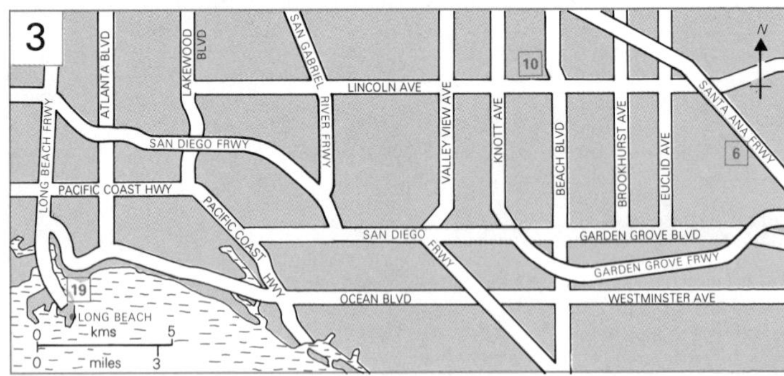
3
N
ATLANTA BLVD
LAKEWOOD BLVD
SAN GABRIEL RIVER FRWY
LINCOLN AVE
10
SANTA ANA FRWY
LONG BEACH FRWY
SAN DIEGO FRWY
VALLEY VIEW AVE
KNOTT AVE
BEACH BLVD
BROOKHURST AVE
EUCLID AVE
6
PACIFIC COAST HWY
PACIFIC COAST HWY
SAN DIEGO FRWY
GARDEN GROVE BLVD
GARDEN GROVE FRWY
19
OCEAN BLVD
WESTMINSTER AVE
LONG BEACH
0 kms 5
0 miles 3

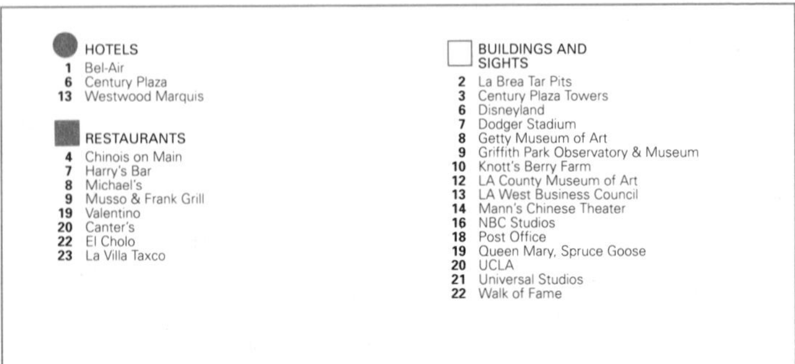
HOTELS
1 Bel-Air
6 Century Plaza
13 Westwood Marquis
RESTAURANTS
4 Chinois on Main
7 Harry's Bar
8 Michael's
9 Musso & Frank Grill
19 Valentino
20 Canter's
22 El Cholo
23 La Villa Taxco
BUILDINGS AND SIGHTS
2 La Brea Tar Pits
3 Century Plaza Towers
6 Disneyland
7 Dodger Stadium
8 Getty Museum of Art
9 Griffith Park Observatory & Museum
10 Knott's Berry Farm
12 LA County Museum of Art
13 LA West Business Council
14 Mann's Chinese Theater
16 NBC Studios
18 Post Office
19 Queen Mary, Spruce Goose
20 UCLA
21 Universal Studios
22 Walk of Fame

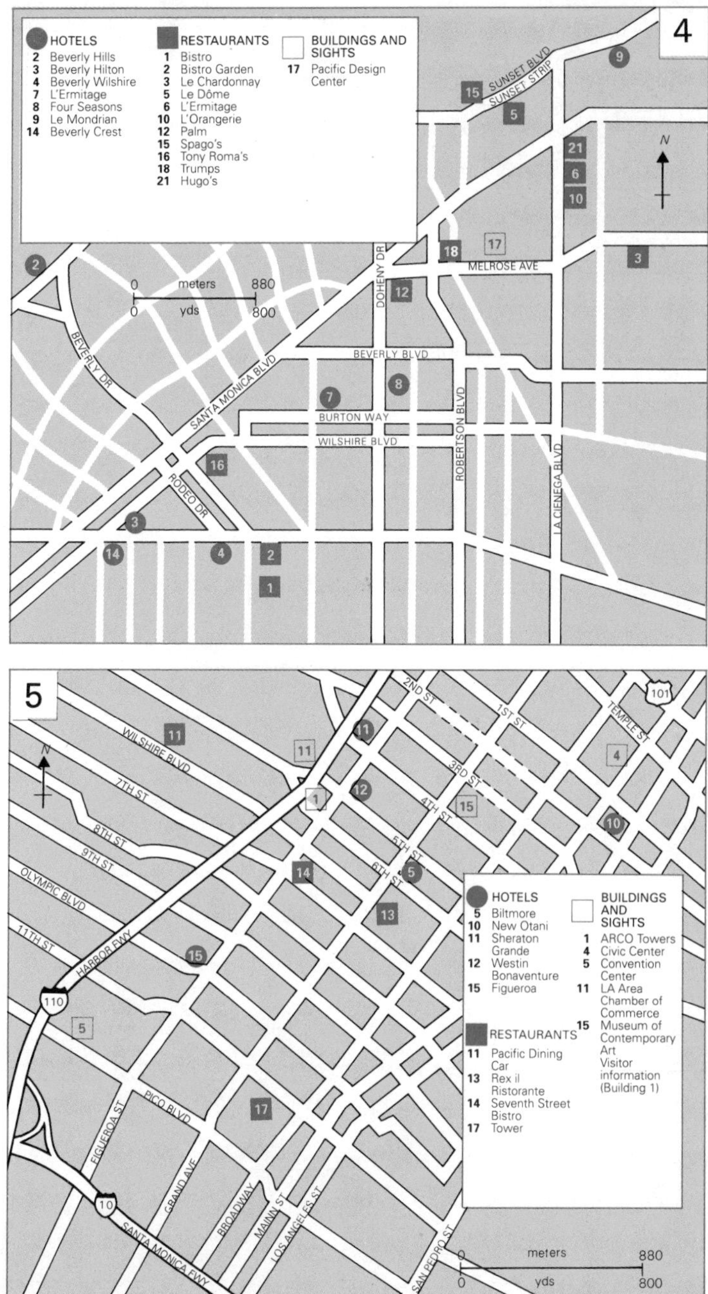
4
HOTELS
2 Beverly Hills
3 Beverly Hilton
4 Beverly Wilshire
7 L'Ermitage
8 Four Seasons
9 Le Mondrian
14 Beverly Crest
RESTAURANTS
1 Bistro
2 Bistro Garden
3 Le Chardonnay
5 Le Dôme
6 L'Ermitage
10 L'Orangerie
12 Palm
15 Spago's
16 Tony Roma's
18 Trumps
21 Hugo's
BUILDINGS AND SIGHTS
17 Pacific Design Center
SUNSET BLVD
SUNSET STRIP
MELROSE AVE
DOHENY DR
BEVERLY BLVD
BURTON WAY
WILSHIRE BLVD
ROBERTSON BLVD
LA CIENEGA BLVD
SANTA MONICA BLVD
BEVERLY DR
RODEO DR
meters 0 880
yds 0 800
5
HOTELS
5 Biltmore
10 New Otani
11 Sheraton Grande
12 Westin Bonaventure
15 Figueroa
RESTAURANTS
11 Pacific Dining Car
13 Rex il Ristorante
14 Seventh Street Bistro
17 Tower
BUILDINGS AND SIGHTS
1 ARCO Towers
4 Civic Center
5 Convention Center
11 LA Area Chamber of Commerce
15 Museum of Contemporary Art
Visitor information (Building 1)
2ND ST
1ST ST
TEMPLE ST
3RD ST
4TH ST
5TH ST
6TH ST
WILSHIRE BLVD
7TH ST
8TH ST
9TH ST
OLYMPIC BLVD
11TH ST
HARBOR FWY
PICO BLVD
FIGUEROA ST
GRAND AVE
BROADWAY
MAIN ST
LOS ANGELES ST
SAN PEDRO ST
SANTA MONICA FWY
101
110
10
meters 0 880
yds 0 800

Century City West of Beverly Hills, Century City has an opulence of its own. When 6th Street and Wilshire Boulevard began to lose their luster as fashionable business addresses, many of LA's advertising and design agencies – for example, J Walter Thompson – moved west. The area also has many entertainment-associated firms (lawyers, accountants and management specialists), along with Tri-Star Pictures, HBO cable channel, talent agency CAA and Blake Edwards. The eye-catching twin Century Plaza Towers is the center for several publishers and show business agents, as well as executive head-hunters, and banking and insurance conglomerates and the ABC Entertainment Center are also there. Across the street are the Century Plaza Hotel and smart outdoor Century City Shopping Center.

Bel-Air Heavy with Hollywood money and prestige, Bel-Air is the fortress home of America's show business elite.

Westside generally refers to anything west of the San Diego Freeway (405) and includes Westwood, West LA, Brentwood, Santa Monica and Venice. The area is heavily residential, peopled primarily by young professionals who seek the cleaner air and outdoor activities the beach brings. Most of the area's businesses are small and service-oriented, but there are pockets of corporate activity.

Next to 405 and adjacent to Beverly Hills and Century City, *Westwood* has a handful of residential high-rises and a large federal complex. At night the streets of Westwood Village, a 12-block shopping, eating and movie-going district, are packed with UCLA students, and others seeking entertainment.

West LA is primarily a middle-class renters' high-rise residential neighborhood. To the north is *Brentwood*, wealthy and "suburban" in feel, and home to the World Bank and many celebrities who shun Beverly Hills. Although primarily a beach resort, *Santa Monica* has some corporate enterprises, law firms and high-tech companies.

Malibu, Venice, Marina Del Rey To the north of Santa Monica, on the coast, is Malibu, where celebrities, entertainment executives and others who are simply wealthy live in beachfront homes. South of Santa Monica, Venice – the focal point for hippies in the 1960s and artists in the 1970s – is now a trendy-but-funky amalgam of characters. The boardwalk (on ocean's edge) is the weekend showplace for bikers, skaters and beachers. There is no real business presence but farther south, Marina Del Rey, LA's main boating center, has many boating/nautical support-product companies as well as high-tech industries. Its proximity to LA International Airport makes Marina Del Rey an appealing alternative to staying within the airport area.

Other areas

North of LA, the *San Fernando Valley*, a massive residential overspill, has developed a personality of its own, although many residents still drive into the city daily to work. Route 101, which starts as the Hollywood Freeway and becomes the Ventura Freeway, has the Universal City complex, which includes Universal Studios, the Universal Amphitheater and MCA Records.

South of LA, orange groves have been transformed into the metropolis of *Orange County*, with the reputation of being one of the richest counties in the whole US. It is an endless housing and shopping mall development, spacious and attractive. High-tech, electronics and aerospace/defense-related industries have a significant presence.

Hotel and restaurant price bands
For the meanings of the price symbols, see page 7.

Hotels

Most of the hotels listed are clustered in Beverly Hills or downtown. If your business takes you to the suburbs, downtown, with its access to freeways, is the best choice.

Bel-Air [$]/////
701 Stone Canyon Rd 90077
☎ 472-1211 [TX] 674151 fax 476-5890 • AE DC MC V • 92 rooms, 32 suites, 1 restaurant
This secluded hotel in LA's wealthiest area attracts the international patrician set who value understated luxury, intimacy and personal service. Each room in the mission-style building has its own fireplace and exterior entrance, and most have walled patios useful for small meetings. The elegant dining room is especially popular for afternoon tea and Sunday brunch. Florist • pool • 1 meeting room.

Beverly Hills [$]////
9641 Sunset Blvd 90210 ☎ 276-2251 [TX] 691459 fax 271-0319 • AE DC MC V • 325 rooms, 2 restaurants, 1 coffee shop
The pink stuccoed Beverly Hills offers a prestigious base for top-drawer executives and movie moguls. Many rooms have patios, and there are also small poolside cabanas ideal for business entertaining or meetings. The Polo Lounge is *the* place to spot celebrities and is a favorite for important business deals. Pharmacy, florist, jeweler, barber, car rental • tennis, pool • 7 meeting rooms, screening room, translation.

Beverly Hilton [$]///
9876 Wilshire Blvd 90210 ☎ 274-7777 [TX] 194638 fax 285-1313 • AE DC MC V • 579 rooms, 47 suites, 5 restaurants, 2 bars, 2 coffee shops
Although it has less cachet than the Beverly Wilshire and is less convenient for central Beverly Hills, the Hilton is very efficient, with an extensive range of services and facilities, including a good business center. Many entertainment and social functions are held here, and Trader Vic's is popular with the entertainment crowd; Mr H does a thriving Sunday brunch. Boutiques, hairdressers, florist • pool, health club • 24 meeting rooms, notary public, translation, teleconferencing, computers, computer modems, business reference library.

Beverly Wilshire [$]////
9500 Wilshire Blvd, Beverly Hills 90212 ☎ 275-5200 [TX] 698220 fax 274-2851 • AE DC MC V • Regent International Hotels • 453 rooms, 76 suites, 2 restaurants, 3 bars, 1 coffee shop
Across Rodeo Drive, the Beverly Wilshire is favored by celebrities and high society, as well as by senior executives. Rooms are well-appointed and dignified; those in the newer wing both vary in style and cost more. The Hideaway, serving traditional and Mexican cuisine, is a popular luncheon spot for the business community. Florist, hairdresser, jeweler, bookstore • pool • 8 meeting rooms.

Biltmore [$]///
506 South Grand Avenue 90071 ☎ 624-1011 [TX] 677686 fax 612-1545 • AE DC MC V • 660 rooms, 40 suites, 4 restaurants, 3 bars
LA's *grande dame* hotel is beautifully appointed, well-maintained and has an extensive art collection throughout the rooms and halls. Adjacent to the 24-story Biltmore Tower office building and only a block's walk from the ARCO Towers, it is nearer California Plaza than other downtown hotels. Its wide range of services and facilities make it popular with those who want something more personal than the Bonaventure. Bernard's has long been one of LA's greatest hotel restaurants, and it is much used by lunching bankers, lawyers and PacTel

executives. Bank, gift shop, pastry shop • tennis at adjacent racquet club, pool, jacuzzi, massage • 18 meeting rooms.

Century Plaza $////
2025 Ave of the Stars, Century City 90067 ☎ 277-2000 TX 698664 fax 551-3355 • AE DC MC V • 1,072 rooms, 75 suites, 4 restaurants, 3 bars, 1 coffee shop
Although principally a convention center, this is the LA hotel that has been used by politicians, diplomats and every US president since it opened in 1966. It is Century City's only hotel, and its Tower complex houses one of LA's best hotel business centers, offering fax, telex, multilingual personnel, business library, computerized airline info system, secretarial, word-processing and transcription services, typewriter, dictaphone and personal computer rental, modems, VCRs, copy service, MCI Mail, Dow Jones reports and Federal Express. La Chaumière is a good French restaurant with incongruous but appealing country inn decor. Shopping arcade, car rental counters • 2 pools, outdoor jacuzzi, guest privileges at adjacent health club, tennis and golf nearby • 30 meeting rooms.

L'Ermitage $/////
9291 Burton Way, Beverly Hills 90210 ☎ 278-3344 TX 698441 fax 278-8247 • AE DC MC V • 114 suites, 1 restaurant, 1 bar
The emphasis here is on individualism, high-quality accommodation, service and luxury. The public rooms are graced with Chagalls, Renoirs, Van Goghs, and Miró sculptures. All the suites have separate sleeping areas, wet bar, private terraces, fully equipped kitchen and multi-line telephones and can accommodate small business meetings. A European-style hotel in a residential area. Complimentary limo • rooftop pool, mineral water spa, solarium • 2 meeting rooms, teleconferencing.

Four Seasons $////
Burton Way at Doheny Dr 90048 ☎ 273-2222 TX 194364 fax 859-3824 • AE DC MC V • 300 suites, 2 restaurants, 1 bar
In company with its prestigious neighbors, the refurbished Los Angeles Four Seasons provides superb views, a background of lush tropical vegetation and a cool elegance in its lounges and spacious suites. Friendly and relaxed service make this a welcoming place to stay. Gift shop • outdoor pool, fitness center, tennis, access to golf. 10 meeting rooms.

Le Mondrian $////
8440 Sunset Blvd, West Hollywood 90069 ☎ 650-8999 TX 182570 fax 650-5215 • AE DC MC V • 188 suites, 2 restaurants, 1 bar
Named after the Dutch artist Piet Mondrian, this 12-story suites-only hotel has little chance of ever blending into Hollywood's Sunset Strip backdrop. Its façade sports a huge surrealistic mural and the arty feel is continued into the lobby with a display of works by contemporary artists. Each suite has three telephones with up to five lines, and all are suitably adapted for business meetings or entertaining. Beauty salon for both men and women, complimentary limo • pool, jacuzzi • 3 meeting rooms.

New Otani $///
1st and Los Angeles 90012 ☎ 629-1200 TX 4720429 fax 622-0980 • AE DC MC V • 448 rooms, 10 suites, 3 restaurants, 2 bars, 1 coffee shop
Appropriately located in the center of Little Tokyo, the luxurious New Otani caters especially to Japanese executives. It has traditional Japanese suites and a delightful half-acre garden. The Thousand Cranes serves *tempura* and *sushi*; Commodore Perry's specializes in steaks and seafood. The Music Center, City Hall and the courts are within walking distance. Sauna, jacuzzi, massage • 8 meeting rooms.

Sheraton Grande [$]////

333 S Figueroa St 90071 ☎ 617-1133 [TX] 677003 fax 617-6055 • AE DC MC V • *470 rooms, 68 suites, 2 restaurants, 2 bars*

Popular with upper management, the Grande has unusually high standards for a Sheraton. Rooms are spacious and well-equipped for working, and there is a butler on every floor. Like the Bonaventure, the Sheraton is connected to some of LA's high-rises by walkways. Errand service • pool, arrangements with nearby health club • 23 meeting rooms, teleconferencing, and audio-visual facilities.

Westin Bonaventure [$]////

404 S Figueroa St 90071 ☎ 624-1000 [TX] 677628 fax 612-4800 • AE DC MC V • *1,474 rooms, 64 suites, 18 restaurants, 3 bars*

Designed by John Portman, the Bonaventure is one of downtown LA's most distinctive landmarks. Its five futuristic glass cylinders are linked by skywalks to the twin ARCO Towers, the Wells Fargo Building and the World Trade Center. A convention hotel with extensive facilities, the Bonaventure has a five-level mall, a maze of freeway-like passages and more than 50 shops and boutiques. There are five executive floors and two for nonsmokers. The views from the rotating Top of Five Restaurant on the 35th floor are exceptional, perhaps more memorable than the food. Tennis at adjacent racquet club, pool • 24 meeting rooms, exhibit hall.

Westwood Marquis [$]/////

930 Hilgard Ave 90024 ☎ 208-8765 [TX] 181835 fax 824-0355 • AE DC MC V • *256 suites, 2 restaurants, 2 bars*

Westwood's premier hotel is located in a residential neighborhood within walking distance of the Village. The ambience is European and intimate, the service attentive and discreet. Guests tend to be in advertising or entertainment. Florist, hairdresser, complimentary limo • 2 pools, sundeck, hydrotherapy tubs, massage, sauna, jacuzzi • 6 meeting rooms.

OTHER HOTELS

Beverly Crest [$]// *125 S Spalding Dr ☎ 274-6801 fax 372-6614* • AE DC MC V. A comfortable low-profile hotel in which to escape Beverly Hills excesses.

Figueroa [$] *939 S Figueroa St 90015 ☎ 627-8971 fax 689-0305* • AE DC MC V. Comfort, facilities (including pool) and ambience make this attractive old downtown hotel good value.

Motels There are a few motels in the beach cities just south of LAX and lots near the big theme parks in Anaheim and Buena Park. Advance reservations are advisable during the summer.

Clubs

Established powerbrokers belong to the city's oldest gentlemen's club, the *California Club* ☎ 299-2929, which does not admit women. The *University Club* ☎ 627-8651, open to anyone who has a college or university degree, does a brisk lunch and dinner business. So does the *Petroleum Club* ☎ 626-8616, where the membership now extends beyond the petroleum, oil and gas industries. In mid-Wilshire, the *Los Angeles Club* ☎ 381-7011, one of the city's biggest, is much used by the local Korean business set. The *Regency Club* ☎ 208-1443 in Westwood has some top names from politics and entertainment.

Of the numerous suburban country clubs, the oldest and most prestigious is the *LA Country Club* ☎ 276-6104. It has many members in common with the California Club: the only women admitted are member's wives, and they have to use a separate entrance. South of Beverly Hills, the *Hillcrest Country Club* ☎ 553-8911 was established by Jews who could not join the LACC. The *Bel-Air Country Club* ☎ 472-9563 is the place that positively welcomes people from the entertainment industry.

Restaurants

LA's casual atmosphere and abundance of restaurants means that business can and does go on all day – at lunch, dinner and breakfast. Lunch venues are generally determined by geography, so although most of the best restaurants are in West Hollywood, downtowners tend to eat at a few local restaurants and clubs. The entertainment industry goes to Sunset and Santa Monica Boulevards, and suburban industries like aerospace and high-tech have their own neighborhood favorites.

Bistro [$]//
246 N Canon Dr, Beverly Hills
☎ 273-5633 • closed Sun • AE DC MC V *• jacket preferred*
An old Beverly Hills standard, the Bistro caters to the political, business and Hollywood communities, and is the venue for many parties, charity functions, and society affairs. The interior is attractive, the dining room open but discreet. Food is very good French/Continental.

Bistro Garden [$]/
176 N Canon Dr ☎ 550-3900 • AE DC MC V
Sister to the Bistro, but trendier, this eating house is priced lower and does a hefty business lunch trade.

Le Chardonnay [$]//
8284 Melrose Ave, West Hollywood
☎ 655-8880 • closed Sun • AE DC MC V
A lovely turn-of-the-century bistro whose French/Californian cuisine is made distinctive by the wood rotisserie and mesquite grill. Le Chardonnay's lunch is dominated by both the entertainment and advertising industries.

Chinois on Main [$]//
2709 Main St, Santa Monica
☎ 392-9025 • closed Sat L–Tue • AE DC MC V *• reservations essential*
Chinois, Wolfgang Puck's second restaurant, opened in 1982 to the same kind of outrageous success as his first – Spago's. This "experiment" combines French and Chinese cuisine, producing delightful results. The irridescent green and maroon interior, designed by his wife, is as beautifully exotic as the food. Tables are somewhat close together, and the place gets noisy at night. Reservations four weeks in advance are usually necessary.

Le Dôme [$]//
8720 Sunset Blvd, West Hollywood
☎ 659-6919 • AE DC MC V
A tasteful restaurant featuring good French food influenced by California cuisine. Le Dôme's Sunset Strip location makes the restaurant popular with agencies, production companies and celebrities. Tables offer enough privacy for quiet conversations. The lunch and after-hours drinks are workmanlike; things get more elegant after 8.

L'Ermitage [$]/////
730 N La Cienega Blvd ☎ 652-5840 • closed L • AE DC MC V *• jacket*
This is the place for a special celebration. The fine menu at this excellent Californian-style French restaurant will appeal to any bon viveur. Specialties include lobster salad with zucchinis and truffles. The classic French decor is complemented by extravagant floral arrangements.

Harry's Bar [$]//
2020 Ave of the Stars ☎ 277-2333 • closed L Sat & Sun • AE MC V
Related to the Harry's in Venice, Florence and San Francisco, this is the premier restaurant in Century City. Fine northern Italian food is served in casual, elegant surroundings. The intimate and quietly chatty dining room is popular.

Michael's [$]///
1147 3rd St, Santa Monica
☎ 451-0843 • AE DC MC V

Everybody who's anybody has eaten at Michael's, still one of the most important dining rooms in Greater LA. White umbrellas in a garden setting are the backdrop to the Californian/French cuisine, which includes a variety of char-broiled meats, fish, and fowl. The wine list has many classics. A good choice for business discussions.

Musso & Frank Grill [$]//
6667 Hollywood Blvd, Hollywood ☏ 467-7788 • closed Sun • AE DC MC V
This, the oldest restaurant in Hollywood, caters mainly for the lower-profile, older showbiz crowd, as well as businessmen who value the restaurant's lack of trendiness. The specialty is American food served with a minimum of fuss. Spacious wooden enclosed booths afford privacy and discretion.

L'Orangerie [$]///
903 N La Cienega Blvd, West Hollywood ☏ 652-9770 • closed L • AE DC MC V
An impressive restaurant, both in its traditional French food and the opulent surroundings. Seafood and delicacies are flown in from France. Formal ambience is heightened by exotic plants and high ceilings. Open for dinner only, L'Orangerie is best for social or celebratory meals. The clientele includes wealthy people from all walks of life.

Pacific Dining Car [$]//
1310 W 6th St ☏ 483-6000 • MC V
One of LA's few 24hr restaurants, the Dining Car attracts downtown regulars for early breakfast as well as dinner. Steak is its main feature. Large tables and booths and unfussy service make it a good place to spread papers and linger.

Palm [$]///
9001 Santa Monica Blvd, West Hollywood ☏ 550-8811 • AE DC MC V
Food and atmosphere are modeled on the New York original, with sawdust on the floor, a crowded dining room and slightly hyper service. Old Hollywood stalwarts and city powerbrokers eat here; excellent steaks and French fries are the pick of the menu.

Rex il Ristorante [$]////
617 S Olive St ☏ 627-2300 • closed Sat L, Sun • AE DC MC V • jacket required • reservations essential
Located in the glamorous Oviatt Building, and reeking of old money from places like San Marino and Hancock Park, the Rex has a discreet atmosphere. The Italian cooking is *nouva*, delicate and attractively presented, complementing the smoked etched glass and shining black decor, with its Art Deco Lalique touches.

Seventh Street Bistro [$]//
815 W 7th St ☏ 627-1242 • closed L Sat & Sun • AE DC MC V
A hot downtown spot at both lunch and dinner, the Bistro is the favorite of many top executives and show-business types. Its French-style food and its popularity have contributed to the growth of the downtown scene.

Spago's [$]////
1114 Horn Ave, West Hollywood ☏ 652-4025 • closed L • AE DC MC V • reservations essential
Wolfgang Puck, who is both chef and owner, has greatly influenced Californian cooking with his creative combinations of fresh and unusual herbs and vegetables with grilled meat, fish and fowl. Located on the Sunset Strip, Spago's is one of LA's biggest celebrity hangouts. Big and noisy, it is a place to see and be seen. But even with a reservation you may have to wait.

Tony Roma's [$]/
9404 Brighton Way, Beverly Hills ☏ 278-1207 • AE DC MC V
Part of an international chain, Tony Roma's has reliably good ribs and delicious onion rings. The Beverly

Hills location offsets the decidedly funky, proletarian feel, but you come here for the spicy sauce, not the snob appeal. Lunch is busy, and Tony's is open until 1.30am.

Tower [$]///
Transamerica Center, 1150 S Olive St ☎ 746-1554 • AE DC MC V • jacket
The Tower is a well-respected French restaurant atop the 32-story Transamerica Center. Fish is the house specialty, and there is an ample wine cellar. A lunchtime favorite for downtown executives, where business can be discussed without being overheard.

Trumps [$]//
8764 Melrose Ave ☎ 855-1480 • closed Sun except for afternoon tea • AE V
A chic art-gallery-land spot with a striking interior and appealing French/Californian cuisine, Trumps is impressively contemporary but too noisy for serious talk.

Valentino [$]//
4313 Pico Blvd, Santa Monica ☎ 829-4313 • closed Fri L, Sun • AE DC MC V
Owner Piero Selvaggio's charm and enthusiasm have made this one of the best Italian restaurants in LA, with inventive food and a wine list of more than 1,100 varieties from France, Italy and California. Valentino is a popular choice for Fortune 500, IBM and McDonnell Douglas executives.

Working breakfasts
Breakfast is an important meal in LA. Most high-profile industry breakfasts take place in the city's top hotels; senior studio executives get together in the pink recesses of Beverly Hills' Polo Lounge or on the terraces of the Bel-Air. In the "others" category, *Hugo's*, 8401 Santa Monica Blvd ☎ 654-3993, is popular and *Canter's*, 419 N Fairfax Ave ☎ 651-2030, a 24hr deli in the heart of the traditional Jewish district, is an LA institution.

Mexican eating
California has many good, cheap Mexican restaurants. Two of the best are *El Cholo*, 1121 S Western Ave ☎ 734-2773 (there's always a wait of at least 20mins, but the lounge is comfortable), and *La Villa Taxco*, 4444 Sunset Blvd ☎ 665-5751.

Bars
Los Angeles, by and large, is not a city renowned for bars. The *Polo Lounge* at the Beverly Hills Hotel, 9641 Sunset Blvd ☎ 276-2251, is the haunt of Hollywood moguls, and the *Grande Avenue Bar* ☎ 624-1011 at the Biltmore, is the smartest of the downtown hotel bars. A few restaurants have good or interesting bars – for example *The Gingerman*, 369 N Bedford Dr, Beverly Hills ☎ 273-7585, owned by film duo Patrick O'Neal and Carroll O'Connor. Out in Santa Monica is the rowdy *Kings Head*, 116 Santa Monica Blvd ☎ 451-1402, an English-style pub frequented by the substantial local British émigré population.

Entertainment
The best source for news of what's on is either of two free weeklies, the *LA Weekly* and the *LA Reader*. *Ticketmaster* ☎ 480-3232 and *Ticketron* ☎ 216-6666 sell tickets to all entertainment and sporting events. *Equity Ticket Agency* ☎ 629-1241 and *Murray's* ☎ 234-0123 are ticket brokers who can arrange choice seats, at higher prices.
Theater and music The biggest, most luxurious stage theater is the *Shubert* in Century City ☎ 553-9000 where Broadway shows appear. Downtown, the *Music Center* ☎ 972-7211 has three venues, the largest of which – the Dorothy Chandler Pavilion – hosts the LA Philharmonic Orchestra. In Hollywood, *Pantages*, 6233 Hollywood Blvd ☎ 642-4242, puts on plays and musicals; *Doolittle Theater*, 1615 N Vine St ☎ 410-1062 specializes in classics.

One unique feature of LA is the large number of equity waiver theaters, which because they seat 99 or less can ignore union restrictions. For struggling actors, writers and directors, they offer a chance to work in legitimate theater. The *Greek Theater*, 2700 N Vermont Ave, ☎ 216-6666 is an impressive outdoor bowl built into the side of a hill; it has top musicians Apr–Oct. For rock'n roll, there is the Art Deco *Palace* ☎ 462-3000.

Cinemas Impressive theaters include the *Mann Chinese* (see *Sightseeing*), the *Pacific Cineramadome*, 6360 Sunset Blvd ☎ 466-3401, and the *Cineplex Theater Center* in Century City ☎ 553-4291.

Nightclubs Many clubs – most notably, the *Comedy Store*, 8433 Sunset Blvd ☎ 656-6225, and the *Improvisation*, 8162 Melrose Ave ☎ 651-2583 – feature comedians every night. The Improv has dancing Sun and Mon. The *Vine St Bar & Grill*, 1610 Vine St ☎ 463-4375, is a supper club with top-class vocal and jazz acts.

Shopping

Rodeo Drive and *Wilshire Boulevard* in Beverly Hills are the most exclusive shopping districts, with some stores open only by appointment. *Melrose Avenue* is the city's liveliest, most contemporary shopping area. New-wave and second-hand clothing mix with smart shops such as Olivia Newton-John's Koala Blue, and there are others selling gifts, records and 1950s furniture. At night, their neon signs are pure art. The *Beverly Center* at La Cienega and Beverly Boulevards ☎ 854-0074 is a major shopping mall, with department stores and boutiques, as well as 25 restaurants and a 16-movie theater complex. The *Westside Pavilion*, Pico Blvd and Overland St in West LA, is one of the city's newest malls. Some of the restaurants, like Crayons on the street level, have unique, wild decor, and the Samuel Goldwyn Theater has impressive neon.

Downtown The wholesale *jewelry district* is clustered around the International Jewelry Center on Hill St at 6th; the *garment district* is around the Cooper Building on Los Angeles and 9th St; and there are the *wholesale flower market* on San Pedro at 7th and the *product market* south on San Pedro. High-rise lobby malls include the *Bonaventure* at 404 S Figueroa, the *ARCO Plaza* at 505 S Flower, and the *Broadway Plaza* at 700 S Flower. In Little Tokyo, traditional vendors, at the *Japanese Village Plaza* on 2nd and Central, merge with luxurious high-tech toy and electronic stores (at Weller Court on 2nd and San Pedro).

Movie memorabilia *Larry Edmunds Book Shop*, 6658 Hollywood Blvd ☎ 463-3273, has one of the area's most extensive collections of film reference books and memorabilia.

Sightseeing

Hollywood landmarks Only the most avid movie buff will not be disappointed by the famous Hollywood landmarks. The only must is *Mann's Chinese Theater* (formerly Grauman's), 6926 Hollywood Blvd ☎ 464-8111, where Cary Grant, Jimmy Durante and Trigger have left their respective foot, nose and hoof prints in the cement pavement; there, too, is the *Walk of Fame*, where bronze stars are inlaid in the pavement to commemorate Hollywood's greatest.

Studio tours North over the Hollywood Hills are studio tours: the *Universal Studios Tour*, 3900 Lankershim Blvd, Universal City ☎ (818) 508-9600, is more of an amusement park ride than "peek-behind-the scenes"; and the *NBC TV Studio*, 300 W Almeda Ave, Burbank ☎ (818) 840-4444, is more technical and less anecdotal.

Griffith Park For a spectacular, panoramic view of LA, Griffith Park's Observatory can't be matched. The Observatory has a set of museum-like displays, while the Planetarium's telescope is open from sunset until late, with three shows a night at 6.30, 9.15 and 10.30 ☎ 664-1191. The park (Visitors Center ☏ 665-5188) offers a wide selection of activities, from golf and tennis to hiking, a bird sanctuary and the Zoo. *Observatory, Vermont Ave ☏ 664-1191. Opens 11.30am, Mon–Fri; 12.30, Sat and Sun.*

Museums Below Hollywood in mid-Wilshire are the *La Brea Tar Pits*, 5801 Wilshire Blvd ☏ 936-2230, a wellspring of natural tar that still seeps onto surrounding roads; fossils found in the tar are on show. Next to the Tar Pits is the city's major museum, the *LA County Museum of Art*, 5905 Wilshire Blvd ☏ 857-6000. The *Getty Museum of Art*, 17985 Pacific Coast Hwy, in Malibu ☏ 459-7611, is one of the richest in the USA; car reservations required a week in advance, or get in free with your bus ticket. The recently established *Museum of Contemporary Art*, 250 S Grand Ave ☏ 626-6222, a striking adjunct to California Plaza, houses 20thC art. South of downtown are the *Museum of Science & Industry*, 700 State Dr ☏ 744-7400, with "touch" displays, NASA-loaned space and satellite equipment and IMAX (image maximation) films which project onto a five-story screen with a six-channel stereo system.

Theme parks Nothing is quite like *Disneyland*, 50 miles/80kms south in Orange County. Allow a whole day; 1313 Harbor Blvd, Anaheim ☏ (714) 999-4565. *Knott's Berry Farm*, 8039 Beach Blvd, Anaheim ☏ (714) 220-5200, is a good second. In Long Beach, you can visit the *Queen Mary*, Pier J ☏ 435-3511, now permanently docked alongside *Spruce Goose*, the world's largest all-wood aircraft, built by Howard Hughes.

Guided tours

Starline Tours, 6845 Hollywood Blvd ☏ 463-3131, offer the best combination of tours and service. *Gray Line Tours Co*, 6333 W 3rd St ☏ 481-2121, are a national chain. Hollywood tours include *Fantasy Tours*, 1721 N Highland Ave ☏ 469-8184, whose open double-decker buses cruise the landmarks. *Hollywood on Location*, 8644 Wilshire Blvd ☏ 659-9165, publishes a daily listing of TV and film shoots with detailed maps. Walking tours through the lands of LA heritage are conducted by the *LA Conservancy*, 849 S Broadway ☏ 623-2489.

Spectator sports

Baseball Dodger Stadium, 1000 Elysian Park Ave ☏ 224-1500, is home to the LA *Dodgers*; the California *Angels* play at the Anaheim Stadium, 2000 State College Blvd, Anaheim ☏ (714) 937-6700.

Basketball The *Lakers* appear at the Forum ☏ 419-3100; the *Clippers* at the Sports Arena ☏ 748-6131.

Football The LA *Raiders* kick off at the Coliseum, 3911 S Figueroa St ☏ 747-7111; LA *Rams* play at Anaheim ☏ (714) 937-6767.

Horse-racing *Santa Anita Park*, Huntington Dr and Baldwin Ave, Arcadia ☏ (818) 574-7223, has a heavy schedule of winter racing and is a social highspot. *Hollywood Park*, Century Blvd ☏ 419-1500, also has winter racing. Summer racing is at *Del Mar*, Jimmy Durante Drive off Hwy 5 ☏ (619) 755-1141, right on the beach.

Soccer The LA *Lazers* can be seen at the Forum, Manchester Blvd, Inglewood ☏ 674-6000.

Keeping fit

Most hotels have extensive private facilities and/or arrangements with specialized clubs. The *Wilshire YMCA*, 225 S Oxford Ave ☏ 386-8570, has limited facilities, but the very smart *Downtown YMCA*, 401 S Hope St ☏ 624-2348, provides a full service. Both sell daily passes. *Nautilus Plus*, 888 International Tower at Figueroa and 9th ☏ 488-0095, has an extensive range of facilities, including weight machines.

Beaches From Malibu to the highly populated South Bay and beyond, there is a string of large public beaches. *Will Rogers Beach*, north on the Pacific Coast Hwy at Topanga

Canyon Blvd, has a large parking lot and a comfortable mixed crowd. Southward, *Santa Monica Beach*, the easiest to get to at the end of Route 10, usually sees a colorful ethnic crowd. *Venice Beach* has a discreet topless bathing area, but watch the boardwalk for muggers and avoid late in the day. *Manhattan Beach* and those to the south, like Huntington, are popular with surfers and families.
Cycling The bike path that runs down along the ocean's edge from Santa Monica to Palos Verdes is the area's favorite biking spot. Cyclists are also permitted in Griffith Park, though some of the hills are steep.
Golf There are a dozen LA municipal courses. If you can't get into *Rancho Park*, 10460 W Pico Blvd ☎ 838-7373, try *Wilson* or *Harding*, Griffith Park Dr ☎ 663-2555. The *Riviera Country Club*, 1250 Capri Dr, Pacific Palisades ☎ 454-6591, home of the PGA Championship Open, is one of the few private clubs that allows nonmembers.
Jogging Alongside the oceanfront bike path is a pedestrian path popular with joggers but watch out for the skaters. Other options are the clifftop *Pacific Palisades Park*, overlooking the ocean (Ocean Blvd in Santa Monica); *San Vicente Blvd* (extending from Ocean Blvd 4 miles/6.5kms to Brentwood Center); and a 4-mile/6.5km hilly path at *UCLA*. In the city itself, both *Griffith Park* and *Echo Park Lake* are used by joggers.
Racquet sports The *Sports Connection* chain ☎ 652-7440 rents courts by the hour. Public tennis courts include *The Tennis Place*, 5880 W 3rd St ☎ 931-1715, and *Riverside Tennis* at Griffith Park ☎ 661-5318.

Local resources

Business services

Several LA-based firms offer a full range of services. *Fingerprint*, 8467 Melrose Pl ☎ 653-2082, is an electronic page-processing center providing comprehensive desktop publishing facilities. *Modern Secretarial*, 2813 La Cienega Blvd ☎ 870 5882, offers a full range of services, while *California Transcribing*, 6010 Wilshire Blvd ☎ 857-5566, includes in-house dictation machines, and word-processing and optical scanning facilities.
Photocopying and printing *Charlie Chan Printing* is a reliable chain with an office in the Union Bank Bldg, 445 S Figueroa ☎ 622-1231, that does pick-up and delivery; there are two more downtown sites on Wilshire Blvd ☎ 381-1301 and 380-6121; and dozens throughout the city.
Secretarial *Electronic Office Personnel* ☎ 934-8211, *Olsten Temporary Services* ☎ 614-1488 and *Stivers Temporary Personnel* ☎ 386-3440 are reliable firms.
Translation *Academie Language Center* ☎ 651-1670, *Inlingua Language & Translation* ☎ 386-9949 and *Berlitz Language Center* ☎ 380-1144.

Communications

Long-distance delivery *Federal Express* ☎ 687-9767; *DHL* ☎ 973-7300.
Local delivery *Rocket* ☎ 469-7155 is reliable.
Post office The *Worldway Postal Center* at LAX, 5800 W Century Blvd, is open 7am–8pm, but the Express Mail window is open 24hrs. The *Terminal Annex* downtown is at 900 N Alameda St ☎ 617-4641 open 7am–9pm. The office in Beverly Hills is 469 N Crescent Dr ☎ 276-3161.
Telex *ITT World Communications* ☎ 269-9191; *Nanosec* ☎ (800) 227-4247; *West Coast Telex & Secretarial* ☎ 463-0903.
Fax *Nanosec* ☎ (800) 227-4247; *Action Telex* ☎ 653-9361.

Conference/exhibition centers

Most hotels have meeting facilities, and several specialize in conventions. Downtown LA also has the *Convention Center*, 1202 S Figueroa St ☎ 741-1151, a municipal facility with a large main exhibition hall, 2 smaller halls and 19 other rooms, restaurants and parking.

Emergencies

Hospitals *Good Samaritan*, 616 S Witmer St ☎ 977-2121; *Cedars Sinai*, 8700 Beverly Blvd ☎ 855-5000; *UCLA Medical Center* ☎ 825-9111.

For dental emergencies, the *LA Dental Society* ☎ 481-2133 makes referrals; the *USC Medical Center*, 12300 N State St ☎ 226-2622, offers short-term, 24hr assistance.

Pharmacies *Horton & Converse* has about a dozen stores; some stay open late, all deliver. The downtown store is at 201 S Alvarado St ☎ 413-2424, open 9–5; mid-Wilshire, 3875 Wilshire Blvd ☎ 382-2236, open until 2am.

Police *Downtown*, 251 E 6th St ☎ 485-2681; *Beverly Hills*, 450 N Crescent Dr ☎ 550-4951.

Government offices

City of LA information ☎ 485-5595; *California Dept of Commerce/Business Development* ☎ 620-2560; *Immigration and Naturalization* ☎ 894-2119.

Information sources

Business information *LA Area Chamber of Commerce*, 404 S Bixel St 90017 ☎ 629-0602 fax 629-0708, covers downtown; *Wilshire Chamber of Commerce*, 3875 Wilshire Blvd, Suite 200, 90010 ☎ 386-8224, includes Hollywood; *Los Angeles West Business Council*, 10880 Wilshire Blvd, 31103 ☎ 475-4574, has good information on Westside and Greater LA.

Local media LA's most comprehensive and international magazine and newspaper store is the *Universal News Agency*, 1655 N Las Palmas Ave ☎ 467-3850. The *Los Angeles Times* has a business section daily (including weekends) with complete stock listings. The *Los Angeles Herald Examiner* is smaller in size and circulation. *Los Angeles* is a glitzy regional magazine; *California* is a well-written monthly. *KNX* (1070 *AM*) and *KFWB* (98 *AM*) are all-news radio stations.

Visitor information *Greater Los Angeles Visitors and Convention Bureau*, 515 S Figueroa St ☎ 624-7300; *Visitors Information Center*, ARCO Plaza ☎ 689-8822; *Hollywood*, 6541 Hollywood Blvd ☎ 461-4213.

Thank-yous

Florists *Pete's Flowers*, 6260 Sunset Blvd ☎ 466-4060, services entertainment corporations like MCA and Motown and supplies fruit packs and gourmet baskets, locally and abroad. *Downstairs Greenery & Florists* ARCO Plaza ☎ 485-1171, Bonaventure ☎ 620-0601 and California Mart ☎ 628-0107.

Gift baskets A corporate favorite is *San Antonio Winery*, 737 Lamar St ☎ 2123-1401, for wine, pâté and cheeses. *Ultimate Nut & Candy*, Farmer's Market, 3rd and Fairfax ☎ 938-1555.

MEMPHIS

Area code ☏ 901

Memphis, an old southern city with an easy tempo, is a market and distribution center, a launching pad for entrepreneurs, a center for medical research, and the crucible of rock 'n roll. The city sits on a high bluff beside the Mississippi River in the extreme southwestern tip of Tennessee. It is the urban center of an agricultural region that includes parts of Mississippi, Arkansas, Missouri, and Tennessee, and its economic base is closely tied to agriculture, with companies such as Holly Farms based here. It also houses the headquarters of such national corporations as Holiday Inns and Federal Express.

Arriving

Memphis International Airport

MIA has few international flights, but busy domestic services operate daily 6.30am–11.30pm. The three-concourse terminal building has a business center (in the center concourse across from TWA) offering secretarial, computer, telex and telecopying services, Mon–Fri, 7–5. A travel agency is open Mon–Fri, 7–7; Sat, 8–5, and Western Union, money order and travelers' cheque services are available.

Nearby hotels *Little Hotel in the Airport*, on the mezzanine level of the airport's west and east concourses ☏ 345-3220. *Sheraton Airport Inn*, 2411 Winchester Rd 38130 (in airport grounds) ☏ 332-2370 fax 398-4055.

City link The airport is about 20mins in rush hours by road south from the city's major business centers. Most major hotels offer a courtesy car service, with direct telephones in the baggage claim areas.

Taxi Cabs stand outside the baggage claim areas. There is a $5 minimum charge for airport trips, and it is advisable to negotiate in advance.

Car rental All the major companies have booths near baggage claim in each concourse: Avis ☏ 345-2849; Hertz ☏ 345-5680.

Getting around

The best way to get around in Memphis is by car. The city is spread out, and taxis are relatively expensive. Buses are slow and rarely run late at night.

Taxi You cannot hail a cab on the street. Try *Yellow Cab* ☏ 577-7777.

Limousine Cadillac limousines may be hired from *Yellow Cab* ☏ 577-7700.

Driving Parking is not a major problem, but there is occasional rush-hour traffic congestion in major business areas, 7.30–8.30am and 4–5.30pm. In most areas, roads form a grid pattern with streets running north–south and avenues east–west. For information on hazardous road conditions or for emergency help, contact the *Tennessee Highway Patrol* ☏ 386-3831.

Bus The routes of the municipally owned bus system (MATA) are not useful for business travelers. For information ☏ 274-6282.

Area by area

Memphis began as two separate ports, Memphis and South Memphis, which were merged in 1840. The major business, government and financial center is in downtown along the Mississippi River. Development and restoration have been progressing for some time, and a section within Parkways Boulevard in downtown has been developed as a medical and research zone. Farther east, a second major business center has grown up at the intersection of the interstate ring and Poplar Avenue. Residential areas spread throughout the city. Some of the most fashionable include Central Gardens, homes built mainly in the early 1900s; East Memphis, homes built primarily in the 1940s and 1950s; and new areas farther east, among them River Oaks.

Hotels

The city where Holiday Inns were born is still the headquarters of the international chain and has six Holiday Inns, including the flagship Crowne Plaza and Holiday Inn East. For traditional ambience and prestige, however, the choice is the Peabody.

Crowne Plaza [$]/
250 N Main St 38103 ☎ 527-7300 fax 526-1561 • AE DC MC V • Holiday Inn • 406 rooms, 14 suites, 2 restaurants, 2 bars
Designed primarily as a convention hotel, the 18-story Crowne Plaza overlooks the Mississippi River and is connected to the Convention Center. Executive level floor. Shops • indoor pool, whirlpool, sauna, fitness room • 6 meeting rooms.

French Quarter Inn [$]/
2144 Madison Ave 38104 ☎ 728-4000 fax 278-1262 • AE DC MC V • 106 suites, 1 restaurant, 1 bar
Modern, all-suite and luxurious, this hotel is adjacent to the restaurants, bars and shops of Overton Square in midtown. It draws much of its clientele from the Medical Center. All suites have jacuzzis, many have private patios or balconies. Weight room, pool, good location for jogging • 2 meeting rooms.

Omni Memphis [$]/
939 Ridgelake Blvd 38119 ☎ 684-6664 [TX] 533299 fax 762-7411 • AE DC MC V • 380 rooms, 10 suites, 1 restaurant, 1 bar
This contemporary 27-story hotel is in a beautifully landscaped office development in the city's eastern business section. Rooms have minibars and coffee-making equipment. Car rental desks • pool, access to local health spa • 31 meeting rooms.

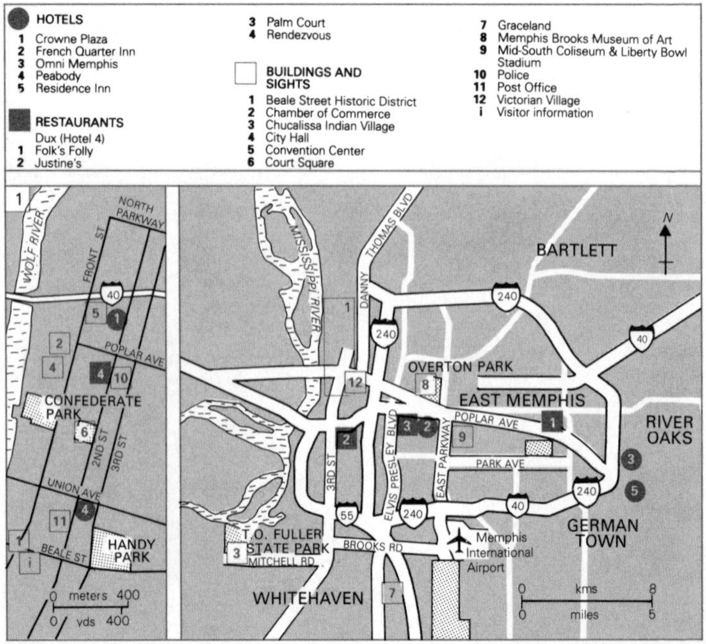

Peabody [$]///
149 Union Ave 38103 ☎ 529-4000
[TX] 558503 fax 529-9600 • AE DC MC V • 454 rooms, 24 suites, 4 restaurants, 3 bars
A few decades ago the Peabody was *the* hotel in the region. It then fell on leaner times and was closed for renovation in the 1970s. Now listed in the National Register of Historic Places, it is again *the* place to stay. Its elegance, ambience, and service make it important in city social life; and the specially trained mallard ducks, which file across the carpet into the lobby for their daily swim in the marble fountain are a sight to see!

Chez Philipe, an expensive, prestigious, formal French restaurant with excellent food, is open for dinner daily except Sunday. Dux is a highly recommended spot for regional dining (see *Restaurants*). The Lobby Bar is perfect for afternoon tea or after-work cocktails (see *Bars*). Mallards is popular with the downtown crowd for lunch and offers the best in evening entertainment (see *Entertainment*). Shopping arcade • pool, whirlpool, sauna, health club • 23 meeting rooms.

Residence Inn [$]//
6141 Poplar Pike Rd 38119
☎ 685-9595 fax 685-9595 ext 4001 • AE DC MC V • 106 suites
The Residence all-suite complex offers the long-term business visitor apartment-like living. The longer you stay, the cheaper the rate. In the city's eastern business sector, the suites are in modern four-story townhouses. Each has a living room with fireplace, dining area, equipped kitchen, and a separate bedroom or bedrooms. Penthouse suites have bath with jacuzzi. Grocery service • sports court • 2 meeting rooms.

OTHER HOTELS

Memphis has many moderately priced hotels and motels clustered in the downtown area, around the Medical Center, near the airport and in the city's eastern business area near I-240 and Poplar Avenue. They include four *Hampton Inns* (reservations ☎ 363-7777), *Holiday Inns* no-frills city hotels ☎ 362-2180, and three *La Quinta Inns* at the Airport and the Medical Center ☎ (800) 531-5900.

Clubs

Memphis restaurants and bars have been able to serve alcohol only since 1969. As a result, much entertaining was done at home or in private clubs, a pattern that still holds. The *Memphis Country Club* (old-line club with a few guest rooms) ☎ 452-2131, *Chickasaw Country Club* ☎ 323-6216, *Colonial Country Club* ☎ 388-6151 and *Ridgeway Country Club* ☎ 853-2247 are exclusive and offer golf, tennis, swimming and dining. The *Memphis Hunt and Polo Club* ☎ 685-8296 and *University Club* ☎ 722-3700 are in the same category, but have no golf course. The *Racquet Club of Memphis* ☎ 765-4400, hosts the US National Indoor Tennis Championships.

Restaurants

Although a lot of business entertaining takes place in clubs, the city does have a wide variety of restaurants, including traditional simple lunchtime cafés, serving "down home" Southern turnip greens, cornbread, and meat and vegetable specials. Try one of the following if you want a change: the *Cupboard* (midtown) ☎ 276-6577, the *Little Tea Shop* (downtown) ☎ 525-6000, or *Fourway Grill* (South Memphis) ☎ 275-2351.

Dux [$]//
Peabody Hotel ☎ 529-4000 ext 199 • AE DC MC V
Since the Peabody Hotel re-opened, the Dux has been acclaimed for its food beyond the confines of Memphis.

Its attractive contemporary decor, regional specialties, and well-spaced tables make it a favorite with the business set from breakfast to dinner.

Folk's Folly [$]//
551 S Mendenhall ☎ 762-8200 • closed L • AE DC MC V • jacket recommended
The best steaks in town are reputed to be served in this small, unpretentious converted house. It is popular for after-work business discussions.

Justine's [$]//
919 Coward Pl ☎ 527-3815 • closed L, Mon, Sun • AE DC MC V • jacket
If you are in town for only one night and looking for an elegant dinner, Justine's is the place. Its Continental cuisine is served in the elegant and formal atmosphere of the Old Coward Place, built in 1843 in French colonial style.

Palm Court [$]/
2101 Overton Sq Ln ☎ 725-6797 • closed L, Mon • AE DC MC V
Located in the center of Overton Square, a midtown area noted for its restaurants, shops and nightlife, Palm Court serves northern Italian cuisine to local *cognoscenti*. The atmosphere is pleasant and lively.

Rendezvous [$]/
52 S 2nd St (enter through back of Gen Washburn Alley) ☎ 523-2746 • closed L Tue, Wed & Thu; Sun, Mon, last 2 weeks in Jul, Dec • AE DC MC V • beer only; take your own wine
Memphis claims to offer the world's best pork barbecue – and even has an annual international barbecue contest to prove it! The Rendezvous is one of the city's leading barbecue joints: it is undergound, filled with memorabilia and has a festive atmosphere.

Bars

The city's bars have developed only since 1969. Overton Square, at the intersection of Madison and Cooper in midtown, has several types: *Paulette's* ☎ 726-5128 for a quiet drink, *La Chardonnay* ☎ 725-1375 for wine, and *Madison Avenue* ☎ 274-1144 for the younger set who want to dance. The eastern business section along Poplar Avenue, east of Perkins, is dotted with bars for after-work drinking; and Beale Street, downtown, offers lively nightlife for the later hours. The *Peabody Lobby Bar* is the best spot for conversation, quiet piano music, an after-work drink, weekday afternoon tea (3–4.30pm) or a nightcap in opulent surroundings; open 11am–1am daily (see *Hotels*).

Entertainment

Memphis and music are inseparable. This was where black blues were first written down by WC Handy; it was also where blues and country & western melded to form 20thC rock'n roll. Elvis Presley lived here. Outdoor festivals and concerts are held throughout the year, and several bars are also good for live music. *Mallard's*, Peabody Hotel, is a favorite with both locals and visitors; Tue–Sat, 9pm–1.30am. *Rum Boogie Café*, 182 Beale St ☎ 528-0150, is just as loud and packed.

The city has several good regional theater companies and is a stopping point for touring productions. The Symphony and Opera are also big attractions. For listings, consult *Memphis Magazine* or Friday's *Commercial Appeal*.

Shopping

Malls Three top-quality small downtown malls and two big regional malls provide for most needs. The small malls are: *Chickasaw Oaks Plaza*, between Poplar Ave and Walnut Grove, just east of Tillman; *Park Place Mall*, Park Ave and Ridgeway; and *Peabody Galleria*, inside the Peabody Hotel (see *Hotels*). The two large regional malls are: *Hickory Ridge Mall*, on Winchester between Hickory Hill and Ridgeway, and *Mall of Memphis*, I-240, Perkins Rd and American Way.

Specialty shopping Good shops for special regional items are: *Alice Bingham Gallery*, 24 S Cooper ☏ 683-6200, regional art; *Patt Kerr Inc*, 200 Wagner Pl ☏ 525-5223, lace designer clothes, phone for appointment; *Strings and Things*, 1492 Union ☏ 278-0500, music store that does custom work for many stars; and *Woman's Exchange*, 88 Racine ☏ 327-5681, handmade children's clothing.

Sightseeing

Beale Street In the early 1800s it was the main street of South Memphis; at the turn of the century the birthplace of the blues; and today it is an entertainment and shopping district of renovated buildings.

Chucalissa Indian Village Choctaw Indians demonstrate crafts in this reconstructed Indian village and museum operated by Memphis State University, 6 miles/10.5kms south of downtown. Several different settlements of the temple-mound culture lived on the site from 1000–1500. *1987 Indian Village Dr ☏ 785-3160. Open Tue–Sat, 9–5; Sun, 1–5.*

Court Square This two-acre park has been the symbolic center of Memphis for generations. It is surrounded by landmark buildings, including the Porter Building, Lincoln American Tower and the Tennessee Club Building. *Between 2nd St and Mid-America Mall on Court.*

Dixon Gallery and Gardens Set in 17 acres of gardens, this 1940s house has antique furniture, silver, crystal, porcelain, carpets, and a collection of French and Impressionist paintings. *4339 Park Ave ☏ 761-5250. Open Mon–Sat, 11–5; Sun, 1–5.*

Graceland Elvis Presley lived here from 1957–77 and is buried with his parents in the gardens. Guided tours of the house, Elvis Museum and other memorabilia last 90mins. *3717 Elvis Presley Blvd ☏ 332-3322. Open Jun–Aug, 8–6; May–Feb, daily 9–5.*

Memphis Brooks Museum of Art The city's fine arts museum features the Kress Collection of Renaissance art and 16th–20thC paintings, prints and sculpture. *Overton Park ☏ 722-3500. Open Tue–Sat, 10–5pm; Sun, 1–5.*

Victorian Village The impressive townhouses in the 600 block of Adams were built during the second half of the 19thC when cotton was king and Memphis was booming. Two are public museums: *Fontaine House*, a restored French Victorian mansion built about 1871, features period antiques and clothing. *680 Adams ☏ 526-1469. Open Apr–Dec, Mon–Sat, 10–4; Sun, 1–4; Jan–Mar, daily, 1–4. Mallory-Neely House*, an Italianate Victorian mansion built about 1852, modified 1883, contains original family antiques and furnishings. *652 Adams ☏ 523-1484. Open Tue–Sat, 10–4; Sun, 1–4.*

Guided tours

Boat tours *Memphis Queen Excursion Boats* ☏ 527-5694; 90min scheduled cruises on a paddlewheeler.

Bus tours *Gray Line Tours* ☏ 942-4662. Half or full-day city, Elvis, riverboat, and nightclub tours.

Spectator sports

Baseball The *Chicks*, a farm team of the Kansas City Royals, play in Chicks Stadium near the intersection of Central and E Parkway ☏ 272-1687.

Basketball The Memphis State University *Tigers* are at Mid-South Coliseum ☏ 678-2331.

Football This is the real craze in Memphis, Liberty Bowl Stadium ☏ 272-1214.

Keeping fit

Most hotels have pools and fitness facilities. While private clubs are usually the setting for business across the net or on the green, public facilities are available. The *Memphis Park Commission*, 2599 Avery ☏ 454-5759, runs the city's 9 golf courses, 17 swimming pools and 8 tennis centers. The most convenient public courses are: *Audubon*, 4160 Park Ave ☏ 683-6941, *Overton Park*,

2080 Poplar Ave ☏ 725-9905, and *Galloway*, 3815 Walnut Grove Rd ☏ 685-7805. The most convenient public tennis courts are: *Rodgers*, 1123 Jefferson Ave ☏ 523-0094. The *Memphis Area Chamber of Commerce* (see *Information sources*) produces a free fishing guide to the area listing 90 fishing sites.

Local resources

Business services

Photocopying and printing *Kinko's Copies* ☏ 327-2679 has the best prices and will pick-up and deliver. *Clarke's Quick Print* has branches city-wide.
Secretarial *Diversified Services Agency* ☏ 794-5385.
Translation *Memphis State University Foreign Languages Dept* ☏ 678-2506 or *Memphis Public Library* ☏ 725-8825 can suggest translators.

Communications

Long-distance delivery *Federal Express* ☏ 345-5044.
Local delivery *M&M Package Express Inc* ☏ 722-8118.
Post Office Main branch, 555 S 3rd St at Calhoun, lobby with stamp machines and pick-up; open 24hr.
Telex and fax *Western Union* ☏ (800) 325-6000.

Conference/exhibition centers

For information contact *Memphis Convention and Visitors Bureau* ☏ 576-8181. *Memphis Convention Center*, 255 N Main St ☏ 576-1200; *Agricenter International* ☏ 757-7777 specializes in agribusiness conventions and trade shows; *Mid-South Coliseum* ☏ 274-7400; and *Shelby Farms Showplace Arena* ☏ 756-7433.

Emergencies

Hospitals Most Memphis hospitals have several locations and each has 24hr emergency room service. The largest are: *Baptist/Central*, 899 Madison Ave ☏ 522-5511; *Methodist/Central*, 1265 Union ☏ 726-7600; *Regional Medical Center*, 877 Jefferson ☏ 575-8181, public; all major credit cards accepted. For ambulance ☏ 458-3311. Doctor or dentist referral ☏ 527-3311.
Pharmacies *Super D* and *Walgreen's* have locations city-wide. In-hospital pharmacies are open 24hr.
Police 201 Poplar ☏ 528-2222.

Government offices

Mayor's Action Center ☏ 576-6500 provides business information.

Information sources

Business information *Memphis Area Chamber of Commerce*, Suite 200, 22 N Front ☏ 575-3500, supplies economic data on the community and works with businesses considering expanding or relocating in the area.
Local media *The Commercial Appeal* is the city's major daily; *The Daily News* is the daily business paper; *Memphis Business Journal* is the weekly business paper.
Visitor information *Visitors Information Center*, 207 Beale St ☏ 526-4880 open Mon–Sat, 9–5. LINC ☏ 725-8895 is a human services, recreation and education information and referral service run by the public library.

Thank-yous

Florist *John Hoover Flowers* ☏ 274-1851; same day delivery.

MIAMI

Area code ☎ 305

Long famous for its resorts, Miami is now an international banking hub (with one of the largest international banking communities outside New York), a leading import-export center and a major cruise base. It is America's gateway to the Caribbean and to Central and South America; many corporations have their Latin American divisions in the city, or nearby. In the 1960s Miami began to develop a decidedly Latin flavor. (Of the 1.85m who now live in the city, nearly half are of Latin origin and nearly 20% are black.) South Florida is still a haven for retirees, but in Miami they are concentrated in the northern suburbs.

Arriving

Miami International Airport

MIA is almost constantly under construction. International passengers use the international satellite terminal, linked by automated shuttle to Customs and Immigration. Passengers collect their baggage at street level, near car rental desks, taxi stands and stations. There is a 24hr multilingual information service (Concourse E ☎ 871-7000), currency exchange and snack bars.

Nearby hotels *Doral Resort and Country Club*, 4400 NW 87th Ave 33178 ☎ 592-2000 fax 592-2000 ext 2321. *Marriott*, 1201 NW Le Jeune Rd 33126 ☎ 649-5000 fax 642-3369. *Miami Airport Hilton*, 5101 Blue Lagoon Dr 33126 ☎ 262-1000 fax 262-5725. *Radisson Mart Plaza*, 711 NW 72nd Ave ☎ 261-3800 fax 261-3800 ext 499. *Sheraton River House*, 3900 NW 21st St 33142 ☎ 871-3800 fax 871-3800 ext 7188.

City link It is about a 15min drive from MIA in North Miami to downtown (8 miles/13kms), 30mins to Miami Beach (14 miles/22kms).

Taxi Cabs are plentiful and the journey to downtown costs about $12; to Miami Beach about $18.

Supershuttle vans ☎ 871-8488 are half the price of cabs.

Car rental Most major firms have offices at the airport, but cars may be in short supply during holiday periods. For collection on arrival, reserve in advance. Rental car costs in Florida are the lowest in the country. Avis ☎ 526-3200, Budget ☎ 871-3053, Hertz 871-0300.

Getting around

An air-conditioned rental car gives the most freedom and comfort. But the highway system is confusing and clogged, so hire a cab until your business is done, then rent a car to go exploring. With the exception of Coral Gables and Coconut Grove, the city follows a grid pattern: avenues run north–south and streets run east–west. Miami Avenue divides east from west; Flagler Street north from south. Streets and avenues are numbered from the dividing lines, and street numbers are followed by NW, NE, SW or SE. Miami is a dangerous city to walk in at night.

Taxi Cab drivers are tightly regulated. They must speak English, load and unload baggage, turn on the air conditioning upon request, and know significant Miami destinations. They are not allowed to recommend specific businesses or to solicit tips. *Central Cab* ☎ 532-5555; *Metro* ☎ 888-8888; and *Yellow Cab* ☎ 444-4444.

Limousine *Limousines of South Florida* ☎ 940-5252.

Car rental *Avis* ☎ 377-2531 (open daily, 8.30–5); *Hertz* ☎ 931-7904 (Miami Beach).

Rail The *MetroRail* elevated train ☎ 638-6700 links downtown Miami to Hialeah and Kendall/South Miami and connects with the elevated *MetroMover*, on which motorized cars circle the downtown area every 90 seconds daily, 6am–midnight.

Bus *Metrobus*, covering most of Dade County, is not recommended for the business visitor.

Area by area

Downtown Philip Johnson's Mediterranean-style Cultural Arts Center and IM Pei's CenTrust Tower are the most striking buildings; others are the Arquitectonic Condominiums along Brickell Avenue, the Southeast Financial Center and its Chopin Plaza neighbors, the Bayside Specialty Center (a market place around the Miamarina) and Isamu Noguchi's computerized fountain on Biscayne Boulevard in the redesigned Bayfront Park. The Dade County Courthouse, the City of Miami offices and the Federal Building are downtown. Major businesses in Miami include law, import-export, banking, agricultural industry and jewelry.

Dodge Island Freight handling and the cruise business are centered in the port on Dodge Island, just east of downtown. The Metro Dade Cultural Center (housing the impressive Center for the Fine Arts, the South Florida Historical Museum and the public library), the James L Knight Conference Center and the Gusman Cultural Center are close by the port. International banks, lawyers, accountants, and luxury condominiums share the waterfront along Brickell Avenue. A few blocks to the north the Omni Plaza Venetia Complex has a major shopping mall, top-class hotels, restaurants and bars, apartments and a yacht basin.

Calle Ocho Cuban culture has revitalized the once deteriorating area to the west of Miami along SW 8th Street, called "Little Havana."

Miami Beach Across Biscayne Bay by causeway is Miami Beach, a narrow, 8 mile/13km-long island. The beach is now being rebuilt, hotels have been refurbished and the Art Deco South Beach area is enjoying a renaissance.

Bal Harbour Along ten blocks of Miami Beach's Collins Avenue, this upmarket area contains hotels, condominiums, a shopping complex and restaurants.

Other areas Light manufacturing,

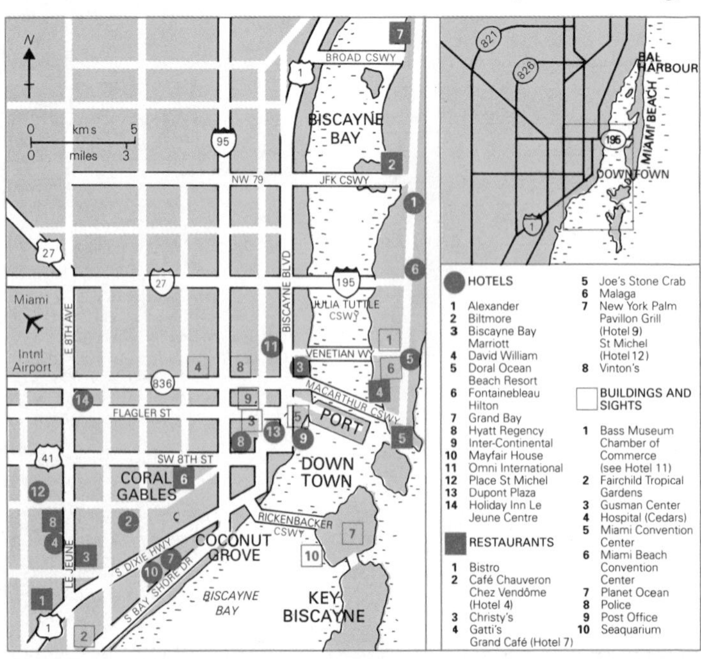

clothing and interior design firms are based in an area 15 blocks north of downtown. South of downtown, along Biscayne Bay, is *Coconut Grove*, one of the oldest and most unusual of Miami communities. It is a gentle blend of black and white, gay and straight, business-minded and bohemian Miamians occupying rustic, shady neighborhoods around the bay.

Wrapped around Coconut Grove to the west and south is *Coral Gables*, home of more than 100 international businesses. *Key Biscayne* is across a bridge from Coconut Grove. It is divided equally among residences, top-class oceanfront hotels and public recreational facilities, including miles of tree-lined beach, a woody park, a golf course and a marina.

Hotels

Greater Miami is a tourist destination of such magnitude that you can find a comfortable, reasonably priced, air-conditioned hotel room near your business; nearly all have freshwater pools and cable television.

Alexander [$]/////
5335 Collins Ave, Miami Beach 33140
☎ 865-6500 TX 808172 fax 864-8525
• AE DC MC V • 211 suites, 2 restaurants, 3 bars, 1 coffee shop
This is the preferred business address in Miami Beach: a luxurious, low-key, oceanfront hotel with tropical gardens, and antique furniture in the lobby and suites. Dominique's serves mostly French cuisine and is noted for its unusual appetizers, which include rattlesnake. Two pools, 4 jacuzzis, marina, jogging, watersports, golf and tennis nearby • 8 meeting rooms, teleconferencing.

Biltmore [$]////
1200 Anastasia Ave, Coral Gables 33134 ☎ 445-1926 fax 448-9976 • AE DC MC V • 240 rooms, 35 suites, 3 restaurants
A $50m renovation has restored this famous 1920s hotel to luxurious splendor and elegance. In Coral Gables and near the airport, it is set beside its own 18-hole golf course. Health club, pool • 11 meeting rooms.

Biscayne Bay Marriott [$]///
1633 N Bayshore Dr 33132
☎ 374-3900 TX 525840 fax 375-0597
• AE DC MC V • 605 rooms, 21 suites, 2 restaurants, 2 bars
This Marriott overlooks the hotel's marina and Biscayne Bay. Veronique's, with inventive American dishes, is a decidedly genteel restaurant with chandeliers and fresh flowers. The marina has 220 boatslips. Pool, tennis and golf nearby, health club • 20 meeting rooms.

David William [$]//
700 Biltmore Way, Coral Gables 33134
☎ 445-7821 • AE DC MC V • 88 rooms, 2 restaurants
A European-style hostelry with a mostly Latin American clientele, the David William is noted for its restaurants. The 700 Club is quiet and has wood paneling and large bar; popular for business lunches. Chez Vendôme is elegantly French (see *Restaurants*). 1 meeting room.

Doral Ocean Beach Resort [$]///
4833 Collins Ave, Miami Beach 33140
☎ 532-3600 TX 518928 fax 534-7409
• AE DC MC V • 420 rooms, 42 suites, 3 restaurants, 4 bars, 1 coffee shop
On the beach with views of both the Atlantic Ocean and Biscayne Bay, the luxurious Doral caters to the convention and tourist trade. Alfredo's rooftop restaurant is related to the original in Rome. Health club, jogging track, pool, aquasports club, access to Doral Country Club • 16 meeting rooms.

Fontainebleau Hilton [$]////
4441 Collins Ave, Miami Beach 33140
☎ 538-2000 TX 519362 fax 534-7821

• *AE DC MC V* • *1,163 rooms, 61 suites, 13 restaurants, 4 bars*
The Fontainebleau is a convention hotel with a range of restaurants, from an Art Deco steak house to an outdoor café with a Calypso band. Rooms have a video network, minibar and jacuzzi. Hairdresser, pharmacy, jeweler • health club, 2 pools, watersports, tennis • 45 meeting rooms, translation.

Grand Bay [$]////
2669 S Bayshore Dr, Coconut Grove 33133 ☎ *858-9600* [TX] *441370 fax 858-1532* • *AE DC MC V* • *181 rooms, 42 suites, 1 restaurant, 4 bars*
The Grand Bay, a CIGA hotels franchise, is just three blocks from the Mayfair Mall. The service is excellent and unobtrusive. Regine's fashionable rooftop disco, part of the international chain, is open to members and hotel guests only. The Grand Café restaurant (see *Restaurants*) has a light and airy dining room. Hairdresser • health club, pool, golf • 6 meeting rooms.

Hyatt Regency [$]//
400 SE 2nd Ave 33131 ☎ *358-1234* [TX] *514316 fax 358-1234 ext 3138* • *AE DC MC V* • *615 rooms, 36 suites, 2 restaurants, 3 bars*
Downtown, with views of Biscayne Bay and the city skyline, this hotel is a favorite for conferences. Its Esplanade restaurant is a cosmopolitan spot serving fresh pompano and swordfish daily. Pool, arrangements with nearby health club • 28 meeting rooms.

Inter-Continental [$]//
100 Chopin Pl 33131 ☎ *577-1000 fax 577-0384* • *646 rooms, 34 suites, 5 restaurants, 1 bar, 1 coffee shop*
Luxurious hotel centrally located at Biscayne Bay. The Pavillon Grill (see *Restaurants*) serves superb food. Health club, pool, jogging, tennis • 13 meeting rooms, teleconferencing.

Mayfair House [$]/////
3000 Florida Ave, Coconut Grove 33133 ☎ *441-0000* [TX] *153670 fax 447-9173* • *AE DC MC V* • *181 suites, 2 restaurants, 3 bars*
In the top two floors of a chic shopping arcade designed by artist/owner Ken Triester. The individually decorated suites have dining areas, hot tubs, and private terrace gardens. The Grill has three dining rooms, each decorated with French and Oriental art. Rooftop pool • 6 meeting rooms.

Omni International [$]//
1601 Biscayne Blvd 33132 ☎ *374-0000* [TX] *515005 fax 374-0020* • *485 rooms, 50 suites, 2 restaurants, 2 bars, 1 coffee shop*
Favored by business travelers, especially from Latin America and the Caribbean, the Omni is part of the Omni Plaza/Venetia Complex. It has 46 club-level rooms overlooking Biscayne Bay. Dentist, hairdresser, optician • arrangements with nearby health club, rooftop pool, tennis • 21 meeting rooms.

Place St Michel [$]//
162 Alcazar Ave, Coral Gables 33134 ☎ *444-1666 fax 447-1318* • *AE DC MC V* • *25 rooms, 3 suites, 2 restaurants, 1 bar*
This small hotel has a comfortable inn-like atmosphere. There are vaulted ceilings, tiled and parquet floors, and individually decorated rooms. The Restaurant St Michel (see *Restaurants*) has a very Parisian tone. The hotel bar is popular with the after-work crowd. 1 meeting room.

OTHER HOTELS

Dupont Plaza [$]/ *300 Biscayne Blvd Way* ☎ *358-2541 fax 377-4049* • *AE DC MC V*.

Holiday Inn Le Jeune Centre [$] *950 NW Le Jeune Rd* ☎ *446-9000 fax 441-0725* • *AE DC MC V*.

Clubs

Miami Club ☎ 374-7300, the oldest of the downtown luncheon clubs, is also the most exclusive. The *City Club of Miami* ☎ 373-2600, the newest of the business clubs, is conservative in membership selection; good for working lunches. The *Bankers Club* ☏ 374-1448, with stunning views of the bay, has world-wide reciprocity with more than 150 clubs. Representing the growing Latin influence in the business community are the *American Club* ☏ 642-5900 and the *Big Five* ☏ 226-2569, a consolidation of the five social clubs that dominated Havana society for 100 years. The *Standard* ☏ 379-1976 is one of the oldest of the downtown clubs. The *University Club* ☏ 371-8666 is the stronghold of Miami's young male professionals. The traditional establishment recreational clubs are the *Indian Creek Country Club* ☏ 866-5751 and Coconut Grove's *Biscayne Bay* ☏ 858-6303 and *Coral Reef* ☏ 858-1733 yacht clubs.

Restaurants

For business dining, look to Coral Gables, Coconut Grove, and Bal Harbour in the evenings; downtown becomes a desert after 5pm. At lunch, lawyers use *Sally Russell's* ☏ 373-4800 and the *Standard* ☏ 379-1976 and *Bankers* ☏ 374-1448 clubs. Brickell Avenue executives walk to lunch at *Cye's Rivergate* ☏ 358-9100, the *Brickell Emporium* ☏ 377-3354 or *Tobacco Road* ☏ 374-1198.

Bistro [$]//
2611 Ponce de Leon Blvd, Coral Gables ☏ 442-9671 • AE DC MC V
Small and friendly, the Bistro specializes in personalized service; it has many regular customers. Good, moderately priced wine list.

Café Chauveron [$]///
9561 E Bay Harbor Dr, Miami Beach ☏ 866-8779 • closed Jun–Oct • AE DC MC V • jacket
Chauveron is one of southern Florida's very best restaurants, run by André, the son of Roger Chauveron (of New York's Chambord). Serving French cuisine in the grand manner, it is noted for soufflés; it also features duck and rack of lamb.

Chez Vendôme [$]///
David William Hotel, Coral Gables ☏ 445-7821 • AE DC MC V
This classy French hotel restaurant, popular with business and finance executives, has red velvet booths and elaborately framed paintings. Successful dishes include steak Diane, rack of lamb, duck with sherry and several good snapper recipes. The wine list is extensive.

Christy's [$]/
3101 Ponce de Leon Blvd, Coral Gables ☏ 446-1400 • AE DC MC V
Well-liked by local business people, Christy's has an elegant Victorian decor like a gentlemen's club. The cooking is conservative: prime rib, fresh fish, and Caesar salad are specialties.

Gatti's [$]//
1427 West Ave, Miami Beach ☏ 673-1717 • closed Mon, May–Oct • AE DC MC V • reservations essential
Featuring northern Italian cuisine, Gatti's has been a family operation for 60 years. Housed in a stucco building, it is a haven for pasta fanatics. Canneloni, tortellini, fresh fish, and scallops are specialties.

Grand Café [$]////
Grand Bay Hotel, Coconut Grove ☏ 858-9600 • AE DC MC V
The Grand Café has a striking, open dining room and an attentive staff. Mediterranean dishes such as *cioppino* Grand Café (seafood in broth), grilled fish and an assortment of pastas highlight the menu. It also has splendid lamb chops and good crab soup.

Joe's Stone Crab [$]/
227 Biscayne St, Miami Beach
☎ 673-0365 • closed Mon L, mid-May–Oct • AE MC V • no reservations
Diners at this big, high-ceilinged South Beach restaurant run the risk of having to stand in line for an hour or two, particularly during the early crab season in the fall. Joe's is a Miami institution, noisy and ebullient, and famous for its stone crabs, which are brought in from the Florida Keys by Joe's fishing fleet.

Malaga [$]/
740 SW 8th St ☎ 854-9101 • AE DC MC V
Captures the flavor of Hispanic Miami in a traditional Spanish setting; there are two indoor dining rooms and a few tables in a romantic outdoor courtyard area. Located in Little Havana, Malaga specializes in Cuban cuisine, including fish dishes, *paella* and squid casserole.

New York Palm [$]//
9650 E Bay Harbor Dr, Bay Harbor ☎ 868-7256 • closed L, May–Sep • AE DC MC V • reservations essential
Ever since it opened in 1986, local business, political and showbusiness celebrities have used the Palm to entertain, discuss deals and impress. The menu is international, the decor elegant, the wine list extensive.

Pavillon Grill [$]//
Inter-Continental Hotel ☎ 372-4494 • AE DC MC V
The Pavillon Grill offers French cuisine, an extensive wine list, and an elegant interior with green marble columns, leather chairs, and mahogany paneled walls. Its specialties include trout stuffed with seafood, spinach and scallop salad and chicken with crabmeat and goat's cheese.

St Michel [$]//
Place St Michael Hotel, Coral Gables ☎ 446-6572 • AE DC MC V
This café restaurant is a lunch favorite of Coral Gables executives. Specialties include rack of lamb, duck with blackcurrants and poached salmon with lobster.

Vinton's [$]///
116 Alhambra Circle, Coral Gables ☎ 445-2511 • closed Sun and holidays • AE DC MC V
Situated in the La Palma Hotel, the very romantic Vinton's serves Continental cuisine; on Monday there is a "gourmet night," with a multicourse *prix fixe* dinner. Bouillabaisse, salmon in sorrel sauce, and duck with raspberry are the menu's highlights. No spirits, but a fine wine list.

Entertainment

Miami is noted for its extravagant floor shows, pari-mutuel wagering (horses, dogs and jai-alai) and, more recently, for sophisticated cultural attractions. In the winter season, the large beach hotels have headline acts and touring companies, from rock groups to symphony orchestras.

Theater and music *Coconut Grove Playhouse*, 3500 Main Hwy ☎ 442-4000, offers regional theater; *Miami Beach Theater of the Performing Arts* ☎ 673-7300 stages Broadway productions; and the *Gusman Center for the Performing Arts*, 174 E Flagler St ☎ 372-0925, has a wide range of stage shows. In addition, the Gusman houses the *Philharmonia Orchestra of Florida* ☎ 945-5180 and the *New World Symphony* ☎ 371-3005. *Greater Miami Opera*, 1200 Coral Way ☎ 854-1643, is at Dade County Auditorium nearby.

Nightclubs The top hotel clubs are the *Fontainebleau Hilton*, *Sheraton Bal Harbour*, 9701 Collins Ave, Miami Beach ☎ 865-7511, *Eden Roc*, 4525 Collins Ave, Miami Beach ☎ 531-0000, and *Grand Bay*. Other clubs include *Biscayne Baby*, 3336 Virginia St, Coconut Grove ☎ 445-3752, for rock'n roll; *Casanova's*, 740 E 9th St, Hialeah ☎ 883-8706, for Latin salsa/disco, with a mixed, dressy crowd; *Ciga Lounge*, on the mezzanine level of the Grand Bay Hotel, has an elegant jazz piano bar; *Les Violins*, 1751 Biscayne Blvd ☏ 371-8668, has extravagant Latin dance numbers and continuous entertainment; *Tobacco Road*, 626 S Miami Ave ☏ 374-1198, has top-name blues bands.

Shopping

From Bloomingdale's at *The Falls* in South Miami to Macy's almost at the county line of Dade and Broward, Miami is one vast shopping center. The Falls is a delightful indoor/outdoor mall enclosing a series of ponds and waterfalls. Off Kendall Drive, there is *Dadeland Mall*; and *Coconut Grove* is good for stylish, offbeat or bohemian fashion and artifacts. *Bal Harbour Shops*, 9700 Collins Ave, is an elegant mall with branches of top US department chains. *Miracle Mile* in Coral Gables is lined with expensive designer shops and boutiques; the *Miracle Center* opened in 1989. The *Omni Hotel and Mall* is favored by the fashionable, both for shopping and eating; *Mayfair Mall* is also chic.

Sightseeing

Ticketmaster ☏ 654-3309 sells tickets for events.

Ancient Spanish Monastery The oldest building in the western hemisphere, lifted from Segovia in Spain where it was first erected in 1141. *16711 West Dixie Hwy, North Miami Beach. Open Mon–Sat, 10–5; Sun, 12–5.*

Bass Museum of Art European paintings, sculpture and tapestries from the Renaissance to the 20th century. *2121 Park Ave, Miami Beach. Open Tues–Sat, 10–5; Sun, 1–5.*

Fairchild Tropical Gardens America's largest botanical garden has more than 5,000 exotic plant varieties and a rain forest; take the guided tram ride. *10901 Old Cutler Rd, Coral Gables. Open daily, 9.30–4.30.*

Metrozoo An outstanding zoo with animals in natural habitats. *12400 SW 152nd St, Kendall. Open 10–4.*

Planet Ocean A multimedia science center devoted to the oceans of the world. *3979 Rickenbacker Causeway, Virginia Key. Open 10–6.*

Seaquarium Across the causeway from Planet Ocean, this tropical marine aquarium has seals, manatees, whale and dolphin shows. *Rickenbacker Causeway, Virginia Key. Open 9.30–6.30.*

Out of town

Disneyworld in Orlando is Florida's top tourist attraction. The flight takes only 30mins, the drive 4hrs.

Everglades National Park, 40 miles/65kms south of Miami, is a tropical swamp and animal preserve.

Guided tours

The coastal mansions and Biscayne Bay's islands can be seen on short cruises. *The Island Queen* leaves from Miamarina, 5th St and Biscayne Bay ☏ 379-5119; *Nikko's Gold Coast* is at 10800 Collins Ave ☏ 945-5461. *American Sightseeing Tours*, 11077 NW 36th Ave ☏ 688-7700 run bus tours.

Spectator sports

Baseball The *Miami Miracle* plays at the Miami Stadium, University Park ☏ 220-7040.

Basketball *Miami Heat* plays at the new Miami Arena, 721 NW 1st Ave ☏ 577-4328.

Football The *Dolphins* and the University of Miami *Hurricanes* are at the Orange Bowl, 1501 NW 3rd St, and at the Joe Robbie Stadium, both ☏ 620-2578.

Horse-racing *Hialeah Park*, 4 E 25th St ☏ 885-8000, has pink flamingos and a beautiful setting. Other courses are *Gulfstream Park*, US-1 at Hallandale ☏ 944-1242, and *Calder Race Course*, 21001 NW 27th Ave ☏ 625-1311.

Jai-alai During winter, gamblers try their luck at jai-alai, a fast court game played at the *Miami Fronton*, 3500 NW 37th Ave ☏ 633-6400.

Keeping fit

Beaches *Hobie Beach, Crandon Park*

(Rickenbacker Causeway) and *Bill Baggs Cape Florida State Park* are on Key Biscayne. The *Venetian Pool* and *Matheson Hammock Park* (Old Cutler Rd) are in Coral Gables.
Bicycling There are more than 100 miles/160kms of year-round paths. Rent from *Dade Cycle Shop*, 3043 Grand Ave, Coconut Grove ☎ 443-6075, and *Key Biscayne Bicycle Rentals*, 260 Crandon Park Blvd, Key Biscayne ☎ 361-5555.
Golf Many hotels offer guests golf privileges at private courses including the *Biltmore* in Coral Gables; the *Key Biscayne*, Crandon Blvd, Key Biscayne ☎ 361-9120; and *Palmetto*, 9300 Coral Reef Dr ☎ 238-2922.
Jogging Among the favorite jogging courses is *David T Kennedy Park* at 220 S Bayshore Dr.
Tennis Public tennis and raquetball courts are numerous at universities, schools and parks ☎ 579-2676.
Water sports and boating Most of the many marinas have rental facilities for surfing, skiing, diving and sailing.

Local resources

Business services

Stephan Secretarial Service, Ponce de Leon Blvd ☎ 444-8311, offers complete services.
Photocopying and printing *Sir Speedy* ☎ 592-7590 provides a convenient service citywide.
Secretarial *Adia* ☎ 279-7111; *Advantage* ☎ 264-7060.
Translation *Berlitz Translation Services* ☎ 371-3686 and *Interamerican Translating* ☎ 371-4283 are convenient for most areas.

Communications

Long-distance delivery *Federal Express* ☎ 371-8500; *DHL* ☎ *592-8795.*
Local delivery *Choice Courier* ☎ 949-0909; *Crown Courier* ☎ 592-4000.
Post office The post office at MIA is open 24hrs for express mail. The downtown office is at 2200 NW 72 Ave ☎ 470-0222.
Telex and fax *Hotelcopy* ☎ 651-5176. *ITT Communications* ☎ 591-1065.

Conference/exhibition centers

Many of the larger hotels provide conference facilities. For other needs, consult the *Convention and Visitors Bureau* ☎ 539-3000.

Emergencies

Currency exchange Available at Bank America International at the airport Concourse E 24hrs, and American Express, 9700 Collins Ave, Bal Harbour, Mon–Sat, 10–6.
Hospitals *Cedars Medical Center*, 1400 NW 12th Ave ☎ 325-5511; *Jackson Memorial Hospital*, 1611 NW 12th Ave ☎ 325-7429; *Mount Sinai Medical Center*, 4300 Alton Rd, Miami Beach ☎ 674-2121.
Pharmacies *Eckerd Drugs* has many stores, several open 24hrs.
Police *Metro-Dade Police* ☎ 595-6263 (headquarters at 1390 NW 14th St); *City of Miami Police*, 400 NW 2nd Ave ☎ 579-6111.

Government offices

Metropolitan Dade County ☎ 375-5900; *Florida Dept of Commerce/International Trade Division* ☎ 446-8106; *US Dept of Commerce* ☎ 536-5267; *Customs* ☎ 536-5810; *Immigration and Naturalization Service* ☎ 536-5741.

Information sources

Business Information *Greater Miami Chamber of Commerce* ☎ 350-7700, in the same complex as the Omni International (see *Hotels*), is one of many chambers in Miami.
Local media The *Miami Herald* gives good local and regional coverage; the Spanish-language *Diario Las Americas* serves the Latin community; *Miami Review* provides business coverage.
Visitor information *Greater Miami Convention and Visitors Bureau*, 4770 Biscayne Blvd 33137 ☎ 539-3000.

Thank-yous

Florists *Buning the Florist, Inc*, 2125 Biscayne Blvd ☎ 945-0843; *Exotic Gardens, Inc*, 4800 Biscayne Blvd ☎ 661-8638.
Gift baskets *The Sweet Treat*, 1565 Sunset Dr, Coral Gables ☎ 665-0233.

MINNEAPOLIS/ST PAUL

Area code ☎ 612

The twin cities of Minneapolis/St Paul are spread across the Mississippi River, the waterway that helped to build fortunes in lumber and flour milling. Today these interests are represented by General Mills, Pillsbury, Bemis, Pentair and International Multifoods. The technology titans Control Data, Medtronic, Cray Research and Minnesota Mining and Manufacturing (3M), have headquarters here. Minneapolis is also the home of Northwest Airlines and the seat of the University of Minnesota, which has strong business, engineering and medical schools. It has close commercial and cultural ties with Canada.

The roots and lifestyles of the two cities are distinctly different. Minneapolis has a strong Scandinavian heritage, a dominant work ethic and a dislike of conspicuous alcohol consumption. St Paul, the smaller of the two, has the area's oldest names and oldest money, derived from railroad and lumber interests, plus a conservative Irish Catholic population. Its powerbrokers entertain in their homes and clubs rather than in restaurants and bars, as Minneapolitans do. St Paul is the seat of state government but it has traditionally relied on its twin for arts, dining, shopping and business, although new commercial complexes are bringing money and activity back to the once-stagnant city center.

Arriving

Minneapolis/St Paul International Airport

Most flights to and from MSP in Bloomington are domestic. Customs, for those that arrive from abroad, are at a secondary terminal, a quarter mile from the main building, making baggage claim a slow process. Facilities include currency exchange 6am–6pm, executive lounge, restaurants and car rental offices; all are in the main terminal ☎ 720-7171.

Nearby hotels *Embassy Suites Bloomington*, 2800 W 80 St ☎ 884-4811 fax 884-8137. *Registry*, 7901 24th Ave S ☎ 854-2244 fax 854-4421.

City link It is about 10 miles/16kms to both downtown areas. Allow about 15mins, 45mins in the rush hours.

Taxi Cabs line up at the main terminal. The fare is about $18.

Limousine The Airport Express ☎ 726-6400 provides shared vans leaving the airport every 15 mins; cost $7.50.

Car rental Most agencies have airport offices but a taxi or limousine is preferable, unless you need to drive frequently between the two cities or to the suburbs; Avis ☎ 726-5220, Hertz ☎ 726-1600, National ☎ 726-5600.

Getting around

Minneapolis is laid out in a grid pattern with avenues – divided by Washington – running north–south and streets – divided by Nicollet – running east–west. Downtown St Paul is less orderly, but its avenues consistently run east–west and streets north–south.

Taxi It is usually possible to hail a cab in either downtown, but they must be ordered by phone elsewhere; expect a wait in bad weather. *Airport Taxi* ☎ 721-6566, *Blue and White* ☎ 333-3331 and *Yellow* ☎ 331-8294.

Limousine *Candlelight Chauffeur Service* ☎ 690-3212.

Car rental *Budget* ☎ 888-0718 (in Bloomington). See also *City link*.

Walking In Minneapolis, most downtown hotels, stores, and office buildings are connected by a skyway system of covered walks and escalators at second-floor level. Any area is safe during daylight, but

downtown streets are deserted after office hours. After dark, avoid walking around Hennepin Avenue, the city's nightlife area, and Loring Park, and Selby–Dale in St Paul.
Bus Minneapolis has no subway, and the *MTC* bus service ☎ 827-7733 is generally of little help to the business visitor, except for commuting to St Paul or the University.

Area by area

The *downtown Minneapolis* skyline is dominated by the 50-story Investors Diversified Services (IDS) in Nicollet Mall. Nearby are Cesar Pelli's Norwest Bank Tower, Saks Fifth Avenue and City Center, a 90-store shopping complex. The Mall stretches southwest past the Orchestra Hall, towards Loring Park and the Guthrie Theatre and Walker Art Center. Nicollet Avenue joins it from the south at Grant St. To the east are the city's financial institutions, government buildings and prestigious legal offices. The recently gentrified arts-and-dining *Warehouse District* is to the west. Just across the Mississippi is *Riverplace*, a waterfront shopping and entertainment complex, and historic *St Anthony Main*, now a restored shopping–dining area. International Market Square, a five-building showcase for interior design firms, lies just west of downtown.

Sandwiched between the industrial and shipping compounds along the Mississippi riverbank to the east and the dual domes of the State Capitol and the cathedral, *downtown St Paul* is the home of prominent banks and insurance companies. The area includes Town Square, a shopping/dining/hotel complex, and Galtier Plaza, in the chic *Lowertown* arts-cum-warehouse district. Rice Park, just south, is a pretty square bordered by St Paul's showcase buildings: the Ordway Music Theater, St Paul Hotel, Landmark Center, the public library, and Civic Center.

St Paul's upper crust occupy the imposing mansions on *Summit Avenue*. Young lawyers and upper management types live in *Crocus Hill*'s Victoriana. *Highland Park*, a neighborhood to the southwest, houses the more conservative, independent business executives. Big money, but not necessarily old, buys an estate in super-exclusive *North Oaks*.

Other areas

The University of Minnesota's East and West Bank campuses are bordered by *Prospect Park*, a coveted riverside neighborhood inhabited mainly by the University faculty. Doctors, lawyers and the town's intelligentsia are based in *Kenwood*, an enclave of smart homes surrounding several lakes 3 miles/5kms south of downtown Minneapolis. At night its focal point, the S Hennepin and Lake Street intersection – known as *Uptown* – is alive with shopping and socializing young professionals.

An address in *Edina*, an inner-ring suburb 15mins from downtown,

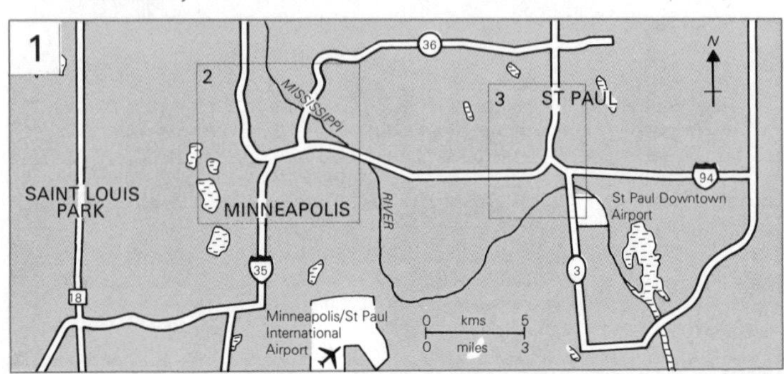

denotes first-generation wealth. Farther out lie the wealthy *Wayzata* and *Orono* communities of chief executives.

Hotels

In preparation for the completion in Spring 1990 of the expanded Convention Center, Minneapolis hotels were remodeled and refurbished. Except for a cluster on The Strip (Hwy 494 to the south and west), they are mostly downtown. St Paul has two main business-class hotels.

Hyatt Regency [$]//
1300 Nicollet Mall, Minneapolis 55403
☎ 370-1234 [TX] 290413 fax 370-1463
• AE DC MC V • 534 rooms, 23 suites, 6 restaurants, 2 bars
Because of its size and location this is a popular choice for conferences and conventions. Behind the awesome fountain in the vast lobby is The Willows, a contemporary restaurant with the genteel atmosphere of a private club (see *Restaurants*). Bank, travel agency, florist, nonsmoking floor • use of Greenway Athletic Club (see *Keeping fit*) • 21 meeting rooms.

Marquette [$]//
710 Marquette Ave, Minneapolis 55402
☎ 332-2351 [TX] 9105761686
fax 332-7707 • Hilton • AE DC MC V
• 266 rooms, 16 suites, 3 restaurants, 2 bars
This modestly understated hotel, offering unusually spacious rooms, each with steam bath, is where VIPs receive Minneapolis's most deferential

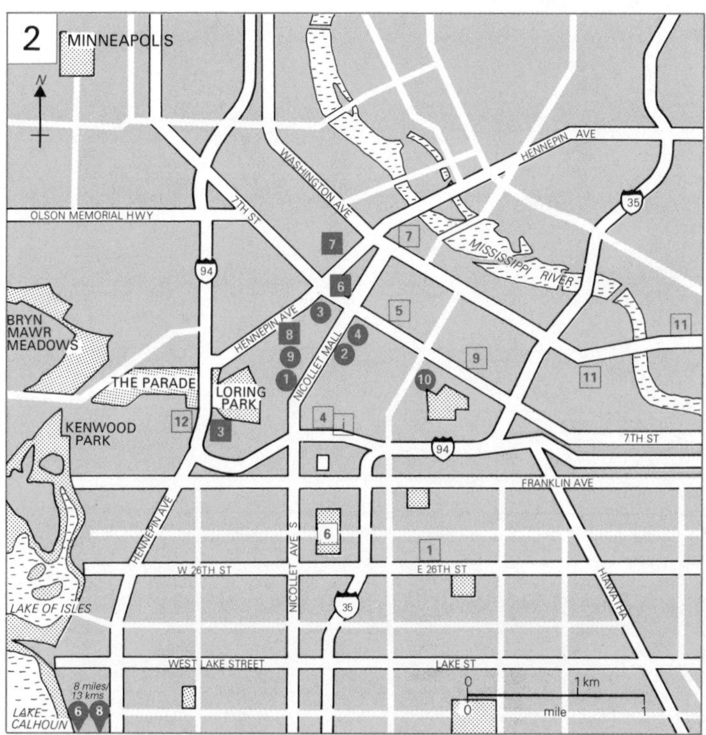

and accommodating service. Located on the 3rd–21st stories of the IDS pinnacle, it is connected by skyway to other business towers. Businessmen are attracted to the dark Marquis bar and the tiny, quiet Marquis restaurant, with its polished and tactful service. The Orion Room, on the 50th floor, offers the most spectacular view of the city. Fitness center • 12 meeting rooms, teleconferencing.

Marriott City Center [$]//
30 S 7th St, Minneapolis 55402
☎ 349-4000 fax 332-7165 • AE DC MC V • 584 rooms, 96 suites, 3 restaurants, 2 bars
The Marriott sits atop the shops of City Center and is connected to adjacent downtown buildings by skyway. Its atrium is a good spot for quiet discussion. The Fifth Season (see *Restaurants*), a greenhouse room serving what is arguably the city's finest cuisine at well-spaced tables, ensures uninterrupted business conversations. Rooms on the executive floor have jacuzzis. Sauna, weight-training • 18 meeting rooms.

Northstar [$]/
618 2nd Ave S, Minneapolis 55402
☎ 338-2288 fax 338-2288 ext 318 • AE DC MC V • Omni • 226 rooms, 2 suites, 2 restaurants, 1 bar
Located on the seventh story of the Northstar Building, this has a chinoiserie-laden lobby; a clubby restaurant, the Rosewood Room, much used by local bankers and attorneys; and the circular Rosewood bar which attracts the same clientele in the early evening. Discounts at two athletic clubs • 6 meeting rooms.

Radisson St Paul [$]/
11 E Kellogg Blvd, St Paul 55101
☎ 292-1900 fax 292-1900 ext 6200 • AE DC MC V • 418 rooms, 22 suites, 3 restaurants, 3 bars
A popular choice in St Paul for conventions and conferences, despite its rather anonymous lobby and rooms. Le Carrousel, a Continental dining room on the top floor, offers splendid views as well as music and dancing. Connected to skyway. Nonsmoking floor, hairdresser, gift shop • pool, guest pass to YMCA sports facilities • 18 meeting rooms.

Radisson South [$]//
7800 Normandale Blvd, Minneapolis 55435 ☎ 835-7800 fax 893-8419 • AE DC MC V • 578 rooms, 18 suites, 3 restaurants, 2 bars
Midway between the airport and downtown Minneapolis, the Radisson South caters to the convention trade as well as to the individual business traveler. Its remodeled marble lobby, elegant with scatter rugs and period furniture, leads to the Spectator Lounge, offering piano music in a homey living-room setting, a good

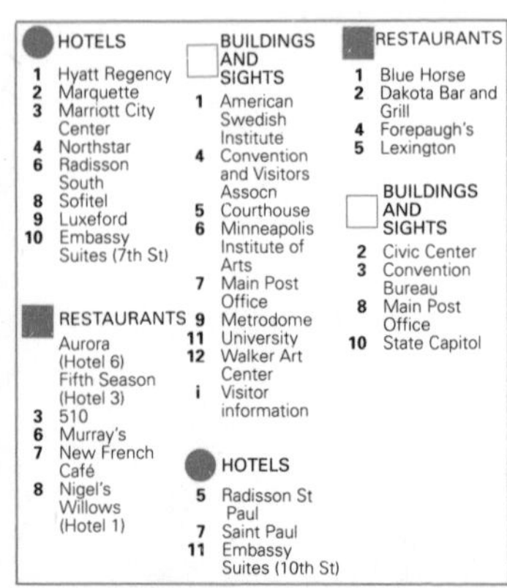

quiet discussion spot, and Aurora, the flagship dining room (see *Restaurants*). Travel agency, car rental, hairdresser, gift shop, poolside cabana suites • pool, sauna, putting green • 17 meeting rooms.

Saint Paul [$]/

350 Market St, St Paul 55102
☎ 292-9292 TX 297008 fax 228-9506 • AE DC MC V • 253 rooms, 30 suites, 2 restaurants, 1 bar

This once-prestigious property had fallen on seedier times but is now splendidly renewed, with gilt, Persian carpets and marble in its intimate lobby. Its Rice Park location and link to the skyway system are major bonuses, as is the fine Franco-American restaurant, L'Etoile. Gift shop • nearby health club • 9 meeting rooms.

Sofitel [$]//

5601 W 78th St, Minneapolis 55435
☎ 835-1900 TX 290215 fax 835-2696 • AE DC MC V • 287 rooms, 11 suites, 3 restaurants, 1 bar

Only 10mins from the airport, 15mins from downtown Minneapolis, the Sofitel has a cosmopolitan air and a dedication to service that suggests its French parentage. It attracts more foreign business guests than most other area hotels. There is a six-story garden atrium, and its spacious rooms can be used for small meetings. La Terrasse, a chic, informal sidewalk café/bar, is famed locally for its onion soup. French deli/bakery, gift shop, hairdresser • indoor pool, sauna, whirlpool • 13 meeting rooms.

OTHER HOTELS

Hotel Luxeford [$]/ *1101 La Salle Ave ☎ 332-6800 fax 332-8246 • AE DC MC V*; and **Embassy Suites** [$]/ *425 S 7th St ☎ 333-3111 fax 333-7984 • AE DC MC V*: both centrally located in Minneapolis, with suites only. **Embassy Suites** [$]/ *175 E 10th St ☎ 224-5400 fax 224-0957 • AE DC MC V*. In St Paul, convenient to the State Capitol.

Clubs

Members of the *Minneapolis Club* ☎ 332-2292 are old names and old money, while the *Minneapolis Athletic Club* ☎ 339-3655 attracts aspiring young achievers. The *Tower Club*, atop the IDS ☎ 349-6277, is favored by academics, and the *Greenway Athletic Club* ☎ 343-3131 is for young professionals.

Across the river, an invitation to the prestigious *Minnesota Club* ☎ 227-8761 usually means lunch with St Paul's monied patricians and executive officers. The *St Paul Athletic Club* ☎ 222-3361 attracts the new entrepreneur as well as the sons of older business families; the *University Club* ☎ 222-1751 is more social than business-oriented.

Restaurants

Minneapolis financiers tend to lunch in the city's top-class hotel restaurants; in St Paul, business dining is generally conducted in private clubs. Socializing dominates the evening hours.

Aurora [$]//

Radisson South Hotel, Minneapolis
☎ 835-7800 • closed L • AE DC MC V

Set piece of the hotel, the Aurora provides superb service and classy, creative food, often in Californian style.

Blue Horse [$]///

1355 University Ave, St Paul
☎ 645-8101 • closed Sat L, Sun • AE DC MC V

St Paul's finest restaurant has long been a favorite of powerbrokers and politicians. The professional staff understands the requirements of a private and perhaps protracted business meal. The menu features seafood and the California wines are a specialty.

Dakota Bar and Grill [$]
1021 Bandana Blvd E, Bandana Sq, St Paul ☎ *642-1442* • AE DC MC V
In a renovated railroad roundhouse, the Dakota serves innovative Californian dishes. After 9, the room grows loud with live jazz.

Fifth Season [$]//
Marriott City Center Hotel, Minneapolis ☎ *349-4000* • *closed L, Sun* • AE DC MC V • *jacket*
Well-spaced tables in a garden atmosphere off the Marriott Hotel's atrium, combined with discreet service and outstanding food, make this a highly desirable business eating place.

510 Restaurant [$]//
510 Groveland Ave, Minneapolis ☎ *874-6440* • *closed Sat L, Sun* • AE DC MC V
The club preferred by the grand old Minneapolis names. An aura of quiet formality, underscored by pale gray walls and chandeliers, sets the tone for French-style dining. The wine list is excellent and staff helpful.

Forepaugh's [$]/
276 S Exchange, St Paul ☎ *224-5606* • AE DC MC V
Top executives from 3M often escort visiting associates to this quaintly restored Victorian mansion overlooking charming Irvine Park. The French-style food is served superbly.

Lexington [$]//
1096 Grand Ave, St Paul ☎ *222-5878* • *closed Sun* • *no credit cards*
If St Paul's leaders are not at the Blue Horse, look for them here at their other neighbourhood club, known as the Lex. Steaks and martinis are favored choices.

Murray's [$]//
26 S 6th St, Minneapolis ☎ *339-0909* • AE DC MC V
Little has changed since this steakhouse opened in the 1940s, including its locally renowned silver butter knife steak, its career waitresses, and its afternoon teas. The crush of patrons includes everyone from visiting celebrities to celebrating locals.

New French Café [$]//
128 N 4th St, Minneapolis ☎ *338-3790* • AE DC MC V
The decor is aggressively stark in this warehouse hotspot, the service chatty, the food *nouvelle cuisine*, the clientele eager to see and be seen. A food temple for those in the monied arts.

Nigel's [$]/
15 S 12th St, Minneapolis ☎ *338-2235* • AE DC MC V
British and Canadian business travelers as well as the local upper crust favor this informal, garden-level café mainly because of its British-born owner, Nigel. Decor and menu are select American.

Willows [$]//
Hyatt Regency Hotel, Minneapolis ☎ *370-1263* • AE DC MC V
This de luxe restaurant is New York-style chic, and polished servers respect the requirements of a business meal. Ask for a banquette or wall table for extra privacy. Don't miss the duck or salad buffet.

Bars

Hotel bars are preferred for business meetings, but for socializing try *Figlio*, 3001 Hennepin Ave S ☎ 822-1688, much frequented by Uptown's young professionals; the *Monte Carlo*, 219 3rd Ave N ☎ 333-5900 (no credit cards), where wheeler-dealers mix with theatrical types; the *New French Bar*, around the corner from the café at 127 N 4th St ☎ 338-3790, very "in" with the city's bohemians; or *The Loon*, 500 1st Ave N ☎ 332-8342, packed with aspiring singles. In St Paul's, *Dixie*, 695 Grand Ave ☎ 222-7345, draws in mainly Crocus Hill WASPs; *Sweeney's* champagne bar at 96 N Dale ☎ 221-9157 attracts a young sophisticated crowd.

Entertainment

Minneapolis has always been the entertainment mecca for the area, especially at *Orchestra Hall*, 1111 Nicollet Mall ☏ 371-5656, but the building of the *Ordway Music Theater*, 345 Washington St ☏ 224-4222, has given St Paulites a top-class venue of their own. The weekly *Twin Cities Reader* covers what is on in both cities.

Theater and music In Minneapolis, the *Guthrie Theater* in Loring Park ☏ 377-2224 presents vivid stagings of classics and contemporary works in repertory. *Chanhassen Dinner Theater* 501 W 78th St, Chanhassen, west of Minneapolis ☏ 934-1500, is noted for comedies and musicals. *Dudley Riggs' Theaters* ☏ 332-6620 offer fringe comedy. Musical director of the *Minnesota Orchestra* ☏ 371-5656 is Dutch-born Edo di Waart; the *St Paul Chamber Orchestra* ☏ 291-1144 is led by artistic director and violinist Pinchas Zukerman; both play at the Ordway Theater, which is also the permanent home of the *Minnesota Opera*. The *Civic Center* stages rock and pop concerts.

Nightclubs *Rupert's*, 5410 Wayzata Blvd ☏ 544-5035, the area's classiest club, features jazz and big band music. *First Avenue*, 701 1st Ave N ☏ 332-1775, hosts funkier rock and jazz groups. Both are in Minneapolis.

Shopping

Riverplace is the newest Minneapolis shopping complex; next to it, a brick factory building, *St Anthony Main*, has been converted into specialty shops. *Southdale*, a shopping mall south of downtown, is adjacent to the pricier and more exclusive offshoot, *The Galleria*; *Ridgedale*, its counterpart on the west of the city, has spawned the equally smart *Bonaventure*. The *Nicollet Mall* in downtown has scores of clothing and gift shops, all dominated by Dayton's department store. Across the street is *City Center*, a 90-shop complex ranging from exclusive models to mass-market wares. *Byerly's Food Store* at St Louis Park, one of Minneapolis's major tourist attractions, has a cooking school, 24hr restaurant, ice cream, candy and bakery shops and an interesting gift gallery stocked with Limoges and Lalique china and glass.

St Paul's downtown *Carriage Hill Plaza*, 14 W 5th St, is a good source of jewelry, fine chocolates and designer fashions. *Town Square*, in the city's center, has 70 mid-price shops and cafés as well as a branch of Dayton's. The *Victoria Crossing* complex at Grand and Victoria Avenues is an intriguing warren of gift shops, bookstores and boutiques.

Sightseeing

Alexander Ramsey House Home of Minnesota's first territorial governor, affording a glimpse of cultivated Minnesota family life in the 1880s. *265 S Exchange St, St Paul ☏ 296-0100. Open Mon–Fri, 10–4; Sat & Sun, 1–4.30.*

American Swedish Institute Art and artifacts of Swedish heritage in Minnesota in an ornate 33-room mansion. *2600 Park Ave, Minneapolis ☏ 871-4907. Open Tue–Sun, noon–4.*

Minneapolis Institute of Arts An eclectic collection; strong points are the Rembrandts, Chinese jade collection and French Impressionists. *2400 3rd Ave S ☏ 870-3131. Open Tue–Sun, 10–5.*

Walker Art Center First-rate display of avant-garde art, plus superb giftshop and cafeteria with skyline vista. *Vineland Pl, Minneapolis ☏ 375-7600. Open Tue–Sat, 10–8; Sun, 11–5.*

Spectator sports

Baseball The *Twins* play at the Hubert H Humphrey Metrodome, 900 S 5th St ☏ 332-0386 and 375-1366.

Football The *Vikings* ☏ 333-8828 and University of Minnesota *Gophers* ☏ 373-3181 are based at the Hubert H Humphrey Metrodome.

Hockey The *Northstars* are at the Met Center, 8100 Cedar Ave S ☏ 853-9300.

Horse-racing *Canterbury Downs* is the local racetrack, at Shakopee ☎ 445-7223.

Keeping fit

Most hotels offer some form of fitness facilities. Open to the public and offering short-term membership is the *Greenway Athletic Club*, 1300 Nicollet Mall ☎ 343-3131, with squash, tennis, fitness center, and pool.
Golf Public courses are found at the larger parks, such as *Highland Park* at Snelling and Montreal Ave, St Paul ☎ 699-3650. Minneapolis courses include *Hiawatha*, 4553 Longfellow Ave S ☎ 724-7715; *Meadowbrook*, 201 Meadowbrook Rd ☎ 929-2077; and *Theodore Wirth*, Plymouth Ave N and Wirth Pkwy ☎ 522-2817.
Racquet sports There are more than 200 public tennis courts. Indoor courts are available at *Normandale*, 6701 W 78th St ☎ 944-2434, and *Northwest*, 5525 Cedar Lake Rd ☎ 546-5474, both of which are in Minneapolis.

Local resources

Business services

Your hotel is likely to be your best resource. For additional help call *AE Support System*, 430 Oak Grove St ☎ 871-2914, or *Business Support System*, 9921 Lyndale Ave S ☎ 888-5979.
Photocopying and printing *Insty-Print* ☎ 337-9800.
Translation *Berlitz* tel 920-4100 and *Krollkraft* ☎ 934-1300.

Communications

Long-distance delivery *Federal Express* ☎ 340-0887; *DHL* ☎ 727-1100.
Local delivery *Road Runners* ☎ 644-8444.
Post office The main Minneapolis post office is at 100 S 1st Ave ☎ 349-4970. St Paul's main post office is at 180 E Kellogg Blvd ☎ 293-3200. The airport post office ☎ 293-3138 is open 24hrs.
Telex *ITT Communications* ☎ (800) 526-3000.

Conference/exhibition centers

The expanded *Minneapolis Center*, 1301 S 2nd Ave ☎ 335-6000, has 100,000 sq ft of exhibition space and 18 meeting rooms; the final phase is complete in 1990. *St Paul Civic Center*, 143 W 4th St ☎ 224-7361.

Emergencies

The *Minnesota Medical Assn* ☎ 378-1875 supplies lists of physicians, and the *Minnesota Dental Assn* ☎ 646-7454 of dentists.
Hospitals *Hennepin County Medical Center*, 701 Park Ave ☎ 347-2121; *Abbott Northwestern Hospital*, 800 E 28th St ☎ 874-4234; *Mount Sinai Hospital*, 2215 Park Ave ☎ 347-4311. In St Paul: *St Paul-Ramsey Medical Center*, 640 Jackson St ☎ 221-2121.
Pharmacies *Walgreen's*, 533 Hennepin Ave ☎ 333-8898, has a convenient downtown location; the branch at 12 W 66th St ☎ 861-7276 is open 24hrs.
Police 325 4th St S ☎ 348-2345.

Government offices

Minnesota Dept of Commerce ☎ 296-4026; *US Customs* ☎ 725-3689; *US Dept of Commerce* ☎ 348-1638.

Information sources

Business information The best sources are *The Greater Minneapolis Convention and Visitors Association*, 1219 Marquette Ave ☎ 348-4313, and *St Paul Convention Bureau*, 445 Minnesota St ☎ 297-6985.
Local media Minneapolis's daily newspaper is the *Star & Tribune*; St Paul's has the *Pioneer Press-Dispatch*. The weekly *Twin Cities Reader* carries entertainment and dining guides.
Visitor information See *Business information*.

Thank-yous

Florists *Bachmans* ☎ 861-7311; *Minneapolis Floral* ☎ 377-8080; *Holm & Olson* ☎ 222-7335.
Gift baskets *Bob's Produce Ranch* ☎ 571-6620; *Toby Brill Confections* ☎ 332-0008.

NEW ORLEANS

Area code ☎ 504

Located 90 miles/144kms from the Mississippi River's delta into the Gulf of Mexico, New Orleans has long been a busy port, as well as a cultural mix of European, Central and South American, Caribbean and, more recently, Southeast Asian traditions. Spearheaded by offshore oil drilling in the Gulf, petrochemical companies dominate New Orleans's economy despite the fluctuations in oil prices. Numerous oil companies have offices in the city and three large companies, McDermott, Freeport-McMoran, and Louisiana Land and Exploration, have headquarters here. Tourism generates some $2bn annually, about a quarter of which is attributable to the city's growing convention trade.

Arriving

New Orleans International Airport

Moisant Field lies 15 miles/25kms west of the downtown Central Business District (CBD). No gate is more than a 5min walk from the baggage claim area. Useful information booth near the Customs area exit. Inquiries ☎ 464-0831.

Nearby hotels *Hilton New Orleans Airport*, 901 Airline Hwy ☎ 469-5000 fax 466-5473. *Holiday Inn Holidome*, 2929 Williams Blvd ☎ 467-5611 fax 469-4915. *Ramada Inn-Airport*, 2610 Williams Blvd ☎ 466-1401 fax 466-1401 ext 570.

City link A cab is best, and sharing is an accepted practice.

Taxi A taxi can drop you off at your French Quarter or CBD hotel within 25mins, 35mins during the 4–6pm peak and 50mins in the morning rush hour, 7–8.30am. Cabs line up on the ground level to the right of the terminal exit. The fare is $18 per passenger, $6 per person over that.

Limousine London Livery ☎ 944-1984.

Car rental See *Getting around*.

Bus Rhodes Transportation "limousine" ☎ 469-7555 runs a service to major hotels. The journey usually takes 45–60mins; the fare is about $8. The much cheaper airport shuttle does not stop at major hotels and is not recommended at night.

Getting around

New Orleanians do not talk in terms of geographical directions; they are generally given as uptown, downtown, lakeside or riverside, relative to the Mississippi River and Lake Pontchartrain. If your business is restricted to downtown you can easily get around on foot.

Taxi Most hotels have taxi stands. Only in the French Quarter and business district do you have a good chance of hailing a cab on the street. Companies that have air-conditioned cabs include *Yellow Checker* ☎ 525-3311 or 943-2411 and *United* ☎ 522-9771 or 524-9606.

Limousine *London Livery* ☎ 944-1984 and *Uptown Limousine* ☎ 861-7693 are among the best services.

Car rental is not recommended except for out-of-town journeys; New Orleans's multiangle street grid and one-way system can be very confusing. However, the local offices are *Avis* ☎ 523-4317; *Budget* ☎ 466-0892; *Hertz* ☎ 568-1645; and *National* ☎ 466-4335.

Walking For safety, steer clear of dark streets at night. The Bienville housing project near the French Quarter should always be avoided.

Bus *CBD Shuttles* No. 1 and No. 2 (Mon–Fri, 6.30–6) travel in opposite directions along a triangular path, including most important business addresses in Canal and Poydras Streets. The *Vieux Carré Shuttle* (Mon–Fri, 5–7; Sat & Sun, 8–6) is convenient for French Quarter locations on or near Chartres Street (pronounced "*Char*-ters"). The *St Charles Avenue Streetcar* crosses the central district on its way uptown 24hrs a day; avoid it at night.

Area by area

Downtown comprises the French Quarter and Central Business District, where most major hotels, banks, law firms and government and corporate offices are concentrated. Among its landmarks are the venerable Cotton Exchange and Whitney Bank Building and the skyscraper offices of Amoco, Chevron, Exxon and Texaco. The prestigious 53-story Place St Charles is the headquarters of Louisiana's biggest law firm, Jones-Walker.

The district's warehouse area has been revitalized recently by a spate of office and residential renovation. Between the warehouse district and the Mississippi River is the New Orleans Convention Center; and stretching for half a mile back to Canal Street is the new Riverwalk shopping center.

French Quarter Located on the site

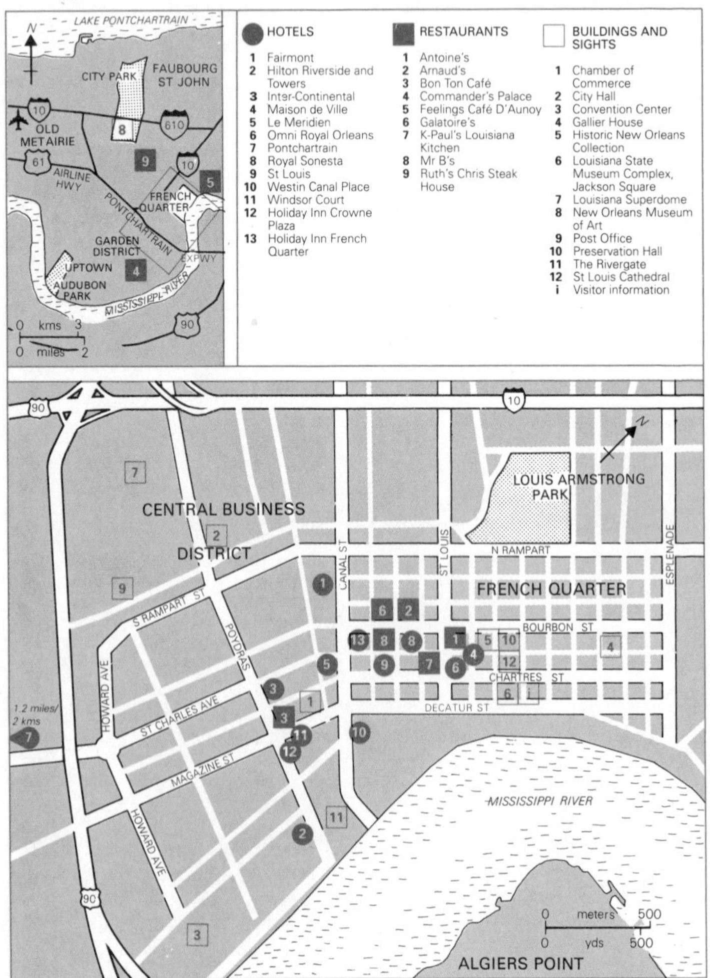

of the original 18thC city, the *French Quarter*, or *Vieux Carré*, still has a European look. Little remains from before the 19th century, but Creole cottages, built flush with the sidewalk around private courtyards – some of them visible from the street – give the area an unmistakable Old World flavor. The daytime hub of the Quarter is Jackson Square, with its permanent population of sidewalk artists; the pedestrian area in front of St Louis Cathedral is the stage for street performers. At night, the action moves to brash and bawdy Bourbon Street. Beyond Jackson Square the Quarter is mainly residential, with a large gay population.

Garden District About 2 miles/3kms west up St Charles Avenue from Canal Street, the Garden District is the most historic of New Orleans's wealthy areas. Many of its mansions date back a hundred years and are raised above ground for protection against flooding.

Uptown A mile or two farther up St Charles Avenue is an area combining the houses of the rich and many modest and even ramshackle dwellings – a legacy of the days when slaves lived on their owners' land.

Other areas

Adjacent to the French Quarter is *Faubourg Marigny*, a small neighborhood that houses many middle-income, old-time New Orleans families and a growing number of young professionals. *Algiers Point*, on a spit of land across the Mississippi River, is also being gentrified. The *Lakefront* area on Lake Pontchartrain north of the French Quarter is typical modern suburbia, with sprawling condominiums and neatly manicured lawns. *Old Metairie* is New Orleans's oldest and most chic suburb.

Hotels

Almost all important hotels are in the downtown area, especially near the foot of Canal Street. Many of the best are ultra-modern, but some retain the city's distinctive European character.

Fairmont $///

123 Baronne St 70140 ☎ 529-7111
TX 8109516015 fax 522-2303 • AE DC MC V • 730 rooms, 60 suites, 4 restaurants, 3 bars

The hotel's block-long lobby, with its gilded Greek Revival columns, opens onto the bustling Central Business District at each end. Rooms vary dramatically in size. The Sazerac is a popular business bar, and at night the Blue Room supper club offers high-quality entertainment. Hairdresser, beauty shops • pool, rooftop tennis • business center, 22 meeting rooms.

Hilton Riverside and Towers $//

2 Poydras St 70140 ☎ 561-0500
TX 6821214 fax 568-1721 • AE DC MC V • 1,516 rooms, 86 suites, 3 restaurants, 4 bars, 2 coffee shops

With its river view and convenient location for the Convention Center, the Hilton is popular with many conventioneers. Its Rivercenter Racquet and Health Club has two pools, a rooftop jogging track, 11 tennis courts, 7 racquetball courts and a squash court. Covered access to the Riverwalk shopping area. Business center, 39 meeting rooms.

Inter-Continental $//

444 St Charles Ave 70130 ☎ 525-5566
TX 58202 fax 532-7310 • AE DC MC V • 462 rooms, 32 suites, 2 restaurants, 2 bars

This imposing St Charles Avenue hotel is a harmonious blend of contemporary and old-time splendor. The hotel has an extensive collection of modern art displayed in its public rooms; a sculpture garden is set into the fifth-floor courtyard. Rooms are modern, spacious and well suited for working, with well-equipped bathrooms. Hairdresser, beauty shops • 30 meeting rooms, teleconferencing.

Maison de Ville $////
727 Toulouse St 70130 ☎ 561-5858 fax 561-5858 • AE DC MC V • 14 rooms, 2 suites, 7 cottages, 1 restaurant
The Maison de Ville caters mainly for clients who value their privacy and who appreciate intimate, Old World surroundings. The main house dates from the mid-19th century; the nearby cottages (former slave quarters) are a century older. All rooms are furnished with antiques. Though the hotel has few in-house business services, its concierge can conjure up almost anything. Pool at the cottages.

Le Meridien $//
614 Canal St 70130 ☎ 525-6500 TX 784465 fax 525-8068 • AE DC MC V • 496 rooms, 6 suites, 2 restaurants, 1 bar
Marble floors, shiny brass railings and a three-story atrium with a water cascade make this Air France-owned hotel one of New Orleans's most luxurious. The well-equipped business center offers back-up secretarial services and a personal computer. Shops • heated pool, health club • 13 meeting rooms.

Omni Royal Orleans $//
621 St Louis St 70140 ☎ 529-5333 TX 58350 fax 529-7089 • AE DC MC V • 351 rooms, 24 suites, 2 restaurants, 4 bars
The huge lobby resplendent with mirrors, marble floors, and beautiful floral arrangements, proclaims the luxurious standard of this French Quarter hotel, which is reflected in the consistently good service. Rooms are on the small side, but are charmingly furnished. The Rib Room is a well-established power-lunching place. Hairdresser, beauty salon, jeweler • rooftop pool • 13 meeting rooms.

Pontchartrain $//
2031 St Charles Ave 70140 ☎ 524-0581 TX 266068 fax 529-1165 • AE DC MC V • 70 rooms, 30 suites, 1 restaurant, 1 bar, 1 coffee shop
Discreetly refined, the Pontchartrain is reminiscent of London's Connaught. It has an international reputation for service, and the Caribbean Room restaurant is an elegant dining room for business entertaining. Café Pontchartrain is the number one breakfasting place for many of the city's business leaders. Arrangements with nearby health club • 1 meeting room.

Royal Sonesta $///
300 Bourbon St 70140 ☎ 586-0300 TX 22361 fax 586-0335 • AE DC MC V • 462 rooms, 32 suites, 2 restaurants, 5 bars
Located in the heart of the French Quarter, the Royal Sonesta caters to the serious business traveler; its 35-room Tower, with concierge and reservation desk, is accessible only by private key. Despite its business orientation, however, the Royal Sonesta appeals also to the tourist, and it has something of a carnival atmosphere all year round. Pool, nearby health club, tennis, golf • 19 meeting rooms.

St Louis $//
730 Bienville St 70130 ☎ 581-7300 fax 524-8925 • AE DC MC V • 68 rooms, 4 suites, 1 restaurant, 1 bar
Small and charming, the St Louis is typically French Quarter in style. All rooms overlook a courtyard with fountain and have antique or reproduction French furnishings. 1 meeting room.

Westin Canal Place $///
100 Rue Iberville 70130 ☎ 566-7006 TX 6711201 fax 523-2549 • AE DC MC V • 398 rooms, 41 suites, 3 restaurants, 2 bars
Among the Westin's attractions are its location, in the smart Canal Place shopping complex, and the magnificent river view from its 11th-floor lobby. Afternoon tea is accompanied by piano music. Shops, hairdresser • pool, access to health club at the Meridien • 8 meeting rooms.

Windsor Court [$]//
300 Gravier St ☎ *523-6000*
[TX] *784060 fax 596-7513* • *AE DC MC V* • *58 rooms, 266 suites, 2 restaurants, 1 bar*
One of the city's newer hotels, the Windsor Court has acquired a loyal clientele, including many senior executives. In the English manor-style lobby afternoon tea is accompanied by classical music. The Grill Room is elegant, the service polished, and the cooking memorable. Many rooms have private balconies and most have refrigerators. The olympic size pool features an underwater music system. Health club, sauna • 8 meeting rooms.

OTHER HOTELS
Holiday Inn Crowne Plaza [$]//
333 Poydras St 70130
☎ *525-9444 fax 581-7179* • *AE DC MC V*. Near CBD and Convention Center.
Holiday Inn French Quarter [$]/
124 Royal St 70112 ☎ *529-7211 fax 566-1127* • *AE DC MC V*. Just across Canal Street from CBD and one block from Bourbon Street.

Clubs

New Orleans society revolves around the annual Mardi Gras celebrations and the 60-plus private clubs or "krewes," each of which sponsors its own parade every year. The most prestigious is *Rex*, whose leader is automatically recognized as the "King of Carnival." In business terms, the city has three important clubs: the Petroleum, the City and the Plimsoll. The *Petroleum Club* ☎ 524-3203 counts among its members top New Orleans's executives from virtually every major American oil company. Across from the Superdome, the *City Club* appeals more to political types, whereas the *Plimsoll Club* ☎ 529-1701, in the World Trade Center, attracts the heavyweights in import-export. More socially-oriented is the *Boston Club*, 824 Canal St ☎ 523-2241.

Restaurants

Often loosely termed "Creole" or "Cajun," New Orleans food is a complex mélange of French, Spanish, Caribbean and African influences. The inhabitants consider eating to be one of life's more important activities and like to take their time over it, although the quick business lunch is growing in popularity, and some hotels provide inexpensive buffets.

Antoine's [$]///
713 St Louis St ☎ *581-4422* • *closed Sun* • *AE DC MC V* • *jacket and tie* • *reservations recommended*
Antoine's has been serving Creole dishes to the moneyed classes since 1840. Huge, with dark wood walls, it is very suitable for quiet conversation. A table in one of the four private dining rooms is a local status symbol. With 35,000 bottles, Antoine's has New Orleans's largest wine cellar.

Arnaud's [$]//
813 Bienville St ☎ *523-0611* • *closed Sat L* • *AE DC MC V* • *jacket and tie for D*
With its tiled floors, beveled glass and ceiling fans, Arnaud's has a turn-of-the-century ambience. Fish is the specialty. The *prix fixe* luncheon is an excellent bargain. Private rooms available.

Bon Ton Café [$]/
401 Magazine St ☎ *524-3386* • *closed Sun* • *AE MC V*
Although primarily a neighborhood restaurant, the Bon Ton is famed throughout town for its Cajun food. Its festive atmosphere is well-suited to off-duty entertaining, but it is also popular for business lunches. Specialties are the shrimp and crayfish dishes, turtle soup and bread pudding, a New Orleans favorite.

Commander's Palace $//
1403 Washington Ave ☏ 899-8221 • closed Sun D • AE DC MC V • jacket and tie requested • reservations essential
Housed in a gracious ante-bellum mansion, this restaurant is popular with the city's upper crust. Dinnertime is always crowded. The cuisine is Creole and American – rated by some as the best in town. A good choice for entertaining important clients.

Feelings Café D'Aunoy $/
2600 Chartres St ☏ 945-2222 • closed Sat L • MC V
The atmosphere is old New Orleans; the service brisk; the food consistently very good. The brick-walled courtyard provides ample privacy for quiet discussion.

Galatoire's $//
209 Bourbon St ☏ 525-2021 • closed Mon • no reservations, no credit cards • jacket and tie after 5pm and Sun
Founded in 1905, Galatoire's is a favorite among old-line New Orleanians. With only a single, tile-floored dining room, the restaurant is charming but noisy and usually crowded, so consider it only for off-duty dining, when you have time to spare.

K-Paul's Louisiana Kitchen $//
416 Chartres St ☏ 942-7500 • closed L Sat & Sun • AE
The line outside the front door of this restaurant proclaims it as one of New Orleans's most popular – considered well worth the wait and the necessity (often) of sharing your table with strangers. Chef Paul Prudhomme's mastery of Creole-Cajun cooking is beyond dispute; but K-Paul's is more suitable for an off-duty meal than for business entertaining.

Mr B's $//
201 Royal St ☏ 523-2078 • AE DC MC V • no smoking
Just two blocks from Canal Street, in the French Quarter, Mr B's is *the* luncheon choice for many CBD professionals. Excellent hickory-grilled Creole-American food, mainly fish; good American wine list.

Ruth's Chris Steak House $/
711 N Broad St ☏ 486-0810 • AE DC MC V
Ruth's is one of the city's busiest business lunch spots, crammed daily with many of the local power-brokers and representatives of the judicial and political fields who come here for steak, seafood and its friendly atmosphere. The surrounding neighborhood is not the best; take a taxi.

Bars

Quite a lot of business is transacted in the city's better hotel bars, especially the *Sazerac* at the Fairmont, the *Rain Forest* atop the Hilton and the Omni Royal Orleans's *Esplanade Lounge*. If you want to combine your business talk with a bit of New Orleans jazz, try the *Bayou Bar* in the Hotel Pontchartrain, a small piano bar much appreciated by locals. The wine bar uptown at *Flagon's*, 3222 Magazine St, is popular with young professionals. Tops among French Quarter bars is the *Napoleon House* at 500 Chartres St. *Pat O'Brien's*, 718 St Peter St, is probably New Orleans's most famous bar, worth exploring in an off-duty moment.

Entertainment

For weekly listings look at the "Lagniappe" (pronounced "lan-*yap*") section in Friday's *Times-Picayune*, or in *Gambit*, a weekly free magazine available in newsstands and restaurants. Tickets can generally be obtained through *Ticketmaster* ☏ 888-8181.

Theater, music and ballet *The Saenger Performing Arts Center*, 143 N Rampart St ☏ 524-2490, a renovated movie palace, stages concerts and touring Broadway plays. The *Orpheum*, 129 University Pl, is the home of the New Orleans Symphony ☏ 525-0500. Local theater productions are performed at the

Contemporary Arts Center, inside the Train Station ☎ 523-1216, and *Le Petit Théâtre du Vieux Carré*, 616 St Peter St ☎ 522-9958. Opera and ballet are staged in the *Theater of the Performing Arts* in Louis Armstrong Park near the French Quarter ☎ 522-0592. The general warning about safety after dark applies to visiting any of these entertainment venues.

Jazz and nightclubs Contemporary jazz clubs include *Snug Harbor*, 626 Frenchman St ☎ 949-0696, and *Tyler's Beer Garden*, 5234 Magazine St ☎ 891-4989. *Preservation Hall*, 726 St Peter St ☎ 522-2841 (day), 523-8939 (evening), is famed for its traditional jazz and ancient musicians who play in a hot, musty, crowded room. Clarinetist Pete Fountain performs with his band in the *Hilton* four days a week ☎ 523-4374.

Shopping

Canal Place, near the foot of Canal Street, is New Orleans's most upmarket shopping center, with Gucci and Saks Fifth Avenue among the noteworthy stores. The popular Riverwalk development (see *Area by area*) is newer and larger. For food and amusing presents, go to *Jackson Brewery*, Decatur and St Peter Streets, which has been transformed into a smart urban mall open 7 days. *Royal Street* in the French Quarter is the place for antiques.

Sightseeing

The St Charles Avenue streetcar is the best way to explore the Garden District and uptown; its 7 mile/11km run takes you past some of New Orleans's most interesting sights.

Beauregard House Once the home of Frances Parkinson Keyes, now a museum with period furniture. *1113 Chartres St ☎ 523-7257.*

Gallier House in the French Quarter offers a view of New Orleans upper-class life in the mid-19th century, with original art and furnishings. *1118-23 Royal St ☎ 523-6722. Open Mon–Sat, 10–4.30.*

Historic New Orleans Collection Ten galleries trace the city's history in documents, antiques, paintings, maps, and memorabilia; a maze of inter-connecting late-18thC houses. *Main gallery at 533 Royal St ☎ 523-4652. Open Tue–Sat, 10–4.45.*

Louisiana State Museum Complex is on Jackson Square in the French Quarter – an historic group of buildings including the old Mint and Arsenal. *Open Tue–Sun, 12–5 ☎ 586-6968.*

New Orleans Museum of Art Located in City Park, NOMA has world-class items from Asia, Africa, Europe and America. The Fabergé egg collection is on display in the City Wing. *Open Tue–Sun, 10–5 ☎ 488-2631.*

Guided tours

Boat tours *Cajun Bayou Cruise* ☎ 484-7801. The *New Orleans Steamboat Company* ☎ 586-8777 has 2hr and half-day cruises. The *Creole Queen*'s 3hr cruise ☎ 529-4567 includes a visit to the Beauregard Plantation House and the site of the War of 1812's Battle of New Orleans; *Honey Island Swamp Tours* ☎ 641-1769 visits one of the country's best-preserved water wilderness areas.

Bus tours *Gray Line Tours of New Orleans* ☎ 587-0861 operates a variety of bus and boat tours.

Limousine tours *Allan's Limousine Service* ☎ 944-1984.

Walking tours *Friends of the Cabildo* ☎ 523-3939 conduct tours of the French Quarter daily except Mon.

Spectator sports

Football New Orleans is deluged each year with fans who come for the Sugar Bowl Classic, held in the Superdome, 1500 Sugar Bowl Dr ☎ 587-3663, on New Year's Day. The professional *Saints* ☎ 733-0255 also play here.

Horse-racing At the *Fairgrounds*, 1751 Gentilly Blvd ☎ 944-5515, from Nov to Apr; and *Jefferson Downs* at 1300 Sunset Blvd ☎ 466-8521.

Keeping fit

Most hotels have pools; some have fitness centers. The outdoor exercise circuit at Audubon Park is a local favorite but is not safe after dark.
Fitness centers *YMCA* ☎ 568-9622 has weight-training rooms and exercise classes for men and women at its Lee Circle and Superdome branches. The Lee Circle Y also has racquetball courts and a gym.
Golf Public courses are at City Park ☎ 483-9397 and Audubon Park ☎ 861-9511.
Tennis Courts are widely available, again at City Park ☎ 483-9383 and Audubon Park ☎ 865-8638. The Hilton's tennis courts (see *Hotels*) are open to guests of any city hotel.

Local resources

Business services

For a comprehensive range of most business services try *Office Masters* ☎ 523-3689.
Audio-visual *AVW Audio Visual* ☎ 522-7937, *Jasper Ewing & Son* ☎ 525-5257.
Printing and photocopying *Accurate Letter Co* ☎ 522-9092; *Kinko's Copies* ☎ 861-8016 is open 24hrs.
Secretarial *Your Girl Friday* ☎ 834-8761.
Translation *Professional Translators and Interpreters* ☎ 581-3122.

Communications

Long-distance delivery *Federal Express* ☎ (800) 238-5355.
Local delivery *Choice Courier* ☎ 522-2678; *Controlled Business Deliveries* ☎ *525-9917.*
Post office *Main Post Office*, 701 Loyola Ave ☎ 589-1111.
Telex and telegram *RCA Global Communications Service*, 2 Canal St ☎ 831-4142; *Western Union*, 334 Carondelet St ☎ 523-5453.

Conference/exhibition centers

New Orleans Convention Center, 900 Convention Center Blvd ☎ 582-3000, and *The Rivergate*, 4 Canal St ☎ 592-2000, both have meeting rooms and big exhibition spaces.

Emergencies

Hospitals *Charity Hospital*, 1532 Tulane Ave ☎ 568-2311; *Tulane Medical Center*, 1415 Tulane Ave ☎ 588-5342. For physician referral call *Touro-MD* ☎ 897-7777. Emergency service (including dental) is provided by *Tuoro Infirmary*, 1401 Foucher St ☎ 897-8250; 24hrs.
Pharmacies *Walgreen Drug Store*, 900 Canal St ☎ 523-7201; a central 24hr drugstore is *Eckerd's*, 3400 Canal St ☎ 488-6661.
Police *New Orleans Police Department*, 715 S Broad St ☎ 821-2222.

Government offices

City Hall, 1300 Perdido St ☎ 586-4311; *US Dept of Commerce's Office of International Trade*, 2 Canal St ☎ 589-6546; *US Immigration and Naturalization Service* ☎ 589-6533.

Information sources

Business information *The Chamber/New Orleans and the River Region*, 301 Camp St ☎ 527-6900, tells visitors what services are available and provides information about potential markets. The Chamber's Economic Development Council ☎ 527-6946 specializes in economic research.
Local media *The Times-Picayune/The States-Item* is New Orleans's only daily newspaper. *Where* and *Go* are useful magazines for visitors; *New Orleans Magazine* is feature-oriented.
Visitor information *The Greater New Orleans Tourist and Convention Commission*, 1520 Sugar Bowl Dr ☎ 566-5011; information center at 529 St Ann St.

Thank-yous

Confectionary Pralines at *Green Orchid*, 626 Chartres St ☎ 529-4900.
Florists *Carrollton Flower Market*, 838 Dublin St ☎ 866-9614; *Harkins the Florist*, 1601 Magazine St ☎ 529-1638.
Wine *Martin Wine Cellar*, 3827 Baronne St ☎ 899-7411.

NEW YORK

Area codes: Manhattan and Bronx ☎ 212; Brooklyn, Queens and Staten Is ☎ 718; New Jersey ☎ 201; Connecticut ☎ 203; Long Island ☎ 516. Telephone numbers in this city guide are in Manhattan and Bronx unless otherwise indicated.

Though New York is not America's capital city, it is without doubt its city of capital. Money – especially the relatively new foreign investment flowing in through the city's exchanges – is the power that has revitalized the city, restructured much of the nation's business through complex financial transactions, and created the 24hr business day. If anything characterizes New York, it is not muggings, subway crime or Central Park after dark; it is the pace that obliges even the most temporary business visitor to seek to shave a minute or so off the walk to the next meeting. New York is the city that invented the power breakfast, an occasion that has little to do with eating, but a great deal to do with winning – contracts, companies, kudos and power.

New York was always a busy place, a bustling seaport; it still is one of the world's busiest ports. But it has lost its manufacturing edge, and many of the best-known corporations have moved their headquarters to the suburbs or to cheaper cities elsewhere. Now New York belongs to the money-movers, the real-estate developers and their supporting communications, image-making and advertising.

Away from the wharves, Manhattan thoroughfares have given their names to entire industries. Seventh Avenue – Fashion Avenue – is the center of American fashion, and Madison Avenue means advertising and promotion. Wall Street, of course, has been the seat of the nation's financial activity since the forerunner of the New York Stock Exchange was founded under a buttonwood tree on that street in 1792.

The pursuit of success and self-advancement has produced a business culture renowned for its extreme pressures, tough standards and high compensation. New MBAs or young lawyers at the foot of a long corporate ladder routinely work 80hr weeks with starting salaries of more than $65,000. But life in New York is more expensive than anywhere else in the USA. City taxes are high, and rents easily top $2,000 a month for a one-bedroom apartment in a doorman-protected building on a good Manhattan block. Good dinners for less than $40 a head are rare, and maintaining the proper corporate wardrobe is expensive. Even play is intense in the Big Apple. City health clubs are full of weight-lifting bankers; Central Park full of jogging media planners. Few high-powered executives are to be found in Manhattan on Friday afternoons in summer; they are headed for weekend homes out of town. Younger strivers, when they can escape their offices early enough, make for whatever is the latest fashionable nightspot to socialize, dance, drink and impair their efficiency for the next morning.

New York is a city of startling contrasts, where extreme wealth flourishes alongside poverty that matches that of many Third World countries. Imported nannies wheel imported baby carriages in elegant little parks just a stone's throw from cacophonous avenues; subway travelers read both the brash *New York Post* and the vastly restrained *New Yorker*. Outside a multimilllion-dollar Broadway musical or the glittering headquarters of a multinational corporation you will find an altogether different kind of financial dealer – the hustler.

Though the old Park Avenue WASP elite has not really ruled New York for any considerable time, one legacy at least of the city's history remains: the enormous bureaucracy which attempts to govern it, accused often of corruption, seldom of efficiency. But after its brush with fiscal disaster and near-bankruptcy in the 1970s, the city has struggled back to solvency and improved many of its municipal services.

New York City is made up of five boroughs: Manhattan, which has over 20% of the city's 7.2m population, the Bronx, Brooklyn, Queens and Staten Island. The metropolitan area also includes counties in New Jersey, immediately across the Hudson River; Westchester County, north of the Bronx; Fairfield County in Connecticut; and Nassau County on Long Island.

Arriving

Three airports serve the metropolitan area: JF Kennedy International (JFK) and LaGuardia (LGA) in Queens, and Newark International (EWR) in New Jersey.

Domestic travelers will find it quicker to get into Manhattan from LaGuardia. International travelers are likely to find that airline schedules dictate their arrival at JFK, even though Immigration and Customs formalities may take less time at Newark. Journey times into town from Newark and JFK are similar; but cab rides from Newark across the state line are much more expensive.

There is a helicopter service from JFK to 34th St, at the East River, about every half hour during the day, which is the quickest way of getting into Manhattan.

By road allow at least 90mins to get between Newark and both the other airports (you have to cross Manhattan). Even the 3mile/5km journey from LGA to JFK may take an hour at peak times. *Carey Transportation* ☏ (718) 632-0500 or (212) 286 9766 operates a half-hourly LGA–JFK bus service. *Salem Transportation* ☏ (718) 656-4511 serves all three airports.

JF Kennedy International Airport

JFK handles international and medium- and long-haul domestic services. International flights arrive at either the International Arrivals Building or the Pan American, American, British Airways or TWA terminals. Major construction work on the TWA terminal begins 1990.

International passengers first go through US Public Health, Immigration and Naturalization formalities, then baggage claim and finally Customs. If you are one of the first off the plane and have only hand baggage, you can be out of the airport in less than 30mins; otherwise, allow an hour. Clearance is usually slowest at the International Arrivals Building; allow up to 2hrs; in summer, it can take much longer.

All terminals have places to eat, drink and buy gifts or duty-free goods. If you expect to have a long wait, the airline executive or VIP lounges are the best places to be. In the International Arrivals Building there is a shared executive lounge and a wide range of services, including a general information counter in the main lobby ☏ (718) 656-7990 and three baggage storage areas ☏ (718) 995-2228. A 24hr currency exchange is on the second floor (other terminals close at 8.30); there is a dental suite between the east and west wings ☎ (718) 656-4747.

Nearby hotels *International Hotel* at JFK 11436 • THF • ☎ (718) 995-9000 TX 4972701 fax (718) 995-9075. *Airport Hilton Inn*, 138-10 135 Avenue, Jamaica, Queens 11436 ☎ (718)322-8700 TX 971962 fax (718) 521-0749. *JFK Airport Marriott*, 135-30 140 St, Jamaica, Queens 11437 ☎ (718) 659-6000 or (800)228-9290 TX 980879 fax (718) 659-4755. *Holiday Inn at JFK*, 14402 135th Ave, Jamaica ☎ (718) 659-0200. All hotels take major credit cards.

City link JFK is 15 miles/24kms east of Manhattan in the borough of Queens. During peak hours (7–10, 3–7) the only quick method of transportation is a helicopter.

Helicopter Most major airlines have arrangements with New York Helicopter Corp ☎ (800) 645-3494 (London, 01-978-5222) which provides free flights from TWA Terminal A for first and business class travelers. The fare, one way, for others is up to $38, depending on the airline. The service is half hourly, 7.50am–7.30pm, and the flight time 10–12mins to the heliport at E 34th St in midtown Manhattan.

Taxi Cabs provide the most convenient way to get into the city and cost only about $28. Taxis wait outside all terminals; there can be shortages during peak arrival periods (late morning and late afternoon). The ride to midtown takes about 30mins with no traffic delays, but can take 90mins during rush hours. After 3pm, the usual route through the Queens-Midtown Tunnel has only one in-bound lane, and many drivers prefer to cross the Triboro Bridge to minimize hold-ups. Because the meter fare is a combination of time and distance, if Triboro is the quicker route, it may not add much to the fare.

Limousine Limousines are often available outside terminals and, shared, should cost less than a cab. Otherwise you can call ahead for a limo to meet you (see *Getting around* for reliable firms).

Car rental A car is almost always an encumbrance in Manhattan, but all the major firms have desks at JFK: Avis ☎ (718) 244-5400, Hertz ☎ (718) 656-7600, National ☎ (718) 632-8300.

Bus Services operated by Carey Transportation ☎ (718) 632-0500 leave every 15–30mins, 6–midnight, fare $8. You can get off at various midtown locations including Grand Central Terminal.

Bus services advertised in hotels often make many stops, and whether your stop is first or last can make a difference of 30mins in travel time.

Subway The JFK Express ☎ (718) 858-7272 leaves every 20mins, 5.30am–midnight, taking 45mins–1hr; fare $6.50. It involves both an airport bus ride (stopping at every terminal) and a long subway trip with frequent stops on the West Side of Manhattan along the IND subway system A, C and E routes. It is useful only in rush hours.

LaGuardia Airport

LGA, named after the former mayor, Fiorello H LaGuardia, is on the East River in Queens, 8 miles/13kms from midtown. The airport is busiest in the early morning, late afternoon and evening, when cabs into town can be scarce and traffic problems are most likely. Long walks to baggage claim are common. Only limited foreign currency exchange is available. The large gift shops offer a wide selection, but do not expect a bargain, nor anything unusual.

Nearby hotels *Holiday Inn*, 100-15 Ditmars Blvd, E Elmhurst, Queens 11369 ☎ (718) 898-1225 fax 898-8337. *Royce Hotel at LGA*, 90-10 Grand Central Parkway, E Elmhurst, Queens 11369 ☎ (718) 446-4800 fax 446-4886. *La Guardia Marriott*, 102 Ditmars Blvd, East Elmhurst, Queens 11369 ☎ 565-8900 or (800) 228-9290.

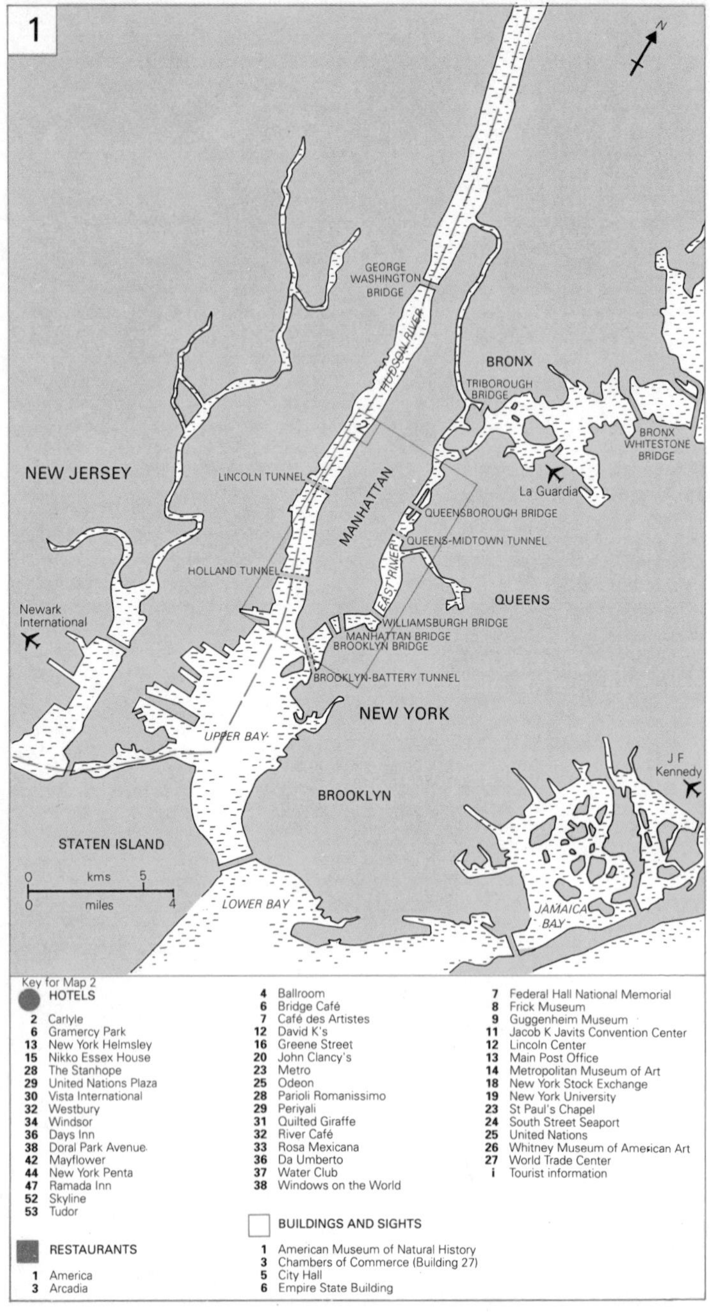
1
N
GEORGE WASHINGTON BRIDGE
HUDSON RIVER
BRONX
TRIBOROUGH BRIDGE
BRONX WHITESTONE BRIDGE
La Guardia
NEW JERSEY
LINCOLN TUNNEL
MANHATTAN
2
QUEENSBOROUGH BRIDGE
QUEENS-MIDTOWN TUNNEL
EAST RIVER
HOLLAND TUNNEL
QUEENS
Newark International
WILLIAMSBURGH BRIDGE
MANHATTAN BRIDGE
BROOKLYN BRIDGE
BROOKLYN-BATTERY TUNNEL
NEW YORK
UPPER BAY
J F Kennedy
BROOKLYN
STATEN ISLAND
0 kms 5
0 miles 4
LOWER BAY
JAMAICA BAY
Key for Map 2
HOTELS
2 Carlyle
6 Gramercy Park
13 New York Helmsley
15 Nikko Essex House
28 The Stanhope
29 United Nations Plaza
30 Vista International
32 Westbury
34 Windsor
36 Days Inn
38 Doral Park Avenue
42 Mayflower
44 New York Penta
47 Ramada Inn
52 Skyline
53 Tudor
RESTAURANTS
1 America
3 Arcadia
4 Ballroom
6 Bridge Café
7 Café des Artistes
12 David K's
16 Greene Street
20 John Clancy's
23 Metro
25 Odeon
28 Parioli Romanissimo
29 Periyali
31 Quilted Giraffe
32 River Café
33 Rosa Mexicana
36 Da Umberto
37 Water Club
38 Windows on the World
BUILDINGS AND SIGHTS
1 American Museum of Natural History
3 Chambers of Commerce (Building 27)
5 City Hall
6 Empire State Building
7 Federal Hall National Memorial
8 Frick Museum
9 Guggenheim Museum
11 Jacob K Javits Convention Center
12 Lincoln Center
13 Main Post Office
14 Metropolitan Museum of Art
18 New York Stock Exchange
19 New York University
23 St Paul's Chapel
24 South Street Seaport
25 United Nations
26 Whitney Museum of American Art
27 World Trade Center
i Tourist information

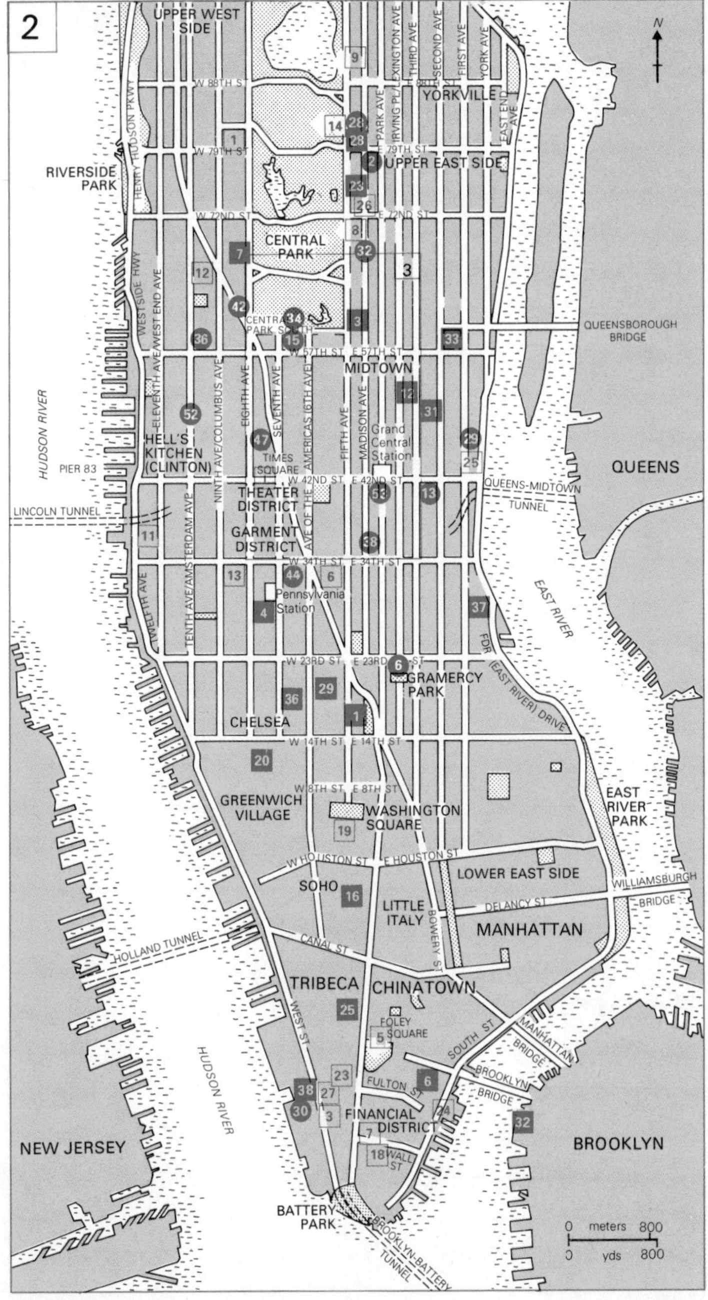
2
UPPER WEST SIDE
RIVERSIDE PARK
HENRY HUDSON PKWY
W 88TH ST
W 79TH ST
W 72ND ST
CENTRAL PARK
CENTRAL PARK SOUTH
YORKVILLE
UPPER EAST SIDE
PARK AVE
IRVING PL/LEXINGTON AVE
THIRD AVE
SECOND AVE
FIRST AVE
YORK AVE
EAST END AVE
E 79TH ST
E 72ND ST
QUEENSBOROUGH BRIDGE
WESTSIDE HWY
ELEVENTH AVE/WEST END AVE
TENTH AVE/AMSTERDAM AVE
NINTH AVE/COLUMBUS AVE
EIGHTH AVE
SEVENTH AVE
AVE OF THE AMERICAS (6TH AVE)
FIFTH AVE
MADISON AVE
TWELFTH AVE
W 57TH ST
E 57TH ST
MIDTOWN
HUDSON RIVER
HELL'S KITCHEN (CLINTON)
TIMES SQUARE
Grand Central Station
PIER 83
W 42ND ST
E 42ND ST
THEATER DISTRICT
QUEENS-MIDTOWN TUNNEL
QUEENS
LINCOLN TUNNEL
GARMENT DISTRICT
W 34TH ST
E 34TH ST
Pennsylvania Station
EAST RIVER
W 23RD ST
E 23RD ST
GRAMERCY PARK
FDR (EAST RIVER) DRIVE
CHELSEA
W 14TH ST
E 14TH ST
W 8TH ST
E 8TH ST
GREENWICH VILLAGE
WASHINGTON SQUARE
EAST RIVER PARK
W HOUSTON ST
E HOUSTON ST
LOWER EAST SIDE
SOHO
LITTLE ITALY
BOWERY ST
DELANCY ST
WILLIAMSBURGH BRIDGE
MANHATTAN
HOLLAND TUNNEL
CANAL ST
TRIBECA
CHINATOWN
WEST ST
FOLEY SQUARE
SOUTH ST
MANHATTAN BRIDGE
BROOKLYN BRIDGE
FULTON ST
FINANCIAL DISTRICT
WALL ST
NEW JERSEY
BROOKLYN
BATTERY PARK
BROOKLYN-BATTERY TUNNEL
0 meters 800
0 yds 800
N

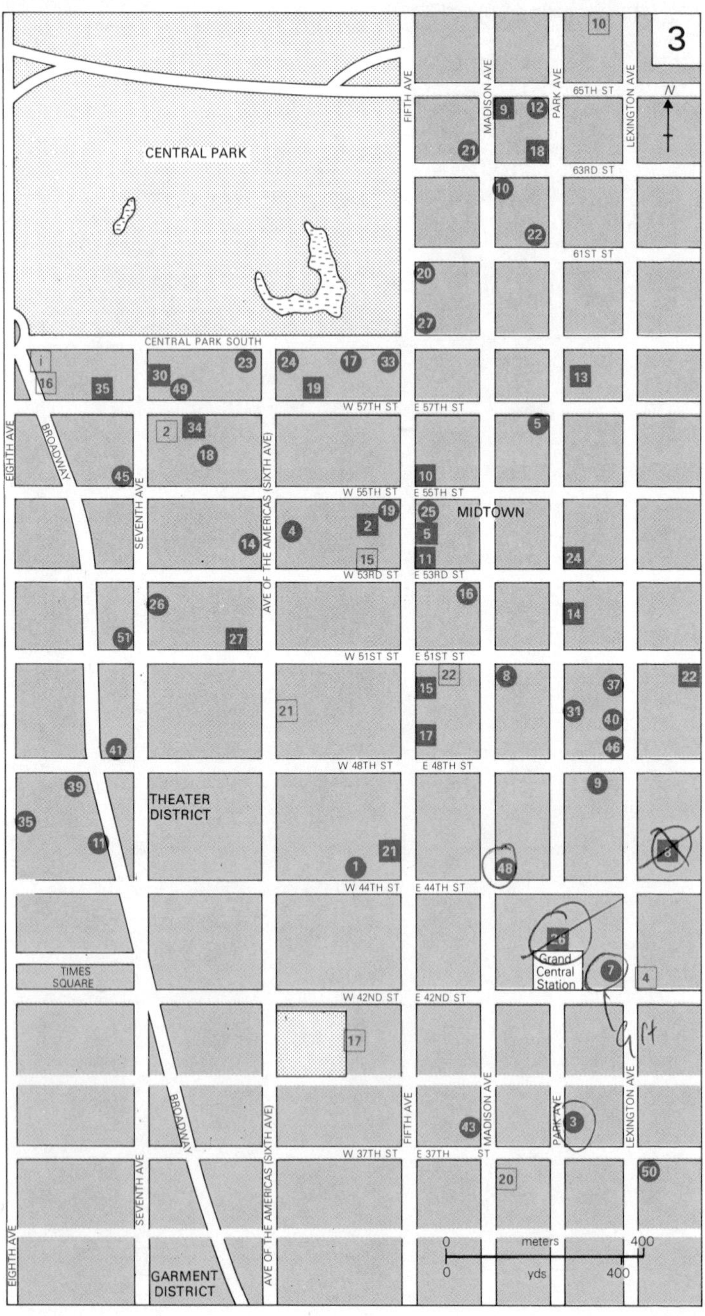

3
CENTRAL PARK
CENTRAL PARK SOUTH
MIDTOWN
THEATER DISTRICT
TIMES SQUARE
GARMENT DISTRICT
Grand Central Station
FIFTH AVE
MADISON AVE
PARK AVE
LEXINGTON AVE
EIGHTH AVE
BROADWAY
SEVENTH AVE
AVE OF THE AMERICAS (SIXTH AVE)
65TH ST
63RD ST
61ST ST
W 57TH ST
E 57TH ST
W 55TH ST
E 55TH ST
W 53RD ST
E 53RD ST
W 51ST ST
E 51ST ST
W 48TH ST
E 48TH ST
W 44TH ST
E 44TH ST
W 42ND ST
E 42ND ST
W 37TH ST
E 37TH ST
N
meters
yds
0
400

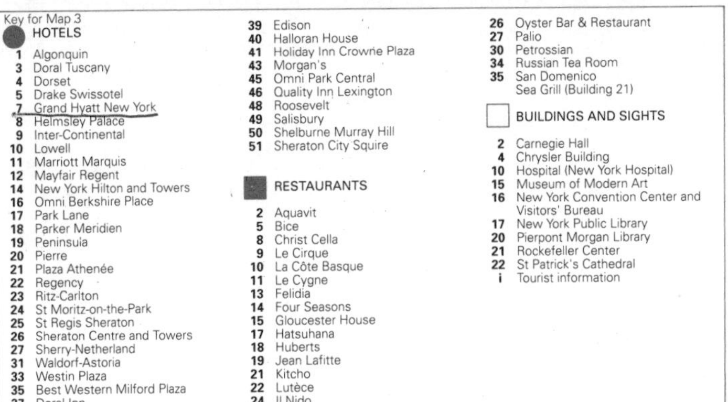

Key for Map 3

HOTELS

1 Algonquin
3 Doral Tuscany
4 Dorset
5 Drake Swissotel
7 Grand Hyatt New York
8 Helmsley Palace
9 Inter-Continental
10 Lowell
11 Marriott Marquis
12 Mayfair Regent
14 New York Hilton and Towers
16 Omni Berkshire Place
17 Park Lane
18 Parker Meridien
19 Peninsula
20 Pierre
21 Plaza Athenée
22 Regency
23 Ritz-Carlton
24 St Moritz-on-the-Park
25 St Regis Sheraton
26 Sheraton Centre and Towers
27 Sherry-Netherland
31 Waldorf-Astoria
33 Westin Plaza
35 Best Western Milford Plaza
37 Doral Inn
39 Edison
40 Halloran House
41 Holiday Inn Crowne Plaza
43 Morgan's
45 Omni Park Central
46 Quality Inn Lexington
48 Roosevelt
49 Salisbury
50 Shelburne Murray Hill
51 Sheraton City Squire

RESTAURANTS

2 Aquavit
5 Bice
8 Christ Cella
9 Le Cirque
10 La Côte Basque
11 Le Cygne
13 Felidia
14 Four Seasons
15 Gloucester House
17 Hatsuhana
18 Huberts
19 Jean Lafitte
21 Kitcho
22 Lutèce
24 Il Nido
26 Oyster Bar & Restaurant
27 Palio
30 Petrossian
34 Russian Tea Room
35 San Domenico
Sea Grill (Building 21)

BUILDINGS AND SIGHTS

2 Carnegie Hall
4 Chrysler Building
10 Hospital (New York Hospital)
15 Museum of Modern Art
16 New York Convention Center and Visitors' Bureau
17 New York Public Library
20 Pierpont Morgan Library
21 Rockefeller Center
22 St Patrick's Cathedral
i Tourist information

City link The fast way into midtown Manhattan by regular helicopter service no longer operates, but helicopters can be rented: New York Helicopter Corp ☏ (800) 645-3494. Otherwise cab or bus is the best method of reaching midtown.
Taxi It takes 20–45mins by cab into midtown and costs about $25 including tolls. The Queens-Midtown Tunnel is the most direct route, but is often snarled with traffic; because the meter fare is a combination of time and distance, the longer Triboro Bridge route may be faster and may not add much to the fare.
Limousine See *Getting around*.
Car rental Having a car in Manhattan is rarely an advantage, but all the major firms have desks at the airport: Avis ☏ (718) 507-3600, Hertz ☏ (718) 478-5300, National ☏ (718) 803-4120.
Bus Carey Transportation ☏ (718) 632-0500 runs buses to Grand Central Station every 20mins, 6.45am–midnight; fare $6. Many hotels have a shared van service; if your hotel is the last stop, it can add 30mins to the trip.
Subway The subway is not a recommended way into town; it is the cheapest ($2) but slowest (at least 2hrs). The Q33 bus connects LaGuardia and the Queens–74th Street subway station, which is on the Flushing line to Grand Central Station and 5th Avenue.

Newark International Airport
Newark, about 16 miles/25kms from midtown, is comparatively uncrowded and problem-free. Terminals A and B and the North Terminal handle domestic flights; international and long-haul domestic flights go through Terminal C. Customs and Immigration seldom take more than 1hr, but long walks to baggage claim are common.

Modern, comfortable facilities are available in Terminals A, B and C. Coffee shops and newsstands are located both landside and airside. Currency exchange is available, but rates are generally poor, especially in Terminal C. Transit buses run between the two. North Terminal has a bookshop, coffee and bar facilities and currency exchange.
Nearby hotels *Howard Johnson*, S Haynes Avenue, Newark, NJ 07114 ☏ (201) 824-4000 or (800) 654-2000 fax (201) 824-2034; very near airport; car rental, pool. *Sheraton Inn Newark Airport*, 901 Spring St, Elizabeth, NJ 07201 ☏ (201) 527-1600 fax (201) 527-1327; limousine service, indoor and outdoor heated pools.
City link The scheduled helicopter service to Manhattan no longer operates, but helicopters can be rented: New York Helicopter Corp. ☏ (800) 645-3495. Otherwise taxi or bus are the best ways into midtown, unless you rent a car.
Taxi Flat rates apply from Newark

into the city. To midtown Manhattan, the fare is about $30. There is an additional charge for East Side destinations above 14th Street. The cab ride takes about 30mins (at least 1hr at peak times).
Limousine See *Getting around.*
Car rental If you must rent the major firms have desks here: Avis ☎ (201) 961-4300 or (201) 961-4340 (nights and weekends), Hertz ☎ (201) 621-2000, National ☎ (201) 622-1270.
Bus Olympia Trails ☎ (212) 964-6233 runs buses to World Trade Center or Grand Central Station, every 20mins, 6am–midnight. NJ Transit ☎ (800 within New Jersey, 201 elsewhere) 460-8444 or 772-2222 operates to Port Authority Bus Terminal every 15–30mins, 24hrs.

Rail stations

The city's two railroad stations – Grand Central and Pennsylvania – are used more by daily commuters from the suburbs than by long-distance travelers. At both, beware of hustlers who will take your bags, offer to get you a cab and then demand several dollars: they are illegal and can be dangerous.
Grand Central Station, on 42nd St at Park Avenue, serves upper New York State and Connecticut. The huge c.1903 Beaux-Arts terminal has many shops and concessions, and it connects with both the Grand Hyatt (see *Hotels*) and the Pan Am Building. The terminal, though generally well organized, is dirty and many homeless people live there. IRT subway trains 4, 5 and 6 stop there, and you can connect with a shuttle train to Times Square. The Oyster Bar (see *Restaurants*) is useful for business lunches. Information ☎ 736-4545.
Pennsylvania Station The modern, underground Penn Station serves Long Island and New Jersey, as well as more distant points on the Amtrak lines. The 7th Avenue, Broadway and 8th Avenue subway lines all stop there. Information: *Amtrak* ☎ 736-4545, *Long Island Railroad* ☎ (718) 454-5477.

Getting around

Manhattan's predominantly grid-like layout is simple to understand outside Greenwich Village and the area below Canal Street. Numbered streets run east–west and numbered avenues run north–south. The east–west street designations are centered on 5th Avenue. Broadway, following an old Indian trail, cuts a long diagonal across the grid. North is referred to as uptown, south is downtown – crucial when asking directions.

Walking is often the quickest and most pleasant way to get around. For longer journeys the subway is quicker during peak hours (7–10, 4–6). At other times, use taxis.
Walking In general, a fit New Yorker with little or no baggage would walk any distance up to 15 blocks – except in bad weather. Calculate walking time at about 1min per north-south block, 2mins per east–west block. Heavy traffic means that you should cross roads as and when the green light shows, rather than sticking to what seems to be the most direct route. Avoid areas with few pedestrians, especially Central Park, after dark. Ask for directions: most New Yorkers are glad to help.
Taxi Going crosstown averages 15mins without traffic problems, but there are ridiculous delays at lunch time and in the rush hours. From midtown to the Financial District takes about 20mins, but at peak times very much longer. Cabs can be hailed in the streets but there are some taxi stands throughout the city.

Many drivers are recent immigrants. They are required to pass language and city knowledge tests, but they may speak English poorly and sometimes do not know their way around. Yellow medallion cabs are subject to city-controlled testing and fare regulations. Nevertheless, many cabs are scruffy, and few are air-conditioned. A cab is available when the center of its roof sign is lit, and medallion drivers must by law take you to any of the city's five boroughs, or to Westchester County, Nassau County or Newark International Airport. Special rates apply on such trips and are posted in each cab. Make a point of being inside the cab before giving your destination, especially if it is outside Manhattan. If a "gypsy" cab (an unregulated ordinary car of any color with a "Livery" or "Car Service" sign on the dashboard) is all you can get, at least make sure to agree the fare in advance.

In the early evening (5–7), cabs are very difficult to find in the street; on Friday evenings, it is almost impossible even to get one by phone. In wet weather, cabs may be found at main hotels, but be prepared for brusque treatment if the driver was hoping for a lucrative airport trip. Cabbies expect a tip of 15–20% of the metered fare. Lost property information ☏ 869-4513.

Radio cabs There are two main types of radio-despatched unregulated cars available, the better of the two being almost limousine standard, although without the stretched body. Although their fares are usually higher than regulated cabs, they are clean, comfortable and air-conditioned: they may be worth the extra cost (except for long trips out to the suburbs). There is a surcharge payable on all journeys between 8pm and 6am.

Reliable, straightforward radio cab services include *Citywide Taxi* ☏ 295-1122; *Utog* ☏ 741-2000 and *XYZ Two Way Radio* ☏ (718)768-7333. The lesser-limousine services include *Salem Transportation* ☏ (718) 656-4511; and *Scull's Angels* ☏ (718) 651-9400.

Limousine Full-scale limo service is available from *Concord* ☏ 230-1600; *London Towncars* ☏ 988-9700; and *Salem Transportation* ☏ (718) 656-4511.

Driving All major car rental companies have facilities at or near the three airports and in midtown, but it is not advisable to drive. Traffic is absurdly bad, and parking expensive.

Subway The subway operates 24hrs, but not all stations are served at all times. Its network covers Manhattan well, particularly in midtown; most of the lines run predominantly north–south.

The IND (Independent) lines (A, C, E, B, D and F trains) seem to have more delays and run less frequently than the IRT (Interborough Rapid Transit) lines (1, 2, 3, 4, 5 and 6 trains). However, IND trains are newer, cleaner and safer.

The BMT line (Brooklyn–Manhattan) runs from lower Manhattan to Brooklyn and Queens and so is less useful to the business visitor than the other two lines.

Distinguishing between local trains, which stop at all stations, and express trains, which do not, is important; generally, express trains run on the tracks in the center of a station, local trains against the walls. Local trains are more often air-conditioned and usually less crowded than express trains, and at rush hours they can also be faster.

The subway is often quickest in rush hours. In the evening, if you are heading for Brooklyn, you can avoid the appalling rush-hour crawl across the bridge by using the east-bound Nassau Street line.

Contrary to the subway system's reputation, its users do not regularly risk loss of life, limb or belongings. However, after 10pm empty trains do offer opportunities to criminals; in rush hours, watch out for pickpockets. If the car you are traveling in begins to empty, move to a fuller one. Always, even in rush hours, avoid deserted or infrequently used exits or entrances, even if they seem more convenient; stick with the crowds. On stations, outside rush hours, you can often wait in designated safe areas.

Free maps of the subway system are available at change booths at stations selling subway tokens either singly or in quantity, including 10 token packs. Some banks also sell token packs. Fares are the same whatever the distance traveled. Subway and bus information ☎ (718) 330-1234.

Buses are the only form of public transportation going crosstown (east–west) in Manhattan; they generally operate on major cross streets (such as 14th, 23rd, 34th) as well as north and south, up and down most major avenues. Stops are frequent (every two blocks on north–south routes; every block crosstown). The exact fare ($1) in coins is required, but subway tokens are acceptable. Passengers may transfer to a connecting line without extra charge, provided they ask the driver of the first bus for a "transfer" when they get on.

City buses tend to be slow-moving, but in the summer most are air-conditioned.

Finding your way around

Use the following information to pinpoint the whereabouts of your next appointment. For north–south avenues the rule is to take the address number, drop the last digit (472 becomes 47), divide by 2 and add or subtract the number shown on the table below. For east–west street addresses see the diagram to find which block a particular address is on.

Central Park occupies the blocks between 5th Avenue and Central Park West and stretches from 59th Street to 110th Street. This means that north of 59th Street, 8th Avenue becomes Central Park West; 9th Avenue becomes Columbus Avenue; 10th Avenue becomes Amsterdam Avenue; 11th Avenue becomes West End Avenue; and 12th Avenue becomes Riverside Drive.

Getting around the USA
For general information on traveling around the USA, and on hotels and restaurants, see *Planning and Reference*.

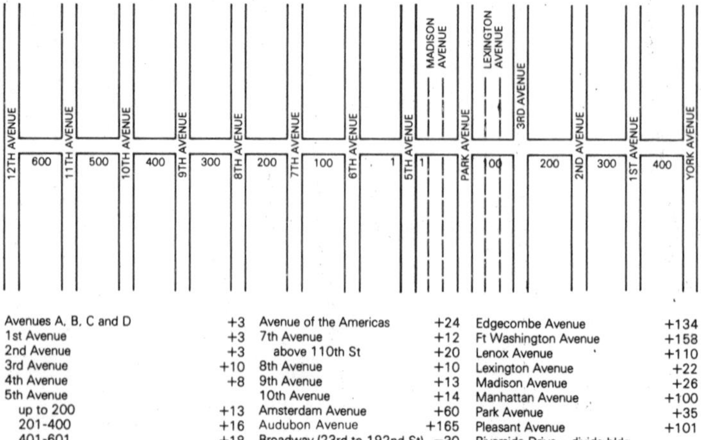

Avenue	
Avenues A, B, C and D	+3
1st Avenue	+3
2nd Avenue	+3
3rd Avenue	+10
4th Avenue	+8
5th Avenue	
up to 200	+13
201-400	+16
401-601	+18
601-775	+20
776-1286 – cancel last figure, then	−18
1287-1500	+45
Avenue of the Americas	+24
7th Avenue	+12
above 110th St	+20
8th Avenue	+10
9th Avenue	+13
10th Avenue	+14
Amsterdam Avenue	+60
Audubon Avenue	+165
Broadway (23rd to 192nd St)	−30
Central Park West – divide bldg no. by 10, then	+60
Columbus Avenue	+60
Convent Avenue	+127
Edgecombe Avenue	+134
Ft Washington Avenue	+158
Lenox Avenue	+110
Lexington Avenue	+22
Madison Avenue	+26
Manhattan Avenue	+100
Park Avenue	+35
Pleasant Avenue	+101
Riverside Drive – divide bldg no. by 10, then up to 165th St	+72
St Nicholas Avenue	+110
Wadsworth Avenue	+173
West End Avenue	+60

Area by area

New York's most important and most prestigious business areas are from 42nd Street to 57th Street and 3rd Avenue to 6th Avenue in midtown, and in the Wall Street area downtown. Certain industries have distinct territories: for example, garment-making is in the west 30s, music in the west 60s, jewelry in the west 40s. Although many city professionals commute from the suburbs, luxurious residential areas still remain on the Upper East Side (on Park and 5th Avenues) and West Side (along Central Park West).

New York developed historically by growing northwards along Manhattan island from the Battery. In the older areas, the grid street plan does not exist, and visitors without a good map may get lost.

Influxes of immigrants in the early part of this century created many ethnic enclaves: Little Italy and Chinatown in lower Manhattan; the German community in Yorkville on the Upper East Side; a Ukrainian outpost in the East Village; black Harlem and Spanish Harlem uptown. With a housing shortage and spiralling rentals, however, today's arrivals tend to settle in the outer boroughs: Greeks and Koreans in Queens; Russians, Jamaicans and Haitians in Brooklyn, for example. Meanwhile, young professionals have gentrified some Manhattan neighborhoods and penetrated Brooklyn areas such as Park Slope, replacing bodegas and numbers shops with upmarket delis and singles bars. In the UN area, Beekman Place and Sutton Place, north of 48th Street, are among the city's most prestigious, most expensive residential neighborhoods, home to some of New York society's oldest families.

Financial District The Financial District, from the Battery north to City Hall, was once home to virtually all the city's banks and brokerage houses. Now, because of the difficulties of expanding in a cramped area and commuting to it, many banks and brokers have moved to midtown. Some firms have moved to the World Financial Center, near the World Trade Center; but many, especially legal firms and those whose business is tied closely to the New York and American Stock Exchanges, securities and commodities, remain downtown. The population has tripled to more than 15,000 since 1975, but the area remains one of the city's most sparsely populated neighborhoods and is deserted after dark and at weekends.

Foley Square and Chinatown East from City Hall, north to Canal Street, is a warren of government buildings around Foley Square, and east and north of that is Chinatown – a maze of busy streets, with oriental restaurants and shops.

TriBeCa and SoHo On the west below Canal Street is the area known as TriBeCa (the TRIangle BElow CAnal), where artists and wealthier trend-followers have converted old factories and warehouses to living and working loft apartments. To the north is SoHo (SOuth of HOuston), similarly transformed into a neighborhood of lofts, wine bars, galleries and expensive shops.

Greenwich Village Between Houston (pronounced House-ton) and 14th Street, from the Hudson to beyond 4th Avenue, is one of the city's most attractive and interesting areas. The low brownstone buildings house upper middle-class families, artists and writers, young professionals and older immigrants. High rents mean that the Village is less bohemian than it was, but its numerous cafés and restaurants still give it an unmatched street life. New York University occupies many buildings in the central part of the Village around Washington Square. The West Village is the center of the city's gay life; East Village, which lies east of Broadway towards Alphabet City (Avenues A, B, C and D), has pink-haired punks alongside old Ukrainians, Indian and macrobiotic eating houses next to old Russian borscht restaurants. The streets of Alphabet City with their after-hours clubs and illicit drug dealing can be dangerous, especially east of Avenue A.

Lower East Side and Little Italy South and east of Houston Street and south of Alphabet City is the Lower East Side, home to millions of mid-19thC European immigrants and refugees. Italians settled around Mulberry Street, creating Little Italy (still full of restaurants, *pasticcerie* and *cafés*). Farther east, European Jews came to crowded tenements and sweatshops; although many moved away when they prospered, the area is still predominantly Jewish, and Orchard Street still the best place in the city to find clothing bargains.

Gramercy Park East Side between 14th and 23rd Streets has some engaging 19thC and early-20thC architecture and two of the city's loveliest small parks, Stuyvesant Square (2nd Avenue at 16th Street) and Gramercy Park (Lexington Avenue at 20th Street). Gramercy Park is open only to residents of its quiet, expensive enclave.

Chelsea To the west lies Chelsea, a mixed neighborhood of young professionals and lower-income families that is rapidly developing.

Garment district Above 23rd Street and Chelsea, above the plant district (6th Avenue in the 20s) and west of the toy district (5th Avenue above 23rd Street) the jumble of decaying buildings, shabby offices and cheap diners meld almost imperceptibly into the garment district, centered on 7th Avenue, above 34th Street. On weekdays, runners rush racks of garments through the streets, groups of people talk and argue at every door, limousines glide to the curbs and disgorge designer passengers. A fifth of the clothing made in the USA comes from this area.

Hell's Kitchen Above the garment district in the west 40s and 50s is what was formerly known as Hell's Kitchen, now officially called Clinton. Its lurid reputation dates from shortly after the Civil War, when the Hell's Kitchen Gang ruled its streets. Although prostitution still thrives, today's residents are mainly Hispanic families, artists and writers. Manhattan Plaza, an apartment tower for musicians and artists at 42nd Street and 10th Avenue, has helped to change the tone of the area.

Theater district Times Square and Broadway, center of New York's legitimate theater, are dazzling by night and sleazy by day. Pornography is still rife along 42nd Street and 8th Avenue, but new office blocks (notably the Klein development) and hotels are changing the emphasis. In the side streets, bars and restaurants cater to Broadway crowds.

Midtown The heart of the midtown business district extends from 42nd to 57th streets, 6th Avenue (Avenue of the Americas) to 3rd Avenue. Glass-sheathed towers along the avenues, virtually all prestige addresses, house the city's top firms in law, advertising, publishing and finance. Addresses east of 3rd Avenue, west of 6th Avenue, and on the side streets generally lack the clout of a tower-top suite or Rockefeller Center. But there are exceptions, such as the Gulf + Western Building at 59th Street and Central Park West, one of the few top addresses outside the usual midtown area. And Park Avenue South and Park Avenue from 23rd to 42nd Streets has experienced a bit of a renaissance, with advertising, publishing and other service firms discovering the charms of the area's quiet streets, good restaurants and office rents.

United Nations area Along the East River from 23rd to 57th Streets, residential neighborhoods succeed one another up to and past the UN. These are generally older, quieter, more established neighborhoods: rentals rise the farther north you go.
Upper East Side The Upper East Side is primarily a residential area; as a rule of thumb, the farther south, the more prestigious. Top executives who choose to live in Manhattan tend to have addresses on 5th or Park Avenues, or in a brownstone or townhouse on one of the side streets.
Yorkville The area above 79th Street and east of Lexington was originally settled by mid-European immigrants. However, in the past 25 years an influx of young, mainly unmarried professionals has changed the area, taking over blocks of nearly featureless high-rises interspersed with blocks of brownstone apartments in the east 70s, 80s and 90s.
Upper West Side Fifteen years ago, only Central Park West was thought respectable. Today, gentrification has transformed the other once-seedy avenues; owner-occupied and restored brownstones line the cross streets; Lincoln Center supports a host of auxiliary industries in the west 60s; and the poor who previously occupied the area have been pushed north towards Harlem. The area's best address is Central Park West, where top-floor apartments can be as costly as those on the more staid East Side. Away from the Park, the population is younger and more mixed.
Central Park Laid out in 1857, the 870-acre park is an oasis of greenery heavily used by joggers, picnickers, sports enthusiasts of all sorts, and families on weekends. It can be dangerous after dark and during less busy weekdays; above 86th Street, be particularly cautious at all times.
Brooklyn The city's largest borough, across the East River, has many lovely neighborhoods restored to residential splendor by young professionals and their families. Brooklyn Heights is now as expensive as Manhattan; Park Slope, farther east near Prospect Park, is evolving in the same way. Williamsburg, at the foot of the Manhattan Bridge, is home to many of the Hasidic Jews who work in the diamond district on W 47th Street.
Queens Most of Queens is traditionally lower middle class or light industrial. But Astoria has been "discovered," and its older ethnic character is changing. Forest Hills, former home of the US Open, is a delightful (and not inexpensive) residential neighborhood; Whitestone seems almost suburban in its greenery.

The suburbs

Many communities in Westchester County north of the city are empty of adults on weekdays. Scarsdale, Rye, Katonah and Mount Kisco are all commuter towns. Generally, towns farther from the city are more desirable but beyond a certain distance their appeal drops sharply. Towns too close, such as Yonkers, are not favored.

Greenwich and Darien, in Fairfield County Connecticut, are the archetypal residences of top corporate executives. Norwalk and Stanford are more middle-class and industrial.

Short Hills and Saddle River, New Jersey, have many middle- and upper-level executives who are driven to the city each day in private cars; others, like gentrified Hoboken and Jersey City, are industrial lower middle class. Generally, the communities farther north and west, away from the Hudson River and the New Jersey Turnpike, are more expensive.

Long Island, like New Jersey, is more diverse than either Fairfield or Westchester. Older areas closer to the city, such as Manhasset and Roslyn, tend to be more expensive. Sands Point and Kings Point are predominantly Jewish; Locust Valley and Oyster Bay are mainly WASP. Huntington and Oyster Bay are home to many professionals.

Hotels

Nearly all New York hotels are geared to business clients, and the best ones are in midtown and the Upper East Side; in the Wall Street area, the only business-class hotel is the Vista at the World Trade Center. Several new hotels are opening on the West Side around Times Square. Expect to pay a minimum of $100 a night, and usually much more. Also, in addition to the usual 8 1/4% state tax levied on your hotel bill, you must also pay the additional taxes: a $2-per-room occupancy charge plus a 5% New York City tax. Bear in mind that rooms on low floors are generally noisier; those without windows looking onto streets are generally quieter. Few city center hotels have in-house health club facilities or swimming pools: those that do have been noted.

Algonquin [$]//
59 W 44th St (5th Ave) 10036
☎ 840-6800 [TX] 66532 fax 944-1419
• AE DC MC V • 165 rooms, 23 suites, 3 restaurants, 1 bar

The great attractions of this turn-of-the-century hostelry are its midtown location (near Grand Central), paneled lobby lounge (a venerable meeting place crowded with sofas and wing chairs) and amiable Blue Bar (see *Bars*). Much needed and planned refurbishment will improve the rooms, and a new chef has recently been appointed. Bedrooms are now well-equipped, but if you can, take a suite, which may be charmingly furnished. The lobby, thick with literary and theatrical associations (Sir John Gielgud and the late Lord Olivier were among the hotel's regulars), is ideal for afternoon tea or cocktails, especially with people from publishing or the theater. There is a 3pm check-out. Drugstore • 1 meeting room.

Carlyle [$]/////
35 E 76th St (Madison Ave) 10021
☎ 744-1600 [TX] 620692 fax 717-4682
• AE DC MC V • 114 rooms, 70 suites, 2 restaurants, 2 bars

This is the nearest Manhattan gets to having a European or Far Eastern grand hotel. Testimony to its desirability lies in the large number of permanently leased rooms, leaving barely 20% available to transients. Furnishings and accessories are harmonious blends of 16th–19thC regal conceits, but there are also discreetly concealed minibars, stereos, televisions and VCRs in every room. The staff is alert, attentive, and available. The restaurant is an excellent choice for a business breakfast or lunch, but is probably not gastronomically distinguished enough to entice you for dinner. Bobby Short, singer and focal point of local society, holds court much of the year in the Café Carlyle (see *Entertainment*). Hairdresser • health club • 2 meeting rooms.

Doral Tuscany [$]////
120 E 39th St (Park Ave) 10016
☎ 687-1600 [TX] 968872 fax 779-7822
• AE DC MC V • 135 rooms, 16 suites, 1 restaurant, 1 bar

The relatively peaceful Murray Hill district south of Grand Central and east of 5th Avenue is home to several small, low-pressure hotels that do not treat guests as mobile cash-flow units. The trade-off is slightly greater distance from the fevered midtown core, but this translates into only a few extra minutes' travel time. The Tuscany is exemplary of the breed, with extras including a variety of gadgets: in the lobby, a stock ticker; in the bedrooms, dressing alcoves with sinks and refrigerators, VCRs, three telephones, electric shoe-polishers and reclining lounge chairs. Rooms are spacious, with large desks, and most have exercycles. Eighty have recently been renovated. Use of nearby health club • 2 meeting rooms.

Dorset [$]///
30 W 54th St (6th Ave) 10019
☎ 247-7300 fax 581-0153 • AE DC MC V • 200 rooms, 1 restaurant, 1 bar
The discreet and stylish Dorset is an ideal choice for the business traveler who wants to visit the nearby Museum of Modern Art or the boutiques on 5th Avenue. The rooms (ask for one on the courtyard side) are pleasantly furnished and of a good size. The bar-café is a favorite with stars from nearby ABC at lunch time.

Drake Swissotel [$]///
440 Park Ave (E 46th St) 10022
☎ 421-0900 TX 147178 fax 371-4190 • AE DC MC V • 583 rooms, 51 suites, 2 restaurants, 1 bar
The once-drooping reputation of this older hotel sparkles again under its new Swiss owners. The Park Avenue address was desirable, and the private rooms of the former apartment building always spacious. But the Swiss have opened up the cramped lobby, brightened the decor and improved the dining rooms. While the result isn't flashy, neither is it sedate. The Restaurant Lafayette is a pleasant place for lunch. Complimentary limo to Wall Street. Use of health club • 7 meeting rooms.

Gramercy Park [$]//
2 Lexington Ave (E 21st St) 10010
☎ 475-4320 TX 668755 fax 505-0535 • AE DC MC V • 350 rooms, 157 suites, 1 restaurant, 1 bar
Europeans have a particular fondness for this downtown hotel in a genteel neighborhood, though New Yorkers think it out-of-the-way and a little worn at the edges. But when image is unimportant or the expense account on the tight side, it is an amiable stopover with adequate rooms and a warm and friendly atmosphere. Ask for a room overlooking the Park. Use of health club • 5 meeting rooms.

Grand Hyatt New York [$]////
42nd St and Park Ave 10017
☎ 883-1234 TX 645616 fax 697-3772 • AE DC MC V • 1,320 rooms, 87 suites, 3 restaurants, 4 bars, 1 coffee shop
The Grand Hyatt's spectacular four-story atrium near Grand Central Station is as wide and long as a football field. It encloses a stepped waterfall, groves of potted trees and a huge hanging wire sculpture, all overwhelming the reception area, lobby and glassed-in bar cantilevered over the street. For the business traveler two floors are given to the Regency Club, with its private lounge, elevator and concierge. On another floor, 14 rooms provide combined conference and sleeping spaces. There is also a huge selection of high-class clothing, gift and jewelry shops. Bookstore, Federal Express • tennis courts/fitness center in Grand Central • 8 meeting rooms.

Helmsley Palace [$]/////
455 Madison Ave (between 50th and 51st Sts) 10022 ☎ 888-7000 TX 640543 fax 355-0820 • AE DC MC V • 859 rooms, 105 suites, 3 restaurants, 2 bars
Harry Helmsley was prevailed upon to preserve and restore the Palace's existing late-19thC Italianate terraces, and his craftsmen did a superb job. Even if you are staying elsewhere, try the Gold Room for tea and Le Trianon for dinner; a pianist plays nightly in Harry's Bar. Bedrooms are comfortable, and all have remote-control TVs, electric shoe-polishers, minibars and clock radios. Guests in the special Tower suites have full kitchens, special elevators and their own check-in area. Hairdresser, jeweler, boutique, antique shop • health club by arrangement • 7 meeting rooms.

Inter-Continental [$]////
111 E 48th St (Lexington Ave) 10017
☎ 755-5900 TX 968677 fax 644-0079 • AE DC MC V • 604 rooms, 88 suites, 2 restaurants, 1 bar
Superbly situated for easy access to the UN and east midtown offices and restaurants, the former Barclay was erected in 1926 at the behest of the

Vanderbilt family and was much favored by Gloria Swanson, Henry Cabot Lodge and Papa Hemingway. It has a measured European character, including the distinctive lobby birdcage and the high ceilings and generous proportions. Discriminating business people and notables from the creative and performing arts appreciate its serenity and privacy. Florist, pharmacy, men's shop, hairdresser • health clubs • 14 meeting rooms, cable facilities, translation, interpreters, secretarial facilities.

Lowell $////
28 E 63rd St (Madison Ave) 10021 ☎ 838-1400 TX 275750 fax 319-4230 • AE DC MC V • 8 rooms, 52 suites, 2 restaurants, 1 bar
The Lowell is a leader in the Manhattan trend toward small, elegant inn-like hotels. An Art Deco façade on a tree-lined Upper East Side street insulates a clientele that includes corporate satraps, upper-level government officials and the occasional film and rock star. All rooms have kitchenettes (when making reservations, tell them what you'd like in the refrigerator). Suites are perfect for small meetings followed by a meal laid out on the marble table. Many of the rooms have working fireplaces, a rare status symbol. Service is highly personalized and includes a knowledgeable, multilingual concierge. 1 meeting room.

Marriott Marquis $//
1535 Broadway (45–46th Sts) 10036 ☎ 398-1900 TX 6712057 fax 704-8930 • AE DC MC V • 1,876 rooms, 141 suites, 3 restaurants, 4 bars, 1 coffee shop
This ungainly, futuristic fortress looming over Times Square does have a certain giddy bravado and no lack of amenities. The lobby is on the 8th floor; there is a revolving restaurant and a theater. Health club, sauna, games room • 23 meeting rooms, business center, teleconferencing.

Mayfair Regent $/////
610 Park Ave (65th St) 10021 ☎ 288-0800 TX 236257 fax 737-0538 • AE DC MC V • 59 rooms, 142 suites, 1 bar
The predominance of suites, many of them permanently leased, suggests the select clientele of this gracious building. The deliberate association with the patrician townhouses of London's Mayfair is entirely fitting. Instead of conventional bars and dining rooms, it offers cocktail service and afternoon tea in the lobby lounge, complete with fireplace. Adjacent to the entrance is the very fashionable Le Cirque (see *Restaurants*), which, although independently operated, functions as *de facto* dining room to the hotel's residents as well as to such regulars as Sylvester Stallone. The suites can accommodate small meetings. 2 meeting rooms.

New York Helmsley $///
212 E 42nd St (between 2nd and 3rd Aves) 10017 ☎ 490-8900 TX 127724 fax 986-4792 • AE DC MC V • 781 rooms, 9 suites, 1 restaurant, 1 bar
Although far less grand than her Palace, it has been a particular pet of the notorious Leona Helmsley, who renamed it after her spouse and partner, as she did the off-lobby Harry's Bar. In truth, it is a rather conventional operation, enlivened by such trademark touches as the harpist in the "gourmet" restaurant and the 25" color TVs with remote control in the bedrooms. The UN is three blocks east; Grand Central one block west. Health club by arrangement • 5 meeting rooms.

New York Hilton and Towers $///
1335 Ave of the Americas (53rd St) 10019 ☎ 586-7000 TX 238492 fax 757-7423 • AE DC MC V • 1,965 bedrooms, 156 suites, 1 restaurant, 3 bars, 1 coffee shop
In the middle of a prairie, this colossus would constitute a good-sized town by itself. When all the rooms are occupied, the combined total of

staff, guests and conventioneers can exceed 7,000. The six-story Executive Tower has its own express elevator, 24hr check-in and check-out, concierge, fully equipped boardroom, and private lounge. Tower bedrooms have three telephones – one on the bedside table, another in the bathroom, a third on the working-size desk. Beauty salon, hairdresser, gourmet shop, drugstore, florist, jeweler • fitness center • 49 meeting rooms, business center with video teleconferencing, translation, computer modems, library, delivery service.

Nikko Essex House $////
160 Central Park S (6th Ave) 10019
☎ 247-0300 TX 7105815730
fax 315-1839 • AE DC MC V • 651 rooms, 64 suites, 1 restaurant, 1 bar
First-class, if not de luxe, the Essex House is owned by Japan Airlines. With its prime location, a staff said to speak 18 languages, good housekeeping and the usual in-room gadgets, it is a notch above many chain hotels. Hairdresser • complimentary passes to nearby racquet club • 14 meeting rooms.

Omni Berkshire Place $////
21 52nd St (5th Ave) 10022
☎ 753-5800 TX 7105815256
fax 355-7646 • AE DC MC V • 415 bedrooms, 23 suites, 2 restaurants, 1 bar
The entrance opens onto a handsome lobby of tinkly mirrors, faceted glass and an emerald-green backdrop. To one side are the popular Rendez-vous bistro, the Atrium bar and a quiet formal restaurant, La Galerie. The pleasantly furnished bedrooms have large desks and telephones. Bathrobes, cable TV, morning coffee and newspaper and complimentary shoeshine are extra touches. 1 meeting room, computer rental.

Park Lane $////
36 Central Park S (5th Ave) 10019
☎ 371-4000 TX 668613 fax 319-9065 • AE DC MC V • Helmsley • 640 rooms, 22 suites, 1 restaurant, 1 bar
This is the Helmsley hotel that Harry and Leona make their home. Despite that, it is unexceptional, but worth considering for its views of Central Park from good-sized rooms. Expect first-class, though not grande luxe, comforts and appointments. The staff can be distant, but are usually helpful and efficient. Do not dine in the restaurant or use room service.
4 meeting rooms, computer rental.

Parker Meridien $////
118 W 57th St (6th Ave) 10019
☎ 245-5000 TX 6801134
fax 307-1776 • AE DC MC V • 600 rooms, 100 suites, 2 restaurants, 1 bar
The opening of this Air France hotel was greeted with exultation by local Francophiles. The ambitious Chez Maurice restaurant and informal Le Patio were immediate successes. Rooms, although often small, are carefully conceived, including spa baths and minibars. The public rooms have a cool, Grecian look, warmed by flowers and feathery plants, and the in-house health facilities are exceptional, with pool, jogging track and racquet ball courts in addition to the usual features of sauna and weight equipment. 8 meeting rooms, translation.

Peninsula $/////
700 5th Ave (at 55th St) 10019
☎ 247-2200 TX 4976154 fax 903-3949 • AE DC MC V • 250 rooms and suites, 2 restaurants, 1 bar
With all the grandeur of the famous Peninsula in Hong Kong, this entirely refurbished hotel (formerly the Gotham and then, briefly, Maxim's) offers a splendid location. Bedrooms have been custom-decorated in Art Nouveau style with luxurious marble bathrooms; the restaurant also evokes the turn of the century. The clientele is mainly senior executives. Health club, pool • 6 meeting rooms, audio-visual equipment in all rooms.

Pierre [$]/////
2 61st St (5th Ave) 10021 ☏ 838-8000 [TX] 127426 fax 758-1615 • AE DC MC V • Four Seasons • 141 rooms, 56 suites, 1 restaurant, 1 bar
In character and clientele, the Pierre is akin to the Carlyle. Both count aristocrats and plutocrats among their enthusiasts; both aspire to the best of what we think of as European standards of service; both go to considerable lengths to protect the privacy and security of their guests. The Pierre falls shorter of the mark, however, with a costly renovation that is more 5th Avenue than French. Reception varies from cheerful to occasionally aloof. Still, it is 15 blocks closer to midtown than the Carlyle and manages to project a convincing facsimile of the gracious era between the world wars. Florist, jeweler, hairdresser, beauty salon • 7 meeting rooms, notary public.

Plaza Athenée [$]////
37 E 64th St (Madison Ave) 10021 ☏ 734-9100 [TX] 6972900 fax 772-0958 • THF • AE DC MC V • 124 rooms, 36 suites, 1 restaurant, 1 bar
One of the best of New York's newer hotels. Rooms and suites are uncommonly comfortable, with reproductions of French-period styles. Television sets are hidden behind armoire doors, and among the conveniences are room safes, shoe trees, tie racks and individual temperature controls. Suites have kitchenettes, and some have terraces or solariums and extra bathrooms. Extraordinarily swift and comprehensive room service is aided by the placement of pantries on every floor. The ground-floor Le Regence restaurant is a sumptuous rendition of *belle époque* Paris.

Regency [$]/////
540 Park Ave (61st St) 10021 ☏ 759-4100 [TX] 147180 fax 826-5674 • AE DC MC V • Loews Hotels • 300 rooms, 93 suites, 1 restaurant, 1 bar
The city's powerbrokers have made the Regency's 540 Park restaurant a fashionable breakfast venue. Otherwise, the hotel maintains the low profile preferred by people who do not require, or who abhor, visibility. Yet it is sheathed in marble, hung with rich tapestries, ablaze with huge vases of flowers, furnished with antiques and replicas of the fancies of Louis XV and lavished with gilded neo-baroque flourishes. All rooms have work desks and safes; many have kitchenettes, some have terraces. Meeting and banquet facilities are among Manhattan's most elegant. Excellent health facilities • 3 meeting rooms.

Ritz-Carlton [$]/////
112 Central Park S (6th Ave) 10019 ☏ 757-1900 [TX] 971534 fax 757-9620 • AE DC MC V • 237 rooms, 30 suites, 1 restaurant, 1 bar
One of the growing number of small luxury hotels, the Ritz-Carlton has the air of an old-line East Coast club, with bleached pine, chintz, leather and mahogany as material for wing chairs and four-poster beds. In the Jockey Club restaurant, wood fires are accompanied by genre paintings of horses and overindulgent squires. The artful mock-rusticity attracts mainly a privileged but hard-working international set who are joined in conference by their New York peers in the restaurant and in the meeting rooms overlooking Central Park. Every bedroom has three telephones, with two lines. Drawbacks are the small lobby, limited public rooms and congested elevators. 4 meeting rooms.

St Moritz-on-the-Park [$]///
50 Central Park S (6th Ave) 10019 ☏ 755-5800 [TX] 66884 fax 751-2952 • AE DC MC V • 682 rooms, 90 suites, 1 coffee shop, 2 restaurants, 1 bar
Apart from its very central location, the best things about this old-timer are its street-level enterprises. Rumplemayer's is essentially an ice cream emporium, banked with stuffed animals. The sidewalk café looking down 6th Avenue and across to Central Park is one of the city's

oldest. Upstairs, however, expect often cramped rooms, indifferently decorated. Choose it for tariffs lower than the name hotels in the immediate vicinity, especially when little time is to be spent in the room. Ask for a higher floor with a park view. 5 meeting rooms.

St Regis Sheraton [$]////
2 E 55th St (5th Ave) 10022
☎ 753-4500 [TX] 148368 fax 758-2514 • AE DC MC V • 348 rooms, 58 suites, 2 restaurants, 1 bar
The builder of this genteel turn-of-the-century hotel was John Jacob Astor, the fourth-generation multimillionaire who went down with the *Titanic*. It was intended as a direct challenge to the original Waldorf-Astoria, and its regal Edwardian tone has been retained through many renovations, the latest complete early in 1990. Rooms have been enlarged, bathrooms graced with marble baths. The King Cole Restaurant/Bar, with its famed Maxfield Parrish mural, is an enormously popular rendezvous for natives as well as tourists. No Manhattan hotel has a more exclusive roster of on-premises shops, including Bijan, Fred jewelry and Godiva. Conference and banquet rooms observe established standards of opulence. Its 5th Avenue location couldn't be better. Health club by arrangement • 10 meeting rooms.

Sheraton Centre and Towers [$]////
811 7th Ave (53rd St) 10019
☎ 841-6400 [TX] 421130 fax 262-4410 • AE DC MC V • 1,816 rooms, 67 suites, 2 restaurants, 2 bars, 1 coffee shop
Only the Hilton in New York is significantly larger than this vast, bustling, efficient hotel, and the two have much in common – in this case The Towers (express elevators to the 46th floor, a private lounge for breakfast and cocktails, and refrigerators and terrycloth robes in the bedrooms are the extras). The in-house bars and restaurants are filled with tourists and conventioneers; meet clients elsewhere. Pharmacy, gift and clothing shops, hairdresser • health facilities at nearby Sheraton City Squire • 36 meeting rooms, translation, recording facilities.

Sherry-Netherland [$]/////
781 5th Ave (59th St) 10022
☎ 355-2800 fax 319-4306 • AE • 54 suites, 46 rooms, 1 restaurant, 1 bar
Given its splendid site at the southeast corner of Central Park, its majority of privately owned apartments and its reputation for civility and discretion, this is one hotel that feels no compulsion to keep up with the Carlyles and Pierres. Captains of industry and notables of the silver screen find it the perfect bastion, as they hide in vast suites with working fireplaces and vistas of grass and skyscrapers glinting in the sun.

The Stanhope [$]/////
995 5th Ave (81st St) 10028
☎ 288-5800 [TX] 6720662 fax 517-0088 • AE DC MC V • 117 rooms, 94 suites, 3 restaurants, 1 bar
It's amazing what $26m can do to a pleasant but formerly unremarkable hotel. In 1986, the new owner cut the number of rooms by nearly half to create suites, and then filled them with buttery leather, silks, marble, Baccarat crystal and bath amenities by Chanel. All the suites have kitchenettes, two-line phones with hold buttons, and audio cassette players. Staff outnumbers clients by two-to-one, as well they should since this is the city's most expensive hotel. 6 meeting rooms.

United Nations Plaza [$]///
1 United Nations Plaza (44th St at 1st Ave) 10017 ☎ 355-3400 [TX] 126803 fax 702-5031 • AE DC MC V • 444 rooms, 35 suites, 1 restaurant, 1 bar, 1 coffee shop
The striking angular blue-green towers that house the hotel have won architectural awards. They also contain offices and apartments, which

is why rooms begin on the 28th floor and all have panoramic views. Given its association with and proximity to the UN, it is to be expected that the clientele and staff reflect that diversity. Many languages and dialects are spoken at the front desk, and that may account for the occasionally confused registration and check-out processes. Rooms are sleekly comfortable, with few surprises beyond those expected of a de luxe establishment. Complimentary limo service to Wall Street, garment district and theater engagements • pool, tennis, health club • 6 meeting rooms, notary public.

Vista International [$]////

3 World Trade Center 10048
☎ 938-9100 [TX] 661130 fax 321-2237 • AE DC MC V • Hilton International • 797 bedrooms, 24 suites, 3 restaurants, 3 bars

This 1980s development is the only major local hotel conveniently placed for Wall Street visitors and is every bit equal to its contemporary uptown cousins. The smallest structure in the World Trade Center complex, it is only a few blocks from the two major stock exchanges and contains two of Wall Street's best restaurants – the American Harvest and The Greenhouse. On the 22nd floor, its health club has the best views to be obtained from the seat of an exercycle. Two executive floors provide a private lounge for breakfast and cocktails and an attendant to arrange airline, restaurant and hotel reservations. Since at least 85% of its customers are business people, every appropriate service is available including extensive conference facilities. Pool, fitness center, racquetball, sauna, jogging track • 16 meeting rooms.

Waldorf-Astoria [$]////

301 Park Ave (50th St) 10022
☎ 355-3000 [TX] 666747 fax 758-9209 • AE DC MC V • Hilton International • 1,692 bedrooms, 183 suites, 4 restaurants, 1 bar, 1 coffee shop

Long a synonym for New York glamor and sophistication, the Waldorf in later years slipped perceptibly, but the decline has been arrested by a $150m reclamation. Art Deco details have been buffed and restored to former glory, the generally spacious rooms primped and brought to standard. Choose one of the 50 rooms in The Towers, a separate luxury section similar to those in the Hilton and Sheraton Centre, though with greater cachet. The lower floors are crowded with enough cafés and shops to fill a large village. The east midtown location is very desirable. 25 meeting rooms, translation, teleconferencing, computer rental, computer modems, recording facilities.

Westbury [$]////

15 E 69th St (Madison Ave) 10021
☎ 535-2000 [TX] 125388 fax 535-5058 • THF • AE DC MC V • 197 rooms, 40 suites, 1 restaurant

Erected as a post-Great War apartment house, the Westbury's conversion to hotel means spacious bedrooms with sometimes cramped baths. Public rooms are understated plush, glinting with cut-glass chandeliers and antique tapestries. It has the look, but not the attitude, of a London gentlemen's club that has reluctantly admitted women. There are few more distinguished addresses, and the Polo Lounge is one of most accomplished of the city's hotel dining rooms, an especially good choice for brunch on Sunday. 5 meeting rooms.

Westin Plaza [$]////

5th Ave (59th St) 10019 ☎ 759-3000 [TX] 236938 or 620179 fax 759-3167 • AE DC MC V • 747 rooms, 88 suites, 6 restaurants, 3 bars

New Yorkers regard the Plaza with a sentimental affection that ignores the reality that it is no longer the epitome of gracious living. But the times, not the Plaza, have changed. Tea in the Palm Court is accompanied, as ever, by violins; the Oak Room continues to fill each evening with managers, entrepreneurs and "executive groupies." The restaurants are dated, still to undergo the trendy transformation of other hotel dining rooms. The location is still the best in New York. Florist, hairdresser, clothing, jewelry and gift shops, cinema, art gallery • reduced rates at nearby health club • 11 meeting rooms.

Windsor [$]//
100 W 58th St (6th Ave) ☎ *265-2100 fax 315-0371* • AE DC MC V • *Helmsley* • *300 rooms*
This is one of Helmsley's less expensive hotels, but it is thoroughly acceptable for the business traveler who wants a good-sized, comfortable room without the full services of a grander establishment. No room service.

OTHER HOTELS
Regular visitors who are not worried about being flashy sometimes find that clubs like the Harvard Club (you need to be the guest of a member) provide everything you can get at, say, the Algonquin, and are cheaper. Among the several hotels being built is the luxury Royal Concordia at 151 W 54th St, due to open in 1990.

The following hotels provide acceptable accommodation, usually at lower prices than most of the hotels given full entries.

Best Western Milford Plaza [$]// *270 W 45th St (by 8th Ave) 10036* ☎ *869-3600* [TX] *177610 fax 944-8357* • AE DC MC V. In the theater district, not far from the garment district.

Days Inn [$]// *440 W 57th St (10th Ave) 10019* ☎ *581-0139* [TX] *960473 fax 581-8719* • AE DC MC V. Near West Side television studios.

Doral Inn [$]// *541 Lexington Ave (49th St) 10022* ☎ *755-1200* [TX] *236641 fax 319-8344* • AE DC MC V. Ask for a room on an upper floor as the 49th Street location can be noisy.

Doral Park Avenue [$]/// *70 Park Ave (70th St) 10016* ☎ *687-7050* [TX] *968872 fax 808-9029* • AE DC MC V. Simple, modern and efficient, this hotel is convenient to midtown and lower midtown districts.

Edison [$]/ *228 W 47th St (between 7th and 8th Aves) 10019* ☎ *840-5000* [TX] *238887 fax 719-9541* • AE DC MC V. Close to the Rockefeller Center and theater district.

Halloran House [$]/// *525 Lexington Ave (48th St) 10017* ☎ *755-4000* [TX] *668844 fax 486-6319* • AE DC MC V. Convenient to midtown banks and Park Avenue; near the United Nations.

Holiday Inn Crowne Plaza [$]// *Broadway at 48th and 49th Sts* ☎ *977-4000* [TX] *213786 fax 333-7393* • AE DC MC V. New flagship chain hotel with leisure and business facilities.

Mayflower [$]// *15 Central Park W (61st St) 10023* ☎ *265-0064* [TX] *968872 fax 265-5098* • AE DC MC V. Close to Lincoln Center, Carnegie Hall and West Side businesses, it offers large, comfortable and quiet rooms.

Morgan's [$]/// *237 Madison Ave (37th St) 10016* ☎ *686-0300* [TX] *288908 fax 779-8352* • AE DC MC V. Small hotel with up-to-the minute decor; convenient for the Madison Avenue crowd.

New York Penta [$]// *401 7th Ave (33rd St) 10001* ☎ *736-5000* [TX] *9672643 fax 502-8798* • AE DC MC V. Near Madison Square Garden and the Jacob Javits Convention Center.

Omni Park Central [$]/// *870 7th Ave (55th St) 10019* ☎ *247-8000* [TX] *42434 fax 757-3374* • AE DC MC V. Charmless but efficient and with easy access to West Side and theater district business locations.

Quality Inn Lexington [$]// *511 Lexington Ave (48th St) 10017* ☎ *755-4400* [TX] *426257 fax 751-4091* • AE DC MC V. Convenient to midtown and the United Nations.

Ramada Inn [$]// *790 8th Ave (48th St) 10019* ☎ *581-7000* [TX] *147182 fax 974-0291* • AE DC MC V. Close to Broadway theaters and midtown, near Rockefeller Center.

Roosevelt [$]// *45 E 45th St 10017* ☎ *661-9600* [TX] *646229 fax 687-5064* • AE DC MC V. Near Grand Central, with extensive conference facilities and the popular Crawdaddy's restaurant, which the business community seeks out for its New Orleans-style seafood and gumbo, as well as for after-work drinks.

Salisbury [$]/ *123 W 57th St 10019* ☎ *246-1300* [TX] *668366 fax 977-7752* • AE DC MC V. Across from Carnegie Hall, convenient to Lincoln Center. Good, spacious rooms but not smart.

Shelburne Murray Hill [$]// *303 Lexington Ave (37th St) 10016* ☎ *689-5200* [TX] *225666 fax 779-7068* • AE DC MC V. The all-suite arrangement is convenient for longer visits and provides workspace as well. Situated in a quiet neighborhood south of midtown.

Sheraton City Squire [$]/// *790 7th Ave (51st St) 10019* ☎ *581-3300* [TX] *640458 fax 582-5379* • AE DC MC V. Close to Broadway theaters and midtown.

Skyline [$]/ *725 10th Ave (50th St) 10019* ☎ *586-3400* [TX] *262559 fax 582-4604* • AE DC MC V. This Best Western is close to the theater district, with easy access to the upper West Side.

Tudor [$]/ *304 E 42nd St 10017* ☎ *986-8800 fax 808-4717* • AE DC MC V. Close to United Nations and Grand Central.

Clubs

Clubs play a very important part in New York's business life. Members use them for lunchtime or after-hours discussions with colleagues and business visitors, and they are popular, especially with the financial community, for group meetings. Most of the principal clubs are in midtown. Some have been established especially for business users; others are for the alumni of the Ivy League colleges with rooms that members and their guests can stay in at much lower rates than those charged by midtown hotels; and there are the old-line social clubs, many of which still exclude women and minorities from membership.

All except the business clubs have strict rules about conduct: guests are not allowed to pay for anything; tipping is forbidden; business papers are not to be displayed in public areas. Among those catering specifically to the business community are: the *Boardroom*, 280 Park Ave ☎ 687-5858; the *Atrium*, 115 E 57th St ☎ 826-9640; and *Sky*, 200 Park Ave ☎ 867-9550.

Alumni of all ages use the Ivy League clubs: *Yale*, 50 Vanderbilt Ave ☎ 661-2070; *Harvard*, 27 W 44th St ☎ 840-6600; *Princeton*, 15 W 43rd St ☎ 840-6400; and the *University*, 1 W 54th St ☎ 247-2100. The old-line clubs, the *Union League*, 38 E 37th St ☎ 685-3800, and *Century*, 7 W 43rd St ☎ 944-0090, have prestige, but so, too, do the *New York Yacht Club*, 37 W 44th St ☎ 382-1000, *New York Athletic Club*, 180 Central Park South ☎ 247-5100, and the *Brook Club*, 111 E 54th St ☎ 753-7020. The Upper East Side's *Links Club*, 36 E 62nd St ☎ 838-8181, is highly rated. Downtown clubs of note include the *Downtown Association*, 60 Pine St ☎ 422-1982, and *India House*, 1 Hanover Sq ☎ 269-2323.

Restaurants

For New Yorkers, business meals are primarily lunches, few with anything stronger than a glass of wine, and power breakfasts, often starting as early as 7.30. Dinners – generally more lavish – are mainly for out-of-town clients or those who live in Manhattan. Lunch starts generally at

12.30, and dinners often end early (9–9.15) to allow commuters to get home. The city has an estimated 17,000 eating places, offering all types of cuisine, service, atmosphere and price. Most checks do not include a service charge; consider 17% a minimum, 20% standard. New Yorkers simply double the sales tax for a quick guide to what should be the minimum tip. If a captain has done more than simply take a meal order, he should be tipped separately – say, 25% of the basic tip. Many restaurants do not allow cigar and pipe smoking, though an increasing number offers nonsmoking areas.

The city's ceaseless quest for novelty can be bewildering to the first-timer. Unconventional menus, custom or decor can cause some people to bristle, others to become expansive. There are still restaurants where a woman executive could be made uncomfortable by relentlessly masculine traditions. Beware, also, of unwittingly inviting a contact to dine at a place where he or she has a regular table: a new relationship can be badly hit by such a gaffe.

The listings here are dominated by established restaurants of sturdy reputation. They are primarily French, Italian or, the catchall hybrid, Continental.

America [$]/
9-13 E 18th St ☎ 505-2110 • AE MC V
This popular eating stable takes its name seriously: it is huge, flashy, exuberant and overwhelming. Most customers are young professionals in advertising and PR, and the 200-plus items on its menu include every real or contrived regional and ethnic cuisine from the Atlantic to the Pacific. Think of it as a visit to a natural phenomenon like Niagara Falls, and to hear yourself think, go at lunch. The standard of cooking is variable.

Aquavit [$]/////
13 W 54th St ☎ 307-7311 • closed Sat L, Sun • AE MC V • reservations advisable
Aquavit signals the welcome return to New York of a restaurant offering traditional Scandinavian dishes interpreted with flair and served in a superb setting overlooking the gardens of the Museum of Modern Art. It is especially popular for business lunches; reserve a table downstairs to ensure you avoid the more informal, crowded and noisy upper floor.

Arcadia [$]//
21 E 62nd St ☎ 223-2900 • closed Sun • AE MC V • reservations essential
Featuring an idyllic Paul Davis mural of the seasons on three walls of the 50-cover dining room, Anne Rosenzweig's Arcadia quickly became one of New York's hottest restaurants. The kitchen produces thoughtful dishes of deceptive simplicity. Getting a table is a serious problem, although you may be luckier at lunch. The lobster sandwich snack is legendary.

Ballroom [$]///
253 W 28th St ☎ 244-3005 • closed Mon • AE DC MC V
Superior Spanish tavern snacks called *tapas* are featured at the magnificent bar out front, where whole hams hang overhead: an excellent choice for pre-dinner drinks. The restaurant's slightly inconvenient location, not far from the garment district, often mandates dinner, as well; besides *tapas*, there are conventional entrées, the creations of chef Felipe Rojas-Lombardi. The separate nightclub at the back is popular for its jazz and cabaret.

Bice [$]////
7 E 54th St ☏ 688-1999 • AE • reservations advisable
A chic offshoot of the Milanese original, Bice opened here in 1987, and could scarcely cope with the crush. Now it has settled down, and is becoming a New York institution, especially for lunch. Food is reliable, often excellent, and there are reasonably priced wines to match. Not the place for quiet conversation; and beware overbookings.

Bridge Café [$]//
279 Water St ☏ 227-3344 • AE DC • no reservations
Ed Koch, noted trencherman, is a regular patron of this winningly ramshackle tavern near the South Street Seaport. Once a disreputable sailors' bar, the 1801 woodframe building predates City Hall, a short walk away. Politicians, bureaucrats and Wall Streeters predominate at lunch. The informal bistro menu is supplemented by daily specials, brought to table by sometimes amateurish young people. Arrive early or late or expect a wait.

Café des Artistes [$]///
1 W 67th St ☏ 877-3500 • AE DC MC V • jackets required
There are few dining spots in Manhattan that can claim the graciousness of this café-restaurant. Leaded windows behind banks of greenery look out upon a tree-lined West Side street, while buffed wood paneling sets off large mirrors and Howard Chandler Christy's famed murals of voluptuous female nudes. There is a masculine tenor to the surroundings, though not aggressively so. The food is agreeable rather than *haute,* and tables are close, but the noise level is usually no more than a contented buzz. The middle-level executives (day) and neighborhood couples and concert-goers (evening) are sprinkled with stars and technicians from the nearby ABC studios. For greater privacy, choose the back room.

Christ Cella [$]///
160 E 46th St ☏ 697-2479 • closed Sun • AE DC MC V
This is a plain, aggressively masculine restaurant, serving extraordinary steaks, chops and onion rings to those with no expense account problems. Fish and lobster are also excellent. Unfortunately the wine list is no match for the food.

Le Cirque [$]///
58 E 65th St ☏ 794-9292 • closed Sun, Jul • AE DC • jacket and tie
Powerhouse business people, politicians and scions of multi-generational fortunes mingle here with butterflies whose principal occupations are charity balls and shopping. Its closely set tables allow snatches of gossip about the mighty as well as the possibility of dipping an elbow into a neighbor's *pasta primavera*. The Franco-Italian-Continental cuisine is entirely secondary to the patrons, who are concerned more with forming proposals and skewering rivals. A place for top executives to entertain their counterparts, it is within the Mayfair Regent Hotel but under separate management.

La Côte Basque [$]///
5 E 55th St ☏ 688-6525 • closed Sun, Jul • AE DC MC V • jacket and tie • reservations essential
Owner-chef Jean-Jacques Rachou, who made his mark in Manhattan with the stylish, now-closed Café Lavandou, has returned La Côte Basque to the pinnacle of the city's French restaurants. His clientele are the same prosperous folk who lunch at Lutèce, Le Cirque and Le Cygne. Bernard Lamotte's naturalistic murals of the Basque coast are delightful, and there is even breathing space between tables. You should make reservations at least three days in advance for weekday meals and at least two weeks for Saturday dinner, which draws celebrants from a wider and somewhat less monied circle. The *prix fixe* lunch menu is good value.

Le Cygne [$]///
55 E 54th St ☎ 759-5941 • closed Sat L, Sun, Aug • AE DC MC V • jacket and tie
It may have a smidgen less cachet than its peers – Le Cirque, La Côte Basque and their ilk – but that merely enhances the serenity of dining in this highly acclaimed spot, where you can make points and consider ripostes without raising your voice. Tables are well-spaced in a post-modernist setting of pearly grays and blues; service is attentive yet unobtrusive. The second floor is even more tranquil; one flight down from the main floor, the private room, with its racks of rare vintages, is perfect for highest-level dinner meetings requiring confidentiality.

David K's [$]//
1115 3rd Ave ☎ 371-9090 • AE DC • reservations advisable
The best choice for "modern" Chinese cooking: healthy, monosodium glutamate free and original. At the same address is David Keh's Café, serving more informal dishes and snacks.

Felidia [$]///
243 E 58th St ☎ 758-1479 • closed Sat L, Sun • AE DC MC V • jacket
Menus without English translation require patrons to listen very closely to the waiters' explanations, but as the northern Italian specialties trundled from the kitchen can be excellent, they are worth the effort. If you prefer, make friends with the paternal captain and leave decisions to him. The game and *porcini* are notable, and the wine list is good. A convivial place to meet clients or prospects. Private room if you need quiet.

Four Seasons [$]/////
99 E 52nd St ☎ 754-9494 • closed Sun, major hols • AE DC MC V • jacket, no denims • reservations essential for Fri & Sat D
The venerable and very expensive Four Seasons has skilfully adapted to stay in the main current of the volatile New York dining scene by providing an acceptable backcloth for people enjoying their power and glory. Ensconced in a towering space in the landmark Seagram Building, it is now into its fourth decade. Menus have been adjusted to cater to the calorie- and health-conscious executive; the famed Grill Room is where mega-players in the "communications game" court each other at lunch, around the massive four-sided bar. Don't invite someone likely to have a regular lunch table, and don't go for dinner, when tourists and out-of-towners take over. In general, go only if invited, and not for the food.

Gloucester House [$]////
37 E 50th St ☎ 755-7394 • AE DC MC V • jacket and tie
The conventions of the traditional steakhouse are observed at this venerable fish house, through whose doors pass executives and millionnaires of a decidedly Establishment stripe. An unshowy lot, they betray no dismay with either the quasi-nautical decor or the breathtaking tariffs for seafood no better than that offered at Grand Central's Oyster Bar. What they want and get is the assurance of tranquility. Middleaged and older businessmen dominate what amounts to a gentlemen's club.

Greene Street [$]//
101 Greene St ☎ 925-2415 • AE DC MC V
Situated in artsy, gentrified SoHo, the large bar features wine by the glass, and the great brick-walled main room serves meals deviating from the *nouvelle* canon primarily in the size of the portions. Nightly jazz, pop and cabaret performances follow at a loud amplification. Waiters and waitresses are generally well-trained and attentive, although most look ready to bolt at the first audition call. Best suited for off-duty drinks or dinner, or to celebrate wrapping up a deal.

Hatsuhana [$]//
17 E 48th St ☎ 355-3345 • closed Sat L, Sun • AE DC MC V
Consensus and its handy midtown location elevate this spot to most-favored *sushi–sashimi* status. Waiting for a table or a seat at one of the *sushi* bars is inevitable, especially at lunch when no reservations are accepted. The presence of many Japanese nationals among the customers is reassuring, and patrons can see for themselves the supreme freshness of the ingredients as these are adroitly sliced, scooped and packaged by the solemn young chefs. Cooked entrées are also available.

Huberts [$]//
575 Park Ave ☎ 826-5911 • closed Sat L, Sun • AE MC V • reservations essential
Both the sylish setting and the original cooking at this fashionable new uptown location, where La Périgord Park used to be, owe something to the Orient, as well as to European tradition. Well-orchestrated space and lighting allows concentration on both business and the clever creations of chef Len Allison.

Jean Lafitte [$]//
68 W 58th St ☎ 751-2323 • closed Sun L • AE DC MC V
The modern French bistro atmosphere and acceptable provincial fare make this a good alternative midtown choice.

John Clancy's [$]//
181 W 10th St ☎ 242-7350 • closed L • AE DC MC V
Clancy's open grills, fueled by mesquite or hickory coals, allow customers to witness the chefs at work, skewering or grilling whole shrimp, scallops, tuna, and, it seems, just about any other aquatic creature that takes the chef's fancy. Desserts are legendary. The only flaw in this attractive and popular Greenwich Village spot is the service, which can be slow. The upstairs room is quieter.

Kitcho [$]//
22 W 46th St ☎ 575-8880 • closed Sun L, Sat • AE DC
Well before Americans were persuaded that raw fish was good to eat, Kitcho was garnering praise for the delicacy and authenticity of its Japanese cooking. While the *sashimi* and *sushi* are admirable appetizers here, there is more on offer, and mysterious combinations are prepared and served with understated artistry in a tranquil environment that abhors flash. Novices are guided gracefully through the unfamiliar enticements of the menu, and you can confidently leave decisions to the waitress. For extra privacy, book one of the *tatami* rooms.

Lutèce [$]/////
249 E 50th St ☎ 752-2225 • closed Sun, major hols, Aug • AE DC • jacket and tie • reservations essential
The stage for André Soltner's virtuoso *haute cuisine* performances (for which reservations must be made two or more weeks in advance) is a converted terrace house in midtown. Downstairs, the fabled Garden Room is the place to be seen; upstairs is good for relative privacy. The maestro moves easily among his patrons, with a word of welcome here, an off-menu suggestion there. His staff serves with neither *hauteur* nor unctuousness. The fixed-price lunch is the time to establish the parameters of a deal, the more ambitious and thrice-as-costly dinner to celebrate its closing.

Metro [$]//
23 E 74th St ☎ 249-3030 • closed Sat L, Sun D • AE DC MC V
A sophisticated new rival to the Odeon and the Café Luxembourg, founded by the same chef, Patrick Clark. The Metro has a casual, club-like atmosphere and the clientele includes gallery-goers at lunch time and East Side locals in the evenings. Savoury dishes are generally more successful than sweet, and service can take a long time.

Il Nido $$$$

251 E 53rd St ☎ 753-8450 • closed Sun • AE DC MC V • jacket and tie • reservations essential

Jockeying for position among the most honored Italian eateries in town, Il Nido is still in the running, judging by the hum of satisfied conversation and the relaxed attitudes of the conservatively dressed patrons that fill its rooms day and night. If they notice that they are swirling their pasta in surroundings that hint more of a Brittany farmhouse than Bolognese trattoria, it doesn't seem to matter. Seats are rare at lunch *or* dinner, even past closing hours. Make sure you reserve at least a day or two ahead.

Odeon $$$

145 W Broadway ☎ 233-0507 • closed Sat L • AE V

With many of the area's best chefs engaged exclusively in corporate dining rooms, the downtown financial district is notoriously short of public restaurants of much verve or style. One solution lies in a brisk stroll north, to gentrified TriBeCa. This chrome-and-marble relic of the Depression–World War II era now offers lighthearted American/French dishes. The crowd is a giddy mix of stockbrokers and lawyers in three-piece suits, bearded and tweedy middleaged artists and avant-gardists in fashion and the performing arts. Consider it for both low-pressure business lunches and off-hours diversion. In the same style, and with 1930s decor, is Café Luxembourg, on the West Side, at 200 W 70th St ☎ 873-7411.

Oyster Bar & Restaurant $$$$

Lower Level, Grand Central Terminal ☎ 490-6650 • closed Sat, Sun • AE DC MC V

The now-fading European tradition of superior railway hotel restaurants was rarely copied in the USA, but the remarkably expensive Oyster Bar is the exception. The specialty seafood, served in cavernous, vaulted rooms, is whatever was available from the wholesalers that morning. The buyer's reach is wide, including fresh turbot flown in from the North Sea and salmon from the Pacific Northwest. Most of the regulars, including Japanese diners, come here for the oysters or clams at the Bar, which starts serving at 11.30am. The main kitchen begins to run out of ingredients by mid-afternoon, so go after 1.30pm to avoid peak eating time, but before 2.30 to avoid shortages. The Saloon room is smaller and marginally quieter.

Palio $$$$

151 W 51st St ☎ 245-4850 • closed Sat L, Sun • AE DC MC V

Entrance to this sparkling Italian eatery is off the covered arcade of the Equitable Center. Inside the doors is a stunning horseshoe-shaped marble bar, flanked by the vivid murals of Sandro Chia which are worth a visit for themselves. The kitchen has a light *nuova cucina* touch, and all the bread and pasta is freshly made. A good choice for business lunches, with a heavy representation from the financial crowd. Dinners are social. Private rooms available.

Parioli Romanissimo $$$$$

24 E 81st ☎ 288-2391 • closed L, Sun, Mon • AE DC V • jacket and tie • reservations essential

The quintessential Upper East Side Italian restaurant has several distinguishing marks – including an avoidance of Sicilian tomato sauces, a recognizable face or two every night, several limos in waiting, a large number of gents in black silk suits with silver in their hair and gold in their shirt cuffs, an interesting decor that goes no farther than manly comfort, and daily specials unmentioned in the menu and revealed by the captain only after prodding. Treatment of strangers is as evenhanded as is possible in a place with so many regular customers.

Periyali [$]/

35 W 20th St ☏ 463-7890 • closed Sat L, Sun • AE MC V

The best Greek taverna in town, Periyali opened in 1988. The rustic Mediterranean decor and innovative but authentic cooking make this a popular venue for informal lunches or off-duty dining.

Petrossian [$]///

182 W 58th ☏ 245-2214 • closed Sun • AE DC MC V • reservations essential

This sumptuous Art Deco café offers an ideal light lunch or after-dinner snack comprising a few ounces of pearly Beluga caviar accompanied by papery-thin leaves of smoked salmon or perhaps a thick circle of *foie gras* embedded with truffles. The whole is best washed down with premium champagne or icy tumblers of Russian vodka. Convenient in central midtown, it attracts a meticulously tonsured and attired custom of international travelers and high-level corporate executives.

Quilted Giraffe [$]/////

550 Madison Ave ☏ 593-1221 • closed Sat, Sun, Jul • AE • jacket and tie • reservations essential

Chef Barry Wine has proclaimed that this is an "elegant luxurious businessman's restaurant to celebrate the closing of a multimillion-dollar transaction" – and the cost will be entirely appropriate. The restaurant's success and acclaim have ensured some of the highest prices in New York, and you need to reserve two to three weeks in advance. To some the *nouvelle* dishes have glorious flourishes that have been refined by maturity and experiment, to others the cuisine has been extravagantly over-praised.

River Café [$]//

1 Water St, Brooklyn ☏ (718) 522-5200 • AE DC MC V • jacket and tie • reservations essential

Built on a barge moored in the East River beneath Brooklyn Bridge, the River Café provides an unobstructed vista of its magnificent span and of the lower Manhattan skyline. During lunch hours a launch shuttles customers from Wall Street, and open-air dining is available in good weather; ask about both when making your reservation. Its cuisine is inventive New American, which now equals the view. Very popular with Wall Street financiers.

Rosa Mexicana [$]//

1063 1st Ave ☏ 753-7407 • AE DC MC V

Mexican cookery once had scant representation in New York, where aficionados were obliged to settle for watery guacamole and flaccid tortillas with fillings of uncertain origin. This sprightly *fonda*, much loved by the younger professional league, offers south-of-the-border dishes that do not involve blistering seasonings. Accept a table in the back room, to which no stigma is attached. Reservations are advisable but a wait in the ever-jolly bar is softened considerably by ingratiating house margaritas.

Russian Tea Room [$]///

150 W 57th St ☏ 265-0947 • AE DC MC V • jacket

Once a rendezvous for the rich and famous, the Tea Room's clientele still includes a fair sprinkling of renowned concert artists and ballet masters, agents and movie stars. The emerald jewel box of a room glints with the polished brass of dozens of clocks and samovars, and crimson banquettes do visual battle with rosy-pink napery. The emphasis is on blinis, caviar, herring, *shashlik* and borscht; quality is uneven. Make every effort to get a booth in the main arena downstairs.

San Domenico [$]///

240 Central Park S ☏ 265-5959 • AE DC M V • jacket

An exciting new contender in the Italian restaurant race, San Domenico is of impeccable pedigree, being the New York version of the top restaurant of the same name in Italy. There have been criticisms of the loud decor, but mainly praise for the chefs, both trained at the original in Imola, and experts with north Italian food in general and fish in particular. Their cooking is complemented by the creations of an American pastry chef.

Sea Grill $//
Rockefeller Center, 19 W 49th St
☎ 246-9201 • AE DC MC V • jacket • reservations essential
When the sunken iceskating rink that is centerpiece of the Rockefeller Center complex was rejuvenated, room was made for restaurants of greater ambition and pizzaz. This strikingly appointed room accommodates both business people and well-heeled tourists. Tables are well-spaced and the leather chairs uncommonly comfortable. The glassed-in kitchen with open grill produces chowders and seafood salads as well as charcoal-striped tuna steaks, sea bass and chicken.

Da Umberto $//
107 W 17th St ☎ 989-0303 • closed L Sat, Sun • AE • reservations advisable
Chelsea trattoria popular with the advertising set. Tuscan and Ligurian cooking is consistently good, but best is the antipasto buffet of vegetables and salads. The back room is marginally quieter than the front.

Water Club $///
30th St (on the East River)
☎ 683-3333 • AE DC MC V • reservations essential
This two-decked, permanently moored barge has a working fireplace and outside dining deck, and a large yacht for dining and sightseeing is tied alongside in summer. The chef skilfully fabricates regional American cooking styles, including New England clam chowder, Connecticut rabbit stew, seafood gumbo and Maryland baby chicken. During the week, the regular crowd comprises business people and senior medics from the nearby hospitals, especially at lunch.

Windows on the World $////
1 World Trade Center (107th floor)
☎ 938-1111 • closed L Mon–Fri • AE DC MC V • jacket and tie • reservations advisable
The Center has three distinct dining areas. *The Restaurant* has a tiered, starship character with superb views of the city and competent Continental cuisine. At midday, it is a membership club, although outsiders can sometimes get in by paying a surcharge. At dinner and weekends, crowds are inevitable and so are waits, even with reservations. The adjacent *Hors d'Oeuvrerie* specializes in international appetizers, alternately highlighting Spanish *tapas*, Chinese *dim sum*, Indonesian *satay* and similar snacks. The *Cellar in the Sky*, the showcase for Kevin Zraly's wine selections, serves the best food of the three restaurants, including a seven-course *prix fixe* banquet.

Power breakfasts
For a substantial number of top executives power breakfasts play a key role in New York business life. Since coffee shops are too noisily plebeian and conventional formal restaurants rarely open before noon, spacious hotel dining rooms profit from the phenomenon. The *Regency*, where the waiters will also make photocopies, and the *Carlyle*, used by investment brokers, are still the tops. A good breakfast can be had at the *Algonquin*. Other possibilities are joining the broadcast network biggies at the *Dorset*, or the tycoons and cosmopolites at Le Patio or Chez Maurice in the *Parker Meridien*. Reservations are generally essential. For addresses and phone numbers, see *Hotels*.

Afternoon tea
Now that many hotels serve afternoon tea – usually from 3 to 6 – executives are discovering its virtues as an alternative to working breakfasts, and as a way to escape office distractions. In the Gold Room of the *Helmsley Palace*, Devonshire cream and scones

lend an authentic touch. In the Palm Court of the *Plaza*, violinists are the musical backdrop. The splendid lobby of the *Mayfair Regent* offers "teas" that can include cappucino and pastries. Other possibilities are the lounges of the *Stanhope, Carlyle, Pierre, Algonquin* and *Inter-Continental* and the Gotham Lounge of the *Peninsula*.

Wall Street dining

Good business-populated eateries scattered across lower Manhattan include *Tenbrooks*, 62 Reade St ☏ 349-5900; *Ye Olde Chop House*, 111 Broadway ☏ 732-6119; *Morgan Williams*, 55 Broadway ☏ 809-3150; *Harry's at Hanover Square*, 1 Hanover Sq ☏ 425-3412; and *Delmonico's*, 56 Beaver St ☏ 422-4747. On the eastern edge of the island is the South Street Seaport, riddled with dozens of bars, cafés and bistros. Some with loyal clientele are *Sloppy Louie's*, 92 South St ☏ 509-9694; *Sweet's*, 2 Fulton St ☏ 825-9786; and *Coho*, 11 Fulton St ☏ 608-0470.

Yet more French

Despite Manhattan's gastronomic diversity, the list of restaurants preferred by business people is overwhelmingly French. *Le Bernardin*, 155 W 51st St ☏ 489-1515, is a very expensive and formal seafood restaurant in the Equitable Center. The acclaimed *Chanterelle* is now at 2 Harrison St ☏ 966-6960. Both require advance reservations of at least a month. Useful alternatives to the restaurants given full entries are: *Aurora*, 60 E 49th St ☏ 692-9292; *Bonley*, 165 Duane St ☏ 608-3852; *Terrace*, 400 W 119th St ☏ 666-9490; *La Reserve*, 4 W 49th St ☏ 247-2993; *Montrachet*, 239 W Broadway ☏ 219-2777 and *Le Périgord Park*, 405 E 52nd St ☏ 755-6244.

Steak houses

When you can't get to or into *Peter Luger*, the best of the steak houses at 178 Broadway in Brooklyn ☏ (718) 387-7400, choices include *The Palm*, 837 2nd Ave ☏ 687-2953, which is expensive and noisy with a less desirable annex *Palm Too* across the street; *Pietro's*, 232 E 43rd St ☏ 682-9760, which is Italianate; downtown, *Moc's*, 112 Duane St ☏ 406-1043; *Spark's*, 210 E 46th St ☏ 687-4855, known *inter alia* for its excellent wine list; *Keens*, 72 W 36th St ☏ 947-3636; *Smith & Wollensky's Grill*, 205 E 49th St ☏ 753-1530; and *Pen & Pencil*, 205 E 45th St ☏ 682-8660.

Grills

Besides *John Clancy's* and the *Sea Grill*, you should try the designer burgers at *Hamburger Harry's* in TriBeCa, 157 Chambers St ☏ 267-4446 and 145 W 45th St ☏ 840-2756; the dashing *Gotham Bar & Grill*, 12 E 12th St ☏ 620-4020; Tex-Mex *El Rio Grande*, 160 E 38th St ☏ 867-0922; or the smoke-barbecued ribs at *Carolina*, 355 W 46th St ☏ 245-0058.

Chinatown

Chinatown's 200-plus eateries tend to be gaudy and cramped or gloomy and cramped, but their cooks are often as skilled as those in the fancier uptown establishments. Prices are much lower, however, and Chinatown is handy for the financial district and the municipal and federal governmental offices of lower Manhattan. These restaurants are definitely not places to bring associates you wish to impress, but are admirable for working lunches or after-hours meals. Among the best are *Canton*, 45 Division St ☏ 226-4441; *dim sum* specialist *Hee Seung Fung Teahouse* a.k.a. HSF, 46 Bowery ☏ 374-1319; *Hwa Yuan Szechuan*, 40 E Broadway ☏ 966-5534; and the Shanghai-style *Say Eng Look*, 5 E Broadway ☏ 732-0796. All are near Chatam Square. Convenient for lunches on the East Side is *Chin Chin*, 216 E 49th St ☏ 888-4555, which offers original oriental food in a modern American setting.

Other ethnic restaurants

Among the city's thousands of ethnic eating places the most agreeable for casual business or off-hours meals are the Cuban *Sabor*, 20 Cornelia St in Greenwich Village ☏ 243-9579; Brazilian *Cabana Carioca II*, 133 W 45th St ☏ 730-8375; Afghan *Pamir*, 1437 2nd Ave near 74th St ☏ 734-3791; Indonesian *Tamu*, 340 W Broadway in SoHo ☏ 925-2751; *Tibetan Kitchen*, 444 3rd Ave near 30th St ☏ 679-6286; Central Asian *Bukhara*, 148 E 48th St ☏ 838-1811; and Indian *Raga*, 57 W 48th St ☏ 757-3450; *Dawat*, 210 E 58th St ☏ 355-7555; or *Darbár*, 44 W 56th St ☏ 432-7227.

Delicatessens

For fast food with an unmistakable New York flavor, try the overstuffed *pastrami* and corned beef sandwiches of its delis. Some are devoutly kosher, others not; but they all share a Jewish heritage. Convenient in midtown are the celebrity-studded *Stage*, 834 7th Ave; the nearby *Carnegie*, 854 7th Ave; *Kaplan's*, 71 W 47th St; and *Fine & Shapiro*, 138 W 72nd St. Most are open seven days and do not accept credit cards.

Bars

Manhattan's thousands of watering holes are packed from late afternoon to early morning. (They can legally remain open until 4am.) Most have clear identities and specific attractions. Few cater exclusively to business people, though many are used by executives unwinding after a long day, or meeting a contact before or instead of dinner. Unaccompanied men or women should feel comfortable in any of the following.

Originally a Prohibition speakeasy, the *21 Club*, 21 W 52nd St, never a great place for the food itself, was for decades *the* single New York bar and eating spot for the power brokers. Its claim (true) was that it could perform any service for its clients. Nor were outsiders made to feel less than grand and privileged, even if they were assigned by rank to one of the three parts of the restaurant – in Nos 17, 19 or 21. Now it just doesn't matter. Although the 21 Club exercises a greater pull on the collective social imagination of gastronomic America than any other place, under new ownership and with many of the key staff gone, 21 is just another terribly expensive restaurant with uneven standards of cooking and service.

Although better known as a restaurant, *Elaine's*, 1703 2nd Ave, is undoubtedly a bar in which to see some of America's big names. Its eponymous doyenne has always been fiercely protective of her pet clients – writers. Long before most of them became literary household names, she coddled and teased such lions as William Styron, Joseph Heller and George Plimpton. They have been augmented, over the years, by such diverse personalities as country singer Willie Nelson, Luciano Pavarotti, Albert Finney and Andy Warhol. To bask in such starlight – but not to stare or approach – arrive after 10 and snuggle up to the long bar right inside the door. If you are denied entrance, many of the same luminaries pass the fancier front-room bar of the *Russian Tea Room* (see *Restaurants*).

Celebrity-watching is also a preoccupation of the drinkers at the long mahogany bar of *Mortimer's*, 1057 Lexington Ave. The objects of their attentions tend to be high-profile fashion designers, musicians and Hollywood superagents. The other, yet-to-be-famous patrons are an attractive bunch, graduates of very select universities and amenable to conversation.

Hotel bars are often refuges for those out-of-towners too timid or listless to venture far from their rooms, and therefore are scorned by natives. Among the exceptions is the *Blue Bar* of the Algonquin, a haven for the theatrical and literary set; and the *Oak Room*, Westin Plaza, home to regulars talking in terms as sleekly groomed and wrinkle-free as their clothes. *Bemelman's* reflects the clientele of the adjacent *Café Carlyle*, 35 E 76th St ☏ 570-7189. On the East River, the *South Street Seaport* complex has bars and cafés crammed with up-and-coming lawyers and brokers.

Beer aficionados should know about the *Peculier Pub*, 182 W 4th St ☏ 691-8667, which has more than 250 brews from across the USA and around the world.

Shopping

New York is the shopper's paradise. You can buy literally anything you might ever want at almost any time of the day or night, and you can buy it at almost any price. New York is a city where someone always knows someone who "has it wholesale": discount stores abound, so much so that it is virtually unknown to pay the list price for, say, a camera or some electronic goods. It pays to ask your native contacts. In general, however, it is best not to be overwhelmed by the vastness of the options, and either shop by neighborhood – going to a district, like 7th Avenue on the Lower East Side for designer clothing bargains, because of what you want to buy; or, like W 34th or E 59th Streets, because there is a famed department store conveniently near your hotel or business. But if you are really in a rush, stick to 5th Avenue where you can buy everything from exotic chocolates to books, furs to cigarettes and rare tobaccos, high fashion to extravagant jewelry, luggage to household goods, watches to wigwams. On the other hand, be aware that some 5th Avenue shops prey on tourists and unsuspecting visitors. The stores and boutiques get more exclusive the farther north you walk from 34th Street.

Most shops open 10–6, with some of the large department stores staying open until 9 at least two nights a week. Most of the department stores are open Sundays, 12–5. Weekday mornings are the best times to shop; lunch times and Saturdays are extremely crowded. Even small shops usually accept at least some credit cards, although a minimum purchase may be stipulated.

Shopping by area

Antiques and art Madison Avenue between 57th and 80th. SoHo is good for avant-garde galleries. Columbus Avenue on the Upper West Side is where you will find trendy shops selling bizarre items.
Books To find bookshops for browsing go to 5th and Madison Avenue, Broadway and Greenwich Village.
Cameras and electronics 32nd Street near 6th Avenue (Camera World) and 32nd near 7th Avenue (Willoughby's – New York's largest camera store); 34th Street near Herald Square.
Clothes 5th and Madison Avenues for high fashion, 7th Avenue for bargains, SoHo and Greenwich Village for the more unusual.
Diamonds and jewelry Look around the stores on 47th Street between 5th and 6th.

Shopping by name

Most of the well-known exclusive names are on Madison or 5th Avenues or on 57th Street. Among these are Tiffany's, Cartier, Bijan, Saks (5th Avenue); Henri Bendel and Courièges (57th Street); Yves St Laurent, Sonia Rykiel and Brooks Brothers (Madison).

Department stores and malls

Macy's, the world's biggest single store, is at W 34th and Broadway. Also in 34th Street at 6th Avenue is the city's largest shopping mall, a multilevel high-rise with each separate level bearing the name of traditional New York shopping meccas, Herald Square, 5th Avenue, Madison and Broadway among them. *B Altman*, 5th Ave at 34th St, *Lord & Taylor*, 424 5th Ave, on ten floors at 39th Street, and *Bergdorf Goodman*, 754 5th Ave at 58th St, are three other old-established department stores with a decidedly upmarket stock.

Bloomingdale's occupies the square block bounded by 59th and 60th Streets and between 3rd and Lexington Avenues. *Trump Tower*, at 725 5th Avenue, has a selection of exclusive shops including *Bonwit Teller*.

Entertainment

New York offers every variety of entertainment imaginable, from the sublime, at Lincoln Center and Carnegie Hall, to Times Square and 42nd Street sleaze. A key rule is to call ahead, even if you think the event or spot will be uncrowded: unexpected publicity could draw throngs, stars change their plans, and ticket prices change at a moment's notice. Most hotels' concierge staff will arrange reservations.

For listings of events, plays, concerts, films and other performances, check *The New Yorker* and *New York* magazines, *The New York Times* Friday "Weekend" section and the *Village Voice*; or pick up a copy of the Visitors Bureau calendar of events.

Theater ticket agencies The Shubert organization, which owns most Broadway theaters, operates the *Telecharge* agency, 330 W 42nd St ☏ 239-6200, which handles tickets for shows in any Shubert-owned venue (with a small service charge per ticket). Telecharge accepts major credit cards and will send tickets or have them held at the box office. Half-price tickets for Broadway and Off-Broadway shows are available on the day at TKTS, Broadway at 47th St or Times Square ☏ 354-5800 (small service charge and long lines). *Ticketron* has outlets throughout the city ☏ 399-4444, cash only; major credit cards accepted on ☏ 947-5850.

Broadway Broadway shows continue to attract the crowds despite rising prices. Tickets to the long-running musicals most popular with visitors are usually the most difficult to get, and discounted seats are seldom available.

Ballet, opera and classical music The main centers are *Carnegie Hall*, 57th St at 7th Ave ☏ 247-7800; *Metropolitan Opera*, Lincoln Center, Broadway at 64th St ☏ 362-6000; *New York State Theater*, *New York City Ballet* and *New York City Opera*, Lincoln Center ☏ 870-5570; and *Avery Fisher Hall*, Lincoln Center ☏ 874-2424.

Cinema New York has hundreds of cinemas, both first-run and art houses. Check the publications cited above for listings.

Piano bars and clubs For a less structured evening, many midtown hotels have piano bars with sophisticated musical entertainment, including Bobby Short's long-running Cole Porter-era act at the *Carlyle*, 35 E 76th St ☏ 744-1600. Jazz clubs such as the *Village Vanguard*, 178 7th Ave S ☏ 255-4037, and the *Blue Note*, 131 W 3rd St ☏ 475-8592, feature well-known artists and rising stars.

Nightclubs Hot discos in New York generally come and go in less than a year. Longer-lived exceptions include *Limelight*, 47 W 20th St ☏ 807-7850, in what used to be an Episcopal church, and *Palladium*, 126 E 14th St ☏ 473-7171. Expect cover charges of at least $15 and very high drink prices. For comedy, try the *Improvisation Restaurant*, 358 W 44th St ☏ 765-8268.

Sightseeing

New York's main "sight" is, of course, Manhattan itself. Many American cities have impressive skylines, but none has the stunning impact of Manhattan's prodigious forest of towers. Spectacular views of Manhattan can be enjoyed from the tops of the buildings themselves, from the water – on one of the ferries or tour boats – or from the opposite shores of the Hudson and East rivers; the view of the Financial District from Brooklyn Heights or the Brooklyn Bridge, an attraction in its own right, is especially to be recommended.

Many of the more familiar sights,

such as the Statue of Liberty, cannot be visited quickly, but museums and the Wall Street area's historic sites are easily sampled by the traveler on a tight schedule.

American Museum of Natural History Four floors of exhibits illustrate the diversity of animal and human life – from a simple mollusk to the elaborate customs and sophisticated craftsmanship of the world's peoples. Realistic life-size dioramas show animals in their natural habitats, including a herd of African elephants and some formidable reptiles. The museum also has an outstanding collection of gems and minerals.

The adjacent *Hayden Planetarium* is the museum's department of astronomy. Its Theater of the Stars presents an hour-long show of celestial phenomena on a huge hemispheric screen; also "cosmic laser concerts." *Central Park West at 79th St ☏ 769-5100; Planetarium ☏ 769-5920. Open Mon, Tue, Thu, Sun, 10–5.45; Wed, Fri, Sat, 10–9.*

Cloisters The building skilfully incorporates parts of several cloisters from southern French medieval monasteries – of which the most famous is St Michel-de-Cuxa – as well as fountains, doorways and the apse of a ruined Spanish chapel. The collection (part of the Metropolitan Museum of Art) includes reliquaries and other liturgical objects. Among its chief treasures are the 15thC Unicorn Tapestries. It is located a long way uptown in Fort Tryon Park, 62 acres of greenery which starts at W 192 Street and overlooks the Hudson. *Open Tue-Sun, 9.30–5.15 (4.45 winter) ☏ 923-3700.*

Federal Hall National Memorial This Greek Revival building, dating from 1842, occupies a site with many historical associations. The English City Hall was founded here in 1699; and it's where the Stamp Act Congress later met to plan a response to British tax policies. Reconstructed after the Revolution, it became Federal Hall, the nation's first capitol, and George Washington was sworn in there as the first President. His statue overlooks Wall Street from the steps of the present building, which was built as a Custom House, later used as a subtreasury of the Federal Reserve Bank, and is now a museum of New York history. *26 Wall St ☏ 264-8711. Open Mon–Fri, 9–5.*

Frick Collection Perhaps New York's most beautiful and visitable museum, the Frick has the advantage – if you are pressed for time – of being quite small; it is possible to view the collection in about an hour. It is also a good place to sit and think or plan your schedule in safety. Built in 1913 as the home of industrialist Henry Clay Frick, the mansion affords a glimpse of the life enjoyed by New York's millionaires in the early 20th century. Frick's outstanding collection of Old Masters – including masterpieces by Bellini, Titian, Holbein, Rembrandt, Vermeer, El Greco and Turner – are superbly displayed. There are delightful Boucher and Fragonard rooms and a collection of 16th–17thC Limoges enamel. *1 E 70th St ☏ 288-0700. Open Tue–Sat, 10–6; Sun, 1–6; closed Mon.*

Guggenheim Museum Of interest for its architecture as much as for the art it contains, the building – completed in 1959 – was designed by Frank Lloyd Wright and commissioned by Solomon R Guggenheim, who used the fortune he made in copper to support nonrepresentational art. The building's design is a continuous oval spiral ramp which becomes smaller in diameter as it moves down; take the elevator to the top and move downwards along the ramp. The Guggenheim features the world's largest Kandinsky collection. *1071 5th Ave between 88th and 89th Sts ☏ 360-3513. Open Tue, 11–7.45; Wed–Sun, 11–5.*

Lincoln Center Dedicated to the performing arts, this impressive, classically inspired complex houses the Metropolitan Opera, the New

York City Opera, the New York City Ballet, the Lincoln Center Theater Company and the Juilliard School (music, dance and drama). Backstage tours of the Met are bookable in advance ☏ 582-3512. The Library and Museum of the Performing Arts is open free to the public and offers a variety of films, concerts and exhibitions. *140 W 65th St and Broadway ☏ 877-2011.*

Metropolitan Museum of Art The 236 galleries include collections of Greek, Roman and Egyptian antiquities, Islamic art, medieval European art, costume, arms and armor, prints and drawings, musical instruments, European painting and sculpture and decorative arts – including several furnished rooms. A new three-story wing is devoted to American art. It is impossible to get a comprehensive view on a single visit. Instead, choose two or three areas of special interest.

The medieval section on the first floor is particularly fine and includes a magnificent Spanish baroque wrought-iron choir screen and Romanesque chapel.

An outstanding attraction of the Egyptian collection is the largely intact Temple of Dendur. In the Greek and Roman section, the Euphronios Krater, bought for $1m, is a superb example of red-figured pottery.

The Met's collection of European painting and sculpture includes masterpieces from all periods and schools. Among them are a *Madonna and Child* by Bellini, *Venus and the Lute Player* by Titian, El Greco's *View of Toledo*, and 33 works by Rembrandt, including *Aristotle with a Bust of Homer*. The 19thC collection in the André Meyer Galleries contains works by David, Delacroix, Turner and Rodin and many Impressionist and Post-Impressionist painters.

The Michael C Rockefeller Wing of Primitive Art has 3,500 pieces donated by Nelson Rockefeller when his son died on an expedition to New Guinea in 1961. The exhibits cover Africa, the Pacific and the Americas.

The Lehman Pavilion contains a fine collection of Italian Renaissance and 19th and 20thC French art.

The American Wing houses the museum's extensive collection of American art, from colonial times to the present. Among the painters represented are Winslow Homer, Frederic Remington, Mary Cassatt, James Whistler, Georgia O'Keeffe and John Singer Sargent. American decorative arts are displayed in a series of period rooms, including a Duncan Phyfe Greek Revival parlor, a room furnished in the austere Shaker style and an earth-toned Frank Lloyd Wright living room overlooking Central Park. The spacious garden court that forms the entrance to the wing is embellished with Tiffany stained-glass windows. *5th Ave at 82nd St ☏ 535-7710 for recorded information. Open 9.30–5.15 (to 8.45 Tue–Sun); closed Mon.*

Museum of Modern Art This extensive collection of modern art runs from Impressionism to Pop Art and includes paintings, sculptures, prints and drawings, architectural models, graphic design and films.

Among the museum's most important acquisitions are: Van Gogh's *Starry Night*; Toulouse-Lautrec's *La Goulue at the Moulin Rouge*; several fine Cézannes; Picasso's *Les Demoiselles d'Avignon*; Chagall's poetic *I and the Village*; Piet Mondrian's abstract geometric compositions; and masterpieces by Matisse. There are also works by the Russian Constructivists and by Latin American painters, as well as by the more familiar School of Paris artists such as Modigliani and Braque and the Americans Edward Hopper and Andrew Wyeth (*Christina's World*). The exhibition of Braque and Picasso cubist pieces side by side is particularly impressive. Dado and surrealism are well-represented by such artists as Arp, Magritte and Dali; abstract expressionism by Pollack, Kline and De Kooning. The museum's sculpture garden includes works by Rodin, Giacommeti and Louise Nevelson. A self-service restaurant overlooks the garden; in warm weather you can eat outside. The museum shop is particularly good for books and gifts. *11 W 53rd Sts ☏ 708-9480. Open Thu–Tue, 11–6 (to 9 Thu); closed Wed.*

New York Stock Exchange Descended from an organization founded in 1792 under a buttonwood tree at Wall and William Streets, the New York Stock Exchange now deals in the shares of nearly 1,600 companies. From the Visitors' Gallery one can watch the chaotic activity on the Trading Floor. Exhibits, recordings and guides explain the Exchange's history and workings. *2 World Trade Center ☏ 321-3977. Open Mon–Fri, 9.30–3.30.*

Pierpont Morgan Library Originally the home of millionaire JP Morgan, this elegant building is now a museum housing his collection of rare books (including a Gutenberg Bible), illuminated manuscripts and medieval and Renaissance works of art. Like the Frick, its tranquil but imposing atmosphere makes it perfect for a breather. *29 E 36th St at Madison Ave ☏ 685-0610.*

Rockefeller Center This city-within-a-city includes 19 buildings, with a working population of 65,000. In 1989 Mitsubishi bought a controlling interest in the Center from the Rockefeller family.

For visitors, the main attractions of the Center are the General Electric Building, the Lower Plaza, which serves as an outdoor café in summer and an iceskating rink in winter, and Radio City Music Hall, an Art Deco palace famed for its elaborate stage shows. Tours of the Center, and of the radio and television studios of NBC (a subsidiary of General Electric), leave from the Guided Tour office on the main floor of the General Electric Building, daily except Sun, 9.30–4.45 and 10–4 respectively ☏ 489-2947. Few television programmes originate in New York; however, it is possible to attend some of those that do; information ☏ 664-3055. Tours of Radio City Music Hall only, including backstage areas, start from the lobby; for information call ☏ 246-4600. The public areas of the Music Hall are included in the general tour of the Center. *General Electric Building*: 30 Rockefeller Plaza, between 49th and 50th Sts; Radio City Music Hall: 1260 Avenue of the Americas at 6th St ☏ 753-3100.

St Patrick's Cathedral This graceful Neo-Gothic church presents a striking contrast to the massive modern towers that surround it. The bronze doors have bas-reliefs depicting notable American Catholics; the stained-glass windows, some made in France, are especially noteworthy. *5th Ave between 50th and 51st Sts.*

St Paul's Chapel The oldest church in Manhattan, St Paul's Chapel was completed in 1766. George Washington worshipped here while President; his pew is in the north aisle. It is now a chapel of *Trinity Church*, the third on the site, which, when it was designed by the English-born architect Richard Upjohn in 1846, established Gothic as the dominant US church style. *Broadway at Vesey St ☏ 602-0874.*

South Street Seaport This complex of piers, museums, galleries, shops, markets and restaurants on the East River is a redevelopment of the area that was the heart of New York's 19thC shipping industry. Carefully restored waterfront warehouses face a small fleet of sailing ships, some of which can be boarded, and there is an exhibition gallery. The schooner *Pioneer* offers 2 and 3hr cruises of the harbor, mid-May–mid-Oct. *South Street Venture Visitors Center, 207 Water St. Ships and gallery open Mon–Sat, 10–6; Sun, noon–6.*

Statue of Liberty This 225-ton, 151ft statue, depicting Liberty holding the light of Freedom and the book of Justice, trampling the chains of Tyranny, was dedicated in October 1886. A gift from the French nation, it symbolized the promise of America

to the newly arrived during the nation's greatest wave of European immigration. Tourists crowd the statue, which was completely refurbished for the 1986 centenial celebrations. If you have two hours, it is worth visiting, especially for the view from the crown. *Circle Line Statue of Liberty Ferry* ☎ *269-5755.*
United Nations Headquarters One of New York's major landmarks, the UN comprises five buildings, of which the most familiar are the slab-like Secretariat, and the General Assembly Building with its gracefully sloping roof. There is plenty to see, including exhibitions, gardens with views of the East River, shops and restaurants. Guided tours of the UN start from the Main Lobby of the General Assembly Building and are conducted in many languages. At the Information Desk one can obtain tickets (free) to some UN meetings. *United Nations Plaza, 405 E 42nd St. Guided tours* ☎ *963-7713.*
Whitney Museum of American Art Marcel Breuer's cantilevered, granite-faced fortress contains an important collection of 20thC American painting and sculpture, including works by Hopper, Neveson, Warhol, and Calder. The museum's acquisitions policy is adventurous and its exhibitions controversial. The Whitney's program includes film showings and avant-garde dance. The museum now has branches in the Equitable Center on 7th Ave, where the murals of Thomas Hart Benton are featured; in the Philip Morris Building at 120 Park Ave; and downtown, 384 Broadway. The main building is *945 Madison Ave at 75th St* ☎ *570-3676. Open Tue, 1–8; Wed–Sat, 11–5; Sun, 12–6; closed Mon.*

Bird's eye views

Empire State Building Once the world's tallest building, this graceful skyscraper still provides spectacular views from the 87th-floor observatory (open) or the 102nd floor (glassed-in). *350 5th Ave between 33rd and 34th Sts* ☎ *736-3100. Open daily, 9.30–midnight.*
General Electric Building In Rockefeller Center, the heart of midtown, with a mere 70 stories, but its views of Manhattan are superb. *30 Rockefeller Plaza, between 49th and 50th Sts. Open Apr–Sep, 10–9; Oct–Mar, 10.30–7.*
World Trade Center The twin towers of the Center, each with 110 stories, are the second tallest buildings in the world (after the Sears Building, Chicago). From the enclosed observation deck on the 107th floor or (weather permitting) the open rooftop promenade, you can see 75 miles/120kms or more on a clear day. ☎ *466-7377. Open daily, 9.30–9.30.*

Guided tours

Boat trips *Circle Line* ☎ 563-3200. Boats make a circuit of Manhattan Island, departing from and returning to Pier 83 at W 42nd St. The cruise, which operates mid-Mar–Nov, takes about 3hrs and includes running commentary. In summer, twilight cocktail cruises can be spectacular on clear nights. A time-saving alternative is the *Staten Island Ferry*, which leaves from the Whitehall St pier, Battery Park ☎ 806-6940 every 20–30min, night and day, all year round. There's no commentary, but at 25 cents for a round-trip it offers good views of the Statue of Liberty, the Verrazano-Narrows Bridge and Lower Manhattan.
Bus tours *Gray Line* ☎ 397-2600. Bus tours, taking 2–8hrs, cost $15–$30. Most leave from the terminal at 900 8th Ave (53rd St). Gray Line also organizes yacht cruises and helicopter tours.
Individual tours *Accent on Language*, 16 E 52nd St ☎ 355-5170, provides tours in all major languages; all guides are licensed and experienced, and tours can be tailored to particular interests.

Spectator sports

Tickets for all metropolitan area professional sporting events can be bought in person at the *Ticketron* outlets around the city ☏ 399-4444, cash only; midtown in Grand Central Terminal by Track 37, Mon–Fri, 9–5; downtown at J&R Music world, 23 Park Row, Mon–Fri, 9.30–5.30.

Baseball The city has two baseball teams and loyalties are sharply divided. The New York *Mets* (National League) play at Shea Stadium, Flushing Meadow, Flushing, Queens ☏ (718) 507-8499; the New York *Yankees* (American League) at Yankee Stadium, River Ave at E 161st St, Bronx ☏ 293-6000.

Basketball New York *Knicks* play at Madison Square Garden, 7th Ave at 33rd St ☏ 563-8300. The *New Jersey Nets* are at Byrne Meadowlands Arena, East Rutherford, NJ ☏ (201) 935-3900.

Football New York *Giants* and *Jets* play at Giants Stadium, Meadowlands ☏ (201) 935-8222.

Horse-racing There is thoroughbred racing at *Aqueduct Race Track*, Rockaway Blvd, 110 Ozone Park, Queens ☏ (718) 641-4700 and *Belmont Park Race Track*, Hempstead Turnpike at Plainfield Ave, Elmont, Long Island ☏ (718) 641-4700. Harness races are held at *Roosevelt Raceway*, Old Country Rd, Westbury, Long Island ☏ (516) 936-3055, and *Yonkers Raceway*, Central and Yonkers Avenues, Yonkers ☏ (914) 968-4200. *Meadowlands Racetrack*, Meadowlands, East Rutherford, NJ ☏ (201) 935-8500 features both types.

Ice hockey New York *Rangers* play at Madison Sq Garden, 7th Ave at W 33rd St ☏ 563-8300; New Jersey *Devils* at Byrne Meadowlands Arena, East Rutherford, in New Jersey ☏ (201) 935-3900.

Keeping fit

Few reasonably priced sports facilities exist for visitors. Hourly court rates for racquet sports can be high and private reservations are difficult, but many hotel concierges can make arrangements with either nearby health clubs or outlying golf clubs. Some hotels have indoor sports facilities and health clubs.

Bicycling Central Park is the best area. Consider bicycling around the city only on weekends. Many large bicycle stores have bikes to rent: *Midtown Bicycle*, 360 W 47th St at 9th Ave ☏ 581-4500; *A&B Bicycle World*, 663 Amsterdam Ave at 92nd St ☏ 866-7600; or *Metro Bicycles*, 1311 Lexington Ave at 88th St ☏ 427-4450.

Golf Manhattan has no golf courses, but there are NYC-owned clubs in some of the outlying boroughs including Brooklyn and Queens ☏ 397-3100 for information.

Racquet sports Many of the city's public tennis clubs also have racquetball courts and offer instruction in both; most squash clubs, however, are private. For tennis courts, expect to pay $25–50 an hour. *Wall Street Raquet Club*, Wall St at the East River ☏ (718) 769-5167; *Village Courts*, 110 University Pl ☏ 989-2300; *Crosstown Tennis*, 14 W 31st St ☏ 947-5780; *Tennis Club at Grand Central Terminal*, 15 Vanderbilt Ave ☏ 687-3841; *Columbus Racquet Club*, 795 Columbus Ave ☏ 663-6900.

Riding *Claremont Riding Academy*, 175 W 89th St ☏ 724-5100. Horses, saddles and bridles provided, but riders must have boots and helmets. No beginners.

Running Runners flock to Central Park in good weather and bad but don't run if the area is deserted; a favorite route of many circles the reservoir, just above 86th Street. *New York Road Runners Club* ☏ 860-4455.

Soccer and softball At weekends, many pick-up softball and soccer games happen spontaneously in Central Park; most welcome visitors. For *soccer*, walk towards the center of the park at 100th Street and look for the North Meadow soccer fields. For *softball*, try the area near the Sheep Meadow, below 72nd Street.

Local resources

Business services

The concierge at most business-class hotels can either supply or – more likely – arrange services such as photocopying, printing, fax and secretarial and translation services. Bear in mind that some hotels tend to over-describe their in-house facilities. *Adia Personnel Services*, 41 E 42nd St ☎ 682-3438, and *International American Executive Business Center*, 14 E 60th St ☎ 308-0049, both offer an extensive range of services.

Photocopying and printing *Mid-City Duplicating* specializes in legal work and has binding, offset printing and blueprint facilities. Free pick-up and delivery. Main office at 222 E 45th St ☎ 687-6699 open 24hrs. Also at 519 Madison Ave (51st St) ☎ 980-8585 and 136 William St ☎ 349-0880, both open 9am–midnight. *Pandick Technologies*, 150 Broadway ☎ 513-7335 and 114 5th Ave ☎ 929-1600, is open 7 days, 24hrs, and offers pick-up and delivery. *Xerox Reproduction Centers*, 200 Madison Ave (36th St) ☎ 561-6700 and 516 W 34th St ☎ 929-9100, offer complete copying, offset duplicating, color prints, transparencies and microfilm.

Secretarial and translation *Accent on Language*, 16 E 52nd St ☎ 355-5170 offers foreign language typing and interpreting and translation services in all major European, Asian and Middle-Eastern languages. *Berlitz*, 866 3rd Ave (53rd St) ☎ 702-3511 or 61 Broadway ☎ 425-3866 offers multi-lingual word-processing and translation services.

Security *Burns International Security Services*, 1501 Broadway ☎ 764-3110 provides bodyguards.

Communications

Long-distance delivery Major firms such as *Federal Express* ☎ 777-6500 and *DHL*, JFK International Airport ☎ (718) 917-8000, offer next-day delivery. *Air Couriers International*, 40B W 24th St ☎ 242-1160, has 24hr door-to-door service.

Local delivery Major banks and law firms use *Archer Services*, 855 6th Ave ☎ 563-8800, and *Bullit Courier*, 42 Broadway ☎ 952-4343 and 405 Lexington Ave ☎ 893-5100.

Post office The *General Post Office* at 421 8th Ave (33nd St) ☎ 330-2908 or 330-2011, is open 24hrs. The 90 Church St post office ☎ 330-5297 is open for Express Mail until midnight.

Telex and fax *ITT Communications Services*, 322 8th Ave ☎ 741-9700.

Conference/exhibition centers

Most of the city's business-class hotels offer conference facilities. The *New York Convention Center and Visitors Bureau*, 2 Columbus Circle ☎ 397-8200, offers help and advice on convention facilities. The *Jacob K Javits Convention Center*, 655 W 34th St (11th Ave from 34th St to 39th St) ☎ 216-2000, is one of the city's newest and largest exhibition centers.

Emergencies

Currency exchange Practically all New York business-class hotels can provide 24hr currency exchange for their guests, though their rates are not usually the best available. Most of the banks at Rockefeller Center offer limited exchange facilities; others include *Bank Leumi*, 120 Broadway ☎ 602-9320, 579 5th Ave at 47th St ☎ 382-4407, and other locations; and branches of the *Chemical Bank* ☎ 310-6161. *American Express* travel service offices are open normal business hours: 65 Broadway ☎ 493-6500; 150 E 42nd St ☎ 687-3700; 374 Park Ave ☎ 421-8240; and 822 Lexington Ave ☎ 758-6510.

Hospitals Virtually all New York hospitals have 24hr emergency rooms. The main ones include *New York Hospital*, 525 E 68th ☎ 472-5454 AE V; *Beth Israel Medical Center*, 1st Ave and 16th St (Stuyvesant Sq) ☎ 420-2840; *Lenox Hill Hospital*, 77th St and Park Ave ☎ 439-2424 AE MC V; *St Luke's Hospital*, 114th

Amsterdam ☏ 523-4000 AE MC ; *Roosevelt Center*, 428 W 59th St ☏ 544-7000 AE MC. For dental emergencies call the *Dentist Emergency Service*, 200 Madison Ave ☏ 213-2004.
Pharmacies *Kaufman Pharmacy*, Lexington Ave at 50th St ☏ 755-2266, open 24hrs, accepts credit cards (AE MC) and will deliver.
Police For all emergencies (ambulance, fire or police) call 911. *Travelers' Aid*, 158 W 42nd St ☏ 944-0013, helps crime victims who are in town for less than four weeks. Also at JF Kennedy International Arrivals Building ☏ (718) 656-4870.

Government offices

New York City, general information ☏ 566-4446; *New York State Department for Economic Development*, 1515 Broadway, 51st Floor, 10036 ☏ 827-6100; *Immigration and Naturalization Service* ☏ 206-6500; *US Dept of Commerce*, 26 Federal Plaza ☏ 264-0634.

Information sources

Business information *Chamber of Commerce for Industry*, 200 Madison Ave, 3rd Floor, 1006 ☏ 561-2030. *US Chamber of Commerce*, Room 1702, 711 3rd Ave, 10017 ☏ 370-1440. Nearly every country in the world maintains a chamber of commerce in New York. *British-American Chamber of Commerce*, 275 Madison Ave (39th St) ☏ 561-2020; *French-American Chamber of Commerce*, 509 Madison Ave, Suite 1900 ☏ 371-4466; *Italy–America Chamber of Commerce*, 350 5th Ave (33rd St) ☏ 279-5520; *Japanese Chamber of Commerce*, 115 E 57th St, 6th Floor, 10022 ☏ 935-0303; *Spain–US Chamber of Commerce*, 350 5th Ave (33rd St) ☏ 967-2170.
Local media The *New York Times* gives national, international and local coverage, with good features and a business section every day. The *Wall Street Journal* specializes in business and financial reporting, Mon–Fri. The *New York Post* is a tabloid afternoon daily, but it also carries the late stock market prices. The *New York Daily News*, also tabloid, is less lurid than the *Post*. *Village Voice*, available weekly on Wed, gives left-of-center political and social coverage, and excellent entertainment listings. *Manhattan, Inc* and *The Atlantic* (a national magazine) are monthlies aimed at the young, ladder-climbing business community. The *New Yorker* gives literary reviews, general commentary, cartoons and entertainment listings. *New York* has good entertainment listings.
AM radio stations WABC 770 news/talk; WCBS 880 all-news; WINS 1010 all-news; WMCA 570 phone-ins/talk/news; WNYC 830 information/talk; WOR 710 talk. WOXR 1560 *New York Times* station, classical/news.
FM radio stations WBAI 99.5 listener-sponsored, no commercials; WECD 97.9 classical/talk; WNYE 91.5 educational/talk. WNCN 103.4 classical; WQXR 96.3 *New York Times* station, classical/news.
Television stations WCBS ch 2, WNBC ch 4, WNYW ch 5, WABC ch 7, WOR ch 9, WPIX ch 11, WNET ch 13.
Tourist information *New York Convention and Visitors Bureau*, 2 Columbus Circle ☏ 397-8222 (open Mon–Fri) has helpful brochures, but staff are often busy. *Times Square Information Center*, 42nd St and Broadway ☏ 397-8222, is open Wed–Fri and weekends.

Thank-yous

Florists *Flora Plenty*, 1135 1st Ave (62nd St) ☏ 254-7777; *Tiffany Florist*, 162 E 23rd St ☏ 254-2758.
Wine merchants *Gourmet Liquor Shop*, 1118 Madison Ave (83rd St) ☏ 734-1400. *Park Lane Liquor Store*, 16 E 58th St ☏ 534-5346. *Sherry-Lehmann Inc*, 679 Madison Ave (60th St) ☏ 838-7500. Liquor stores in New York do not accept credit cards.
Special gifts Most department stores package and deliver gifts; try *Bergdorf Goodman* (see *Shopping*).

PHILADELPHIA

Area code ☏ 215

As the birthplace of the Declaration of Independence and the US Constitution, Philadelphia is the country's most historically important city. Yet though it once vied with London and other world centers of influence, much of the city's status and sense of urgency faded as the seat of government moved away, leaving it with little more than WC Fields's tombstone epitaph – "All in all, I'd rather be in Philadelphia."

Recent commercial real estate construction and retail development have done much to transform what had become a quaint Quaker haven into a forward-looking, economically vital city. Today it is the second largest city on the East Coast, an expanding metropolitan area of universities, colleges, and medical schools and a major center for international enterprises, particularly those involved in health care, energy, pharmaceuticals, high-tech, publishing, accounting and even, still, some "smokestack" industries. The area's big companies include Sun Co., CIGNA, Bell Atlantic, Du Pont, Campbell Soups, Alco Standard, Unisys, SmithKline Beckman, Scott Paper, Rohm & Haas, Commodore International, CertainTeed, Lea and Febiger, WB Sounders and Crown, Cork and Seal.

Though nearly 90 miles/144kms from the Atlantic, Philadelphia's seaport has a busy oil and cargo trade, and the local Navy repair yard is a major employer.

Arriving

Philadelphia International Airport
PHL is served by all major domestic carriers and a few international airlines such as TWA, British Airways, Lufthansa, Air France, Mexicana Airlines and Air Jamaica. Passengers on other international carriers make domestic connections to Philadelphia after first clearing Customs at a major gateway airport such as New York.

PHL has two sections, a modern domestic facility and a single-story international terminal half a mile/1km away, linked by a free 24hr shuttle bus running every 5mins. There are four domestic terminals (B, C, D and E). A new $75m combined domestic/international terminal (A) opens in 1990.

The international terminal has multilingual staff; general (as well as airport) information is available daily 6am–midnight; and you can arrange car rental, obtain snacks and flight insurance and get currency changed

The four domestic terminals, connected by a main corridor, offer flight insurance, currency exchange (6.30am–9.30pm) and multilingual information facilities (6am–midnight), mailing, American Express banking machines, and a full-service dining room with cocktail lounge open 11.30–8. All terminals have bars, snack stands and gift shops. General airport information ☏ 492-3181.

Nearby hotels *Airport Hilton Inn*, 10th St and Packer Ave 19148 ☏ 755-9500 fax 462-6947. *Airport Ramada Inn*, 76 Industrial Hwy, Essington 19029 ☏ 521-9600 fax 521-9388. *Guest Quarters Suites*, 1 Gateway Center, 4101 Island Ave 19153 ☏ 365-5500 fax 492-9858. *Philadelphia Airport Marriott*, 4509 Island Ave 19153 ☏ 365-4150 fax 365-3875.

City link Center City or downtown Philadelphia is approximately 8 miles/13kms north of the airport, 15mins by road in non-rush hour traffic, 45mins in morning and evening rush hours (7–8.30, 4.30–6). Best options are to take a taxi or, if you have only a small amount of

baggage, the SEPTA Hi-Speed Rail line.
Taxi A taxi ride into Center City will cost about $16. Taxis are readily available at all terminals.
Limousine Van limos can be shared for about $12 per person. For limousine service call Knights's Limousine ☏ 333-1333 or Casino Limousine ☏ (609) 429-1000.
Car rental Courtesy phones at street level in the baggage claim area of the domestic terminal connect directly to nearby offices of Hertz ☏ 492-7200, Avis ☏ 492-0900, National ☏ 567-1760, Budget ☏ 492-9442 and Dollar ☏ 365-1605.
Rail SEPTA's high-speed rail line to Center City takes about 20–25mins and runs daily from the domestic terminal via 30th Street Station (30th and Market Streets), Suburban Station (16th St and John F Kennedy Blvd) and Market Street East Station (10th and Market Streets) from 6.10am to 12.10am for about $4. For information ☏ 574-7800.

Rail station

30th Street Station Though most business travelers arrive by air, 30th Street Station ☏ 824-1600 handles a good deal of business traffic, with its excellent Amtrak links to New York, Washington, Boston, Atlantic City and other major East Coast cities. Located right in Center City, the station is a cavernous Art Deco building. Cabs are readily available outside; most downtown destinations are within 5–15mins.

Getting around

The city's streets are laid out on a grid pattern, developed by William Penn more than 300 years ago. Numbered streets run north–south, named streets east–west.
Walking Philadelphia is a very walkable city, and most of the major

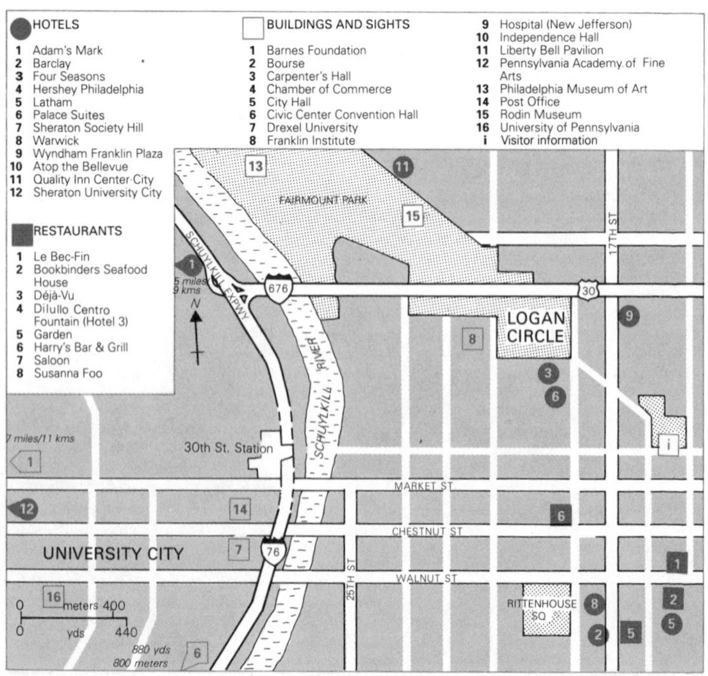

business, entertainment, historical and cultural areas are within easy reach of each other. To go from City Hall, at Broad and Market, to Independence Hall, at 6th and Chestnut, is a brisk 20min walk.

Many of the major office buildings are located between Broad and 20th, an area just six blocks wide.

Taxi It is safer to negotiate some parts of downtown – for example, Market Street just east of City Hall and the area just east of Broad Street – by taxi, daylight or dark. Cabs are plentiful on the streets before 5pm, but later it is advisable to call for one about 30mins in advance: *Yellow Cab* ☎ 922-7186, *Quaker City Cab* ☎ 728-8000 and *United Cab Association* ☎ 625-9170.

Car rental Drivers unfamiliar with the city may have problems, for signposting is confusing and sparse; but if your business takes you to the outlying regions, a car is advisable.

Public transportation SEPTA operates commuter rail lines, buses, trolleys and subways to all parts of the city and suburbs. Base fare is about $1.25 (exact change is required and tokens are available), although traveling to outlying suburbs costs more. Avoid all forms of public transportation at night in favor of taxis. Don't ever use the subway.

Area by area

In the city center, the main areas divide along financial, historical or sociological lines. Elsewhere there are distinct ethnic neighborhoods – for example, South Philly (Italian), Roxborough and Kensington (Polish and Irish), North Philadelphia (black) and Chinatown.

Center City Downtown has both commercial and residential interests. It houses most of the city's major corporations, banks, publishing houses, law and accounting firms, advertising agencies, and government institutions. But in addition to high-rise office buildings, hotels and shopping areas, Center City's tree-bordered streets and grand avenues have historic sites, smart restaurants, apartment complexes, condominiums and townhouses. City Hall stands at the very core, at the intersection of Broad and Market Streets, topped by a statue of city founder, William Penn. Prestigious Center City areas are the Rittenhouse Square area and Society Hill.

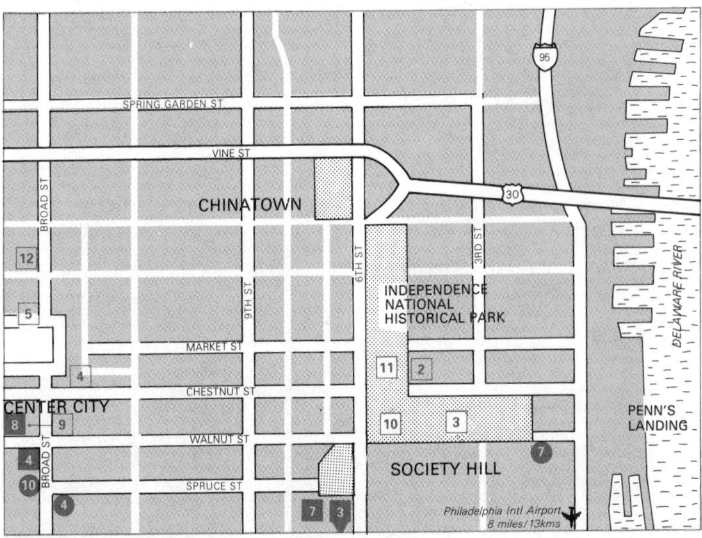

Chestnut Hill A suburb northwest of Center City and bordering Germantown, Chestnut Hill is a residential bastion of money and class, with big, graceful mansions, good restaurants and elegant shops overlooking the elite Chestnut Hill College.
Chinatown A huge and ornately oriental gateway marks the entrance to this neighborhood, northeast of City Hall and bordering the site of the planned $450m Convention Center. The area offers a crowded array of colorful shops and restaurants.
Fairmount An established working-class area, Fairmount is now much sought after by young professionals for its Victorian mansions, townhouses, and gracious, tree-shaded streets. It is also a fast-developing commercial area.
Germantown/Mount Airy The site of the colonial army's last battle with the British in 1777 is today an area of stately old houses and churches, favored by successful entrepreneurs.
Main Line Named after the railroad link to Center City, this affluent and highly regarded area of the western suburbs is the traditional home of Philadelphia's established society families. Main Line residents have a huge influence on the business and political dealings of the city.
Society Hill Years of restoration have made this area a living example of how Philadelphia looked in its colonial days. Elegant Georgian and Federal townhouses line the narrow, cobbled streets lit by old-fashioned Franklin streetlamps. Though largely residential, inhabited by some of the city's wealthiest and most powerful politicians, lawyers and corporate executives, Society Hill also has Philadelphia's major historic attractions, including Independence National Historic Park (see *Sightseeing*). Penn's Landing – where William Penn first set foot in the New World – is now a burgeoning tourist area with residential and commercial development.
University City Student and community life meet on the west bank of the Schuylkill River (pronounced Skoo-kull). The area includes 30th Street Station, the Ivy League University of Pennsylvania, the Wharton School of Business, the Civic Center, Drexel University, and the city's major urban high-tech research and development center, the University City Science Center.

Hotels

Philadelphia's old mainstays such as the Ben Franklin have gone, replaced by modern, high-quality hotels, many of them along the Ben Franklin Parkway, west of Broad Street, convenient for the major Center City offices.

Adam's Mark [$]//
City Ave and Monument Rd 19131
☎ 581-5000 [TX] 7106701953
fax 581-5069 • AE DC MC V • 515 rooms, 67 suites, 2 restaurants, 3 bars
Philadelphia's second largest convention hotel (after the Wyndham), Adam's Mark is outside Center City on City Line Avenue, about 6 miles/10kms. Nonetheless, its attention to individual guests' needs makes it a firm favorite with business visitors. The decor is modern, and health facilities are extensive, with jacuzzi, saunas, health club, racquetball courts and two indoor/outdoor pools. 9 flexible meeting rooms.

Barclay [$]///
Rittenhouse Sq, 18th and Locust 19103
☎ 545-0300 [TX] 7106701009
fax 545-2896 • AE DC MC V • 240 rooms, 30 suites, 1 restaurant, 1 bar
Luciano Pavarotti, Bob Hope and Zubin Mehta are among those who enjoy the Barclay's prestigious location in Rittenhouse Square,

convenient to Center City and the theater district. Its Old World charm, elegant lobby and well-proportioned rooms are among its other attractions. Nearby health club • 12 meeting rooms.

Four Seasons $/////
1 Logan Sq 19103 ☎ 963-1500 TX 00831805 fax 963-9562 • 371 rooms, 7 suites, 2 restaurants, 2 bars
The Four Seasons is Philadelphia's best and most prestigious hotel. With its beautifully landscaped garden and courtyard, numerous fountains and spacious, richly appointed lobbies, it is the place to stay if you want to make an impression. The good-sized rooms, furnished in Federal-period style, are easy to work in; the Fountain Room restaurant is often crowded with the city's corporate elite. Indoor pool, whirlpool, sauna, massage, health club • 13 meeting rooms.

Hershey Philadelphia $//
215 South Broad St (at Locust) 19107 ☎ 893-1600 TX 834374 fax 893-1663 • AE DC MC V • 420 rooms, 8 suites, 2 restaurants, 2 bars
In the heart of the theater and business district, the Hershey is immediately recognizable by its four-story, black-enameled, steel and glass atrium. The hotel has a private executive floor with its own lounge, concierge and sitting area. Year-round pool, health club • 11 meeting rooms.

Latham $//
135 South 17th St (at Walnut) 19103 ☎ 563-7474 TX 831438 fax 563-4034 • AE DC MC V • 141 rooms, 3 suites, 1 restaurant, 1 bar
The Latham offers a quieter and more intimate atmosphere than any other city hotel, though it doesn't stint on luxury. The tiny lobby is extremely ornate, and the very comfortable rooms have Louis XIV writing tables and sybaritic bathrooms. Nearby health club • 4 meeting rooms.

Palace Suites $///
18th St and Benjamin Franklin Pkwy 19103 ☎ 963-2222 TX 902585 fax 963-2299 • AE DC MC V • THF • 285 suites, 1 restaurant, 1 bar
An impressive guest register bears such names as President Gerald Ford, James Stewart and the late Princess Grace of Monaco. The all-suites complex is well equipped for business visitors. Each suite has a foyer, separate meeting/dining area, a bar, a sitting area with balcony and a bedroom with balcony. Outdoor pool, arrangement with nearby health club • 7 meeting rooms, business reference library, translation, teleconferencing.

Sheraton Society Hill $///
1 Dock St 19106 ☎ 238-6000 fax 922-2709 • AE DC MC V • 348 rooms, 17 suites, 1 restaurant, 2 bars
The red brick façade of this relatively new Sheraton complements the colonial architecture of surrounding historic Society Hill. The lobby, which includes a cocktail bar, is used for informal business get-togethers. Indoor pool, health club • 17 meeting rooms.

Warwick $//
17th and Locust 19103 ☎ 735-6000 TX 5106005742 fax 790-7766 • AE DC MC V • 180 rooms, 15 suites, 2 restaurants, 1 bar
The Warwick's 1920s lobby, with ornate Persian carpets and well-upholstered sofas, is an elegant place for informal business chat. Just a block from Rittenhouse Square, the Warwick is well placed for the city's main offices, shops and theaters. The hotel's Caribbean-style Polo Bay disco is popular with younger professionals. 6 meeting rooms.

Wyndham Franklin Plaza $//
2 Franklin Plaza, 17th and Vine 19103 ☎ 448-2000 TX 00834572 fax 448-2864 • AE DC MC V • 760 rooms, 53 suites, 2 restaurants, 2 bars, 1 coffee shop
Philadelphia's largest convention

hotel, the Wyndham, is just by City Hall in the heart of Center City. The size and price of single rooms can vary dramatically, so check thoroughly before making a reservation. First-rate health club. Hair salon, gift shops • indoor pool, health club, tennis, raquetball, squash • 22 meeting rooms.

OTHER HOTELS

Atop the Bellevue [$]////
1415 Chancellor Court (at Broad and Locust Sts) 19102 ☏ 893-1776 fax 893-9868 • AE DC MC V. Restored hotel at the top of the historic Bellevue, with modern health facilities.

Quality Inn Center City [$]//
501 N 22nd St 19130 ☏ 568-8300 fax 557-0259 • AE DC MC V. Recently renovated, with a pool.

Sheraton University City [$]/
36th and Chestnut Sts 19104 ☏ 387-8000 fax 387-8000 ext 605 • AE DC MC V. Next to the University of Pennsylvania.

Clubs

Until recently, most of Philadelphia's noteworthy clubs were open to men only, but now even the ultra-conservative Union League accepts women members. Philadelphia is staunchly clubby, and many locals prefer to conduct business and entertain clients "at the club." Founded in 1834, the *Philadelphia Club*, 13th and Walnut ☏ 735-5924, is the oldest gentlemen's club in the country and unswervingly maintains its Main Line high society ambience. The distinguished *Union League*, Broad and Sansom Sts ☏ 563-6500, was founded in 1862 to support the Union cause and has evolved into a civic and business-oriented society. Younger professionals are in the majority at the *Racquet Club*, 215 South 16th St, which traditionally aims to "combine the gentility of the manor house with the heroics and sweat of a college gym."

Hotel price bands
For the meanings of the hotel price symbols, see page 7

Restaurants

Philadelphia's restaurants are much patronized by the business community and are extensively used for doing business. For an off-duty treat, try one of the locally famous cheese steaks (thinly-sliced beef served on a roll with melted cheese and fried onions) at *Pat's Steaks*, 9th and Passyunk Avenue.

Le Bec-Fin [$]////
1523 Walnut St ☏ 567-1000 • closed L Fri & Sat, Sun • AE MC DC • jacket • reservations essential
Le Bec-Fin is unbeatable for business dining, especially if an impressive setting and top-class French food are needed. Its opulent surroundings and good service draw a well-groomed crowd of corporate executives and politicians. The lunch menu is much less expensive than the dinner *prix fixe*. Make sure you reserve weeks in advance, especially for Saturday dinner.

Bookbinders Seafood House [$]//
215 S 15th St ☏ 545-1137 • closed Sat L • AE DC MC V
A traditional seafood house crammed with captain's chairs, oak paneling and nautical paraphernalia, Bookbinders is a Philadelphia landmark and an established spot for business lunches. Do not confuse it with the old Original Bookbinders in Society Hill.

Déjà-Vu [$]///
1609 Pine St ☏ 546-1190 • closed L, Sun, Mon • AE DC MC V

This small restaurant serves classic French cuisine using seasonal ingredients. The service is elegant, the decor elaborate.

DiLullo Centro [$]/
1407 Locust St ☏ 546-2000 • AE DC MC V • jacket and tie recommended • reservations advisable
With an elegantly comfortable atmosphere in a renovated theater, DiLullo's has excellent northern Italian dishes. Its interior white wood half-walls allow privacy for business discussions without being claustrophobic. There is an imaginative wine list. With its convenient Center City location, this is a popular lunch spot for the local business community.

Fountain [$]///
Four Seasons Hotel ☏ 963-1500 • AE DC MC V • reservations essential
Undisputedly the cream of Philadelphia's grand hotel restaurants, the Fountain is an excellent spot to be seen in. The tables allow quiet conversation; the French/American cuisine is top-notch. Reserve at least a week in advance for dinner.

Garden [$]//
1617 Spruce St ☏ 546-4455 • closed Sat L, Sun • AE DC MC V
The stylish Garden – another converted Center City townhouse with antique tables and bar – is a traditional meeting place for business lunches; its many small rooms ensure privacy. The menu features aged prime grilled beef, seafood and homemade desserts.

Harry's Bar & Grill [$]/
22S 18th St ☏ 561-5757 • closed Sat & Sun • AE DC MC V • jackets
Popular for both lunch and dinner with the business set, Harry's makes a point of serving straightforward steaks, veal, seafood and pasta in a comfortable club-like atmosphere; there are prints on the walls. Service can be slow. Harry's is also a favorite after-work meeting place.

Saloon [$]/
750 South St ☏ 627-1811 • closed Sat L, Sun • AE
This quaint Italian restaurant off the beaten track in the heart of South Philly is a cozy haven of rich wood paneling, Victorian antiques and brass. It is ideal for private conversation and has first-rate steak as well as Italian dishes.

Susanna Foo
1512 Walnut St ☏ 545-2666 • closed Sun, 2 weeks Jul • AE DC MC V
This city center Chinese restaurant serves dishes influenced by French cuisine. A convenient choice for a working lunch.

Bars

The after-hours bar scene picks up considerably on Wednesdays and Fridays and plays an important role in Philadelphia's business activity. *Downey's*, Front and South Streets ☏ 629-0525, is an Irish pub popular with business executives after working hours; it also serves steak and seafood and late-night fillers. *Carolina's*, 261 South 20th St ☏ 545-1000, is a neighborhood bar-cum-restaurant in the affluent Rittenhouse Square area, very popular with younger professionals, as is *Houlihan's*, 18th St and Rittenhouse Sq ☏ 546-5940. The *Polo Bay* at the Warwick Hotel (good seafood served) is a Friday evening meeting place for the smart set. The *Irish Pub*, 2007 Walnut St ☏ 568-5603, is very often noisy and packed; it is best used as an off-duty watering hole. *Dickens Inn*, 2nd and Pine at New Market ☏ 928-9307, is a cheery English-style pub adorned with sketches, prints and other Dickensiana, serving imported stout and ales and English and Continental food.

Entertainment

Ballet, jazz, and classical music dominate Philadelphia's entertainment attractions. For floor shows or headline acts, Philadelphians go to

Atlantic City, 45mins away. Major concerts and other entertainments are staged at *The Spectrum*, Broad St and Pattison Ave ☎ 389-5000. Check the monthly *Philadelphia* magazine, or the "Weekend" sections in the *Inquirer* or the *Daily News* for what's on. *Ticketron* ☎ 885-2515 or *Chargit* ☎ (800) 223-0120 sell tickets.

Theater and music The *Academy of Music*, Broad and Locust Sts ☎ 893-1930, is home to the Philadelphia Orchestra, the Opera Company of Philadelphia, and the Pennsylvania and Milwaukee Ballet, and also has top guest entertainers. The *Annenberg Center*, University of Pennsylvania, 3680 Walnut St ☎ 898-6791, is an arts center with professional theater, film, music, and other special presentations. The *Forrest Theater*, 1114 Walnut St ☎ 923-1515, features touring Broadway musicals, as well as other short-running plays and concerts. The *Walnut Street Theater*, 9th and Walnut Sts ☎ 574-3586, the oldest English-speaking theater in continuous use, was established in 1809 and now stages dramatic presentations, concerts, lectures, films, dance and experimental theater. The *Wilma Theater*, 2030 Sansom St ☎ 963-0345, stages innovative productions.

Cinema The city has some fine art cinemas, including the *Roxy Screening Rooms*, 2021-23 Sansom St ☎ 561-0114, and the *Ritz Five*, 214 Walnut St ☎ 925-7900.

Nightclubs The *Bourse*, at 5th and Ranstead, is the renovated old Stock Exchange, now housing lots of trendy boutiques and chic restaurants, as well as the *Beverly Hills Bar and Grill* ☎ 627-0778, providing dancing amid high-tech 1950s and 1960s decor. The *Polo Bay* disco, at the Warwick Hotel on 17th and Locust, is Philadelphia's most favored nightclub among young professionals. *Flanigan's*, 2nd and South, is a nightclub/disco which is also popular with younger professionals. *PT's*, 6 S Front St, is much used by the local business community, and offers dancing, backgammon, wine bars and live entertainment. *Spectacles*, in the Sheraton Society Hill, 1 Dock St, has clever, lighthearted decor which lends energy to one of the city's trendiest nightspots.

Shopping

In the Center City area, the *Gallery at Market East* spans Market Street from 8th to 11th streets, with major stores linked by scores of smaller shops and restaurants; open Mon–Sat, 10–6; Sun, noon–5 ☎ 925-7162. The *Bourse*, 21 South 5th St, once the city's Stock Exchange, now has three floors of boutiques, gift shops and restaurants; open daily ☎ 625-9393. *South Street*, a sort of Philadelphian Greenwich Village, has a wide variety of restaurants and shops selling everything from antiques to organic foods. *John Wanamaker's*, 13th St between Market and Chestnut, is Center City's most renowned department store. Other fashionable stores include *Brooks' Brothers* at 15th and Chestnut, *Bonwit Teller* at 17th and Chestnut, *Nan Duskin* at 18th and Walnut, *Bailey, Banks, and Biddle* at 16th at Chestnut, *Saks Fifth Avenue* on City Line Avenue and *Bloomingdale's* in the suburban malls at King of Prussia and Willow Grove. *Jewelers' Row* is on Sansom St between 7th and 9th, and *Antique Row* is on Pine St between 9th and 12th Streets.

Sightseeing

The "musts" among the city's many historic sites are Independence Hall, the Pennsylvania Academy of the Fine Arts, the Museum of Art and the Barnes Foundation.

The Barnes Foundation, in Merion, 7 miles/11kms west of Center City, has a world-class private collection of post-Impressionist art, including works by Matisse, Degas and Van Gogh. Visit by reservation. This museum is a revelation. *300 N Latches Lane, Merion ☎ 667-0290. Open Fri & Sat, 9.30–4.30; Sun, 1–4.30; closed Jul & Aug.*

Franklin Institute Four floors of science and technology exhibits, America's largest public observatory, Fels Planetarium, and a walk-through replica human heart. *20th St and Ben Franklin Pkwy ☏ 448-1200. Open Mon–Fri, 9.30–5; Sat & Sun, 10–5.*
Independence National Historical Park The area has more than 50 historically interesting attractions, including the *Betsy Ross House*, 239 Arch St; *Carpenters' Hall*, 320 Chestnut St; *Christ Church*, 2nd St above Market St; *Congress Hall*, 6th and Chestnut Streets; *Independence Hall*, 5th and Chestnut; and the *Liberty Bell Pavilion*, Market St between 5th and 6th. Most sites are open daily, 9–5; all are free. For additional information contact the Visitor Center, 3rd and Chestnut ☏ 597-8974.
Pennsylvania Academy of the Fine Arts is the oldest museum and art school in the USA, exhibiting three centuries of American art. *Broad and Cherry ☏ 972-7600. Open Tue–Sat, 10–4.*
Philadelphia Museum of Art has more than 500,000 paintings, sculptures, drawings, prints and other examples of the decorative arts. *26th St and Ben Franklin Pkwy. Open Wed–Sun, 10–5 ☏ 763-8100.*
Rodin Museum has the largest collection of Rodin sculptures and drawings outside France. *22nd St and Ben Franklin Pkwy ☏ 787-5476. Open Tue–Sun, 10–5.*

Guided tours

Centipede Tours ☏ 735-3123 provides candlelight tours through Old Philadelphia and Society Hill beginning at historic City Tavern, 2nd and Walnut at 6.30pm. *76 Carriage Company* ☏ 923-8516 give horse-drawn carriage tours of Philadelphia's historic areas starting from Independence National Historical Park, 5th and Chestnut St, daily from 10 to 5; tours of Society Hill and Head House Square are from 7pm to midnight. *Fairmount Park Trolley Bus* ☏ 636-1666 offers guided tours of Fairmount Park, Society Hill and Independence National Historical Park in motorized recreations of Victorian trolleys.

Out of town

Atlantic City with its casinos, health and sports facilities, convention hotels, 6-mile long boardwalk and beaches is 60-miles/98kms east.
Valley Forge National Historical Park is about 25 miles/40kms west of the downtown area in King of Prussia, where General Washington's army spent the grueling winter of 1777-8.

Spectator sports

Philadelphians are sports-happy, and the Phillies (baseball) and the Eagles (football) are very popular teams; games are usually sellouts.
Baseball The *Philadelphia Phillies* play at The Vet, Broad St and Pattison Ave, Apr–Oct ☏ 463-1000.
Basketball The *76ers* play at the Spectrum, across from The Vet, Oct–Apr ☏ 339-7676.
Football The *Eagles* play at The Vet, Aug–Dec ☏ 463-5500.
Horse-racing *Garden State Park*, off Rte 70, Cherry Hill, NJ ☏ (609) 488-8400; thoroughbred season mid-Feb–mid-Jun, Mon–Fri; harness season Mar–Sep, Wed–Sun.
Ice hockey The *Flyers* play at the Spectrum from Oct–Apr ☏ 755-9700.

Keeping fit

Fitness center *Clark's Uptown Racquet Swim & Health Club* ☏ 864-0616.
Bicycling *Fairmount Park Bike Rental*, 1 Boat House Row ☏ 236-4359, daily Mar–Nov, weekends Dec–Feb.
Golf Municipal courses are open year-round, weather permitting: *JF Byrne*, 9500 Leon St ☏ 632-8666; *Juniata*, M and Cayuga Sts ☏ 743-4060; *Karakung*, 72nd and Lansdowne Ave ☏ 877-8707; *Franklin D Roosevelt*, 20th St and Pattison Ave ☏ 467-2418.
Jogging Most popular routes are along Kelly Drive and West River

Drive in Fairmount Park.
Tennis There are over 100 free public tennis courts throughout Fairmount Park ☏ 686-2176.

Local resources

Business services

For comprehensive business services, convenient locations and prompt turnaround try *Philadelphia Business and Technology Center*, 5070 Parkside Ave ☏ 879-8500.
Photocopying and printing *The Printer's Places*, Walnut St ☏ 546-6562 and at 15th St ☏ 567-1400, and *Minuteman Press* ☏ 629-8505, throughout the city. Most will pick up and deliver.
Secretarial services *Kelly Services* ☏ 564-3110 and *Olsten Services* ☏ 568-7795.
Translation *Language Bank* ☏ 879-5248; *Berlitz Translation Services* ☏ 735-8500; and *International Visitors Center* ☏ 823-7261.

Communications

Long-distance delivery *Federal Express* ☏ 923-3085 and *Quick Courier Service* ☏ 592-9942.
Local delivery *Heaven Sent* ☏ 923-0929 and *Kangaroo Couriers* ☏ 561-5132.
Post office The post office at 30th and Market ☏ 895-8000 is open 7–7 daily; the 9th and Market location ☏ 592-9610 is open Mon–Sat, 7–5.
Telex *World-Wide Business Centers*, 714 Market St ☏ 238-7000; *Western Union* ☏ (800) 527-5184.

Conference/exhibition centers

Many of the larger hotels provide good conference and meeting facilities. For other needs, call the *Convention & Visitors Bureau* ☏ 636-3300.

Emergencies

Currency exchange Money can be changed during normal office hours at *American Express Travel Service*, 2 Penn Center Plaza ☏ 587-2342, and the *Visitor Information Center at the Bourse*, 215 5th St ☏ 923-6317.
Hospitals For specific health referrals, call the *Philadelphia Medical Society* ☏ 563-5343; *Philadelphia County Dental Society* ☏ 925-6050; *Hahnemann University*, Broad and Vine ☏ 448-7000; *New Jefferson University*, 11th and Walnut ☏ 928-6000; *University of Pennsylvania*, 34th and Walnut ☏ 898-5000.
Pharmacies *CVS Pharmacies*, *Thrift Drug* and *Rite Aid Discount Pharmacies* have many stores.
Police At 6 111th St and Winter ☏ 686-3060.

Government offices

City Commerce Dept ☏ 686-3646; *Mayor's Office Information* ☏ 686-2250; *Pennsylvania Dept of Commerce* ☏ (717) 787-3003; *US Dept of Commerce* ☏ 597-4603; *US Customs Service* ☏ 597-4605; *Immigration and Naturalization Service* ☏ 597-3961.

Information sources

Business information *Chamber of Commerce of Greater Philadelphia*, 1346 Chestnut St, Suite 800 ☏ 545-1234.
Local media Of Philadelphia's two daily newspapers, *The Philadelphia Inquirer* provides the best local and regional coverage. *Focus* and the *Philadelphia Business Journal* are the major business-oriented magazines, *Philadelphia* lists events.
Visitor information The *Philadelphia Visitors Center*, 16th St and John F Kennedy Blvd ☏ 636-1666, is the main information source. The *Philadelphia Convention and Visitors Bureau*, 1515 Market St ☏ 636-3300 is especially useful for groups planning conventions, trade shows or exhibitions.

Thank-yous

Florists *Flower World*, South Broad St ☏ 567-7100; *Society Hill Florist*, 713 Walnut St ☏ 925-5715.
Gift baskets *Stein*, 7059 Frankford Ave ☏ 338-7100.

PHOENIX

Area code ☏ 602

Set in Arizona's Valley of the Sun, Phoenix is a city of tourism and high-tech. The sprawling network of individual communities remains a favored retirement zone and a fruit growing center, but its erstwhile kingpins, agriculture and copper, are on the decline, and electronics and publishing have moved in. The city has attracted many Midwest and East Coast corporations to its affordable land, magnificent climate and very healthy economy, among them McDonnell-Douglas (20mins southeast in Mesa); Greyhound; and the Best Western International and Ramada Inns hotel chains. Phelps-Dodge, America West Airlines, Circle K and Western Savings and Loan Association have their headquarters here. It is also an important military center, with Litchfield Park's Luke Air Force Base, Williams Air Force Base in Chandler and the Army and Air National Guard State Headquarters nearby.

Arriving

Sky Harbor International Airport

Sky Harbor has three terminals, and a $170m fourth terminal is planned for 1990. Traffic is mainly domestic, and the airport is easy to negotiate; inquiries ☏ 273-3300.

Nearby hotels *Doubletree Suites at the Gateway Center*, 320 N 44th St 85008 ☏ 225-0500 fax 225-0957. *E-Z-8*, 1820 S 7th St 85034 ☏ 254-9787.

City link It is a 10min drive to the heart of downtown, 15mins during the 8–9am and 5–6pm rush hours. Since Phoenix is very spread out, most travelers rent a car at the airport.

Taxi Cabs are available at all three terminals; agree a fare in advance.

Limousine Arizona Chauffeur Exclusive Limousines ☏ 461-9907.

Car rental is available from all three terminals: Avis ☏ 273-3222, Hertz ☏ 267-8822, Dollar ☏ 275-7588, and American International ☏ 273-6181.

Bus The 24hr Super Shuttle ☏ 244-9000 operates a door-to-door service throughout the Valley.

Getting around

Phoenix is an easy city to find your way around; except for Grand Avenue, the streets follow a grid system. Central Avenue is the dividing line, with avenues to the west and streets to the east.

Taxi Cabs do not cruise the city's streets, so reserve ahead. Be sure to negotiate the fare in advance. Reliable firms are *Courier Cab* ☏ 232-2222; *Yellow Cab* ☏ 252-5252; *Checker Cab* ☏ 257-1818; *AAA Cab* ☏ 253-8294; *Village Cab* ☏ 994-1616.

Limousine *La Limousine Service* ☏ 242-3094; *Arizona Limousines* ☏ 267-7097.

Car rental If your business takes you to nearby communities like Scottsdale, Tempe and Mesa, a rented car is the most efficient way to get around (see *City link*).

Public transportation There is no subway, no rail service, and the bus service is slow.

Area by area

Phoenix's financial district is on Central Avenue, between McDowell and Camelback Roads, just minutes from downtown. The residential area closest to downtown is Encanto Park, which has the city's oldest houses, built 30–50 years ago. They have been gentrified and are now owned by lawyers and business leaders. The big-money homes are in Biltmore and Paradise Valley (to the north). As a rule of thumb, north and east are home to affluent professionals; south and west are areas of blue-collar workers and minorities. Academics live in Tempe, close to Arizona State University campus. Mesa, farther east, is a strongly Mormon area.

Hotels

The best hotels are in north Phoenix or Scottsdale, with golf courses, tennis courts, Olympic-size swimming pools and extensive meeting space. Between late May and mid-September hotel prices can be cut by as much as 70%.

Arizona Biltmore [$]////
24th St and Missouri Ave 85106
☎ 955-6600 [TX] 165709 fax 954-0469
• Westin • AE DC MC V • 500 rooms, 78 suites, 5 restaurants
With a design inspired by architect Frank Lloyd Wright, this is the best of the Valley's top resort hotels. Occupying 39 acres of immaculate landscaped grounds, the Biltmore attracts celebrities, while its substantial business clientele appreciates the central location between downtown and Scottsdale. The Orangerie (see *Restaurants*) is highly recommended. Gift and beauty shops, hairdresser • 3 pools, health club, golf, tennis • 15 meeting rooms.

Camelback Inn [$]////
5402 E Lincoln Dr, Scottsdale 85253
☎ 948-1700 [TX] 9109501198
fax 951-8469 • 423 rooms, 22 suites, 4 restaurants, 2 bars
A pretty resort hotel, the pueblo-

inspired Camelback provides dramatic views of the nearby mountains. Guest rooms are not particularly lavish, but the public rooms are agreeably rustic. Health spa, pools, golf, tennis • 20 meeting rooms, recording facilities, teleconferencing.

Embassy Suites Biltmore [$]//
2630 E Camelback Rd 85016
☏ 955-3992 • 232 suites, 1 restaurant, 1 bar, 1 coffee shop
Located next to Biltmore Fashion Park, this hotel has a distinctive Art Deco look and a greenhouse-style lobby. The all-suite arrangement is good for work or small meetings. Easy access to downtown Phoenix, Scottsdale and the airport. Arrangements with nearby golf club, pool • 8 meeting rooms.

Executive Park [$]/
1100 N Central Ave 85004
☏ 252-2100 fax 252-4674 • AE DC MC V • 105 rooms, 1 restaurant, 1 bar
This quiet hotel has a relaxed and homey atmosphere. Rooms are equipped with spacious desks and access for computer hook-up. Complimentary transportation downtown • pool, jacuzzi • 11 meeting rooms.

Hilton Pavilion [$]/
1011 W Holmes Ave, Mesa 85202
☏ 833-5555 fax 649-1886 • AE DC MC V • 212 rooms, 60 suites, 2 restaurants, 3 bars
Decked out in white Italian marble flooring, tile fountains and Hawaiian koa wood, with an eight-story atrium lobby sprouting 50ft palm trees, the Hilton conference resort is well placed for the outlying southeast suburbs. Pool, golf • 13 meeting rooms, teleconferencing.

Hyatt Regency [$]//
122 N 2nd St 85004 ☏ 252-1234
[TX] 668347 fax 254-9472 • AE DC MC V • 711 rooms, 44 suites, 2 restaurants, 3 bars, 1 coffee shop
The Hyatt is frequently used by local corporations for important visitors. Its revolving rooftop restaurant, Compass, affords a grand view of both desert and mountains, and Catina's bar is popular for business meetings. Access to health club, pool, tennis courts • 24 meeting rooms.

Marriott's Mountain Shadows [$]///
5641 E Lincoln Dr, Scottsdale 85253
☏ 948-7111 fax 948-7111 ext 1898 • AE DC MC V • 339 rooms, 3 restaurants
At the base of Camelback Mountain and set in 70 acres of desert gardens, the Marriott blends contemporary with Spanish and Indian design. Often used for conventions, it is also a good place to relax. 3 pools, tennis, golf, fitness center • 11 meeting rooms.

Pointe at Squaw Peak [$]//
7677 N 16th St 85020 ☏ 997-2626
[TX] 4953529 fax 997-2391 • AE DC MC V • 600 suites, 4 restaurants
A luxury resort hotel given entirely over to suites and villas. Suites are spacious, and the large dining tables in the de luxe villas are useful for small meetings. Golf, 6 pools, riding, racquet sports, exercise room • 14 meeting rooms, teleconferencing.

Ritz-Carlton [$]/
2401 E Cambelback Rd 85016
☏ 468-0700 fax 468-0793 • AE DC MC V • 286 rooms, 15 suites, 2 restaurants, 1 bar
The modern Ritz-Carlton opened in October 1988. There is elegant dining in The Grill and cocktails in the lobby lounge. Rooms are comfortable and traditional, with luxurious marble bathrooms. Executive floor. Health club, pool, tennis, arrangements with nearby golf clubs • 7 meeting rooms.

Sheraton Phoenix [$]//
111 N Central Ave 85001 ☏ 257-1525 fax 253-9755 • AE DC MC V • 450 rooms, 84 suites, 2 restaurants, 1 bar, 1 coffee shop
Convention-oriented, this Sheraton provides a high standard of prompt, professional service. The public areas have been redecorated since Sheraton

took over from Hilton in 1988. A popular meeting place for the downtown business crowd. Health club, pool, jogging track • 18 meeting rooms, teleconferencing.

OTHER HOTELS

Ramada Inn Metrocenter [$]/ *12027 N 28th Dr 85029* ☎ *866-7000 fax 942-7512* • AE DC MC V.

Westcourt [$]/ *10220 N Metro Pkwy E 85051* ☎ *997-5900* TX *706629 fax 997-1034* • AE DC MC V.

Clubs

Top people from all walks of life can be found at the sedate *University Club*, 39 E Monte Carlo ☎ 254-5408, on a residential, palm-lined street. The *Arizona Club* – 3550 N Central ☎ 264-3441 and 100 W Washington ☎ 253-1121 – has a largely civic and corporate membership.

Restaurants

Downtown executives usually head uptown or over to neighboring Scottsdale for business meals, though they may use the *Golden Eagle* ☎ 257-7700 on the 37th floor of the Valley Bank Center and the Phoenix Hilton's *Sand Painter* ☎ 257-1525. Attorneys and judges from the nearby courthouse prefer the more casual *Greenhouse* ☎ 252-2742 or *Plaza Café* ☎ 279-1450. Another good choice is the historic *1895 House* ☎ 254-0338, with innovative dishes and an intimate atmosphere.

La Chaumière [$]//
6910 E Main St, Scottsdale ☎ *946-5115* • *closed Sun May–Dec* • AE DC MC V
A Scottsdale institution, serving top-class French creations. Service is impeccable, and the numerous small dining rooms afford privacy for quiet conversation. Good wine list.

El Chorro Lodge [$]/
5550 E Lincoln Dr, Scottsdale ☎ *948-5170* • *closed mid-Jan–mid-Sep* • AE DC MC V
In a scenic desert oasis with dramatic views of Camelback and Mummy Mountains, the Lodge offers 1930s decor with fireplaces and wood beams, and casual dining on the outside patio. Western art is an appropriate accompaniment to American food. Much favored for working lunches and Sunday brunch.

Durant's [$]/
2611 N Central Ave ☎ *264-5967* • AE DC MC V
Durant's has catered successfully for business entertaining for more than 30 years. It offers generous portions of American food, with steak and prime ribs a specialty.

Orangerie [$]///
Arizona Biltmore Hotel ☎ *955-6600* • AE DC MC V
The Orangerie has a reputation for excellence. The Continental menu is both varied and imaginatively prepared; game is a specialty. Good wine list.

Le Relais [$]////
8711 E Pinnacle Peak Rd, Scottsdale ☎ *998-0921* • *closed L, Sun & Mon in summer* • AE DC MC V • *reservations essential*
Le Relais is *the* place to take a client you want to impress. The atmosphere is elegantly European; the food is French. Dress is more formal than in most Valley restaurants.

Bars

Phoenix bars are lively, but they tend to be frequented mainly by students, off-duty young professionals and tourists. Local executives use the bars of the main hotels, particularly the *Oasis Lounge* at the Camelback, *Catina's* in the Hyatt Regency and *Adams Lounge* at the Sheraton. *Oscar Taylor's*, 2420 E Camelback Rd, is a restaurant-bar also much used for talking over a drink.

Entertainment

To find out what's on and where, call the *Jazz Hotline* ☎ 254-4545, *Select Box Office* ☎ 267-1246 or the *Scottsdale Center for the Arts* ☎ 994-2787.

Theater, music, dance and opera The *Celebrity Theater* ☎ 267-1600, *Phoenix Symphony Hall*, 225 E Adams St ☎ 264-4754, *Gammage Center*, Arizona State University, Tempe ☎ 965-3434, *Scottsdale Center for the Arts*, 7383 Scottsdale Mall ☎ 994-2787 and the *Sundome*, 19403 R H Johnson Blvd, Sun City ☎ 975-1900, all attract the big names. *Phoenix Little Theater*, 25 E Coronado Rd, Civic Center ☎ 254-2151, has series of hit plays, while dinner theater is available at *Max's* ☎ 937-1671. *Ballet Arizona* at the Scottsdale Center ☎ 381-0184 gives classical and modern dance performances. *Arizona Opera Company* at 225 E Adams ☎ 254-1664 and the *Arizona State University Lyric Opera Theater* ☎ 965-3398 both present operatic performances.

Nightclubs Local and nationally known jazz musicians play at *Chuy's*, Mill Ave, Tempe ☎ 968-5568, while top-40s and country & western tunes alternate at *Studio West*, 4029 N 33rd Ave ☎ 279-3800. The cabaret show at *Yesterday's*, 9035 N 8th St ☎ 861-9080, features waiters, waitresses and audience participation, and a commendable menu. *Mr Lucky's*, 3660 Grand Ave ☎ 246-0686, has country bands upstairs, rock 'n roll downstairs. *Seekers Comedy Nite Club*, 4519 N Scottsdale Rd, Scottsdale ☎ 949-1100, features stand-up comics.

Shopping

The *Borgata*, 6166 N Scottsdale Rd, is styled after a medieval Italian village, with some 50 luxury boutiques and gourmet restaurants. One of the best shopping locations is the *Biltmore Fashion Park*, 2470A E Camelback Rd, with exclusive stores including I Magnin and Saks Fifth Avenue. Scottsdale's *Fifth Avenue Shops* include rows of art galleries, restaurants and specialty stores. A major renovation has improved midtown's open-air *Park Central Mall*, 3121 N 3rd Ave, home of Miracle Mile, a terrific Jewish deli. North Phoenix's *Metrocenter*, 9617 Metro Pkwy W, has close to 400 stores and eateries. Mesa's popular *Fiesta Mall* features top chain stores, specialty shops, restaurants and bars.

Sightseeing

Desert Botanical Garden More than 10,000 desert plants; continuous guided tours. *1201 N Galvin Pkwy ☎ 941-1225. Open 9–sunset.*

Heard Museum Anthropology and primitive arts, with an attractive selection of Indian crafts in the shop. *22 E Monte Vista Rd ☎ 252-8881. Open 10–4.45; Sun, 1–4.45.*

Phoenix Zoo Over 1,000 animals in carefully reconstructed environments in a desert mountain preserve. *5810 E Van Buren ☎ 273-7771. Open daily, 9–5.*

Guided tours

Jeep tours The spectacular Arizona desert is well worth exploring by jeep. Recommendations include *Arizona Awareness* ☎ 947-7852 and *Arizona Bound Jeep Tours* ☎ 994-0580.

Bus and van tours *Windows on the West Tours* ☎ 840-8245. *Scottsdale Stages* ☎ 947-4256 can accommodate large groups as well as customized tours.

Aerial tours Take a leisurely view of the Valley with the *Unicorn Balloon Company of Arizona* ☎ 991-3666 or for a swifter ride *Sky Cab of Arizona* ☎ 998-1778.

Out of town

Grand Canyon is a 5–6hr drive from Phoenix. Reservations are a must if you plan to stay overnight; call Grand Canyon National Park Lodges ☎ 638-2631. For air tours by plane or helicopter try *Kenai Helicopters* ☎ 638-2412.

Spectator sports

Baseball The *Phoenix Firebirds* play minor league ball at Phoenix Municipal Stadium, 5999 E Van Buren ☏ 275-4488.
Basketball The *Suns* play Oct–May at Veterans Memorial Coliseum, 1826 W McDowell ☏ 263-7867.
Horse-racing *Turf Paradise*, 1501 W Bell Rd ☏ 942-1101, Oct–mid-May.

Keeping fit

Golf Popular courses include *The Phoenician Golf and Tennis Resort*, 6255 E Phoenician ☏ 941-8200; *Arizona Biltmore*, 24th St and Missouri Ave ☏ 955-6600; *Orange Tree Golf Resort*, 10601 N 56th St ☏ 948-3730; and *Papago Golf Course*, Papago Park ☏ 275-8428.
Tennis Public courts are at *Encanto Park*, 15th Ave and Encanto Dr ☏ 262-4539; *Hohokam Tennis Center*, 1235 N Center St, Mesa ☏ 834-2149; and *Indian School Park*, 4289 N Hayden Rd, Scottsdale ☏ 994-2740. Or try the *Village Tennis Club* ☏ 840-6412.

Local resources

Business services

Photocopying and printing *Alphagraphics* ☏ 252-7002.
Secretarial *Manpower* ☏ 264-0237; *Employers Overload* ☏ 264-4080; *Northwest Secretarial* ☏ 866-0017.
Translation *Berlitz Translation Services* ☏ 265-7333; *Professional Interpreters Corp* ☏ 998-8915.

Communications

Long-distance delivery *Federal Express* ☏ 254-4662; *DHL Worldwide Express* ☏ 244-9922.
Local delivery *Moody's Quick Courier Service* ☏ 861-2121; *Express Delivery* ☏ 274-6060.
Post office 4949 E Van Buren ☏ 225-3434 and downtown at 522 N Central Ave ☏ 253-4102.
Telex *Western Union* ☏ (800) 325-6000.

Conference/exhibition centers

For large-scale conventions contact *Phoenix Civic Plaza* ☏ 262-6225; see also *Business information*.

Emergencies

Hospitals *Phoenix General Hospital*, 1950 W Indian School ☏ 279-4411; *St Joseph's Hospital and Medical Center*, 350 W Thomas Rd ☏ 285-3000; *St Luke's Center*, 1800 E Van Buren ☏ 251-8100; *Good Samaritan Medical Center*, 1111 E McDowell Rd ☏ 239-2000; *Scottsdale Memorial Hospital*, 7400 E Osborn Rd ☏ 994-9616.
Pharmacies *Walgreen's* (downtown ☏ 264-0848), *Long's* and *Drug Emporium* all have several locations in the area. Also *24 Hour Drugs*, 1023 E Indian School Rd ☏ 274-5981.
Police The main office is 620 W Washington St ☏ 262-6151.

Information sources

Business information The *Phoenix Chamber of Commerce*, 34 W Monroe St ☏ 254-5521. For information about a specific area, contact the *Arizona Chamber of Commerce* ☏ 248-9172. A helpful source of data is the *Phoenix and Valley of the Sun Convention and Visitors Bureau*, 505 N 2nd St, Suite 300 ☏ 254-6500.
Local media *The Arizona Republic* and the *Phoenix Gazette* are morning and afternoon daily papers. The *Business Journal* is a weekly tabloid. The monthly *Phoenix Metro Magazine* lists local entertainment and other events.
Visitor information *Arizona Office of Tourism*, 1100 W Washington St ☏ 542-8687. *Phoenix and Valley of the Sun Convention and Visitors Bureau* (see above).

Thank-yous

Florists *Phoenix Flower Shops*, 5012 E Thomas ☏ 840-1200; *My Florist, Inc*, 534 W McDowell ☏ 258-7401.
Gift baskets For gift baskets filled with native products try the *Sphinx Date Ranch*, 6802 E McDowell Rd, Scottsdale ☏ 941-3468, or *The Basket Case*, 5037 N 7th Ave, Scottsdale ☏ 266-3818.

PITTSBURGH

Area code ☎ 412

Once a gritty steel town, Pittsburgh is now a center of business, finance and education and the home of such corporations as Westinghouse Electric, USX, Heinz, Bayer USA and National Intergroup. As the steel industry has declined, a service-oriented economy has emerged. Carnegie-Mellon University spearheads Pittsburgh's advances in computer software. But the city is still blue-collar in attitude despite the increase in white-collar workers and young professionals.

Arriving

Greater Pittsburgh International Airport

All international travelers arrive at Gate 45; baggage collection and Customs are just steps away. You can expect to be on your way in 30–45mins. For those arriving on domestic flights, baggage collection can be as far as 10mins from the arrival gate. Currency can be changed at *Tele-Trip* ☎ 472-0241, open daily 6am–8.30pm in the main concourse (*Mutual of Omaha Service Center*). Pittsburgh National Bank has a branch in the main terminal, open 9.30–4. There is a full range of airport services; most close by 9pm but a restaurant is open 24hrs. For airport information ☎ 778-2525.

Nearby hotels *Airport Hilton*, 1 Hilton Dr 15231 ☎ 262-3800 fax 695-1068. *Airport Hotel*, GPIA Mezzanine Level 15231 ☎ 264-8000 fax 264-3354. *Holiday Inn Airport*, 1406 Beers School Rd 15108 ☎ 771-6500 fax 771-6500 ext 1190. *Royce Hotel*, 1160 Thorn Run Rd, Coraopolis 15108 ☎ 262-2400 fax 264-9373.

City link It is a 30min drive to Pittsburgh's downtown Golden Triangle, though the morning and evening rush hours (7–9, 4–6) can add 30mins.

Taxi Taxi stands are just outside both airport terminals; fare to downtown Pittsburgh averages around $25–$30.

Limousine Limo Center ☎ 923-1650.

Car rental Avis ☎ 262-5160, Hertz ☎ 262-1705, Dollar ☎ 262-1300, Budget ☎ 262-1500 and National ☎ 262-2312 operate desks on the lower level of the main terminal.

Bus Airport Limousine Service ☎ 471-8900 operates half-hourly in the morning and evening and every 20mins in the afternoons, from 7am to 1am. Buses leave from the lower level of the main terminal and stop at most of the major downtown hotels; cost is around $8.

Getting around

Because Pittsburgh streets tend to follow topography, finding your way around the hills and rivers can be confusing. The downtown section is not large, however, and a visitor can easily cover most of it on foot.

Taxi There are not many cabs available on the street, so plan on phoning, with a 15–30min wait. Recommended firms include *Yellow Cab* ☎ 665-8100 and *Colonial Taxi* ☎ 833-3300.

Car rental See *City link*.

Subway The *Light Rail Transit System* operates only for three downtown stops, but is quick, reliable and free (before 7pm).

Bus The bus network mainly links the suburbs with downtown; it is not useful for the city center.

Area by area

Downtown The downtown business area is known as the Golden Triangle and is bordered by the Allegheny and Monongahela Rivers. Its skyline is dominated by Philip Johnson's neo-Gothic glass tower for PPG Place, which holds numerous smart boutiques. Other older and no less extravagant architectural confections are scattered about, legacies from industrialists such as Frick, Carnegie and Mellon. The city's financial activity is centered on Grant Street.

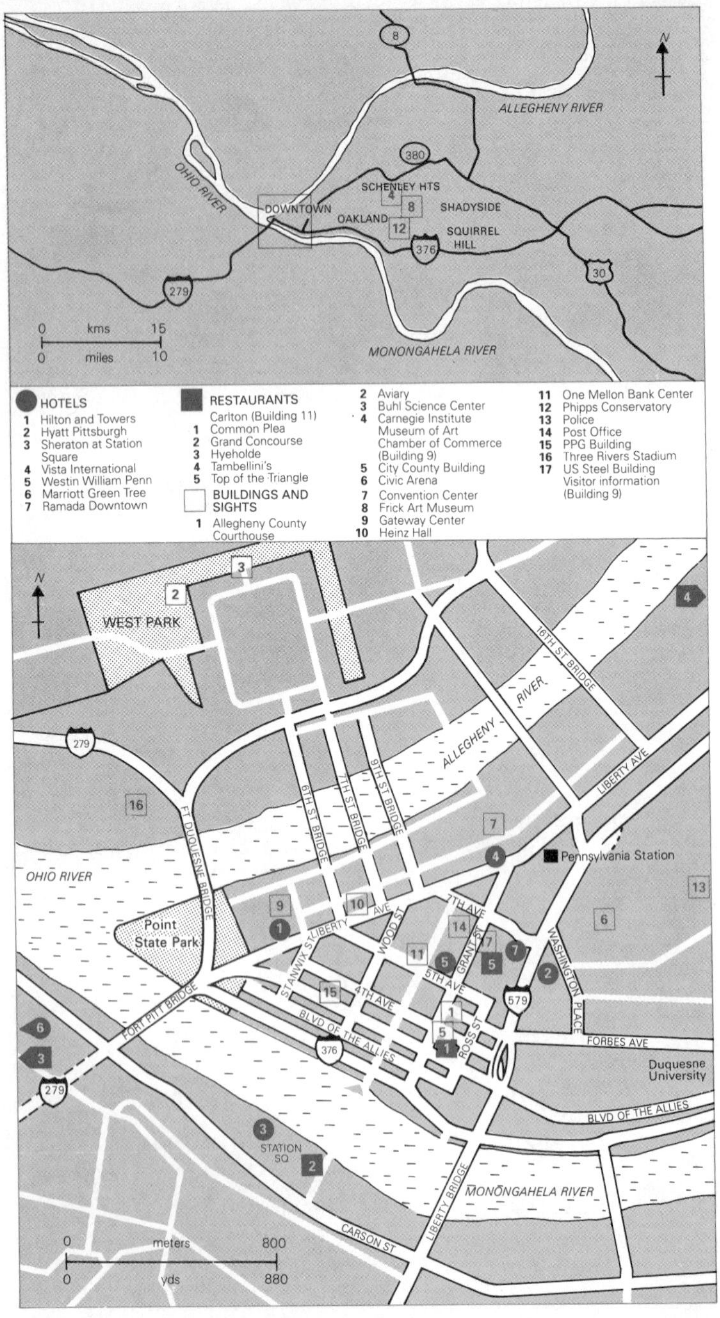
8
ALLEGHENY RIVER
380
OHIO RIVER
SCHENLEY HTS
4
8
SHADYSIDE
DOWNTOWN
OAKLAND
12
SQUIRREL HILL
376
30
279
0 kms 15
0 miles 10
MONONGAHELA RIVER
HOTELS
1 Hilton and Towers
2 Hyatt Pittsburgh
3 Sheraton at Station Square
4 Vista International
5 Westin William Penn
6 Marriott Green Tree
7 Ramada Downtown
RESTAURANTS
Carlton (Building 11)
1 Common Plea
2 Grand Concourse
3 Hyeholde
4 Tambellini's
5 Top of the Triangle
BUILDINGS AND SIGHTS
1 Allegheny County Courthouse
2 Aviary
3 Buhl Science Center
4 Carnegie Institute Museum of Art Chamber of Commerce (Building 9)
5 City County Building
6 Civic Arena
7 Convention Center
8 Frick Art Museum
9 Gateway Center
10 Heinz Hall
11 One Mellon Bank Center
12 Phipps Conservatory
13 Police
14 Post Office
15 PPG Building
16 Three Rivers Stadium
17 US Steel Building
Visitor information (Building 9)
WEST PARK
16TH ST BRIDGE
ALLEGHENY RIVER
279
LIBERTY AVE
16
6TH ST BRIDGE
7TH ST BRIDGE
9TH ST BRIDGE
FT DUQUESNE BRIDGE
Pennsylvania Station
OHIO RIVER
Point State Park
LIBERTY AVE
STANWIX ST
WOOD ST
7TH AVE
GRANT ST
WASHINGTON PLACE
5TH AVE
4TH AVE
FORT PITT BRIDGE
BLVD OF THE ALLIES
ROSS ST
579
376
FORBES AVE
Duquesne University
BLVD OF THE ALLIES
STATION SQ
MONONGAHELA RIVER
LIBERTY BRIDGE
CARSON ST
0 meters 800
0 yds 880

Just across the Monongahela River is Station Square, a converted railroad terminal with shops, restaurants and bars. This area also has a number of computer software firms. Also in the downtown area is Point State Park, 36 acres of gardens, where the Monongahela and Allegheny Rivers converge to form the Ohio.

Oakland Just east of downtown is Oakland, site of the University of Pittsburgh and Carnegie-Mellon University, two of the city's seven major educational institutions. Most of Pittsburgh's high-tech industry is clustered around the university area. Just across Forbes Avenue from the Pitt campus's Cathedral of Learning is the Carnegie Institute (see *Sightseeing*).

Shadyside and Squirrel Hill Continuing east on Forbes Avenue will take you to Shadyside and Squirrel Hill, both fashionable neighborhoods which have recently seen a huge influx of young professionals. The area has many smart shops and restaurants, along with some of the city's most popular nightspots.

The suburbs

Old money and established families can be found in *Sewickley* and *Sewickley Heights*, two of the most affluent neighborhoods in eastern United States. Both are to the north of Pittsburgh on the Ohio River. Also in the north is *Fox Chapel*, another desirable residential area, with woodland and quiet country roads. Fashionable addresses south of Pittsburgh include *Mount Lebanon* and *Upper St Clair*.

Hotels

Pittsburgh has only a limited selection of hotels, most of which cater mainly to business travelers. All of the hotels listed below are within easy walking distance of most major corporation offices.

Hilton and Towers [$]//

Gateway Center 15222 ☎ *391-4600 fax 391-0927* • *AE DC MC V* • *717 rooms, 31 suites, 2 restaurants, 2 bars*

On a downtown site overlooking the "big three" rivers, the Hilton is especially convenient for those with business in the towering Gateway Center. Sterling's restaurant, in the main lobby, is often filled with business diners. Hairdresser, drugstore • health club • 21 meeting rooms, teleconferencing, translation.

Hyatt Pittsburgh [$]//

112 Washington Pl 15219 ☎ *471-1234* [TX] *812364 fax 355-0315* • *AE DC MC V* • *400 rooms, 20 suites, 1 restaurant, 1 bar*

Commanding a fine view of downtown Pittsburgh, the Hyatt is convenient to corporate headquarters and to the nearby Civic Arena. The Regency Club's two executive floors provide some of the city's choicest business-oriented accommodation; make sure you are given a room with adequate work space. Health club, pool, sauna, whirlpool • 14 meeting rooms.

Sheraton at Station Square [$]/

7 Station Square Dr 15219 ☎ *261-2000 fax 261-2932* • *AE DC MC V* • *293 rooms, 53 suites, 2 restaurants, 2 bars*

Just across the river from downtown, the Sheraton, with its futuristic lobby, is a favorite with business travelers dealing with the Station Square area's high-tech companies. Hairdresser, florist • pool, sauna, fitness center • 8 meeting rooms.

Vista International [$]///

Liberty Ave at 10th St 15222 ☎ *281-3700 fax 281-2652* • *AE DC MC V* • *571 rooms, 44 suites, 2 restaurants, 1 bar*

This luxury hotel, across the street from the Convention Center, offers first-class business facilities, including three executive floors. Fitness center • 18 meeting rooms.

Westin William Penn [$]//
530 William Penn Way, Mellon Sq 15219 ☎ *281-7100* [TX] *866380*
fax 281-3498 • AE DC MC V • *595 rooms, 47 suites, 2 restaurants, 1 bar*
Wide corridors, wood paneling and lovely old furniture make the Westin the choice of visiting dignitaries and high-level executives. Its location is unbeatable, virtually across the street from 18 major corporate headquarters. The Terrace Room, the city's number one spot for business breakfasts, is well suited also for business lunches and dinners. Access to nearby health club, jacuzzi • 35 meeting rooms.

OTHER HOTELS

Marriott Green Tree [$]//
101 Marriott Dr, Crafton 15205
☎ *922-8400* [TX] *7106442016*
fax 922-8981 • AE DC MC V.
Convenient for business in the southwest suburbs.

Ramada Downtown [$]///
Bigelow Sq 15219 ☎ *281-5800*
fax 281-1448 • AE DC MC V. All-suite hotel with health club and pool.

Clubs

Old money and local powerbrokers can be found at the *Duquesne Club* ☎ 391-1500 downtown or the *Pittsburgh Athletic Association* ☎ 621-2400 in Oakland. The *Rivers Club* ☎ 391-5227 has reciprocal membership with other health clubs.

Restaurants

Eating out in the city is mainly a lunchtime activity, since Pittsburgh's nightlife proceeds in the outskirts and suburbs. On pleasant days, many business lunchers walk to the numerous restaurants at Station Square.

Carlton [$]//
One Mellon Bank Center, 500 Grant St ☎ *391-4099* • *closed Sun* • AE DC MC V
The Carlton specializes in prime meat, charcoal-broiled seafood, Cajun dishes and veal. Tables are close together, but the restaurant remains a favorite with Pittsburgh business people.

Common Plea [$]//
308 Ross St ☎ *281-5140* • AE MC V
Near the courthouse, the Common Plea is another established luncheon spot. Seafood and veal are specialties. Space on the ground floor is limited; tables upstairs offer more privacy.

Grand Concourse [$]//
1 Station Sq ☎ *261-1717* • *closed Sat L* • AE DC MC V
One of the city's most attractive restaurants, the Grand Concourse is a renovated railroad station, with soaring ceilings and stained-glass skylights. Its booths and secluded areas are ideal for private lunches or dinners. Seafood is the specialty.

Hyeholde [$]//
190 Hyeholde Dr, Coraopolis ☎ *264-3116* • *closed Sat L, Sun* • AE DC MC V
Occupying an old country mansion, the classy Hyeholde offers expert cooking and excellent wines. Near the airport.

Tambellini's [$]//
860 Saw Mill Run Blvd ☎ *481-1118* • *closed Sun* • AE DC MC V • *no reservations*
An attractive restaurant on the south shore of the Allegheny River which specializes in seafood – lobster, crab, oysters and sole – with some Italian specialties.

Top of the Triangle [$]//
600 Grant St ☎ *471-4100* • AE DC MC V • *reservations essential*
The view – from the top floor of the US Steel Building – is superb; but

the restaurant's main advantage for business people is its spaciousness, with large tables and booths designed for privacy. Cuisine is Continental.

Bars

Many say that the best drinks in town are found at *Froggy's*, 100 Market Street ☎ 471-3764, a favorite of young professionals. Local executives tend to head across the Monongahela River to *Chauncy's* at Station Square, South Side ☎ 232-0661. Another popular after-hours spot is *Tramp's*, 212 Blvd of the Allies ☎ 261-1990, a former bordello; the *Top of the Triangle* bar (see *Restaurants*) is a good choice for working discussions. In the Southside, the Marriott Green Tree's *Cahoots* bar has a loyal clientele.

Entertainment

Information about events can be found in the daily newspapers or in the weekly *In Pittsburgh*. Tickets can be bought at box offices or at the *Tix Booth*, USX Plaza ☎ 642-2787.

Theater and music The Pittsburgh Symphony Orchestra is at *Heinz Hall*, 600 Penn Ave ☎ 392-4800; ballet and opera are performed at the *Benedum Center*, Liberty St ☎ 456-2600. The *Pittsburgh Public Theater*, 1 Allegheny Sq ☎ 321-9800, and the *Playhouse Theater Center*, 222 Craft Ave ☎ 621-4445, offer a range of entertainment.

Jazz/nightclubs Most of the best jazz spots are bars and restaurants. The best-known is *Balcony* ☎ 687-0110 in Shadyside. In Oakland are *Hemingway's* ☎ 621-4100, *Graffiti* ☎ 682-4210, which offers a variety of jazz, classical, folk, rock and comedy, and for straight rock'n roll the *Decade* ☎ 682-1211.

Shopping

The two established downtown department stores are *Kaufmann's*, at 5th and Smithfield, and *Horne's*, at 501 Penn Ave. The smart shops at *Oxford Center Tower*, at Grant and 4th Ave, and *PPG Place*, off Stanwix St, sell a wide and original variety of clothing, gifts and gadgets. Other stylish boutiques can be found at *Station Square* and along *Walnut Street* in Shadyside.

Sightseeing

Aviary A fine collection of tropical and domestic birds in natural settings. *W Ohio and Arch St ☎ 323-7234. Open daily, 9–4.30.*

Buhl Science Center Includes science exhibits, a planetarium, a laser show, and (during the winter) a huge model train exhibit. *Allegheny Sq ☎ 237-3300. Open Sun–Thu, 1–5; Fri, 1–9.30; Sat, 10–5.*

Carnegie Institute Museum of Art A main Pittsburgh attraction, with a collection of paintings, sculpture, furnishings and other works of art. *4400 Forbes Ave, Oakland ☎ 622-3131. Open till 5; closed Mon.*

Frick Art Museum Fine collection including Old Masters in an Oakland mansion. *7227 Reynolds St and S Homewood Ave ☎ 371-0600. Closed Mon & Tue.*

Phipps Conservatory Exhibits of orchids, cacti and tropical plants; also seasonal shows. *Schenley Park ☎ 622-6914. Open daily.*

Guided tours

Boat tours The *Gateway Clipper Fleet* ☎ 355-7980 offers sightseeing and dinner-dance cruises. Boats leave from Monongahela Wharf at Station Square.

Bus tours *Lenzner Coach Lines*, Mt Nebo Rd, Sewickley ☎ 761-7000.

Spectator sports

Baseball The *Pittsburgh Pirates* play at Three Rivers Stadium, 400 Stadium Circle on the North Side ☎ 323-5000.

Football Three Rivers Stadium is also the home of the *Steelers* ☎ 323-1200. Many businesses have boxes in the stadium.

Hockey The *Penguins* play downtown at the Civic Arena, Washington Pl, Center and Bedford Avenues ☎ 642-1800.

Keeping fit

Most major hotels have facilities of their own or arrangements with local health clubs. The many parks are well used for jogging, walking and impromptu softball or soccer games.
Fitness centers *The Rivers Club*, 1 Oxford Center, Grant St ☎ 391-5227, and *The City Club*, 119 6th St ☎ 391-3300, both offer a full range of facilities, including racquet sports. Both clubs will make arrangements with out-of-town visitors.
Bicycling Rental from *North Park* ☎ 935-1971 and *South Park* ☎ 835-5710.
Golf Some hotels have arrangements with local country clubs. *Schenley Park* in Oakland ☎ 622-6959 is one of the best public courses.
Jogging Two of the largest city parks, *Schenley Park* in Oakland and *Frick Park* in Squirrel Hill, have extensive jogging paths and are reasonably safe during daylight hours.
Tennis There are many public tennis and racquetball courts at local parks (for example Mellon Park).

Local Resources

Business sources

Photocopying and printing *Quik Print Copy Shop* has five locations downtown, including 545 Liberty Ave ☎ 456-1060, 903 Liberty Ave ☎ 456-1059 and 207 Smithfield St ☎ 456-1067.
Secretarial *Stivers Temporary Personnel* ☎ 566-2020. *Quick Print* (see above) will do typing, word-processing and will send faxes.
Translation *Berlitz* ☎ 471-0900 and *Inlingua* ☎ 391-3181.

Communications

Long-distance delivery *Federal Express* ☎ 765-8900 and *DHL Worldwide Express* ☎ 262-2764.
Local delivery *Mercury Messenger Service* ☎ 391-2016.
Post office The main Post Office is on the north side at 1001 California Ave ☎ 359-7895, open 8am–10pm. There is a downtown post office at Grant and 7th ☎ 642-4472.
Telex *Western Union* ☎ (800) 325-6000.

Conference/exhibition centers

The city's major convention venue is the *David L. Lawrence Convention Center*, 1001 Penn Ave ☎ 565-6000.

Emergencies

Hospitals *Allegheny General Hospital*, 320 E North Ave ☎ 359-3252, is the closest hospital to downtown Pittsburgh. Also *Mercy Hospital*, 1400 Locust St ☎ 232-7555. Dental treatment is available at *Kaufmann's* department store, 5th and Smithfield ☎ 232-2978.
Pharmacy *Thrift Drug*, Penn and 6th Avenues ☎ 391-0969.
Police 2000 Centre Ave and Dinwiddie ☎ 255-2827.

Government offices

Pittsburgh Government Printing Office ☎ 644-2721 provides useful literature; *US Dept of Commerce* (International Trade Administration), Federal Building ☎ 644-2850; *Immigration and Naturalization Service* ☎ 644-3356.

Information sources

Business information The *Greater Pittsburgh Chamber of Commerce*, 3 Gateway Center ☎ 392-4500, will provide information on businesses.
Local media The two local dailies are the morning *Pittsburgh Post-Gazette* and the evening *Pittsburgh Press*. The weekly *In Pittsburgh* is available free.
Visitor information The *Greater Pittsburgh Convention and Visitors Bureau*, 4 Gateway Center ☎ 281-7711. Visitor Information Center, Gateway 3, Liberty Ave ☎ 281-9222; open Mon–Fri, 9.30–5; Sat & Sun, 9.30–3. For information on current activities ☎ 391-6840.

Thank-yous

Florists *Flowers by Salvy and Tom*, 813 Liberty Ave ☎ 281-1300; *Lubin and Smalley*, 126 5th Ave ☎ 471-2200; and *John McClements*, 925 Penn Ave ☎ 261-1041.

ST LOUIS

Area code ☏ 314

St Louis sits at the heart of the Midwest, at the confluence of the Missouri and Illinois Rivers with the Mississippi; the city is in Missouri, but parts of the metropolitan area are in Illinois. Despite the song and the city's French fur-trading settler origins, you don't meet people in "St Louie" – you pronounce the "s"! St Louis has always been an important transportation hub – as an inland port, as a railroad center, and more recently as the intersection of four cross-country interstate highways and the site of a busy airport. Today its principal industries are aerospace, transportation and medicine. Major companies that have their world and corporate headquarters here include Monsanto, Ralston Purina, Emerson Electric, General Dynamics, McDonnell-Douglas, Jefferson Smurfit, Kellwood and Interco.

Arriving

Lambert-St Louis International Airport

STL is located 15 miles/24kms from downtown St Louis. Its four passenger concourses lead to the main terminal's baggage claim area, adjacent to parking and public transportation: allow 30–60mins for the whole operation. Hotel information can be obtained and reservations placed by using free phones in the baggage area. Other services include a bank (7.30–5; Canadian, British, French and German currencies) and various shops, restaurants and bars. For general and freight information ☏ 426-8000.

Nearby hotels *Henry VIII*, 4690 N Lindbergh 63044 ☏ 731-3040 fax 731-3040 ext 6125. *Park Terrace Airport Hilton*, 10330 Natural Bridge Rd 63134 ☏ 426-5500 fax 426-5500 ext 438. *St Louis Airport Marriott*, I-70 at Lambert Airport 63134 ☏ 423-9700 fax 423-0213.

City link St Louis is a city in which a car is no handicap. All the major firms have desks at the airport.

Taxi Laclede Cab is the largest and most frequently available taxi service ☏ 652-3456; Country Cab ☏ 991-5300. Fares to downtown average $12–$18.

Limousine Airport limousine vans operate a 15min schedule to downtown and Clayton hotels for about $7 per passenger ☏ 429-9240.

Driving Expect about a 20min drive to downtown, 15mins to the Clayton business district.

Bus The Bi-State Bus Co ☏ 231-2345 has an express service that leaves every 45mins.

Getting around

St Louis has excellent freeways and secondary highways, and most districts can be reached easily and quickly by car or cab. The city bus service is adequate, but slow. Roads lead into downtown like spokes on a wheel. Downtown's streets running north–south are numbered; east–west streets have names.

Taxi *Yellow Cabs* are available by phone ☏ 361-2345.

Car rental *Avis* ☏ 426-0277, *Hertz* ☏ 421-3131, *National* ☏ 426-6272.

Walking The downtown business area is easily walkable; but take care after dark.

Area by area

Downtown is the city's hub and Central Business District (CBD). In addition it has St Louis's major hotels and best restaurants. Bounded by Market Street on the west, Convention Plaza Drive on the north, the Mississippi River to the east and US Highway 40 to the south, the downtown business area is the location for major companies such as Ralston Purina, near Busch Stadium, and Southwestern Bell Telephone, in the heart of the CBD.

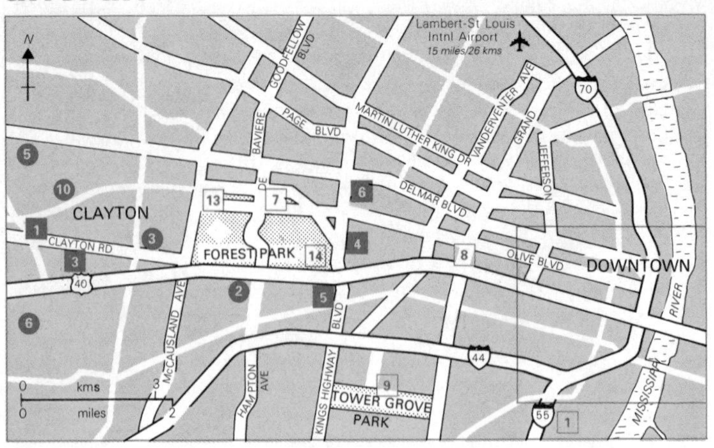

HOTELS

1 Adam's Mark
2 Breckenridge Frontenac
3 Cheshire Inn and Lodge
4 Clarion
5 Daniele Hilton
6 Doubletree
7 Embassy Suites
8 Hyatt Regency St Louis
9 Marriott Pavilion
10 Radisson Clayton
11 Stouffer Concourse
12 Day's Inn at the Arch
13 Holiday Inn Downtown Convention Center
14 Holiday Inn Downtown Riverfront
15 Majestic

RESTAURANTS

1 Al Baker's
2 Anthony's
3 Busch's Grove
4 Café Balaban
5 Dominic's
6 Tenderloin Room
7 Tony's

BUILDINGS AND SIGHTS

1 Anheuser - Busch Brewery
2 Busch Memorial Stadium
3 Cervantes Convention Center
4 City Hall
5 Convention and Visitors Bureau
6 Gateway Arch
7 The History Museum
8 Hospital (St Louis)
9 Missouri Botanical Garden
10 Old Courthouse
11 Police
12 Post Office
13 St Louis Art Museum
St Louis RCGA (Building 5)
14 Science Center

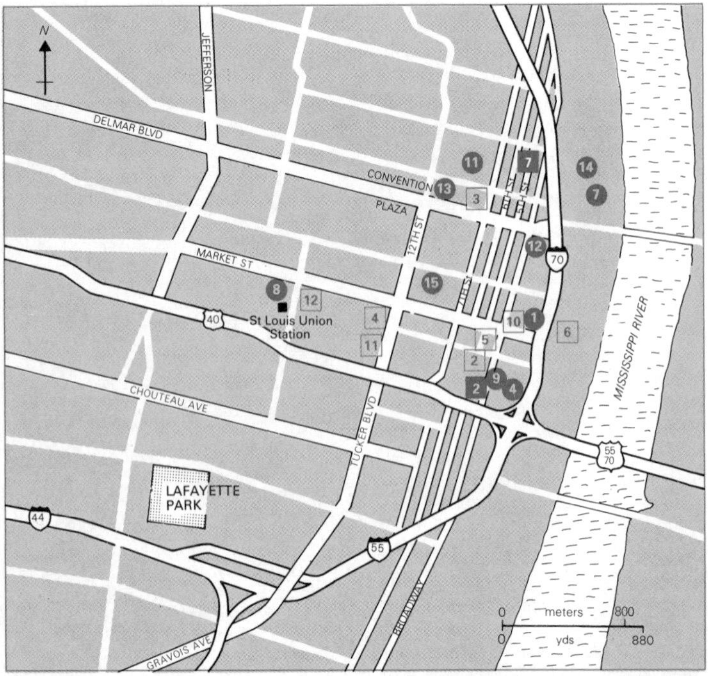

Clayton Just 10mins from downtown and 15mins from the airport, Clayton is both a business and wealthy residential area. General Dynamics is among the top-rank corporations here. It has good hotels and eating places.

West Port The West Port area, about 20 miles/32kms from downtown, has retail stores, restaurants, hotels, office/warehouse buildings and light-industrial plants. The new West Port Plaza has European-style boutiques and a range of restaurants and entertainment, all in an Alpine setting.

Highway 40 Another business district is the corridor along Highway 40, southwest of the residential West Port area.

Hotels

St Louis is fast developing as a convention center, and as a result there has been a considerable growth in the number of hotels offering special services for the business visitor. A new Ritz-Carlton hotel is opening in Clayton in 1990.

Adam's Mark [$]II

314 N 4th St 63102 ☏ 241-7400 TX 9107640890 fax 241-9839 • AE DC MC V • 910 rooms, 96 suites, 6 restaurants, 2 bars

A relatively new luxury hotel with fine furnishings, the Adam's Mark has indoor health facilities and a special level for VIPs, including private lounge and dining room. 2 pools, exercise equipment, racquetball • 30 meeting rooms.

Breckenridge Frontenac Hotel & Conference Center [$]I

1335 S Lindbergh 63131 ☏ 993-1100 TX 434383 fax 993-8546 • AE DC MC V • 257 rooms, 13 suites, 2 restaurants, 1 bar

This elegant French-style hotel is adjacent to the distinctive Plaza Frontenac shopping center and is convenient for visitors to IBM, Citicorp and Monsanto. Luxury level floors with lounge and concierge. Health club, pool • 24 meeting rooms.

Cheshire Inn and Lodge [$]I

6306 Clayton Rd 63117 ☏ 647-7300 fax 647-0442 • AE DC MC V • 108 rooms, 10 suites, 2 restaurants, 2 bars

A splendid re-creation of an old English country inn, including the heavy wooden beams, the midtown Cheshire is beautifully furnished with English antiques in every room. Pool, health club • 6 meeting rooms.

Clarion [$]I

200 S 4th St 63102 ☏ 241-9500 TX 2911010 fax 241-9500 • AE DC MC V • 825 rooms, 50 suites, 1 restaurant, 2 bars, 1 coffee shop

Expanded and redecorated in the last five years, the Clarion is between Busch Stadium and the Arch downtown. Top of the Riverfront, the hotel's 28th-floor revolving restaurant, offers a spectacular view of the Mississippi. Pools, health club/spa and games room • 20 meeting rooms.

Daniele Hilton [$]II

216 N Meramec, Clayton 63105 ☏ 721-0101 fax 721-0101 ext 666 • AE DC MC V • 90 rooms, 6 suites, 1 restaurant, 1 bar

Elegant, yet cozy, the Daniele has stylish European decor, a good restaurant and a piano lounge. Pool, health club access • 2 meeting rooms.

Doubletree [$]II

16625 Swingley Ridge Rd, Chesterfield 63107 ☏ 532-5000 fax 532-9984 • AE DC MC V • 223 rooms, 6 suites, 2 restaurants, 3 bars

A modern sprawling complex designed for business meetings, the Doubletree is set in a secluded spot, ideal for concentration and relaxation. Sports include racquetball, tennis, handball, fitness center, swimming and nearby golf. 32 meeting rooms, lecture theater.

Embassy Suites [$]//
901 N 1st St, Laclede's Landing 63102 ☎ *241-4200 fax 241-6513* • *AE DC MC V* • *300 suites, 1 restaurant, 1 bar*
This all-suite hotel on Laclede's Landing, is a good place for dining and nightlife and easily accessible to downtown. Each suite has a refrigerator and bar, two telephones and two TVs. Complimentary breakfast and cocktail hour • pool, health club • 6 meeting rooms.

Hyatt Regency St Louis [$]//
Union Station 63103 ☎ *231-1234* [TX] *5006103807 fax 436-6827* • *AE DC MC V* • *542 rooms, 29 suites, 2 restaurants, 1 bar*
The crown jewel of the refurbished Union Station and the most prestigious address in St Louis. Some rooms are in the station, some in the old train shed; all are well-appointed. Gift shop • pool, health club, sauna • 22 meeting rooms.

Marriott Pavilion [$]//
1 Broadway ☎ *421-1776* [TX] *9107611029 fax 331-9029* • *AE DC MC V* • *670 rooms, 12 suites, 2 restaurants, 1 bar*
The Marriott is as popular with the sports crowd as with corporate executives. Health club, indoor pool • 23 meeting rooms, business reference library, teleconferencing facility.

Radisson Clayton [$]/
7750 Carondelet Ave, Clayton 63105 ☎ *726-5400 fax 726-6105* • *AE DC MC V* • *220 rooms, 12 suites, 1 restaurant, 2 bars*
This modern hotel provides good service, large rooms (all with work space) and fine facilities. Convenient for business in the Clayton area. Health club, racquetball, 2 pools • 12 meeting rooms.

Stouffer Concourse [$]//
9801 Natural Bridge Rd 63134 ☎ *429-1100* [TX] *709107 fax 429-3625* • *AE DC MC V* • *400 rooms, 18 suites, 2 restaurants, 2 bars*
This ultra-modern luxury hotel, near the airport, is popular with many of the city's business visitors. Health club, pool, tennis • 30 meeting rooms.

OTHER HOTELS

Day's Inn at the Arch [$] *4th and Washington 63102* ☎ *621-7900 fax 621-7900 ext 7215* • *AE DC MC V*. Comfortable and convenient.

Holiday Inn Downtown Convention Center [$]/ *9th at Convention Plaza 63101* ☎ *421-4000 fax 421-5974* • *AE DC MC V*. Across from the Convention Center.

Holiday Inn Downtown Riverfront [$]/ *200 N 4th St 63102* ☎ *621-8200 fax 436-8030* • *AE DC MC V*. Close to many downtown businesses and attractions.

Majestic [$]/// *1019 Pine St* ☎ *436-2355 fax 436-2355* • *AE DC MC V*. Fairly new luxury hotel in 75-year old building; European ambience.

Clubs

St Louis's business network flourishes through the area's many country clubs. Most are in St Louis County, but the *Missouri Athletic Club* ☎ 231-7220 is a downtown club with elegant dining, meeting and health facilities. The most prestigious and exclusive "old money" clubs are *St Louis Country Club* ☎ 994-0011, *Bogey Golf Club* ☎ 946-6250, *Old Warson Country Club* ☎ 968-0840 and *Westwood Country Club* ☎ 432-2311. Members of these include the city's businessmen and politicians. An invitation to lunch, dinner or a round of golf can be considered a mark of honor.

Restaurants

St Louis is well supplied with good restaurants, especially Italian ones; and a great deal of business is done in them – not only at lunch time and in the evening, but also in the morning at breakfast.

Al Baker's [$]//
Clayton and Brentwood, Clayton
☎ *863-8878 • closed L, Sun •* AE DC MC V *• jacket requested*
Well regarded for its Continental cuisine, fresh seafood, long wine list and elegance, Al Baker's is good for an important business dinner.

Anthony's [$]///
10 S Broadway ☎ *231-2434 • closed L, Sun •* AE MC V
A favorite with locals and visitors alike, Anthony's is a four-star restaurant specializing in light Continental cuisine, fresh seafood and excellent wine. The outstanding service and elegant, ultra-modern atmosphere make it equally suitable for a private business discussion or a romantic dinner.

Busch's Grove [$]/
9160 Clayton Rd ☎ *993-0011 • closed Sun and Mon •* MC V
A St Louis County favorite since the 1890s, Busch's specializes in prime ribs. Besides the main restaurant there are individual screened cabins for outdoor dining.

Café Balaban [$]//
405 N Euclid ☎ *361-8085 •* AE DC MC V
Considered *the* place to be seen in the Central West End, Balaban's features French dishes, Continental cuisine and fresh seafood in the dining room. The downstairs level gives added privacy. The glass-enclosed café provides an *à la carte* menu.

Dominic's [$]///
5101 Wilson on the Hill ☎ *771-1632 • closed L, Sun •* AE DC MC V *• jacket and tie*
Dominic's serves sophisticated Italian cooking in opulent surroundings featuring marble statues and oil paintings. Tables are widely spaced. One of the best restaurants in St Louis.

Tenderloin Room [$]/
Kings Highway and Lindell
☎ *361-1414 •* AE DC MC V *• reservations advisable*
Known for its prime steaks, the Victorian-style Tenderloin Room is a St Louis tradition. Chops, seafood and a dessert tray are all specialties. Formerly in the Chase Hotel.

Tony's [$]///
826 N Broadway ☎ *231-7007 • closed L, Sun •* AE DC MC V *• reservations before 7pm Tue–Fri*
Tony's is generally acknowledged to be number one in St Louis. Superb Italian food (try the lobster Albanello) is served here in an elegant setting. The perfect choice for a celebratory meal.

Bars

There is no shortage of lounges and bars in the St Louis area. Besides those in the major hotels, some popular bars for talking business include *Laclede's Landing, Central West End, West Port Plaza* and *Union Station*. The "hot spots" include two *Houlihan's*, one in Union Station and one in the Galleria in Clayton.

Entertainment

Classical music, open-air theater, Broadway shows and, of course, Dixieland jazz are all important features of St Louis nighttime entertainment.
Theater On the riverfront, *Goldenrod Showboat* ☎ 621-3311, 700 N Leonor K Sullivan Blvd, is a floating dinner theater, staging vaudeville, melodrama and musical revues and in June the National Ragtime Festival. The *Muny* ☎ 361-1900, a 12,000-capacity outdoor amphitheater in Forest Park, is the venue for music and plays in summer, with appearances by entertainment's biggest names. The refurbished *Fabulous Fox Theater*, 527 N Grand Blvd ☎ 534-1111, and old movie theater, is as much of an attraction as the shows it stages; it consistently hosts top-name stars and shows. *Westport Playhouse*, 600 W Port Pl ☎ 275-8787, is a newish theater in

the round, where no seat is more than 30ft from the revolving stage. It offers mainly comedy and musicals.
Music The *St Louis Symphony Orchestra* ☎ 534-1700 is America's second oldest. Its season runs from fall to spring, and it usually performs at Powell Symphony Hall, 718 N Grand Blvd.
Nightclubs Laclede Landing is a redeveloped nine-block area by the river where clubs, pubs and discotheques put on anything from jazz to nostalgia.

Shopping

St Louis is well-served with shopping malls. Two popular suburban centers are *Northwest Plaza* at St Charles Rock Rd at Lindbergh and the *Plaza Frontenac*, Clayton Rd at Lindbergh, which includes high-fashion stores such as Saks Fifth Avenue and Neiman-Marcus. *St Louis Centre* is a huge mall in the central business district. If you have time to spare you should see *St Louis Union Station*, restored and redeveloped as a shopping and entertainment center.

Sightseeing

Anheuser-Busch Brewery Tours A 1hr tour of the world's largest brewery includes the famous team of Clydesdales, a look at the old brewhouse and a sampling of the products. *Broadway and Pestalozzi ☎ 577-2626. Open daily, 9–4, exc Sun and holidays.*
The History Museum Colorful exhibits focus on the history of St Louis, Missouri and the American West. Housed in the Jefferson Memorial Building, displays include advertising, firearms, and the 1904 World's Fair and Charles Lindbergh memorabilia. *Forest Park ☎ 361-1424. Open Tue–Sun, 9.30–4.45; closed Mon.*
Gateway Arch, the symbol, by Finnish architect Eero Saarinen, of St Louis delicately poised on the Mississippi levée, is America's tallest memorial; observation room, 630ft up. *11 N 4th St ☎ 425-4465.*
Missouri Botanical Garden, which has North America's largest Japanese Garden, also houses the Climatron, a domed greenhouse, and Mediterranean and desert houses. *4344 Shaw Blvd ☎ 577-5125. Open daily.*
Old Courthouse, dating back to the 1820s, was both the site of slave auctions and the location of the 1847 Dred Scott trial which further inflamed the controversy between North and South on slavery. It also houses the Museum of Westward Expansion. *At Gateway Arch ☎ 425-4465. Open Tue, 1.30–8.30; Wed–Sun, 10–5.*
St Louis Art Museum A fine building in its own right, the St Louis Art Museum has more than 70 galleries of art treasures. *Forest Park ☎ 721-0067. Open Tue, 1.30–8.30; Wed–Sun, 10–5; closed Mon.*
Science Center comprises the McDonnell Planetarium, Museum of Science and Natural History, and Medical Museum and Science Park. *Forest Park ☎ 289-4400.*

Spectator sports

Baseball The *St Louis Cardinals* play at Busch Memorial Stadium, Broadway at Walnut, downtown ☎ 421-3060.
Ice hockey The *Blues* play their home games at the Arena, midtown, 5700 Oakland ☎ 781-5300.

Keeping fit

Fitness center The YMCA downtown, 1528 Locust ☎ 436-4100, has an indoor pool, track, racquetball, and exercise equipment. *Vic Tanny International* ☎ 576-5300 has eight health clubs throughout the area.
Bicycling Forest Park in the city and Queeny Park in the country have bicycle paths. *Freewheelin'*, 6388 Delmar ☎ 361-5854, has bikes to rent.
Golf Two good public courses are in *Forest Park*, 9 and 18 holes ☎ 367-6848; and *Ruth Park*, 9 holes ☎ 373-4800.
Jogging *Forest Park* has numerous

paths. Starting on *Wharf Street* below Gateway Arch, you can trek 2 miles/ 3kms along the river.
Tennis The *Dwight F Davis Tennis Center* ☎ 367-0220 in Forest Park is open during daylight hours.

Local resources

Business services

Firms that offer complete business support services include *Bradlie Business Service*, 222 S Bemiston, Clayton ☎ 726-2496.
Photocopying and printing *Quick Print*, in Clayton ☎ 726-1110 and West Port ☎ 569-0994, offers free pick-up and delivery. Another choice is *PIP*, whose downtown location is at 620 Olive St ☎ 962-1086.
Secretarial *Kelly Services* has eight offices ☎ 576-7787.
Translation *Berlitz Translation Services*, 200 Hanley ☎ 721-1070, and the *World Affairs Council of St Louis*, 212 N Kingshighway ☎ 361-7333.

Communications

Long-distance delivery *Federal Express* ☎ 367-8278.
Local delivery *Jiffy Express Package Delivery* ☎ 725-3995 has 24hr service in a 200-mile radius.
Post office The main post office is downtown at 1720 Market ☎ 436-4418.
Telex *Western Union* ☎ 421-3967 or *Postal Center Telex International* ☎ 725-8300.

Conference/exhibition centers

For large groups or exhibits, contact the *St Louis Convention and Visitors Commission*, 10 Broadway ☎ 421-1023. The *Cervantes Convention Center*, Convention Pl at 7th, has an L-shaped exhibit area containing 240,000 sq ft ☎ 342-5036. *Kiel Auditorium* has five assembly halls, 1400 Market ☎ 622-3600. Midtown's *Arena*, 5700 Oakland ☎ 644-0900, seats almost 20,000.

Emergencies

Currency exchange Most banks exchange foreign currency during normal banking hours, including *Centerre Bank*, 510 Locust, downtown ☎ 554-6000.
Hospitals *Washington University Medical Center* ☎ 362-5000 includes the Jewish Hospital of St Louis and Barnes Hospital. *St Louis University Hospital* ☎ 771-6400.
Pharmacies *Walgreen's* ☎ 534-7707 and *Medicare Glaser* ☎ 569-1100 have several locations, some open 24hrs.
Police *Police Dept–St Louis*, Clark and Tucker, downtown ☎ 231-1212.

Government offices

US Dept of Commerce District Office/ International Trade Administration, 120 S Central Clayton ☎ 425-3302; *US Customs Service*, 120 S Central ☎ 425-3136.

Information sources

Business information The *St Louis Regional Commerce and Growth Association* (*RCGA*), 100 St 4th St, is a major source of information ☎ 231-5555.
Local media *St Louis Post-Dispatch* is the daily newspaper, with global and local coverage. The *St Louis Business Journal* reports area business and financial news. *St Louis Magazine* is a monthly featuring entertainment and cultural events.
Visitor information *St Louis Convention & Visitors Commission*, 10 S Broadway, Suite 300 63102 ☎ 421-1023 or (800) 325-7962, helps with planning trade shows.

Thank-yous

Florists Credit card telephone orders are taken by *Tom Carr Florist*, 442 Mansion House Center, downtown ☎ 421-3769; *Town & Country Flowers*, 8127 Maryland, Clayton ☎ 862-2800; *Walter Knoll Florist*, 5501 Chippewa ☎ 352-7575.
Gift baskets *Pfeifer's Party Pastries and Fine Wines*, 8021 Clayton Rd ☎ 725-2572.

SAN ANTONIO

Area code ☏ 512

Once little more than a historic tourist resort, the old Spanish city of San Antonio – site of the battle of the Alamo – is developing as an industrial and business base. The city was out-distanced in the 1920s by oil-booming Dallas and Houston; but its diversified economy (government, tourism and services industries) spared it the worst of the Texas downturn of the mid-1980s, and new businesses have been moving here. Five military bases, including Lackland, the US Air Force's basic training facility, are important to the economy, and corporate America is represented by Diamond Shamrock, Valero Energy and Associated Milk Producers. The population of over 1m is young – average age about 28 – and mainly Hispanic.

Arriving

San Antonio International Airport
SAIA is served by 15 major and numerous commuter airlines. Terminal 1, where most domestic flights arrive, is relatively new and efficient, and baggage can usually be claimed in less than 15mins. International flights arrive at Terminal 2, where it may take travelers up to an hour to retrieve baggage and clear Customs.

Both terminals have restaurants and snack bars. There are duty-free facilities in both terminals, but they open only during normal business hours and when flights from Mexico come in. Information ☏ 821-3411.

Nearby hotels *Amerisuites North*, 10950 Laureate Dr ☏ 691-1103 fax 691-2180. *Embassy Suites Airport*, 10110 Hwy 281 ☏ 525-9999 fax 525-0626. *La Quinta Airport East*, 333 NE Loop 410 ☏ 828-0781 fax 826-3445. *Radisson Airport*, NW Loop 410 at San Pedro ☏ 340-6060 fax 340-7174.

City link In normal traffic it takes about 15mins to drive downtown. All the hotels listed provide courtesy cars. Otherwise take a taxi (about $11–$13) or the Supervan Shuttle ☏ 344-7433. All major car rental firms have counters in both terminals: Avis ☏ 826-6332, Budget ☏ 828-5693, Hertz ☏ 826-0651.

Getting around

Downtown is compact, and you can walk to most destinations. But for business beyond the city center, a taxi, limo or car is essential.

Taxi There are usually lines of cabs at all major hotels and taxi stands on the Paseo del Rio (Riverwalk) between E Commerce and Buena Vista. Taxi companies include *Yellow Cab* ☏ 226-4242, *United Taxi* ☏ 733-0852 and *Checker Cab* ☏ 222-2151.

Limousine *Fiesta* ☏ 431-5466.

Car rental See *City link*.

Walking The compact downtown area is safe for walking, and it takes only 15–20mins on foot from, say, the Main Plaza east to HemisFair.

Bus *VIA Metropolitan Transit* runs many routes out into the suburbs. Downtown, the *VIA* San Antonio streetcars run a service on five routes; bus information ☏ 227-2020.

Area by area

The city is clustered around a horseshoe bend of the San Antonio River. From the center, the main streets fan out, following old Spanish roads. Superimposed on these are interstate expressways.

Downtown San Antonio is marked by district boundaries – Market Square on the west and HemisFair Park on the east. The city center, at the Alamo and Paseo del Rio, is a mix of business and tourist attractions. Its 1920s and 1930s skyscrapers, such as the copper-roofed Tower Life and ornate brass-decorated Nix Professional Building, are still the city's prestigious office addresses, with the newer glass-curtain wall buildings, Interfirst, One Riverwalk and Republicbank Plaza.

North Star Mall and Loop 410 The mile-long enclosed North Star Mall is the focus of expansion to the north of the city. New business development is also spreading rapidly north along the interstate highway to San Pedro and out west along Loop 410.

Northwest suburbs The northwest is growing, with new housing areas and several high-tech businesses, such as Sea World and Texas Research Park. The South Texas Medical Center, near Loop 410 to the northwest, and the university nearby have been the catalyst for expansion in this area.

Residential areas Prime residential areas include King William, its splendid 19thC mansions just three blocks south of the city center. Monte Vista is distinguished and equally affluent north of downtown; and Alamo Heights, Terrell Hills and Olmos Park, just 10mins to the northwest of Monte Vista, are the prestige suburbs, collectively known by their zip code ending: "09."

Other areas The west and south sides of the city are predominantly working class and Hispanic. Eastside is mainly working class.

Hotels

Business hotels are becoming extremely competitive, and even the luxury establishments often have promotional packages. Most of the following have been chosen for their convenient locations.

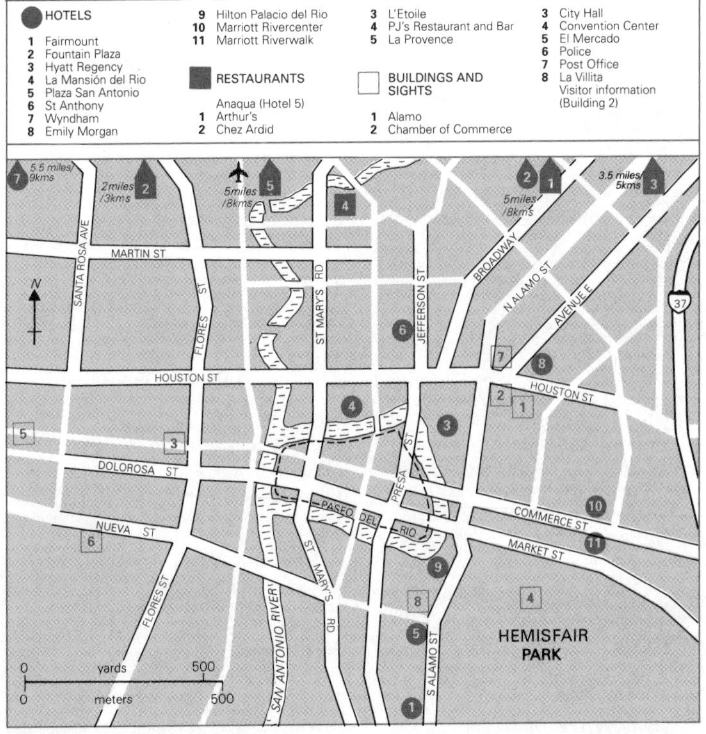

Fairmount [$]//
401 S Alamo 78205 ☎ *224-8800*
[TX] *5106018532 fax 224-2767* • AE DC MC V • *20 rooms, 17 suites, 1 restaurant, 1 bar*
This meticulously restored three-story Italianate Victorian building garnered international attention as the heaviest building ever moved. The splendid lobby has lots of Italian marble; the rooms are the best-appointed in San Antonio and have four-poster beds. 2 meeting rooms.

Fountain Plaza [$]/
37 NE Loop 410 78216 ☎ *341-3535*
[TX] *767478 fax 341-0410* • AE DC MC V • *292 rooms, 2 restaurants*
For visitors doing business around the airport and the South Texas Medical Center, this is a convenient and comfortable option. The hotel has a fountain courtyard, complete with palms and banana plants. Pool • 8 meeting rooms, secretarial service.

Hyatt Regency [$]///
123 Losoya 78205 ☎ *222-1234*
[TX] *767249 fax 227-4925* •
AE DC MC V • *632 rooms, 30 suites, 3 restaurants*
Modern and luxurious, the Hyatt is admirably located for downtown business and has a wide range of business facilities. Rooftop pool, corporate health club • 17 meeting rooms.

La Mansión del Rio [$]//
112 College St 78205 ☎ *225-2581*
[TX] *767478 fax 226-0389* • AE DC MC V • *337 rooms, 11 suites, 2 restaurants, 2 bars, 1 coffee shop*
A hacienda-style hotel, La Mansión has excellent rooms overlooking the river. The inner courtyard, with its pool and scarlet bougainvillea is a pleasant retreat. Pool • 11 meeting rooms.

Plaza San Antonio [$]///
555 S Alamo 78205 ☎ *229-1000*
fax 229-1000 ext 7826 • AE DC MC V • *242 rooms, 10 suites, 1 restaurant, 1 bar, 1 coffee shop*
The Plaza San Antonio, set in a 6-acre garden, has an aura of serene elegance. Rooms have balconies overlooking tiled courtyards and lush grounds harboring pheasants. Heated outdoor pool, health club, saunas, tennis courts, golf nearby • 14 meeting rooms, recording facilities and secretarial services.

St Anthony [$]///
300 E Travis 78298 ☎ *227-4392*
[TX] *203481 fax 227-0915* • AE DC MC V • *227 rooms, 83 suites, 2 restaurants*
Old-fashioned and distinguished, this lovingly restored turn-of-the-century hotel specializes in traditional, personal service. Roof garden • pool, weight-training room • 19 meeting rooms, translation and secretarial services.

Wyndham [$]//
9821 Colonnade 78238 ☎ *691-8888*
fax 691-1128 • AE DC MC V • *328 rooms, 3 suites, 2 restaurants*
Its polished granite façade and marble interior, furnished with chandeliers, Oriental rugs and masses of fresh flowers, give the Wyndham an air of *grande luxe*. It is just 10mins from the airport and the Medical Center. 2 pools and jacuzzi, sauna, nearby racquetball club • 16 meeting rooms, secretarial services.

OTHER HOTELS

Emily Morgan [$]// *705 E Houston 78205* ☎ *225-8486 fax 225-7227* • AE DC MC V. An elegant hotel near the Alamo and Convention Center.

Hilton Palacio del Rio [$]// *200 S Alamo 78205* ☎ *222-1400 fax 270-0761* • AE DC MC V. A large, modern hotel just across from the Convention Center.

Marriott Rivercenter [$]// *101 Bowie St 78205* ☎ *223-1000 fax 223-6239* • AE DC MC V. New hotel connected to River City Mall.

Marriott Riverwalk [$]// *711 E Riverwalk 78205* ☎ *224-4555 fax 224-2754* • AE DC MC V. Convenient for downtown business.

Clubs

Top of the list for those in business are the *City Club* ☏ 732-8145 and the *Plaza Club* ☏ 227-4191 – opposite City Hall and the resort of many top government officials. Both have reciprocal membership privileges within the Club Corporation of America. The atmospheric *Club Gireau* ☏ 271-7777 is up-and-coming; the *Argyle* ☏ 824-1496 is in the smart "09" suburb. The *San Antonio Country Club* ☏ 824-8865 is the oldest and most exclusive in town.

Restaurants

San Antonio has many informal Mexican restaurants, but for important business meals top executives choose one of the city's more conventional eating places.

Anaqua [$]|
Plaza San Antonio Hotel ☏ *229-1000* • *AE DC MC V*
The setting, in restored 19thC houses, and food -- Continental/French – are superlative. Ring-neck pheasants stride through the tropical gardens and cool courtyards.

Arthur's [$]|
4001 Broadway ☏ *826-3200* • *closed L* • *AE MC V*
An elegant glass box overlooking the 300-acre Brackenridge Park, Arthur's has Oriental decor and Continental/French cuisine. Specialties include fillet stuffed with fried oysters and *béarnaise* sauce.

Chez Ardid [$]|
1919 San Pedro ☏ *732-3203* • *AE MC V* • *jacket required at D*
An Italianate house with a skylit atrium and intimate, elegant side rooms. Its restrained elegance and mainly French cuisine are popular with a young business clientele.

L'Etoile [$]|
6106 Broadway ☏ *826-4551* • *AE DC MC V*
L'Etoile has a Parisian brasserie atmosphere, with brass ceiling fans and wooden balconies. The French menu is innovative, and the service is excellent.

PJ's Restaurant and Bar [$]|
700 N St Mary's Rd ☏ *225-8400* • *AE DC MC V*
A favorite business lunch and dinner place overlooking Riverwalk, PJ's specializes in Continental/French cuisine. Fine wine list and inventive menu.

La Provence [$]|
206 E Locust ☏ *225-0722* • *closed L* • *AE DC MC V*
Expect conservative, classic French cuisine and excellent service in this converted 1920s mansion. The lamb is particularly good.

Bars

San Antonio's bar life is concentrated in hotels and restaurants. Downtown there are numerous spots on the Paseo del Rio where you can sip a

Tex-Mex

No visitor to San Antonio should leave without sampling the local Texan brand of Mexican food, "Tex-Mex" – which features gooey, chili-smothered enchilladas. Be prepared for incredibly hot and spicey concoctions. Downtown, the best places to find Tex-Mex are *Mi Tierra*, 218 Produce Row ☏ 225-1262, open 24hrs, or *La Margarita*, 102 Produce Row ☏ 227-7140, in El Mercado. Also downtown are the *Cadillac Bar*, 212 S Flores St ☏ 223-5533, fashioned after its famous counterpart in Nuevo Laredo, Mexico, and *Mario's*, 325 S Pecos St ☏ 223-9602, the late-night spot for politicians.

margarita. The city's young professionals flock to a revived area in the 3000 block of N St Mary's Street, where there is a row of trendy restaurants and bars. The new *River City Mall* is just establishing itself as a pleasant place for off-duty excursions.

Entertainment

Nightclubs offer dancing and live music, from country-and-western to jazz. Jim Cullum's Jazz Band is a permanent feature of the Hyatt Regency (see *Hotels*) from Fri to Sun. There is also jazz at *Arthur's*, and for soft rock it's *PJ's Band* at One Riverwalk Place (see *Restaurants*).
Theater and music The *San Antonio Performing Arts Association*, Suite 230, 110 Broadway ☏ 224-8187, has a good record for attracting a variety of internationally known performers. The *San Antonio Symphony Orchestra*, 111A Lexington Ave ☏ 223-5591 (box office), also imports major stars and conductors. It also plays at the Majestic Theater, 214 E Houston St ☏ 226-2626, which has recently been converted from a 1920s cinema to a magnificently ornate Spanish baroque amphitheater.

Shopping

In San Antonio the obvious shopping attractions are Mexican and Central American items. *Market Square, El Mercado*, west of downtown, is ideal for curios and ceramics. Out of town, *North Star Mall* on Loop 410 has major stores, including Saks Fifth Avenue and Marshall Field's.

Sightseeing

The Alamo, an early 18thC mission where Davy Crockett, Col James Bouvier and 184 Texans fought off 5,000 Mexicans in the 1836 struggle for Texan independence, is on Alamo Plaza between Crockett and Houston Streets. *La Villita* ("the little town"), opposite the 1968 World's Fair site, HemisFair Park ☏ 299-8610, is a restored village reflecting San Antonio's Spanish origins. *King William* district is an area of exquisitely restored Victorian mansions along the river, just south of the city center. If you have time, you can follow the *Mission Trail* south, which takes in four of San Antonio's 18thC missions including *Mission Concepción* (807 Mission Rd), the oldest, and *Mission San José* (600 Lone Star Blvd), the best preserved. Missions open daily 9am–6pm ☏ 229-5701.

Guided tours

Bus tours *Alamo Tours* ☏ 735-5019, and *Grayline Sightseeing Tours* ☏ 227-5251 offer a variety of package tours to all major tourist sites.
Boat Tours The *Paseo Del Rio River Boats* ☏ 222-1701 provide daily, 30min trips.

Out of town

The *LBJ Ranch* on US-290, 75 miles/120kms from San Antonio, is a 200-acre ranch donated by President and Mrs Johnson and run by the National Park Service ☏ 644-2241. Bus tours include Johnson City and the working ranch. About a 30min drive from San Antonio is the *Guadalupe River*, a cypress-lined waterway in the still unspoiled heartland of Texas.

Spectator sports

Baseball The *Mission*, a Class AA farm team for the Los Angeles Dodgers, play at VJ Keefe Field ☏ 434-9311, Apr–Aug.
Basketball *Spurs* play home games at the Convention Center Arena, HemisFair Park ☏ 224-9578.

Keeping fit

The downtown *YMCA*, 903 N St Mary's ☏ 227-5221, has facilities to rival private health clubs – swimming, aerobics, weight-training room and sauna.
Bicycling Bikes can be rented from the Plaza San Antonio (see *Hotels*) and at *Brackenridge Park*. A 10 mile/25km Hike and Bike Trail passes the missions. Parts of it are isolated,

so you will want company.
Golf Municipal courses include one at *Brackenridge Park* ☏ 226-5612 and *Oak Hills Country Club* ☏ 349-5151.
Jogging *Friedrich Park*, 21480 Milsa Rd, has splendid wilderness trails. Do not jog alone.
Racquet sports *McFarlin Tennis Center*, 1503 San Pedro ☏ 732-1223, has a nominal fee.
Water sports and boating There are 15 lakes around San Antonio, but the closest is a 30min drive, and the largest, *Canyon Lake*, is an hour away by car. It is the best for sailing and windsurfing.

Local resources

Business services

For comprehensive services, the downtown best is *Headquarters Co* ☏ 226-7666.
Photocopying and printing *Kwik-Kopy Printing* has shops all over town – downtown ☏ 224-5589, northside ☏ 340-3488. They will pick up and deliver.
Translation *Berlitz Translation Services* ☏ 681-8944.

Communications

Long-distance delivery *Federal Express* ☏ 271-0561.
Local delivery *VIANET* ☏ 342-6217.
Post office The downtown post office is at 615 E Houston ☏ 227-3399. Special delivery ☏ 821-5232. All post office hours: 8.30–5.
Telex *Telex Communiqué* ☏ 341-5248.

Conference/exhibition centers

The *San Antonio Convention Center* ☏ 299-8500, is in HemisFair Park. The *Arena* next to it seats 15,389, and the *Theater of Performing Arts*, Suite 230, 110 Broadway ☏ 224-8187, can pack in 2,731.

Emergencies

Hospitals Downtown area, *Santa Rosa Hospital*, 519 W Houston St ☏ 228-2011; Northside area, *Methodist Hospital*, 7700 Floyd Curl Dr ☏ 692-4040.
Pharmacies *Eckerd Drugs* has branches in all areas. For 24hr service, *Revco* ☏ 690-1616.
Police *San Antonio Police Dept*, 214 W Nueva St ☏ 299-7484.

Government offices

San Antonio City Hall, Military Plaza ☏ 299-7011; *Customs*, International Airport ☏ 822-0471; *Immigration and Naturalization Service*, 727 E Durango ☏ 229-6350.

Information sources

Business Information *Greater San Antonio Chamber of Commerce*, 602 E Commerce ☏ 229-2100, publishes a guide to San Antonio.
Local media San Antonio has two major daily newspapers: *San Antonio Light*, is serious and business-oriented; *Express-News* is more sensational but also has good business coverage. The best business magazine is the *San Antonio Magazine*.
Visitor information *Convention and Visitors Bureau*, 210 S Alamo St ☏ 299-8123. *Visitors Information Center*, 317 Alamo Plaza ☏ 299-8155.

Thank-yous

Florists *The Rose Shop*, 1903 San Pedro ☏ 732-1161, and *Kelly-Scherrer*, 326 W Josephine ☏ 735-6184, both near downtown.
Gift Baskets *Creative Alternatives*, 2520 N Main Avenue ☏ (800) 284-0276 delivers. *Allen's Flowers and Gifts*, 2101 McCullough ☏ 734-6441, does food and wine baskets.

SAN DIEGO

Area code ☎ 619

Just a 30min drive from the Mexican border, San Diego is California's oldest city, its third largest and one of its fastest-growing. Discovered by the Portugese explorer Juan Cabrillo in 1542, it still continues to attract new residents. Today's city is predominantly one of young people, mostly under 30, who enjoy a near-perfect climate and an easy southern Californian way of life. Aerospace giant Rohr Industries has its headquarters in Chula Vista, and General Dynamics in Kearny Mesa. Tourism contributes more than $2bn a year to the area's economy, and the Pacific Fleet injects even more. Other important business sectors are electronics, agriculture and research institutes like the Salk Institute of Biological Studies and the Scripps Institution of Oceanography.

Arriving

San Diego International Airport

SAN, known locally as Lindbergh Field, has two adjacent terminals, and the farthest gate in either is a 5min walk from the baggage claim. Baggage cart rentals are available. *Tele-Trip Company* ☎ 295-1501 operates a currency exchange and Western Union service daily, 6.30–5. *Union Bank* (East Terminal ☎ 230-4340) is open Mon–Thu, 9–4; Fri, until 6, and there is a 24hr American Express cash dispenser outside the west end of East Terminal. Air freight services are listed in *Flighttimes*, free in the airport.

Nearby hotels *Sheraton Grand on Harbor Island*, 1590 Harbor Island Dr 92101 ☎ 291-6400 fax 296-5297. *Travelodge Harbor Island*, 1960 Harbor Island Dr 92101 ☎ 291-6700 fax 291-6700.

City link *Taxi* Cabs are available 24hrs at both terminals. The fare to downtown is about $6.

Car rental It is a 5–10min drive to downtown. All major rental firms have desks in both terminals.

Bus Airporter Express ☎ 231-1123 provides 24hr transportation to all major hotels from both terminals.

Getting around

Taxi Taxis have to be ordered by telephone. *Checker Cab* ☎ 234-4477 and *Yellow Cab* ☎ 234-6161 are major companies.

Limousine *VIP Limousine* ☎ 299-7000 and *Capitol Limousine* ☎ 296-8373.

Car rental A car is by far the best method to get around. You can rent at the airport, and the major firms also have offices downtown: *Avis* ☎ 231-7171, *Hertz* ☎ 231-7000, *National* ☎ 231-7100. Parking in downtown is easy, more difficult along the coast in summer.

Area by area

Downtown In the legal, financial and governmental heart of the city, old buildings are being replaced by attractive hotels, office blocks, condominiums and boutiques. Many Victorian buildings are being restored, especially in the Gaslamp Quarter, south of Broadway and between 3rd and 6th Avenues – the hub of all downtown activity. The $160m bayfront San Diego Convention Center was completed in the fall of 1989.

Balboa Park Bordering downtown to the northeast, this site of two world fairs in 1915 and 1935 is where many of San Diego's museums, galleries, theaters and its Zoo are now located.

La Jolla San Diego's leading research institutes, high-tech research and development firms are located in this residential and business area 10 miles/16kms northwest of Balboa Park.

Point Loma, one of the more desirable neighborhoods, spreads over the hills of almost the entire peninsular between the ocean and San Diego Bay.

Coronado A 2 mile/3km bridge connects this island to the mainland. Naval Air Station North Island occupies nearly half the area.
Mission Valley is the major shopping center. It stretches northeast of Old Town and Mission Hills and is the site of San Diego's Jack Murphy Stadium.
Mission Bay, 10mins north of downtown, includes Mission Beach, a wealthy residential area, Pacific Beach and Mission Bay Park, a 4,600 acre aquatic park. In summer, the whole area is very crowded.
Other areas Many computer companies are located in Sorrento Valley, east of La Jolla.

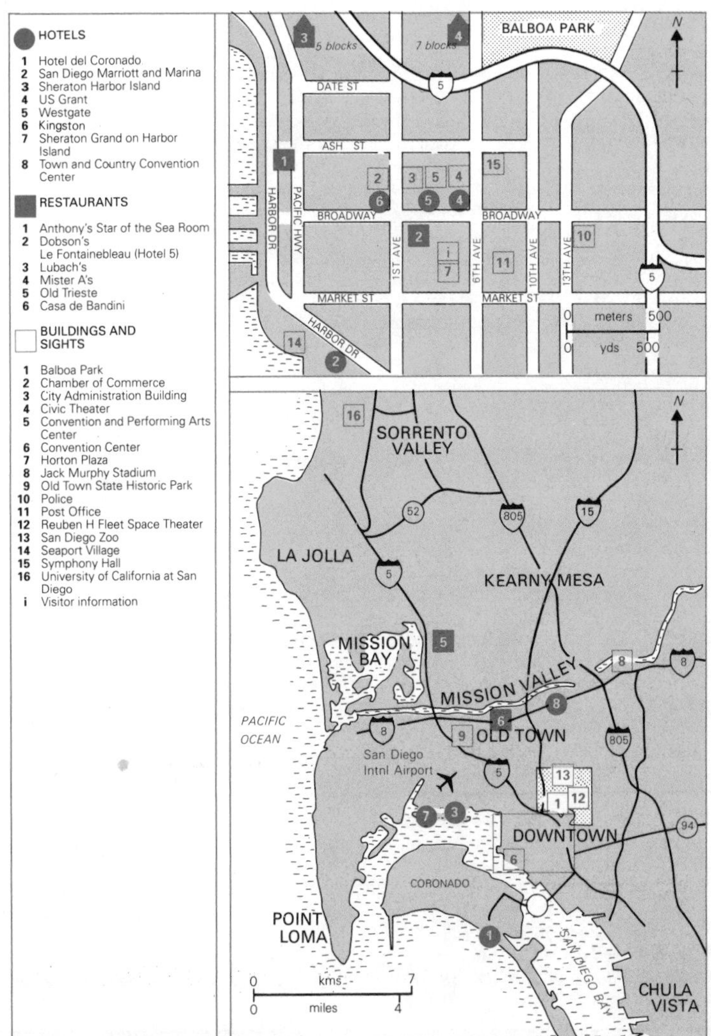

Hotels

Most of San Diego's top hotels are concentrated downtown, in Mission Valley or near the airport. Several have a very extensive range of sports facilities.

Hotel del Coronado [$]////
1500 Orange Ave 92118 ☎ 522-8000 fax 522-8239 • AE DC MC V • 643 rooms, 37 suites, 3 restaurants, 2 bars, 2 coffee shops
Long popular with US presidents, visiting celebrities (including the Duke and Duchess of Windsor) and business travelers, this 19thC hotel is also where Marilyn Monroe made the movie *Some Like It Hot*. It is a graceful, turreted building with a perpetually busy lobby, paneled floor-to-ceiling in dark wood. Suites in the newer beachfront towers are particularly suited to business visitors who want room to work. Nearby golf course, health clubs, 2 pools, tennis, power and sailboat rentals at adjacent Glorietta Bay Marina • 30 meeting rooms.

San Diego Marriott and Marina [$]///
333 W Harbor Dr 92101 ☎ 234-1500 [TX] 695425 fax 234-8678 • AE DC MC V • 1,355 rooms, 40 suites, 2 restaurants, 1 bar
The striking Marriott (previously the Inter-Continental), with its curved, mirrored façade, stands at the edge of San Diego Bay, beside its own 19 acre marina on the waterfront, and by the Convention Center and Seaport Village. Oriental ceramics and other artworks decorate the marbled lobby and lounges; in the inner courtyard pathways meander beside trickling waterfalls. The rooms, which overlook the bay, are modern and comfortable. Hairdresser, gift shops • marina, 2 pools, 3 mile/5km jogging track, tennis, jacuzzi, sauna • 23 meeting rooms.

Sheraton Harbor Island [$]///
1380 Harbor Island Dr 92101 ☎ 291-2900 [TX] 697120 fax 294-3279 • AE DC MC V • 669 rooms, 40 suites, 2 restaurants, 2 bars
The contemporary Sheraton East overlooks the multimillion dollar Harbor Island marina, and its Tower Club business center has the widest range of facilities of any hotel in the city. Rooms are furnished to a very high standard, and its Nautilus club complex has lighted tennis courts, health club, sauna, pool and a 5 mile/8km jogging track. 40 meeting rooms, recording facilities, notary public.

US Grant [$]////
326 Broadway 92101 ☎ 232-3121 [TX] 183881 fax 232-3626 • AE DC MC V • 280 rooms, 60 suites, 1 restaurant, 1 bar
Built in 1910, this restored hotel in the financial district downtown has a distinctly monied atmosphere. Its marble floors, handsome furnishings and the high standards of individual rooms are a strong magnet for its mainly business clientele. The formal Grant Grill and casual Grant Grill Lounge are both quiet and intimate, good for food and conversation. Complimentary limo to nearby health club, airport and golf course • 15 meeting rooms.

Westgate [$]///
1055 2nd Ave 92101 ☎ 238-1818 [TX] 695046 fax 232-4526 • AE DC MC V • 233 rooms, 11 suites, 2 restaurants, 2 bars
Opulently elegant, this is the hotel with cachet in San Diego. Rooms have Louis XV and Louis XVI style furnishings and the bathrooms are in Italian marble. The lobby has Baccarat crystal chandeliers and a Steinway grand piano. White-gloved waiters serve the mainly business and international clientele in Le Fontainebleau (see *Restaurants*). Complimentary limo to nearby health clubs • 14 meeting rooms.

OTHER HOTELS

Kingston [$]/ *1055 1st Ave 92101 ☎ 232-6141 fax 232-0118 • AE DC MC V.*

Sheraton Grand on Harbor Island [$]/// *1590 Harbor Island Dr 92101 ☎ 291-6400 fax 294-9627 • AE DC MC V.*

Town and Country Hotel-Convention Center [$]// *500 Hotel Circle N 92108 ☎ 291-7131.*

Clubs

Downtown, the exclusive *Cuyamaca Club* ☎ 232-2386 and less smart *University Club* ☎ 234-5200 are both much used by judges, lawyers, and finance executives. The prestigious old-money *San Diego Yacht Club* ☎ 222-1103 is in Point Loma. The *La Jolla Beach and Tennis Club* ☎ 454-7126 has a celebrity membership.

Restaurants

Many of San Diego's excellent seafood restaurants are on the waterfront downtown with superb views. The Old Town is best for Mexican food.

Anthony's Star of the Sea Room [$]///

1360 N Harbor Dr ☎ 232-7408 • closed L • AE MC V • jacket and tie • reservations essential

Much used for business entertaining, Anthony's caters to an older, affluent clientele. Floor-to-ceiling windows look out on San Diego Bay. Seafood only, abalone a specialty.

Dobson's [$]//

956 Broadway Circle ☎ 231-6771 • closed Sat L, Sun • AE MC V • reservations essential

A restored turn-of-the-century pub, this busy restaurant is much used by powerbrokers, politicians and leading lights of the local arts scene. Ask for a table upstairs to overlook the crowded bar.

Le Fontainebleau [$]//

Westgate Hotel ☎ 238-1818 • closed Sat L • AE DC MC V • jacket • reservations 1 week in advance for Sat and Sun

Antique French decor and excellent service make this San Diego's most elegant and formal restaurant, popular for business lunches, entertaining, and Sunday brunch. The classic French menu, with the emphasis on seafood, includes an excellently priced *prix fixe* meal.

Lubach's [$]//

2101 N Harbor Dr ☎ 232-5129 • AE MC V • jacket • reservations advisable

Popular for business lunches, Lubach's has been a top San Diego restaurant for more than 30 years and has a menu ranging from lobster thermidor to hamburgers.

Mister A's [$]/

2550 5th Ave ☎ 239-1377 • AE DC MC V • jacket

Atop the 5th Avenue Financial Center, Mister A's commands a magnificent view of Balboa Park, downtown and San Diego Bay. Its exclusive air, leather upholstery and wood paneling make it a popular choice for business entertaining. It has an extensive and good wine list.

Old Trieste [$]//

2335 Morena Blvd ☎ 276-1841 • closed Sat L, Sun, Mon • AE DC MC V • jacket • reservations essential

Much favored by San Diego's uppercrust, this intimate restaurant serves excellent northern Italian cuisine with an emphasis on fish and veal. The service is also first-class.

Mexican food

Casa de Bandini, 2660 Calhoun St ☎ 297-8211, which specializes in Mexican seafood, is the best outdoor Mexican restaurant in Old Town.

Bars

Popular with top executives are the *Grant Grill Lounge* (see *Hotels*),

Dobson's (see *Restaurants*) and *Frenchy Marseilles*, 801 C St ☎ 233-3413. *The Butcher Shop*, 5255 Kearny Villa Rd, Kearny Mesa ☎ 565-2272, which is also a restaurant, is a favorite with the aerospace and high-tech industry.

Entertainment

Good sources of information about current entertainment are *San Diego* magazine and the Sunday arts and the Friday weekend sections of the *San Diego Union*. For tickets, contact *Ticketron* ☎ 268-9686 or *Arts Tix* ☎ 238-3810 for half price, day-of-performance tickets.

Music and theater The *San Diego Opera* ☎ 236-6510 attracts top international artists. Performances are at the Civic Theater, *Convention and Performing Arts Center* ☎ 236-6510, which also hosts trade shows, ballets, plays, musicals and rock concerts. The *Old Globe Theater* is a replica of Shakespeare's Globe Playhouse ☎ 239-2255. The *Simon Edison Center for the Performing Arts* in Balboa Park ☎ 239-2255 includes the *Cassius Carter Center Stage*, the outdoor *Lowell Davis* and *Festival Stage*.

Nightclubs *Pal Joey's*, 5147 Waring Rd ☎ 286-7873, has Dixieland jazz.

Shopping

Downtown's open-air *Horton Plaza* has movie theaters, art galleries, restaurants, four major department stores and more than 150 shops. Designer boutiques, trendy eateries and art galleries line the streets of La Jolla near Girard Avenue and Prospect Street. *Bazaar del Mundo* and the *Galleria* in Old Town have shops selling everything from South American textiles to gaily painted Mexican pottery. *Seaport Village* is a bayside shopping and entertainments complex, also with restaurants.

Sightseeing

Balboa Park, covering more than 1,000 acres at the edge of downtown, contains the San Diego Zoo and most of the city's museums, including the important Museum of Art (with works by Rembrandt, Picasso and the Impressionists ☎ 232-3821), Natural History Museum ☎ 232-3821, the Reuben H Fleet Space Theater and Science Center and the Air Space Museum ☎ 234-8291.

Old Town Part of San Diego's original settlement can be visited in the Old Town State Historic Park. Guided 1hr tours leave daily at 2pm ☎ 237-6770.

Reuben H Fleet Space Theater and Science Center features astronomy displays, simulated space flight, and a giant screen OMNIMAX theater. *1875 El Prado ☎ 238-1233. Open Sun–Thu, 9.15–9.30; Fri–Sat, 9.15–10.30pm.*

San Diego Zoo One of the finest zoos in the world set in 125 acres of grounds. Tours by the Balboa Park bus (40mins) cover ground that would otherwise take a day to see. *Zoo Dr ☎ 234-3153.*

Guided tours

Boat tours *Harbor Excursion*, 1050 N Harbor Dr ☎ 233-6872, and *Invader Cruises*, 1202 Kettner Blvd ☎ 234-8687, operate daily cruises and popular whale-watching trips in winter.

Out of Town

Tijuana, an unattractive town, is just over the Mexican border in Baja California, 30mins south of the city. In addition to its ethnic shopping market, bullfights are a big draw.

Spectator Sports

Baseball The *San Diego Padres* ☎ 283-4494 play in San Diego Jack Murphy Stadium, 9449 Friars Rd.

Football The *Chargers* ☎ 280-2111 are at the San Diego Jack Murphy Stadium.

Horse-racing *Del Mar Racetrack* ☎ 755-1141 has thoroughbred racing late Jul–mid-Sep; closed Tue.

Keeping fit

Many hotels have fine sports facilities.

Beaches *La Jolla Cove* has the most

beautiful beach. *Coronado Beach* has excellent swimming.
Bicycling There are marked bike trails in Balboa Park and around Mission Bay. You can rent from *Bicycleville*, 740 10th St, Imperial Beach ☎ 424-5565.
Golf San Diego County has over 60 golf courses, of which *Torrey Pines Municipal*, 11480 N Torrey Pines Rd, La Jolla ☎ 453-8148, is the best of those open to the public.
Jogging Balboa Park has a marked course, and there is a popular run at E Mission Bay and Clairemont Dr.
Tennis The *Balboa Tennis Club* ☎ 295-4242 at the end of Texas St in Balboa Park, has public tennis courts. *North Park Recreation Center*, 4044 Idaho St ☎ 296-4747, has outdoor racquetball and tennis courts.

Local resources

Business services

Headquarters Co, 701 B St (Imperial Bank Tower) ☎ 231-0206, and *The Total Office*, 964 5th Ave ☎ 544-1433, offer full facilities.
Photocopying and printing *Sir Speedy*, 444 West C St ☎ 231-2799, and *PIP*, 923 6th Ave ☎ 239-2079.
Secretarial *Victor Temporary Services* ☎ 279-7310 and *A Personal Touch* ☎ 238-1623.
Translation *Berlitz Translation Services* ☎ 297-8392.

Communications

Long-distance delivery *Federal Express* ☎ 295-5545 and *DHL* ☎ 275-3890.
Local delivery *Ambassador Courier* ☎ 296-8501 and *Courier Express* ☎ 292-4668.
Post office Downtown office at 815 E St ☎ 232-5096; main office at 2535 Midway Dr ☎ 221-3310.
Telex and telegram *ITT Communications* ☎ (800) 922-0184 and *Western Union*, 941 Broadway ☎ 236-0777.

Convention/exhibition centers

San Diego Convention Center on Harbor Drive opened late 1989. *Convention and Performing Arts Center*, 202 C St 92101 ☎ 236-6500. For information contact *San Diego Convention and Visitors Bureau*, 1200 3rd Ave, Suite 824 ☎ 232-3101.

Emergencies

Currency exchange *Deak-Perera*, 177 Horton Plaza ☎ 235-0900. At 531 C St ☎ 232-1488, Mon–Fri, 9–5.
Hospitals Doctors on call: ☎ 275-2663. *Hillside Hospital*, 1940 El Cajon Blvd ☎ 297-2251, provides emergency dental treatment; cash payment required. During business hours, the *Dental Society Referral Service* ☎ 223-5391 helps locate dentists. *Mercy Hospital*, 4077 5th Ave ☎ 294-8111, and *UCSD Medical Center*, 225 Dickinson St ☎ 294-6222, for emergencies.
Pharmacies *Kaiser Hospital*, 4647 Zion Ave ☎ 584-5555, has a 24hr pharmacy. *Long's Drug Store*, Horton Pl, is open Mon–Fri, 7.30–11 (9.30pm, Mon); Sat, 9–11; Sun, 9–7.
Police 1401 Broadway ☎ 531-2000.

Government Offices

San Diego Government Information ☎ 236-5555; *US Dept of Commerce/International Trade Administration* ☎ 293-5395; *US Customs* ☎ 293-5360; *Immigration and Naturalization Services* ☎ 557-5570.

Information Sources

Business information The *Greater San Diego Chamber of Commerce*, 110 West C St, suite 1600 ☎ 232-0124.
Local Media The *San Diego Union* and *San Diego Tribune* are the best dailies for local news.
Visitor information *International Visitor Information Center*, 11 Horton Plaza ☎ 236-1212. The *Visitors Information Center*, 2688 E Mission Bay Dr ☎ 276-8200.

Thank-yous

Florists *Snyder's*, 825 4th Ave ☎ 233-0779, and *Broadway Florists*, 800 Broadway ☎ 239-1228.
Gift baskets *Westgate Gourmet Shop* at the Westgate Hotel ☎ 233-4475.

SAN FRANCISCO

Area Code ☏ 415

First settled by the Spanish in the 18th century, San Francisco was acquired by the United States in 1847. It was a major Pacific Coast port from the 1849 Gold Rush until the 1960s, when Oakland made a successful bid for the containerized shipping business. Today, San Francisco's economy is dependent largely on the $1bn brought to the area by tourists and business travelers; government and service industries are the largest employers. Several of the nation's biggest corporations have major offices or headquarters in the city; among these are Chevron, BankAmerica, Union Bank, Transamerica, Wells Fargo, McKesson, Levi Strauss, Potlatch and Shaklee. The Bay Area, which includes the cities of Oakland, Berkeley and Richmond and the Santa Clara (Silicon) Valley, is dotted with big corporations, such as Safeway Stores, Intel, Apple Computer, Clorox, and Advanced Micro Devices. Stanford University and the University of California at Berkeley are the region's major institutions of higher learning.

San Francisco is one of the most distinctive and appealing American cities. The natural beauty of its setting, overlooking San Francisco Bay and the Pacific; its temperate climate; and its relaxed, yet sophisticated, lifestyle attract millions of visitors annually, as well as many permanent settlers. Always a cosmopolitan city, it has the largest Chinese community outside Asia; in recent years many Hispanics, Filipinos and blacks have settled here. The city's large homosexual population is significant, both politically and economically.

Arriving

The Bay Area has three international airports – San Francisco, Oakland and San Jose – all within 1hr driving time of San Francisco. There is a helicopter connection between San Francisco International and Oakland International Airports; services operate Mon–Fri every 30–45mins, 6am–10pm; Sat and Sun, 9.20–7.30.

San Francisco International Airport

SFO's three terminals are connected by covered walkways, and it takes no more than 15–20mins to walk from one end to the other. A free inter-terminal shuttle service circles the upper level (6am–midnight every 5mins).

Domestic flights come into either the North Terminal – which has the airport's only restaurant, a video games room, a Christian Science reading room, and a Bank of America cash machine – or the South Terminal. Clearing Customs and Immigration at the International Terminal takes 30–60mins, sometimes longer. Citibank and Bank of America branches are open for foreign currency exchange 7am–11pm, and there is a 24hr Citibank cash machine on the lower level. An AT&T Communications Center includes a conference room with teleconferencing capability and a fax machine; you can make long-distance calls 8am–10pm. The staff is multilingual.

The airport has many bars and coffee shops; barber and shower facilities are available during regular business hours. Hotel information, bus schedules, limousine and car rental services are opposite baggage claim areas. Airport information ☏ 761-0800.

Nearby hotels *Clarion*, 401 E Millbrae Ave, Millbrae ☏ 692-6363 fax 697-8735. *Hilton Inn*, San Francisco Airport 94128 ☏ 589-0770 TX 172239 fax 489-4696. *Marriott*,

1800 Old Bayshore Hwy ☎ 692-9100 fax 692-8016. *Sheraton Inn*, 1177 Airport Blvd, Burlingame ☎ 342-9200 fax 342-9200 ext 1700. All take major credit cards.
City link There is no direct rail or subway connection to San Francisco, but the 16 miles/26kms can be driven in under 20mins – 40mins in the 6-9 morning peak period. All bus, van and taxi stands are on the lower level near baggage claim. Car rental parking lot and inter-terminal shuttles are on the upper, departure level.
Taxi The fare to downtown is about $25.
Limousine Try Executive Limousine Service ☎ 362-6550 or Armadillo Limousine ☎ 665-1234.
Car rental Parking in San Francisco is either difficult or expensive, and a car is unnecessary for appointments in the downtown or financial districts. If you must rent, try Alamo ☎ 347-9911 or Hertz ☎ 771-2200.
Bus Airporter buses leave every 20mins for five hotels downtown; fare about $6 ☎ 495-8404. SuperShuttle vans (maximum 7 passengers) deliver to any area in the city for $8; many hotels operate courtesy shuttle services. The Bay Area Rapid Transit (BART) subway system is also viable for East Bay destinations – look for a SamTrans bus No. 3B to get to the Daly City station.

Oakland International Airport

Oakland handles mainly local and domestic flights. Both terminal buildings have a bar and coffee shop; Terminal 1 has a cocktail lounge. Information ☎ 577-4000.
Nearby hotels *Hilton Inn*, 1 Hegenberger Rd, Oakland ☎ 635-5000 fax 635-0244. *Hyatt*, 455 Hegenberger Rd, Oakland ☎ 562-6100 TX 335374 fax 569-5681.
City link The airport is 18 miles/29kms from downtown via the Mimitz Freeway and the Bay Bridge. The drive should take no more than 25mins, 10am–3pm and after 9pm; add 30mins for the morning peak, 6–9am.
Taxi Yellow Cab ☎ 444-1234; Metro Yellow Taxi ☎ 444-4499. The fare to downtown is about $30.
Limousine Ambassador Limousine Service ☎ 881-0800.
Car rental See *San Francisco International Airport*.
Bus Oakland's limited bus service is not a serious option.
Subway During the day, the BART subway train is a quick alternative to driving – there is an Air BART shuttle connection to the Coliseum BART subway station (every 10mins, Mon–Sat, 6am–midnight; Sun, 9am–midnight.)

Getting around

The best strategy is to rent a car for out-of-town, but walk or use taxis and public transportation in town.
Walking The city center is compact, and walking is the best and most enjoyable way to get around, though it is often worthwhile to take a bus or cable car for a few blocks to avoid tramping up one of San Francisco's many hills. For longer distances, or in wet weather, take a taxi, bus or cable car.
Taxi You may not always be able to hail a taxi in the street; call ahead. Fares are about $3.00 for the first mile, $1.50 thereafter. *Yellow Cab* ☎ 626-2345, *Veteran's* ☎ 552-1300, *De Soto* ☎ 673-1414.
Limousine *Armadillo Limousine* ☎ 665-1234.
Driving San Francisco has a serious shortage of on-street parking spaces, especially in the downtown and financial districts by day and North Beach at night. However, its simple grid pattern is easy to follow, and despite the hills, the direct route is often the quickest. Elevated freeways connect North Beach and the financial district to the Bay Bridge and both peninsular freeways (Hwy 101, Interstate-280), but peak-hour traffic is heavy, and there are jams every weekday 4–7pm at the approaches to the Bay Bridge. Delays are frequently caused by accidents or, in winter, by heavy rainfall. Parking

HOTELS
- 6 Hyatt Regency
- 18 Park Hyatt

RESTAURANTS
- 1 Cadillac Bar
- 3 Chez Panisse
- 7 Ferry Plaza
- 8 Greens
- 9 Harris's
- 10 Hayes Street Grill
- 12 MacArthur Park
- 13 Mandarin
- 15 Max's Diner
- 17 Tadich Grill

BUILDINGS AND SIGHTS
- 1 Alcatraz Island
- 2 Asian Art Museum
- 6 City Hall
- 7 Coit Tower
- 8 Embarcadero Center
- 9 Federal Reserve Bank
- 10 Ferry Building
- 11 Ghirardelli Square
- 12 Hospital (Pacific)
- 13 Main Post Office
- 14 Maritime Museum
- 15 Moscone Convention Center
- 16 Musuem of Modern Art
- 17 Pier 39
- 18 Police
- 21 De Young Memorial Museum

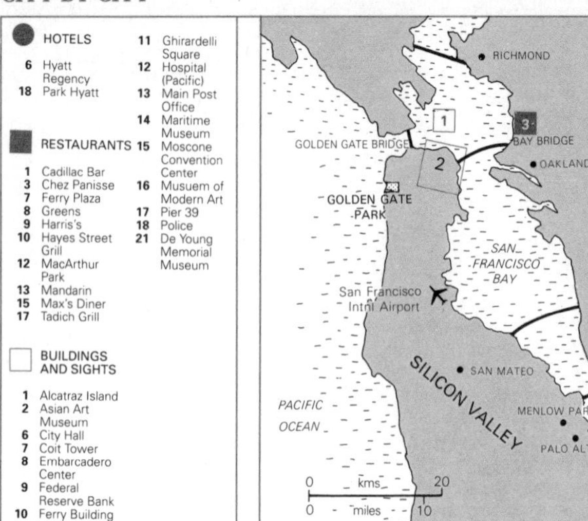

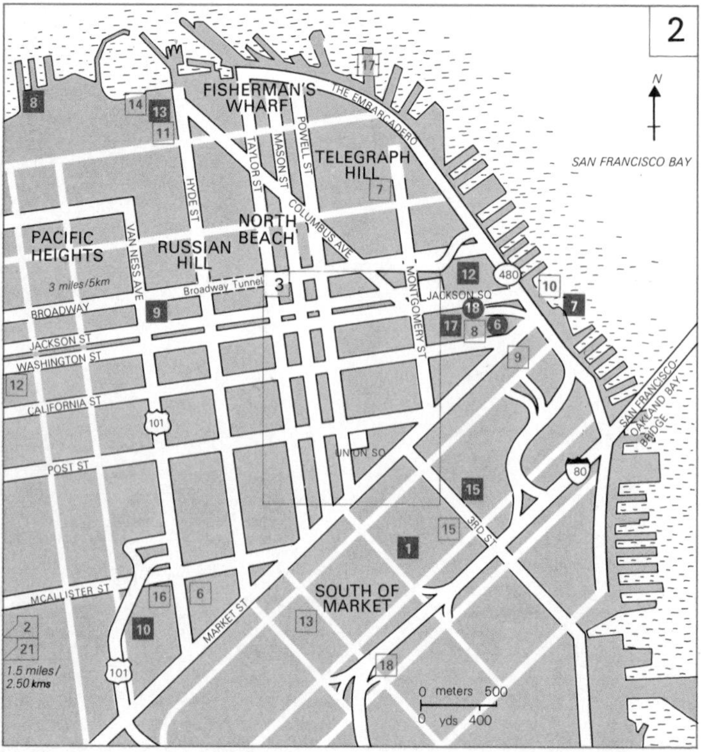

2
N
FISHERMAN'S WHARF
THE EMBARCADERO
TELEGRAPH HILL
SAN FRANCISCO BAY
TAYLOR ST
MASON ST
POWELL ST
HYDE ST
NORTH BEACH
COLUMBUS AVE
PACIFIC HEIGHTS
VAN NESS AVE
RUSSIAN HILL
3 miles/5km
Broadway Tunnel
MONTGOMERY ST
JACKSON SQ
480
BROADWAY
JACKSON ST
WASHINGTON ST
CALIFORNIA ST
101
SAN FRANCISCO-OAKLAND BAY BRIDGE
UNION SQ
POST ST
80
3RD ST
SOUTH OF MARKET
MCALLISTER ST
MARKET ST
1.5 miles/ 2.50 kms
0 meters 500
0 yds 400

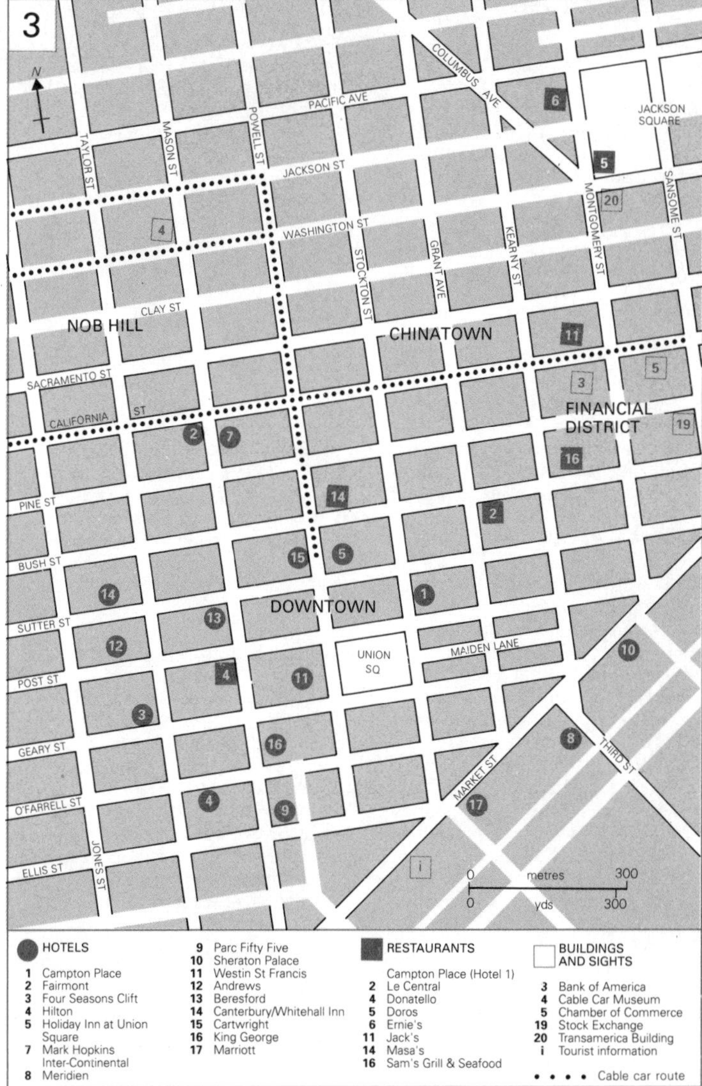

is expensive, but the following municipal garages are relatively cheap: *Civic Center Plaza* (enter on McAllister), *5th and Mission* (enter on 4th), *Portsmouth Square* (enter on Kearny, between Clay and Washington), *Sutter/Stockton* (enter on Bush), *Union Square* (enter on Post), and *Vallejo Street* (between Powell and Stockton).

Bus and cable car Cable cars operate between the financial district and the hotel area of Nob Hill. For advice on routes ☎ 673-6864. Bus services to

Marin, Alameda and San Mateo counties are operated by *Golden Gate Transit* ☎ 332-6600, AC *Transit* ☎ 839-2882 and *SamTrans* ☎ 761-7000 respectively. Each has its own bus stops, or you can board at the Transbay Terminal on Mission at 1st Street.

Subway The *Bay Area Rapid Transit* (BART) ☎ 788-2278 connects San Francisco to East Bay communities. It is practical, fast and uncrowded outside peak hours. Avoid empty cars and exits at night.

Rail A passenger train service connecting the peninsula cities between San Francisco and San Jose is run by *Caltrain* ☎ 557-8661. San Francisco terminus is at 4th and Townsend. It is advisable to call ahead to have a taxi meet your train.

Area by area

San Francisco's neighborhoods are neatly delineated and easily identified. Business and commerce are concentrated in the northeast corner, residential neighborhoods and suburbs to the west and south.

Financial district This area, a compact wedge between downtown and the Bay, extends from the Transamerica "pyramid," the tallest building in the city, to Market Street, with its easily identifiable high-rises. Montgomery Street is the district's historical center, and the 52-story Bank of America Building sits squarely at the intersection with California Street. The Embarcadero Center is at the bottom of California; the Stock Exchange is on Pine Street at Sansome; and the Federal Reserve Bank is on Market at Drumm.

Downtown San Francisco's main shops, hotels and theaters are downtown. Macy's, Neiman-Marcus, Saks, Nordstrom's and I Magnin's department stores surround Union Square; Sutter Street and Maiden Lane nearby have scores of galleries and boutiques.

"Jackson Square" There *is* no Jackson Square; the area is in fact a few city blocks of Gold Rush-era buildings preserved around Jackson at Sansome. The handsome brick warehouses, built before the 1906 earthquake, are now occupied by lawyers, advertising agencies, decorators and art dealers. A few blocks north, TV stations, advertising agencies and health clubs surround the all-brick offices of Levi Strauss at the foot of Telegraph Hill.

Chinatown Narrowly confined between the high-rises of the financial district and the slopes of Nob Hill, the densely populated residential and business area of Chinatown is a pedestrian corridor between downtown and North Beach and Fisherman's Wharf. It is customarily defined as lying within the eight blocks between Bush and Broadway, bounded by Kearny to the east and Powell to the west. Its Grant Avenue stores cater mainly to the tourist, but on Stockton Street the language, food and customs are authentically Chinese.

North Beach Most of the city's nightlife happens in North Beach's clubs, restaurants and cafés – many of them owned by descendants of the Italian immigrants who once dominated the area. Many architects and graphic designers have their offices here, and the area has a European café-society air by day. At night Broadway is a glittering array of contrasting neon signs advertising the entertainment and sex industry wares; but the street scene is good-natured and inoffensive.

South of Market Business concerns have begun to move in and upgrade this once low-rent district. It is the center for the city's photographic, printing and audio-visual businesses. Interior design, furnishing and gift trade showrooms occupy the renovated warehouses of Showplace Square; marine repair and shipping businesses operate from the piers and dry docks south of the Bay Bridge.

Other areas

The expensive houses and apartments on the north slopes of *Telegraph Hill*,

Nob Hill and *Russian Hill* have superb views of the Bay. *Pacific Heights* and *Presidio Heights* are considered the city's best addresses, despite the foggy summer weather. North of Lombard Street – "the crookedest street in the world" – the Mediterranean-style houses of the *Marina*, the only area to suffer much damage in the 1989 earthquake, face the Golden Gate Bridge, Alcatraz and the expensive yachts moored in St Francis Yacht Club. Across the Bay are the wooded hills of affluent *Marin County*, famous for its sybaritic, fashion-conscious lifestyle. The surroundings are bucolic, and the view of the city as one approaches the Golden Gate Bridge is striking: *Larkspur*, *Tiburon* and the charming former fishing village of *Sausalito* are convenient commuter areas. *East Bay* commuters have fine views of the city and the Golden Gate Bridge but the drawback of a long, slow journey into town. To the south of San Francisco, the *Pensinsula* cities line El Camino Real, the original Spanish road which linked the 18thC missions. Some commuters make the trip each working day from as far away (1hr drive) as *Atherton* and *Menlo Park*, on the northern edge of Silicon Valley.

Hotels

Most of the city's major business hotels are conveniently within a 10min walk of Union Square – but walking in the area near the Hilton, for example, is not recommended at night. Because of San Francisco's popularity as a tourist and convention center, its room rates are generally comparable to those of New York and Los Angeles, and hotels are often booked up a month or more in advance.

Campton Place [$]/////
340 Stockton St 94108 ☎ *781-5555*
[TX] *6771185 fax 955-8536 • AE DC MC V • 113 rooms, 10 suites, 1 restaurant, 1 bar*
A block from Union Square and two blocks from the financial district, this small, well-appointed hotel woos the discriminating traveler with tasteful furnishings, fine art, personalized "anything-is-possible-at-any-time" service and an award-winning restaurant of the same name (see *Restaurants*). Membership at San Francisco Tennis Club and Nob Hill Club • 2 meeting rooms.

Fairmont [$]/////
950 Mason St 94108 ☎ *772-5000*
[TX] *9103726002 fax 772-5086 • AE DC MC V • 540 rooms, 60 suites, 6 restaurants, 4 bars, 1 coffee shop*
This *grande dame* of San Francisco is familiar to TV viewers as the St Gregory of the *Hotel* series. A popular convention hotel, it is also a suitable choice for the individual business traveler. Hairdressers, shops, travel agency, bank • spa and fitness center • 19 meeting rooms, teleconferencing via the hotel's own satellite dish.

Four Seasons Clift [$]////
495 Geary St 94102 ☎ *775-4700*
[TX] *340647 fax 441-4621 • AE DC MC V • 304 rooms, 25 suites, 1 restaurant, 1 bar*
After a $5.5m refurbishment, the classically stylish, 15-story Clift is fast becoming the most fashionable place to stay in San Francisco. Spacious rooms, excellent service, a fine French restaurant (with an alternative low-calorie, low-cholesterol menu) and the civilized Redwood Room bar are among its attractions. There are seven floors set aside for nonsmokers. Arrangement with nearby health club • 8 meeting rooms, computer modems, translation, teleconferencing.

Hilton [$]////
One Hilton Sq 94102 ☎ *771-1400*
[TX] *176180 fax 771-6807 • AE DC MC V • 1,911 rooms, 393 suites,*

4 restaurants, 2 bars, 1 coffee shop
Close to the financial, theater and shopping districts, this is a major convention hotel. Concierge level with separate registration. One of the restaurants, Kiku of Tokyo, offers traditional Japanese dishes. Heated outdoor pool, fitness center • 64 meeting rooms with supporting clerical services.

Holiday Inn at Union Square [$]//
480 Sutter 94108 ☎ 398-8900
[TX] 9103722009 fax 989-8823 •
AE DC MC V • 400 rooms, 51 suites, 1 restaurant, 1 bar
One of the more luxurious Holiday Inns, this is only one block from Union Square and three blocks from the financial district. The bells of passing cable cars make the lower rooms on Powell Street noisy. Nonsmoking rooms • 9 meeting rooms.

Hyatt Regency [$]////
5 Embarcadero Center 94111
☎ 788-1234 [TX] 9103721018
fax 989-7448 • AE DC MC V • 711 rooms, 44 suites, 2 restaurants, 3 bars, 1 coffee shop
This modern hotel is the focal point of the Embarcadero Center business and shopping complex, at the edge of the financial district. The 20-story atrium lobby is filled with plants, trees, cafés and shops; the revolving rooftop bar and restaurant are good for conversation over a drink or meal. The two Regency Club floors, each with its own concierge, provide the business traveler with office facilities and luxury accommodation. Hairdresser, florist, shops • jogging and exercise courses • 35 meeting rooms.

Mark Hopkins Inter-Continental [$]///
1 Nob Hill 94108 ☎ 392-3434
[TX] 340809 fax 421-3302 • AE DC MC V • 393 rooms, 29 suites, 2 restaurants, 2 bars, 1 coffee shop.
The Mark has long been one of San Francisco's most renowned hotels, and its top-floor bar is particularly popular with business people and well-heeled tourists. Less extravagant than its Nob Hill neighbor, the Fairmont, the Mark has an air of quiet refinement. The cable car to the financial district stops outside the front door. Hairdressers, gift shops, drugstore • membership at Nob Hill Club • business service center, 14 meeting rooms.

Meridien [$]///
50 3rd St 94103 ☎ 974-6400
[TX] 176910 fax 543-8268 • AE DC MC V • 585 rooms, 26 suites, 2 restaurants, 2 bars
Two blocks from Union Square and one from the Moscone Center, the Meridien caters mainly for business visitors. The restaurant menu is excellent. Membership at SF Tennis Club • 8 meeting rooms.

Parc Fifty Five [$]//
55 Cyril Magnin St 94102 ☎ 392-8000
[TX] 755982 fax 543-8268 • AE DC MC V • 886 rooms, 90 club rooms, 39 suites, 2 restaurants, 2 bars
Opened in 1984 as the Ramada Renaissance, the 32-story Parc Fifty Five has more than $1m worth of art throughout its public areas. Unfortunately it is on the edge of the sleazy Tenderloin district, where walking during the day is not enjoyable and at night quite unnerving. Gift shops • health club, membership at SF Tennis Club • 20 meeting rooms.

Sheraton Palace [$]//
2 New Montgomery St 94105
☎ 392-8600 [TX] 4977003 fax 543-0671 • AE DC MC V • 545 rooms, 20 suites, 2 restaurants, 2 bars, 1 coffee shop
The 100-year-old Victorian-style Sheraton, at the bottom of Montgomery Street at Market, caters mainly for business travelers, who appreciate the larger-than-average rooms, the high ceilings and the proximity to the financial district and Moscone Center. The Palace was once the favorite of presidents and leading

stars, such as the legendary Sarah Bernhardt. Major renovation is planned for completion in the mid-1990s. Shops, hairdressers • health clubs • business center with 23 meeting rooms.

Westin St Francis [$]////
335 Powell St 94102 ☎ *397-7000* [TX] *278584 fax 774-0124* • AE DC MC V • *1,125 rooms, 75 suites, 4 restaurants, 5 bars, 1 coffee shop*
Statesmen, politicians, literary lions and other celebrities stay at the St Francis, a quick three-block walk from the financial district and across the street from Union Square. Gift shops, hairdressers, ticket agency, airport transport • fitness center • 24 meeting rooms.

OTHER HOTELS

Andrews [$]// *624 Post St 94109* ☎ *563-6877 fax 928-6919* • AE MC V. Small, modern hotel two blocks from Union Square. Award-winning restaurant features American cuisine.

Beresford [$] *635 Sutter St 94102* ☎ *673-9900* [TX] *176088 fax 474-0449* • AE DC MC V. European-style hotel with small but comfortable rooms.

Canterbury/Whitehall Inn [$]// *750 Sutter St 94109* ☎ *474-6464 fax 474-5856* • AE DC MC V. Lots of antiques and an English decor, including a pub-style lounge.

Cartwright [$]// *524 Sutter St 94102* ☎ *421-2865* [TX] *176579 fax 421-2865* • AE DC MC V. The rooms are small, but attractive, and the hotel has a loyal business clientele.

King George [$]// *334 Mason St 94102* ☎ *781-5050 fax 391-6976* • AE DC MC V. The European atmosphere attracts many overseas visitors.

Marriott [$]/// *785 Market St 94103* ☎ *896-1600 fax 777-2799* • AE DC MC V. Vast new downtown hotel near Moscone Convention Center, with convention facilities, health club and pool.

Park Hyatt [$]//// *Embarcadero Center, 333 Battery St 94111* ☎ *392-1234 fax 421-2433* • AE DC MC V. Smaller and less impersonal than the Hyatt Regency but in the same complex and geared to the requirements of business travelers.

Clubs

The *Bohemian Club* ☎ 885-2440 is one of San Francisco's most exclusive establishments and was once the haunt of literary and theatrical figures – today it is oriented more to the conservative senior businessman and politician. The *Commonwealth Club* has more than 15,000 members, most of them lawyers, accountants and business people interested in current affairs. The club holds informative luncheon meetings every Friday to which visitors are welcomed; for information ☎ 543-3354. The *Press Club*, which now admits women, takes its members mainly from public relations and the press. *St Francis Yacht Club* ☎ 563-6363 is the city's quintessential business/social club.

Restaurants

San Franciscans eat out a lot, and restaurants come and go almost as quickly as the fog. But in this food- and fashion-conscious city there are restaurants that have survived the test of time. Many are relaxed, in West Coast style; some are indisputably "establishment," all meet the sophisticated standards of cuisine that locals consider a hallmark of the city. Note that most stop seating patrons by 10–10.30.

Cadillac Bar [$]//
1 Holland Court ☎ *543-8226* • AE DC MC V

A short walk from downtown and a block from Moscone Center, this popular luncheon spot is also open for dinner and features mesquite-grilled seafood, Mexican dishes and loud music. A very noisy, but entertaining experience. Long, well-stocked stand-up bar, and a large after-work business crowd.

Campton Place $////

Campton Place Hotel ☎ 781-5155 • AE DC MC V • jacket and tie requested
A comfortable, sophisticated restaurant offering imaginative, award-winning American food, served with considerable style. Breakfast is available daily.

Le Central $/

453 Bush St ☎ 391-2233 • closed Sun • AE MC V
This Parisian-style bistro/brasserie is still a favorite of local politicians, corporate executives and media personalities, though it has lost some of its ultra-fashionable status. Closely spaced tables discourage confidential business discussions.

Chez Panisse $///

1517 Shattuck Ave ☎ 548-5525 • closed L, Sun & Mon • AE DC MC V
With a menu that changes daily, Alice Waters has attracted diners who appreciate French and Californian cooking to this restaurant in Berkeley. Less formal and less expensive café upstairs.

Donatello $///

Donatello Hotel, 501 Post St ☎ 441-7182 • closed L Sat, Sun • AE DC MC V
A favorite with senior business people. The classic Italianate surroundings may be too imposing for a casual business lunch but just right if a high-stakes business transaction is pending. Excellent northern Italian cuisine expertly prepared and served.

Doros $///

714 Montgomery St ☎ 397-6822 • closed Sat L, Sun • AE DC MC V
This award-winning restaurant serves excellent Continental cuisine. It is a popular haunt of advertising and media types, and its quiet atmosphere is very suitable for business conversations.

Ernie's $///

847 Montgomery St ☎ 397-5969 • D only • AE DC MC V • jacket and tie
This red-plush, early Victorian restaurant specializes in French cuisine and has one of the best wine lists in the city. Formal yet pleasant service and exceptionally good food attract a loyal clientele, many of them from the financial district.

Ferry Plaza $//

1 Ferry Plaza, behind the south end of Ferry Building ☎ 391-8403 • closed Sun–Tue D, Sat L • AE DC MC V
A superb view of San Francisco Bay is a feature of this spacious restaurant, which attracts a large business clientele. Champagne brunch on Sunday.

Greens $//

Building A of Fort Mason Center ☎ 771-6222 • closed Sun D, Mon • no credit cards
With a good view of the Golden Gate Bridge, Greens sits on a pier in the Bay and serves fresh and imaginative vegetarian meals to a good mix of local residents and visitors, including many non-vegetarians. It is popular with businesswomen at lunch time, although it is a 10min drive from downtown, but has abundant free parking.

Harris's $//

2100 Van Ness Ave ☎ 673-1888 • closed L Sat & Sun • AE MC V • jackets
This is San Francisco's best place for a steak dinner with all the trimmings. Aged beef is perfectly cooked and expertly served in a comfortable old-style San Francisco dining room. Private dining rooms are available for groups.

Hayes Street Grill $/

320 Hayes ☎ 863-5545 • closed Sat L, Sun • MC V

Located in the Civic Center area, this fine, reliable seafood restaurant attracts a loyal crowd of city and government employees and politicians during the day and opera, symphony, and ballet-goers at night. However, the tables are too close together for really private conversation.

Jack's [$]//

615 Sacramento St ☎ 421-7355 • closed L Sat & Sun • AE • jacket and tie

Established in 1864, this financial district institution specializes in French/Continental cuisine and caters largely to a business luncheon clientele. A place that is "famous because it is famous," it tends to offer better service to steady customers than to newcomers, so accept an invitation from a regular, but look elsewhere if you are the host. Close seating makes conversation difficult, but private rooms are available.

MacArthur Park [$]//

607 Front St ☎ 398-5700 • closed Sat L • AE MC V

California game and tasty barbecued ribs are the house specialties. Good local wines, an oakwood smoker and mesquite grill add up to a better-than-average California-style meal at a reasonable price. The bar is popular with the financial district crowd, especially right after work.

Mandarin [$]///

900 North Point in Ghirardelli Sq ☎ 673-8812 • AE DC MC V

With an extensive variety of northern Chinese specialties, beautifully prepared and served amid Oriental antiques and museum-quality art, this is an impressive place to entertain a client. It has great views of the Bay, and its outstanding service has earned it a fine local reputation as one of the best Chinese restaurants in a town noted for them.

Masa's [$]////

648 Bush St ☎ 989-7154 • closed L Sun & Mon • AE DC MC V • jacket requested • reservations advisable

The fine French *haute cuisine*, beautifully presented and served, is a San Francisco delight, but you must reserve early: three weeks ahead for a weekend, 1–3 days during the week. One of the few restaurants offering a traditional French cheese course. To enjoy it at room temperature, ask to have it set out when you order your entrée, since local health laws dictate that all dairy products be kept refrigerated.

Max's Diner [$]

311 3rd St ☎ 546-6297 • AE MC V • no reservations

Huge quantities of the type of home-cooked food that much of America grew up on – meatloaf, mashed potatoes, roast turkey with stuffing and gravy – are served here very efficiently at very reasonable prices. Its nostalgic 1950s decor is complemented by the sound of jukebox "golden oldies." Breakfast is served from 7.30 during the week.

Sam's Grill and Seafood [$]//

374 Bush St ☎ 421-0594 • closed Sat, Sun, holidays • MC V

Financial district workers appreciate the ample portions, reasonable prices and good, no-nonsense service here. It has been a favorite luncheon spot since 1867. Similar to the Tadich Grill in style and appeal – with polished wood and private rooms. It closes at 8.30.

Tadich Grill [$]//

240 California St ☎ 391-2373 • closed Sat & Sun • no credit cards • no reservations

The granddaddy of business lunch restaurants, Tadich Grill is the oldest restaurant in California – it was established in the legendary year of 1849, the year of the Gold Rush. Its varied menu features charcoal-broiled fresh seafood, steaks and chicken. The huge counter bar – where you can eat if you are in a hurry – makes the wait bearable. It closes at 9.

SILICON VALLEY

Silicon Valley – real name, Santa Clara Valley – stretches about 50 miles/80kms from the quiet and intellectual community of Palo Alto, home of Stanford University, 25 miles/40kms south of San Francisco, to San Jose, 30 miles/48kms farther. It was here that the silicon chip was developed – and multiplied. Today, what was once a quiet farming community of almond and orange groves is now the home of more than 3,000 electronics companies.

Arriving

From San Francisco International Airport it is 30mins by car to Palo Alto and 40–50mins to San Jose. Follow the signposts south on Highway 101 to San Jose; or the Interstate 280. *Helicopters Unlimited* ☎ (415) 632-9422; or you can fly to the busy San Jose International Airport. Car rental is a must: *Hertz* ☎ (408) 297-9495, *Avis* ☎ (408) 993-2224, *Budget* ☎ (408) 288-8800.

Nearby hotels *Holiday Inn Airport*, 1355 N 4th St ☎ (800) 453-5340. *Hyatt San Jose*, 1740 N 1st St ☎ (800) 993-1234 TX 357408. *Le Baron*, 1350 N 1st St ☎ (408) 288-9200. All are in San Jose.

Hotels

Most of the Valley's hotels are in San Jose or Palo Alto, convenient for Sunnyvale, Cupertino, Santa Clara and Mountain View. All are geared to business needs.

Hyatt Palo Alto [$]/
4290 El Camino Real, Palo Alto 94306 ☎ (415) 493-0800 TX 334477 fax (415) 493-5877 • AE DC MC V • 200 rooms, 1 restaurant, 1 bar

Across the street from the Hyatt Rickey's, with slightly less expensive and less luxurious accommodation. The Echo restaurant is informal Italian, and Tempo's bar is popular for after-work drinks. Exercise room, pool, tennis.

Hyatt Rickey's [$]///
4219 El Camino Real, Palo Alto 94306 ☎ (415) 493-8000 TX 334477 fax (415) 424-0836 • AE DC MC V • 350 rooms, 1 restaurant, 1 bar

The better of the two Hyatts, Rickey's is *the* choice of regular Valley visitors. Sprawling across 22 acres of ponds, pools, a croquet lawn, putting green and cabanas, it has Californian charm. The rooms are de luxe, the conference facilities comprehensive. Both J Patrick's bar and Hugo's restaurant are popular meeting places. Exercise room, pool, tennis.

Red Lion Hotel [$]//
2050 Gateway Plaza, San Jose 95110 ☎ (408) 453-4000 fax (408) 437-9507 • AE DC MC V • 515 rooms, 10 suites, 1 restaurant, 1 coffee shop, 1 bar

Beside San Jose Airport, well-appointed and a good business address, the Red Lion offers standard rooms and adequate restaurants. Pool, health club, disco • 20 meeting rooms.

Stanford Park Hotel [$]///
100 El Camino Real, Menlo Park 94025 ☎ (415) 322-1234 fax (415) 322-0975 • AE DC MC V • 164 rooms, 12 suites, 1 restaurant, 1 bar

This smart hotel near Stanford University is popular for business presentations. Service is quiet and efficient. Each room is decorated in quasi-New England style with exposed wood. The lobby bar is a comfortable meeting area with unobtrusive piano entertainment. Pool, health club • 3 meeting rooms.

Restaurants

Good eating places tend to be very crowded and the food may not compensate for the long wait. For a special occasion San Francisco is only 45mins by car, but some of Silicon Valley's restaurants are worth trying.

Lion and Compass $//
1023 N Fair Oaks Ave off Hwy 101, Sunnyvale
☎ (408) 745-1260 • closed L Sat & Sun • AE DC MC V
The pride of Silicon Valley, patronized by senior executives. A tickertape service keeps the busy entrepreneur in touch with his investment portfolio over a glass of good California wine.

MacArthur Park $/
27 University Ave, Palo Alto
☎ (415) 321-9990 • closed Sat L • AE MC V • casual
A favorite of the local business community for lunch, drinks and dinner, this noisy restaurant is always buzzing. The large vaulted room used to be a part of the Palo Alto railroad station, but its computerized order-entry system puts it clearly in today's Silicon Valley; waiters and waitresses carry handheld computers. The atmosphere is jovial and relaxed; private rooms are available.

Le Mouton Noir $//
14560 Big Basin Way, Rte 9, Saratoga ☎ (408) 867-7017 • closed L, Sun • AE MC V
A French country-style restaurant with an unassuming but charming atmosphere. The menu changes frequently, and the wine list is comprehensive. Reserve a week in advance.

Plumed Horse $///
Rte 9, Saratoga
☎ (408) 867-4711 • closed L, Sun • AE MC V • no jeans
Often crowded, so reserve a day in advance. The cuisine is Continental, and the wine list includes good California labels.

Relaxation and resources

Business information *San Jose Convention and Visitors Bureau*, 333 W San Carlos St, Suite 1000, 95110 ☎ (408) 295-9600.
Business services Available from *Adams Joyce Secretarial Service* ☎ (415) 854-6800, in Menlo Park, and *Letter Shop*, 1573 Samedra, Sunnyvale ☎ (408) 275-1667.
Keeping fit *Decathlon Club*, 3250 Central Expressway, Santa Clara ☎ (408) 738-8743; most companies have a membership policy.
Long-distance delivery *Federal Express* ☎ (415) 877-9000 or *Purolator Courier* ☎ (800) 645-3333.
Local delivery *Ultra Express* ☎ (800) 858-7299; *US Courier* ☎ (415) 495-0200.
Photocopying and printing *Copy Shop*, 581 University Ave, Palo Alto ☎ (415) 328-1272; *Kinko's*, 299 California, Palo Alto ☎ (415) 328-3381, and 1285 El Camino Real, Menlo Park ☎ (415) 321-4202.
Secretarial *Adia Personnel Services* Sunnyvale ☎ (408) 733-2882 has offices throughout Silicon Valley. *Kelly Services*, Palo Alto ☎ (415) 852-9922.
Translation *Berlitz Translation*, Palo Alto ☎ (415) 323 0076; *Japanese Linguistic Service*, Redwood City ☎ (415) 321-9832.

For the meanings of hotel and restaurant price symbols, see page 7.

Bars

Bars play an important role in San Francisco's business life; and there is a wide variety of establishments from which to choose. For example, there are the young professionals' bars near Union Street, such as *Perry's* and *Balboa Café*; the conservative hotel bars downtown, such as *One-Up Lounge* at the Hyatt on Union Square and *S Holmes Esq Public House* at the Holiday Inn at Union Square; the gay-oriented bars and dance clubs south of Market Street around Folsom Street, such as *The Stud Bar* and *Febe's*; the after-business bar/restaurants in the financial district and the Embarcadero Center, such as *The Royal Exchange* and *Harrington's*; the noisy and colorful neighborhood bars in North Beach, such as *The Savoy-Tivoli* and *The Adler Museum* ('Specs"); and the racier places on Broadway, such as *The Condor*. *Washington Square Bar and Grill*, 1707 Powell St ☎ 982-8123, is a popular spot in North Beach for media personalities and politicians; it also serves fine Italian food.

The *Carnelian Room*, 345 Montgomery, is perched on top of the Bank of America Building, 52 stories above the financial district; its recessed bay-window table seating provides a spectacular view and a measure of privacy. Expensive, but impressive. The *Cirque Room* at the Fairmont, 950 Mason St, serves cocktails, California wines and specialty coffee drinks in a splendid Art Deco lobby-level lounge. Perfect for afternoon tea or a quiet, early evening drink away from the crowds; the piano player's arrival at 9.30pm makes conversation difficult. The *Compass Rose*, in the Westin St Francis, is an attractive, fairly large bar which also serves a light lunch until 2.30, Mon–Sat. *Equinox*, in the Hyatt Regency, 5 Embarcadero Center, is San Francisco's only revolving rooftop lounge where you can overlook the Bay. The seating is designed for one-to-one conversations.

Businesswomen from the financial district frequent the civilized *London Wine Bar*, 415 Sansome St, which serves excellent local wines by the glass and fine light lunches. A good place to relax and enjoy great Dixieland jazz on the waterfront is the *Pier 23 Café*, Pier 23 at The Embarcadero. The *Buena Vista*, 2765 Hyde St, at Fisherman's Wharf, claims to have invented Irish coffee.

One of the most relaxing and elegant bars in the city, the *Redwood Room* in the Four Seasons Clift, 495 Geary St, is a classic Art Deco cocktail lounge with original carved redwood panels and stylish light fixtures. At the top of Nob Hill, the famous *Top of the Mark*, in the Mark Hopkins Hotel, was the world's first "skyroom" with a stunning panoramic view of the whole of San Francisco and the Bay Area.

Entertainment

The "anything goes" spirit of the Barbary Coast which attracted Gold Rush miners, sailors and settlers a century ago still pervades today's "Baghdad-by-the-Bay." The greatest concentration of nightlife is in the North Beach/Broadway district, but nightclubs, discos and live music/dance clubs can be found in almost every section of the city. Yet San Francisco is not an all-night, nonstop town. Most restaurants stop seating guests at 10-10.30 and close by midnight. Last call is 1.30, and there are few after-hours clubs; those that do stay open stop serving alcohol at 2. A recording of entertainment highlights is available 24hrs from the Convention and Visitors Bureau – English ☎ 391-2001, French ☎ 391-2003, German ☎ 391-2004, Japanese ☎ 391-2101 and Spanish ☎ 391-2122.

Ticket agencies Both BASS ☎ 262-2277 (tickets) or 835-3849 (recorded information) and *Ticketron*

☎ 546-7400 handle tickets for sport, theater and concert events. *STBS*, on Stockton St downtown ☎ 433-7827, provides half-price unsold tickets for day-of-performance events as well as a full range of ticket services, for a small charge.

Theater and ballet San Francisco has a rich theatrical tradition which is continued today by highly regarded repertory companies such as the American Conservatory Theater (*ACT*) company at the *Geary Theater*, 415 Geary St ☎ 673-6440, the *Curran Theater*, 445 Geary St ☎ 673-4400, the *Golden Gate Theater*, 25 Taylor St ☎ 474-3800, and the *Orpheum*, 1192 Market St ☎ 474-3800. "*Beach Blanket Babylon*" at *Club Fugazi*, 678 Green St ☎ 421-4222, is a cabaret-style production – no minors except on Sunday afternoon. The San Francisco Ballet, the oldest in the country, is at the *War Memorial Opera House*, Van Ness Ave and Grove St ☎ 621-3838.

Music Tickets for the *San Francisco Symphony Orchestra*, Davies Hall, Van Ness Ave at Grove St ☎ 431-5400, are often available in front of Davies Hall for subscription series performances on the day. The opera season extends from September to December and features one of the world's finest companies performing at the War Memorial Opera House, Van Ness Ave and Grove St ☎ 621-6600.

Nightclubs The *Venetian Room* at the Fairmont Hotel ☎ 772-5163 and the *Plush Room* at the York Hotel, 940 Sutter St ☎ 885-6800, are two good places to hear top-name entertainers perform in an intimate, supper club/cabaret atmosphere. Comedy clubs are a San Francisco specialty, and one of the best is the *Punch Line*, above 445 Battery Street ☎ 397-7573, which features top local and national talent. *Finocchio's*, 506 Broadway ☎ 982-9388, is world famous for its 14 female impersonators. Top local and international jazz musicians perform at *Kimball's* Restaurant, 300 Grove St ☎ 861-5555.

Shopping

San Francisco's main shopping district, *Union Square*, has major department stores such as *Macy's*, Stockton at O'Farrell, and *Saks Fifth Avenue*, 384 Post. Art galleries line both sides of Sutter Street; *Gumps*, 250 Post Street ☎ 982-1616, is world famous for its jade and high-quality contemporary wares; *Shreve & Co*, Post at Grant ☎ 421-2600, has fine jewelry and a courteous, knowledgeable staff; *Brooks Brothers*, 201 Post ☎ 397-4500, is a must for high-quality, classic men's clothing; stylish, beautifully tailored and expensive designer clothes can be found at *Wilkes Bashford*, 375 Sutter ☎ 986-4380. On the other side of the financial district, the four-building office/shopping complex *Embarcadero Center* has more than 175 retail shops, restaurants and art galleries. Farther down the Embarcadero is *Pier 39*, a collection of more than 130 specialty shops and restaurants only two blocks east of Fisherman's Wharf. Just west of the Wharf are three more main shopping complexes: *The Cannery*, *The Anchorage* and *Ghirardelli Square* (pronounced *Gear*-ar-delly).

Sightseeing

No sightseeing tour of San Francisco is complete without experiencing the city's historic cable cars, renovated in 1982. Cars operate 6am–1pm daily.

Alcatraz Island A mile and a half/2.4kms from Fisherman's Wharf, Alcatraz sits in the middle of San Francisco Bay and was once a federal prison. Excellent tours of the island, conducted by National Park Service rangers, afford views of the city and the Golden Gate Bridge. Make sure to wear a warm coat, since it is always cold on the Bay.

Asian Art Museum The exhibits here include the priceless Avery Brundage collection of Oriental antiquities. *Golden Gate Park ☎ 668-8921. Closed Mon & Tue.*

California Palace of the Legion of Honor Art museum with 16th–20thC paintings, prints and sculpture.

Rodin's *The Thinker* collection is at the entrance. *Lincoln Park ☏ 750-3614. Closed Mon and Tue.*

Chinatown A walk along Grant Avenue between Bush Street and Columbus Avenue introduces the visitor to the most famous and colorful of San Francisco's ethnic neighborhoods. Separating the financial district from North Beach, Chinatown offers a fascinating mix of exotic shops, restaurants, food markets, temples, museums and businesses. The steadily growing community is spreading north into North Beach, buying up old-established buildings and businesses and extending the Chinese culture into a predominately Italian neighborhood.

Coit Tower Shaped like a fire hose nozzle, this cylindrical tower stands atop Telegraph Hill and was built in 1933 as a monument to San Francisco's volunteer firemen. An observation platform at the top provides an excellent view of the city and the North Bay. *North Beach. Open 9–4.30; Mar–Sep, 10–5.30.*

Fisherman's Wharf Though it ranks as San Francisco's most popular attraction, the Wharf is a mere shadow of its former self and is more a tourist trap than a working fishing community. Excellent year-round 75min sightseeing boat tours leave from Pier 39 (*Blue and Gold Fleet* ☏ 781-7877) and Pier 41 (*Red and White Fleet ☏ 456-2800*.

Golden Gate Bridge San Francisco's most famous Art Deco landmark was completed in 1937. Measuring 6,450ft across, the bridge is the world's second largest suspended structure. Pedestrians and cyclists can cross free and enjoy an inspiring, if somewhat chilly, view of the Pacific Ocean on one side and San Francisco on the other.

Golden Gate Park Once a wasteland of sand dunes, these 1,017 acres/4.1sq kms are now the world's largest man-made park. Within its boundaries are the Steinhart Aquarium, Morrison Planetarium, California Academy of Sciences, MH de Young Memorial Museum, Asian Art Museum, Japanese Tea Garden, Conservatory of Flowers, Strybing Arboretum and Botanical Gardens, and the Chinese Pavilion. *Between Fulton St and Lincoln Way.*

MH de Young Memorial Museum contains collections of European and American art. *Golden Gate Park ☏ 750-3614. Closed Mon and Tue.*

Museum of Modern Art This collection includes works by many major artists, such as Klee, Calder and Matisse, as well as a fine collection of photographs. *War Memorial Bldg, Civic Center ☏ 863-8800. Closed Mon.*

Guided tours

Boat tours *Hornblower Yachts* ☏434-0300 offer regular dinner, lunch and brunch cruises in San Francisco Bay, from Pier 33 on the Embarcadero.

Bus tours *Agentours* ☏ 661-5200 has daily 4hr narrated tours in several languages. *American Express* ☏ 981-6293 has daily narrated tours including an 8hr tour of the wine country. Twelve tour plans are available from *Gray Line* ☏ 896-1515; they provide free pick-up and return to downtown hotels.

Limousine tours *Armadillo Limousine* ☏ 665-1234 offers personal – and expensive – tours of San Francisco and the wine country. Limos are equipped with telephones for travelers who need to combine business with pleasure.

Out of town

The Wine Country Located 44 miles/71kms north of San Francisco, the vineyards of Napa and Sonoma counties comprise one of the best wine-growing regions of the world. Most wineries are geared to visitors, and many include restaurants and even accommodation.

Spectator sports

Baseball The *San Francisco Giants* play at Candlestick Park, 8 miles/

13kms south of the city off the Bayshore Freeway ☏ 467-8000. Downtown box office: 170 Grant Ave ☏ 982-9400. The *Oakland Athletics* are at Oakland Coliseum, across the Bay – a subway ride from the financial district – ☏ 638-0500. Tickets are also available in San Francisco through BASS ticket agency ☏ 762-2277.
Football The *49ers* are three-time champions in recent years and are *the* hottest sports ticket in town. They kick off at Candlestick Park; box office ☏ 468-2249.
Horse-racing *Bay Meadows Racecourse*, off Hwy 101, 20 miles/32kms south of San Francisco ☏ 574-7223, has thoroughbred racing, Friday evening racing and quarter horse racing. *Golden Gate Fields*, PO Box 6027, Albany ☏ 526-3020, across the San Francisco-Oakland Bay Bridge, 12 miles/19kms from downtown San Francisco, has thoroughbred racing.

Keeping fit

Many hotels provide free temporary membership at various health and tennis clubs with reasonable day rates. Among these clubs are *Physis*, 1 Post St ☏ 989-7310, the *San Francisco Tennis Club*, 5th and Brannan St ☏ 777-9000, the *Nob Hill Club*, at 950 California ☏ 397-2770, and *Symmetry*, 1 Market Plaza ☏ 495-3434.
Bicycling Most of the city's bike rental shops are located on Stanyan St at the east end of Golden Gate Park.
Golf The city has four public golf courses: the 9-hole, par 27 "pitch and putt" course in *Golden Gate Park* ☏ 751-8987; the 9-hole, par 27 *Fleming Course* ☏ 664-4690 in Harding Park; an 18-hole, par 72 course, and a 9-hole, par 32 course also in *Harding Park* ☏ 661-1865; and *Lincoln Park Course* ☏ 221-9911, which offers 18 holes, a par 68, some fairly rough greens and magnificent views of the Pacific Ocean and the Golden Gate Bridge.
Tennis *The SF Park Dept* ☏ 558-4532 maintains over 100 free tennis courts throughout the city. The Campton Place, the Meridien and the Parc Fifty Five Hotels have arrangements with the San Francisco Tennis Club (see *Hotels*).

Local resources

Business Services

Complete business services can be provided on short notice by *Adia Personnel Services*, 44 Montgomery St, Suite 1250 ☏ 434-3810, which has 16 offices in the Bay Area; *Kelly Services*, 1 Post St, Suite 2150 ☏ 982-2200; and *Office Overload*, 44 Montgomery St, Suite 860 ☏ 896-0345.
Photocopying and printing The *Copy Factory*, 1 California St ☏ 781-2990, caters to convention and business persons' needs and is open 24hrs Mon–Fri and 9–5.30 on weekends. *Postal Instant Press* (*PIP*) has several locations downtown, including 44 Montgomery ☏ 421-7703 and 35 Taylor ☏ 441-1844.
Translation *Berlitz Translation Services*, 660 Market St, 4th floor ☏ 986-0233; the *International Translation Center*, 1550 California St, Suite 1 ☏ 771-3411, can translate from and into 55 languages.

Communications

Long-distance delivery For overnight delivery of documents and packages under 150lbs to all states, *Federal Express* ☏ 877-9000. For international delivery, *Emery Worldwide* ☏ 877-1833 or *DHL Worldwide Express* ☏ 345-9400. The *US Postal Service* ☏ 550-5240 offers express mail of up to 70lbs overnight, to major US cities. Open 8am–5pm.
Local delivery *Quicksilver Messenger Service*, 550 Beale ☏ 495-4360, guarantees a 1hr downtown delivery. Also offering 24hr, 7-day service via bicycle and van is *Special "T" Messsenger/Delivery Service*, 322 6th St ☏ 861-2225. Also *Aero Special Delivery Service*, 242 Steuart ☏ 982-1303.
Post office The main post office is at 7th and Mission ☏ 550-0100.

Telex and fax The *HQ-Headquarters Companies* ☎ 781-5000 provides domestic and international telex and fax facilities in the financial district.

Conference/exhibition centers

San Francisco has three major convention facilities. The city's premier meeting place, *Moscone Center*, 747 Howard St ☎ 947-4000, is within walking distance of more than a third of the city's top hotels. The *Brooks Hall/Civic Auditorium* complex, 99 Grove St, Civic Center ☎ 974-4000, is the second largest facility downtown. The *Cow Palace*, Geneva Ave and Santos ☎ 469-6000, is a huge clear-span structure with a 100ft ceiling and 14,500 permanent seats. Another choice nearer downtown is the *San Francisco Concourse*, 635 8th St ☎ 864-1500.

Emergencies

Currency exchange The *Bank of America Foreign Exchange Office* at the airport keeps the longest office hours: 7am–11pm daily. Downtown, *Deak-International* is at 100 Grant Ave ☎ 362-3452, Mon–Fri, 9–5.
Hospitals *Pacific Presbyterian Medical Center*, Clay and Buchanan ☎ 563-4321, is close to downtown. *San Francisco Dental Office*, 132 Embarcadero ☎ 777-5115, offers immediate treatment of emergencies and is open 6 days a week, early mornings and evenings.
Pharmacies *Walgreens* has 21 stores in the city, including one open 24hrs at 3201 Divisadero ☎ 931-6415, and two locations downtown at 500 Geary Blvd ☎ 673-8411 and 135 Powell ☎ 391-4433, open Mon–Fri, 8am–9pm; Sat, 9am–5pm; Sun, 10am–6pm.
Police The main police station is south of Market at 850 Bryant ☎ 553-1551.

Government offices

For *City and County of San Francisco* information ☎ 554-4000; *California State Governor's Office* ☎ 557-3326; *US Government* general information ☎ 556-6600; *US Customs* ☎ 556-0067.

Information sources

Business information *San Francisco Chamber of Commerce*, 465 California ☎ 392-4511, provides valuable information and assistance to nonresidents interested in doing business in the city. The *San Francisco Convention and Visitors Bureau*, at Hallidie Plaza, Powell and Market ☎ 391-2000, maintains a multilingual staff to aid the business traveler with literature and information.
Local media *Eastern Newsstand* carries a wide selection of newspapers and magazines and has five locations in the greater downtown area. One is at 3 Embarcadero Center ☎ 982-4425; another is in the Galleria Shopping Center at 50 Post St ☎ 434-0531. The *San Francisco Chronicle* is the morning paper (Herb Caen's column is a must); the *San Francisco Examiner* comes out in the afternoon. The *San Francisco Business Journal*, published every Monday, covers industry, business trends, events and people in the Bay Area. *San Francisco Business* is a monthly magazine published by the San Francisco Chamber of Commerce ☎ 392-4511. *Key Magazine*, available free in many hotels, describes the weekly events in the city.
Visitor information Visitor Information Center, Hallidie Plaza (lower level), Powell and Market Streets ☎ 974-6900; open Mon–Sat, 9–5.30 (till 3 on Sat); Sun, 10–2.

Thank-yous

Florists/gift baskets *Podesta Baldocchi*, 1 Embarcadero Center ☎ 346-1300. There are many street-corner flower carts downtown.
Wine merchants Knowledgeable downtown merchants include *John Walker and Co*, 175 Sutter St ☎ 986-2707; *London Wine Bar*, 415 Sansome St ☎ 788-4811; and the *Wine and Cheese Center*, 205 Jackson St ☎ 751-4242.

SEATTLE

Area code ☏ 206

Standing on Puget Sound in the extreme northwest of the USA, Seattle – which began as a logging camp 150 years ago – is today a major import/export shipping terminal to the Far East. American President and Hanjin Container Lines are its largest port customers, and shipbuilding and repair are important to the region. Lockheed and Todd Shipyards are the field leaders. Other dominant corporations include the spacecraft and airplane giant, Boeing; the heavy equipment manufacturer PACCAR in the high-tech city of Bellevue just to the east; and lumber corporations Weyerhaeuser and Boise Cascade. Traditional industries like fishing and mining (the headquarters of Burlington Resources are here), have recently been joined by computer design specialists such as Microsoft, ensuring the area's continued economic growth. As the economic hub of the Pacific Northwest and Alaska, Seattle is high on the national job-creation table.

Arriving

Seattle-Tacoma International Airport

Sea-Tac, 13 miles/21kms south of downtown Seattle, has five arrival concourses surrounding the main terminal, and two satellite concourses connected to it by regular subway service; cars run every 2mins. International flights arrive at South Satellite, which has Customs and Immigration services, interpreters in 21 languages, and currency exchange. Even at non-peak periods, it can take an hour to clear Customs. Moving sidewalks and escalators make it easy to get to the baggage claim area, which also has major car rental counters, telephone booths and Western Union. Desks, telephones and copy and telecopier machines are available in the business communications center in North Satellite. Bars close at 2am, but a cafeteria-style restaurant is open 24hrs. Airport information ☏ 728-3400.

Nearby hotels *Sea-Tac Red Lion Inn*, 18740 Pacific Hwy S ☏ 246-8600 fax 242-9727. *Radisson* Pacific Hwy S 17001 ☏ 244-6000 TX 320074 fax 246-6835.

City link *Taxi* The most convenient way to get into downtown Seattle is by cab, which generally takes only 20–30mins in morning and evening rush hours. The fare is about $20.

Limousine Shuttle Express (vans) ☏ 622-1424, Park Place Limousine ☏ 363-9902.

Car rental The major car rental agencies have desks in the main terminal, but a car is useful only if you have business in outlyng areas; Dollar Rent A Car ☏ 433-5825.

Bus The Airport Express, which leaves every 20mins, costs approximately $6 ☏ 626-6088. There are also frequent Metro bus services.

Getting around

The city's main business community, hotels, restaurants, shopping and entertainment are all conveniently located within the compact downtown area, though the city is quite hilly.

Taxi The most reliable firms are *Farwest* ☏ 622-1717 and *Yellow Cabs* ☏ 622-6500.

Limousine *Elite Limousine Service* ☏ 575-2332 operates 24hrs.

Car rental *Avis* ☏ 448-1700; *Hertz* ☏ 682-5050.

Bus *Metro Transit* operates frequent services and has an 18-block free zone downtown, from the waterfront to 6th Street and from Jackson to Blanchard streets; information ☏ 447-4800.

Monorail A monorail runs between the downtown shopping area at 4th Street and Pine and the Seattle Center.

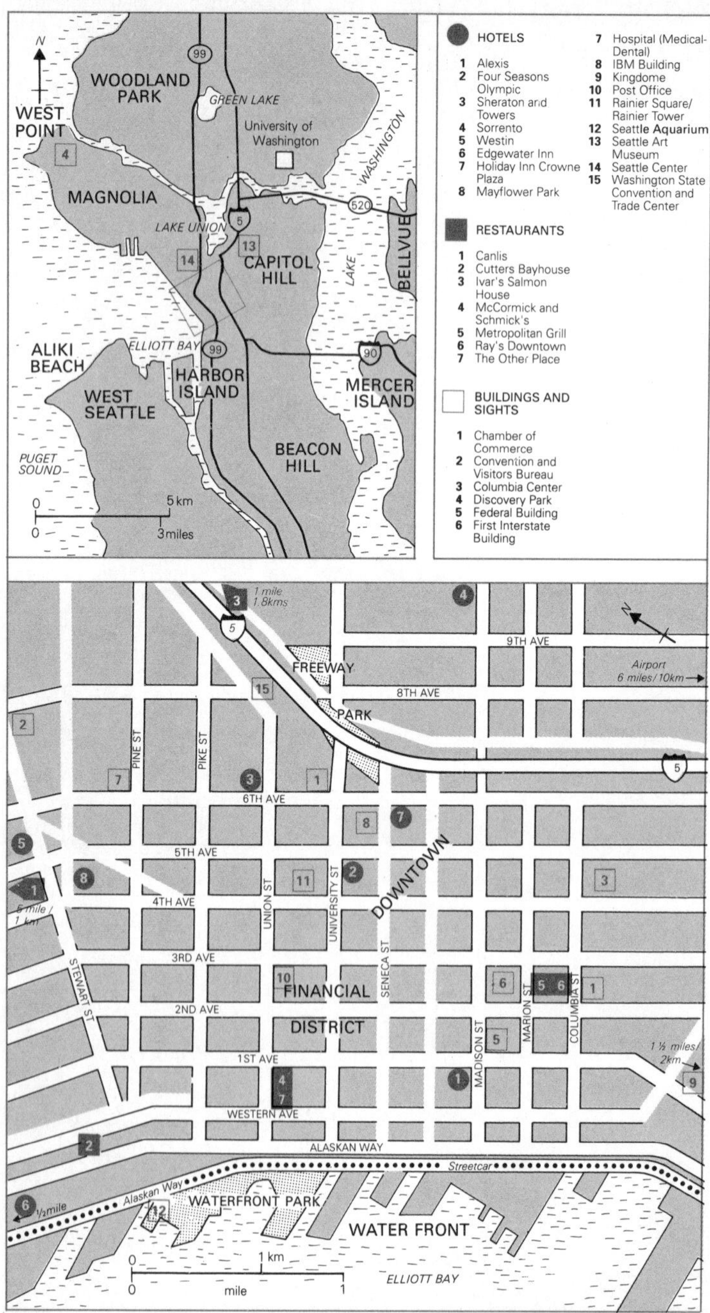
HOTELS
1 Alexis
2 Four Seasons Olympic
3 Sheraton and Towers
4 Sorrento
5 Westin
6 Edgewater Inn
7 Holiday Inn Crowne Plaza
8 Mayflower Park
RESTAURANTS
1 Canlis
2 Cutters Bayhouse
3 Ivar's Salmon House
4 McCormick and Schmick's
5 Metropolitan Grill
6 Ray's Downtown
7 The Other Place
BUILDINGS AND SIGHTS
1 Chamber of Commerce
2 Convention and Visitors Bureau
3 Columbia Center
4 Discovery Park
5 Federal Building
6 First Interstate Building
7 Hospital (Medical-Dental)
8 IBM Building
9 Kingdome
10 Post Office
11 Rainier Square/Rainier Tower
12 Seattle Aquarium
13 Seattle Art Museum
14 Seattle Center
15 Washington State Convention and Trade Center
WOODLAND PARK
GREEN LAKE
WEST POINT
University of Washington
MAGNOLIA
LAKE UNION
CAPITOL HILL
LAKE WASHINGTON
BELLVUE
ALIKI BEACH
ELLIOTT BAY
HARBOR ISLAND
WEST SEATTLE
MERCER ISLAND
BEACON HILL
PUGET SOUND
5 km
3 miles
1 mile 1.8kms
FREEWAY PARK
9TH AVE
8TH AVE
6TH AVE
5TH AVE
4TH AVE
3RD AVE
2ND AVE
1ST AVE
WESTERN AVE
ALASKAN WAY
Airport 6 miles/10km
PINE ST
PIKE ST
UNION ST
UNIVERSITY ST
SENECA ST
MADISON ST
MARION ST
COLUMBIA ST
STEWART ST
DOWNTOWN
FINANCIAL DISTRICT
1 ½ miles/ 2km
Streetcar
Alaskan Way
WATERFRONT PARK
WATER FRONT
½mile
1 km
mile
ELLIOTT BAY

Area by area

Seattle is built on six hills, with views over water and mountains from vantage points all over the city.
Downtown Most of the city's business headquarters are in the lively downtown area, with its plazas and parks (generally streets run east–west, avenues north–south). The 76-floor Columbia Center, Rainier Square/ Rainier Bank Tower, the First Interstate Building at 1111 3rd Avenue and the IBM Building are among the most prestigious business addresses.
Other areas Old-money residential estates are the Highlands, north of downtown, and Broadmoor, east on Lake Washington. Windermere, Innis Arden, and Laurelhurst are other areas with cachet. Young professionals have settled by Lake Washington.
Suburbs Immediately north of Seattle, Ballard was founded by Scandinavians and still retains its ethnic heritage. To the east across Lake Washington, and linked by bridge, is Bellevue, a high-tech area known as "Silicon Valley North."

Hotels

Most of the better hotels are downtown within easy reach of the business headquarters, restaurants, and entertainment. Many have in-house business facilities. The hotels listed have meeting rooms for large groups, plus trained staff to make arrangements for conferences.

Alexis [$]//

1st and Madison 98104 ☎ 624-4844 fax 621-9009 • AE DC MC V • 27 rooms, 27 suites, 2 restaurants, 1 bar
An attractive, turn-of-the-century building decorated with discreet good taste, the Alexis puts great emphasis on personal service. Rooms, furnished with antiques, are large enough to work in, and many have stoves or fireplaces. The Café Alexis is one of Seattle's top restaurants and a favorite meeting ground for big-league executives. Guest membership to Seattle Athletic Club and Rooftop Tennis • 2 meeting rooms.

Four Seasons Olympic [$]///

411 University 98101 ☎ 621-1700 [TX] 152477 fax 623-2271 • AE DC MC V • 450 rooms, 48 suites, 3 restaurants, 1 bar
Opened in the mid-1920s, the Olympic was considered one of the best hotels in western America; now absorbed into the Four Seasons empire it is grander than ever. Just five blocks from the waterfront, it caters mainly for leaders of Seattle society, top executives and their visiting counterparts. Its de luxe, elegantly furnished rooms are highly suitable for working in or for small meetings. The health club is one of the city's best, and the Georgian Room is a much-favored and impressive corporate meeting place. Solarium, health club, sauna, massage • 13 meeting rooms, translation.

Sheraton and Towers [$]//

1400 6th (and Pike) 98101 ☎ 621-9000 [TX] 152981 fax 621-8441 • AE DC MC V • 880 rooms, 46 suites, 3 restaurants, 1 bar
A fine collection of works by Northwest artists is this Sheraton's *pièce de résistance.* As important for the business visitor are the Tower's well-equipped third-floor executive rooms. Indoor pool, health club, weight room • 26 meeting rooms.

Sorrento [$]//

900 Madison 98104 ☎ 622-6400 fax 625-1059 • AE DC MC V • 76 rooms, 40 suites, 1 restaurant, 1 bar
Overlooking downtown and Puget Sound, this small hotel will appeal to guests who prefer personal service and ambience to high-tech hustle. The comfort of its antique-filled rooms is complemented by the readiness of the concierge to arrange

business services. The Hunt Club is a good choice for business dining, with a wide range of seafood. Guest membership to Seattle Athletic Club • 2 meeting rooms.

Westin $//
1900 5th Ave 98101 ☎ 728-1000 TX *152900 fax 728-1653 • AE DC MC V • 865 rooms, 47 suites, 3 restaurants*
The twin 47-story towers of this downtown giant give panoramic views of the locale, and its sleekly renovated interior attracts much convention trade. The Palm Court restaurant is commendably opulent, and Trader Vic's is popular with local corporate leaders. Indoor pool, fitness center, sauna • 27 meeting rooms.

OTHER HOTELS

Edgewater Inn $/ *2411 Alaskan Way 98121* ☎ 728-7000 *fax 441-4119 • AE DC MC V.*

Holiday Inn Crowne Plaza $// *6th and Seneca 98101 ☎ 464-1980* TX *152032 fax 340-1617 • AE DC MC V.*

Mayflower Park $// *405 Olive Way 98101 ☎ 623-8700 fax 382-6997 • AE DC MC V.*

Clubs

The *Rainier Club* ☎ 296-6848 is Seattle's oldest and most prestigious. The *Washington Athletic Club* ☎ 622-7900 offers accommodation, athletic facilities and excellent dining. The exclusive men-only *101 Club*, on the top of the WAC building, has the best view in town. The *College Club* ☎ 622-0624 has a mixed membership and *Women's University Club* ☎ 623-0402, women only.

Restaurants

Much of Seattle's business entertaining takes place in the better hotel restaurants such as the Café Alexis, the Sorrento's Hunt Club, Fullers in the Sheraton and the Georgian Room in the Four Seasons.

Canlis $///
2576 Aurora Ave N ☎ 283-3313 • closed L Sun • AE DC MC V • jacket
Splendid views of Lake Union, Northwest seafood and charcoal-grilled steaks are the main attractions of this well-known restaurant. Private dining rooms available.

Cutters Bayhouse $/
2001 Western Ave ☎ 448-4884 • AE MC V
Looking out over Elliot Bay, Cutters has become so popular for business get-togethers that reservations are advised. The fantastic view of Puget Sound and the Olympic Mountains, the casual ambience and light pasta make this ideal for a working meal.

Ivar's Salmon House $/
401 NE Northlake Way ☎ 632-0767 • AE MC V
A visitor to the Northwest will enjoy this new experience: eating alder-smoked salmon, Indian-style, in a replica of a tribal longhouse beside Lake Union. Best for informal meals.

McCormick and Schmick's $/
1103 1st Ave ☎ 623-5500 • closed L Sat & Sun • AE DC MC V
A comparatively new restaurant, though with the look and feel of a long-established one, McCormick and Schmick's specializes in seafood and grilled meats. Look especially for the oysters and Manila clams in season.

Metropolitan Grill $/
818 2nd Ave ☎ 624-3287 • closed L Sat & Sun • AE MC DC V
In midtown, the Metropolitan is crowded with the elite of the Seattle business community; reservations are advisable. Steak is a specialty.

Ray's Downtown $/
950 2nd Ave ☎ 623-7999 • closed Sat L, Sun • AE MC V • D reservations essential
Ray has two excellent restaurants, but

this is the one most used by local executives for weekday lunches. His Boathouse Shilshole is a 20min drive away on the waterfront at Shilshole ☏ 789-3777, but its stunning location on the Sound makes it well worth the effort. Top-rate seafood and prime rib.

The Other Place $//

96 Union St ☏ 623-7340 • closed Sun L • AE DC MC V • reservations recommended

Recently moved from farther along Union, this favorite spot has taken over an old building near Pike's Market, but retains its old elegance and quality of service. Even so, the style is sufficiently casual to appeal also to the younger professional. Now with a view of the water, its emphasis has moved from game to seafood. A separate lounge provides a good private spot for pre-dinner discussion.

Bars

Hiram's at-the-Locks, 5300 34th NW ☏ 784-1733, overlooks the canal, a scenic place to watch the boats, meet the younger professional crowd, and dine on seafood. *J&M Café* ☏ 624-1670, in the Pioneer Square area, is a turn-of-the-century saloon. The long bar of the *Metropolitan Grill*, 818 2nd St ☏ 624-3287, downtown, is also popular for after-work drinks.

Entertainment

The Friday "What's Happening" in the morning *Seattle Post-Intelligencer* and the "Tempo" column of the evening *Seattle Times* give listings. *Ticketmaster Northwest* ☏ 628-0888 takes MC and V telephone orders.

Theater and music Broadway shows and stars come to the *5th Avenue Theater*, 1308 5th ☏ 625-1418. *Pioneer Square Theater*, 512 2nd ☏ 622-2016, and the *Empty Space Theater*, 95 Jackson ☏ 467-6000, are more experimental. The *Gilbert and Sullivan Society* and *Seattle Repertory Theater* both perform at the Seattle Center's *Bagley Wright Theater* at 305 Harrison Street ☏ 443-2222. Also at the Center is the *Seattle Opera House* ☏ 443-4711, home to the Seattle Symphony Orchestra. The Pacific Northwest Ballet also performs here.

Nightclubs *Backstage*, 2208 NW Market, presents groups ranging from rock to folk music. *Celebrity Bar & Grill* is a favorite with the younger professionals. In Pioneer Square under Swannie's Bar & Restaurant, *Comedy Underground*, 222 S Main ☏ 628-0303, has stand-up comedy acts. *Windjammers*, 7001 Seaview NW ☏ 784-4070, has live bands.

Shopping

I Magnin, *Nordstrom* and *Frederick & Nelson* are on Pine Street at 5th and 6th. Expensive specialty and clothes shops, such as *Littler's* and *Talbot's*, are in Rainier Square, 4th and Union. *Pioneer Square*, around 1st and Yester, is another specialty shop haven, for fruit, vegetables, seafood, handmade craft items and antiques.

Sightseeing

Discovery Park, site of the *Indian Cultural Center*, has a 2 mile/3km beach with hiking trails. *3801 W Government Way ☏ 285-4425.*

Seattle Aquarium, one of the city's major attractions, has a variety of historical nautical exhibits as well as marine life. The underwalk dome is surrounded by water and fish. *Pier 59, Waterfront Park ☏ 386-4320.*

Seattle Art Museum Specializes in African and Asian art; at Volunteer Park. *1400 E Caler, adjacent to the city's Conservatory ☏ 625-8901.*

Seattle Center Covering more than 70 acres in downtown, it was built for the 1962 World's Fair, and includes the towering 605ft Space Needle and the Pacific Science Center, with hands-on exhibits. *305 Harrison.*

Guided tours

Seattle Harbor Tours, Pier 55 ☏ 623-1445, make trips Apr–Oct. *Tillicum Village and Tours*, Pier 56 ☏ 329-5700, travels twice daily May–Sep to Blake Island, a state park; also visits Northwest Coast Indian Cultural Center. *Underground Tours* ☏ 682-4646 offer 2hr 30min walks along the now subterranean streets of 1899 in the Pioneer Square area.

Spectator sports

Baseball The *Seattle Mariners* ☏ 628-3555 play in the Kingdome, 201 S King St.
Basketball The *Supersonics* ☏ 281-5800 are at the Seattle Center.
Football The *Seahawks* ☏ 827-9777 play at the Kingdome. The University of Washington team, the *Huskies* ☏ 543-2200, is also popular.

Keeping fit

Metropolitan Health Club, 1519 3rd Ave ☏ 682-3966, and *Nautilus Northwest Athletic Club*, 2306 6th ☏ 443-9944.
Bicycling Rentals from the *Bicycle Center* ☏ 523-8300.
Golf *Bellevue Municipal Golf Course*, 5500 140th St NE, Bellevue ☏ 451-7250; *West Seattle Golf Course*, 4470 35th St SW ☏ 935-5187.

Local resources

Business services

Photocopying and printing *Kinko's Copy Center*, 1335 2nd Ave ☏ 692-9225 (free pick-up and delivery); *Superior Reprographics*, 1925 5th Ave ☏ 443-6900.
Secretarial *Globe Secretarial*, 306 6th Ave ☏ 448-9441, open 8–5.30 Mon–Fri, weekends by appointment.
Translation *Red Cross Language Bank* ☏ 323-2345 offers 24hr interpreting.

Communications

Long-distance delivery *Federal Express* ☏ 282-9766. *National Courier System* ☏ 682-9315 operates 24hrs.
Local delivery *Farwest Taxi* ☏ 292-0569 or *Overland Transportation Service* ☏ 441-4555.
Post offices Downtown at 3rd and Union ☏ 442-6340; or at the airport, 16601 Air Cargo Rd ☏ 284-3302.

Conference/exhibition centers

The Washington State and Trade Convention Center, 800 Convention Plaza ☏ 447-5000, opened in 1988. The *Seattle Center* has two auditoriums; *Kingdome*, the sports arena, is also available for large gatherings. The Seattle-King County Convention and Visitors Bureau ☏ 461-5840 gives information.

Emergencies

Currency exchange *Check Mart*, 1206 1st Ave ☏ 622-2274, is open Mon–Fri, 8am–9pm; Sat, 9–9; Sun, 11–7.
Hospitals *Swedish Hospital Medical Center*, 747 Summit ☏ 386-6000; *Virginia Mason*, 925 Seneca ☏ 223-6490; and *Saint Cabrini*, Terry and Madison ☏ 682-0500, all have 24hr emergency services. *Medical-Dental Building*, 509 Olive Way, Suite 1062 ☏ 623-4096 (24hr emergencies).
Pharmacies *Kelley-Ross* ☏ 622-3565. *Fred Meyer*, 401 Broadway E ☏ 323-5256.
Police At 610 3rd Ave ☏ 625-5011.

Government offices

Federal Information Center ☏ 442-0570; *US Customs* ☏ 442-8274; *Passport Information* ☏ 442-7945.

Information sources

Business information *Greater Seattle Chamber of Commerce*, 600 University St, Suite 1200, 98101 ☏ 461-7200; *Economic Development Council* ☏ 386-5040.
Local media City news is supplied by the morning and evening *Seattle Times*. The *Seattle Daily Journal of Commerce* and the weekly *Seattle Business Journal* cover business.
Visitor information *Seattle-King County Convention and Visitors Bureau*, 660 Stewart ☏ 461-5840.

Thank-yous

Florists *Crissey*, 416 University at 5th ☏ 728-6661; *Chas E Sullivan* ☏ 624-1300 open seven days.
Gift baskets *Au Delice* ☏ 747-7541; *Totem Smokehouse Gourmet Seafood* ☏ 443-1710; *Cheers & Chocolates* ☏ 454-7780.

WASHINGTON DC

Area code ☎ 202; codes for nearby Virginia and Maryland are 703 and 301 respectively. Telephone numbers in this city guide are in Washington DC (District of Columbia) unless otherwise indicated.

As the nation's capital, Washington is, in many ways, the USA's most important city for business, given the role of government as a regulator of all commerce and industry, national and international. Virtually every major US corporation has an office of some sort in the Washington area, and nearly all US trade associations are headquartered here. In the past, Washington was dominated by government; Capitol Hill and Embassy Row were the city's major centers. Today, however, the private sector – corporations, lobbying groups and the like – predominates. Washington is a city obsessed by power, where lobbyists and politicians vie for influence, yet it is also a city relatively open in terms of access, especially by European standards. It is, above all, a town of bureaucrats and lawyers. Major employers are government, national trade associations, government contractors and the law. Because of its importance, many major US corporations maintain a presence, even head offices, in the city: defense contractors such as Martin Marietta, Atlantic Research Corporation and Fairchild Industries; communications giants – like COMSAT, INTELSAT, Gannett, and MCI; and financial institutions. Washington is an important center of learning, with several major universities, including George Washington, Catholic and Georgetown. Among the city's numerous tourist attractions are the White House, the Capitol, the Washington Monument, the Lincoln Memorial, and some of the best museums in the world.

Arriving

Washington is served by Washington National Airport, Dulles International and Baltimore-Washington International. Because National is nearer downtown, it is the preferred airport for domestic flights. International travelers have the choice of Dulles or BWI, both about a 45min drive from the city.

Washington National Airport

National is situated just over 4 miles/6.5kms from downtown Washington, across the Potomac River in northern Virginia. Handling about 40,000 passengers a day in cramped conditions, it is usually congested in the late afternoon and on Sunday night, but is nevertheless an easy airport to find your way around. Recent renovation has been extensive and facilities have been improved. Passengers collect their baggage at street level; car rental desks, taxis and shuttle buses to car rental lots, long-term parking, and the Metrorail are all nearby. From plane to car can take only 15min, but baggage delays can double that during heavy traffic in late afternoon. A full banking service is available, Mon–Sat, 9–7; currency exchange, secretarial services, photocopying, telex/telegram and conference rooms are provided in a business services center, open 6am–9.30pm daily. Information ☎ (703) 685-8000.

Nearby hotels *Crystal City Marriott*, 1999 Jefferson Davis Hwy, Arlington, VA ☎ (703) 521-5500 fax (703) 685-0191. *Holiday Inn, National Airport*, 1489 Jefferson Davis Hwy, Arlington, VA ☎ (703) 521-1600 fax (703) 920-1236. *Marriott Crystal Gateway*, 1700

Jefferson Davis Hwy, Arlington, VA ☎ (703) 920-3230 fax (703) 979-6332.
City link *Taxi* The best way downtown is by taxi. It takes 15–20mins, 35mins in the rush hour 3.30–6. The fare is about $10. A cab ride from Dulles International costs about $30; from Baltimore-Washington Airport, closer to $40. It is advisable to agree the fare with the driver beforehand.
Car rental Since cabs are readily available and relatively cheap to downtown (while parking lots are expensive), a cab is the better choice, but rental companies have desks at the airport: Avis ☎ (800) 739-4810; Hertz ☎ (800) 979-6300; National ☎ (800) 328-4567; Budget ☎ (800) 920-3360; and Dollar ☎ (800) 421-6868.
Subway The Metrorail station is only a short ride away on a free shuttle bus which runs from outside the baggage area.
Bus The Washington Flyer ☎ (703) 685-1400 services downtown Washington, Dulles International Airport, suburban Maryland and northern Virginia. A one-way ticket to downtown hotels is $5; round-trip $8. For Dulles International, the fares are $10 and $18.

Dulles International Airport

Dulles is in northern Virginia, a 40–50min ride via the Dulles Access Road to downtown; in rush hours, it can take 15mins more. The strikingly beautiful terminal, designed by Eero Saarinen, is easy to negotiate, and exiting usually takes about 15mins (45mins if you have to go through Customs and Immigration), though construction work can cause Customs delays.

For international travelers, Dulles has a business center on the ground floor; domestic travelers are catered for on the main floor at the east and west ends, 7am–11pm daily. Services include currency exchange, secretarial, photocopying, telex/telegram and conference rooms. There is a bank on the ground floor ☎ (703) 661-8861 and (703) 471-7498, open Mon–Fri, 9–1, 3–5. Concorde passengers to and from London can use British Airways' First Class lounge. Airport information ☎ (703) 471-7838.
Nearby hotels *Marriott-Dulles*, Dulles International Airport, 33 West Service Rd, Chantilly ☎ (703) 471-9500 fax (703) 661-6785. *Ramada Renaissance Dulles*, 13869 Park Center Rd, Herndon, VA ☎ (703) 478-2900 fax (703) 478-9286, 15mins from the airport. *Holiday Inn*, 1000 Sully Rd, Sterling, VA ☎ (703) 471-7411; limousine provided for the 10min ride. *Holiday Inn*, Fair Oaks Mall, 11787 Lee-Jackson Hwy, Fairfax County VA ☎ (703) 352-2525; limousine provided for the 25min ride.
City link If you are staying in downtown Washington, take either a cab or the Washington Flyer bus. Driving can be frustrating, and parking is expensive. There is no Metrorail from Dulles.
Taxi Cabs to downtown Washington are available 24hrs ☎ (703) 471-5555. The fare is about $35.
Car rental Major companies include Avis ☎ (800) 661-8874; Budget ☎ (800) 437-9373; Hertz ☎ (800) 471-6020; National ☎ (800) 328-4567; and Dollar ☎ (800) 421-6868.
Bus The Washington Flyer ☎ (703) 685-1400 provides a fast bus service to downtown every 30mins, fare $10 one way, $17 round trip to downtown. To National Airport, the fares are $10 and $18 respectively. The Flyer also serves northern Virginia and suburban Maryland.

Baltimore-Washington International Airport

BWI lies about 10 miles/16kms south of Baltimore and 30 miles/48kms north of Washington on the Washington-Baltimore Parkway (Interstate 95). It handles domestic and international traffic. Currency exchange, notary services, photocopying, secretarial services,

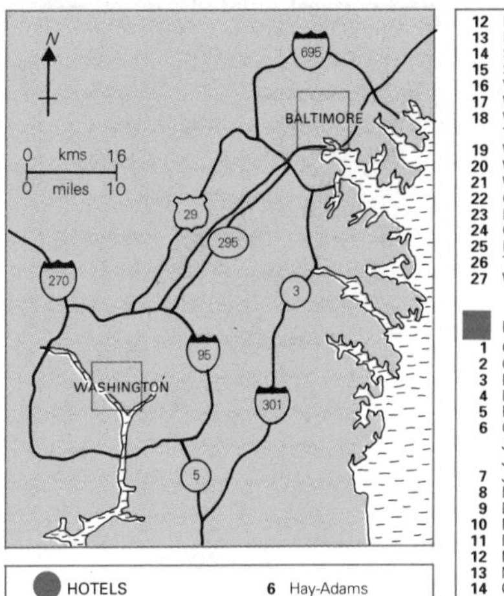

HOTELS
1 Capital Hilton
2 Embassy Row
3 Four Seasons
4 Grand
5 Hampshire
6 Hay-Adams
7 Jefferson
8 Madison
9 JW Marriott
10 Mayflower
11 Omni Shoreham

12 Park Hyatt
13 Ritz-Carlton
14 Sheraton Carlton
15 Sheraton Washington
16 Vista International
17 Washington Court
18 Washington Hilton and Towers
19 Watergate
20 Westin
21 Willard Inter-Continental
22 Georgetown Dutch Inn
23 Henley Park
24 Quality Inn Downtown
25 Ramada Inn Central
26 Tabard Inn
27 Washington

RESTAURANTS
1 Cantina d'Italia
2 City Café
3 Dominique's
4 Duke Zeibert's
5 Fourways
6 Germaine's
Jean-Louis (Hotel 19)
Jockey Club (Hotel 13)
7 Joe and Mo's
8 Le Lion d'Or
9 Maison Blanche
10 McPherson Grill
11 Mr K's
12 Morton's of Chicago
13 Nora
14 Occidental
15 Old Ebbitt Grill
16 Le Pavillon
17 Sichuan Pavilion
18 Vincenzo's
19 Washington Palm

BUILDINGS AND SIGHTS
1 Arlington National Cemetery
2 Capitol
3 Convention Center
4 Corcoran Gallery of Art
5 Diplomatic Reception Room
6 Dumbarton Oaks
7 Georgetown University
8 Hillwood Estate
9 Hospital (George Washington)
10 Jefferson Memorial
11 John F Kennedy Center
12 Library of Congress
13 Lincoln Memorial
14 National Gallery of Art
15 National Zoological Park
16 Pentagon
17 Phillips Collection
18 Post Office
19 Smithsonian Institution
20 US Supreme Court
21 Washington Cathedral
22 Washington Monument
23 White House
i Visitor information

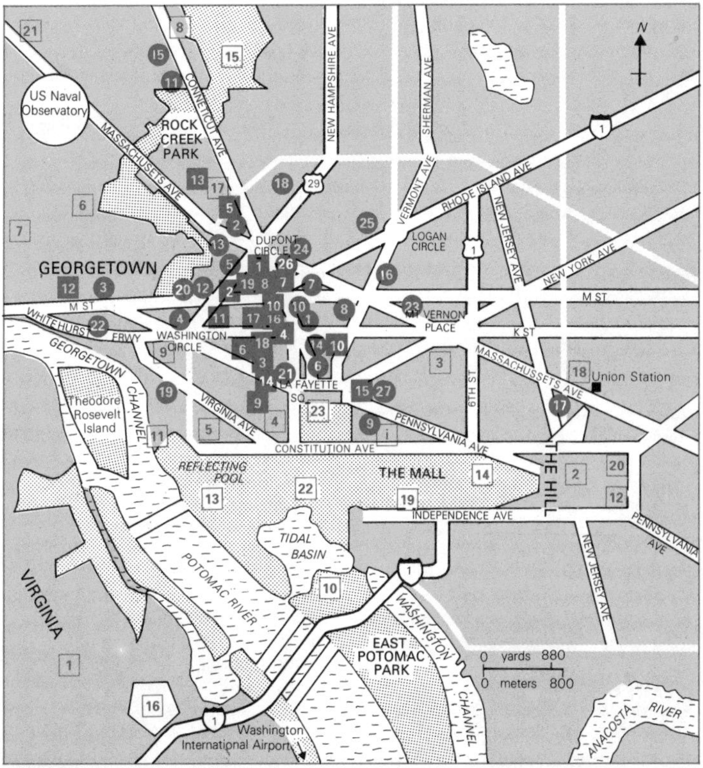

communication services and emergency cash are available at the Mutual of Omaha Service Center, Pier C ☏ (301) 859-5997. Information ☏ (301) 859-7100.
Nearby hotel *International BWI*, 7032 Elm Rd 21240 ☏ (301) 859-3300 fax (301) 859-0565; free shuttle bus.
City link *Taxi* Downtown Washington is a 45min drive from BWI; the center of Baltimore is just 15mins by taxi. The fare to Washington is about $40, to Baltimore $12.
Limousine BWI LIM ☏ 441-2345 provides a limo/bus service to the Washington Hilton, Capital Hilton and Greenbelt Terminal every 60mins, 4.30am–midnight. The fare is $10 one way, $18 round trip.
Car rental Five car rental firms are represented at BWI: Avis ☏ (301) 859-1680; Budget ☏ (301) 859-0850; Dollar ☏ (301) 859-8950; Hertz ☏ (301) 850-7400; and National ☏ (301) 859-8860.
Rail Amtrak ☏ (800) 872-7245 provides services to Washington and Baltimore and other East Coast connections. Commuter rail service is provided by MARC ☏ (800) 325-7245. Free shuttle bus service is provided between the terminal and rail station.

Rail station

Union Station Amtrak trains from points north, south and west, including an almost-hourly service from New York, Boston and other Eastern Seaboard cities, arrive at this imposing station near the Capitol, on Massachusetts Ave ☏ 484-7540 (reservations). Union Station has been completely renovated and now contains, in addition to the Amtrak national headquarters, 120 shops, 9 movie theaters, a Metrorail station and several fine restaurants and fast-food eateries. The 1907 building has emerged as Washington's newest tourist attraction and shopping mall.

Getting around

Washington is designed in the shape of a wheel, with the Capitol building in the center and the streets radiating out like spokes. For the newcomer, driving can be a nerve-racking experience; and illegal parking is heavily penalized. The city is divided into four quadrants, and streets are numbered and lettered consecutively; the diagonal streets are named after US states. If the numerous circles and squares cause driving difficulties, they also make walking a pleasure; it is practically impossible to get lost once you know the system. The best way to get around is on foot (although the city is spread out and many streets are long) or by taxi, especially on "the Hill," where parking is almost exclusively by permit.
Taxi Cabs are readily available downtown. Drivers may not understand much English, though they do generally know their way around. Fares are reasonable and are calculated on a zone basis. (Virginia and Maryland taxis, however, are metered.) Do not be surprised if your driver stops to pick up another fare going in the same direction; likewise, do not hesitate to hail an occupied cab. New passengers have to pay the full zone fare, but additional members of the original party pay only a small premium. If you cannot hail a cab, you can call *Capitol Cab* ☏ 546-2400; *Diamond Cab* ☏ 387-6200; *Imperial Cab* ☏ 543-2222; *Yellow Cab* ☏ 546-7900.
Limousine *Carey Limousine* ☏ 892-2000; *Admiral Limousine* ☏ 554-1000; and *International Limousine* ☏ 388-6800.
Car rental Major car rental companies have downtown offices: *Avis* ☏ 467-6588; *Budget* ☏ (703) 920-3360; *Dollar* ☏ 296-3095; *Hertz* ☏ (800) 628-6174.
Subway The Metrorail's stations and trains are clean, quiet and comfortable; lines run throughout Washington and into northern Virginia and suburban Maryland. Ticket-selling is fully automated, occasionally making for annoying

difficulties. You can buy a fare card for various amounts, but the minimum is $1. Crisp dollar bills are needed for the ticket machines. The system operates Mon–Fri, 6am–midnight; Sat, 8am–midnight; Sun, 10–6 with trains running every 10mins on average. Information ☏ 637-2437.

Bus Metrobus ☏ 637-2437 operates in DC and in the Virginia and Maryland suburbs. It has 1,600 routes, and fares range from 75 cents to $1. Exact change or tokens are needed but transfers between routes are free.

Area by area

When the French architect Major Pierre Charles L'Enfant was asked by President Washington to design the city in 1791, he placed the US Capitol building on the Hill to be the focal point of the city at one end of the 2-mile vista known as the Mall; the other is the Lincoln Memorial. The Capitol remains one of Washington's most visible and evocative landmarks.

Downtown Capitol Hill and Pennsylvania Avenue, which leads west to the White House, are dominated by huge Neo-classical government buildings. On the Hill, young Congressional staffers rub shoulders with countless tourists. Farther down Pennsylvania Avenue are the soberly dressed bureaucrats from the Department of Justice, Treasury, FBI and Federal Trade Commission buildings. Non-government businesses are concentrated around K Street and Connecticut Avenue, where lawyers, lobbyists and national trade associations throng the area – and its many business hotels and restaurants. The Washington Convention Center occupies an entire block bounded by 9th, 11th and H Streets and New York Avenue.

Old Downtown is the city's fastest growing commercial sector, extending from just east of the White House almost to Union Station. In recent years it had become somewhat run-down, but its department stores and new businesses, including quite a few luxury hotels, are thriving.

Georgetown Once a busy seaport with a thriving tobacco trade, Georgetown has many fine old Georgian and Federal-period townhouses where the city's social and political elite live and entertain. The area also has an array of ethnic restaurants strung along M Street and Wisconsin Avenue, plus a fine selection of fashion shops. To the east of Georgetown, Massachusetts Avenue runs into Dupont Circle, which has many lively boutiques and restaurants, art galleries and bookshops. The Washington Harbour development includes condominiums and offices and is a good spot for strolling, with lovely views of the Kennedy Center.

Massachusetts Avenue The majestic stretch of this avenue running from Dupont Circle out past Rock Creek Park is known as Embassy Row. Here, and in the surrounding neighborhood, you will find most of Washington's embassies, many surrounded by spacious gardens. The area is also home to many senior executives and politicians.

Other areas Foxhall Road, in the Wesley Heights and Spring Valley area, is another prestigious address. Other expensive neighborhoods are scattered throughout Chevy Chase, Potomac and Bethesda in Maryland and across the river in McLean, Virginia. Alexandria is another gentrified Virginia enclave, home to many Washington professionals. Its ambience is similar to that of Georgetown, with gracious 18th and early-19thC houses, gardens and tree-shaded streets. King Street, in particular, contains numerous chic restaurants and trendy shops.

Hotels

Washington's top hotels cater well for the business traveler, with support services such as secretarial help and meeting and conference rooms readily available. All the hotels listed are in NW, not far from the Convention Center at 9th and H Streets. Many have useful restaurants for business entertaining. Most have good security systems (the city's crime rate is high).

Capital Hilton [$]///
16th and K Sts ☎ 393-1000
[TX] 7108229068 fax 393-7992 •
AE DC MC V • 549 rooms, 25 suites, 2 restaurants, 1 bar
The fine location, just two blocks north of the White House, makes this hotel convenient for business discussions in the center. Rooms are unusually spacious. Two health clubs • 16 meeting rooms.

Embassy Row [$]///
2015 Massachusetts Ave NW 20036
☎ 265-1600 [TX] 892650 fax 328-7526
• AE DC MC V • 196 rooms, 28 suites, 1 restaurant, 1 bar
Just off Dupont Circle, the Embassy Row is used by diplomats and CEOs seeking security and personable, attentive service. Its subdued Ambassador Grill serves *nouvelle cuisine*. Pool, nearby health club • 5 meeting rooms.

Four Seasons [$]////
2800 Pennsylvania Ave NW 20007
☎ 342-0444 [TX] 904008 fax 944-2076
• AE DC MC V • 167 rooms, 30 suites, 1 restaurant, 2 bars
Hard by Georgetown and just 12 blocks from the White House, on the edge of Rock Creek Park, this luxurious hotel is held to be one of the world's finest; be sure to get a room overlooking either the Chesapeake and Ohio Canal or the park. The handsome Aux Beaux Champs restaurant offers alternative calorie-, sodium- and cholesterol-reduced menus, as well as first-class Continental fare. Afternoon tea in the lobby (3–4.30) is a local favorite. Complimentary weekday limousine transportation • personalized exercise program, jogging path, health club • 5 meeting rooms, teleconferencing, business reference library.

Grand [$]////
2350 M St NW 20037 ☎ 429-0100
[TX] 904282 fax 429-9759 • AE DC MC V • 231 rooms, 31 suites, 3 restaurants, 1 bar
A European-style hotel, formerly the Regent, the Grand has a fine reputation, although service is thought to have slipped somewhat lately. Each bathroom has floor-to-ceiling marble panels, a large sunken tub, a separate shower and TV. All rooms have three telephones. Some of the suites have fine paintings, a jacuzzi and fireplace. The Promenade overlooking the courtyard is pleasant for tea or cocktails, and the Mayfair restaurant is smart and expensive. Health club, outdoor pool • 8 meeting rooms.

Hampshire [$]//
1310 New Hampshire Ave at N St 20036 ☎ 296-7600 [TX] 7108229343 fax 293-2476 • AE DC MC V • Taj • 54 suites, 36 rooms, 1 restaurant
This elegant small hotel prides itself on personal service. The 36 front-facing rooms all have balconies, and the decor is 18thC European. The Hampshire has a good Creole restaurant, Lafitte. Breakfast is original, with spicy Creole omelets and *pain perdu*. Arrangements with nearby health club • 3 meeting rooms.

Hay-Adams [$]///
1 Lafayette Sq NW 20006 ☎ 638-6600
[TX] 8229543 fax 638-2716 • AE DC MC V • 140 rooms, 18 suites, 3 restaurants, 2 bars
The Hay-Adams boasts that it is "an island of civility in a sea of power"; and the fashion publication *W* has said it is "as close as one can get to staying at the White House, short of being invited by the President." The

rooms, some with a fireplace, are tastefully furnished, and the view from the windows and balconies is of Lafayette Square and the White House or the Washington Monument. The gentlemen's club-style English Grill and the John Hay Room offer good Continental food (the former is a preferred eating place of Washington's financial community), but for breakfast try the Adam Room. Health club, jogging track • 3 meeting rooms.

Jefferson [$]/////
1200 16th St NW 20036 ☎ 347-2200 [TX] 248879 fax 331-7982 • AE DC MC V • 69 rooms, 35 suites, 3 restaurants
Small, but distinguished, and just four blocks from the White House, the Jefferson was an apartment building until 1941. Its spacious rooms are attractively decorated; some have antique furnishings, including canopied beds. The Walter Annenbergs, Helen Hayes and Leonard Bernstein are among the hotel's discriminating guests. The staff are personable and attentive. The Hunt Club restaurant provides American cuisine in a warm, clubby atmosphere. 2 meeting rooms.

Madison [$]/////
15th and M St NW 20005 ☎ 862-1600 [TX] 64245 fax 785-1255 • AE DC MC V • 353 rooms, 35 suites, 2 restaurants, 2 bars, 1 coffee shop
Not far from Dupont Circle and directly across the street from the *Washington Post* headquarters, the Madison has a 23-year record of good service and accommodation. All suites are furnished with antiques. The Montpelier Room serves traditional Continental dishes at rather elevated prices. Health club nearby • 14 meeting rooms.

JW Marriott [$]///
1331 Pennsylvania Ave NW ☎ 393-2000 [TX] 7108229638 fax 626-6991 • AE DC MC V • 773 rooms, 51 suites, 3 restaurants, 1 bar
The flagship of the Marriott chain, the JW is big – and because of that, slightly impersonal; nevertheless, it is luxurious and conveniently located. The imposing lobby features expanses of marble flooring and gigantic crystal chandeliers. Plants and fresh flowers abound. The hotel connects with National Place, a popular shopping mall. Its smartest restaurant, the Celadon, features French/Chinese dishes. The National Café ranges from light snacks to full entrées, while the Garden Terrace has a jazz band. Health club • 22 meeting rooms.

Mayflower [$]///
1127 Connecticut Ave NW 20036 ☎ 347-3000 [TX] 892324 fax 347-3000 ext 2187 • Stouffer • AE DC MC V • 641 rooms, 83 suites, 2 restaurants, 1 bar
A $65m renovation in the mid-1980s restored to this Washington landmark the Old World charm and status it had upon first opening in 1925. The Mayflower is ideal for engagements in the city's business district. Its airy Café Promenade does daily lunchtime buffets, but Nicholas is more intimate and stylish. Nonsmoking rooms, gift shop, jeweler, hairdresser, beauty shop • 17 meeting rooms.

Omni Shoreham [$]///
2500 Calvert St NW 20008 ☎ 234-0700 [TX] 7108220142 fax 234-0700 ext 3117 • AE DC MC V • 770 rooms, 47 suites, 1 restaurant, 1 bar, 1 coffee shop
The Art Deco Shoreham lies in Washington's NW district, just a short distance from the tranquil Rock Creek Park. Service is both courteous and efficient. Pool, tennis, basketball • 22 meeting rooms.

Park Hyatt [$]////
24th and M St NW 20037 ☎ 789-1234 [TX] 897105 fax 457-8823 • AE DC MC V • 224 rooms, 132 suites, 2 restaurants, 2 bars
This hotel has a full health club and 16,000 sq ft of conference and banquet space. The handsome suites

and rooms have king-size beds, TV in the bathroom and multiline telephones. Afternoon tea is served in the Tea Lounge 3–5; champagne and caviar are offered later. Nonsmoking floor, hairdresser • pool, jacuzzi, sauna, fitness room • 23 meeting rooms, business center.

Ritz-Carlton $////
2100 Massachusetts Ave NW 20008
☎ 293-2100 TX 263758 fax 293-0641 • AE DC MC V • 230 rooms, 30 suites, 1 restaurant, 1 bar
Formerly the Fairfax, the Ritz-Carlton has warmth and charm. Its Jockey Club (see *Restaurants*) and Ritz bar are as popular now as they were in the Kennedy era. Regulars include distinguished Europeans, corporate chiefs and media personalities. Nearby health facilities • 9 meeting rooms.

Sheraton Carlton $////
923 16th St NW 20006 ☎ 638-2626 TX 440650 fax 638-4231 • AE DC MC V • 196 rooms, 38 suites, 1 restaurant, 1 bar
The Carlton is a throwback to a more gracious era, with a palm court lobby for afternoon tea and a wood-paneled wine bar frequented by K Street executives for after-work drinks. The dining room has an excellent reputation. Hairdresser • arrangements with nearby health club • 7 meeting rooms, translation.

Sheraton Washington $//
2660 Woodley Rd NW 20008
☎ 328-2000 TX 892630 fax 234-0015 • AE DC MC V • 1,352 rooms, 117 suites, 3 restaurants, 2 bars, 1 coffee shop
A giant of a hotel, the Sheraton Washington contains a mini-village of shops. The Sunday brunch buffet is a veritable *grande bouffe*, with nearly 200 different items. Hairdresser, post office • health club, 2 pools • 38 meeting rooms.

Vista International $///
1400 M St NW 20005 ☎ 429-1700 TX 440237 fax 785-0786 • AE DC MC V • Hilton • 368 rooms, 29 suites, 2 restaurants, 3 bars
Soft background music – string quartet, piano or harpist – in the greenery-filled lobby sets the tone here, though the Vista's location is less than ideal; be wary of walking to the north or east after sunset. The American Harvest restaurant is Continental; the more casual Verandah does a good Sunday brunch. Executive level floors. Gift shop, health club • 13 meeting rooms.

Washington Court $///
525 New Jersey Ave NW 20001
☎ 628-2100 TX 4970525 fax 879-7918 • AE DC MC V • 265 rooms, 32 suites, 2 restaurants, 1 bar, 1 coffee shop
As the only new luxury hotel on Capitol Hill, the Washington Court (formerly the Sheraton Grand) is ideal if your business is with Congress or one of the many associations, unions and government agencies nearby. The salmon-colored marble lobby has a glass atrium with a three-story garden trellis and waterfall. The rooms, including two floors for nonsmokers, all have exercise equipment, personal computers, and telephones in bedroom and bathroom. 7 meeting rooms.

Washington Hilton and Towers $///
1919 Connecticut Ave NW 20009
☎ 483-3000 TX 248761 fax 265-8221 • AE DC MC V • 1,150 rooms, 82 suites, 2 restaurants, 2 bars, 1 coffee shop
About seven blocks north of Dupont Circle, the convention-oriented Washington Hilton is both modern and efficient. It has recently been remodeled and has one luxury level floor. The health-conscious traveler is well catered for here, for the hotel offers an outdoor pool, jogging track, tennis courts and bike rental, plus a health club and game room. Business center, 31 meeting rooms.

Watergate $////
2650 Virginia Ave NW 20037
☎ 965-2300 TX 197691 fax 337-7915
• AE DC MC V • 238 rooms, 3 restaurants, 2 bars
Part of the notorious Watergate complex, this Cunard hotel is just across the street from the Kennedy Center. The award-winning Jean-Louis (see *Restaurants*) is generally considered the city's finest hotel restaurant. The Watergate Terrace, downstairs from the lobby, is popular with the Kennedy Center crowds in the evening, and Les Champs is good for a quick light meal. Complimentary limousine to downtown 7–10am, hairdresser, boutique shops • health club, pool • 7 meeting rooms.

Westin $////
2401 M St NW 20037 ☎ 429-2400 TX 4979801 fax 457-5010 • AE DC MC V • 378 rooms, 38 suites, 2 restaurants, 1 bar
Perhaps the Westin's strongest point is its fitness center, with exercise equipment, squash courts, lap pool, saunas, steamroom, whirlpool, massage and aerobic classes. The hotel also has conference facilities, including a soundproof theater equipped for worldwide video-conferencing. Nonsmoking rooms • 15 meeting rooms.

Willard Inter-Continental $////
1401 Pennsylvania Ave NW 20004
☎ 628-9100 TX 897099 fax 637-7326
• AE DC MC V • 395 rooms, 62 suites, 1 restaurant, 2 bars, 1 coffee shop
Oliver Carr, a prominent Washington developer, restored the Willard to its 1901 splendor, besides adding offices and boutiques. Two blocks from the White House, this was once the gathering place for presidents, politicians and literary figures, including Mark Twain and Charles Dickens. Its block-long lobby, Peacock Alley, where special-interest groups would gather in hopes of cornering politicians, is where the term "lobbyist" was coined. The turn-of-the-century wood-paneled Willard Room serves American food. The Round Robin Bar is a replica of the c.1850 black marble original. Adjacent shopping complex • 15 meeting rooms, translation, recording facilities.

OTHER HOTELS

Georgetown Dutch Inn $// *1075 Thomas Jefferson St NW 20007 ☎ 337-0900 fax 333-6526 • AE DC MC V.* Off M Street, near the Chesapeake and Ohio Canal.

Henley Park $// *926 Massachusetts Ave NW 20001 ☎ 638-5200 fax 638-6740 • AE DC MC V.*

Quality Inn Downtown $/ *1315 16th St at Massachusetts Ave NW ☎ 232-8000 fax 667-9827 • AE DC MC V.*

Ramada Inn Central $// *1430 Rhode Island Ave NW 20005 ☎ 462-7777 fax 332-3519 • AE DC MC V.*

Tabard Inn $// *1739 N St NW ☎ 785-1277 fax 785-6173 • MC V.*

Washington $/// *15th St and Pennsylvania Ave NW 20004 ☎ 638-5900 TX 7108220105 fax 638-6740 • AE DC MC V.* Famous for its rooftop terrace, where from May to October you can admire the finest views in Washington, drink strawberry daquiris and have a snack or light meal.

Clubs

Washington clubs provide hidden, but powerful, opportunities to forge important business relationships – but mainly for men. The *F Street Club* is an exclusive dining club in the downtown area ☎ 331-0020. For prominent scientists, such as Carl Sagan, and literary figures, there is the all-male *Cosmos Club* ☎ 387-7783 in a distinguished building on Massachusetts Avenue near Embassy Row. The traditional business, legal and banking community belongs to the all-male *Metropolitan Club* ☎ 835-2500. The *University Club*, established in 1904, is on 16th Street

☎ 862-8800. It recently opened its membership to women and has meeting rooms as well as dining and athletic facilities. For women only, there is the *Sulgrave Club* on Massachusetts Avenue ☎ 462-5800.

In Georgetown, the traditional *City Tavern Club* provides its members with an intimate townhouse atmosphere. Situated downtown on I Street, the discreet men-only *Alibi Club* is very exclusive ☎ 298-7788.

Restaurants

Dining in Washington has moved away from steak and potatoes to more sophisticated fare, although quality does not always match prices. Many restaurants around K Street and Connecticut Avenue specialize in the business lunch, and prices in these establishments are equivalent to those in New York City. There is an ever-expanding range of ethnic restaurants. Georgetown's numerous exotic offerings lean towards the mass market, but those in Adams Morgan just northwest of Dupont Circle are, for the most part, good value.

Cantina d'Italia [$]//
1214A 18th St NW ☎ 659-1830 • closed L Sat, Sun • AE DC MC V • reservations essential
A northern Italian restaurant, popular for 20 years with business people, the media and the diplomatic corps. The intimate atmosphere is maintained in a series of dimly-lit small dining rooms, and the changing menu offers good fish, veal and pasta. Extensive wine list.

City Café [$]///
2213 M St NW ☎ 797-4860 • closed Sat L, Sun • no credit cards
Less formal and less expensive than its associated restaurant, the Nora. City Café's chic, modern decor is a suitable background for its healthy new American dishes based on organically grown produce from small local farms in Virgina, West Virginia and Maryland. A good choice for lunch.

Dominique's [$]//
1900 Pennsylvania Ave NW ☎ 452-1126 • closed L Sat, Sun • AE DC MC V
Just two blocks from the White House Dominique d'Erno has created an unusual restaurant featuring a rather gaudy mélange of paintings and other Washington memorabilia. In times past, this was a real showplace, though in recent years it has been surpassed by other, newer restaurants. It is still a favorite with Kennedy Center performers, however. The menu ranges from the traditional to the bizarre – including ostrich and rattlesnake.

Duke Zeibert's [$]//
Washington Square Bldg, 1050 Connecticut Ave NW ☎ 466-3730 • closed Sun L • AE DC MC V • jacket
The owner came out of retirement a few years ago to move his well-established restaurant into a new building with a view of Connecticut Avenue – though, that said, if you get the view, you are not in the preferred room. For over 30 years he has made his reliable steak and seafood house a home for politicians, business leaders, athletes and media personalities, though the food is easily bettered in other nearby restaurants.

Fourways [$]//
1701 20th St NW ☎ 483-3200 • closed L Sat, Sun • AE DC MC V • jacket and tie
The French food at Fourways is attractive, as is the building itself – a grand oak-paneled mansion that is a historic landmark.

Germaine's [$]///
2400 Wisconsin Ave NW ☎ 965-1185

• closed L Sat, Sun • *AE DC MC V* • *reservations essential*
Serving well-prepared Asian dishes – incorporating Vietnamese, Korean, Chinese, Thai, Indian and Japanese influences, among others – Germaine Swanson's spectacularly successful restaurant is one of the best in Washington. The daily specials are the thing to watch for, as is the house specialty, pine cone fish. Good wine list.

Jean-Louis [$]////
Watergate Hotel ☏ *298-4488* • *closed 2 weeks in Aug* • *AE DC MC V* • *reservations essential*
Regulars feel that you cannot beat the *nouvelle* creations prepared here by Jean-Louis Palladin, one of America's most inventive and talented chefs. Go here for a special evening; expect to be pampered, and to pay plenty for it. Pastel peach walls and mirrors make the small room seem spacious. There are two seatings per night with three-, four- and five-course meals available, and you can choose wines by the glass to accompany each course.

Jockey Club [$]//
Ritz-Carlton Hotel ☏ *659-8000* • *AE DC MC V* • *jacket and tie*
This old Kennedy favorite has a warm, clubby atmosphere, with red leather banquettes and English hunting prints on the walls; and it remains well patronized by politicians and media types. Its crabmeat is renowned; its service laudable.

Joe and Mo's [$]//
1211 Connecticut Ave NW
☏ *659-1211* • *closed Sat L, Sun* • *AE DC MC V* • *L reservations essential*
An Old Downtown institution, this steakhouse has a loyal following among the city's leaders, although one goes here to be noticed, not for the food, which is occasionally disappointing. On the other hand, the staff are courteous and efficient. Ideal for breakfast – imaginative and well-prepared – as well as for lunch.

Le Lion d'Or [$]///
1150 Connecticut Ave NW
☏ *296-7972* • *closed L Sat, Sun* • *AE DC MC V*
Chef-owner Jean Pièrre Goyenvalle has maintained consistently high standards. Duck, quail and pigeon are specialties of his kitchen; the seafood and soufflés are also noteworthy. Dishes are classic French rather than *nouvelle*. The wine list is fairly priced. Original art and antiques grace this elegant and well-known restaurant.

Maison Blanche [$]///
1725 F St NW ☏ *842-0070* • *closed L Sat, Sun* • *AE DC MC V* • *jacket and tie*
A favorite of the Reagan and Bush administrations, the Maison Blanche is consistently rated as one of the better restaurants; a good table here undoubtedly lends status. The setting is plush. The waiters are helpful in guiding you to the excellent daily specials, and the long wine list offers some good things.

McPherson Grill [$]//
950 15th St NW ☏ *638-0950* • *closed L Sat, Sun* • *AE DC MC V*
Attorneys and White House staff are among the clientele at this latest of Oliver Carr's ventures. The Grill formula has been updated: a bright and airy Art Deco interior (but with the traditional crimson leather banquettes) and subtle variations to standard steaks, seafood and side orders. There is also a bar, and a private dining room.

Mr K's [$]//
2121 K St NW ☏ *331-8868* • *AE DC MC V* • *jacket and tie*
Two white marble lions guard the entrance to this elegant restaurant in the city's business district. The food is Chinese, while the plush dining room (which includes a nonsmoking area) has a pleasant European feel. The giant shrimp, quail and frogs' legs are splendid, and the service is gracious.

Morton's of Chicago $////
3251 Prospect St NW ☏ 342-6258 • closed L and Sun • AE DC MC V
Morton's is undoubtedly Washington's best steakhouse, and its white-walled dining room is always crowded with politicians, lobbyists and business people. It takes no reservations after 7pm. Huge portions.

Nora $////
2132 Florida Ave NW at R St ☏ 462-5143 • closed L and Sun • no credit cards
Fine American *nouvelle cuisine* is served here in a cozy setting with lace curtains and turn-of-the-century furniture. Typical dishes include smoked trout with horseradish sauce and roast chicken with mustard cream sauce; all produce is organically grown. The meat served is only from animals reared in stress-free conditions.

Occidental $///
475 Pennsylvania Ave NW ☏ 783-1475 • closed Sat L, Sun • AE DC MC V
Renovated and reopened in 1987, the Occidental has made a dramatic comeback to the Washington restaurant scene. Upstairs is the formal main dining room; downstairs the paneled, club-like Grill Rooms lined with photographs of famous patrons and testifying to the slogan of 1906, "Where Statesmen Dine." Famous faces are still seen. The cooking is now modern American.

Old Ebbitt Grill $///
675 15th St NW ☏ 347-4801 • AE DC MC V
Founded in 1856, Ebbitt's is the city's oldest saloon, although the present building is a recent reconstruction. It has Persian rugs, oak beams, marble floors and gas lamps. There is an oyster bar, the Old Bar and Grant's Bar, as well as two dining areas. There is a varied menu – everything from hamburgers to pasta, good fish, excellent desserts. It is also popular for breakfast.

Le Pavillon $//////
Washington Sq Bldg, 1050 Connecticut Ave NW ☏ 833-3846 • closed L Sat, Sun • AE DC V • jacket • reservations requested
A Lalique table stands in the foyer of this favorite of Washington society. Exquisite *nouvelle cuisine* is served here, and Chef Yannich Cam checks every dish as it leaves the kitchen. The service is attentive and discreet, and tables are suitably spaced for privacy. However, some people feel the prices are too high and the portions on the small side. For a celebratory dinner.

Sichuan Pavilion $///
1820 K St NW ☏ 466-7790 • AE DC MC V
Although the restaurant is US-owned, the Sichuan's chefs are recruited from the People's Republic of China Chungking Service Bureau, which operates hotels and restaurants for visiting dignitaries and prepares state banquets. This is the best Chinese restaurant in Washington – elegant yet unpretentious. The food is always beautifully presented, and the service discreet.

Vincenzo's $///
1606 20th St NW ☏ 667-0047 • closed Sun • AE MC V
This pleasant Italian seafood restaurant serves excellent fresh fish,

Out of town
If time permits and you want a special treat, head for *Windows* ☏ (703) 527-4430, across Key Bridge in Rosslyn, Virginia, which offers a panoramic view of DC. The menu is also excellent. *L'Auberge Chez François* is a pleasant 45min drive through Virginia hunt country to Great Falls. Note, however, that you have to make your reservation two weeks ahead. The food is Alsatian, the atmosphere that of a French country inn.

grilled or fried, and pasta – but no meat or cream sauces. The simple Adriatic decor features tiled floors and whitewashed walls.

Washington Palm [$]////
1225 19th St NW ☎ *293-9091* • *closed Sat L, Sun* • AE DC MC V • *reservations essential*
A southern cousin of New York's Palm restaurant, this is yet another stronghold of the city's business and political communities. The steaks are good, the lobsters succulent and truly jumbo-sized, the service friendly and reasonably efficient. Well recommended for working lunches.

Bars

Washington's hotel bars and lounges are much in use as work spills over from offices. The business elite favor the *Fairfax Bar* at the Ritz-Carlton, the classiest bar in town, with 18thC English paintings on the walls. Other favorite bars include *Bullfeathers*, 410 1st St SE, *the* gathering place for Hill staffers; the *Hawk & Dove*, 329 Pennsylvania Ave SE, close to the Capitol, with an old Irish tavern atmosphere; and *Jenkins Hill*, 223 Pennsylvania Ave SE, one of the longest bars in DC.

In the business district, the *Sign of the Whale*, 1825 M St NW, is an attractive English-style pub, popular with young professionals. *Rumors*, 1900 M St NW, is always crowded. Besides its two bars, it has an enclosed sidewalk café overlooking busy 19th Street.

In Georgetown, *Clyde's*, 3236 M St NW, is frequented by Washington politicoes and their staff. Art Deco design and lively 1960s music make *F Scott's*, 1232 36th St NW, a local favorite. *Mr Smith's*, 3104 M St NW, is a Georgetown landmark, with an old tavern atmosphere.

Entertainment

The best sources of information are the "Weekend" section of Friday's *Washington Post* and the monthly *Washingtonian* magazine. For tickets contact *Ticketplace*, 12th and F St NW ☎ 842-5387. Cut-rate tickets are often available on the day of an event.

Music *The John F Kennedy Center for the Performing Arts*, New Hampshire Avenue at Rock Creek Pkwy ☎ 254-3600, is a stunning building overlooking the Potomac River. With five halls, including the Opera House and the Concert Hall, it is the cultural hub of Washington. Its restaurant, The Roof Terrace, has only mediocre food and an overwhelming decor of red plush and chandeliers, but is convenient. *Blues Alley* ☎ 337-4141 in Georgetown attracts student and diplomat jazz fans. During summer months there is a fine arts and music festival, featuring well-known performers, at *Wolf Trap Park*, about 45mins out of town in the direction of Dulles Airport; for information call ☎ (703) 255-1800. Summertime entertainment is also provided at the *Carter Barron Amphitheatre* in Rock Creek Park ☎ 426-6700.

Theater Washington's principal theaters are the *Warner* 13th St between E and F ☎ 626-1050, and the *National*, 1321 Pennsylvania Ave NW ☎ 628-6161; both stage Broadway productions. The *Folger Theater*, 201 East Capitol St SE ☎ 546-4000, is considered America's top Shakespearean playhouse. *Ford's Theater* ☎ 347-4833 has been restored to the way it was the night President Lincoln was shot. *Arena Stage*, 6th St and Maine Ave SW ☎ 448-3300, is a fine repertory theater.
Comedy and drama are presented at the *Eisenhower* in the Kennedy Center.

Nightclubs The *Marquee Lounge* in the Omni Shoreham Hotel has 1930s and 1940s music; for 1950s, 1960s and 1970s sounds, try *Déja Vu* on M Street.

Shopping

Formerly something of a fashion backwater, Washington has a growing number of smart shops. In the heart of the business district along

Connecticut Avenue, you will find *Elizabeth Arden*, the *Tiny Jewel Box*, *Burberry's* and *Ralph Lauren Polo Shop*. *Kramer Books & Afterwords* is both bookstore and café. At 1840 L St NW there is *Brooks Brothers* men's shop. Department stores such as *Woodward & Lothrop*, known as "Woodies," *Hecht's* and fashionable *Garfinckel's* are in Old Downtown. Shopping malls include *The Shops* at National Place, 1331 Pennsylvania Ave, and *The Old Post Office*, just opposite.

If you have time, Georgetown has something for everyone – especially along Wisconsin and M Streets. *Georgetown Park* has 120 shops and restaurants in an attractive converted warehouse. *Mazza Gallery*, on the border of DC and Chevy Chase, Maryland, on Wisconsin Avenue NW, is popular and has a Metrorail stop. *Neiman-Marcus* is accompanied by an array of boutiques from *Benetton* to *Pierre Deux*. In the same area are *Lord & Taylor*, *Saks Fifth Avenue*, *Saks-Jandel* and *Gucci*. Among Virginia's shopping malls are *Tyson's Corner*, in Vienna (including Bloomingdale's), and *Fair Oaks Mall*, near Dulles Airport.

Sightseeing

Washington's monuments, parks and museums, especially the Smithsonian, could keep a sightseer busy for months.

Arlington National Cemetery Includes the Tomb of the Unknown Soldier, the Kennedy graves and Arlington House, home of General Robert E Lee until the Civil War. *Across the Memorial Bridge, in Arlington ☎ 629-0931. Open Apr–Sep, 8–7; Oct–Mar, 8–5.*

Capitol Half-hour tours of the Capitol set off every 15mins, 9–3.45. US visitors can arrange with their Congressman to get a pass to enter the chambers of the House or Senate to see Congress in action; European visitors will need some form of identification, such as a passport. *East end of the Mall ☎ 224-3121 or 225-6827. Open 9–4.30.*

Corcoran Gallery of Art Founded in 1859, this museum has a fine collection of American art, as well as works by European masters. *New York Ave and 17th St NW ☎ 638-1439. Tours Tue–Sun, 10–4.30; Thu, 10–9.*

Diplomatic Reception Room, Department of State Exquisitely decorated room, with fine 18thC antiques; it is here that the Secretary of State entertains foreign dignitaries. *2201 C St NW ☎ 632-3241. Tours at various times; reservations needed.*

Dumbarton Oaks This splendid Georgetown mansion houses Byzantine and pre-Columbian art. *1703 32nd St NW; gardens at 31st and R St. Open daily, 2–6; museum Tue–Sun, 2–5.*

Executive Office Building This vast gray pile in Second Empire style, just west of the White House, is the home of various governmental offices. Not open to the public, but the exterior is worth a small detour for its architectural interest. *17th St and Pennsylvania Ave NW.*

Hillwood Estate The former estate of Marjorie Merriweather Post, located in the upper reaches of northwest Washington. You can tour her home and see her large collection of Russian decorative arts, including Fabergé. *4155 Linnean Ave ☎ 686-5807. Reservations required. Closed Tue & Sun.*

Jefferson Memorial The graceful, domed monument is especially striking at night. Engraved on its walls are excerpts from Jefferson's writings, including the Declaration of Independence. *Tidal Basin end of 15th St SW.*

Library of Congress Built in 1897, the copper-domed Library contains more than 80m books and is one of the most spectacular buildings in Washington, an ornate Italian Renaissance/Beaux-Arts design modeled after the Paris Opera House. There are exhibits, concerts and lecture tours. Just next to the Capitol. *1st and E Capitol St SE ☎ 707-5458. Open Mon–Fri, 9–4; Sat, 8.30–5; Sun, 1–5.*

Lincoln Memorial Inspired by classical Greek architecture with columns representing the 36 states in the Union when Lincoln died. At the west end of the Mall. *23rd St NW between Constitution and Independence Ave. Open 24hrs daily.*
National Gallery of Art Situated on the Mall, this is one of the world's great art museums. The graceful West Building is a harmonious setting for an outstanding collection of Old Masters, particularly strong in the Italian and Dutch schools. There are also important Impressionist paintings. The acclaimed new East Building contains modern art, including works by Alexander Calder and Henry Moore, and temporary exhibitions. The Museum has a good cafeteria restaurant and presents free concerts on Sunday evenings. *4th–6th Sts on Constitution Ave ☏ 737-4215. Open Mon–Sat, 10–5; Sun, 12–9.*
National Zoological Park Held to be one of the world's finest zoos, this forms part of the Smithsonian Institution (see below), though it is located in an extension of northwest Washington's Rock Creek Park. The giant pandas Hsing-Hsing and Ling-Ling – a gift from China – are major attractions. A pleasant spot to spend a sunny afternoon. *3001 Connecticut Ave NW ☏ 673-4821. Open May–mid-Sep, 8–8 (grounds), 9–6 (buildings); mid-Sep–Apr, 8–6 (grounds), 10–4.30 (buildings).*
Phillips Collection Two blocks northwest of Dupont Circle, this is a fine collection of art, featuring Impressionist and Post-Impressionist painting, in a lovely old red-brick house. *1600 21st St NW ☏ 387-2151. Open Tue–Sat, 10–5; Sun, 2–7.*
Smithsonian Institution The Smithsonian is a federally chartered, nonprofit corporation comprising scientific, educational and cultural interests based mostly in Washington. Most of the buildings are along the Mall. The building known as the *Castle* is the headquarters and has a visitors' center ☏ 357-2700. The *Air and Space Museum*, held to be the world's most popular museum, has some fascinating films, as well as the Wright brothers' first airplane, Lindbergh's *Spirit of St Louis*, various space vehicles, and even the *USS Enterprise*, well known to all *Star Trek* fans. *The National Museum of American Art*, *The National Museum of American History* and *The National Museum of Natural History* all have excellent displays and exhibits. The *Freer Gallery* has the finest Far and Near Eastern art outside the Orient; and the *Hirshhorn Museum*, which displays modern art, has an outstanding sculpture garden. *1000 Jefferson Dr SW. Most museums are open daily, 10–5.*
US Supreme Court This Neo-classical marble structure is one of the Capital's most impressive. The Court's sessions are open to the public. *1st and E Capitol St SE ☏ 479-3000. Cafeteria open Mon–Fri, 9–4.30.*
Washington Cathedral A huge Gothic-style church (Episcopal), also known as the National Cathedral and, more accurately, the Cathedral Church of St Peter and St Paul. Still unfinished (because of the slow traditional construction methods employed), it is a successful blend of French and English Gothic styles. The splendid interior has some fine stained glass, and the square tower is a Washington landmark. *Mt St Alban ☏ 537-6200. Open daily, 10–4.30.*
Washington Monument The world's tallest masonry structure, designed by Pierre L'Enfant. An elevator takes you to the top. *15th St and Constitution Ave. Open daily, Apr–Sep.*
White House This elegant porticoed building is the official home of the President. A popular tour takes visitors through five state rooms. Tickets to the more comprehensive "VIP" tour can sometimes be obtained through congressional contacts. *1600 Pennsylvania Ave NW ☏ 456-7041. Open Tue–Sat, 10–12.*

Guided tours

You can get to the sights by walking,

taking the Metrorail, or hiring your own limousine for the afternoon. *Gray Line* ☏ 386-8300 has set tours such as "Washington After Dark," but one of the most reasonable ways to view major sights is the *Tourmobile* ☏ 554-7950. These blue-and-white canopied shuttle buses operate continuously, so you can get on or off at any one of the 18 stations and stay as long as you please.

Out of town

Colonial Williamsburg lies 150 miles/240kms south of Washington DC in Virginia. Once the capital of the colony of Virginia, it is full of historical interest and has been meticulously restored. Although inevitably somewhat artificial, it successfully captures the atmosphere of 18thC life. *Mt Vernon* lies 16 miles/25kms south of the city on the George Washington Parkway in Virginia. A gracious 18thC house overlooking the Potomac, it was the home of George Washington and is still maintained in the style of an old southern plantation. You can also travel there by boat, Mar–Nov, leaving from Pier 4, 6th and Water Streets NW ☏ 554-8000.

Spectator sports

Baseball Washington does not have its own major league team. But you can watch the Baltimore *Orioles* at Baltimore Stadium ☏ (301) 347-2525.
Basketball The *Washington Bullets* play at the Capital Center, Capital Beltway and Central Ave, Landover, Maryland. For tickets ☏ (301) 350-3900.
Football The *Redskins* are based at the Robert F Kennedy Stadium ☏ 546-2222.
Horse-racing For thoroughbred racing, *Laurel Race Course*, Laurel, Maryland ☏ 725-0400, about 18 miles/28kms away. *Pimlico* lies 40 miles/64kms from Washington ☏ (301) 542-9400.
Ice hockey The Washington *Capitols* play at the Capital Center ☏ 350-3500.

Keeping fit

Fitness centers *JW Marriott Hotel*, 1331 Pennsylvania Ave NW ☏ 393-2000; *Washington Squash and Nautilus Club*, 1220 20 St NW ☏ 659-9570; *Watergate Health Club*, 2650 Virginia Ave NW ☏ 298-4460; *Westin Fitness Center*, 2401 M St NW ☏ 457-5070.
Bicycling Washington's wide boulevards are ideal for cyclists. For rentals, *Big Wheels*, 1004 Vermont Ave NW ☏ 638-3301.
Boating The calm Potomac River is especially suitable for canoes or sailboats. *Thompsons Boat Center*, Virginia Ave at Rock Creek Pkwy NW ☏ 333-4861, rents canoes, sailboats and bicycles.
Golf *Rock Creek* course, 16th and Rittenhouse NW ☏ 882-7332, is open to the public. *East Potomac Park* ☏ 863-9007 has both 18-hole and 9-hole courses. The Maryland and Virginia suburbs have many other open courses.
Horseback riding *Rock Creek Park* has 14 miles/22kms of wooded trails, a bicycle path and a bridle path. For information on rentals, horses and instruction, contact *Rock Creek Park Horse Center*, Military and Glover Roads NW ☏ 362-0117.
Jogging A favorite jogging course is the *Mall*, from the Lincoln Memorial to the Capitol.
Tennis *Rock Creek Tennis Stadium*, 16th and Kennedy NW ☏ 234-5090, and *East Potomac Park* ☏ 554-5962, have more than 20 courts which you can rent. Indoor, clay and hard. Reservations must be made in person.

Local resources

Business services

All of the concierges at the hotels can find you almost any service you may need. Alternatives are *Codus Corporation* ☏ 347-4947 or *Courtesy Associates* ☏ 347-5900.
Photocopying *City Duplicating Service* ☏ 296-0700; *Beaver Press* ☏ 347-6400.
Secretarial *Courtesy Associates* ☏ 347-5900.

Translators *International Visitor Information Service*, Language Bank ☏ 783-6540; *Berlitz Language Center* ☏ 331-1160; *Interpreters Bureau* (used by State Dept) ☏ 296-1346.

Communications

Long-distance delivery *Federal Express* ☏ 953-3333; *DHL Worldwide* ☏ 684-8733.
Local delivery *Metro* ☏ 387-8200; *All State Messenger Service* ☏ 841-9000; *Messenger Express* ☏ 347-7333.
Post office Main branch ☏ 523-2337, Massachusetts Ave and North Capitol St. Open Mon–Fri, 7am–midnight.

Convention/exhibition centers

District of Columbia Armory, 2001 E Capitol St ☏ 547-9077; *Washington DC Convention Center*, 900 9th St NW ☏ 789-1600.

Emergencies

Hospitals *Georgetown University*, 3800 Reservoir Rd NW ☏ 687-5055; *George Washington Medical Center*, 901 23rd St NW ☏ 994-3884; *Columbia Hospital for Women*, 24th and L St NW ☏ 293-6500.
Pharmacies *Peoples' Drug Store*, 14th and Thomas Circle ☏ 628-0720.

Information sources

Business information *Greater Washington Board of Trade*, 1129 20th St NW ☏ 857-5900.
Local media The *Washington Post* gives good local, national and international coverage. The *Washington Times* is not so well thought of. *USA Today* is based in Virginia. The monthly *Regardie's* magazine provides an incisive feature-oriented business commentary, while the *Washingtonian* (also monthly) is very helpful for local information. *Dossier* specializes in the latest Washington gossip.
Visitor information The *Washington DC Convention and Visitors Association* (*WCVA*), 1212 New York Ave NW ☏ 789-7000, provides free brochures on hotels, sightseeing, events, restaurants. It also operates the *Washington Visitor Information Center*, 1455 Pennsylvannia Ave NW ☏ 789-7000, open Mon–Sat, 9–5.

Thank-yous

Florists *The Flower Designers*, 3301 New Mexico Ave NW ☏ 966-3400; *David Ladd & Co*, 1622 Wisconsin Ave NW ☏ 337-0413.
Gift baskets *Sutton Place Gourmet* ☏ 363-5800, on New Mexico Avenue, can deliver a basket of almost any kind of food. Also *Sutton Place Gift Gallery Ltd* ☏ 966-8228 and *Essentially Chocolate* ☏ 387-6994 supply attractive packages.

Planning and Reference

Entry details

Documentation

Visas All travelers to the USA except nationals of Canada, Mexico, Japan and Britain (who have a right of abode in the UK, who will stay up to 90 days only and have a non-refundable return ticket) require a visa. There are various types. The non-immigrant visa is specially designed for temporary business visitors. Application forms can be obtained from travel agents, airlines, or the local US embassy or consulate. Processing visa applications may take four weeks, though it is possible to obtain a visa in a few hours through major travel agencies who run a visa service. Application must be by post or through an agency, not in person. Business visa applicants will require a valid passport and may need some kind of proof – a letter from a US contact or their own firm will do – of the business nature of the trip. Most visas are multiple entry with a maximum of six months per stay, issued for an indefinite period, and do not need to be renewed. Have the still valid visa transferred to the current passport. The Immigration authorities have the right to refuse entry even if there is a valid visa. There is a directory of undesirable aliens.

Health requirements Only travelers from countries where diseases such as cholera and yellow fever are widespread require vaccination certificates; check with the US embassy.

Driver's license To drive in the USA, it is advisable to have an International Driving Permit but sufficient to have a license issued by a country that has signed the 1949 Geneva Motoring Convention. Travelers who do not have such a license must apply for a US license by contacting the Dept of Motor Vehicles in the state of entry to the USA. A test is necessary in most states.

Immigration Among others, you are asked the following questions on the forms you need to fill in before entry. Are you carrying more than $5,000? Have you recently been on a farm or ranch? Are you carrying fruit or vegetables?

Customs regulations

Basic duty-free allowances are for one liter of wine or spirits and either 200 cigarettes or 50 cigars or two kilos of tobacco. Personal gifts totalling up to $100 in value are duty-free, but this can be claimed only once in a six-month period. Some state laws permit less alcohol; check with the embassy or airline.

Prohibitions Entry of meat and meat products, fish, fruit, dairy products, vegetables and plants is restricted. Many such items are banned. Some products are not to be carried across state lines; fruit cannot be taken into California, for example. Visitors carrying medication should bring along a prescription or validating letter from a doctor in case it is a prohibited drug in the USA, where many items, such as codeine, are available only by prescription.

Climate

The USA has many extremes of climate, from deserts and swamps to subtropical forests and permanent glaciers. Some places freeze for months in the winter and bake in the summer. Tornados are an occasional hazard in the Midwest, hurricanes in Florida and the Gulf of Mexico. In summer, the country is almost universally hot, but San Francisco and Seattle are among the exceptions. The winter traveler visiting different regions has to be prepared for all weathers. Remember that offices, restaurants, shops, hotels and homes are centrally heated and air-conditioned, with the result that in summer you go from very hot outside temperatures to over-cool inside. The reverse is true in winter.

The Northeast is a temperate region, with about 3.5in rainfall a month throughout the year. Winds are rarely heavy, though in New York state and New England winter temperatures can be brought down sharply by winds blowing from the north and northeast through Canada. Summers are warm, sometimes hot, and can be oppressively humid in coastal cities such as New York. Daytime temperatures in New York fall to several degrees below freezing, as low as 25°F/-4°C in winter, and remain in the 80s/about 30°C between June and August. Boston is cooler. Snow falls all over the region in winter.

The Midwest The farther west you travel, the drier it gets. Driest are the plains states, in the shadow of the Rockies, with as little as 20in/50cm rainfall a year. Most rain in the region falls in spring and early summer. Winter is very cold in Northern states, with constant and chilling winds keeping temperatures down at 27°CF/-7°C commonplace. More southerly cities, such as Kansas and St Louis, also freeze, with low day air temperatures around 40°F/4°C. Spring and autumn – also called fall – both tend to be short and pleasant, and summers are hot throughout the region, with temperatures in the 80s/about 30°C. It is generally a dry heat, but humidity can be high in the Great Lakes area.

South and Southeast Frosts are relatively rare in the Deep South and Southeast, but they are fairly common in border states such as Virginia and Kentucky. Winters in Florida are positively pleasant, with temperatures rarely going much below 70°F/18°C. Summers are always hot – around 90°F/32°C throughout the region in July and August – and are more pleasant inland. Florida and the Gulf of Mexico often have 90% humidity for weeks at a time, with violent storms bringing only temporary relief. The average monthly coastal rainfall can be as much as 8in/20.32cm. The difference is quite marked in Texas, where inland cities such as Dallas and San Antonio have 30–40% less rainfall than Houston.

Far West The region splits into three climactic zones. In the north, Oregon and Washington can be very wet, often with snow on high ground inland. Winters are fairly mild, especially in the coastal cities like Seattle – where it rarely freezes, and summers are warm and dry. Along the Pacific coast from the Canadian border to below San Francisco fogs are common in summer. California and the Rockies are drier and sunnier, with altitude determining the temperature; the Rockies and Sierra can be numbingly cold in winter. Even relatively sheltered Denver has winter temperatures as low as the Northern cities. The coastal plain is very different. It never freezes in Los Angeles or San Francisco; summer temperatures in LA are around 80°F/27°C, and in San Francisco around 70°F/21°C. Inland, Arizona and New Mexico are the driest regions in the USA, consisting mainly of desert with an annual rainfall of less than 10in/25.4cm. There are occasional frosts in winter, but summer temperatures in Phoenix, for example, are generally well over 100°F/38°C.

Alaska The largest state in the Union, with extremely varied topography, Alaska has great climatic diversity. Summer temperatures, however, are generally pleasant – about 75°F/24°C in the largest city, Anchorage. Winters are cold with temperatures sometimes dropping to –10°F/–23°C. In this part of the state rainfall averages about 25in annually.

Hawaii Despite being situated in the tropical zone, Hawaii has a temperate climate, thanks to cooling trade winds; and the temperature in Honolulu normally ranges between 72°F/26°C and 78°F/26°C. The amount of rainfall varies dramatically throughout the island, with some places receiving about 9in annually and others more than 450in.

Information sources

For general business information about the USA, visitors can contact the commercial department of the US embassy in their own country – or any local association established to promote trade and commerce with the USA. Sources of business information inside the USA include the commercial departments in each state and individual city chambers of commerce. More general, nationwide information can be obtained from the Chamber of Commerce of the United States, 1615 H St NW, Washington DC 20062 ☎ (202) 463-5300, or else from the Council of State Chambers of Commerce, 122 C St NW, Suite 200, Washington DC 20001 ☎ (202) 484-8103. For general tourist information, contact the office of the United States Travel and Tourism Administration (USTTA) in your home country. In the USA, information is available from state and city tourist offices.

Holidays

The main vacation months in the USA are June–early September, when the schools take their summer break; many factories close down during August. But more and more incentive fares are being introduced to encourage the spread of holidays through the year. There are also many official national, regional and state holidays. The following holidays are observed in all states unless otherwise indicated.

Jan 1 New Year's Day
3rd Mon in Jan Martin Luther King Day in most Northern states
Feb 12 Lincoln's Birthday – in 23 Northern states
3rd Mon in Feb Washington's Birthday
Late Mar/early Apr Good Friday
Jul 4 Independence Day
1st Mon in Sep Labor Day
2nd Mon in Oct Columbus Day or Pioneer's Day in 44 states
Nov 11 Armistice Day and Veterans' Day
Tue after 1st Mon in Oct Election Day, even years only
4th Thu in Nov Thanksgiving Day
Dec 25 Christmas Day

Some fixed-date holidays are celebrated on the nearest Monday; in some states, if any holiday falls on a Sunday the following Monday is automatically a holiday. In addition, many cities have their own holidays – for example, Boston observes St Patrick's Day on *Mar 17*.

In cities with a large Jewish population – notably New York – the observances of the major Jewish holidays may affect the business schedule. The dates of these vary slightly from year to year, and the degree of observance also varies, depending upon whether one is Orthodox, Reform or Conservative (the last two being more liberal). The holiday periods are as follows: Passover (commemorating the Exodus from Egypt), eight days mid to late Apr; Rosh Hashanah (New Year), two days end Sep; Yom Kippur (the Day of Atonement – the holiest day of the year), beginning of Oct; Chanukah (celebrating the rededication of the Temple in 165 BC), eight days mid to late Dec.

Money

The US dollar is divided into 100 cents (¢). Coins in circulation are the penny (1¢), nickel (5¢), dime (10¢), quarter (25¢), half dollar (50¢), and dollar ($1); the last two are not in common use. It is useful to keep a good supply of nickels, dimes and quarters for public telephones and vending machines. Notes (called bills) in circulation are $1, $2, $5, $10, $20, $50, $100, $500, and $1,000. Again the last two are very rare. All bills are green and of the same size; large denomination bills may be refused. You should avoid carrying large amounts of cash; credit and charge cards and US$ travelers' checks are the safest and most convenient way to take your money.

Credit and charge cards The major cards are widely accepted throughout the USA in hotels, motels, restaurants, stores and gas stations. Renting a car without a credit or charge card can be very difficult, and most hotels like you to produce one when you check in. Before you leave for the USA, check that your credit card limit is high enough.

Checks US$ travelers' checks can generally be used as if they were cash, though you may need to produce identification. Banks may refuse to cash foreign denomination travelers' checks.

Changing money in the USA is more difficult than in, say, Europe – another reason for relying on plastic cards and US$ travelers' checks. Visitors are advised to calculate how much money they may need for porters, taxis, and so on, and to carry the necessary cash. It is not a good idea to rely on banks. Relatively few banks and hotels will exchange currencies (if they do, the commission is likely to be high), and specialist currency exchange offices are rare outside international airports. Banks open Mon–Fri, 9–3. Some open late one day a week; a few open Sat morning.

Sales taxes

Sales There is no Federal indirect taxation, but cities and states levy sales tax – 2–12% – on most transactions; prices displayed do not include sales tax.

Tipping

Hotels Bellhops expect $1 minimum or 50¢–$1 per bag; in top-class hotels allow $2 per bag or $5 for several bags. There is no need to tip the elevator operator or desk clerk, but regard $1 as the minimum for the doorman on arrival or on leaving – more if he provides some special service. Thereafter, when you need a taxi 50¢ would do. Tip the chambermaid $1.50 per night. Leave the money in an envelope marked "For the maid."

Restaurants Allow 15–20% of the bill before tax. Tipping the maître d'hôtel is usually officially discouraged, but it is often the only way to get a seat in a crowded restaurant.

Bars For waiter service, allow 15–20% of the bill. A tip is expected even if you are served at the bar.

Taxi Drivers expect around 15%, more in New York.

Other situations At railroad stations and airports, 50¢–75¢ a bag, minimum $1. Haircut, shave, 15–20%. Restroom attendant 25¢–$1.

Getting there

Fierce competition between airlines, particularly on North Atlantic and domestic routes, has made it difficult even for skilled travel agents to keep up to date with the options open to the international traveler visiting the USA; and distance is no guide to air fares. Visitor USA (VUSA) fares (see below) are not available to Americans. If price is a major consideration, it may be cheaper to fly into a major gateway and take a domestic flight to the final destination, especially if you plan on three or more flights on one particular carrier; then a 3-(or more) coupon air pass is available, giving substantial discounts. If time is crucial, note that not all "direct" international flights are nonstop. The following cities are major gateways: Atlanta, Boston, Chicago, Dallas/Fort Worth, Denver, Detroit, Houston, Los Angeles, Miami, Minneapolis/St Paul, New York (JFK and Newark), Orlando, St Louis, San Francisco, Seattle and Washington DC.

Getting around

The distances involved usually mean that it is best to fly between major cities, rather than go by road or rail. For some journeys – New York to Washington, for example – train can be quicker and more comfortable.

By air

The domestic air network is extremely comprehensive, and numerous discount and promotional fare schemes make it worthwhile shopping around for a flight. Ask your travel agent for the cheapest possible fare on the flight(s) of your choice. VUSA fares (which must be booked outside the USA) give discounts of up to 40% of the normal fare. Frequent Flyer programs or Mileage Clubs offer upgrades, other benefits such as car rental, hotel discounts, and eventually free flights to regular customers with a US address.

By car

The fastest routes are the multi-lane Interstate highways, indicated on maps and signs by I followed by the number on a shield. They have no traffic lights or cross traffic and only limited access and exit points. US and state highways are similar, but with more entrances and exits and some cross traffic.

Regulations There is a 55mph/88kph speed limit generally on all roads nationwide although it can be 65mph/104kph; built-up areas and school zones have lower limits marked by roadside signs. Other regulations vary from state to state, but some are common to all. Overtaking on the inside is permitted on multi-lane highways, and you are usually allowed to turn right on a red light, if the way is clear – though not in New York City. It is illegal to pass a school bus when it has stopped to pick up or unload children, and to drive while under the influence of alcohol. In some states it is illegal to carry alcoholic drinks in a car, unless they are still sealed. Generally it is illegal to take alcohol across state lines.

Gas stations are numerous, although there may be long distances between them on the interstates. Gasoline is sold by the American gallon, 4/5th of an imperial gallon, equivalent to just under four liters.

Car rental is easy, provided you are over 25, have a valid driving license and a credit or charge card. Rates vary from state to state; Florida's are low, New York's high. Quoted rates do not include collision damage waiver, personal accident insurance or tax. If you want to pick up a car in one place and leave it in another, there is usually a drop-off charge; local companies rarely allow you to do this. Corporate rates are worth investigating, as are fly-drive and other special deals for car rental bookings made outside the USA. Large companies generally cover their staff for insurance. Make sure that you don't give rental companies double profits!

National and international firms with toll-free (800) numbers include:
Avis ☎ 331-1212
Budget ☎ 527-0700
Dollar ☎ 421-6868
Hertz ☎ 654-3131
National ☎ 227-7368.
Thrifty ☎ 367-2277.

Breakdowns and accidents If the car is rented, there will be a leaflet in the glove compartment describing procedures in the case of accident and breakdown. If you break down on a highway, and there is no phone nearby, pull off the road, raise the hood, attach something white – a handkerchief or scarf, for example – to the driver's door handle and wait for a police highway patrol. Walking along a highway, especially at night, is dangerous, and in some states illegal. Unaccompanied women are advised to stay in the car with the doors locked until help arrives.

Officially, all road accidents must be reported to the police.

By rail

The inter-city Amtrak rail network covers 44 states and about 500 cities. Services are most popular up and down the "Northeast Corridor" between Boston, New York and Washington, and on into Florida and New Orleans, and on the West Coast between Los Angeles and San Francisco. Services in the Midwest are minimal and journeys often require more than one change of train, although routes radiate from Chicago to the West, Southwest and South. As a means of seeing the country in comfort, the coast-to-coast lines, with their observation cars, bars and club cars, are unsurpassed. But some of the track is in poor condition, and late running is not unusual.

Reservations can be made at city center stations, at travel agents, at Amtrak offices or by calling the Amtrak toll-free number ☏ (800) 872-7245. Discounts are available on some routes if you make prior reservations.

By bus

Greyhound and Trailways are the two major long-distance bus companies covering the Continental US with scheduled services.

Hotels

The immense hotel-building boom experienced in the USA in the past two decades has been led by the needs of the ever-growing army of national and international business travelers. In all major US cities there is now a wide choice of first-rate hotels offering a range of business facilities and services rarely found in European provincial hotels.

Styles Most US hotels are purpose-built, and few date back more than 100 years. The most prestigious places to stay are the usually the *grandes dames* or the luxury European-style hotels, which pride themselves on their personalized service, but the big de luxe convention hotels will often be a better choice for the traveler who needs access to a wide range of business facilities and services. For those who do not need to adopt a high profile, a room in a mid-range hotel or even a motel is likely to be perfectly adequate for a short stay; in general, price differences between hotels in a city reflect location and the number of restaurants, bars and so on more than the quality of the guest rooms.

Facilities The standard US business hotel room is spacious and has twin beds or a double bed. (Some chains, such as Holiday Inn, provide two double beds, for family use.) All rooms have a private bathroom, a direct-dial telephone (use of which may be charged at above standard rates), a color TV and a desk at which to work. Rooms in de luxe hotels have such extras as refrigerators or minibars (wet bars) stocked with drinks, in-room movies or cable channels and as many as three telephones, one by the bed, one by the desk and one in the bathroom. More and more hotels now have rooms, or entire floors, reserved for nonsmokers.

All business hotels will provide room service, usually 24hrs, and valet or laundry service (usually same day). They all also have a concierge who will help guests with reservations for shows and sightseeing tours, advise on restaurants and shopping, and deal with special requests; however, the extent of such service varies considerably from one hotel (and city) to another. Express check-out or check-in is advertised by many hotels; check-out can usually be expedited by leaving a blank, signed credit card voucher.

Special "executive" or "club" rooms and executive floors are now a fairly common feature of large business hotels in the USA. What you get for the higher price you pay for executive status varies a lot. It may be top-quality accommodation in a self-contained section of the hotel, which has its own lounge and a comprehensive business center (see below) and serviced by its own concierge. Or it may amount to little more than a slightly-above-standard room and complimentary breakfast and newspaper.

Business services Any business hotel should be able to arrange photocopying and secretarial/typing help, and audio-visual equipment for use in meeting rooms. The best-equipped hotels offer just about any in-house service you care to think of – word processing, translation, computers, computer modems, teleconferencing, a business reference library and links with electronic news/

business/stock market information services. However, some hotels' advertising tends to exaggerate the services they offer; so if you know that you will have specific requirements, it is always best to check with the hotel in advance.

Prices and reservations Prices are almost always quoted per single room, excluding tax. Rates vary enormously from city to city. In New York a room in a top-class hotel costs over $300 a night, and a luxury suite can cost more than $600. Such is the expense of hotel accommodation in Manhattan that it is difficult to find acceptable accommodation for under $125 a night. On the other hand, in cities such as Kansas City you can stay in the best hotels for not much more than $100 a night. Corporate rates giving substantial discounts are widely available. These don't always have to be negotiated in advance.

Major credit and charge cards – American Express (AE), Diners Club (DC), MasterCard/Access (MC) and Visa (V) – are accepted by virtually all business hotels. Expect to be asked to give a card number when making a reservation, especially if you will be checking in after 6pm. You may also be asked for a credit card imprint when you check in.

To find out if a hotel has a toll-free (800) reservations number, call the national toll-free information directory ☏ (800) 555-1212.

Hotel groups

Most groups operate a frequent business traveler plan offering preferential service and discounts to those who qualify. Telephone reservations numbers given are toll free (800).

Best Western Marketing group for individually-owned hotels throughout the USA. Gold Crown Club offers discounts. Standards, styles and clientele vary ☏ 528-1234.

Four Seasons Select group of Canadian-owned luxury hotels (flagship Chicago's Ritz-Carlton) which pride themselves on personalized service ☏ 332-3442.

Helmsley Includes some of New York's most luxurious hotels (flagship the Helmsley Palace), as well as those that used to belong to the Harley group ☏ 223-6800.

Hilton More than 260 hotels throughout the USA, including Hawaii. Schemes include Vista Club and Executive Business Service. The group includes not only large luxury hotels but also smaller first-class inns ☏ HILTONS.

Holiday Inns About 1,500 hotels throughout the USA. Reliable standards; large, modern rooms; cable movies. Staff can be offhand. Special privileges for Priority Club members ☏ 465-4329.

Howard Johnson Some 500 budget hotels, mainly in the East, Southeast, and Midwest ☏ 654-2000.

Hyatt About 150 top-class and resort hotels, many with excellent business and/or leisure facilities. Striking architecture and design is a Hyatt feature (although acrophobes should beware the vertiginous glass elevators). Gold Passport holders get special privileges ☏ 228-9000.

Inter-Continental About 10 highly rated, Japanese-owned hotels, mostly on the East Coast. Special privileges (such as room upgrades) for members of Six Continents Club ☏ 33-AGAIN.

Marriott Very large group whose hotels vary widely in size and style. Some city hotels have excellent business facilities ☏ 228-9290.

Omni Over 30 high-quality hotels mainly in cities east of the Mississippi River ☏ 228-2121.

Ramada Over 600 hotels and inns throughout the USA. Reliable but rarely inspiring. Ramada Business Card offers privileges and discounts ☏ 228-2828.

Sheraton Some 300 hotels throughout the USA. Generally high standards but rarely the most prestigious place to stay in town. Privileges and discounts available under Sheraton Executive Travelers Plan and Sheraton Club International ☏ 325-3535.

Stouffer About 30 hotels in major cities (flagship Washington's Mayflower). All are located downtown, and most have special floors with business facilities ☏ 468-3571.
Trusthouse Forte Britain's biggest hotel group used to have a slightly dowdy image, but owns some of the world's premier hotels, such as the George V in Paris. In the USA it owns the budget Travel Lodge chain, as well as a few first-rate city hotels including New York's Westbury ☏ 225-3050.
Westin De luxe hotels in many major cities. Westin Premier frequent guests programs offer special privileges ☏ 228-3000.

Recommended hotels

Hotels given full entries in the guide have generally been selected on the basis of being the most comfortable and stylish and the best-equipped for business travelers.

Listed under "Other Hotels" are establishments that do not achieve the standards of their competitors but which offer perfectly adequate accommodation, usually at a lower price than the hotels given full entries.

The price symbols have the following meanings:

$	under $75
$/	$75–125
$//	$125–175
$///	$175–225
$////	over $225
$/////	well over $225

At the time of going to press these reflect the price (including tax and service) for one person occupying a standard room.

Restaurants

The restaurant business in the USA has enjoyed tremendous growth in recent years both at the top end of the market and in the fast food sector.

Business dining habits vary from region to region and from city to city. In the major cities you will find a wide range of restaurants suitable for every level of business entertaining. Inevitably, in smaller cities the choice is not so wide; and the top restaurant in such cities will not generally be on a par with the top restaurants in New York or Chicago, for example. Descriptions of the recommended restaurants in different cities reflect the standard within each particular part of the city and the choice available.

Traditionally, French restaurants serving classic or *nouvelle cuisine* are favored for high-powered business entertaining, but there are many exceptions to this rule. Italian restaurants – the cooking is usually Northern Italian – rank among the best of many cities' restaurants. California cuisine is now as fashionable on the East Coast as it is on the West. Seafood predominates in cities such as San Diego and Miami, and rib joints and steak houses operate as business people's dining clubs in cities as diverse as New York, Chicago, and Kansas City. In addition, there are numerous restaurants serving many other national cuisines: Chinese, Japanese, Vietnamese, Mexican, Creole, Polish and Russian. In general, however, it is best to avoid taking a business colleague to a foreign restaurant – apart from French or Italian – unless you know that he or she enjoys that kind of food.
Reservations It is always sensible to make restaurant reservations at least 24hrs ahead. If you have any special requirements, such as a private booth or a table in a nonsmoking area, mention them at the time of phoning.

If you are going to arrive late, warn the restaurant or you may lose your table.

Recommended restaurants

The restaurants given full entries in the guide have been selected with the business traveler especially in mind – as well as for the quality of the food – and are those considered by local people to be the best in the city for working meals and business

Vintage chart

Vintage assessments are always a compromise because they have to exclude the talented growers who succeed even in "poor" years. This chart provides guidelines for wine from classic areas.

Very good years are indicated by **bold**

Years to avoid are given in *italics*

Drinkability (n) indicates wines which are not yet ready for drinking; (w) indicates wines which are ready for drinking but which will improve

Red Bordeaux
Médoc/Graves: **88** (n) 87 (n) **86** (n) **85** (n) *84* **83** (n) **82** 81 (w) *80* 79 **78** (n) *77 74 73 72*

Pomerol/St-Emilion: **88** (n) 87 (n) 86 (n) **85** (n) *84* **83** (n) **82** (n) **81** (w) 80 (w) 79 (n) **78** (n) *77 74 72*

Great older vintages: 66 62 61 59

White Bordeaux
Sauternes/Barsac **86** (n) 85 (n) *84* **83** (n) *82* 81 (n) 80 79 78 *77* **76 75** *74 73* **71 70 62 61**

White Burgundy 88 (n) 87 (w) **86** (w) **85** (w) 84 (w) 83 82 81 80 **79 78** *77 76 75 74*

Red Burgundy 88 (n) 87 (n) 86 (n) **85** (n) 84 (w) 83 (n) 82 *81* **80 78 72 71**

Northern Rhône
Côte Rôtie/Hermitage **88** (n) 87 (n) 86 (n) **85** (n) 84 (w) **83** (n) **82** (w) 81 80 79 **78** (w) *75* **69**

Champagne 87 (n) 86 (n) **85** (n) *84* **83** (n) **82** (w) 81 (w) **76 75 71**

Alsace 87 (n) 86 (n) **85** (n) *84* **83** (w) 82 81 (w) 80 79 **76 75 71**

Rhein/Mosel 88 (n) 87 (n) 86 (w) **85** (n) 84 **83** (w) 82 81 80 *78* **75 71**

Barolo 88 (n) 87 (n) 86 (n) **85** (n) 84 (w) 83 (w) **82** (w) 81 **78** (w) 77 **71 64**

Chianti Classico **88** (n) 87 (w) 86 (w) **85** (n) *84* **83** (w) **82 79 77**

Port 85 (n) 83 (n) 82 (n) 80 (n) 78 (n) **77** (n) **70 66**

California Carneros red 88 (n) **87** (n) **86** (n) **85** (n) **84** (w) 82

Napa and Sonoma red 88 (n) **87** (n) **86** (n) **85** (n) **84** (w) 82

California Chardonnay 88 (n) **87** (n) **86** (w) 85 83

Oregon red 88 (n) 87 (n) 86 **85** (w) **83**

Recommendations

For pleasurable drinking in 1989-92 we recommend: 1975 cru classé red Bordeaux, 1976 red Burgundy, 1978 top white Bordeaux, 1975/1976 Sauternes, 1986 white Burgundy, 1978 Chablis, 1978 Côte Rôtie, 1982 vintage Champagne, 1983 Rhein/Mosel, 1978 Barbaresco, 1977 Amarone, 1983 Chianti Classico Riserva, 1986 Sonoma Chardonnay, 1985 Napa Cabernet Sauvignon, 1988 Australian Cabernet Sauvignon, 1982 Rioja Reserva, 1976 Alsace, 1985 Vouvray.

entertaining. A few are recommended for purely social occasions, including celebrations.

The price symbols used in the guide have the following meanings:

- [$] under $20
- [$]/ $20–40
- [$]// $40–60
- [$]/// $60–100
- [$]//// over $100
- [$]///// well over $100

At the time of going to press they reflect the price of a typical dinner for one, including acceptable wine, tax and service. Prices are often lower for lunch.

Bars

It is important for visitors to recognize the growing US antipathy to mixing alcohol with business – especially during the working day. US bars are generally places to relax and unwind in after working hours.

Every city has its own style of bar, with the emphasis on spirits, cocktails and bottled beers; in some there are imitation English or Irish pubs, and these tend to be mainly for entertainment rather than serious talking. Hotel bars are usually the most suitable places to meet if you want a serious discussion over a drink. Alternatively, a local business contact may suggest meeting in the bar of his or her club.

Laws governing bar opening hours and the sale of alcohol vary from state to state.

Shopping

Standard shop opening hours are 9.30–6, Mon–Sat, but most stores have one or more late-opening days; some, especially in shopping malls, are open until 9 or 10 every weekday. Some are even open on Sun, and in large cities there are supermarkets that never close.

Department stores There are no truly nationwide chains of department stores, but high-class stores such as Bloomingdale's, Macy's and Saks Fifth Avenue have branches in many cities. Stores such as Sears Roebuck, JC Penney and Montgomery Ward are more middle-market, with a wide range of products but usually a narrower brand choice.

Shopping malls Every city has its modern shopping malls – usually located in the suburbs or on the periphery. A few are to be found in the heart of town. These modern developments often include leisure, entertainment and restaurant complexes.

Sales tax can be avoided in some states if the goods are to be sent out of the state. It always pays to ask if the shop will mail or ship your purchase direct to your home address. Often it is a matter of balancing the tax saved against the extra shipping charges incurred.

Crime

The United States's reputation for violent crime is due partly to the image presented by its entertainment industry and partly to some genuinely high statistics. States with the highest crime rates are Florida, Arizona, Colorado, California, Nevada, Oregon and Texas. New York has the highest rate for robbery, followed by California, Florida and Maryland.

As in most countries, common sense and safety-consciousness will prevent your being added to the crime statistics. As a precaution against credit card fraud it is wise to remove the carbons after signing a voucher.

In hotels, give valuables to the front desk to keep in a safety deposit box, or put them in the safe in your room.

Keeping safe When walking in any city, keep to the well-populated streets; do not enter deserted areas, especially after dark. In big cities, take a cab at night rather than ride the subway or walk, and call for the cab to collect you rather than go out to look for one. If confronted by someone asking for money, hand it over. Don't resist a robbery, and *never* argue with a gun. It is prudent always to divide any money you are carrying between two wallets. Keep cash and cards separate. Try to avoid looking scared, which can persuade a potential mugger that you are vulnerable and an easy target.

Dealing with the police If you are stopped by a member of the police force, you should be courteous and helpful. Emphasize that you are a visitor and that if you have broken the law it was innocently and inadvertently done. Never attempt to pay a fine on the spot – which could be construed as attempted bribery, a serious charge. If you are arrested, you are allowed to make one telephone call; use it to call your nearest consulate for advice or to contact a friend who can find you a lawyer. Duty lawyers are also available; ask the police for details. You are not required to make any statement to the police.

Embassies

The major foreign embassies are all located in Washington DC (tel area code 202), but most countries have consulates in other principal cities such as Chicago, New York and San Francisco.

Australia, 1601 Massachusetts Ave NW, Washington DC 20036 ☎ 797-3000.
Austria, 2343 Massachusetts Ave NW, Washington DC 20008 ☎ 483-4474.
Belgium, 3330 Garfield St NW, Washington DC 20008 ☎ 333-6900.
Britain, 3100 Massachusetts Ave NW Washington DC 20008 ☎ 462-1340.
Canada, 1746 Massachusetts Ave NW, Washington DC 20036 ☎ 785-1400.
Denmark, 3200 Whitehaven St NW, Washington DC 20008 ☎ 234-4300.
Finland, 3216 New Mexico Ave NW, Washington DC 20016 ☎ 363-2430.
France, 4101 Reservoir Rd, Washington DC 20007 ☎ 944-6000.
Federal Republic of Germany (West), 4645 Reservoir Rd NW, Washington DC 20007 ☎ 298-4000.
Greece, 2221 Massachusetts Ave NW, Washington DC 20008 ☎ 667-3168.
Ireland, 2234 Massachusetts Ave NW, Washington DC 20008 ☎ 462-3939.
Italy, 1601 Fuller St NW, Washington DC 20009 ☎ 328-5500.
Japan, 2520 Massachusetts Ave NW, Washington DC 20008 ☎ 937-6700.
Netherlands, 4200 Linnean Ave NW, Washington DC 20008 ☎ 244-5300.
New Zealand, 37 Observatory Circle NW, Washington DC 20008 ☎ 328-4848.
Norway, 2720 34th St NW, Washington DC 20008 ☎ 333-6000.
Portugal, 2125 Kalorama Rd NW, Washington DC 20008 ☎ 328-8610.
Spain, 2700 15th St NW, Washington DC 20009 ☎ 265-0190.
Sweden, 600 New Hampshire Ave NW Washington DC 20037 ☎ 944-5600.
Switzerland, 2900 Cathedral Ave NW, Washington DC 20008 ☎ 745-7900.
Yugoslavia, 2410 California St NW, Washington DC 20008 ☎ 462-6566.

In addition, there is a *Delegation of the Commission of the European Community*, 2100 M St NW, Washington DC 20037 ☎ 862-9500.

Health care

Health care is a wholly private affair in the USA. It is every individual's responsibility to make sure that he or she is fully insured – US costs for all kinds of treatment are a good deal higher than in most countries.

If you fall ill

Pharmacists A wide range of over-the-counter medicines are available for minor ailments. For other drugs you will need a prescription; overseas prescriptions are not usually accepted, but most doctors will, for a fee, write a copy prescription without examination. Most towns have at least one late-opening or 24hr pharmacy, and most pharmacists will give basic medical advice.

Doctors Medical practitioners' standards are high. The cost of any malpractice suit means that doctors will err on the side of overtreatment rather than neglect. Technical expertise and equipment are generally as modern as you will find anywhere in the world. To find a doctor, ask at your hotel reception desk or seek the advice of the concierge. Most doctors in large US cities have one or two specialties, even in general practice. Some small communities may have no doctor at all if there is not enough business to support a sufficiently lucrative practice.

Emergency treatment For the emergency services and an ambulance ☏ 911; if the 911 number does not apply, call the operator, "0." Standards of care in hospitals are high, and ambulance crews and medical emergency services are equipped to begin treatment on the spot.

Dental treatment is similar to medical treatment in both standards and costs. In choosing a dentist, take the advice of local contacts, the hotel desk or the concierge.

Costs Doctors expect immediate payment by non-US residents, but most accept credit cards. A single visit to a doctor will cost a minimum of $50. Asking a doctor to come to your hotel will cost at least $100; bandages and drugs are all extra. Hospital care can cost $2,000 per day.

Your admission to the hospital may be delayed unless you carry some evidence of your ability to pay – such as your certificate of insurance (credit cards are not necessarily acceptable as proof of ability to pay). It is also advisable to carry some evidence if you are allergic to any drugs used in emergencies – such as penicillin – or suffer from a disease requiring special treatment, such as diabetes.

Communications

Using the telephone All US numbers have a three-digit area code and a seven-digit subscriber code. Do not use the area code when calling a number in the same area. Numbers prefixed with 800 are toll-free nationwide. Telephone dials/buttons have letters as well as numbers; and some businesses' numbers spell out their name or some other appropriate word, for ease in remembering it.

The dialing tone is a continuous tone that should cease when dialing begins. A slow, repeated tone indicates that the number dialed is ringing. A faster repeated tone, the busy signal, indicates that the number dialed is already in use. A very fast rhythmic tone means that all lines are busy. If there is a continuous, high-pitched tone try re-dialing. If the tone persists, call the operator.

Pay phones are widely available in public and semi-public places: hotel and office lobbies, shops, bars and restaurants, transportation depots, gas stations, subway stations and on streets and highways. Most take nickels, dimes and quarters, but many also accept credit cards or special telephone credit cards. All public telephones have a small plaque giving full operating instructions.

International calls may be made from pay phones – provided that you have plenty of change. Most hotels have international direct-dial phones in the rooms, but there is often a sizable surcharge for calls made using these phones. Many countries now operate a "direct" service, whereby you can dial the international operator in your own country and have a call charged to a home-based credit card. An alternative is to ask the person you are calling to accept the charge (known as a "collect" call).

Useful numbers Operator 0 or 00. You can ring the operator for a wide variety of services. Besides dealing with difficulties in connecting a call, the operator will route you to recorded services such as the time and weather forecast and will provide information on local health and dental services, and so on. For telephone information, dial 411 (if within same area code) or 1-(area code)-555-1212 for numbers in other areas. There is a toll-free international inquiries service ☏ (800) 874-4000.

Telegrams and overseas cablegrams can be sent either from your hotel (for which you will pay an additional handling charge) or from any office of Western Union. A further option within the USA is to send a Mailgram, which is delivered the next day for about half the cost of a telegram.

Telex and fax

Most of the larger hotels have telex and/or fax machines which can be used to send and receive messages for guests, but such a service is not normally operable by the guest. Independent operators run telex bureaux in the larger cities (see *City by city: Local resources*).

Mail

The Federal mail service is reasonably efficient. The size of the country means that not all mail can be guaranteed next-day delivery, but first-class letter mail is usually delivered on the second day after posting. New York delivery times can be longer. All long-distance internal mail is sent by air, without extra airmail charge. Overnight Express mail is available at higher cost. Special quick services are also available to many overseas destinations.

Post offices are generally open Mon–Fri, 9–5. Some open until 1pm Sat. Most big cities have at least one 24hr office. Stamps can be bought at drugstores, hotels, bus and rail stations, and other locations. There is a 25% extra charge payable anywhere other than at a post office. Mailboxes are almost as ubiquitous as phone booths. In lobbies, stations and other indoor locations they may be simply a slot in the wall marked "US Mail." Mailboxes in the street are generally dark blue and bear the US mail logo.

Deliveries Federal Express is the leading company for both local and long-distance deliveries in the USA. Internally they guarantee delivery by 10.30 on the second day. Quoted delivery times for overseas delivery are also subject to a money-back guarantee. Other nationwide courier services include DHL, for international delivery, and Airborne and Purolator, for both internal and overseas services. Dial local information (411) for the number of the nearest branch. All courier services are generally quicker than the mail and provide 24hr pick-up.

Dialing codes

US area codes

The United States (apart from Alaska and Hawaii – see below) is divided into four time zones: Eastern (E), Central (C), Mountain (M) and Pacific (P), each one hour earlier than the previous one. In the following list, the time zone of each city is identified by initial.

City (state)	Time zone	Area code
Atlanta (Georgia)	E	404
Atlantic City (New Jersey)	E	609
Baltimore (Maryland)	E	301
Birmingham (Alabama)	C	205
Boston (Massachusetts)	E	617
Buffalo (New York)	E	716
Charlotte (North Carolina)	E	704
Chicago (Illinois)	C	312
Cincinnati (Ohio)	E	513
Cleveland (Ohio)	E	216
Columbus (Ohio)	E	614
Dallas (Texas)	C	214
Denver (Colorado)	M	303
Detroit (Michigan)	E	313
Fort Lauderdale (Florida)	E	305
Fort Worth (Texas)	C	817
Grand Rapids (Michigan)	E	616
Hartford (Connecticut)	E	203
Houston (Texas)	C	713
Indianapolis (Indiana)	E	317
Jersey City (New Jersey)	E	201
Kansas City (Missouri)	C	816
Los Angeles (California)	P	213
Memphis (Tennessee)	C	901
Miami (Florida)	E	305
Milwaukee (Wisconsin)	C	414
Minneapolis (Minnesota)	C	612
Nashville (Tennessee)	C	615
New Orleans (Louisiana)	C	504
New York (New York)	E	212
Norfolk (Virginia)	E	804
Oklahoma City (Oklahoma)	C	405
Philadelphia (Pennsylvania)	E	215
Pittsburgh (Pennsylvania)	E	412
Portland (Oregon)	P	503
Richmond (Virginia)	E	804
Sacramento (California)	P	916
Salt Lake City (Utah)	M	801
St Louis (Missouri)	C	314
San Antonio (Texas)	C	512
San Diego (California)	P	619

San Francisco (California)	P	415
Seattle (Washington)	P	206
Tampa (Florida)	E	813
Toledo (Ohio)	E	419
Tulsa (Oklahoma)	C	918
Washington DC	E	202

Alaska is 5 hours behind Eastern time.
Hawaii is 5 hours behind Eastern time.

International dialing codes

In the following list of selected international codes the time difference is given in relation to Eastern time, + indicating the number of hours later and – the number of hours earlier. When phoning from Central, Mountain and Pacific times, add 1, 2 or 3 hours, respectively, to any "+" time; subtract 1, 2 or 3 hours from any "–" time. All country codes are prefixed by 011.

Area	Country code	Time difference
Argentina	54	(+2)
Australia	61	(+13–15)
Austria	43	(+6)
Bahamas	1 809	(no difference)
Belgium	32	(+6)
Bermuda	1 809 29	(+1)
Brazil	55	(+0–2)
Britain	44	(+5)
Canada	1	(zones correspond roughly to US)
Colombia	57	(no difference)
Costa Rica	506	(–1)
Denmark	45	(+6)
Egypt	20	(+7)
Eire	353	(+5)
Finland	358	(+7)
France	33	(+6)
Germany (West)	49	(+6)
Greece	30	(+7)
Guatemala	502	(–1)
Hong Kong	852	(+13)
Hungary	36	(+6)
Iceland	354	(+5)
India	91	(+10.30)
Indonesia	62	(+12–14)
Iran	98	(+8.30)
Israel	972	(+7)
Italy	39	(+6)
Jamaica	1 809	(no difference)
Japan	81	(+14)
Korea (South)	82	(+14)
Luxembourg	352	(+6)
Mexico	52	(–1)
Netherlands	31	(+6)
New Zealand	64	(+17)
Nigeria	234	(+6)
Norway	47	(+6)
Pakistan	92	(+10)
Panama	507	(no difference)
Peru	51	(no difference)
Philippines	63	(+13)
Portugal	351	(+5)
Saudi Arabia	966	(+8)
Singapore	65	(+13)
South Africa	27	(+7)
Spain	34	(+6)
Sweden	46	(+6)
Switzerland	41	(+6)
Taiwan	886	(+13)
Turkey	90	(+8)
USSR	7	(+8–16)
Venezuela	58	(+1)

Conversion charts

The metric system is not regularly used in the USA, although it is gradually gaining acceptance; the scientific disciplines, for example, use it exclusively. Increasingly, temperatures are given in Celsius (C – also known as Centigrade) in addition to the more commonly used Fahrenheit (F). Shoe and clothing sizes differ from those used in the UK and Continental Europe. Length is denoted in feet and inches (12 inches = 1 foot; 3 feet = 1 yard = 0.91 meter).

Temperature

°F	32	40	50	60	70	75	85	95	105	140	175	212
°C	0	5	10	15	20	25	30	35	40	60	80	100

Mass (weight)

kilograms (kg)		kg or lb		pounds (lb)
0.454	=lb	**1**	kg=	2.205
0.907		**2**		4.409
1.361		**3**		6.614
1.814		**4**		8.819
2.268		**5**		11.023
2.722		**6**		13.228
3.175		**7**		15.432
3.629		**8**		17.637
4.082		**9**		19.842
4.536		**10**		22.046
9.072		**20**		44.092
13.608		**30**		66.139
18.144		**40**		88.185
22.680		**50**		110.231

Length

centimeters (cm)		cm or in		inches (in)
2.54	=in	**1**	cm=	0.394
5.08		**2**		0.787
7.62		**3**		1.181
10.16		**4**		1.575
12.70		**5**		1.969
15.24		**6**		2.362
17.70		**7**		2.756
20.32		**8**		3.150
22.86		**9**		3.543
25.40		**10**		3.937
50.80		**20**		7.874
76.20		**30**		11.811
101.60		**40**		15.748
127.00		**50**		19.685

Volume

liters (l)		liters or US gallons		US *gallons
3.79	=l	**1**	gall=	0.26
7.58		**2**		0.52
11.37		**3**		0.78
15.16		**4**		1.04
18.95		**5**		1.30
22.74		**6**		1.56
26.53		**7**		1.82
30.32		**8**		2.08
34.11		**9**		2.34
37.90		**10**		2.60
75.80		**20**		5.20
113.70		**30**		7.80
151.60		**40**		10.40
189.50		**50**		13.00

* 1 US gallon = 0.83 UK/Imperial gallon
6 US gallons = 5 UK/Imperial gallons

Distance

kilometers (km)		km or miles		miles
1.609	=mi	**1**	km=	0.621
3.219		**2**		1.243
4.828		**3**		1.864
6.437		**4**		2.485
8.047		**5**		3.107
9.656		**6**		3.728
11.265		**7**		4.350
12.875		**8**		4.971
14.484		**9**		5.592
16.093		**10**		6.214
32.187		**20**		12.427
48.280		**30**		18.641
64.374		**40**		24.855
80.467		**50**		31.069

Index